PSYCHOTHERAPY SUPERVISION

PSYCHOTHERAPY SUPERVISION

THEORY, RESEARCH AND PRACTICE

Edited by

ALLEN K. HESS
Auburn University

A WILEY-INTERSCIENCE PUBLICATION

JOHN WILEY & SONS, New York • Chichester • Brisbane • Toronto

Library of Congress Cataloging in Publication Data:
Main entry under title:

Psychotherapy supervision.

   (Wiley series on personality processes)
   "A Wiley-Interscience publication."
   Bibliography: p.
   Includes index.
   1. Psychotherapy—Study and teaching.   I. Hess,
Allen K., 1945–   [DNLM: 1. Psychotherapy—Educa-
tion.   WM18 P979]

RC480.5.P778   616.89′14′07   80–25
ISBN 0–471–05035–0

Printed in the United States of America

10 9 8 7 6 5 4

Contributors

T. JOHN AKAMATSU, PH.D., Associate Professor and Director of the Psychological Clinic, Department of Psychology, Kent State University

JOSEPH F. APONTE, PH.D., Professor and Director of Clinical Training, Department of Psychology, University of Louisville

MICHAEL R. BARNAT, PH.D., Senior Clinical Psychologist, Michigan Headache and Neurological Institute, Ann Arbor

ERNST G. BEIER, PH.D., Professor, Department of Psychology, University of Utah

ANNETTE M. BRODSKY, PH.D., Associate Professor, Department of Psychology, University of Alabama

BARRY R. BURKHART, PH.D., Associate Professor, Department of Psychology, Auburn University

LARRY COHEN, Doctoral candidate, Department of Psychology, Adelphi University

WILLIAM N. CONFER, PH.D., Clinical Psychologist, Wiregrass Mental Health Center, Dothan, Alabama

ROBERT R. DIES, PH.D., Professor, Department of Psychology, University of Maryland

ALBERT ELLIS, PH.D., Institute for Rational-Emotive Therapy, New York City

CRAIG A. EVERETT, PH.D., Assistant Professor and Director, Graduate Program in Marital and Family Therapy, Department of Family and Child Development, Auburn University

DOUGLAS R. FORSYTH, PH.D., Associate Professor and Director of the Division for Human Services and Applied Behavioral Sciences, University of Massachusetts

LAMAURICE GARDNER, PH.D., Professor, Department of Psychology, Wayne State University

DAVID S. GLENWICK, PH.D., Director of the Portage County Children's Services Center, Department of Psychology, Kent State University

LEONARD GREENBERG, Doctoral candidate, Case Western Reserve University

ALLEN K. HESS, PH.D., Associate Professor, Department of Psychology, Auburn University

KATHRYN A. HESS, M.S., East Alabama Mental Health Center, Opelika, Alabama

ALLEN E. IVEY, PH.D., Professor, Division of Human Services and Applied Behavioral Sciences, University of Massachusetts

NORMAN KAGAN, PH.D., Professor, Department of Counseling, Personnel Services and Educational Psychology, Michigan State University

ROBERT G. KAPLAN, Doctoral candidate, Department of Psychology, Case Western Reserve University

CHARLES V. LAIR, PH.D., Professor and Director of Clinical Training, Department of Psychology, Auburn University

MICHAEL J. LAMBERT, PH.D., Associate Professor, Department of Psychology, Brigham Young University

ROBERT J. LANGS, M.D., Editor-in-Chief, *International Journal of Psychoanalytic Psychotherapy*, New York City

MARSHA M. LINEHAN, PH.D., Assistant Professor and Director of the Psychological Services and Training Center, Department of Psychology, University of Washington

MICHAEL J. LYONS, Doctoral candidate, Department of Psychology, University of Louisville

WILLIAM R. MARSHALL, PH.D., Clinical Psychology Faculty, Family Practice Center, Moses H. Cone Memorial Hospital, Greensboro, North Carolina

STANLEY MOLDAWSKY, PH.D., Private practice, Maplewood, New Jersey

JOHN M. REISMAN, PH.D., Professor, Department of Psychology, DePaul University

LAURA N. RICE, PH.D., Professor, Department of Psychology, York University

MARGARET J. RIOCH, PH.D., Professor Emeritus in Residence, The American University, Washington, D.C.

RALPH SLOVENKO, Professor of Law and Psychiatry, Wayne State University

ELIZABETH STEVENS, Doctoral candidate, Department of Psychology, Kent State University

LYN E. STYCZYNSKI, PH.D., Staff Psychologist and Instructor, Tufts-New England Medical Center, Boston

IRVING B. WEINER, PH.D., Vice Chancellor for Academic Affairs and Professor, Department of Psychology, University of Denver

RICHARD L. WESSLER, PH.D., Director of Training, Institute for Rational-Emotive Therapy, New York City

DAVID M. YOUNG, PH.D., Assistant Professor, Department of Psychological Sciences, Indiana University—Purdue University

Series Preface

This series of books is addressed to behavioral scientists interested in the nature of human personality. Its scope should prove pertinent to personality theorists and researchers as well as to clinicians concerned with applying an understanding of personality processes to the amelioration of emotional difficulties in living. To this end, the series provides a scholarly integration of theoretical formulations, empirical data, and practical recommendations.

Six major aspects of studying and learning about human personality can be designated: personality theory, personality structure and dynamics, personality development, personality assessment, personality change, and personality adjustment. In exploring these aspects of personality, the books in the series discuss a number of distinct but related subject areas: the nature and implications of various theories of personality; personality, characteristics that account for consistencies and variations in human behavior; the emergence of personality processes in children and adolescents; the use of interviewing and testing procedures to evaluate individual differences in personality; efforts to modify personality styles through psychotherapy, counseling, behavior therapy, and other methods of influence; and patterns of abnormal personality functioning that impair individual competence.

IRVING B. WEINER

University of Denver
Denver, Colorado

Preface

This book is a collection of original contributions attempting to define the as yet uncharted regions of teaching and learning of psychotherapy. The supervision of psychotherapy is an activity that many mental health professionals engage in; however, as with many high frequency activities, it has gone largely unnoticed. Carl Rogers (1957) came closest to recognizing psychotherapy supervision in his description of experiential techniques and human qualities that encourage psychotherapists to develop. Rogers' early recognition of the issues involved in training psychotherapists has gone unheeded and the current status of the field still can be accurately summarized by his quote, "Considering the fact that one-third of present day psychologists have a special interest in the field of psychotherapy, we would expect a great deal of attention might be given to the problem of training individuals to engage in the therapeutic process. . . . For the most part this field is characterized by a rarity of research and a plentitude [sic] of platitudes." (Rogers, 1957, pg. 76). This is particularly puzzling in view of the time psychologists spend in training psychotherapists. Examination of the articles in *Professional Psychology* shows the increased amount of attention being given to training functions in various settings.

Several trends account for the current investment of time, and indicate that the future will show an increase in such time allocations. One is the Community Mental Health Act that requires community mental health centers to provide education and consultation as one of its five basic functions. A second impetus is the growing recognition of the need for quality control regarding consumer services generally, and mental health services in particular. The growth of the program evaluation area (Guttentag, Kiresuk, Oglesby and Cahn, 1975) and the presence of "how-to-shop-for-your-therapist" guides (Park, 1976; Parloff, 1976) are indicators of the demand for competence in psychotherapists. Thirdly, proposed National Health Insurance programs will likely mandate reimbursement for trained professionals only, and require close supervisory control for mental health workers who have not received the terminal degree in their field. The current movement by health service professions toward requiring continuing education programs for practitioners to maintain licensure will augment the focus on supervisory and training functions. A fourth consideration is the therapists' own need to enhance their skills and self-development. Given this growth pattern, recognition of psychotherapy supervision as a field or area of professional activity is due.

Work on teaching and learning psychotherapy skills can be found in the literature. Ekstein and Wallerstein (1958; 1972) thoughtfully consider issues in teaching and learning psychotherapy. Originating from the psychoanalytic perspective, they provide a model that includes administrative issues as they impinge on supervisor-therapist-client relationships. Bruch (1974), from a Sullivanian, interpersonal approach, illustrates clinically important problems in the progress of the therapist's skill acquisition. Kell and Mueller [1966; and Mueller and Kell (1972)] describe the therapist and supervisor as they encounter each other and the client in their journey toward personal growth. Rioch, Coulter and Weinberger (1976), from an interpersonal perspective, trace the variegated patterns by which therapists developed in training seminars. All of these works, and many of the articles they reference, provide rich sources for supervisors and therapists to understand the complex processes by which people help others to unravel the tangled strands of their relationships.

Despite the considerable sources the above works provide, no one source presents a comprehensive definition of the domain of psychotherapy supervision. As a prime feature, this book presents chapters on the broad areas encompassed in the teaching and learning of psychotherapy. The chapters are intended to provide different authors' conceptual frameworks in order for the reader to begin to recognize issues that recur in different chapters, and to have available various authors' views on the issues. In a sense, this intellectual analogue of the geographer's method of triangulation should provide a richer knowledge of a phenomenon than if there were unanimity of opinions. One example of this emerging focus on an issue is the concept of patient responsibility. Some theorists (e.g. Langs, Chapter 10) believe the patient is the supervisor's responsibility ultimately. Glenwick (Chapter 17) finds that Ohio state law takes that position too, while Weiner and Kaplan (Chapter 4) see the issue clouded by the lines of authority a field agency may exercise.

Secondly, many of the chapters survey available research regarding the state of knowledge of their respective areas. Hopefully, many of the assertions made and questions raised will stimulate advances on both theoretical and empirical levels.

Thirdly, some chapters offer case illustrations or vignettes in an effort to portray the processes underlying the teaching and learning of psychotherapy. The case vignettes will demonstrate both the vagaries and regularities of psychotherapy supervision, providing a guide for the practitioner and a source of hypotheses for the researcher.

The chapters are grouped into nine parts, each intended for particular purposes. Part I, "Conceptual Bases," provides a conceptual framework for clinical work in general, and an overview of the developments in supervision in particular. Part II, "Perspectives in Supervision," presents a variety of experiential viewpoints of the novice supervisee, the novice supervisor, the problems of supervising the new student, and how one uses one's self to change. It provides the raw material or "human stuff" that occurs in supervision, by which the subsequent chapters can be more richly understood. Part III, "Psychotherapies," consists of chapters written by prominent practitioners representing major types of psychotherapy. Each chapter describes how therapists in their respective theoretical orientation are trained. Part IV, "Teaching Formats," provides methodologies which have been developed to define and train those skills essential for successful psychotherapy. This is followed by Part V, "Developmental Perspectives," which details some particular problems that arise in supervision of psychotherapists working with children, adolescents, or the elderly. Part VI, "Special Modalities," explores the training issues related to treating people in crises, groups, and marital couples and families, as well as offering psychotherapy in community agency settings. As these nontraditional treatment modes have become recognized, particular training questions need to be addressed by supervisors. These issues are defined here. Part VII is a chapter that reviews the research bases for supervisory practices, and suggests directions that future research needs to take. Part VIII offers suggestions regarding legal obligations, sex-role, racial, ethnic, and social class issues that arise in both psychotherapy and the supervisory relationship. Part IX offers a summary of the current practice of psychotherapy supervision, and describes the needs for the further development of this field.

The book has been composed with particular reference to the readership. While intended for the professional who supervises in psychotherapy, it appears that this turns out to be quite a large group. Garfield and Kurtz (1976) found supervision to rank fifth out of twelve activities in terms of time spent by a sample of clinical psychologists. This exceeded such activities as group psychotherapy, behavior modification, and research in which a considerable part of the student's academic career is invested, in stark contrast to the attention given to training supervisors. The only activities exceeding supervision were individual psychotherapy, diagnostics-assessment, teaching, and administration. Though only 2% claim supervision as their primary professional identity, it can be asserted that, using some definitions of supervision (see Chapters 2, 28 and 31), all clinicians are involved in the supervisory process. We intend the materials to be relevent to practitioners from the student level through the transition of supervisee to supervisor to experienced and accomplished supervisors wishing to broaden their scope and refine their skills. We intend the book as an aid for teachers to structure both didactic and experiential teaching settings so psychotherapy and supervision both can be taught more effectively and enjoyably. Particular attention has been paid to the theoretical and research developments in psychotherapy supervision. And the practicing clinician can use the material to hone his or her skills by considering the suggestions offered by the authors.

The material has been written principally by psychologists, but it is intended for all practitioners engaged in delivery of human services designed to help people achieve personal change. Thus we hope people from backgrounds such as psychology, nursing, psychiatry, counseling, and social work will find this volume helpful.

A volume such as this is obviously the creation of many people. The authors have reaffirmed my high opinion of their professionalism by their level of scholarship, acceptance (and sometimes the correcting) of my suggestions, and willingness to comply with deadlines and other demands of authorship. Rita Dauber's unflagging secretarial assistance, the availability of several esteemed colleagues who provided enlightened discussion, the care of the Wiley staff, and the myriad types of help provided by my family, especially my daughter Tanya's effervescence and honesty and my wife Kathryn's ineffable Thou-ness, are gratefully acknowledged.

ALLEN K. HESS

Auburn, Alabama
March 1980

Bruch, H. *Learning psychotherapy.* Cambridge, Mass.: Harvard University Press, 1974.

Ekstein, R., and Wallerstein, R. S. *The teaching and learning of psychotherapy.* New York: International Universities Press, 1958; 1972 (Rev. ed.).

Garfield, S. L., and Kurz, R. Clinical psychologists in the 1970's. *American Psychologist,* 1976, *31,* 1–9.

Guttentag, M., Kiresuk, T., Ogelesby, M., and Cahn, J. *The evaluation of training in mental health.* New York: Behavioral Publications, 1975.

Kell, B. L., and Mueller, W. J. *Impact and change: A study of counseling relationships.* New York: Appleton-Century-Crofts, 1966.

Mueller, W. J., and Kell, B. L. *Coping with conflict: Supervising counselors and psychotherapists.* New York: Appleton-Century-Crofts, 1972.

Park, C. C. *You are not alone.* Boston: Atlantic—Little, Brown, 1976.

Parloff, M. Shopping for the right therapy. *Saturday Review,* February 21, 1976.

Rioch, M. J., Coulter, W. R., and Weinberger, D. M. *Dialogues for therapists.* San Francisco: Jossey-Bass, 1976.

Rogers, C. R. Training individuals to engage in therapeutic practice. In C. R. Strother (Ed.), *Psychology and mental health.* Washington, D.C.: American Psychological Association, 1957.

Contents

PART THREE   PSYCHOTHERAPIES

PART FOUR   TEACHING FORMATS

PART FIVE   DEVELOPMENTAL PERSPECTIVES

PART SIX   SPECIAL MODALITIES

PART SEVEN   RESEARCH

PART EIGHT   PROFESSIONAL CONSIDERATIONS

PART NINE   CONCLUSION

PSYCHOTHERAPY SUPERVISION

PART ONE

Conceptual Bases

Part I, "Conceptual Bases," consists of two chapters which serve to introduce the reader to ways of thinking about clinical supervision issues, and to the succeeding chapters in the book. Chapter 1, *Theories and Models of Clinical Psychology* by Allen K. Hess, describes the interplay between the theoretical assumptions one adopts and the nature of the data that both supports and is generated by the theoretical constructions of the clinician. Some functions and limits of theories and models, and a novel theory are presented.

Chapter 2, *Training Models and the Nature of Psychotherapy Supervision* by Allen K. Hess, describes six models that the supervisory relationship can take. The nature of the relationships, the benefits and drawbacks, and the purposes of the models are discussed. These models can be used to understand the perspectives of authors of the subsequent chapters.

CHAPTER 1

Theories and Models in Clinical Psychology

ALLEN K. HESS

I wonder if everyone realizes how quickly doctors get rusty and how great is their need for periodic scouring. And how neat a trick it must be to try to measure a doctor's competence! His command of facts, yes. His judgment, perhaps, with the aid of batteries of computers. But grading him as a healer is something else, his art is so shot through with abstractions, so shaped by attitudes, intuitions, values, and other subtle emanations. (McClenahan, 1978, p. 87).

These abstractions and subtle emanations, attitudes, and values form the essence of therapeutic and supervisory relationships. Often practitioners (and the authors of the chapters that follow this one) work with their assumptions and theories to the point where they become unnoticed, as unnoticed as the air we breathe. On too few occasions do we take the opportunity to scrutinize our values and theories. The authors in the following chapters will present their views of the healing process. The reader is invited to clarify and sharpen his or her own views using the authors' conceptualizations to bring the issues into focus.

In order for the reader to have available a set of conceptual tools that help to analyze the views presented in the chapters, and to synthesize or reconcile differing perspectives of supervision, this chapter reviews the roles of theory and model construction in psychology generally and psychotherapy in particular. The benefits and drawbacks of theorizing are presented, followed by a framework that integrates theoretical and empirical approaches. The definition and deployment of models are outlined with an illustration of a novel model that clinicians and researchers may find particularly useful in reconceptualizing phenomena previously forced into prevailing but ill-fitting dimensional models.

THEORY AND MODELS

General Considerations

The role of theory and model development must be understood in order for the professional psychotherapist to (a) be clear about his or her psychotherapeutic functioning, (b) be aware of the varieties of alternative theories and procedures potentially available, (c) understand the historical lines of development that lead

3

to current practice, and (d) be able to assess the quality and kind of service the client receives. Perhaps the need for a clear conceptual understanding of one's theories is especially great in the helping professions, particularly in an area such as supervision, where the client is purchasing an intangible relationship. Since the psychotherapist is providing a service, and this service is delivered in essence through the medium of the psychotherapist's behavior and structuring of the relationship and client expectancies (Frank, 1973; Kazdin and Wilcoxson, 1976; Strupp, Fox, and Lessler, 1969), the process of psychotherapy is a highly abstract one. In order to identify helpful and harmful elements of the psychotherapy and to refine or modify them, the psychotherapist necessarily engages in construing what he or she is doing vis-á-vis the client. The supervisor, in a sense engaging in a metarelationship (Abroms, 1977) and attempting to facilitate the supervisee's skills, tries to identify the goals that are primary in the supervision and capture the flavor of the psychotherapy which the supervisee is conducting. It is this abstractive activity of therapy and "metatherapy" that differentiates the lay therapist (bartender, hair dresser, spiritualist) from the professional. The professional is committed to the refinement of skills (the identification and augmentation of the "curative" elements), the efficacious teaching of these skills, and the attendant technology (technical terms, and assessment and research activities) required to achieve these first two goals.

The type of conceptualization may vary in a number of ways. Data can be digital (able to be put in binary or in numerical terms) or analogic (couched in metaphors or in configural terms) (Spence, 1974), and quantitative or metrically specific versus qualitative, global, or intuitive. Psychology has had its schisms, with different camps staking out their views of the boundaries of psychology proper. Cronbach (1957) and Meehl (1954) describe the tension between the experimentalist and correlationalist approaches to knowledge and the actuarial and clinical approaches to prediction. In a broader sense, Pepper (1942) describes analytic approaches to understanding, which attempt to divine the "real" elements or invariant lawful relationships between the elements, and the synthetic approaches, which attempt to portray the context, configuration, or the telic or goal striving patterning characterizing phenomena. Pragmatists who wish to avoid abstruse speculations and vexing theoretical ambivalence tend toward (a) selection of one or the other theories to which graduate training exposes them, (b) eclecticism, or (c) denial of theory in favor of a rootedness in "facts" and "common sense."

Selection of a theory inevitably leaves one with a theory that must be lacking in scope, precision, or both (Pepper, 1942). Psychoanalytic theory, as clinically descriptive as a theory can be, lacks the necessary specification to allow precise isolation of variables. Psychometric purists, who have isolated types of traits with unequaled precision, leave us with mosaic or paint-by-the-numbers portraits with the essence of the client not quite captured. Existentialism, behaviorism, and other viewpoints, while admirably taking stands, often find their positions eroding when critically examined. One often needs to leave the setting where the theory is promulgated to see its limits. The intern whose behavioral training is cast aside in favor of more "clinical" theories in the community mental health center is not uncommon.

Training that exposes one to several viewpoints leads one to embrace eclecticism as a welcome theoretical haven. To date, no unified, deliberate, or intentional eclectic theory is compelling. An appealing eclecticism would have to reconcile incompatible "truths" from different theories. It would have to decide the correct admixtures of the various theories. In a sense, each person's eclecticism would be a unique amalgamation, leaving us with no consensual theory at all. Concepts would lose contact with root metaphors (rendering us vulnerable to making the metaphor an empty abstraction, or to reifying the metaphor so as not to lose it). Measurement devices would likely not be isomorphic to the constructs, potentially leaving us with odd situations such as using the MMPI or the galvanic skin response to assess ontological anxiety, or a Thematic Apperception Test (TAT) to assess Reinforcement Value (Rotter, 1954). Fiske (1973) attributes the disappointingly low correlation coefficients usually found between personality traits to the "casually selected procedure[s] for its [the trait's] measurement" (p. 89). Instead he suggests studying the "construct-operation unit," or the delineation of the construct with a "specific measuring operation congruent with the conceptualization" (p. 89). A second type of eclecticism is "accidental." It is the point at which one arrives when reconciling strengths and weaknesses of theories. One tarries long enough to replenish cognitive supplies and then proceeds to further develop and refine a theory.

The problem with "common sense" involves choosing *whose* common sense. For each common sense aphorism, there is one to contradict it. While common sense appears to hold truth value, its terms are vague when one pursues them. This type of problem plagued the original "frustration leads to aggression" hypothesis (Dollard, Doob, Miller, Mowrer, and Sears, 1939). Ill-defined terms are irritating, and when they are refined they no longer belong to the realm of common sense. Refinement of terms leads us to theory building once more.

Since the issue of theoretical speculation versus radical and metaphysical behaviorism has been hotly debated in psychology in the twentieth century (Marx and Hillix, 1973) some attention to this issue seems merited. Those eschewing theorizing claim that such speculation is wasteful at best, and more often is misleading by giving us the illusion that something substantial has been discovered or explained where in fact the theory may not explain the phenomenon at all. Skinner (1953) eloquently states that in our trying to figure out the purpose of behavior and using various concepts to explain behavior (e.g., goals, incentives, and even habits) we needlessly complicate the explanation of behavior, and lead ourselves away from a concise and efficacious explanatory system. To understand why a child turns toward a piece of candy or an executive feels anxiety and depression when promoted, we need not turn to constructs such as intrinsic motivation or fear of success. These explanations, Skinner argues, are actually misleading. When theorizing, he says, we think we know something more than we did before, but these explanations are derived from the phenomenon and unless they are anchored in further empirical networks (Cronbach and Meehl,

1955) relating the constructs to other independently anchored data about the child or executive, the constructs are tautological (MacCorquodale and Meehl, 1948). And *if* they are validated in this fashion, then *do* we know more than before anyway? Or could we have known as much simply by observing the *class* of variables the child has previously responded to in a similar fashion, or the *class* of executives that have responded in a similar fashion to a promotion, and made as accurate a prediction. In fact, knowing the functional relationship between the response and the class of eliciting stimuli, atheoretical proponents say, we can effectively and directly modify behavior by various methods of stimulus and response control, avoiding ambiguous and potentially misleading theories.

While the atheoretical perspective provided a corrective influence for a psychology which had become excessively mentalistic during the first two decades of this century (Chaplin and Krawiec, 1974), the use of theoretical terms is both unavoidable and useful. Theoretical assumptions are implied when one chooses one set of behaviors or facts to attend to rather than other sets. The choice by the experimenter to use pigeons, or by the clinician to inquire about toilet training or about a person's closest current friends, implies particular theoretical frameworks whether or not the experimenter or clinician wishes to recognize or make explicit these guiding frameworks. Thus the clinician who takes an early childhood history is guided by assumptions about human nature, and these will lead the clinician to certain predictions regarding the amenability of the client to a particular treatment, strategy, or model. The theory will affect the psychotherapist's practice in terms of number of sessions per week, amount of time per session, length of treatment, the nature of therapeutic goals, and the focus and nature of the treatment sessions. The psychoanalytic psychotherapist may feel that a detailed inquiry and a working through of childhood losses are critical for improvement of a depressive client, while a psychotherapist who is guided by social learning theory may feel that engineering the client's daily schedule—so that the client is heavily engaged in peer contact that prevents the client from behaving depressively—forms the crux of the treatment.

The language of the psychotherapist is a critical factor in understanding how theory will impact upon practice. An example from the history of psychology is the Structuralists' use of the term observer *(O)* rather than the Behaviorists' use of the term subject *(S),* denoting the *O* as an active participant who is involved in the introspective process rather than the passive subject of the experimenter's manipulation and study. In clinical practice, identifying a person as a "patient," a "case," or a "client" may have quite different effects on the client's and the psychotherapist's attitudes and relationships. A psychotherapist may involve a client in planning the client's future but be less inclined to do so with a case, which is more likely to be "managed" in case management meetings. A person who is called "obsessive," implying a static, trait-like quality, will be more likely to maintain obsessions than one who is told he is obsessing, an action for which he is responsible. The therapist also is subject to the behavioral predispositions promoted by his or her theoretical assumptions. Supervision can explore the explicit theoretical assumptions and implicit metaphors or assumptions about people and about the various labels or syndromes. These assumptions are manifest and can be traced by the therapist's choices, such as at which particular points in the session what types of interventions are made, what choice of terms the therapist uses, and how the duration and frequency of sessions are structured. One supervisee, who was authoritarian in her relationships with people, used the term "children" when working with 14 to 17-year-olds. The resentment it engendered and the consequent acting out and failure of the youths to assume responsibility were difficult for the therapist to relate to the subordination that the term "children" and her other similar belittling actions created. These stemmed from her implicit models of how human relationships work and, parenthetically, were illustrated in supervision by her superficial obeisance to her image of the supervisor's imputed power.

Some Functions of Theory

Theories perform several functions. Theories are conservative and restrict us to a narrow range of phenomena deemed scientifically acceptable (Kuhn, 1962). The use of theories provides the advantages of (Kuhnian) normative science, including the avoidance of conceptual nihilism, the benefits of scientific communication of findings by means of a consensual semeiotic system, the ability to contrast theories with each other, and the orderly progression of knowledge. Wegener's (Hallam, 1975) theory of continental displacement or drift is an illustration of the conservative nature of scientific acceptance of novel theories. In 1915 he published his proposal that the world's land was one primordial continent, Pangaea. He marshaled considerable fossil, geological, and geographical evidence for the articulation of continents with each other. Yet within 15 years his evidence was dismissed, his theory derided, and his reputation suffered various attacks. For geologists and geophysicists to accept Wegener's theory would have been a costly development in terms of "retooling" the scientists' conceptual schemas and reinterpreting the canonical knowledge of the time. When normative science becomes staid, and an alternative perspective develops unavoidable evidence, some of which is anomalous with canonical knowledge and important enough not to be dismissed, then the paradigm shift occurs. The new approach provides a qualitative Gestalt-like shift, according to Kuhn (1962), in the scientists' perceptions of which data are admissible, which phenomena are to be attended to, and which methodologies are proper. Other theorists (Meehl, 1978) contend that theories fade away slowly rather than suddenly dying. Psychology has examples of both suddenly and gradually expiring systems of thought.

Once a paradigm prevails, professionals structure their experiences within this new world view. When criticism toward and discomfort with the medical model of abnormal behavior reaches a crescendo, an alternate model—such as the social psychological approaches emphasizing impression management (Braginsky, Braginsky, and Ring, 1969), facework (Goffman, 1967), or situational or contextual determinants (Rosenhan, 1973)—will become recognized as an acceptable and even quintessential explanation for abnormal behavior.

Perhaps one way for the reader to assess the impact of a new conceptualization is to examine one. One approach that may have a great impact in coming years is catastrophe theory (Zeeman, 1976). The theory of the catastrophe holds that phenomena are often discontinuous and take the form of sudden transformations. Traditionally, mathematical equations—predominantly differential equations— have been the ideal in describing phenomena. Einstein's relativity equation in physics and Hull's hypothetico-deductive system in psychology are examples of theories in the continuity or increment framework. Catastrophe theory holds that the dog's choice to attack or retreat, the mother's abuse of a child, and the patient's decision to call a therapist to initiate psychotherapy are essentially discrete decisions. While underlying dimensions may describe these events in terms of amount of threat to the dog, or frustration tolerance of the mother, or distress felt by the patient, the nature of the events stretches continuity approaches beyond their limits. That is, many phenomena are discrete, all or none events, when we consider the sequential behavior of the organisms, given that the organism exceeded the threshold for a behavior. Thus when a dog has attacked, a greater amount of threat will be needed for it to terminate the fight and to flee instead. Once a client attends an initial session the decision matrix regarding "attending psychotherapy sessions" assumes a different form. A small change in a continuous dimension (client's distress) can result in dramatic qualitative changes (attending therapy). The following simplified illustration of the cusp model of catastrophe theory may help in understanding how this new theory, and theories generally, allow new areas of research to emerge and more accurate prediction statements to develop.

Figure 1, for simplicity's sake, does make a critical assumption. To be sure, initiating psychotherapy is likely to be a function of several parameters, and the control surface may be more complex than depicted below. However, assuming the decision is based on a global feeling of despair versus self-satisfaction, one can see that when a client feels neither distress nor security, no changes in behavior

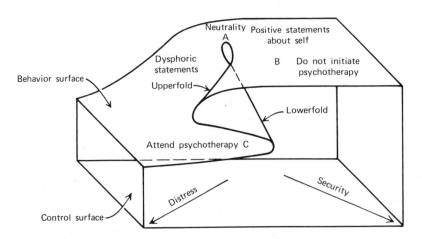

FIGURE 1. The cusp model of catastrophe theory.

will occur and current behavior will continue (position A). As distress or security on the control surface exerts a pull, the person's position on the behavior surface will change. If security increases a person may move to position B. If distress increases a person may reach the upperfold in the behavior surface and be ready for a sudden change in behavior. Given an increment in distress, the person may then be characterized as in position C. A person moves on the horizontal parts of the behavioral surface, jumping from the upper fold to the lower surface and from the lower fold to the upper behavioral surface, without traversing the underside of the cusp. The novel features of catastrophe theory emerge when we consider the client as he or she feels more security. A threshold or a continuity model would have the client not attending psychotherapy at the same point where the previous decision to attend was made. However, the catastrophe model, having the person at point C now, would require the person to traverse to the lowerfold before nonattendance in psychotherapy would occur. Considerably more security would be required to change the behavior, because that person would need to go under the cusp to reach the lowerfold. Catastrophe theory, then, is illustrative of how a theory can present a new, and more predictive framework.

Definitions

Cronbach and Meehl (1955), Harris (1960), Marx (1963), MacCorquodale and Meehl (1948), and Kantor (1957) provide the sources of the following definitions and framework.

When observers can agree that a physically measurable action occurred we can define this occurrence as an *event.* Events are our primary data. Thus a client lapsing into 60 seconds of nonspeaking is an event. Each event is labeled, and by virtue of labeling becomes an abstraction, termed an *intervening variable.* We can label the 60 seconds of nonspeaking as "silence" or "reflection," depending on our theoretical presuppositions. Given several events on the datum plane (Figure 2), we may wish to construe or infer a relationship between the data that involve abstracting, theorizing, or employing constructs in a network.

The following observations of a client in therapy serve to illustrate how a clinical theory is employed. A client came to therapy after a weekend at a resort hotel where he and his wife spent their honeymoon several years earlier. In

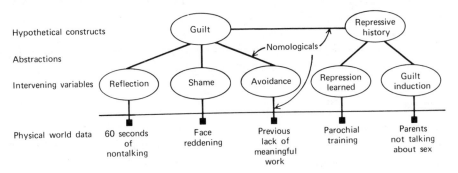

FIGURE 2.   Nomological network.

response to the therapist's statement, "How was your weekend?" the client did not speak for a minute. During the nontalking or silence, the client's face reddened, his eyes glanced upward toward the therapist several times, and the therapist recalled that the previous three sessions were spent with the client avoiding mention of his spouse and sex. From prior information the therapist may have found a strict and repressive childhood training regimen both in school and at home, and he might infer the presence of guilt from the history and the current behaviors of the client. Our concepts are hypothetical. That is, we know them from the data, inductively, or we can begin with them and assess their ability to fit the data deductively. The intervening variables are related to a higher order of abstraction called a *hypothetical construct;* for example, "guilt" in Figure 2. This term differs from the intervening variable in that, as a superordinate construct, it has *surplus meaning.* Invoking a term such as "guilt," "schizophrenic," "nude encounter group," or "psychotherapy" has meaning beyond the particular set of "data-intervening variable-hypothetical construct" chains one is intending in a particular instance.

This scheme is termed a *nomological network.* The lines linking data to intervening variables, intervening variables to hypothetical constructs, and hypothetical constructs to each other are called *nomologicals.* In conventional terms the nomological link between data and the intervening variables is an operational definition. The resulting web or network is usually termed a *theory.* Much of the debate described earlier between atheoretical and theoretical approaches concerns the degree to which superordinate constructs are palpably related to data or events. Kantor (1957) asserts "unless constructs are derived from events, they are likely to be autistic creations" (p. 59). He advises that we keep the events directly before us, so we will not be confused by "licentious products of autistic creation" (p. 59), which unanchored constructs become. This is the problem of the construct's surplus meaning.

Opposing the drawbacks of the surplus meaning problem are the benefits of hypothetical constructs; the ability to understand many events with few constructs. Miller (1959) graphically illustrated that when relating a set of three independent variables with three dependent variables, nine univariate relationships are possible (variable 1 of set A with variables 1, 2, and 3 of set B, variable 2 of set A with variables 1, 2, and 3 of set B, and so forth). With the use of one construct, the number of relationships reduce to six (each variable to the construct). With sets of four or five variables the savings increase geometrically (16 versus 8 and 25 versus 10, respectively). Thus an empirically anchored construct may create a savings in terms of the profusion of the number of relationships and in terms of our parsimonious conceptualization of the events.

Emergence of Models

Psychological theorizing has avoided the construction of "grand old theories" that was characteristic of its earlier years, instead constructing mini-theories and models. This may be due in part to the avoidance of the old "autistic creations" or unanchored constructs, and in part to a more sophisticated stage in psychology's growth as a discipline [as Kuhn (1962) describes the development of scientific disciplines].

Models are essentially analogies which can take any of a wide variety of forms, from a mathematical equation [as in W. K. Estes' (1959) statistical models of learning] to pictorial displays [as in Broadbent's (1957) models of human attention] to physical representations [as in Watson (1968) and Crick's double helix model of DNA]. In the following chapters which describe various models of psychotherapy supervision, the reader may wish to keep in mind both the advantages and limitations, and criteria for the use of models.

Lachman (1960) lists four benefits of model building. Models as a *method of representation* allow us to work with the phenomena. Representing light as particles permits theorizing and perhaps novel conceptions and empirical findings to emerge. Related to this is the use of *rules of inference* with models. In psychotherapy, if an increase in trust in the therapist will be accompanied by increased self-disclosure by the client, then by inference we may postulate that a trust inducing supervisor will elicit more supervisee revelations of errors, allowing supervision to progress rapidly. As seen in the two preceding points, models may help in the *interpretation of data and relating it to theory.* Observing a warm supervisor's high success rate may suggest to us that the fulfillment of the Rogerian model—which includes unconditional positive regard as an essential condition—might have relevance to psychotherapy supervision. Extending client-centered theory to supervision may help, then, in generating a way for us to conceptualize supervision, and can lead to research propositions.

Models can provide pictorial (visual) representation which can aid in the intuitive grasp of the conceptualization of a phenomenon. A diagram of the psychoanalyst's seating position vis-à-vis the psychoanalysand's supine position, or putting students on the couch to experience the encouragement of transference, is a richer way to teach about maximizing transference and the psychoanalytic process than is an hour lecture on transference.

Chapanis (1961) adds that models help us *describe and understand complex phenomena* and *learn complex skills.* The latter can be accomplished when models are operationalized, as in the case of computer simulation of psychotherapy situations and audio-visual techniques in teaching and learning psychotherapy [see especially the chapters by Akamatsu (16), Forsyth and Ivey (18), and Kagan (19)]. The use of models in this literal fashion allows us to *see new relationships,* particularly with the option of repeated playing back of significant interactions captured on tape. Models provide a *framework for experimentation,* both in allowing phenomena to be seen more clearly and in the use of the model both as a research tool and as an object for conceptual refinement. As a data gathering tool, models can be quite cost effective, and allow us to capture previously unattainable evidence. The model allows us to experiment with minimal cost. If we were interested in how much personal revelation by the therapist is necessary to evoke a certain amount of self-disclosure in the client, simulation or role playing in a seminar may provide some information in answering this question, as well as providing a kind of information, direct and experiential, that is essential in the teaching of complex skills such as psychotherapy. Experimenting with the degree to which seating arrangements facilitate self-disclosure in a seminar setting is less costly than trying the seating arrangements with clinic patients. And, of course, models are *fun*. People are attracted by the concise, pictorial presentation of a gestalt that provides an intuitively helpful crystallization of a process or phenomenon.

Models, to be sure, have limitations. Simon and Newell (1963) suspect that models are prone to *Type II errors* or making erroneous assertions broader than the phenomenon. Lachman (1960) notes that a model may invite us to *overgeneralize*, and entice us into *logical fallacies. Relationships discovered in the model may not hold true.* For example, the social psychological model that in a relationship liking increases if a person initially received no reinforcement, but subsequently did receive reinforcement may not hold true for a person in the initial stages of psychotherapy. The therapy situation might call for an immediate positive trusting experience so self revelation could occur quickly and efficaciously. In the face of no reinforcement the client may not return to allow the social psychology model liking process to be manifest.

To the extent that a model is *not deployable,* has *limited scope,* and is *imprecise,* it *diverts useful energy.*

This, then, provides a background that can be used in evaluating the theory and models that are presented by the authors of the following chapters. Some express their constructs explicitly while others more implicitly embed their models and measurement or data bases in their descriptions of psychotherapy and its supervision.

REFERENCES

Abroms, G. M. Supervision as metatherapy. In F. Kaslow (Ed.), *Supervision, consultation and staff training in the helping professions.* San Francisco: Jossey Bass, 1977.

Braginsky, B. M., Braginsky, D. D., and Ring, K. *Methods of madness.* New York: Holt, Rinehart & Winston, 1969.

Broadbent, D. E. A mechanical model for human attention and immediate memory. *Psychological Review,* 1957, *64,* 205–215.

Chapanis, A. Men, machines, and models. *American Psychologist,* 1961, *16,* 113–131.

Chaplin, J. P., and Krawiec, T. S. *Systems and theories of psychology* (3rd ed.). New York: Holt, Rinehart and Winston, 1974.

Cronbach, L. J. The two disciplines of scientific psychology. *American Psychologist,* 1957, *12,* 671–684.

Cronbach, L. J., and Meehl, P. E. Construct validity in psychological tests. *Psychological Bulletin,* 1955, *52,* 281–302.

Dollard, J. Doob, L. W., Miller, N. E., Mowrer, D. H., and Sears, R. R. *Frustration and aggression.* New Haven, Conn.: Yale University Press, 1939.

Erikson, E. H. *Childhood and society.* New York: W. W. Norton, 1950.

Estes, W. K. The statistical approach to learning theory. In S. Koch (Ed.), *Psychology: A study of a science* (Vol. 2). New York: McGraw Hill, 1959, pp. 380–391.

Fiske, D. W. Can a personality construct be empirically validated? *Psychological Bulletin,* 1973, *80,* 89–92.

Frank, J. D. *Persuasion and healing* (Rev. ed.). Baltimore: Johns Hopkins University Press, 1973.

Goffman, E. *Interaction ritual.* New York: Anchor Books, 1967.

Hallam, A. Alfred Wegener and the hypothesis of continental drift. *Scientific American,* 1975, *232,* 88–97.

Harris, J. G., Jr. Validity: The search for a constant in a universe of variables. In M. Rickers-Ovsiankina (Ed.), *Rorschach psychology.* New York: Wiley, 1960.

Kantor, J. R. Events and constructs in psychology. *Psychological Record,* 1957, *7,* 55–60.

Kazdin, A. E., and Wilcoxson, L. A. Systematic desensitization and nonspecific treatment effects: A methodological evaluation. *Psychological Bulletin,* 1976, *83,* 729–758.

Kuhn, T. S. *The structure of scientific revolutions.* Chicago: University of Chicago Press, 1962.

Lachman, R. The model in theory construction. *Psychological Review,* 1960, *67,* 113–129.

MacCorquodale, K., and Meehl, P. E. On a distinction between hypothetical constructs and intervening variables. *Psychological Review,* 1948, *55,* 95–107.

Marx, M. The general nature of theory construction. In M. Marx (Ed.), *Theories in contemporary psychology.* New York: Macmillan, 1963.

Marx, M. H., and Hillix, W. A. *Systems and theories in psychology* (2nd ed.). New York: McGraw-Hill, 1973.

McClenahan, J. Portrait of the doctor as a dying man. *The Atlantic Monthly,* 1978, *242,* 86–88.

Meehl, P. E. *Clinical versus statistical prediction: A theoretical analysis and a review of the evidence.* Minneapolis: University of Minnesota Press, 1954.

Meehl, P. E. Theoretical risks and tabular asterisks: Sir Karl, Sir Ronald, and the slow progress of soft psychology. *Journal of Consulting and Clinical Psychology,* 1978, *46,* 806–834.

Miller, N. E. Liberalization of basic S-R concepts: Extensions to conflict behavior, motivation, and social learning. In S. Koch (ed.), *Psychology: A study of a science* (Vol. 2). New York: McGraw-Hill, 1959, pp. 196–292.

Pepper, S. C. *World hypotheses.* Berkeley, Calif.: University of California Press, 1942.

Rosenhan, D. L. On being sane in insane places. *Science,* 1973, *180,* 356–369.

Rotter, J. B. *Social learning and clinical psychology.* Englewood Cliffs, N.J.: Prentice-Hall, 1954.

Simon, H. A., and Newell, A. The uses and limitations of models. In M. Marx (Ed.), *Theories in contemporary psychology.* New York: Macmillan, 1963.

Skinner, B. F. *Science and human behavior.* New York: Free Press, 1953.

Spence, D. P. Analogic and digital descriptions of behavior. *American Psychologist,* 1973, *28,* 479–488.

Strupp, H. H., Fox, R. E., and Lessler, K. *Patients view their psychotherapy.* Baltimore: Johns Hopkins University Press, 1969.

Vaillant, G. E. How the best and the brightest came of age. *Psychology Today,* 1977, *11,* 34–41, 107–110.

Watson, J. D. *The double helix.* New York: Atheneum, 1968.

Zeeman, E. C. Catastrophe theory. *Scientific American,* 1976, *233,* 65–83.

CHAPTER 2

Training Models and the Nature of Psychotherapy Supervision

ALLEN K. HESS

Essentially, supervision involves two individuals, the supervisor and the supervisee, interacting with each other. Each brings to the situation several manifest agenda, as well as latent agenda from other sources such as prior supervisory experiences. Agenda are imposed also by external sources such as licensing laws (see Slovenko's Chapter 28) and by agency requirements (Ekstein and Wallerstein, 1972) such as practica, internship, and residency placements. In this way many supervision participants find themselves together with goals and needs that may conflict or that are differentially ordered (e.g., the supervisor is trying to ensure high quality service to the client while the supervisee is trying to look competent and earn his or her degree). This can lead to various impasses in supervision.

First, the supervisee may find a number of reasons to be unproductive in supervision. He or she may feel it is wasteful to take valuable time away from a heavy caseload to rehash case material for the benefit of the supervisor. Then, too, a supervisor who may appear younger and less experienced than the psychotherapist (see Styczynski's Chapter 3) may raise doubts in the supervisee as to what the supervisor can add to the supervisee's understanding of the case. When supervision is not progressing, the compulsory aspect of supervision to meet legal or funding or agency needs will produce added resentment. If the supervisee is inexperienced and overwhelmed by being entrusted with an actual clinical case, he or she may view supervision as wholly insufficient to address his or her self doubts. One student asked, "Do they [faculty] realize what they are doing? One of these people could kill themselves. They need help. My degree doesn't mean a thing—it's academic. These patients are hurting real pain!" In summary, the supervisee comes to supervision with a panoply of preconceptions and needs, some of which are unrecognized by both parties.

Second, the supervisor may have various activities he or she would rather be doing. Reward systems for supervisors in academic settings are uncommon despite recommendations by such bodies as the American Psychological Association to reward supervisory activities (1976). Thus academic supervisors may be devoting more time to research and writing than to seeing supervisees. If the supervisor lacks training and didactic or experiential preparation for supervision, he or she may consider it an activity that is puzzling and, in its ambiguity, repellent. The more clinically inclined supervisor may prefer to do psychotherapy than to hear about someone else's cases. Thus many reasons may obstruct the supervisor from operating optimally in supervision.

Should the supervisee and supervisor both bring agenda that dispose them toward recalcitrance, then they may enter into a collusion whereby they pass the time in each other's company, sometimes pleasantly, but neither learning very much. Even if one of them is motivated to discuss pertinent issues, the weight of the dolor of the other may be sufficient to bring the relationship back to one that is inert.

More likely, the pair find themselves in an unstructured human relationship, the rules of which are largely unarticulated. In many cases the task remains unspoken (both *know* they are in supervision, but what this consists of is unsaid), and it may remain so purposefully on the supervisor's part in a misguided effort to see how the student structures the supervision or "handles ambiguity." Instead of this one-sided guessing game, some clear understanding of the tasks (see Rioch's Chapter 6) and models of supervision would provide frameworks for the two to work together and help each other grow (see Barnat's Chapter 5).

The notion that supervision is essentially a dyadic human interaction with a focus on modifying the behavior of the supervisee, so he or she may provide better service to a third person (patient) ordinarily not present, underlies the following models.[1] Each model has three characteristics describing it: (a) its goals, (b) the degree to which the supervisee can choose to attend the sessions, both physically and psychologically, and (c) the nature of the relationship. These are shown in Table 1.

LECTURER

Essentially, this model of supervision is one-sided, and involves an acknowledged master who presents his or her ideas to a group. The goal of the lecturer is to acquaint the audience with his or her views, theories, or techniques. The participants are the lecturer and the audience, members of which may be quite distant from the lecturer, to the extent that some people may hear and see the presentation some time later on audio-visual tape. The members may attend the lecture for various reasons, including increasing their armamentarium of psychotherapy skills, seeing a person whose work they have read and heard about, and for the stimulation value of hearing how someone else handles the cases one struggles with in day-to-day clinical work.

The lecture has numerous advantages. It is economical, allowing many people to attend simultaneously. The exciting lecturer may stimulate discussions, study

[1]Watson (1973) has proposed a similar schema. His has six models: (a) supervisory group, (b) case consultation, (c) tutorial, (d) peer group, (e) tandem, and (f) team, with descriptions of them on several dimensions.

Table 1. Models of psychotherapy supervision

Model	Goal	Choice	Relationship
Lecturer	Convey global conceptual schemes and technique. Generate enthusiam	High	One to mass audience
Teacher	Teach specified content and skills within programmatic scheme	Moderate	Superordinate to subordinate
Case review	Explore ways of thinking and relating to cases.	Low	Elder to younger
Collegial-Peer	Support and gaining a different, unforced view	High	Equals in shared intimacy
Monitor	Maintain at least minimally acceptable levels of service	Low	External censor, evaluator
Therapist	Help psychotherapist grow and reach new levels of adaptiveness with self and clients	Moderate to high	Benign supervisor, trusted model

groups, and new techniques to be tried out on one's clients. This imparting of excitement is hard to overestimate. In relatively rural areas the impact of a visit from a well-known therapist is referred to years later. It provides redirection and enrichment for therapists, often rejuvenating them or preventing them from "burning out." The lecture allows novice therapists to be exposed to concepts and to the clinical inference process in the security of the anonymity that a large audience provides. Often discussions and question-and-answer sessions after the presentation provide a measure of socialization for novices. They can observe the critical processes of advanced professionals who may question the speaker, especially if the theory is not compatible with those of some members of the audience. The subsequent debates show students how a seemingly sensible approach may contain flaws or at least be viewed quite differently by someone espousing a different view.

The lecture allows people to partake or sample a line of inquiry without committing themselves to that view beyond the lecture session. It provides the freedom to explore, and often gives reference materials for further exploration but without the compulsory element common to other models. The lecture allows a practitioner, who has not engaged in formal study for some time, to assess where the field has gone, and some lecturers may offer some measure of relief in the discovery that the field has not left the person far behind.

One disadvantage of the lecture is that one's own questions and agenda items may not be met. If the material and level of presentation of the lecture are too narrow, then some groups—beginners or advanced—will be unsatisfied. In effect, one's time is wasted. Moreover, a poor presentation may discourage members of the audience from pursuing a potentially useful therapy modality. Finally, lectures may give naive listeners the mistaken impression that they have license to practice techniques they have heard about but have not mastered in any professional sense.

Relationships

The relationship between the lecturer and audience is one of a leader to a mass ego (Brown, 1968; Sargant, 1957). The lecturer may experience the power of being in communication with a following, and realize the satisfaction of being on the same "wave length" with a mass and helping them discover new ways to work with their clients. The audience might feel a surprising closeness to the effective lecturer, and feel the social support of having shared the experience with other audience members.

A number of effective lecturers have used this model to teach psychotherapy. Teodoro Ayllon (behavioral), Ernst Beier (communicational), Albert Ellis (rational-emotive), Rollo May (existential-analytic), Albert Scheflin (interactional), Thomas Stampfl (implosive behavioral), and Otto Will (Sullivanian) are particularly effective in presenting their frameworks in this fashion.

Some modifications of the lecture model can include active demonstrations of interviews, as John Rosen (direct analysis) preferred, small group discussions and workshops following the lecture, or even the inclusion of the audience as an active participant in the style of J. L. Moreno (psychodrama). The essence of the relationship is still that of a leader to a large social group. As such, the lecturer may not be aware of the reactions he or she may arouse in the audience. This can be seen when members, perhaps after the lecture, approach the lecturer and make requests or speak in terms of intense closeness, as though the lecturer had been relating to them specifically during the talk.

TEACHER

This model has as its goal the transmission of specific content, and sometimes the imparting of skills by one who is eminently qualified by some sociopolitical structure to one who is less qualified. The teacher, hired and sanctioned by a school, is mandated to cover specific material and skills in a curriculum. The student enrolling in the school is obliged to master the course content, usually in pursuit of a degree or certificate. As such, the student's degree of choice of teachers varies. One instructor may teach a course that is required of all students, several instructors may offer the course at different points in the student's program, or the course may be optional. Students (though unbeknownst to them) may exercise considerable choice by requesting a course by a specific instructor, a fact that does not escape the attention of the head of a department and the other faculty members.

The teacher model has flexibility in the variety of techniques it subsumes. In a large class setting the lecture may be used. More usually in professional training a smaller class is the norm, often taking the form of a seminar. The focus in the seminar may range from didactic reviews of research to presentations of clinical material, and even to the use of microcounseling (see Forsyth and Ivey's Chapter 18), Interpersonal Process Recall (see Kagan's Chapter 19), and other personal skill development exercises with the students in the course. The goal of the course and its method or form should be isomorphic and both should be clear to the teacher and students. If the teacher is unclear about this, the course will likely not reach its goals. The students—as consumers of the course—need to know the goals and the tasks that will be required of them.

In specifying the goals, some clarity in the course's articulation with the curriculum of the program is necessary. While in its extreme form rigid specification can compromise a teacher's academic freedom, this is not usual. Too often the other extreme occurs, and courses in a series fail to build on each other and form an integrated, complementary sequence. Consideration of the program's goals can help in the structuring of courses and course sequences. This will help, too, in guiding the instructor as to which techniques will best suit the course.

Relationship

The teacher and student are in a superordinate-subordinate role relationship. This can be modulated by the specific course structure, the teacher's style, and the dynamics of the group of students. Even if a teacher, in his or her effort to be democratic, feels the students and teacher have managed to become coequals, the students rarely feel this. The structural elements—(a) the sanction of the teacher as a master and the students as learners, (b) the responsibility of the teacher regarding the structure of the course, and (c) the ultimate evaluative responsibility of the teacher to grade or endorse the student—all serve to maintain the superordinate-subordinate relationship (see Rioch's Chapter 6).

The continued relationship between students and teachers can work toward a feeling of coequality. More often the one-up, one-down relationship is maintained and strengthened. However the continuity of the relationship can be effectively used to include the students in course planning as they progress in the program. This can help to tailor the curriculum to the kinds of activities they wish to pursue. For example, a student in a sequence on adult psychotherapy may have interests in existential psychotherapy and correctional psychology. If the instructor knows of the student's interests, he or she could design a section in the course where the student presents material on the life term prisoner's adjustment or coming to terms with his dilemma. The teacher model is flexible enough to accommodate a variety of student needs, given the planning necessary to clarify a course's goals and matching these to concordant techniques.

CASE CONFERENCE

The case review or case conference involves staff members, often in the company of senior staff or consultants, discussing new or ongoing cases in a clinical setting.

New cases involve intake workers presenting data from initial interviews. Questions from the other staff may reflect different theoretical predilections and experience bases, and provide feedback for the intake staff. The questions and subsequent discussion regarding case management and disposition serve to instruct less experienced staff and students, interns, and residents in the clinical decision-making process in terms of gathering, integrating, and presenting data. Case reviews of ongoing cases can provide extensive learning experiences when participants prepare the case for presentation and question openly in a nonthreatening fashion. The therapist can try out suggestions, and can review the results in subsequent case conferences.

The goals of the case conference include helping the participants clarify their clinical decision making, gaining vicarious case experience, and providing the client with the benefits of the collective wisdom and resources of the staff.

Relationship

The relationship of members of the case conference is one of elders and youth. Invariably senior staff and consultants review the work of the junior staff and students. To the extent that this structure is relaxed or minimized in favor of a participatory relationship, the junior status people will be able to state their reasoning in an open, nondefensive fashion. The senior staff will have more material available with which to instruct the staff. This open stance can be augmented by the senior staff sharing experiences and errors, which will promote more open listening by junior staff. Since the experiences of senior staff are limited, and junior staff may have some intriguing cases, the case review often can be rewarding for senior professionals if they can adopt a "learning set" in addition to their teaching set.

All too frequently case conferences are seen as time wasting sessions. This is both regrettable and true. The sessions often have stultifying effects on the students who are required to attend. Senior staff may ponderously pontificate on their views, making the case conference an exercise in exacting doctrinal obeisance from junior staff. Only one rebuke is needed for junior staff to understand the survival value of theoretical orthodoxy. The real, rather than espoused, values of the clinic or agency will be vividly apparent in case conferences.

The benefits of case conferences, in addition to those listed above, can include learning about the persons on the staff as resources for one to consult on various problems. Case conferences can help to keep cases from being "lost in the shuffle" of a clinician's caseload, and to expose one's clinical reasoning in an effort to continue one's professional development.

COLLEGIAL-PEER

This model involves two or more persons who occupy equal role status positions and develop a cooperative relationship. While a friendly competition can exist, the dominant tenor of the relationship is mutual growth. More often than not the choice of partners is made on the basis of personal compatibility, as well as professional respect, and evolves as one person reviews an interesting or troublesome case with a colleague during some free time.

Because of the informality of this model, its goals are often unstated. The satisfaction of talking over clinical issues that are intrinsically interesting to the colleagues is as important as any other factor. Other important goals include gaining a different view of a case, and getting consensual validation about one's reasoning before exposing it to a staff conference or working with one's client on the issue, or after getting feedback which jars one's conceptual base. A peer can gain by recitation of the "facts" of the case to a trusted peer with the result that the psychotherapist who has over—or under—valued a point or even omitted a critical element in the case can be corrected. This was illustrated when a clinician interviewed a couple in the throes of marital trouble and forgot to ask about the circumstances under which they initially decided to get married, which had a great bearing on their unsatisfactory marriage. A peer review quickly disclosed this omission. Often simply "talking a case aloud" to someone will reveal to the psychotherapist how he or she conceptualizes the case, verbalizes the conceptualization, and acts or fails to act in the sessions, particularly when the therapist learns what the colleague does in therapy and is able to compare his or her own style with the colleague's style.

Among the other benefits of the model are greater case exposure for the "helper" in the relationship, the trying on of the consultant-supervisor role for the "helper," and mutual solidification of professional roles and relationships for both.

Two peers can become disruptive to a program when their relationship becomes exclusive of other peers and supervisors and they participate in a "folie a deux." This is an infrequent risk since one or both persons will have "significant other" professionals in their daily activities that will prevent the exclusive and suffocating isolation of the two from occurring.

Relationship

While the relationship is of two equals, often one is more senior than the other. Sometimes they will fluctuate with one being more senior or expert in one area —for example, psychotherapy with families—and the other more expert in another area—say, counseling with the organically impaired. Vaillant (1977) describes more generally how a person in a profession may pair up with a professional several years his or her senior. The senior person can provide personal, professional, and social support for the beginning professional's first few years, acting in a sense as a sponsor.

Personal styles are the critical factor in the collegial relationship. Certainly other peers may have as much or more expertise in the areas the two discuss, but the support and trust developed in their relationship can sustain them in their professional role development as psychotherapists.

MONITOR

The monitor role is one that arises out of legal or bureaucratic fiat. Consumer sensitivity and the increase in third party payments contribute to a recent rise in pressure for review of health services. A particular form of monitoring, the Professional Standards Review Organization (PSRO) has set up guidelines, for example, that psychodiagnostic activities must meet (American Psychological Association, 1976). Similarly, administrations of clinics currently set up record review committees to meet current professional standards or the state legal guidelines and employ the monitor model. Augmenting the trend to adopt this model is the issue of umbrella coverage (see Glenwick and Stevens' Chapter 17, and Slovenko's Chapter 28), or of a professional employing para- or subprofessionals to perform delegated activities. As this increases, the need to document and monitor services will increase.

The goal of the monitor is a conservative one at this point. It is to see that no harm is done. While recommendations can be made by the monitor, his or her essential goal is a protective one where the monitor and agency seek to minimize risk. Although no one would claim to ignore exceptionally novel and positive treatment, in fact the monitor wants to see that minimally acceptable practice is performed. Anything novel then will be seen as a potential risk. The dictum that the healer must cause no harm with the treatment is the focus of the monitor. The agency will claim that high quality service is the goal, but the contingencies employed acknowledge low risks, employ negative sanctions, and have no provisions to recognize superior work.

Relationship

The monitor serves as an external censor and evaluator. As such, much anxiety and hostility may be engendered. Unfortunately, the monitor model has ignored the dispensing of favorable feedback. Including positive options would make the monitor model more of a learning situation, remove the emphasis on conservatism, and lessen the hostility and fear that staff members often express about the monitoring personnel and mechanisms.

The element of choice is absent in this model, augmenting the resentment directed toward the monitors. Some participation by the staff (and perhaps patient groups) in formulating the criteria and selecting the monitors would make the process more acceptable. When monitors are personnel external to the agency, this may be more difficult. One way to make monitoring palatable and accountable, also, would be for evaluations of monitors to be routinely collected from psychotherapists as well as other sources. A form of blind review of cases may be needed so monitors would not be unduly influenced by the psychotherapists' evaluation of the monitor.

The monitor model will be increasing in the future. It behooves patients, psychotherapists, third-party payers, and monitors for this model to include a learning element for the therapists. The model should include a feedback element for monitors, too.

THERAPIST

The therapist model may be the most common for supervisors to assume. This probably occurs by default because the supervisor may not have considered various other supervisory processes and models. Since the supervisor is a psychotherapist now involved in a helping interaction with another human, it is not surprising at all that supervision may become psychotherapy. Moreover a supervisor, either from his or her perspicacity, or from a tendency to overpathologize [cf. Berne (1963), Chap. 14], may see disjunctive elements in the supervisee's personality or interpersonal style that require attention. More explicit reasons to use this model include a focus by some "schools" of psychotherapy on the psychotherapist's personal growth (see Barnat's Chapter 5), on eliminating or making the psychotherapist aware of blind spots, or on the necessity for practitioners to understand the technique (and either calibrate or sensitize the psychotherapist to the techniques' power) by experiencing the treatment (see Wessler and Ellis's Chapter 14).

Ostensibly the goals of the psychotherapy model are to help the therapist grow, free him or her from blindness about the warp and woof of his or her personality and interpersonal skills, and understand the treatment in great depth and intensity. The supervisor may hold vague goals of "helping" the supervisee and may slip into the psychotherapy model in his or her effort to help. Or, feeling the lack of training in supervision in his or her own career, the supervisor may resolve this ambiguity by engaging the supervisee in psychotherapy.

Relationship

It is questionable whether the psychotherapy model is a viable supervisory model. Certain human relationship qualities are similar between supervision and psychotherapy. Trust in the supervisor, or at least the perception of him or her as benign, is essential. The supervisee may need to delve openly into personal and possibly unattractive aspects of his or her history or current feelings, particularly (and perhaps solely) as they relate to the therapist's functioning. However, inherent in the supervisory role is an evaluative component which conflicts with the role of the supervisor as therapist. The supervisor who does therapy as supervision will face a situation during student or trainee evaluations when one or both roles will be compromised. The border becomes blurred between a trainee's self revelations constituting therapy or intense supervision of countertransference. Supervision which focuses on the trainee's skill development—rather than attempting to change the trainee's personality—is supervision with a chance at succeeding. Brodsky, in Chapter 30, and Gardner, in Chapter 29, point out issues (sex role, racial, ethnic, and social class stereotypy) that are personal but are appropriate for supervisory discussion. However, when personality change appears necessary, the supervisor is well advised to refer the supervisee to an independent practitioner who would have no connection with the training program. The supervisor ought to continue the supervision, pursuing countertransference issues up to, but not into, the personal therapy of the supervisee. One pair of universities, in physical proximity but administratively separate, takes each other's students as therapy clients with no feedback expected or forthcoming about the student.

Certainly the supervisor may be attracted to the psychotherapy model when the supervisee replicates a focal interaction that is occurring in the psychotherapy. If the supervisee performs, vis-à-vis the supervisor, as the client does to the student therapist, or the supervisee acts toward the client and supervisor in a nontherapeutic fashion, psychotherapeutic intervention with the supervisee may be indicated. Instead of the supervisor engaging the supervisee in psychotherapy in supervision, he or she may deal with the problem as one of *supervision,* with the focus on the clinical management of the client, given certain resources and limits of the supervisee. For example, one supervisee, who resented his clients when they rejected his nurturance, recalled that his mother was quite forceful in asserting her maternal, caring role. The more personal exploration of this area in the supervisee's life can be dealt with in therapy while the ways in which therapy is structured as a function of his needs, and the alternative ways of conducting therapy, are the proper focus of supervision. When the supervisee is not in ongoing personal therapy more of the supervisee's personal domain is available for exploration. However, this should be done only at the invitation of the supervisee and with the focus and major portion of time still committed to the supervision of the supervisee's therapy practice. If the supervisee has extensive or enduring problems, again, referring him or her to a psychotherapist who will work conjointly and in a nonevaluative fashion would be the preferred alternative. In programs where psychotherapy is required or preferred, the issues of confounding the psychotherapeutic and supervisory processes can be more easily avoided. In fact, Wampler and Strupp (1976) report that 71% of APA-approved clinical psychology training programs recommend (67%) or require (4%) personal psychotherapy for their students.

The issue of evaluation, while important, is secondary to the issue of choice regarding a confound in the psychotherapy model of supervision. When students are assigned supervisors who then use the psychotherapy model, they are put in positions of being forced into revealing themselves to someone with whom they may be incompatible, or even antagonistic. Even if they have been able to engage in a successful psychotherapeutic experience, the forced compliance aspect of the situation that the supervisees feel may stymie the supervisor's best efforts. That is, being compelled to attend psychotherapy may create resistance that diminishes the attractiveness that psychotherapy may have had.

If the supervisee has choice, and the evaluation issue can be successfully resolved, then the psychotherapy model can be a powerful teaching-learning growth experience. The experience of the impact of issues such as time limits, silence, fees, interpretation, reflection, and the power of the psychotherapist role all will become quite real in a way that academic teaching cannot portray. The supervisor as a model psychotherapist is a powerful device for the student to learn how to behave psychotherapeutically. Moreover for the supervisee, the corrective and growth experiences inherent in his or her model are important for the development of a more capable cadre of professionals. Similarly, the amount of time involved in this model can be a demonstration of the program and senior psychologists' concern about the welfare of the newer professionals and the supervisee's clients.

CONCLUSION

The essential premise in this section, then, is that supervision is a quintessential interpersonal interaction with the general goal that one person, the supervisor, meets with another, the supervisee, in an effort to make the latter more effective in helping people in psychotherapy. The models are ways to consider how the relationship may be structured, along with the functions, advantages, liabilities, and role structure of members that are attendant to the relationships. They provide a way of integrating the sections that follow. While each author may expose certain models or elements of models, the schema presented here is a way of ordering their contributions and identifying the models or parts of models they are using.

REFERENCES

American Psychological Association, Board of Professional Affairs, Task Group on Model Criteria Sets. *Model criteria sets.* Washington, D.C.: Author, 1976.

Berne, E. *The structure and dynamics of organizations and groups.* Philadelphia: Lippincott, 1963.

Brown, J. A. C. *Techniques of persuasion.* Middlesex, England: Penguin, 1968.

Ekstein, R., and Wallerstein, R. S. *The teaching and learning of psychotherapy.* New York: Basic Books, 1972.

Sargant, W. *The battle for the mind.* Garden City, N.Y.: Doubleday, 1957.

Vaillant, G. E. *Adaptation to life.* Boston: Little, Brown, 1977.

Wampler, L. D., and Strupp, H. H. Personal therapy for students in clinical psychology: A matter of faith? *Professional Psychology,* 1976, *7,* 195–201.

Watson, K. Differential supervision. *Social Work,* 1973, *18,* 80–88.

PART TWO

Perspectives in Supervision

Part II, "Perspectives in Supervision," consists of seven chapters that present issues in the development of the therapist and supervisor. Chapter 3, *The Transition from Supervisee to Supervisor* by Lyn E. Styczynski, describes the role transition and its attendant tensions that the novice supervisor may experience. Some requisite skills, important choices in supervision, and qualities of the new supervisor are considered. Chapter 4, *From Classroom to Clinic: Supervising the First Psychotherapy Client* by Irving B. Weiner and Robert G. Kaplan, focuses on the special set of learning problems that confront the psychotherapist going from the class into the clinic for the first time. The problems include translating didactic truisms into authentic helping relations—often with the least desirable, most refractory clients—and consolidating some professional identity while this stressful change proceeds. The crucial role the supervisor can play is presented with specific guidelines that can facilitate learning.

Chapter 5, *Psychotherapy Supervision and the Duality of Experience* by Michael R. Barnat, provides a searching account of the psychotherapist's experiencing, and of the ways the experiencing of conflict, limits, feelings and growth can enrich psychotherapy and supervision. Barnat describes how the therapist can affirm his or her personal and professional roles; particularly the supervisory experiences that impede or stimulate this ongoing personal progression, the historical, political, and commercial context of specific supervisions. The supervisee's transition from passively learning "how-to-do-it" (psychotherapy) to experiencing an active integration-of-self, and the problem of separating the supervisee and a supervisor provide illustrations of helpful and harmful supervisory identifications.

In a similar way, Chapter 6, *The Limitations of Supervision in Dynamic Psychotherapy* by Margaret J. Rioch, describes the progression from role produced dynamics ("one up" and "one down" positions) that impede learning to successfully encountering these issues. This enables people in a dynamic relationship to use the human skills of one to increase the human source skills of the other. Rioch extends this process to the group supervision situation.

Chapters 7, 8, and 9 are authored by students with experience in different university training programs and with a variety of supervisors. Chapter 7, *The New Supervisee Views Supervision* by Larry Cohen, describes the intellectual and emotional expectations a supervisee might bring to supervision. Chapter 8, *Super-*

vision from the Perspective of the Supervisee by Leonard Greenberg, focuses on how supervisees can more effectively structure their use of supervisory expertise, especially in the differential use of supervisors who have different areas of strength. Chapter 9, *Psychotherapy Supervision: Supervisees' Perspective* by William R. Marshall and William N. Confer, considers the variety of purposes supervision may serve for the psychotherapist at different points in the psychotherapist's training. The chapters are especially important for students who can gain some perspective on their own exhilaration and trepidation upon entering supervision, and for the supervisor who may need to relearn the students' perspective.

CHAPTER 3

The Transition from Supervisee to Supervisor

LYN E. STYCZYNSKI

The transition from supervisee to supervisor marks an important change in professional identity for the clinician. The student role is relinquished for the role of competent clinician and supervisor. Although there has been much preparation in developing clinical skills, this is rarely the case with supervisory skills. There are no formal courses, processes, or practica through which the clinician learns to supervise, nor are there the rituals or rites of passage which facilitate important role transitions (Sarbin and Allen, 1968). Likewise, literature directly relevant to learning to supervise is sparse. But in spite of this, a significant portion of clinicians' time is frequently devoted to supervision and training (Garfield and Kurtz, 1976). Thus it is important to address the various components of the transition from supervisee to supervisor, first to provide a base for helping future clinicians as they become supervisors, and second to facilitate those who have become supervisors—both recently and in the past—to be more consciously aware of various aspects of the process in which they engage. This paper will provide an examination of these issues by one who has recently made this transition.

What are the major components of the transition to supervisor? First, despite limited formal training for supervising, there are a number of ways through which useful skills can be gained before the transition occurs. Utilizing these past experiences, the new supervisor makes a number of choices, either consciously or unconsciously, as supervising begins. Finally, the supervision ultimately provided by the novice may differ from that of senior colleagues in several predictable ways.

PREPARATION FOR THE SUPERVISORY ROLE

Resources available to new clinical supervisors are varied but limited. Generally, beginning supervisors are able to integrate into their new role skills and experience from a number of previous professional roles, such as supervisee, teacher, therapist, researcher, colleague, and consultant. These experiences are provided by most traditional clinical training programs but are seldom taught for the purpose of developing supervisory skills. Other resources are less readily available. Direct training in supervising is rare, occurring most frequently during postdoctoral training or by private arrangement. Although the practical application of relevant literature within a supervisory situation is of benefit, the literature is often not easily accessible. It seems apparent that none of these resources alone can be adequate in providing the novice with all of the skills required to do supervision. However, each may contribute useful components to be integrated into supervision. A more careful examination of the contributions of each of these resources may be useful in understanding how a clinician formulates the new supervisory role.

Supervisee

As a trainee, the supervisor probably already learned a great deal about the supervisory process. Certain aspects of previous supervision were more useful than others, and this was to some extent influenced by the level of clinical sophistication and the clinical area being supervised. Experience with a number of supervisors has provided a variety of role models from which to choose. The overall theoretical orientation of previous supervisors may also have influenced one's style and goals in supervising as well as one's clinical orientation. For example, within an analytic framework, supervision might focus on the trainee's own personality dynamics and countertransference, with relatively less focus on the nature of the client. However, just as one cannot learn to be a therapist by entering therapy (although it may help), one cannot rely on being supervised to become a skillful supervisor. Role models rarely parallel our own strengths and weaknesses. Future supervisees will have training and personal needs that differ from those the supervisor experienced during training. And certainly there are valid alternative orientations to supervision from those of one's past supervisors.

Teaching

Many new supervisors have done classroom teaching and from this experience and training can develop supervisory skills. This experience enables the new supervisor to be comfortable with the roles of authority and mentor which are common to both teaching and supervision. Teaching also provides experience and skill in the evaluation of the learning needs of students and in the didactic presentation of material. Finally, teaching makes one aware of the limitations of one's impact as an instructor. However, only in tutorial teaching do the intense one-to-one aspects of supervision begin to occur, in which the supervisor or teacher must be keenly attuned to the perspective and responses of the individual student, as well as to the material being taught.

Therapist

Skill as a therapist is a critical resource for the beginning supervisor. Not only is this skill to be imparted to the trainee, but also many of the demands of supervising parallel those of therapy. Most obviously, the supervisor's ability to guide the trainee to successful therapeutic interventions is dependent on the supervisor's own ability to assess the patient's needs and judge appropriate modes of intervention. However, the supervisor's therapy skills are also useful in structuring the supervisory relationship in order to optimize change and development of the student. Careful listening to the trainee's presentation, both verbal and nonverbal, allows the supervisor to obtain necessary information about the patient and to understand what has previously occurred so that modes of intervention most appropriate for the student and patient may be planned. The utilization of therapy skills in supervising allows the supervisor to model the desirable behaviors for the student. Likewise, the students can be helped to observe themselves in various contexts and provided with suggestions and feedback in the context of clinical work and the supervisory relationship. Various models of supervision have, to varying degrees, integrated the roles of therapist and supervisor. In the traditional analytic model the supervisor's functioning might often overlap that of therapist in supervision, while more recent models place greater emphasis on the supervisor using clinical skills to help the student with "learning problems" in supervision (Ekstein & Wallerstein, 1972) or as a base for a more didactic approach (Tarachow, 1963). Thus, although there is some variation in the manner in which the beginning supervisor may choose to utilize clinical skills, competence as a therapist provides an essential component in the development of competence in supervising.

Researcher

Although research skills are less clearly related to supervision, they can nevertheless be very useful to the novice supervisor. Research experience can help develop skills in accurate and reliable observation and integrating observations into testable hypotheses. Participation in research also provides an awareness of the many variables in patients' lives that must be considered in determining change agents. The supervisor experienced in research will probably be more willing to test the hypotheses utilized in formulating a treatment plan and to incorporate new data as it becomes available. Finally, if the supervisor is to incorporate new research in the areas of clinical assessment, intervention, or supervision, it is essential that he or she be skillful in evaluating and integrating studies in appropriate and useful ways.

Colleague and Consultant

Previous experience as a colleague and consultant helps the new supervisor to evaluate and respond to the clinical work of others. Specifically this experience has already placed the beginning supervisor in the position of attempting to understand patients based on the reporting of another person. Likewise, the novice supervisor has experience in critically evaluating the clinical work of other professionals and has learned to express suggestions and opinions in ways which maintain mutual respect. As a colleague participating in training seminars and informal discussions, the new supervisor will have received similar feedback and —ideally—become attuned to his or her own personal strengths and weaknesses, both as a therapist and a consultant. Programs which encourage group participation in training seminars, the use of peers for support, feedback, and clinical input, and openness in assessing one's own strengths, weaknesses, and means of compensation enable students to generalize learning from these experiences to their roles as supervisor.

Literature

There is a useful but sparse literature in the area of supervision which the beginning supervisor can use as a resource. Books by Ekstein and Wallerstein (1972), Bruch (1974), and Tarachow (1963), as well as the present volume, are available to help the new supervisor understand the teaching and learning of clinical skills. Likewise, writers from clinical psychology, psychiatry, counseling, and social work have dealt with a variety of supervisory issues in their respective journals. Unfortunately, the new supervisor is rarely provided supports (e.g., bibliographies or seminars) in exploring this literature, which is often not readily available and which is found in the journals of less familiar disciplines as well as one's own.

Training in Supervision

A limited number of clinicians are able to receive direct training in supervision at the time they begin supervising. This experience is most frequently available in advanced training programs or in settings which utilize hierarchical supervision, with more advanced students teaching their less experienced peers. However, such supervision may also be arranged privately by the beginning supervisor. This training provides the beginning supervisor with feedback from a more experienced and skilled colleague regarding one's style, one's sensitivity, and the appropriateness and usefulness of one's comments in supervision. Such feedback can be an extremely useful component of the new supervisor's development, but there are also limitations. In addition to the patient, trainee, and supervisor, the supervisor's supervisor becomes a fourth person, who is yet another step away from the patient and therapeutic process. This can make communication and role definition within the structure much more difficult, especially for the beginning supervisor. In such a training arrangement, the novice and senior supervisor must also deal with such issues as the extent to which the senior supervisor's views and style should be adopted by the beginner who has distinct personal and clinical attributes. Since the novice probably has not yet integrated the new role as supervisor and may still be developing into a mature therapist, it is important that both the senior and beginning supervisor be aware of the need for new supervisors to develop their own identity—both as supervisors and therapists—if they are to optimally utilize their personal and professional strengths. Nevertheless, such supervising arrangements offer one of the few opportunities available to prepare the clinician specifically for supervising.

The beginning supervisor has a number of potential resources available, including related skills and experience, literature, and direct, ongoing training. Using these limited resources, novice supervisors must then begin to formulate their new roles, making a number of important decisions and choices as they do so.

CHOICES MADE BY THE BEGINNING SUPERVISOR

During the early meetings, the new supervisor makes a number of choices, either conscious or unconscious regarding: (1) modality of supervision, (2) emphasis within supervision, (3) range of focus of supervision, (4) style of supervision, (5) type of role to take with the supervisee, (6) adaptation of training needs of the supervisee, (7) handling of formal evaluations, and (8) accommodating one's own personal and professional limitations as a supervisor. Awareness of these decisions as they occur allows the new supervisor to make well-integrated choices and thus provide optimal supervision.

Modality

The most obvious of these decisions are fairly concrete. A decision must be made regarding the mode of supervision—that is, the format and context of the supervision. The supervisor may utilize process notes, audiotape recording, videotape, direct observation, or cotherapy with the supervisee as the format for supervision. Supervision may be provided in the context of a group, a seminar, or on a one-to-one basis. To some extent, decisions will be influenced by the facilities and orientation of the institution. However, of the choices which remain, the supervisor must select the format and context based on the advantages and disadvantages of each alternative in the context of the trainees' needs and their own skills.

Emphasis

Given the time limitations of supervision, it is impossible to cover all aspects of the clinical material presented. The supervisor must determine where to place the emphasis in supervision. Choices include such areas as case management, theoretical formulation of case material, modes of intervention, or the process occurring in the therapy. Clearly, the emphasis of supervision frequently varies based on the needs of the case and trainee at a particular time.

Breadth of Focus

A decision must also be made regarding the range in which the supervision will be focused. In the context of a broader range, the supervisor might initiate a discussion of general issues presented by such cases. A supervisor taking a narrow focus might discuss specific details of interactions during the therapy hour. The breadth of focus will, in all likelihood, strongly influence choices regarding modality and emphasis.

Style and Role

Decisions regarding more interpersonal aspects of the supervision are also made. The beginning supervisor must determine a general style of supervision—for example, didactic, supportive, authoritative, therapeutic, confronting, or reflective. In selecting a style, the supervisor also determines his or her role in the relationship with the trainee. Supervisors may take on a variety of roles in various combinations, such as administrator, colleague, teacher, role model, consultant, or therapist. The choices of style and role are often limited by the supervisor's own interpersonal modes of relating and are often made unconsciously. However, by making these decisions consciously, the new supervisor can determine in what manner he or she can most comfortably relate to trainees and at the same time be most useful to them. Certainly at times this decision will not only be influenced by characteristics of the supervisor, but also by characteristics of individual trainees—their personalities, expectations of supervision, dependency needs, response to authority, past training, current level of competency, and so on. Thus the supervisor's style and role will need to be sufficiently flexible to negotiate a working relationship with a variety of trainees, but at the same time secure enough to provide useful, consistent structure in the supervision.

Trainee Evaluation

In the early supervisory sessions, the supervisor must make evaluative decisions regarding the trainee. Specifically, the new supervisor must determine the training needs of the student and how his or her own attributes will be used to meet these needs. He or she should decide whether this assessment is to be shared with the trainee. If so, plans for the supervision will involve joint decisions.

The formal evaluation of trainees required by most institutions can be difficult for beginning supervisors. However, at some point a decision must be made, either consciously or unconsciously, about the criteria and process for these evaluations. Will the assessment be based on general competency or development in specific areas? How will various aspects of clinical skills be weighted in the evaluation? How will change and development be assessed? What are the supervisor's expectations for the trainee? Will the trainee be included in the selection of criteria and/or assessment of progress? How and when will feedback be provided to the trainee? Resolution of these questions is often accomplished most easily by making such difficult and complicated decisions early in the supervisory relationship.

Tolerance

Finally, the beginning supervisor must determine the extent to which he or she can tolerate and effectively supervise alternative theoretical orientations and therapeutic styles. It is unrealistic to expect a supervisor to be able to comfortably and effectively supervise any trainee doing any kind of therapy. Honest self-evaluation can help the new supervisor to make initial decisions regarding areas of expertise and personal limitations. When these strengths and limitations are communicated to students, they are able to integrate their own needs with those things the supervisor provides best, thus optimizing their training experiences. Likewise, when these strengths and limitations are communicated to administrators, more appropriate trainees can be assigned. In this way, students who know little about therapeutic technique or who are firmly behaviorally oriented might not be assigned to a supervisor whose skill and emphasis lies in dealing with countertransference. Similarly, beginning students would not be assigned to confrontive, unsupportive supervisors, but rather to more supportive supervisors who may not be as finely critical and sophisticated as the more advanced student needs. And ideally, the novice supervisor might be assigned students who will optimally use his or her areas of expertise but will also be able to tolerate the changes in supervisory style that may occur as the new role evolves.

Influencing Factors

Obviously, none of these decisions are made in a vacuum. The new supervisor is influenced by the agency for which the supervision is provided, and by the facilities, political considerations, and time available for supervision. Personal characteristics of individual supervisors may also strongly influence various aspects of their supervision. The range of supervisory experiences during past training provides the base for their supervisory style. Theoretical biases lead to supervision congruent with the requirements of the orientation. And certainly personality variables influence how supervision decisions are translated into interactions with the trainee.

For example, Dr. C.'s training had been in inpatient treatment and community mental health centers, and his own therapeutic approach emphasized case management and problem solving with the patient. Interpersonally there were few persons with whom he maintained close relationships, and he was most comfortable in situations where he was able to clearly define his role. During his first three years of supervising as Director of Psychology at the local mental health center, he had increasingly come to supervise trainees in small groups, focusing supervision on the management of cases, emphasizing the need to determine the patient's motivation for change early in treatment, and providing minimal personal support to trainees. Trainees found his management suggestions useful but were often anxious and reluctant to spontaneously enlist his help in therapeutic concerns.

A complete discussion of this complex interaction of past experience, theoretical orientation, and personality in formulating a supervisory style would probably warrant an additional paper. However, it should be apparent that all of these components are very much interwoven. A final component is also important in the supervision provided by the beginning supervisor—inexperience in the supervisory role. Since the new supervisor's basis for decision making and integrating differs from that of the more experienced supervisor, it would seem likely that the supervision provided early in the clinician's experience may differ from later supervision in some important ways which warrant further examination.

CHARACTERISTICS OF THE NEW SUPERVISOR

What makes beginning supervisors different from experienced colleagues? Having just made a significant role transition, the novice must consolidate the new role and deal with the anxieties accompanying this transition as the initial supervision is occurring. The supervisor's role is an unfamiliar one, combining various elements (i.e., responsibility, demands, intensity, and limitations) in ways that differ from previous relationships. These components will all influence the beginning supervisor's perspective and lead to differences in more concrete aspects of supervision. It is certainly possible to predict advantages and disadvantages the novice will bring to supervising, issues and tasks which will be especially salient in the new role, and ways in which the new supervisor's perspective may differ from those of senior colleagues.

Advantages

The recent transition from trainee to supervisor provides the beginning supervisor with several potential advantages over more experienced colleagues. Having only recently been on the other side of the desk, the beginning supervisor is able to empathize more readily and respond accurately to the trainee. A second advantage for beginning supervisors is that since memories of being supervised are fresh, both positive and negative aspects of one's own training can be readily employed to orient the supervision so that it will be most helpful to the trainee. Finally, the enthusiasm of the beginning supervisor can be a special advantage. The novice is often willing to invest more time and energy in supervision, and his or her excitement and interest will be readily communicated to the trainee.

Limitations

The recent transition of the new supervisor can also limit some aspects of the supervision. Supervision by a less experienced supervisor may be much like therapy with a less experienced therapist: it is in the lack of elegance and precision of the process that the limitations of the less experienced therapist or supervisor are usually manifest, although the ultimate goals accomplished are essentially the same. For example, since the new supervisor's experience is limited, the use of certain modalities of supervision such as tape recording may be more appropriate than use of modalities in which one must be attuned to the student's interpretation as well as the material presented, certainly a more complex and difficult task. Thus within the supervisory process, options of the new supervisor may be somewhat limited.

If the new supervisor has only recently been a trainee, other limitations may also occur. The supervisor may be so closely identified with the student that this interferes with the supervision. For example, the supervisor may assume that "if I had this problem, of course my trainees will, too." Conversely, the supervisor may be overly supportive and reluctant to confront anxiety laden issues. Thus it is important for the new supervisor to be attuned to difficulties which occurred during his or her own supervision so that distortions in response can be recognized when similar issues arise in supervising.

The new supervisor's own therapy style may still be very much evolving. Although it is probably rare that a clinician feels that his or her therapy style is completely integrated, the young clinician is often still experimenting in a very active way. If this experimenting is actively included in the supervision, it can cause confusion and frustration for the supervisee.

Interpersonal Needs

The interpersonal needs of the supervisor as well as the trainee will inevitably be a part of their relationship (Chessick, 1971; Lower, 1972; Rosenbaum, 1953). Although the effects of this are inherently neither positive or negative, for the new supervisor there are special concerns. First, the beginning supervisor may not yet be aware of how personal needs will enter into this new kind of relationship. For example, achievement needs may be expressed by efforts to be the "most liked," "most difficult," or "most available" supervisor. The newness of the supervisory role may also increase particular needs which will later become less important in supervisory relationships. The beginning supervisor may be especially concerned with proving competence, reassurance of popularity, or establishing power in the relationship, all of which will become less important as security in the new role increases. It is important that the new supervisor be aware of these needs and take care that they not be met at the expense of the trainee.

Perspective as Supervisor

The unique perspective of the supervisor may make the initial experience a difficult one for the novice supervisor. As the third person in the therapy relationship the supervisor must understand the clinical material, suggest interventions, and be ultimately responsible for clinical decisions, usually without having met the patient and with only the information presented by the trainee. The demands of this new perspective may, at first, be uncomfortable and even unrewarding for the beginning supervisor accustomed to direct patient contact. Also unique is the intense one-to-one relationship which often occurs between supervisor and trainee. This may parallel the counselor-client relationship along such dimensions as facilitating behavior change, acceptance, and sensitivity to the student's needs. However, it differs in an important way: it is inherently judgmental. For both the student and supervisor there is an ongoing evaluation of how the student is "measuring up" as a clinician. This is a significant source of anxiety for most trainees. The new supervisor must be aware that this is an inherent element of the relationship and determine how he or she will facilitate the student's development by maintaining this anxiety at an optimal level for learning.

Assessment of the Supervisee

Issues which arise in response to individual differences in trainees may also place new and difficult demands on the supervisor. The novice must first assess the current level of skill and particular training needs of the student and then determine how these needs can best be met in view of the supervision he or she can offer. The supervisor must also attempt to formulate realistic expectations for change and development in the student. Expectations that are too high may lead to frustration and disappointment for all involved, while expectations that are too low may result in the trainee learning less than might have been possible. Without the benefit of previous experience, the beginning supervisor will probably need to remain flexible, utilizing alternative resources to formulate expectations. Mutual goal setting with the student, consulting with colleagues experienced in supervising, and periodic reassessments of students' progress may be useful. Finally, since new supervisors are often assigned students that others do not want, it is likely that the beginning supervisor will encounter trainees whose personal issues interfere with clinical work. Dealing with such situations can be delicate and unpleasant, and even more difficult for one still in the process of establishing a sense of competency and security in the new supervisory role. For example, a young female supervisor who must deal with a trainee who cannot recognize or acknowledge his inappropriately seductive style, can feel much anxiety, awkwardness, and anger, making supervising very difficult. Alternatively, a skillful, confident, but defensive trainee may be initially threatening to the beginning supervisor and unaccepting of the supervisor's help. However, successful resolution of these issues associated with the supervisor's novice status can lead to a stronger learning alliance than might have otherwise occurred.

Feedback Mechanisms

A final characteristic of the beginning supervisor's experience is the limited availability of feedback mechanisms by which to assess strengths and weaknesses as a supervisor. One's own assessment of changes in the students' skills is useful but perhaps biased. Also, since trainees often have several supervisors simultaneously, it is difficult to assess the impact of a single supervisor based on the student's development. Feedback from students can be useful but may be more reliable regarding supervisory style than supervision effectiveness. This is because it is probably easier for students to assess experiential aspects of supervision than it is for students to evaluate their own professional development in response to particular supervisors. It must also be kept in mind that all aspects of students' feedback may be significantly influenced by their desire to please the supervisor. Finally, unless the beginning supervisor is being supervised in this experience, feedback from colleagues will probably be sparse and often based on comments from students. Although this can certainly be helpful, it is perhaps the least reliable of feedback mechanisms. A formalized review of the new supervisor's work by a senior clinician and experienced supervisor can provide a reliable and useful source of feedback, assuming the reviewer is also skillful in gathering and interpreting the information necessary to formulate a fair review. Thus, since each of these feedback mechanisms for supervisors has its limitations, utilization of several feedback mechanisms is probably the best option available to new supervisors.

Although the goals of supervision and the ultimate learning of the student are often not affected by the extent of the supervisor's experience, other aspects of supervision are certainly influenced. The experienced supervisor is more likely to reach goals of supervision with greater ease and via a more direct process. In addition, the novice supervisor must rely on somewhat different personal and professional resources than senior colleagues. An awareness of these differences may be useful in assigning trainees to supervisors.

CONCLUSION

Before efforts can begin to provide future clinical supervisors with consistent and adequate preparation, one must understand the beginning supervisor's needs. This chapter, written from the perspective of one who recently made the transition from trainee to supervisor, represents an effort to describe significant aspects of the new supervisor's experience. Although much work remains to be done in understanding how supports may be most usefully provided to the novice supervisor, it is hoped that the need for preparation and ongoing supports of the clinical supervisor will become increasingly apparent.

Finally, the resources, decisions, and issues discussed in this paper are not unique to the beginning supervisor. As the more experienced supervisor continues to reexamine initial decisions in this role, experiment with alternatives, and evaluate his or her own strengths and weaknesses as a supervisor, the demands of the supervisory relationship and the supports available in responding to them will continue to be of relevance. Ongoing awareness and examination of these issues can do much to insure continued growth of the supervisor long after the initial transition into this role has been made.

REFERENCES

Bruch, H. *Learning psychotherapy: Rationale and ground rules.* Cambridge, Mass.: Harvard University Press, 1974.

Chessick, R. D. How the resident and the supervisor disappoint each other. *American Journal of Psychotherapy,* 1971, *25,* 272–283.

Ekstein, R., and Wallerstein, R. S. *Teaching and learning of psychotherapy.* New York: International Universities Press, 1972.

Garfield, S. L., and Kurtz, R. Clinical psychologists in the 1970s. *American Psychologist,* 1976, *31,* 1–9.

Lower, R. B. Countertransference resistances in the supervisory situation. *American Journal of Psychiatry,* 1972, *129,* 156–160.

Rosenbaum, M. Problems in supervision of psychiatric residents in psychotherapy. *Archives of Neurology and Psychiatry,* 1953, *69,* 43–48.

Sarbin, T. R., and Allen, V. L. Role theory. In G. Lindzey and E. Aronson, *The Handbook of Social Psychology.* Reading, Mass.,: Addison Wellesley, 1968, 488–567.

Tarachow, S. *Introduction to psychotherapy.* New York: International Universities Press, 1963.

CHAPTER 4

From Classroom to Clinic: Supervising the First Psychotherapy Client

IRVING B. WEINER AND ROBERT G. KAPLAN

Beginning psychotherapists face some special learning problems in making the transition from classroom to clinic. Where formerly they had talked in the abstract about working with clients whose hypothetical behavior could be altered at will to meet the needs of the discussion, they now must take professional responsibility in the real world for attempting to be helpful to clients whose behavior is dictated primarily by their own and not the therapist's needs. Three particularly challenging tasks for beginning therapists are (a) learning to integrate treatment techniques with personal authenticity, (b) learning to recognize the boundaries of psychotherapy and of themselves as effective agents of behavior change, and (c) learning to achieve an appropriate sense of professional identity and responsibility.

Supervisors need to appreciate the impact that such learning problems can have on therapists' efforts to relate meaningfully to their initial clients. This chapter will first elaborate some of the circumstances that create these problems and then propose some guidelines for helping new professionals deal with them.

SPECIAL LEARNING PROBLEMS OF BEGINNING THERAPISTS

Learning to be a technician and a real person at the same time is an almost universal difficulty for beginning therapists, regardless of the circumstances in which they work. With the rare exception of naturally gifted people who require little instruction, there is ample reason to believe that good therapists are made, not born (Weiner, 1975, Chap. 3). The other common problems of beginning therapists—learning boundaries of effectiveness and a sense of professional identity—vary in severity as a function of administrative constraints affecting with what patients and under what auspices they do their initial work.

Integrating Treatment Techniques With Personal Authenticity

The key element when therapists make the transition from classroom to clinic is learning to translate the didactic principles of psychotherapy they have learned into specific and personally congruent ways of communicating with clients. Therapists who have learned *what* to do from books and lectures must now learn *how* to do it with the troubled person sitting across from them and looking to them for help. As Reiss (1975) notes, there is often a striking contrast between what young clinicians *know* and what they know *how to do* in treatment situations. In addition to resolving such cognitive uncertainties in a new situation, beginning therapists must learn to select from many possible ways of conducting effective psychotherapy interviews those that are most natural for them, in order to appear as an authentic and genuine person rather than a stilted purveyor of techniques.

As an illustration of translating *what* to *how,* beginners will probably have learned in the classroom that they need to make the client feel comfortable about talking to them. In the treatment room, they must recognize that this desired end is rarely achieved directly by such remarks as "I'm here to help you, so you can trust me and say anything you want without worrying about how I'll take it." Beginning therapists must instead become familiar with the various indirect but more convincing ways of helping clients feel safe and secure in the interview situation (see Weiner, 1975, Chap. 7).

With respect to personal authenticity, consider a client who says, "I want you to know I'm really upset." The therapist may recognize that this statement calls for an expression of interested and understanding concern. For some therapists a simple gesture, such as a facial expression or certain movements of the head or hands, will suffice. For other therapists, whose personality style orients them more toward verbal than nonverbal communication, a gesture in this situation might appear awkward or unnatural and, worse yet, fail to convey clearly the intended interest and understanding. Rather than gesture, these latter therapists will do better to respond to the client who says, "I want you to know I'm really upset," with appropriate words, such as "I understand," or "I hear you," or "You're upset."

As this illustration suggests, there can be no single prescription to guide beginning therapists in selecting their intervention style from alternatives that are equally appropriate in theory. Therapists have to learn about themselves, in the arena of ongoing psychotherapy, to discover the response styles that are sufficiently congruent with their nature to convey both a clear message and a sense of genuineness to the client.

Just as beginning therapists cannot learn the most natural way of expressing themselves from their textbooks, they cannot learn it directly from their supervisors either. What serve as natural styles of verbal and nonverbal communication for the supervisor will not necessarily serve as well for the trainee, unless they happen to be similar kinds of people. Ornstein (1968) compares the pitfalls of beginners' mimicking their supervisor to the plight of the sorcerer's apprentice, who learned from painful experience that successful magic required more than just copying bits and pieces of what he had seen the sorcerer do.

The supervisor can certainly help beginning therapists recognize awkwardness and artificiality in their attempts to communicate and may even be able to suggest alternative ways of communicating that work well. However, only the therapist, through sensitive self-awareness and careful attention to how his or her behavior is perceived by clients, can determine the expressive style that best integrates treatment techniques with personal authenticity.

Recognizing Boundaries of Effectiveness

Reading about the percentage of people with particular kinds of problems who respond well to psychotherapy is one thing; it is quite another to participate in a real-world contract in which one's methods and skill are committed to a person who wants and needs to be helped. Most people who undertake psychotherapy training are highly motivated to help others. For beginning therapists the almost inevitable result is some failure to achieve all they had hoped for on their clients' behalf—followed in the wake by discouragement about psychotherapy as an effective procedure and/or themselves as effective therapists.

As Barnat (1977) notes, being aware of the awkwardness and uncertainty mentioned above can sometimes lead beginners to doubt the efficacy of psychotherapy and of themselves as therapists. Two additional kinds of circumstances frequently complicate learning the boundaries of effectiveness. The first involves clients who cannot be helped or who can be helped only slightly. It is a fact of life that most of the clients assigned to beginners in training centers are those who were considered least "attractive" by staff and more senior trainees. One of the prerogatives of status in the clinical world is being able to select the most attractive and rewarding people with whom to work. In part this administrative feature of clinical training centers can be rationalized by a preference to have beginners cut their teeth in situations where they cannot do much damage.

As a result, novice therapists' clients include a high proportion of chronically disturbed, characterologically disordered, and minimally motivated persons—those who are least likely to participate actively in psychotherapy and benefit from it. Experienced therapists set limited goals for such clients and find satisfaction in modest gains achieved in the face of major obstacles to change. For beginners, however, flushed with enthusiasm and fresh from the classroom with an array of techniques in mind, lack of substantial change can be very disheartening. As psychotherapy proceeds and the client stays the same, beginning therapists often fall prey to nagging doubts that (a) psychotherapy doesn't work or (b) someone else with more talent for doing psychotherapy could be achieving success where they have failed.

The second circumstance involves clients who by all usual criteria have excellent prospects of benefiting from psychotherapy. Here the learning problem relates not to lack of change, but rather to the pace of change. Beginning therapists working with insightful and responsive clients often anticipate that a quick once-through of the techniques they have learned will produce a prompt and meaningful redirection in life style and resolve all previous problems. The extent to which resistances to change and the necessity for working through can slow progress even in the most responsive client are overlooked in the excitement of the treatment room, even when they have been thoroughly discussed in the classroom.

This second circumstance can also generate the twin bugaboos of "Psychotherapy's no good" and "I'm no good" as beginning therapists come to grips with realities that counter their wish to cure the world's psychological problems. The learning task is to avoid the Scylla of unrealistic positive expectations without foundering on the Charybdis of therapeutic nihilism. The classroom provides only the raw materials for such learning to take place. The final product—a reasonable sense of what psychotherapy can do and of one's own assets and limitations as a therapist—is forged in the therapist's workroom.

Achieving a Sense of Professional Identity

Achieving an appropriate sense of identity and responsibility is a learning issue for all professions, and it does not seem appropriate here to deal with it in its broad context. Barnat (1977), Berger and Freebury (1973), Chessick (1971), Schuster, Sandt, and Thaler (1972, Chap. 3), and Tischler (1968), among others, describe new therapists' struggles to gain a firm sense of their professional role identity. Especially important in this regard is the need for beginners to avoid reducing their anxiety in an unfamiliar situation by adopting either a distant, analytical, authoritative role at the expense of communicating warmth, or a friendly, reassuring role at the expense of objective exploration of unpleasant subjects. As noted by Lewis (1978, p. 157), supervision "must address the balance of intimacy and detachment required to be an effective psychotherapist."

Often beginners' needs to feel competent contribute to their having difficulty in assuming an appropriate professional role. Beginning therapists tend to invest heavily in their clients' welfare, in part because doing so gives them a sense of importance that their novice status may otherwise deny. Clients may be all too willing to accept advice and let someone else take care of them, while beginning therapists, in their zeal, may try to make up for all the unhappiness their client has experienced. The result may be a covert deal between beginner and client: "I'll make you feel special and loved if you get better and make me feel special."

Beyond this general problem, there are particular circumstances in which beginning therapists often find themselves that create specific identity issues of which supervisors need to be aware. Because of the nature of training arrangements in many clinical programs, trainees seeing their first client tend to be only minimally engaged as a staff member in the setting where their client has come for help. Often they function as a practicum student whose only contact with a clinic or hospital is in relation to the client they see there once or twice a week. In other instances beginning trainees in a multiservice setting are assigned primarily to inpatient services and visit the outpatient clinic only to keep appointments with their psychotherapy client.

These circumstances make it difficult for beginning therapists to experience the feelings of status and responsibility that come from full-scale participation in a clinical setting. Conferences in which their client is reviewed may be scheduled when they cannot be present, or perhaps even without their knowledge. Messages may not reach them because they are rarely there or, worse yet, because people taking messages do not even know who they are. Emergencies relating to their clients may be referred to someone else in their absence. They may have the experience of arriving for an appointment to learn that their client has been transferred to another therapist or admitted to the hospital without their having been informed or consulted. They may learn that the clinic hours have been changed, so that they can no longer use the appointment time they have contracted for with their client, or that the therapy room they have been using is no longer available.

These and similar administrative insults can make it difficult for beginners to feel that they are qualified professionals-in-training delivering important human services. Instead, they may feel demeaned in their work and may neglect such responsibilities as making sure that they or a designated colleague can be reached at all times in case of emergency. Many if not all of these learning problems can be minimized by adequate coordination between training programs and supervisors on the one hand and training centers on the other.

GUIDELINES IN SUPERVISING BEGINNING THERAPISTS

Supervisors, like therapists, function most effectively when they have settled into modes of communication that are consistent with their personal style. Nevertheless, there are some generally applicable supervisory tactics that can accelerate beginning therapists' progress in mastering the learning tasks just discussed. The translation of didactic principles into actual therapist behavior can be facilitated by preparatory supervisory sessions, anticipatory role-playing, and a continuing focus on how principles can guide what the therapist should say and do. The recognition of the limits of psychotherapy and of one's professional identity can be facilitated through a careful focus on realistic constraints and efforts to expand therapists' awareness beyond their initially limited experience.

Preparatory Supervisory Sessions and Anticipatory Role-Playing

Supervisors who instruct beginning therapists to schedule a first meeting with them after they have had their initial session with their client are already compounding their supervisees' learning difficulties. Supervision should begin *before* the client is seen, and not only for customary purposes of "selecting a case" from several that may be available or of discussing in general terms what the client's major problems seem to be and what directions the therapy is likely to take. Rather, pretherapy supervision should include very specific consideration of who will say what to whom under which circumstances. A supervisor can often best serve a novice therapist's initial learning needs by assuming nothing, not even that the beginner knows how to greet a client and get him or her seated in the interviewing room.

Focused questions and anticipatory role-playing are helpful techniques in preparing beginners to have the right words in their mouths, both for routine purposes and for dealing with special issues that may arise. "What will you say in the waiting room?" "How will you begin the interview?" "What if your client refuses to talk, or asks if everything here is confidential, or objects to your tape-recording the session?" "How will you respond if the client asks if you're old enough to do this kind of work, or how many people with the same problem you've treated before, or whether you're a doctor, or how come you don't have a regular office to use?"

Some problems of these types may need to be addressed by all therapists, whereas others are the special province of beginners, who often in fact look younger and have fewer of the trappings of the status than their clients might have expected or wished. Students who have had a good didactic course in psychotherapy will usually be able to devise an appropriate solution to the problem, given time to sit back and mull it over. Ongoing psychotherapy differs from a classroom examination, however, in that a difficult question cannot be reserved until later. Appropriate words of response must be immediately available; otherwise, either an awkward silence or inappropriate words will ensue, to the detriment of building an effective treatment relationship.

By carrying out anticipatory role-playing for difficult questions that beginning therapists are likely to face, supervisors can help them determine in advance the words that would constitute a useful response. Such preparation not only provides learning but also builds the beginning therapist's confidence with respect to handling sticky nuances in the treatment relationship. To be successful, however, this supervisory technique must be carefully designed as role-playing and not just role-modeling. It is not sufficient for the supervisor to indicate how he or she would deal with a problem. Through anticipatory role-playing, supervisees can experiment until they find the words that achieve a particular purpose while being congruent with their personal style. As noted earlier, supervisors can indicate what the therapists' purpose should be at a particular time and can suggest alternative modes of achieving it through various combinations of words or gestures—but they cannot simply put their words in their supervisee's mouth.

Continuing Focus on Principles

Not even the most astute and ambitious supervisor can anticipate every difficult situation a beginning therapist will encounter. In addition to learning specific responses from role-playing, therapists need to have general principles in mind from which they can derive ways of dealing with new situations that have not been considered in prior supervision. In this regard, research findings indicate that supplementing role-playing with instruction in principles provides more effective supervision, as measured by therapist performance, than either approach used seperately (Stone and Vance, 1976).

Supervisors may be tempted to assume that beginning therapists have already learned in the classroom what they need to know about principles of psychotherapy. However, under the pressure of having to respond to a live and perhaps demanding client, inexperienced therapists easily get caught up in the superficial content of an interview. They may then begin flying by the seat of their pants and overlook how their prior textbook learning applies to the real situation in front of them. In a demonstration of this effect, Cichetti and Ornston (1976) found from a content analysis of intitial interviews that novice therapists tend to become involved in concrete details and lose sight of the broader context of what their client is saying, whereas more experienced therapists are more likely to abstract and integrate what they hear.

Supervisors can help beginning therapists learn to integrate principles and practice by encouraging constant reflection on their *strategy* and *tactics;* "At this point in time, what is it I'm trying to accomplish (strategy) and what is the best way of doing it (tactics)?" To illustrate, consider the client who in an early interview says, "I don't really enjoy coming here." The beginning therapist with a sensitive grasp of dynamic psychology may have the thought, "You're afraid to give up your symptoms." Should he or she express this thought directly to the client?

Beginning therapists can learn a great deal about how actually to conduct psychotherapy by recognizing that the answers to many questions of this kind are readily available from a quick review of principles with which they are already (it would be hoped) familiar. In this case, a therapist's statement that "You're afraid to give up your symptoms" would constitute an interpretation. A widely accepted principle regarding interpretations is that they must be carefully timed to accord with the client's readiness to deal with them and should constitute the end point of a sequence of clarifications and confrontations that gradually paves the way for them (Chessick, 1974, Chap. 9; Fromm-Reichmann, 1950, Chap. 8; Weiner, 1975, Chap. 8).

Hence the answer to the above question is "No." Interpretive leaps for the jugular in early interviews whenever the therapist gets a bright idea are cognitively premature and can undermine the treatment relationship. In this particular instance, the time is right for helping the client explore feelings and for avoiding any foreclosure through premature interpretation. With these principles of interpretation in mind and recognizing that they imply a strategy of encouraging exploration, the therapist can readily select an appropriate response to "I don't really enjoy coming here" from such alternatives as "Oh?", "What's it like?", "You have some concerns about being in therapy," or "Perhaps we could look at the feelings you're having."

Attention to Realistic Constraints

Supervisors of beginning therapists may not be able to alter such realities as a supervisee's low status as a professional or involvement with a limited prognosis client. However, adequate awareness of these special learning problems of beginners is an important first step in helping them recognize that their experiential world does not necessarily represent the way things can and should be.

With respect to professional responsibility, for example, supervisors should impress upon trainees their around-the-clock obligations even when the setting in which they are seeing their first client makes few such demands. Trainees need to appreciate that a treatment contract commits them to new and perhaps unfamiliar aspects of being a clinician. These include making themselves and their whereabouts known to all staff who may have dealings with their client; never being out of telephone contact without having made adequate provision for coverage by a colleague; accepting that traditional school vacations to which they have become accustomed bear no relationship to their obligations as therapists; and discussing with the client the fee for their services, even if all direct financial transactions are being handled between the agency and an insurer.

Education in these responsibilities is often noted to escape adequate attention of the supervisor (Myers, 1976; Pasternack and Treiger, 1976). This is unfortunate, since discussions of professional responsibility and insistence on meeting it can be very helpful to beginners in learning their roles and achieving a sense of identity. If supervisees suffer such ignominies as having their treatment room assigned to someone else or their client discharged without their knowledge, supervisors need to review with them (a) the principles of good therapy that are being violated in these instances (appropriate physical surroundings and adequate continuity of care, respectively); and (b) the fact that such events are rarely the lot of full-time staff in an agency, so that they can look forward not only to better days for themselves, but also to having an opportunity when they become fully credentialed staff to help spare the next generation of trainees such difficulties.

Most beginning therapists will have sufficient personality strength and good judgment to be able to draw on the experience and observations of their supervisor as a means of avoiding low self-esteem and a diffusion of professional identity in the face of such administrative problems. Even though beginning therapists need to avoid mimicking their supervisors, some identification with them is widely observed to help promote a sense of being a competent professional (Halleck and Woods, 1962; Sharaf and Levinson, 1957). Additionally the reactions of beginners to their work with unresponsive or psychologically limited clients can be kept in perspective by pointed efforts of the supervisor to focus on realistic constraints. Trainees will have read a good deal about certain types of people and problems that respond well or poorly to psychotherapy. However, in the natural excitement of starting at last to do the helpful work for which they have been preparing, beginners can easily overlook making this particular transition from classroom to clinic. Consequently, any lack of progress is construed as a reflection on the ineffectiveness of psychotherapy or on their own limitations.

Supervisors need to act as constant testers of reality to help trainees in these situations. If the client is a characterologically disordered, chronically depressed person who has changed little during two previous courses of therapy at the clinic, the supervisor should point out early and often that this is a type of person known to have relatively little potential for benefiting from psychotherapy. While doing their best to help, beginning therapists must recognize that lack of progress in such a case is not generalizable to all cases.

Supervisors should also be sensitive to the reality of certain anxieties and conflicting needs that beginning therapists often experience. Numerous clinicians writing about supervision have commented on beginners' uncertainty in the therapist's role, their struggle with competing needs to improve their skills and to deny any lack of competence, and their wish both to receive help from their supervisor and to impress him or her with how little supervision they need (Ekstein and Wallerstein, 1958; Dewald, 1969; Fleming and Benedek, 1966; Maltsberger and Buie, 1969).

Supervisors can facilitate beginner's coping with realistic constraints by providing a supportive relationship through which they can express their feelings in adjusting to a new role and working with patients. This does not mean that supervision should become psychotherapy. Research indicates that the beginning therapist's performance is enhanced more by instruction during supervisory sessions than by explorations of their personal experience (Hansen, Pound, and Petro, 1976; Payne, Weiss, and Kapp, 1972; Ronnestad, 1974). We would strongly endorse the view of Cohen and DeBetz (1977, p. 59) in this regard: "The trainee's problems in doing therapy with the patient are fair game for supervisory intervention, while personal problems (provided they do not interfere) are not."

To provide support in the face of sources of anxiety that are interfering with learning, supervisors need to reinforce what beginning therapists are doing well along with pointing out their errors in judgment and technique. Such a balanced approach to supervision can help beginners avoid the impression that signs of progress are only incidental to their skills whereas lack of progress must be laid on the doorstep of their ineptness. Although *helpful* therapy is judged by its outcome, *good* therapy is not. Good therapy is what the therapist does, not how the client responds to it. Beginning therapists need to recognize when a lack of progress is not their fault, and supervisors can help them maintain an appropriate sense of their abilities by pointing out whenever and wherever appropriate, "You've done a good job, in terms of all that is currently known about conducting psychotherapy; it's unfortunate that the client could benefit only minimally from your efforts, but it's unlikely that anyone else could have done better."

REFERENCES

Barnat, M. R. Spontaneous supervisory metaphor in the resolution of trainee anxiety. *Professional Psychology,* 1977, *8,* 307–315.

Berger, D., and Freebury, D. R. The acquisition of psychotherapy skills: A learning model and some guidelines for instructors. *Canadian Psychiatric Association Journal,* 1973, *18,* 467–471.

Chessick, R. D. How the resident and the supervisor disappoint each other. *American Journal of Psychotherapy,* 1971, *25,* 272–283.

Chessick, R. D. *Technique and practice of intensive psychotherapy.* New York: Jason Aronson, 1974.

Cichetti, D., and Ornston, P. S. The initial psychotherapy interview: A content analysis of the verbal responses of novice and experienced therapists. *Journal of Psychology,* 1976, *93,* 167–179.

Cohen, R. J., and DeBetz, B. Responsive supervision of the psychiatric resident and clinical psychology intern. *American Journal of Psychoanalysis,* 1977, *37,* 51–64.

Dewald, P. A. Learning problems in psychoanalytic supervision: Diagnosis and management. *Comprehensive Psychiatry,* 1969, *10,* 107–121.

Ekstein, R., and Wallerstein, R. S. *The teaching and learning of psychotherapy.* New York: Basic Books, 1958.

Fleming, J., and Benedek, T. *Psychoanalytic supervision.* New York: Grune and Stratton, 1966.

Fromm-Reichmann, F. *Principles of intensive psychotherapy.* Chicago: University of Chicago Press, 1950.

Halleck, S. L., and Woods, S. M. Emotional problems of psychiatric residents. *Psychiatry,* 1962, *25,* 339–346.

Hansen, J. C., Pound, R., and Petro, C. Review of research on practicum supervision. *Counselor Education and Supervision,* 1976, *16,* 107–116.

Lewis, J. M. *To be a therapist: The teaching and learning.* New York: Brunner/Mazel, 1978.

Maltsberger, J. A., and Buie, D. H. The work of supervision. In J. E. Semrad and D. Van Buskirk (Eds.), *Teaching psychotherapy of psychotic patients.* New York: Grune and Stratton, 1969.

Myers, B. S. Attitude of psychiatric residents toward payment of psychotherapy fees. *American Journal of Psychiatry,* 1976, *133,* 1460–1462.

Ornstein, P. H. Sorcerer's apprentice: The initial phase of education and training in psychiatry. *Comprehensive Psychiatry,* 1968, *9,* 293–315.

Pasternack, S., and Treiger, P. Psychotherapy fees and residency training. *American Journal of Psychiatry,* 1976, *133,* 1064–1066.

Payne, P. A., Weiss, S. D., and Kapp, R. A. Didactic, experiential, and modeling factors in the learning of empathy. *Journal of Counseling Psychology,* 1972, *19,* 425–429.

Reiss, N. B. Problems in the teaching of psychotherapy. *Psychotherapy: Theory, Research and Practice,* 1975, *12,* 332–335.

Ronnestad, M. H. Effects of modeling, feedback, and experiential supervision in beginning counseling students' communication of empathic understanding. *Dissertation Abstracts International,* 1974, *33,* 6985–6986.

Schuster, D. B., Sandt, J. J., and Thaler, O. F. *Clinical supervision of the psychiatric resident.* New York: Brunner/Mazel, 1972.

Sharaf, M. R., and Levinson, D. J. Patterns of ideology and professional role definition among psychiatric residents. In M. Greenblatt, D. Levinson, and R. Williams (Eds.), *The patient and the mental hospital.* Glencoe, Ill.: Free Press, 1957.

Stone, G. L., and Vance, A. Instructions, modeling, and rehearsal: Implications for training. *Journal of Counseling Psychology,* 1976, *23,* 272–279.

Tischler, G. L. The beginning resident and supervision, *Archives of General Psychiatry,* 1968, *19,* 418–422.

Weiner, I. B. *Principles of psychotherapy.* New York: Wiley, 1975.

CHAPTER 5

Psychotherapy Supervision and the Duality of Experience

MICHAEL R. BARNAT

"The Naming of Cats"

> . . . When you notice a cat in profound meditation,
> The reason, I tell you, is always the same:
> His mind is engaged in a rapt contemplation
>   of the thought, of the thought, of the thought
>   of his name . . .*

T.S. Eliot

1888–1965

INTRODUCTION

There is some excellent work in the literature on supervising psychotherapy trainees (Doehrman, 1976; Ekstein & Wallerstein, 1958; Kell and Mueller, 1966; Mueller and Kell, 1972). Less is available on the process of being supervised—that is, participating in a time-bound process that has as its minimal aim one's own establishment as a functional psychotherapist (Barnat, 1974).

While rich in many respects, the literature of experiential growth (e.g., Rogers and Stevens, 1967) fails to provide a language with enough theoretical specificity to illuminate the moments in human development when, for example, social roles, ethics, and technical skills are integrated into the therapist's personality. The same might be said of popular literature (e.g., Viscott, 1972).

Psychoanalysts have provided glimpses into their experience of the therapy process (Reik, 1948; Sachs, 1940). With varying degrees of success, both analysts (Guntrip, 1975) and experimentalists (Boring, 1940; Brown, 1940; Landis, 1940) have examined their personal therapy process and outcome. The role of counter-

---

transference in therapy and theory has also been documented (Guntrip, 1975; Kernberg, 1972).

While a body of student observations would seem necessary to lend meaning to professional ones, there is a void where trainee perceptions are concerned (Barnat, 1977). The following will suggest why there is not more literature mapping the point at which professional identities begin to develop.

This paper addresses itself not so much to the formal elements of supervision (e.g., how much is enough?) but rather to the changing balances within students throughout their training. The issues here are: How is supervision helpful when and where it is helpful and how do we appreciate the word "training"?

For practical reasons my exposition is limited to self-observation and often private experience. That is the best data I have. The technical usefulness of these comments depends, in part, on their being precisely personal. This approach is risky in terms of verifiability but no shakier than the ground we like to call 'hard data' in some other contexts. For example, to fulfill a faculty research requirement, I was once encouraged to "just give some MMPI's and write 'em up!"

Let me set the stage with two other examples.

I once approached a faculty person with the idea of writing a paper on trainee experience. To my inquiry, the senior replied: "Why should people want student observations when they can have professional ones?"

Later, when I had written about neophyte training experiences (Barnat, 1973b) I asked a supervisor to review the manuscript. Graciously, he did and said: "Good. The next time you can write about *doing* therapy."

These were well-meaning folks with valid perspectives. Perhaps too, they were reacting to my naïveté. But if these are general attitudes, then it is easy to appreciate the lack of student literature on early professional development.

These reactions suggest something almost illegitimate about being an apprentice, let alone dwelling on it. The reciprocal attitude is that the state of having arrived is a blessed one. Since I have had trouble in that area too, it seemed all the more important to talk in as precise a way as possible about how "not ready yet" becomes "I've arrived!"—or something that feels to a graduate student like arriving (Barnat, 1977).

One point is that there may be some learning processes that can only be appreciated from the point of view of one who is acted upon. This person is the psychotherapy trainee in the front line of the learning experience. And also, when you try to write about being acted upon, you find out that it is hardly passive at all. It is an interactive and synthesizing process terribly underrepresented as "modeling" (Bandura and Walters, 1963).

Passivity implies inactivity. What I am describing is more like *resourceful receptivity.* The transfer of technical skills (empathy) or a professional ethos (conflict resolution by talking) *is* the transmission of culture. To say that you have accounted for those processes, you have to address the issue of what the trainee does internally with the material he or she is expected to master. The student has to look for a language to put these experiences into words.

Writing about elusive experiences changes those experiences in equally elusive ways (Erikson, 1964, p. 54). I am aware of the risk but I think this is the only way to preserve what seems worthy. I also hope that the five years that have passed since I was in a formal training program do not disqualify me from the effort. There can be a value in trying to say something relevant, even if you never reach the goal.

TRYING TO PRESERVE THE DATA OF CHANGE

I think for many psychotherapy trainees, the first casualty of postgraduate life is the change process itself. Unless you are awfully good at it, self-reflection may be considered immature. The tendency to look inward, as well as the time it takes, gets displaced as the therapist becomes increasingly involved in family and service where the continuing psychic investment must be shared significantly with others. Under the bureaucratic press, the therapist may find that tried and true methods for publications and other career enhancements are best. The kind of scrutiny I am referring to is by definition untried and untrue.

If this were not enough, graduates frequently leave their training programs with just enough scientific reasoning to discount the personal. (I would say that the most useful data I took away from graduate school was a wealth of memories—the afterglow, as it were—of what I felt was a marvelous learning experience.)

Agreed, the mental life is not always cooperative (see Goffman, 1974, p.8 *ff*). Memories are fashioned in part by the struggle to describe exact sequences of events and then by the descriptive words themselves. I risk ending up with general anecdotes that already belong to other therapists and supervisors, or material so specific I wish I could bypass it.

As is true in other branches of the social sciences, our discipline tends to sterilize the data by distilling fact from emergent meaning (Spence, 1973). Except that in clinical psychotherapeutic life, meaning is precious while fact as pure fact plays a more dubious role. So frequently in supervision, it is only the vital momentary meaning that one would want to preserve! So in a way, I run the risk of burying the process I try so hard to put into words. Scarier yet for lovers of fact, as I mature, so does my appreciation of these events.

Trainee change process may remain unexplored for still another reason. If supervision (like therapy) had an impact, then there was probably a painful element to it (Doehrman, 1976; Mueller and Kell, 1972). The pain was necessary. But there is a tendancy to want to let pain rest for comfort's sake.

As if all this pressure were not enough, consider how clumsy it is to live the life you are trying to record! That is what this paper is about. Most trainees are too busy with various requirements to add to their burdens a search for the meaning of every waking moment. And frequently supervision fails to provide an atmosphere that welcomes the trainees' or supervisor's most sensitive material anyway (Barnat, 1973a; Pleck, 1976. See also Jourard, 1971).

So, many factors mitigate against reconstructing the growth process. The importance of trying is illustrated in the following event. At the end of the year, some graduate students asked a popular supervisor what they could give him in return for his investment in their development. He said: "Just pass it on."

This delightful response points to the heart of this paper: How do you pass on intangibles, like meanings? How important will such events or descriptions be to the upcoming generation of students or supervisors? Since such experience is always unique and irreplaceable to the person, what end is served aside from the writer's need to do it? Certainly not mere technical efficiency.

Looking back, I think the supervisor had the Golden Rule in mind, something he felt so precious that he wanted it preserved in and through students. But knowing that supervisor, he probably also meant "Pass it on in *your* way." In fact, I always had a fantasy of sharing later whatever seemed vital at the moment. It was as if those moments were only truly fulfilled in the retelling. In my enthusiasm, I could find no hazards in the prospect.

WHAT MANNER OF DATA IS THIS?

In crucial respects, trainee growth under supervision is not a linear process. Sometimes we write as if it were (Barnat, 1973b; Kell and Mueller, 1966) so it is easier to work with.

But when you write about supervisory impact, the data are spotty: "Oh, I got a little something over here and a little over there and this vital bit I didn't even know till after I graduated."

In synthesizing these experiences, I got most of my clues from scanning my trainee years for bits of humor and wit, or formulae garnered in different times and places.

For example, in a military mental hygiene setting, a psychiatric officer invited me to jointly interview a GI. The client had been arrested for wearing womens' clothes in a public restroom. He was a rather quiet man with a light moustache.

I took a personal history and we joined the psychiatrist. During the interview I was a serious and observant student. Perhaps I was too serious because when the psychiatrist, with delicate candor, asked the man if he had worn his moustache along with the ladies' garments, I had to stifle a laugh that erupted inside.

The GI's answer was instructive. He smiled meekly that he had not. The lesson for me was that if genuine compassion attends the clinical process, then ironies would be less likely to hurt the patient. People were more flexible than I had thought. No supervision has ever been more potent than that unrehearsed episode.

It would be a mistake to take such experiences for granted. These transient events may have a powerful influence on one's training or on the kind of therapist one wants to be.

The word "training" is terribly sterile. For me, training was no abstraction. It was moments of gorgeous irony like the incident above, and the seemingly endless attempt to make sensible choices about the future given what I knew about myself. "Training" was me, evolving. I wanted to avoid becoming a commodity and I hoped that clinical psychology and psychotherapy would not become commodities. I had a subjective time continuum, personal deadlines, and there were times when graduate school felt like one delay right after another. And I had doubt. I could not have been too different from other students in this regard.

More than the doubts themselves, it is the constancy of doubt and anxiety that weighs on a training professional and may lead to depression. The trainee may wonder if he or she will ever feel sufficient. The overabundance of this raw experience is counterbalanced against the exquisite rarity of healing moments of wit and insight that seem to make the burdens of doubt more tolerable. Such restorative experiences cannot be programmed into supervision. But they constitute crucial data.

I sometimes felt that supervision was a kind of ritual relief from doubt. It was a chance to draw strength in part from the transient identification with the supervisor (when I did identify) and also the supportive alliance: "we therapists versus them unpsychological folks." Time was marked by rituals in humor. In this way, the formal aspect of supervision provided a supportive structure that allowed me to test new observations. The ambiguities of clinical experience require a ritual "telling."

This is also to say that there are countless moments that provide clues to the clinical learning process.

I recall myself at the university, sitting in a clinic room. There was a lot of tension between my client and myself. We were not saying anything. My body felt tense and my skin was itchy. I hooked my foot under the rung of the chair. My attention was most clearly on the corner of my mouth, the place where smiles first appear. The slightest muscle movement there seemed to be transmuted into a comforting image of myself emitting and enjoying a sad, rabbinical smile. Then, because I felt that the smile was *in* and *from* me, even while it was *to* me, I felt like I had an emotional surplus which in that immediate context, felt like competence. Then I felt relief.

All this happened in a split second. When I unhooked my foot I knew how tense it had been.

Free of doubt, I posed a direct question to the client. The feedback suggested that I had perceived accurately. I wonder if I would have asked the client a question if the image of a rabbinical smile had not emerged from a muscle twinge. The client's feedback brightened my whole day.

The tape never recorded this part of the supervisory process. Not even video-tape can pick up material that subtle. But such subtleties were always influencing the movement of therapy and supervision. Supervision was defined by personal struggles of the supervisor and myself and how those problems conformed to our shared concept of psychotherapy. It is hard to conceptualize the process in *impersonal* terms. But this is the crucial data that frequently gets lost.

MOOD, AMBIANCE, AND STYLE

Traditionally, studies of supervision (see Doehrman, 1976) focus on a task: "the teaching and learning of psychotherapy" (Ekstein and Wallerstein, 1958). This task orientation implies a proscribed process of skills, but misses those elements of training that reflect the trainee's and supervisor's life drama and social realities. It would be important to know, for example, how therapy skills are integrated with other strengths of the trainee (e.g., how well they adapt to married life).

It seems to me that the major share of my clinical learning involved what would be called by learning theorists "incidental learning" (Dollard and Miller, 1950). Mood refers to the general "feeling" of a historical period (e.g., the "Vietnam period"). Ambiance suggests everything: the collective "happenings" in the all-around at any given moment. Varieties of supervisory and professorial character models define style. This is the field for incidental learning. In other words, more often than not, what I needed to solve a personal or technical problem was in the periphery of my awareness, not the center.

To give an example, I could even take some therapeutic cues from the way my supervisor said "Excuse me!" after he sneezed. This is what I mean by ambiance. Did therapists sneeze? Was "Gesundheit" forgiveness? I think that as a trainee I was always putting together a conceptual scheme of ethics and treatment from sources this random. This felt urgent to me, in part because the amount of material I felt responsible for mastering sometimes seemed overwhelming.

Political or campus moods provided a fluid and stimulating environment which, every now and then, some commentator brought into sharp focus. A *New Yorker* cartoon showed legions of marching patients, each group under the banner of its therapeutic guru. These comments sometimes put therapy in a new philosophical perspective.

The mutual expectations of supervisors and trainees were molded by such extraneous variables. One of the best examples I can think of occurred when an analyst explained to me the "infiltrative" nature of psychoanalytic procedure. How I responded to that had something to do with how old I was and the war going on. To my Vietnam generation, the word "infiltrate" was politically charged with insidious implications—notwithstanding meanings it had with respect to the healing potentials of a therapeutic alliance.

Our psychological *Zeitgeist* combined with my 25-year-old idealism, Beatles lyricism, confusion over the moral status of violence (and corresponding faith in the morality of psychotherapy), the impact of Masters and Johnson, guruism in the pop-psych culture (Perls, Laing, and Leary), and a lot of interest (all scientific, of course) in sexual indulgence as it related to psychotherapy services. All the while I was riding the wave of economic support for education stimulated by Sputnik and Kennedy idealism. This is not to look back and say that my training was faulty because of a lot of commercial and ideological noise. Many of the perspectives generated then only became invalid when they were put clumsily into literal practice (e.g., open marriages and some communal life styles).

For these and more personal reasons, supervision was "holy." Anything seemed holy that involved a ritual tête-à-tête of two people certain of their special insight. The transference and countertransference in supervision is clear enough (see Benedek, 1963). The issue to be researched would be to what degree what happens historically leads to the exploitation of transferential vulnerabilities. We all played little games with each other from time to time. We even delighted in having our games exposed (Berne, 1964). The mood of the time sanctified our rituals (love and closeness were big sellers). If distortion existed, it was shared by supervisors and trainees from this cultural perspective.

My supervisor and I eagerly incorporated into our relationship what 'felt right.' For example, my expectations of supervisory wisdom were tremendous. These were the standards we allowed ourselves and our rapport to be judged by.

For another example, the popular word "growth" seemed to be marvelously adaptable to the needs of the moment. It could mean anything from barking at your thesis advisor to adopting a new theoretical perspective. If I went to a porno movie, my peers called it psychological growth. (I preferred to think of it as perverse.) These emerging fads (the evolving ethos) influenced the values we were willing to buy and sell and what personal impasses we felt responsible for mastering.

Many other factors influenced what the supervisory relationship meant or could mean to us, and therefore which relationships succeeded in my eyes and which failed. How old was my supervisor and how long had he or she been supervising? How long had certain ideas been in circulation? Was the rumor out that someone's idea had fallen short of its original promise? (See Lazarus, 1977.) Who were the satirists biting in those days? Who was the department hiring? I needed to figure out which values were really in departmental operation and which were being paid lip service. Divorces were of high interest: was my supervisor getting divorced? Who and how many wanted post-doctorates in our department? How was the department rated nationally? Who was complaining? What about? I peeked a few times to find out to whom dissertations were dedicated. And so important, what transcendence of all these influences could I hope to achieve? Supervision cannot really be abstracted from all of these.

COMPOUNDING THE PROBLEM: THE DUALITY OF EXPERIENCE

This title refers to my simultaneous status as subject and object, agent and host (Bassos, 1976). When I try to account for change experiences in my supervised training, I come to the conclusion that, at any point, I was probably chasing myself.

That is, I did not just "decide" to seek a degree, or "interpret" to my practicum client, or "take" my orals. I watched myself do all these things or at least "do like" what others seemed to be doing. I measured my progress, feared my anticipations of failure, and applauded my achievements. One supervisor captured my obsessiveness by saying that when I had cause to celebrate something, I went "Whew!" instead of "Whee!"

If all this reflexive self-observation was not the greater part of my training, it was certainly a large part. When I say it, it seems embarrassingly obvious. The point to underscore is that it did not seem obvious then, and it follows that clinical growth is the *way* things come to be obvious.

Supervision seemed crucial because identification with qualities of supervisory character allowed me to experience getting beyond reflexive self-spectatorship into feelings associated with spontaneous clinical action. Resolving somehow the paradox of self-involvement was my highest hope for myself. Supervision that focuses on "how to" frequently misses problems at this narcissistic level (Kernberg, 1972). My peers and I were vociferously invested in being "good" therapists (whatever that meant at the time). To me, being a good therapist had to do with technical proficiency only insofar as proficiency included inward resolution. To be a good craftsman was not enough and, in fact, it seemed like a sham if it concealed an unhappy person.

An adequate reconstruction of my professional growth has to account for the development of my self-reflectiveness, the way I watch myself.

All the observations in this paper make crucial reference to an inner seeing (c.f., Jaynes, 1977) that goes on all the time during training. Whatever the monitor turns out to be, without it, identification and other forms of social learning would be very limited. Schafer (1968) calls this the "reflective self representation." Bassos (1976) writes about reflective and nonreflective modes in psychotherapy. Hilgard demythologizes the "hidden observer" in experimental form (Hilgard, 1977). Erikson (1977) makes an issue out of the primacy of vision—that our language of apperception and comprehension is intimately related to the language of sight. Meltzoff and Moore (1977) report an experiment with neonates. They attempt to employ the explanatory model of a supra-modal body representation to account for some facial mimicry in infants. And, in describing I-Thou relatedness, Buber (1970) recalls being, momentarily "eye to eye" with his cat.

I think that I am talking about the same general phenomenon in discussing my evolution as a therapist. A homey way to say it would be that whatever my mind is, it has some pretty changeable body images "in it" (refer to Schilder, 1950) and that a lot of my social thinking makes reference to "seeing" one body area or another. Schafer (1968) describes the primary process presence. I do not have a better language, really, to talk about my more or less acute sense, as a trainee, of being "occupied" much of the time. If I felt occupied by somebody I admired, then I felt wonderful (buoyancy, relief, "future-is-now"). If I felt like my corporeal self housed somebody I did not want to be like, then I became preoccupied with inner distress and hard to get along with.

I think this is the stuff of identification. I worked my way through a lot of therapists and theorists this way. I do not know to what degree other students were aware of this inner feedback. I describe it because I want to make the point that to say "life is lived as a duality" is not just to voice a lyrical truism. Such a statement has proprioceptive and object relational referents (Friedman, 1975; Guntrip, 1973). The transient identifications which can be fostered during supervision provide insights into these processes.

This duality seems to make talking about my supervision exponentially more complex. But other models of the learning process miss a lot in this regard.

I know that when I was eighteen, looking forward to a long term of education, my sense of duality (division) was bound up in the somewhat sad imagery of the "well-wisher" and the "sojourner": being, doing, and always dimly aware of the shifting, transmutable relationships between the two.

Let me give an example. No place like the military can give you the feeling that you are "lost and forgotten" and "present and accounted for" at the same time. However, a sense of survival can be generated by the recognition of someone important to you. A psychiatric officer in the Mental Hygiene Center where I was assigned stopped me in the hallway with the question: "Who are you in real life?"

Blessed be he! He wanted to know! His remark made possible a momentary rededication of the hope that we two were somebody whose truer natures were beyond that place. It may have had something to do with the vigor I invested in getting into graduate school. I wonder if the best moments in therapy are any more than that.

I am trying to share how important the sense of "other eyes watching" can be in keeping a personal balance, or losing it, particularly when the eyes are subjectively "inside." This perceptual split, so important in the notions of identity and the self, is probably what sustains chronic feelings of "not yet" and "something else." Paradoxically, while it can be a powerful motivator, it can be psychically absorbing because its result is a feeling of inner disharmony and incompletion. Supervisory identification may heal this feeling of division from one's self.

MORE ON SUBJECTIVE DUALITY

This disharmony was probably the chief motivator behind my interest in psychotherapy. The reactor, or reactive watcher, refers to my preconscious mode of experiencing. It is how I know what it means to live with myself. As my subjective shadow, it puts together from mood, ambiance, and style the conceptual schemes that help me navigate the clinical world.

It is hard to resist borrowing constructs from object relations theory (Fairbairn, 1954; Guntrip, 1973) to speak for me. It is also hard, as Goffman warns (1974, p. 8 *ff.*), to avoid the trap of infinitely regressive self-pursuit. Nevertheless, intuiting, deciphering, and labeling these inner observational entities occupied a lot of my time and interest during training.

Part of my neophyte dilemma was this: my best self seemed to be the least self-conscious. Not a mime. A doer, an actor, plain and simple. But a nearly reflexive feeling of being nagged or haunted by my own subjectivity meant to me that I could only *watch* and *wait* to see myself act. This felt like a dual destiny and it felt unfair. (Others seemed to *act.*)

Every supervisory and client hour bore the brunt of this internal division, of watching and waiting. And the success of every transaction with a client or supervisor depended in part on whether imagery generated in those hours suggested that my completion was imminent or my waiting perpetual.

(The irony is that I kind of liked it that way. Now that I am older, with some suburban respectability, enough time in analysis to say I at least tried it, and have worked through a paper on "passive" experience, I fear I am losing the old reactor. In a paper like this you run some risk of success. If I actually say what is important to say about my training, I will forfeit some of that sense of personal uniqueness which is bound up in the magic of inexpressibility. These are the hazards of trying to "pass it on.")

The final statement of any circular process (self-consciousness) will always be as elusive as it is intriguing. But a few things become clearer in the telling. During neophyte hours it was the *reactor* that sat with the client, aware of shifting moods or an itchy foot, or the sometimes incredible demand to regard the client benignly. It was to the reactor that the client was scoldingly waving a kleenex or canceling sessions. The reactor could not reach the client. Only the actor could have reached out. The reactor seemed as scolding as the client! The reactor could only mime and mimic, taking its cues from therapeutic actors.

(Occasionally I get the feeling that other trainees do not experience these things. Then they whisper in other contexts that they do, like a neophyte therapist who, with a delightfully ambivalent laugh, admitted he had farted in the client hour. It is comforting to consider that discomforting self-spectatorship may be a universal people simply do not talk about.)

I believe that no matter how confusing it may be to try to talk about these mental processes, some stabilities are recordable. For instance, the watcher seems to have a dual character. On the one hand it has a kind of detached neutrality, alive but inert. It is not hooked to any judgments or imperatives (Hilgard, 1977). More specifically, I saw and heard a lot of things in the client hour that I never processed.

On the other hand, my observant seer is "bound to me," not neutral at all. I am reminded of the phrase "stuck on myself." That is why I frequently was not a very spontaneous therapist during training; why I sought models of unselfconscious action in theorists, supervisors, and peers. Of course I had analogues of such spontaneity in me. I was once a child. But during early training there were only brief periods of time (Barnat, 1973a; 1973b) when I felt so natural that what I did or said to clients could be accounted for without reference to my imagery of someone else. And the cultural scene provided numerous therapeutic prototypes and stereotypes to refer to!

Let us say, to illustrate, that my client says: "I'm angry!" I respond with something gratuitous, uncalled for by theory or client needs. I say: "It's healthy to be angry some of the time!" Instantly I recognize that I am only meeting some need of my own.

In the next moment my neutral observer assumes a scornful face. After that, I am left with the feeling that my facial features belong to or serve somebody who does not like me, or who *I* feel is pathetic. I am not using metaphor here, at least not any more than I have to. I am talking about what I see with my inner sensors (Schilder, 1950). I also wish to point out the theoretical bias that these phenomenon are mentally determined rather than being primarily a function of language (see Jaynes, 1977).

Quite a battle might ensue as I suffered through a feeling of shame. My bodily features would be the disputed ground as far as my inner eyes could see. Engrossing as it might be, this experience would still be marginal (preconscious), and if I brought it up in supervision, it would only be in the most general terms.

Rapport with the client would suffer as my reactive self was given over to the dispute. If the shame were bothersome enough, I might feel the need to disprove the latent accusation that I was foolish. I might do so by pretending—portraying to myself—some character quality of a supervisor who had been supportive to me. From the adoption of an incompatible identification, the feeling of shame would be diffused: once again I could feel okay and on the offensive.

All this has to be placed in the context of my subjective time continuum, the deadlines or feelings of "leeway" (Erikson, 1977) that were actually part of being in my twenties. I waited: for courses, for intern placements, for a galley proof. I waited to take my place as an actor and for the actor to act. This tension is illustrated in one graduate student's lament: "They expect you to be an expert in human relations, but they don't give you time for any!"

QUESTING FOR UNITY: THE ACTOR

Permit me to repeat my theme: the self-spectatorship necessary for meaning, modifying, and a hundred other functions left me vulnerable at the same time because of the implied perceptual division.

I experienced this vulnerability as doubt about my own purposes. One of my most acute dilemmas of doubt was feeling that negative impulses—like some hostile ones—made lies out of positive impulses—like caring ones. When such painful juxtapositions became a problem, I could usually find some supervisor or theorist whose benign sarcasm or faultless logic provided me with the reassurance that seemingly alien urgings could belong in and to the same person. Harmony was possible.

Consider another reconstruction. Once I sat with a practicum client and was somewhat embarrassed by the fleeting urge to grit my teeth. Perhaps they were playing a game with me. On a subjective level, I was only concerned at the moment that the tape sound good to the supervisor.

Emerging internally was a dim vision of a sweetly reassuring face. Part of me began to wonder if it were mocking me. Then the contradictory impulses to kick and kiss the client got confused and my fragile rapport was suspended. I was "in my head."

I had a more or less perpetual urge to *"portray."* When I got myself in a mental or interpersonal dilemma, in an attempt to feel better, I almost reflexively portrayed someone who I had reason to believe was deft at getting out of that very dilemma. A sense of harmony can be purchased on short order in this fashion. What I had to portray with were the internalized qualities of character by which my sponsors seemed to manifest their joy in triumph over doubt. This observation about portrayal ties together many of the observations in this paper (Barnat, 1977).

My portrayal amounted to "hearing" the supervisor's favorite phrase: "You can deliver love in an armored car!" I had a picture of a cement wall crumbling on an armored vehicle with flowers in it. Then I saw myself "humorously" booting the client in the rear. Then I had a feeling that I liked the client. And after all these mental shifts had readjusted my perspective, I said: "I don't think we're getting anywhere." Then the client looked guilty and we talked about our purposes.

(Note that the actor had to wait for the impatient reactor who was always waiting for it.)

If, in these examples, I was just putting on masks, I was not alone. One well-liked supervisor was noted for his characteristic grin. A student reflected a criticism of that supervisor by saying that at the end of the year there were always "a half dozen students walking around with that grin on their face!"

Was this *just* guruism? I think it is a mistake to dismiss processes like this because they are not "pure." This seems to me to be a kind of play (Erikson, 1977) necessary for learning. Yes, it was fun to identify with someone I liked and admired and who may have admired me. But if the internalization process worked through to usable identifications, then I had something more than a warm feeling of borrowed peace. I had a logic which was the beginning of a real sense of harmony (competence).

It must have felt good to my supervisor to grin his warm, comical grin. When I could wear that grin in my inner face, then I could intuit the struggle and resolution that only that grin could convey. I hesitate to think of this as simply "identification with the aggressor" (Freud, 1946). Perhaps this is because as a graduate student, identification was one of the few things I was really good at! I think this is where my empathic potency was! These inner sensory processes allowed me to take away something from supervision.

What else is Schafer (1968) talking about when he defines internalization as "all those processes that transform" outer into inner mechanisms for regulating impulses and self esteem? What better place than the supervisory relationship to study these processes? I think that the best and least of us were somehow in love with being mimics of the therapists and professors who had given us affirmative winks—snappy one-liners, unconditional positive regard, and all.

Let me put this more personally. When I was younger, I made no distinction between psychologist and psychotherapist. But now I think that the psychologist is the superordinate identity. (The danger to me is that being a therapy technician leaves one with a skill that is no more than a clerical excercise, with no historical consciousness, not even good craft. I am aware that this is an idiosyncratic bias.)

But a psychologist is an observer once removed from the "action." The observer looks, hears, comprehends.

I believe now that my interest in becoming a psychologist has been related to a need to project and concretize the implied perceptual division that alienates myself (agent) from itself (host) leading to chronic angst and sadness.

The hucksters aside for a moment, people who become healers want to heal (i.e., "put together"). By making my complexities my business I can grapple with them in hopes of finding a balm for soreness of spirit. It is turning host into agent, refusing simply to bear the human condition but insisting on a commanding view.

Note the delicious paradox: my desire was to occupy a social role that I believed meant a perpetual state of self-healing. A therapeutic vocation could absorb conflict, allow me to work in my most comfortable perceptual sphere, share companionship, and lay claim to a certain amount of naive cultural regard. The unique qualities of the therapy hour actually help me put together the active, passive, nurturant and assaultive, solitary, and communal elements making up myself.

Yet, whether journeyman or neophyte, to watch one's self means to perpetually aggravate one's feeling of aloneness. It has been said satirically that "psychoanalysis creates the disease for which it is the cure." Maybe it does. But without such scrutiny, how else would we define our humanity, or know how supervisors supervised or clients learned from us?

Supervision at its best was a mutuality supporting the notion that I could transcend these struggles.

Let me give a final example of the supervisory relationship "in action," not in the tutorial hour but in the client hour.

A practicum client glanced at me ambiguously and I got tense. Almost immediately, I was enjoying a feeling of sponsorial presence. Now, I must have known at some level what was going on. Otherwise it would be hard to explain why I would have conjured up that particular imagery of that particular supervisor in response to that ambiguity. But right then I would have disavowed any notion of what to say.

I began to feel a kind of merging (Schafer, 1968) with my image of the supervisor: my image of the supervisor's body occupied the same proprioceptive "space" and the same geometric plane as mine. My supervisor had a way of leaning forward and putting his hand on his knee. I was sensing in myself "knee," though I did not put my hand on my knee.

The supervisor's mannerism was no empty gesture, and I sensed the logic to it. I expected that some insightful response would be forthcoming from it. Some wonderful insights had emerged from the supervisor when he put his hand on his knee. But I found myself unable to extrapolate that meaning and offer it to the client, unable to *portray the moment to its logical conclusion.*

I had perhaps introjected an element of supervisory character (knee touch) but I had not yet worked through some of the declarative statements that the seemingly self-evident mannerism may have substituted for in the supervisor's subjective world. But the effort was supervision in action.

It takes time for probable opinions (corollaries) to evolve from some internalized image, whether we are talking about facial features, gestures, voice qualities, or other "partial objects." (Refer to Scheflen, 1972 for a communicational approach to these behaviors.) What I got from supervisors, I often got by walking around portraying their uniqueness, for example, muttering the punchline to their favorite joke or their laughter, until what was self-evident to them was self-evident to me. (Now, because of my own makeup, I sometimes had trouble getting *rid* of some person's features with whom I had identified. This extended sense of cohabitation probably influences how much I make out of this aspect of training.)

These kinds of identification experiences stand in contrast to "being yourself." (See Jourard, 1971.) However, it is unlikely that the processes would be successful without the spontaneities of the supervisor already being part of the self that walked around looking for them all the time. These qualities just rarely seemed to evolve spontaneously a lá Zorba the Greek.

The actor one hopes to internalize is *wholesome*. It is a sense of self that is not morally compromised or challenged. It is me when I experience a unique congruence of breath and muscle, aim and resources, naive receptiveness and readiness to laugh. Proprioceptively speaking, the actor is forward leaning, out reaching, and in bringing. It is telling the client what I really believe about the life he is portraying for me. The actor is available to be needed; it spends and expends. It takes its cues from time but it never bickers with time or any of the characters that occupy my object world. It cannot mime or mimic and its energies are only in the service of intention.

The exquisite paradox for me as a writer, learner, and therapist is that the robustness described above is sacrificed by a simple perceptual shift, as when Orpheus made Eurydice disappear with a backward glance. That image conveys the feeling of frustrating delicacy associated with mental states that seem to embody the most wholesome resilience.

Some pains and doubts are chronic simply because there are no words to express them. Some supervisors had found unique ways to express them, and I wanted to know what they knew, to know why some things seemed to make sense to them that did not yet make sense to me. As a source of the reassurance that emotion could be intuited [in the way that Gendlin (1969) invites you to intuit], supervised training was a quest for a disciplined way of being a self healer.

(IN)CONCLUSION: THE HERE AND NOW

Concluding a paper that has as its focus processes that are perceptually circular and developmentally inconclusive is difficult. I think these observations have meaning beyond their meaning to me. I do not think that that is a simple summary meaning.

Rather than conclude, I will resort to a logical interruption by quoting a favorite supervisor. In a moment that combined simplicity and vision he said: "What you're doin's where you're at."

That sentence is more rigorous than it sounds. It is true of every therapist or supervisor. I would only add one element. Your unique style is probably having more of an impact than you are aware of.

As might be inferred from this exercise, the change process is a continuous one.

Supervision of trainees serves as a continual reminder of the ways my values change with age and other pressures. But I am also reminded of the genius who put identity in a nutshell when he observed that the more things change, the more they stay the same.

Since ambiguity, like desperation, is a chief parameter of clinical life, I can only wonder: some trainees never seem to get the point. Others bend over backward to repeat what I have said. What they may learn will depend in part on the degree to which identification with me has altered some troubling misalignment in themselves. Perhaps just their self-awareness is sharpened. One hates to close on such a tentative note, but what I have to give trainees may amount to little more than the mastery I have achieved over myself. I always have to wonder: for whom am I the sponsor? For whom am I the naysayer?

One would like, though, to help trainees feel more confident in nurturing and confronting those clients who feel threatened by their own inner divisions and uncharitable images.

REFERENCES

Bandura, A., and Walters, R. *Social learning and personality development.* New York: Holt, Rinehart and Winston, 1963.

Barnat, M. Student reactions to supervision: Quests for a contract. *Professional Psychology,* 1973, *4*(1), 17–22. (a)

Barnat, M. Student reactions to the first supervisory year: Relationship and resolutions. *Journal of Education for Social Work,* 1973, *9*(3), 3–8. (b)

Barnat, M. Some characteristics of supervisory identification in psychotherapy. *Psychotherapy: Theory, Research and Practice,* 1974, *11*(2), 189–192.

Barnat, M. Spontaneous supervisory metaphor in the resolution of trainee anxiety. *Professional Psychology,* 1977, *8*(3), 307–315.

Bassos, C. Two modes of consciousness and their pseudomodes. *Psychotherapy: Theory, Research and Practice,* 1976, *13*(4), 335–342.

Benedek, T. Countertransference in the training analyst. *Bulletin of the Menninger Clinic,* 1963, *11,* 12–16.

Berne, E. *Games People Play.* New York: Grove Press, 1964.

Boring, E. Was this analysis a success? *Journal of Abnormal and Social Psychology,* 1940, *35*(1), 4–10.

Brown, J. Was this analysis a success? *Journal of Abnormal and Social Psychology,* 1940, *35*(1), 29–44.

Buber, M. *I and Thou.* New York: Charles Scribner's Sons, 1970.

Doehrman, M. Parallel processes in supervision and psychotherapy. *Bulletin of the Menninger Clinic,* 1976, *40*(1).

The author is indebted to Allen K. Hess for the opportunity to participate in the supervision issue project; to Rhonda Barnat for help in the preparation of the manuscript and to Howard Wolowitz of the University of Michigan for fruitful discussion.

Dollard, J., and Miller, N. *Personality and Psychotherapy: An analysis in terms of learning, thinking and culture.* New York: McGraw-Hill, 1950.

Ekstein, R., and Wallerstein, R. *The teaching and learning of psychotherapy.* New York: Basic Books, 1958.

Erikson, E. *Insight and responsibility: Lectures on the ethical implications of psychoanalytic insight.* New York: Norton, 1964.

Erikson, E. *Toys and reasons: Stages in the ritualization of experience.* New York: Norton, 1977.

Fairbairn, W. *An object relations theory of the personality.* New York: Basic Books, 1954.

Freud, A. *The ego and the mechanisms of defense.* New York: International Universities Press, 1946.

Friedman, L. Current psychoanalytic object relations theory and its clinical implications. *International Journal of Psychoanalysis,* 1975, *56*(2) 137–146.

Gendlin, E. Focusing. *Psychotherapy: Theory, Research and Practice,* 1969, *6*(1), 4–15.

Goffman, E. *Frame analysis: An essay on the organization of experience.* New York: Harper and Row, 1974.

Guntrip, H. *Psychoanalytic theory, therapy and the self.* New York: Basic Books, 1973.

Guntrip, H. My experience of analysis with Fairbairn and Winnicott: How complete a result does psychoanalytic therapy achieve? *International Review of Psychoanalysis,* 1975, *2*, 145–156.

Hilgard, E. *Divided consciousness: Multiple controls in human thought and action.* New York: Wiley, 1977.

Jaynes, J. *The origins of consciousness in the breakdown of the bicameral mind.* Boston: Houghton Mifflin, 1977.

Jourard, S. *The transparent self.* New York: Van Nostrand, 1971.

Kell, B., and Mueller, W. *Impact and change: A study of counseling relationships.* New York: Appleton-Century-Crofts, 1966.

Kernberg, O. *Borderline conditions and pathological narcissism.* New York: Jason Aronson, 1972.

Landis, C. Was this analysis a success?: Psychoanalytic phenomena. *Journal of Abnormal and Social Psychology,* 1940, *35*(1), 17–28.

Lazarus, A. Has behavior therapy outlived its usefulness? *American Psychologist,* 1977, *32*(7), 550–553.

Meltzoff, A., and Moore, M. Imitation of facial and manual gestures by human neonates. *Science,* 1977, *198* (4312), 75–78.

Mueller, W., and Kell, B. *Coping with conflict: Supervising counselors and psychotherapists.* New York: Appleton-Century-Crofts, 1972.

Pleck, J. Sex role issues in clinical training. *Psychotherapy: Theory, Research and Practice,* 1976, *13*(1), 17–19.

Reik, T. *Listening with the third ear.* Garden City, N.Y.: Garden City Books, 1948.

Rogers, C., and Stevens, B. *Person to person: the problem of being human.* Lafayett, Calif.: Real People Press, 1967.

Sachs, H. Was this analysis a success?: Comment. *Journal of Abnormal and Social Psychology,* 1940, *35*(1), 11–16.

Schafer, R. *Aspects of internalization.* New York: International Universities Press, 1968.

Scheflen, A. *Body language and social order: communication as behavioral control.* Englewood Cliffs, N.J.: Prentice-Hall, 1972.

Schilder, P. *The image and appearance of the human body.* New York: International Universities Press, 1950.

Spence, D. Analog and digital descriptions of behavior. *American Psychologist,* 1973, *28* (6), 479–488.

Viscott, D. *The making of a psychiatrist.* New York: Arbor House, 1972.

CHAPTER 6

The Dilemmas of Supervision in Dynamic Psychotherapy

BY MARGARET J. RIOCH

When we speak of the dynamics of something, we mean, first and foremost, something which does not appear on the surface, something which is not obvious. Artists knew of these things a long time ago. Now scientists know about them, too. A desk, for example, is not, from a scientific point of view, a solid piece of wood, but a whirling mass of molecules, atoms, electrons, and of even smaller particles. Things are *not* what they seem, least of all from the point of view of modern physics, to say nothing of dynamic psychology. In the mid-twentieth century Fred Hoyle already said that no literary imagination could have invented a story one hundredth part as fantastic as the sober facts that have been unearthed.

The Freudian metaphor of the iceberg, with the most important part hidden under the water, is still a good and useful one. If we are to look at the dynamics of anything, it means that we must look beneath the surface, into the depths, to discover the parts that give trouble and may even sink a large ocean-going vessel. We assume that something goes on beneath the outward forms which both enriches them and makes them questionable. It is into the depths that we look for truth and also for trouble. Surely we need a third dimension of depth to give truth to our perceptions of space. When a picture, for example, gives us a sense of space and of depth, we think that the painter has mastered the technique of perspective and has given us the illusion of truth. We may *see* only two dimensions but we know there is a third. It was Freud who first described in detail how we usually see only the tip of the iceberg; but under the surface strange things occur which are hinted at in dreams and myths, in slips of the tongue, etc. And it was Jung, that connoisseur of myths, who taught us to look not only at the trouble beneath the surface, but at the origin there of the great creative drives in human life.

Since Freud it is a matter of popular knowledge that things go on beneath the surface. Not only mental health professionals, but even the man in the street knows that if he is worried about something, mysterious processes may occur in his body which result in a cold in the head or a skin rash or wherever else his Achilles' heel is located. And the manifestations do not have to be somatic, in the sense of a physical illness. It may be that he does not sleep well because he is worried about something even though he does not admit to himself consciously that he is worried. It may be that he forgets an important appointment which he had every intention of remembering. Or he may find himself spending an inordinate amount of time rearranging his desk drawers and neglecting to do important things when unpleasant decisions are required which he prefers to forget.

Dynamics give life its richness and color. At the same time they make it hazardous even if one stays encased in the cocoon of one's own house without venturing abroad upon the highways and byways where the "real" dangers appear. So it is, too, with supervision. It would seem like a fairly innocuous way to spend one's time, and it plays a large part in most training programs. This is in itself interesting and indicates that we are dealing with something, namely psychotherapy, which we do not understand very well and which is an art or a skill rather than a science. If psychotherapy were really a science, it could be spelled out carefully in a book and would need to be updated only when there was a new finding which was recognized by other scientists. The cumulative nature of science would be the cumulative nature of psychotherapy. Someone would make new discoveries. They would be recognized as valid and they would be incorporated in the work of all upstanding psychotherapists. But it is not so. We consider that the best way to learn, like the best way to learn to play the piano, for example, is by the apprenticeship method. Usually one has more than one teacher. One may in fact look around a bit before finding "the teacher who is the right one for me." This implies that the teacher may be all right for someone else, but not for me. In other words, there is not one right way to do the thing, but several ways, perhaps many, many ways. It is considered a good idea to have more than one supervisor. The right one may never exist but one finds one's way as a therapist among the many ways offered. Sometimes one is lucky enough to find the right model. Sometimes one has to put together "the right way for me" out of the various pieces that are offered.

To come to the specific topic of this paper (the dilemmas of supervision in dynamic psychotherapy), we see the outward surface of a process called supervision in our ordinary lives, but we are more deeply concerned with what lies beneath that surface. The term "beneath" is not derogatory. "Beneath" may imply the driving force without which no motion would occur. Or it may be that "beneath" implies an important struggle while the outer surface remains calm.

In supervision we are dealing with two main characters: the supervisor and the supervisee. In group supervision the latter is multiplied by the number of supervisees present. This complicates the phenomenon but still there remain two major persons: the supervisor and the supervised. The usual case in group supervision is that the latter of these is a group which takes turns presenting cases; or group supervision may take the form of a continuing case seminar. But the main characters remain the same.

The process of supervision, like all human relationships, is fraught with hazards. On the surface, a trainee or supervisee comes to a supervisor and arranges time, place, and money. Or in a training program, students go to classes arranged by the program and they sign up and pay for the courses. The instructor, as one of the people selected to train students, is reimbursed by the university or other training institute.

Let us begin with something which is fairly near the surface, so near that it can really be *seen*. The supervisor or the teacher often sits in a special place. If it is his office he takes his accustomed chair and the supervisee comes to visit him, not vice versa. If it is a classroom, again the teacher often has his special place or seat—for example, at the head of the table—and it is rare that a student will take the teacher's place. These phenomena depend on the special position of the supervisor in relation to the supervised.

The thesis of this paper rests on the proposition that there are two forces in America, one operating from above down and one operating from down upward. This is not a general truth but one which holds in America today. The statement holds for "today in America" or "today in the West," but it was not always thus. The caste system in India existed for many generations without much movement from above downward and from below upward. The same holds true of the classes in feudal society and indeed until perhaps the twentieth century. But today there is a strong tendency for what is down to move up. And also for what is up to be stricken with such a bad conscience that it moves down. This process of movement is what is referred to first of all as the dynamics of supervision. Later the definition of dynamics will be expanded to include more complex phenomena, such as dependency and pairing, both in anti-work functions and in the service of work. But for the moment let us consider this matter of up and down.

If one glances at the dictionary definition of "supervise" one sees immediately that it comes from Latin "super" and "video"—to oversee. Webster's goes on to define the word as "to oversee for direction, to superintend, to inspect with authority."

Not many upstanding young people want to be inspected with authority. There are also those, including many supervisors, who do not greatly enjoy being in the role of the person with the authority to inspect, because one knows very well what the thoughts of the supervisee are almost bound to be. He or she can barely wait for the day when he will "oversee for direction, superintend, and inspect with authority" some other victim.

The "you are up; I am down" situation is not likely to obtain for very long. The balance is untenable. Something has to be done to bring things into equality. How can that be done? Many ways spring immediately to mind. The simplest one is to bring the supervisor down. One can do this easily, if the supervisor is not clever and careful, by noting his errors and telling him, kindly and patiently, that the patient in question did not respond favorably to his suggested treatment. One can lead him on to think he is wonderful, only to tell him that the patient, for whom he was so hopeful, committed suicide. The reverse works equally well; if he is very pessimistic, the patient makes marvelous strides and recovers brilliantly. One can do all these things and more, very quietly, so that the supervisor is unaware that anything untoward is going on. One simply sits out the supervision, passes the course, or puts in a required number of hours, pays one's bill, says thank you and tells one's peers that Dr. X. is a nice fellow, but that one really gets nothing out of supervision with him.

Another way to redress the balance is for the supervisee to be a brilliant therapist himself, so brilliant that he is really not in need of and not interested in what the supervisor has to say. Perhaps the supervisee has thought of all this already. Or what the supervisor suggests cannot be done. Or the supervisee does not change in any way, shape, or manner during the supervision. This last is perhaps the best way of all to bring him down, for the supervisor, being human, likes to think he is having an effect.

But the supervisee, if he starts "one down," is not the only one who tries to correct the balance. The supervisor, especially in these days of egalitarian tendencies, is likely to be uncomfortable in his role of superior. He wants to be a helper rather than an overseer; one who assists rather than one who tells someone what to do. A very good supervisor once reported that he got out of this uncomfortable position by sharing his doubts about the therapeutic process with his trainee. He freely admitted that he was not omniscient, that he often made mistakes, that he did not know what to do, and so on. Probably no one was fooled by this. Surely if one does not make fewer mistakes than the supervisee one should not be taking his money or one should not be in the position of teacher while the supervisees are the taught. But this supervisor was neither unperceptive nor stupid. He was referring to a situation of reduced or optimal anxiety in which people are not so anxious that they cannot hear anything, but anxious enough to be very alert. Even quite gentle supervisors have been told by students that they heard nothing the supervisor had said, but the students continued to be convinced that the supervisor was a great therapist and that they themselves were not very good. Some supervisors have tried to get out of this situation by asking the student to think what it is that he wants to know, what question is troubling him just now about his patient. Students have told quite reasonably what seemed to be troubling them. For example, a young woman said she felt that a particular patient's excursions into her family background were, at a certain point in the treatment, simply a way to avoid talking about a pressing problem, but she wanted to feel more sure of this before bringing it to the patient's attention. It was pointed out by the supervisor that the patient's excursion into her family background could be an avoidance *and also* have a certain meaning—in this particular case the supervisor thought that talking about her family was a self-justification for the patient's feelings of guilt for not satisfying her partner sexually—and that the talk about her family represented both an avoidance of the actual problem and a means of saying "I surely can't help it because etc., etc." When this had been said, the student a minute later could not remember what the supervisor had told her, though it was on a topic which had presumably occupied her mind more than any other in the past week.

The situation of "I am up; you are down" is stressful for both supervisor and supervisee. Furthermore it is ineffective. The supervisee does not learn anything. Only the most venal of supervisors can stand this. If the supervisor puts or pretends to put himself on the same level with the supervisee, some kind of work can proceed. Out of gratitude the supervisee can put or pretend to put the supervisor in the position of teacher—at least he does so temporarily so long as the supervisor is being so amiable and pretending that there is no difference in competence between the two parties.

While the up-down pull is being exerted, other dynamic forces come into play which may indeed never be mentioned except by those people impolite enough to want to look into the depths and see the fantastic creatures that live there.

One of them is the phenomenon of "pairing" as described by Wilfred Bion (1961). Although Bion speaks of it here as a group phenomenon, it may occur when supervisor and supervisee are the only people in the room. Sexual pairing of people of opposite sexes and similar ages facilitates such pairing, but is not necessary for it to occur. It is, of course, encouraged when the teacher or supervisor is imagined or perceived by students to be attracted by one student's therapeutic gifts, his brilliance, his sensitivity, his tact, his perfect timing, and the like. The supervisor is imagined or perceived by the student in the pair as possessing great wisdom, modesty, and perceptiveness in teaching just the right things at the right time.

In one seminar a male student, not without the collaboration of the instructor, saw himself as the catalyst of the group, and thus as the instructor's (a woman) right hand man—saying things which would be inappropriate for her to say. He offered himself up as a sacrifice to the group in ways which the instructor was saved from doing, by bringing up unpleasant subjects, admitting that he was bored by certain people's case presentations, challenging the competence of his fellow students; in other words, by taking on himself all the unpleasant duties which in his heart of hearts he thought were really hers, and by making himself cordially disliked by many of his classmates, pushing himself thus into partnership with the instructor.

The essence of this pairing, the thing which gives it its force and its zest, is the hope invested in it. Bion identifies this as the hope for a Messiah who will bring salvation. It is not always identified consciously as such by participants in the pairing. There is, however, about the two an air of hopefulness which rests on the illusion that the pair will bring about things which neither one could do alone. This is illusory because either one *could* do it alone. The illusion is that it can be done solely by a pair. If only two persons are in the room together the illusion consists in an overestimation of the power of the other; "only he could appreciate me this much." "Only he could bring out the best in me the way he does."

Once two male students "appreciated" each other in similar ways, as if neither could function without the other. The fact that they functioned very well at a distance of almost a thousand miles from each other the following year should, of course, not be considered as evidence against the illusion.

Still more deeply hidden in the depths of the unconscious is the student's tendency to dependency which indeed is often fostered by the supervisor's wish to be depended upon.

There are occasionally situations in which students like the one up-one down position and remain in it. This occurs when the student or students are operating on what Bion would call the basic assumption dependency. In other words, the student likes being one down because it rids him of the necessity of thinking or acting for himself. He then assumes that the supervisor is one who can infinitely protect him and think for him. He himself knows nothing and depends solely on the great wisdom of the supervisor to enlighten him. Some of this attitude occurs in all fruitful supervision, but it does not obtain very frequently and not for very long. The student wants to try his own wings. In fact, the good supervisor wants him to. And so, while this dependency may be a comfortable situation for a beginning therapist, it is not long before the position of one up, one down, begins to feel very uncomfortable to the student, if not indeed to the supervisor as well. He—the student—begins to fight against it.

Strangely, the fight-flight basic assumption, to use Bion's terminology once more, seems more in evidence than any other. Even supervisors who have no particular valency for fight-flight notice this. The prevalence of the fight-flight phenomenon has to do with the one up, one down position. It is often amazing to see how nice decent people become devious, sulky, or even untruthful in the situation of supervision.

For example, a student realizes that she has avoided confronting a patient on the issue of who was to take the initiative in starting the session and bringing up topics. An opportunity for discussing this in a supervisory hour was present but not used. The student frankly admitted that she had to do this herself without interference of the supervisor or the supervisory seminar. She felt that what she would get from both would be "interference" with the treatment process. If she was to do her best with the patient she wanted to be unencumbered by the supervision.

Another student showed by his sulky facial expression how little he liked bringing an account of what he had done with a recalcitrant patient to the seminar. The student's behavior was indeed unconventional and would probably have been questioned by the supervisor. He had several times telephoned a patient who showed his unwillingness to keep appointments by simply not showing up. Finally the patient came for an interview and this was considered by the student to be a therapeutic triumph. At least he did succeed in seeing him several more times and in getting him to discuss his sexual problems which the patient had been loathe to do before. The supervisor would probably have questioned the wisdom of pursuing a patient who showed so clearly a reluctance to be in therapy.

The predicament of the supervisor who takes his work seriously is indeed formidable. He has a duty to society to let the supervisee know when he finds his work unacceptable. But who is he to judge? Society has made provisions whereby anyone with a few years of experience may be licensed to call himself a psychiatrist or psychologist or social worker. If one supervisor disapproves, it is easy for the student to find another. And anyway, how can the supervisor be sure that the patient is not profiting by simply having a listening ear to hear his troubles? What kind of mess may he be stirring up and what kind of destruction may he be bringing about if he tells this supervisee he thinks his work with patients ought to be stopped. He knows very well what havoc can be wrought by anxiety. It may be indeed that he is not getting an accurate picture of the therapy by the report of the supervisee and that the work is much better than he thinks. This is the place where a recording, audio or video, may be useful.

But let us suppose that the student's work is not too terrible and that there is no real question in the supervisor's mind that he ought to stop it. Then the problem becomes "how to help." How can the student learn to go more deeply, more effectively into the patient's problem?

I have elsewhere (Rioch, Coulter, and Weinberger, 1976, pp. 231–33) outlined the three main kinds of supervision. Let me summarize what I think they are.

First, the supervisor tells the student what he would do if he were there. The obvious disadvantage of this method is that he is not there. These days there are, I hear, ways in which the supervisor can be there behind a one-way screen, and pipe into the therapist what he thinks should be done. Aside from the fact that this is prohibitively time consuming, entailing the supervisor's presence at every therapeutic hour, I find it an abhorrent procedure from everyone's point of view. The patient does not really know whether he is listening to his therapist or to a voice from the rear. The therapist must either depend on the supervisor or must feel the interventions as a foreign body. And the supervisor who intervenes places himself in a position of God on high who knows what is right to do at every moment. If we do not have such gadgets available, it is even more dangerous to tell a student what the supervisor would do, for the simple reason that the student is not the supervisor, and what makes sense for one person does not necessarily at all make sense for another. In spite of this obvious fact, supervisors, including myself, go on telling students what they would have done. And occasionally this can even be useful—by providing a model which the student can use later at his discretion when perchance the opportunity seems ripe.

Second, the supervisor explains the patient more deeply to the student than he had been able to see him before. Students are often dazzled by the brilliant performance of their supervisors who have supposedly seen 100 such clients and who can consequently predict their behavior. Aside from the bedazzlement, it is often extremely useful to a student to have a better understanding of the person who is sitting before him. The supervisor's greater breadth of experience makes it possible for him to see aspects of the patient not visible to the neophyte. Puzzling symptoms or behavior patterns suddenly make sense which they had not done before. This is a real gift which the supervisor can give to the student. But he cannot tell what the student will make of it. Sometimes the student takes the gift and its wrappings and deposits it before the patient, who is ill prepared to receive it. Sometimes, he takes and hoards the gift, not knowing where or how to use it effectively. Occasionally this may be because the supervisor's picture, dazzlingly brilliant though it was, does not really help the student in finding a way to relate to his patient therapeutically.

The group situation is even more difficult. I have described (Rioch, Coulter, and Weinberger, 1976, p. 219) the anti-therapeutic effects of a case seminar in psychotherapy in which the students took turns presenting cases. They had then not only the supervisor to contend with, but their fellow students as well. One student illustrates the problem neatly. He says with regard to a patient he is presenting: "I kept thinking that Ellen would say it had all been very superficial and Doug would say it was unclear and that I seemed to him very confused. I don't know what you would say, Dr. Rioch, except that I shouldn't have let her go over time. Gail would say I couldn't work with her if I didn't know what she wanted. And everybody would say she had walked over me, so I kept her on and practically shouted at her that I had to find out what her problem was. She got quite annoyed and said she had been telling me about it all this time. So I said, "We have to stop now. Tell me next time so that I can understand it. And I got up and walked out."

This student had correctly sized up his colleagues and could predict what they would say. What they would say was not exactly favorable to him. A student in a group, for example in a clinical case seminar, has to deal with the approval or lack of it of his colleagues as well as the instructor. He has to act as if he knew the answers when he is probably still quite unsure of the questions.

Third, the supervisor attempts to work with the student's anxieties and his defenses against them. The reason why I am in favor of the third kind of supervision is simple: it stands a chance of stirring up anxiety. I think there is no greater teacher than this in the whole wide human world, especially if it is what has been referred to as reduced or optimal anxiety. But the student must give permission for this kind of work to occur. Even if he gives lip service to wanting to understand and penetrate his own defenses he may be incapable of seeing what he is doing, not because of intellectual incompetence, but because his defenses are too well entrenched. But, I am in favor of this kind of supervision, simply because it does allow a chance for anxiety to occur if it will, and thereby for students to learn something.

A sound track of a supervisor's thoughts as he supervises goes something like the following: a million questions arise. The foremost may be: When shall I interrupt? Students often, in an effort to impress by completeness of report, or in an unconscious effort to stop the penetration of the supervisor, leave little time for the supervisor to get in. Shall I ask every time a point is unclear or shall I wait hoping that clarity will emerge? Shall I point out that one cannot work without knowing where this man's life has been lived or does the student know this and has he simply neglected to inform me? Let us assume that the questions of fact and the question of when to intervene have been answered. Then the most important question is *how* to intervene. The supervisor is torn in the same way the student is. He can impress the student with his brilliance or he can be useful. An excellent therapist burst out once with an exclamation after a group session, "Oh, I was brilliant tonight, absolutely brilliant. But they learned nothing—really nothing. I should have kept my mouth shut." How often one is in the quandary of saying something perhaps brilliant, perhaps not, but knowing that it is useless. One has indications that the student cannot hear. Perhaps he is making the same mistake for the second or third time. Perhaps he is clearly impatient with the supervisor's statement which comes as an interruption of his train of thought.

In order for the supervisor to make sense to the supervisee, his intervention must not only be comprehensible, it must come at the right time for the student. He must be ready to use it. This means that the student must be speaking with a question in mind. If he is in the mode of reporting, he will want to get on with his job and interventions are at best interruptions, usually unwelcome ones.

It is the custom in some group supervision to ask the students to formulate a question which they want the seminar to discuss. This works well a few times, but soon ways are found to formulate questions to which either no answers can be found, or the supervisee knows them already, or the question is so irrelevant that it is surely not going to affect the work. Students, as well as others, are very clever at formulating questions that they are not interested in.

Unless the supervisor and the supervisee have a very unusual relationship or have already worked for a long time together the usual anxieties stirred up by strangers are likely to appear in both. "How am I impressing this fellow?" is almost certain to be in both their minds.

Group supervision is by and large a more likely arena for productive work than individual supervision. There are, of course, exceptions to this when the pair of supervisor and supervisee can forget about who is up and who is down. The thing that facilitates the group work is the fact that the supervisor is outnumbered. The weight of the peer group is some compensation for the supposed expertise of the instructor or supervisor who actually finds himself sometimes to be in a very lonely position opposite faces which often, in their inscrutability, conceal hostility, boredom, or some other variation of how to move up when someone senses that he is down.

The question may well be raised as to how, when all these forces are operative, any effective work is done at all in supervision. The answer is that often it is not. In fact, more often, nothing is accomplished, work is not done, and supervisees sit through the interminable hours because there are certain requirements in the program which gives them certificates that they need in order to make a living. The less we have of required "sitting through" the better. But just as in learning to play the piano, the most important thing is to practice, and to have the stimulation of a teacher to whom one can go once a week or so and show what one has done. In learning to practice and to present one's work to a teacher, one also learns to listen to oneself. This is probably the most important aspect of teaching the piano and of supervising psychotherapy that there is. One learns to listen to oneself. The fact of the supervisor's being present is not really so important as it would seem. A spark may be struck by an occasional supervisor. That is the *un*usual rather than the usual case. Much more common is the case of the student who says truthfully that he remembers nothing of what the supervisor said to him. But in the practice of psychotherapy he has learned, first of all, confidence in himself, and second of all, that most important element—listening to oneself while one is also listening to the other, a neat trick which all therapists must discover for themselves.

There is another way to get out of the bind which I have called the one-up and one-down situation. But it is not very often found. More often the supervisee comes upon the path—albeit a lonely one—in which he learns to listen to himself. The way is described by Krishnamurti (1976),

> A disciple is one who learns all the time, and the word 'discipline' comes from the word 'disciple'—one who is learning. Now if you are learning all the time, there is no need to conform, there is no need to follow any one. Therefore, the division ceases because both the teacher and the disciple are learning. Both are moving in the same direction at the same time. Disorder means the lack of discipline, the lack of capacity to learn. When you are learning, there is no disorder. Disorder comes when you merely conform to what has been said or what will be (Krishnamusrti, (1976) p. 7).*

In other words, if one is interested in learning, rather than in one's own position, whether that is one up or one down, then there is *order* which comes not from whether one is above or below the other, but springs only from the movement of knowledge and learning. But in America at the present time I have my doubts, as you may indeed have yours, as to whether this state as described by Krishnamurti obtains very often. We are more likely to settle for the lonely path of the supervisee who learns to practise and to hear himself in spite of the supervisor. Only occasionally and with great good luck do we find a supervisor or a teacher who is moving in the same direction as we are. Then there is real learning and no disorder in either supervisor or supervisee.

REFERENCES

Bion, W. *Experience in groups.* New York: Basic Books, 1961.

Krishnamurti, J. *Bulletin, Krishnamurti Foundation of America,* Autumn 1976, *30.*

Rioch, M. J., Coulter, W. R., and Weinberger, D. M. *Dialogues for Therapists,* San Francisco: Jossey-Bass, 1976.

*©Krishnamurti Foundation Trust Ltd., 1976.

CHAPTER 7

The New Supervisee Views Supervision

LARRY COHEN

Most people entering supervision—both supervisees and supervisors—are looking for an experience that is rewarding both intellectually and emotionally. That the new supervisee will find the experience anxiety-provoking seems undeniable and unavoidable given the importance with which it is imbued at the early stages of a therapist's career. Some understanding of the bases of this anxiety will hopefully serve to reduce it to a level at which it can be used effectively to make supervision a rewarding experience in both personal and professional growth.

The literature on psychotherapy supervision is typically written almost exclusively by supervisors, reflecting the point of view of only one member of the supervisory relationship. Although the supervisor was once a supervisee too, we may assume with reasonable certainty that his or her major identification at the time of writing on the subject is with the role of supervisor. The aim of this paper is to elucidate the process of supervision from the student's perspective. It is an attempt to take supervisors back in time to the days when they too knocked at the profession's door. It is intended as well to provide new supervisees with some conceptual grasp of the experience they are grappling with.

In good measure, the success of doctoral programs in clinical psychology in training clinicians will reflect the quality of supervision provided to budding therapists. Through course catalogue, intuition, or the "grapevine", students who have never been supervised and who may have virtually no idea of what the supervisory experience entails, are quick to realize this. Almost as soon as they enter training they begin to hear about this mysterious process. They may know that it is conducted behind closed doors and that it is something that they are not quite ready to experience. They will have to earn it by going through a period of classes and evaluations. All the upper-classpeople talk about it with great emotion, whether they view it as a transcendental interaction or purgatory. It is the place where a "real" therapist starts to teach you how to do therapy. Each new list of assignments of supervisors to students is a cause for celebration, despair, or outrage, depending in part about what one has heard about Dr. X. While the concern about getting a good supervisor—and there *are* good and bad supervisors, at least in terms of the match of two personalities—is an important one, given that supervision is where a lot of learning takes place, why is the experience of supervision so often highly charged and anxiety-provoking for new therapists?

To begin with, the nature of the relationship the student therapist is entering is unclear. Will I be an apprentice? A peer? Student? Friend? Lover? Patient? Some combination of the above? In short, the parameters of behavior and the limits to which the interaction may soar or sink are unknown entities, and though they will certainly differ among varying individuals, both supervisees and supervisors, the student therapist does not have the advantage—or disadvantage—of a previous history in supervision, which is to say, no personal road map. How the student responds to supervision will be the natural result of his or her personality interacting with that of the supervisor. There may be, for example, an initial period of cautiousness, a tentative testing of the waters with a new supervisor. Or, anxiety may show itself in counterdependency, resulting in a student who is less open to supervision. Regardless of how the student therapist responds to supervision it is the supervisor's reaction to the beginning therapist which proves crucial to the effectiveness of the supervision. While the analogy to psychotherapy is clear, the supervisor may or may not respond as a therapist would to the needs of the supervisee. Much has been written about the pros and cons of supervision as psychotherapy (e.g. Meerloo, 1952; DeBell, 1963). The question here, however, is not the value of supervisors as therapists, but rather that within this issue one thing is certain—supervisees ask themselves if supervision will turn out to be psychotherapy. Whether students want such "psychotherapy" or not, they are keenly attuned to the supervisor's behavior in this regard, and such behavior sets the tone for this aspect of the relationship.

Nobody really likes to be evaluated. While constructive criticism may be sought after in supervision, supervisees are often uncomfortable with the evaluative aspects of the relationship. This is especially true in supervision because the judgment of the student's performance as a psychotherapist is inextricably intertwined with a student's self-image. Early in training, "becoming" a therapist is what the student is about. Being rated as a therapist is often tantamount to being rated as a person at this point in the young therapist's career. To add to the anxiety, the party doing the evaluation is a recognized, experienced "judge" of personality. This personality assessment will also influence accuracy of reporting what occurred in treatment sessions, and openness to process in the relationship with the supervisor.

Another feature of the supervisor's evaluation (typically made at the request of the training institution as one aspect of a complex system of "quality control" of professionals entering the field) is that it may have a highly significant impact on the student's hopes, aspirations, and economic future. A glowing end-term report will help to assure that the supervisee can continue in training and advance toward his or her degree. Students, knowing that they will be evaluated, are often reluctant to say what they really think, in short, to "push" supervisors. A thorough airing of differences between supervisee and supervisor regarding dynamics and techniques of therapy is an under-used resource in training therapists, especially at the doctoral level. That it is underused is largely due to the new therapist's reticence in the face of uncertain relationship parameters and very certain knowledge that an important evaluation is forthcoming.

The role of narcissism in psychotherapy has also been looked at largely in terms of the supervisor. Emch (1955) and Lower (1972) have written about the supervisor's narcissism in terms of creating disciples in their own image. This phenomenon, for better or for worse, has real effects upon student therapists. Do they want to be like their supervisor? Do they feel obliged to be like their supervisor? This may refer solely to theoretical orientation or to the whole personality constellation of the supervisor. In any case, there is no doubt that the supervisory relationship will be modified by the degree to which the supervisor is seeking to create therapists who work in a way that is similar to his or her own and the degree to which a student is willing to go along with what is being demonstrated. The supervisee's need to develop his or her own autonomy will also determine the degree to which he or she will emulate the supervisor. That is to say that the beginner, despite the lack of technical skills and no matter how new to therapy, will certainly have some ideas, some notions of what needs to be done and how he or she wants to work as a therapist. This may be based in philosophy, previous experience as a patient in psychotherapy or, at very least, a sense of comfort or discomfort with certain types of intervention. Whatever the basis, and despite the fact that most teachers want simply to teach, and students to be taught, the degree to which the supervisor needs to train others to be like him or her, and the degree to which the student therapist is seeking to develop into an individual and unique therapist rather than a disciple is another important factor in the supervisory experience. DeBell (1963) has also written about supervisors' ambivalence in training new psychotherapists who will then compete with them for a fixed population of treatment patients. Perhaps on some level, students themselves are reluctant to enter into competition—the competition of differing ways of doing therapy—with the more experienced, knowledgeable, and "powerful" supervisor.

Another area of concern for the new therapist is the need to see his or her patient "improving," "getting better," or "being cured." This too is based in part upon the student's narcissism, but has other sources as well. How skillful the supervisor is in actually rendering the new therapist more effective in interactions with the patient as well as to what degree the supervisee can be convinced that he or she is in fact being effective in promoting patient growth are important factors in supervision. While failure of treatment is a reality to be dealt with, feeling successful will help the new supervisee, who may not feel at all sure that he or she is really a therapist, to begin to develop a therapist role syntonic with his or her skills and temperament. In addition, how free the student therapist feels to express satisfaction, dissatisfaction, frustration, rage, and so on, at the supervisor for fulfilling or not fulfilling the student's perceived expectations in carrying out therapy is of paramount importance to the student's experience of supervision, and ultimately to the success or failure of the treatment being conducted by the supervisee. Spotnitz (1976) includes among the major goals of supervision the concept of helping the student therapist communicate appropriately with the patient. Combining Doehrman's (1974) view of parallel processes in psychotherapy and supervision with the construct of modeling from learning theory, it becomes clear that the supervisor who can foster "progressive communication" (again Spotnitz) in the supervisee, in terms of relating feelings regarding the patient and the supervisor, will be facilitating student growth as well as improved treatment. In a relationship with such a supervisor a student is also more likely to feel free to express dissatisfaction with his or her own performance as a therapist. Supervisees are quick to appreciate a climate where they can see their own anxiety on the wane because their feelings are tolerated, accepted, and solicited as useful. They begin to see such an environment as useful in itself, by analogy, in the treatment situation in which they are so much involved.

Typically, the new therapist is seriously confronted with role conflict (Sarbin, 1969). The student who is at the point of commencing his or her actual practical experience as a therapist is often at the same time deeply involved as a patient in a personal therapeutic experience. Identification at the early stages may be more with the role of patient than with that of therapist. Additionally, in some training centers, upper-class students who are beginning therapy practica and thus being supervised for the first time may also be involved in supervision of incoming students in clinical areas such as psychological report writing. A day of rushing from an analyst's couch to a therapist's chair to supervising psychodiagnostic reports to being supervised in conducting therapy may be excellent as an exercise in personal flexibility but may also be a source of insecurity and identity conflicts for many students. "Am I really a therapist or am I just the machine which carries out my supervisor's suggestions? Will I ever be like my own therapist? Know as much as my supervisor, or the four previous supervisors, all of whom had different viewpoints? Be able to do it myself? After all, I'm still lying on the couch two times a week. Who am I to be tampering with other people's problems in living when I haven't resolved my own yet?" Sorting out the distinctions in all these roles is part of what confronts the therapist-in-training, and, to the beginner especially, the confusion is formidable.

After having been in supervision for a while, having felt some of the feelings (both joyful and sad), anxieties, and conflicts associated with that process, and growing a little more comfortable with the idea of involving themselves in therapy, students will ask themselves what role they want to serve as a therapist (hopefully they've already spent some time examining what they want out of the therapeutic relationship in which they play the role of patient). It is not a long step from this point to the juncture at which the student begins to examine his or her needs in relating to a supervisor. These will vary among students. Some will move one step further and think about the motivations of their teachers for doing supervision. It is a commonplace to say that therapists need their patients. Can it be true, the new therapist may wonder, that supervisors need their supervisees too? Why are they doing supervision? He or she may ask, What needs am I expected to fulfill for Dr. X? Can I fulfill these? Do I want to? What if I don't? The extent to which supervisors communicate their needs to their students will influence the supervisory relationship. While some students may view such communications as burdens to be borne (likely to be the case when such communications are indirect and where the students themselves are needy), some student therapists will view them as attempts to make supervision a peer situation (when communication of such needs is reasonable and direct, and made to more mature students) and may enjoy and be comforted by such messages.

However, how accurately the student therapist will report what occurred in a session with a patient, especially what he or she as the therapist said in the way of intervention, will depend a great deal upon how the supervisor is seen. Is this someone who will accept my errors? Can I let on how I actually feel about a patient? Can I say what I feel about my supervisor? To what extent is the supervisor threatened by me? How much can I reveal and to what extent am I risking attack, both personal and professional, by doing so? While the answers to these questions may depend as much upon the student's maturity and world view as upon real characteristics of the supervisor, they are the "data" which a student will use in determining how deeply to participate in supervision (see Rioch's Chapter 6). The supervisee's openness to commentary and suggestion, whether psychotherapeutic or didactic in nature, will result in different course of action by the supervisor in realizing training goals. Emphasizing parallel processes in the treatment and supervisory situations, for example, can be expected to be fruitful only in cases with student therapists who are willing and able to deal with process in the supervisory situation itself.

Finally, it is important to look at the role of dependency in terms of its effect on the new supervisee and the supervisory relationship. Student therapists are sometimes compared to apprentices. They learn from their supervisors the vast majority of skills, theory, and techniques they will need. In some sense, their dependency upon supervisors, especially in the earlier stages of conducting therapy, is total. Concurrent development will come through lectures, independent reading, and experience. Clearly, such a state of dependence will produce different effects in different students. There may be an appreciation for the lifting of ultimate responsibility. There may be a resentment for lifting that responsibility. Perhaps the students will question whether this responsibility can ever be lifted, to be borne by the supervisor. There is likely to be gratitude for sharing knowledge and experience, and usually the student will experience a combination of those and other feelings as his or her supervision progresses. Whatever the response to the experience of dependency may be, the new therapist knows that he or she will ultimately be working more independently, and will have more clearly acknowledged responsibilities. The student therapist, in his or her relationship to a supervisor, is very often contending with the issue of dependency and attempting to find some resolution for it. Insofar as the student is helped to be dependent while necessary but encouraged to grow towards a state of more independent thought and action based on solid theory and skills, supervision will be achieving one of its major aims and the supervisee will experience supervision as satisfying and rewarding.

REFERENCES

DeBell, D. E. The critical digest of the literature on Psychoanalytic supervision. *Journal of the American Psychoanalytic Association,* 1963, *11,* 546–75.

Doehrman, M. Parallel processes in supervision and psychotherapy. *Bulletin of the Menninger Clinic,* January 1976, *40*(1).

Emch, M. The social context of supervision. *International Journal of Psychoanalysis,* 1955, *36,* 298–306.

Lower, R. Countertransference resistances in the supervisory situation. *American Journal of Psychiatry,* 1972, *129*(2), 156–60.

Meerloo, J.A.M. Some psychological processes in the supervision of therapists. *American Journal of Psychotherapy,* 1952, *6*(3), 467–470.

Sarbin, T. Role theory. In *Handbook of Social Psychology,* (2nd ed.) G. Lindzey and E. Aronson, Eds. Reading, Mass: Addison-Wesley, 1969.

Spotnitz, H. Trends in modern psychoanalytic supervision. *Modern Psychoanalysis,* 1976, *1*(1), 201–217.

SUPPLEMENTARY REFERENCES

Ackerman, N. Selected problems in supervised analysis. *Psychiatry,* 1953 *16,* 283–90.

Arlow, J. A. The supervisory situation. *Journal of the American Psychoanalytic Association,* 1963, *11*(3), 576–594.

Barnat, M. Student reactions to supervision: Quests for a contract. *Professional Psychology,* 1973, *4*(1) 17–22.

Carkhuff, R. R. and Truax, C. B. Training in counseling and psychotherapy: An evaluation of an integrated didactic and experiential approach. *Journal of Consulting Psychiatry,* 1965, *29*(4), 333–336.

Ekstein, R. and Wallerstein, R. S. *The teaching and learning of psychotherapy.* New York: Basic Books, 1958.

Fleming, J. Teaching the basic skills of psychotherapy. *Archives of General Psychiatry,* 1967, *16,* 416–26.

Fleming, J. and Benedek, T. *Psychoanalytic supervision: A method of clinical teaching.* New York: Grune and Stratton, 1966.

Gaoni, B. and Neumann, M. Supervision from the point of view of the supervisee. *American Journal of Psychotherapy,* 1974, *23,* 108–114.

Goin, M. K., and Kline, F. Supervision observed. *Journal of Nervous and Mental Diseases,* 1974, *158*(3), 208–213.

Gray, J. J. Methods of training psychiatric residents in individual and behavior therapy. *Journal Behavior Therapy and Experimental Psychiatry,* 1974, *5,* 19–25.

Grotjahn, M. Problems and techniques of supervision. *Psychiatry,* 1955, *18,* 9–15.

Haigh, G. V. Alternative strategies in psychotherapy supervision. *Psychotherapy: Theory, Research and Practice,* 1963–1965, *1*(2), 42–3.

Hogan, R. A. Issues and approaches in supervision. *Psychotherapy: Theory, Research and Practice,* 1963–1965, *1*(2), 139–141.

Hora, T. Contribution to the phenomenology of the supervisory process. *American Journal of Psychotherapy,* 1957, *11,* 769–73.

Kubie, L. Research into the process of supervision in psychoanalysis. *Psychoanalytic Quarterly,* 1958, *27*(2), 226–236.

Langer, M., Puget, J., and Teper, E. A methodological approach to the teaching of psychoanalysis. *International Journal of Psychoanalysis,* 1964, *45,* 576–73.

Levine, F. M., Tilker H. A. A behavior modification approach to supervision of psychotherapy. *Psychotherapy: Theory, Research and Practice,* 1974, *11*(2), 182–88.

Lewin, B. D. and Ross, H. *Psychoanalytic education in the United States.* New York: Norton, 1960.

Muslin, H. L., Burstein, A. G., Gedo, J. E., and Sadow, L. Research on the supervisory process. *Archives of General Psychiatry.* 1967, *16,* 427–431.

Perlman, G. Change in "Central Therapeutic Ingredients" of beginning psychotherapists. *Psychotherapy: Theory, Research and Practice,* 1973, *10*(1), 48–51.

Poser, E. G.. Training behavior-change agents: A five-year perspective. *Proceedings of the Third Banff International Conference on Behavior Modification.* April, 1971.

Schlessinger, N. Supervision of psychotherapy: A critical review of the literature. *Archives of General Psychiatry,* 1966, *15,* 129–34.

Searles, H. The informational value of the supervisor's emotional experience. *Psychiatry.* 1955, *18,* 135–46.

Searles, H. Problems of psychoanalytic supervision. *Science and Psychoanalysis,* Vol. 5. New York: Grune and Stratton, 1962.

Selfridge, Fred, et. al. Sensitivity-oriented versus didactically-oriented in-service counsellor training. *Journal of Counsel Psychiatry,* 1975, *22*(2), 56–9.

Styczynski, L. Transition from supervisee to supervisor. Paper presented at the 1977 Convention of the APA.

Thoresen, C. Training behavioral counselors. *Banff International Conference on Behavior Modification.* April, 1971.

Truax, C. B., Carkhuff, R. R., and Douds, J. Towards an integration of the didactic and experiential approaches to training in counseling and psychotherapy. *Journal of Counseling and Psychiatry,* 1964, *11,* 240–247.

Vickers, K. Supervisory effects on novice therapists' therapeutic style and orientation. Doctoral Dissertation. Adelphi University, 1974.

Wagner, F. F. Supervision of psychotherapy. *American Journal of Psychotherapy,* 1957, *11*(4), 759–768.

Weiss, S. and Fleming, J. Evaluation of progress in supervision. *Psychoanalytic Quarterly,* 1975, *44*(2), 191–205.

Wolstein, B. Supervision as experience. *Contemporary Psychoanalysis,* 1971, *8,* 165–172.

CHAPTER 8

Supervision from the Perspective of the Supervisee

LEONARD GREENBERG

It is a difficult task for someone who no longer assumes a role to recollect completely what that experience was like. While most supervisors are former supervisees, it is likely that they have forgotten or become less sensitive to what it is like to be a supervisee. Not only is a supervisee's experience of supervision different, but also the way he or she conceptualizes supervision is unique to that role.

While supervisees have limited clinical knowledge, they are exposed to the entirety of their own clinical efforts. Supervisors can view a trainee's work in the context of extensive clinical experience, but only see a limited portion of the supervisee's work. A trainee usually has several supervisors in a given year and changes supervisors annually. As a result, each supervisor usually has time only to understand and work with particular aspects of a trainee's skills. While frequently supervisors may consider themselves to be supervising an entire person, supervisees can and frequently do see themselves as picking what is useful to them from a variety of supervisory settings.

Trainees also may feel especially responsible for determining what is important for themselves to learn, since they can see their skills in a broader perspective. These differences make a supervisee's experience of supervision different than that of a supervisor.

This chapter will examine what is particular to a supervisee's perspective. Emphasis will be placed on the effect of the supervisee's being simultaneously trained by several supervisors and how this leads to supervisors being utilized differentially according to their strengths and weaknesses. Finally the paper will examine several conflicts for supervisees, deriving from their at times contradictory goals and the limitations inherent in supervision.

TRADITIONAL VIEWS OF THE SUPERVISEE'S ROLE

Beckett (1969), a psychoanalytic trainee writing on supervision, describes a supervisory relationship which strongly parallels a traditional psychotherapy relationship. According to him the raw material of supervision is mostly the emotional reaction of the trainee to the patient. In the process of learning how to identify, utilize, and compensate for those feelings, the supervisee is assumed to form a "working alliance" and develop "transference reactions" to the supervisor. Conflicts about the trainee's adequacy and situationally generated fears and anxiety are expected to be acted out in supervision where they eventually are analyzed and worked through.

While this perspective has some merits particularly for psychoanalytic supervision, many supervisory experiences differ. Supervision need not center around analysing one's own personality or exploring feelings about what went on in a therapy session; instead, supervision may function on a more didactic level. A supervisee may focus on developing a variety of responses and interpretations to specific situations, or focus on filling in the gaps between general principles, gathered in texts and classrooms, and individualized problems encountered with one's clients.

Gaoni and Neumann (1974) in another article on the point of view of the supervisee, describe supervision as serving differing functions at different points in training. They describe initial supervisions as didactic, with the supervisee looking for directions, wanting to be told what to do. Gradually the supervisory focus is expected to change from the client to the supervisee. The focus on the supervised therapist is initially on his techniques and only later on experiences as a therapist. Eventually supervision may develop into a consultative experience.

While Ganoi and Neumann recognize several supervisory tasks, they separate them in a logitudinal sequence; this implies that the later focus on the trainees' reactions to his or her clients is the most sophisticated and important aspect of training. While this may fit for supervisees who are only trained by a single, analytically oriented supervisor, such pure cases are probably not common. Instead one might expect a trainee to have several supervisors, each of whom places different emphasis on various aspects of the supervisees' experience or on techniques. The current variety of techniques and therapies increases the probability of being supervised on new techniques late in training. This makes it difficult to conceptualize an overall sequence of clinical development, except in training programs limited to a single technique.

FACTORS THAT DETERMINE WHAT IS LEARNED IN SUPERVISION

Multiple supervisors for a given supervisee are almost universal, yet the effects of this have received limited attention in the theory on supervision. Since learning is divided among many supervisory relationships, what then determines what is available in a given supervisory relationship? Aspects of the training institution, the supervisor, and the supervisee are all likely to contribute.

Setting

Supervisory settings may be seen as providing limits to supervision, such that within a given setting there is a distinct set of therapy experiences available. The type of clients who come to that setting, with their expectations and background, influence the type of therapy possible. Supervision may be limited by the nature of the clients, by the availability of opportunities for recording and observations, as well as the expectations of the setting for both the therapist and the supervisor.

Supervisors

The supervisor's knowledge and experience, both of clinical material and of supervision are certainly important factors in determining what may be learned in supervision. While a supervisee may be allowed considerable freedom in choice of therapy techniques, opportunities for learning are not equal for all choices. The supervisee can expect to optimally benefit from supervision when using the techniques that are most familiar to the supervisor—specifically, those techniques that are used by the supervisor. In this way the trainee is encouraged to work primarily within the supervisor's area of competence. He or she is also further discouraged from straying from the supervisor's preferred areas by a higher probability of criticism when utilizing methods that the supervisor has not found worthwhile to learn.

As a supervisee, one assumes that it is not just the supervisor's knowledge that directs the focus of supervision, but the current interests of the supervisor as well. Thus a supervisor who is currently interested in nonverbal communications might be expected to focus, with the supervisee, on nonverbal communications during the trainees' therapy session. A supervisor's interests may even determine which clients as well as what aspects of therapy are focused on.

Lastly, a supervisor's personality is likely to influence the nature of the supervisory process. Typically, a supervisor's personality has been considered relevant only when it is "interfering" with what a given author would consider the proper work of supervision (e.g., Grinberg, 1970).

This perspective originates from a model of supervision akin to therapy, so that a supervisor's personality is relevant only as a countertransference type phenomenon. Alternatively, a supervisor can be assumed to have a more direct role in influencing the content of supervision. A supervisor can offer training in various types of therapy, each requiring that different skills be acquired by the trainee. With such a variety of tasks to be learned, a supervisor's personality may be assumed to determine which of many options are emphasized in supervision. Even within a given type of therapy there are many choices of focus which may be effected by the supervisor's personality. For example, a relatively authoritarian supervisor might stress authoritarian aspects such as the setting of limits with clients (e.g. regular attendance at sessions); in supervision the same supervisor might be more prone to make explicit criticisms, and be more likely to dictate the handling of particular clients.

Supervisees

Supervisees, like supervisors, are biased by their personalities, interests, knowledge, and theoretical orientation. Although trainees differ on many of these variables, because of commonalities in their experiences there are some attributes believed to be shared by most supervisees. Specifically, trainees are assumed to be and feel ignorant and inexperienced, and are pressured by the demands of working with emotionally laden material. They are expected to expose themselves in supervision; to form a relationship with an authority figure who may be critical. This relationship is complicated by the likelihood of the trainee's transferring associations from other authority relationships, and therefore likely to invoke defenses which have characterized those relationships in the past (Beckett, 1969; Chessick, 1971; Kadushin, 1968).

While this description of supervisees is probably accurate, it is incomplete. A supervisee's self-disclosures in supervision are likely to vary as a function of all the factors which affect perceived safety in supervision. While a supervisee's perceived safety is influenced by past experience, the supervisor's behavior may be an even more important influence. The supervisor can realistically affect the trainee's sense of safety by how he or she relates in supervision; particularly important in determining safety is how much the supervisor is confrontive, how the supervisor confronts, how consistent and fair the supervisor is. For the supervisee, the expectation (realistic or otherwise) of negative consequences for disclosure is likely to limit that disclosure. Such expectations may range from fear of the loss of the supervisor's favor as a result of demonstrated incompetence to fear of damaging one's likelihood of succeeding professionally by receiving negative evaluations.

WHAT THE SUPERVISEE WANTS FROM SUPERVISION

The variety of experiences available with different settings, supervisors, and supervisees, allows for the fullfillment of quite a range of goals in supervision. While the basic goal of supervision is the learning of the technique of psychotherapy, it may also serve other functions. Supervision may be used by supervisees to evaluate strengths and weaknesses in their skills. Supervision may serve as a source of support over difficulties encountered with clients, or an opportunity to ventilate about therapy experiences. Furthermore, problems novice therapists identify in their own work may be utilized as areas for personal growth—that is, when problems as a therapist and as a person coincide. Supervisory sessions may at times serve to help validate or evaluate a theoretical perspective by examining it in the context of the trainee's ongoing cases. Supervision also provides an opportunity for positive reinforcement of one's accomplishments as a therapist. Also important, supervision is a source for evaluations and recommendations which affect one's professional future.

HOW SUPERVISEES ATTEMPT TO UTILIZE SUPERVISION

A supervisee has been described herein as a person with a variety of complicated and possibly conflicting goals, who is to be supervised by different people in different situations. Within the range of available experiences a supervisee attempts to choose so as to maximize the chances of achieving his or her goals. This is complicated by a supervisee's sometimes limited knowledge of what resources are available (e.g., what a supervisor's strengths are), as well as by not having clearly conceptualized goals for supervision. Yet, even with imperfect knowledge, supervisees do make choices. The clearest and most straightforward choices are those in which one chooses where (placements and training institutions), by whom, or in what (type of therapy) one is supervised. In these situations a trainee may not know exactly what is being chosen, but usually enough information is available to make relatively well informed decisions.

Less clear are those decisions a supervisee makes in determining how to utilize supervision. While one's awareness of making decisions in supervision may vary, decisions are clearly being made. Thus, one may choose to present varying aspects of one's work, or choose to focus on particular clients. One may ask a supervisor to focus on particular problems that one identifies, or seek help in some specific aspect of therapy. Extra help may be sought for special difficulties. Even what intervention is attempted with a given client may be a function of both a supervisor's expectations and the risks one is willing to take with that supervisor.

Ideally, what happens in supervision would be mutually decided upon by both participants, on the basis of what is most useful for the supervisee. However, even if an accurate and mutually agreeable appraisal of a trainee's strengths and weaknesses were available, how to focus supervision would still not be clear. This is because a supervisee's goals are complex and overlapping. What is available is limited by the supervisor's biases and skills as well as the problems presented by one's clients. So instead of a mutual decision, both supervisor and supervisee make independent, covert or unconscious decisions as to the focus of supervision.

CONFLICTS INHERENT IN SUPERVISION

When the multiple functions of supervision are taken into account, it seems inevitable that decisions by supervisees would involve conflicts. One such conflict occurs when a supervisee feels forced to choose between focusing on what a supervisor is interested in (and therefore most effective in supervising) and what the supervisee feels is an area where he or she needs help. For example, such a difficulty might occur when a supervisor who is a behavior therapist concentrates supervision on the mechanics of an operant program, while a supervisee is not sure if the relationship with the client is strong enough to support effective compliance. The conflict between a trainee's perceived needs and what is most available in supervision may affect how closely he or she attempts to imitate a supervisor's style. Thus, if a supervisor best supervises interventions that are most like those with which he or she has had personal experience, then the trainee must choose between stylistically imitating the supervisor's style and what is most consistent with his or her own style.

Another conflict for supervisees is the choice between presenting what makes them look good, and what makes them look bad (i.e., where help is most needed). This issue was alluded to earlier in the context of the supervisee's sense of safety in disclosure. The decision to disclose is frequently made by balancing the costs of exposing areas of weakness with the gains accrued through being supervised in those areas. Clearly factors such as recommendations to be written by supervisors along with amount of help one is likely to receive affect such disclosures. Even when working with a supervisor with whom disclosure is relatively safe, there are times when it is less functional to expose difficulties. Consequently, toward the end of a supervisory relationship a trainee is likely to attempt to appear improved in the areas on which supervision focused, especially in areas which were identified as weaknesses. In fact, a supervisee may have difficulty determining if improvement has really occurred or if he or she has only succeeded in doing or presenting his or her work more consistently with a supervisor's biases.

Many of the conflicts in supervision reflect the fact that the supervisor functions both as mentor and as evaluator. The role of evaluator (critic, judge, source of recommendations) is sufficiently important to affect much of what goes on in supervision. The influence of evaluations is least when the supervisee feels confident that the effects of evaluation will be benevolent; this leaves the supervisee free to pursue whatever is perceived to be most instructional in supervision and beneficial to the client. However, to whatever degree an evaluation is seen as potentially threatening, the supervisee is proportionally likely to be pushed toward performing for and pleasing the supervisor. This is most often done by concealing mistakes and attempting to imitate the supervisor's style of intervention. While the threat of negative evaluation may be functional in changing the supervisee's behavior, it may also create anxiety, further fostering less open interactions with the supervisor. While some anxiety is functional in providing motivation for change, too much anxiety may restrict the supervisee's openness and initiative, making the process of supervision unpleasant for all concerned. Therefore, a supervisee may be expected to learn best when there is an expectation of a moderate amount of criticism, and evaluations in which the positive outweigh the negative.

Deciding whether to accept a supervisor's criticisms, suggestions, or perspectives can be a difficult task for a supervisee. Such decisions are perhaps most difficult when working with knowledgeable supervisors whose personality style differs markedly from that of the supervisee. What should a supervisee do when a supervisor, who is perceived as distant, criticizes a trainee as being too involved with his or her clients? How does one respond to a supervisor who is perceived as aggressive, when encouraged by that supervisor to be more aggressive with one's clients? Thus, it seems particularly difficult when a supervisee must make decisions in areas biased by both the supervisor's and the supervisee's personality.

IMPLICATION

In this paper, supervision is conceptualized as an imperfect process, subject to multiple strengths, limitations, and objectives of supervisors and supervisees. These various elements inevitably generate conflicts, which are often not overtly attended to; should the conflicting interests and goals be made more overt than logical choices in those supervisory situations would be easier. Identification and communication of a supervisor's biases would be helpful. Explicit contracting around the focus of supervision might simplify decisions, while careful attention to the effects of evaluations may minimize their ill effects. Hopefully, attention to the supervisee's perspective will make such communication and contracting easier to execute.

REFERENCES

Beckett, T. A candidate's reflections on the supervisory process. *Contemporary Psychoanalysis,* 1969, *5,* 169–179.

Chessick, R.D. How the resident and the supervisor dissappoint each other. *American Journal of Psychotherapy,* 1971, *25,* 272–283.

Gaoni, B., and Neumann, M. Supervision from the point of view of the supervisee. *American Journal of Psychotherapy,* 1974, *28,* 108–114.

Grinberg, L. The problems of supervision in psychoanalytic education. *International Journal of Psychoanalysis,* 1970, *51,* 371–383.

Kadushin, A. Games people play in supervision. *Social Work,* 1968, *13,* 23–32.

CHAPTER 9

Psychotherapy Supervision: Supervisees' Perspective

WILLIAM R. MARSHALL AND WILLIAM N. CONFER

Our supervision experiences of varying lengths have included training under behavioral, cognitive, communication, dynamic, and Gestalt orientations in individual, couple, group, and family settings during our graduate and internship placements. Despite wide procedural and theoretical differences, a few essential commonalities surfaced for us in our development as psychotherapists. The purpose of this chapter is to focus on these intrapersonal and interpersonal supervision experiences across supervisor orientation. Therefore, we do not espouse any "right way" to supervise; but by communicating shared perplexities, stresses, and triumphs during this ongoing process, we hope to acknowledge those components of our training that we found encouraging and valuable. In addition, our experiential account of being supervised may suggest ways for supervisors to augment their present teaching methods.

Our discussion will summarize our phenomenological experience of being supervised before addressing the issue of supervisee and supervisor contributions to traditional supervision that encourage successful development of the trainee. Finally, we shall develop the theme of the supervisory experience serving in many respects as an analogue to therapy itself.

THE PHENOMENOLOGY OF BEING A SUPERVISEE

Initially, our understanding of the psychotherapy process was that gleaned from textbooks rather than personal experience, and we had to accept on faith that therapy could be effective in helping patients change their lives. Journal case presentations often seem to imply that therapeutic breakthroughs were quickly achieved with only moderate effort by both patient and therapist. However, only several months of practicum experience were required to dispel this myth.

The caustic jokes about patient craziness and lack of appreciation which, in retrospect, appear to be defensive in nature, signaled the future realization that the veneer of altruism and goodwill was based upon a personal investment in a career of helping people. Patient no-shows, setbacks, and successes were often taken personally under the implied assumption that a therapist *would* have vast control of the patient's life. When expectations for drastic and demonstrable change were frustrated, anxiety increased as the result of a tendency to measure professional worth by patient movement. In an attempt to mollify the feelings of frustration and find the "correct" answers for patient problems, additional books and articles were read; and frequently, technique and instrumentality—that is, demanding that the patients change immediately, accept responsibility for their lives, and so on—were overemphasized. Only further experience and supervision would engender the understanding that patients' behaviors were, more often than not, signs of personal strength or components of their pathology.

Audio-playbacks were impressive in pointing out how stilted and unproductive many therapists' comments were. Therapy one-liners—gleaned from books—which were intended to stimulate the patient (and impress the supervisor) did not seem authentic or useful. Various personal reactions accompanied such play-backs. "I sound so anxious!" "How could I have so blatantly missed what this individual was saying to me?" "It is obvious I should have gone in this direction here and kept silent there." "I applied this technique in such a haphazard manner!" "I'm not even listening to the person here!" "This patient is getting angry at me now just like s(he) does when anyone gets too close to her/him."

The playback sessions also provided feedback about our progress as therapists. Hopefully, comparison of current tapes with those of past sessions would illustrate improvement in a never ending process of "becoming" a psychotherapist. The thought that today's belly laugh resulted from yesterday's session, but today's session would produce tomorrow's belly laugh, is both comforting and frustrating. As will be expanded below, the psychotherapist's growth as a therapist is analogous, in many ways, to that of our patients—the process never ends.

As experience increased, the process of supervision was continually reframed. The fledgling "therapist" had very limited skills and the supervisor was often required to take an active role as teacher. From the supervisee's perspective, supervision at this stage was the opportunity to elicit the answers from the master at the cost of having one's efficacy as a human being questioned. Even though this perception was often more imagined than real, it was nevertheless a very compromising position.

Later the supervisee's augmented skill permitted the supervisor to assume the task of guiding the therapist's development. A parallel change in the therapist's task was also evident. As a result of learning and increased confidence, supervision was not nearly as threatening so that previously untried avenues of patient-therapist interaction could be explored. The supervisor and supervisee eventually developed an open camaraderie between two professionals working to assist a patient to understand and alter the puzzle—her/his life. Personal reflections of differences in style could be explored and changed as necessary. Supervision then became a process of skill refinement and horizon expansion for the therapist (and supervisor?).

This brief synopsis suggests many of the misconceptions about patients, treatment, and supervision that are born out of the shaky wedlock of supervisee personality and professional inexperience. Supervisors may recognize these as some characteristic errors and pitfalls of fledgling therapists.

THE NATURE OF TRADITIONAL PSYCHOTHERAPY SUPERVISION

Obviously, the misconceptions cited above are issues for clarification during the supervision experience. At least two factors which might interfere with the training potential of the supervision experience need further emphasis. First, the supervisor/supervisee relationship has an unequal power/authority distribution. The student is faced with a dilemma of displaying her/his attempts at therapy (particularly those aspects where she/he feels inadequate, unhelpful, or incorrect) in order to develop greater sophistication within an evaluative context. The student is aware that she/he is to be graded for performance and evaluated as a person as well; yet the student must risk professional and personal disclosure to improve as a therapist.

The second issue concerns the traditional structure of psychotherapy practicum experiences which require the student to interview/treat a client/patient and then present the case material to a supervisor for critique, assistance, and direction. This typical procedure is fraught with difficulties, the most obvious of which is that the supervisor is expected to know the client with only second-hand information reported by the supervisee. The supervisor has only limited contact with the client, and consequently the accuracy and usefulness of her/his conclusions and suggestions are contingent upon the inexperienced supervisee's report of evaluation and treatment efforts. In addition to suggesting ethical dilemmas, this arrangement seems to compromise therapeutic effectiveness. Muslin, Burstein, Gedo, and Sadow (1967) asked experienced judges to rate patient functioning from audio tapes of trainee-patient interviews and of trainee-to-supervisor presentations. The results indicated that in the early stages of supervision, supervisees are unreliable reporters of patient functioning because (a) important themes were missing from student presentations, (b) patient affect was inadequately reported, (c) the patient-therapist relationship was unclear, and (d) students tended to cut off patient exploration. Furthermore, supervisors agreed that their formulations based on student reports were in error.

Stein, Karasu, Charles, and Buckley (1975) compared the influence of two methods of supervision on ratings of patient pathology, motivation for treatment, level of insight, and prognosis. In the first method (traditional), the supervisee evaluated the patient and then verbally reported the findings to the supervisor, whereas in the second condition, the supervisor directly observed the supervisee's interview with the patient. Both the supervisor and supervisee in each condition independently rated the patient on the four variables. The results indicated that the supervisors' and the supervisees' ratings were more comparable when both observed the patient whereas the supervisor rated the patient lower on the four variables, particularly psychopathology, when her/his assessment was based upon the supervisee's report. The authors suggest that the supervisors' lower rating on motivation, insight, and prognosis might be particularly detrimental to the patient in that the supervisor's attitude might tend to lessen the supervisee's enthusiasm and indirectly have a negative influence on the patient's treatment.

The above studies suggest that training and supervision are integral to the development of effective therapists, yet this same priority does not appear to have been reflected in academic training programs. Lubin (1962) polled APA Division 12 (Clinical) and found that 20% of the respondents had not received any supervised training in psychotherapy, and over half of those psychologists who received supervision did so as post-doctoral fellows under the tutelage of psychiatrists. Jorgensen and Weigel (1973) mailed questionnaires to the training directors of the 106 APA-approved and provisionally approved programs in clinical and counseling psychology. For the 97 directors who responded, psychotherapy practicum experiences were reported as being of primary importance by 25% of the respondents, and another 32% considered the internship to be the major psychotherapy training site. For the remaining 43%, psychotherapy training was acquired from formal course work or post-graduate experiences.

Since only one-fourth of the training directors in the Jorgensen and Weigel (1973) study considered practicum experiences to be crucial for psychotherapy training, it would be interesting to know what psychotherapists considered as important in their own training. Henry, Simms, and Spray (1973) partially answer this question. Their sample of approximately 7000 psychotherapists included not only psychologists but also psychiatrists, psychoanalysts, and psychiatric social workers. The summary comment of this sample was the criticism that their training programs overemphasized academic work and provided insufficient clinical experiences. Our experiences suggest that students might have to assume the responsibility to seek out many and varied therapy/supervision opportunities rather than limit their training to formal course work.

SUPERVISEE AND SUPERVISOR CONTRIBUTIONS TO A PRODUCTIVE WORKING ALLIANCE

As previously mentioned, several characteristics of therapists in their early stages of supervision are often evident. The student is plagued by treatment misconceptions; she/he unreliably reports case data, feels inadequate (or at least uninformed and uncomfortable) in the new role as therapist, and feels somewhat threatened by the evaluative aspects of her/his supervision. In light of these—and undoubtedly other—roadblocks, the atmosphere of supervision must be conducive to facilitating the arduous task of therapist development. Upon completion of a practicum, a supervisee summarized the experience with the supervisor as "I heard what I wanted to hear, but hadn't heard before; and I learned what I already knew, but didn't!" However, all too often after months of supervision, other supervisees flatly state "I just can't do therapy that way," "I don't feel comfortable with her/his approach," or "the patients just don't respond when I do it her/his way." Why is one supervision experience enriching and another worthless or even devastating? Obviously, there are many potential answers to that question. However, our experience suggests that one important component of the satisfactory supervision experience for the trainee is the development of a compatible working relationship with the supervisor.

The responsibility of this relationship appears to be shared by both supervisee and supervisor.

The Supervisee

The trainee can facilitate this compatability and her/his professional growth as a therapist in several ways. First, the student's subjective goals for the practicum may provide only fragmentary help in supervisor selection since the inexperienced therapist's orientation is likely quite malleable. However, the potential supervisee may find it useful to request a brief interview with a potential supervisor to ascertain the latter's therapy orientation and supervision approach. During the interview, the student can acquire an intuitive feel for whether she/he can work with that supervisor. Second, we have found it to be extremely beneficial to request multiple supervisory experiences from therapists of diverse orientations. This exposure forced us to question the assumptions and evaluate the effectiveness of alternate therapeutic approaches. In addition, each orientation can provide ideas, techniques, and a conceptualization framework that might be integrated into one's developing style. Third, during the course of supervision we have found that we could enhance our learning experience by thoroughly reviewing case material and therapy tapes before supervisory sessions in an attempt to minimize distorted reporting. Portions of the taped interview where we felt unsure or lost could be marked for quick retrieval and playback. We also found that we could profit by communicating to the supervisor how we felt in response to a patient, the patient's body language, and any other potential data the supervisor could not obtain from the tape itself. Fourth, the supervisee can attempt to seek a variety of patients in order to broaden the scope of her/his professional experience and tap supervisor proficiency in dealing with a variety of pathological states. Fifth, the supervisee can be interested enough to shape provocative and penetrating questions based on her/his growing experience as a therapist that not only increase the depth of her/his understanding but also provide a degree of structure for supervisor responding and direction. Finally, as many others have stressed (cf. Hammer, 1972), the importance of personal growth and psychological health of the therapist is extremely important. For some potential psychotherapists, personal psychotherapy is probably valuable, important, and even necessary. At the very least however, potential psychotherapists should have some exposure to the patient role in order to have the opportunity to experience firsthand the therapeutic relationship from the point of view of a patient. This is not to suggest that all psychotherapists need therapy. For many therapists, personal psychotherapy was of little value for their professional lives (Henry, Sims, and Spray, 1973).

The Supervisor

In at least four ways the supervisor can contribute to a maximal supervisor/supervisee working alliance: (1) afford an atmosphere that encourages trainees to grow as therapists by communicating and resolving insecurities in their role; (2) adopt a style of communicating suggestions and corrections that will enhance supervisee confidence, acceptance, and satisfaction; (3) devise methods to close the gap between student report and actual patient behavior; and (4) avoid debilitating attitudes that detract from her/his working relationship with a supervisee. Each of these considerations will be discussed in more detail.

Pierce, Carkhuff, and Berenson (1967) have elucidated the conditions that facilitate the professional growth of counselors-in-training. Seventeen volunteers who were enrolled in a Mental Health Counselor Training Program were rated on the dimensions of empathy, respect, genuineness, concreteness, and self-disclosure. The volunteers were then randomly assigned to one of two supervisors who had been previously rated high or low on the above dimensions. A second rating of the trainees occurred upon completion of the training program. The results of the pre-post comparison indicated that trainees assigned to the high functioning supervisors evidenced the most gain in functioning as measured by those dimensions.

Supervision style also appears to be a pertinent variable in the supervisor-supervisee relationship. A recent study (Cherniss and Equatios, 1977) addressed the effect of various styles of clinical supervision upon supervisees in terms of (a) supervisee satisfaction with and acceptance of supervision and (b) supervisee self-confidence as a clinician. The results indicated that supervisor styles stressing (a) advice, suggestions, and interpretations concerning client dynamics and clinical techniques (the "didactic-consultative" style), (b) asking questions designed to stimulate the supervisee to think through and solve problems on her/his own (the "insight-oriented" style), or (c) encouraging the supervisee to question emotional responses to the clinical process (the "feeling-oriented" style) were rated much higher on both measures than were the orientations where the supervisor (d) left the supervisee alone most of the time and was rarely available for consultation (the "laissez-faire" style), or (e) where the supervisee was told in specific terms what to do and how to do it (the "authoritarian" style). Goin and Kline (1974) video taped supervisory sessions and then asked both supervisors and supervisees to rate the supervisors on a continuum from outstanding through poor. Content analysis of the sessions revealed that outstanding supervisors made more didactic comments about patients and technique and also were neither extremely passive nor authoritatively directive, but seem to find a middle ground of activity. Their trainees heard them as making more helpful, information-giving comments about the technique, process, and practice of psychotherapy.

A supervisor can extend her/his limited contact with the patient of the supervisee by participating in the initial session(s), viewing the session(s) by either a visual recording or observation mirror, or at least listening to an audiorecording of the session. The supervisor can gain an appreciation for the patient's status, the therapist's skill, and the patient-therapist interaction; furthermore, the observation data is a rich source of constructive feedback for the supervisee. As the supervisor becomes familiar with the therapist and is able to rely upon her/his evaluations, the need for this close contact may be somewhat diminished.

While many supervisor attitudes and needs can enhance the supervisor-supervisee relationship, other attitudes and needs can lessen the quality of the supervision experience. An obvious, yet often forgotten, detraction is supervisor inattentiveness. One of the authors recalls the frustration and irritation induced by a supervisor who took the tape playbacks as an opportunity to read his mail. Although he professed to be listening as well, the supervisor communicated a lack of interest and a poor model of attending and responding, both of which he asserted to be at the heart of his therapeutic process.

As Kadushin (1968) has observed, the supervisor has needs that are met by the supervisee because supervisor satisfaction stems from the growth of the trainee. Gratification of these needs may enhance the working alliance; however, at least two debilitating attitudes can arise from supervisor needs: (a) the demand that the supervisee be a protégé or carbon copy of the supervisor (see Lower 1972) and (b) subtle condescension. As supervisees want and need to personalize their approaches, a supervisor's demand for conformity or a poor tolerance for supervisee autonomy can seriously interfere with supervision. Subtle condescension can arise from the supervisor's superior knowledge and skill, her/his position of power over the supervisee (i.e. rating both the supervisee's person and performance), and the supervisee's vulnerability as a novice. Potentially valuable exercises couched in statements such as "of course you *know* what so and so says about that" or "read these ten books and *then* we'll discuss it" can be interpreted as one-upmanship and breed either resentment or sycophants.

SUPERVISION AS A THERAPY ANALOGUE

In our experiences it appears that across supervisors a common thread often emerged; namely, our relationship with a particular supervisor, in many respects, was analogous to the supervisor's approach with patients. As the relationship with a supervisor developed we felt comfortable enough to permit modification of our dysfunctional thoughts, feelings, behaviors, attitudes, and conceptions regarding therapy process and technique. Interestingly, we could only recognize the extent of our dysfunctional practices after we had made the changes and saw the impact on the patients with whom we worked. This notion of patient-therapist and supervisee-supervisor parallel is not altogether unique with us (Fleming and Benedek, 1966); however, it may prove instructive to carry this analogy between supervision and therapy a bit further.

Keen (1976) has proposed that the universal components of psychotherapy are support and confrontation, regardless of the therapist's orientation. Similarly, we perceive our training in psychotherapy as well-paced doses of encouragement and challenge. Supportive measures included: empathic understanding of our intrapersonal struggles highlighted earlier; plaudits for our correct/productive interventions (although our positive contributions may have been meager initially); constructive critiques worded such that we could hear, retain, and use them (i.e. not devastating); and encouragement with the stresses of suicidal, homicidal, seductive, or manipulative patients.

While we resented what appeared to be undue criticism, we appreciated challenges that compelled us to justify our interventions or substantiate our procedures. Some of the most profitable (for us) interventions by our supervisors were those which permitted us to experience the pitfalls of our efforts. An example of this strategy is "therapeutic alter ego" whereby the supervisor wears out his fingertips on the "stop" button of the tape recorder to inquire "why did you say this?", "what are you leading to?", and "how do you think the patient received that?". An essential aspect of this technique is the opportunity to explore alternatives, although premature stoppages of the tape can impede this process.

Just as psychotherapy is an opportunity for change, our supervision allotted us the necessary environment to modify and develop our professional skills. Supervisor flexibility in response to the supervisee's changing needs seems to be of paramount importance. Gaoni and Neumann (1974) discuss four stages of supervisee development and the resultant demands on the supervisor.

First, the student expects the supervisor to assume responsibility for patient care and provide continuous treatment suggestions. During the second stage the supervisee becomes an apprentice and attempts to learn the "tools of the trade" by imitating the supervisor. As the trainee develops professionally, she/he looks for the supervisor to help her/him work through patient-therapist relationship issues (Stage 3). Finally, supervision moves into stage four once the supervisee is skilled and has largely developed her/his "therapeutic personality". At this point the supervision relationship is one of mutual consultation about cases.

Initially, we needed the supervisor to assume the expert role to help us cultivate such basic skills as assessing pathology, learning how to listen, opening and closing the hour, and so on. As we developed our inner resources and gained greater confidence in our role, we favored exercising our creativity in problem solving. Consequently, the task of our supervisor became one of refining developing skills, assisting in advance conceptualizations, and assessing the possible consequences of our proposed treatment strategies.

At that point supervision approaches that afforded the occasion to reconstruct the situation, perhaps experience it as the patient might, and lead to "spontaneous" solutions for therapy predicaments were valuable. Like any patient, we incorporated what seemed appropriate, and filed away the rest for future reference as necessary.

For us as supervisees, the supervision process was an interesting, valuable, and even necessary component of our training as psychotherapists. Obviously many diverse supervision approaches and styles can effectively accomplish the goal of facilitating therapists' professional growth. Our intent in this paper was to discuss those aspects of supervision that, we felt, should be emphasized. Supervisees might share some of our perceptions and, we hope, supervisors can learn and improve by understanding our and their own supervisee's viewpoint.

REFERENCES

Cherniss, C., and Equatios, E. Styles of clinical supervision in community mental health programs. *Journal of Consulting and Clinical Psychology,* 1977, *45,* 1195–1196.

Fleming, J., and Benedek, T. *Psychoanalytic Supervision.* New York: Grune and Stratton, 1966.

Gaoni, B., and Neumann, M. Supervision from the point of view of the supervisee. *American Journal of Psychotherapy,* 1974, *23,* 108–114.

Goin, M.K., and Kline, F.M. Supervision observed. *Journal of Nervous and Mental Disease.* 1974, *158,* 280–213.

Hammer, M. To students interested in becoming psychotherapists. In M. Hammer (Ed.), *The theory and practice of psychotherapy with specific disorders.* Springfield, Ill.: Charles C. Thomas, 1972.

Hansen, S.C., & Barker, E.N. Experiencing and the supervisory relationship. *Journal of Counseling Psychology,* 1964, *11,* 107–111.

Henry, W.E., Sims, J.H., and Spray, S.L. *Public and private lives of psychotherapists.* San Francisco: Jossey-Bass, 1973.

Jorgensen, G.T., and Weigel, R.G. Training psychotherapists: Practices regarding ethics, personal growth, and locus of responsibility. *Professional Psychology,* 1973, *4,* 23–27.

Kadushin, A. Games people play in supervision. *Social Work,* 1968, 23–32.

Keen, E. Confrontation and support: On the world of psychotherapy. *Psychotherapy: Theory, Research and Practice,* 1976, *13,* 308–315.

Lower, R.B. Countertransference resistance in the supervisory situation. *American Journal of Psychiatry,* 1972, *129*(2), 70–74.

Lubin, B. Survey of psychotherapy training and activities of psychologists. *Journal of Clinical Psychology,* 1962, *18,* 252–255.

Muslin, H.L., Burstein, A.G., Gedo, J.E., and Sadow, L. Research on the supervisory process. I. Supervisor's appraisal of the interview data. *Archives of General Psychiatry,* 1967, *16,* 427–431.

Pierce, R., Carkhuff, R.R., and Berenson, B.G. The differential effects of high and low functioning counselors upon counselors-in-training. *Journal of Clinical Psychology,* 1967, *23,* 212–215.

Stein, S.P., Karasu, T.B., Charles, E.S., and Buckley, P.J. Supervision of the initial interview. *Archives of General Psychiatry,* 1975, *32,* 265–268.

PART THREE

Psychotherapies

Part III, "Psychotherapies," presents supervision of various psychotherapies. While commonalities between the approaches exist, the differences in approaches toward supervisory issues are noteworthy.

Chapter 10, *Supervision and the Bipersonal Field* by Robert J. Langs describes the flow of the interactional process between the patient, the psychoanalyst, and the supervisor. The concepts of the bipersonal field are applied to the supervision of a therapy case.

Chapter 11, *Psychoanalytic Psychotherapy Supervision* by Stanley Moldawsky, is an account of supervision from a psychodynamic viewpoint, including the establishment of a learning alliance with the therapist.

Chapter 12, *A Client-Centered Approach to the Supervision of Psychotherapy* by Laura N. Rice, presents a model for growth of the therapist. Particular attention is paid to the match between a therapists' values and his or her suitability to adopt the client centered approach.

Chapter 13, *Supervision of Behavior Therapy* by Marsha M. Linehan, suggests that behavioral approaches may appear easy to master, resulting in a lack of attention to training. The chapter reviews training models that have developed and proposes a comprehensive model of behavioral therapy training.

Chapter 14, *Supervision in Rational-Emotive Therapy* by Richard L. Wessler and Albert Ellis, specifies the particular skills that the rational-emotive therapist brings to bear in therapy, and the variety of techniques the RET training program uses.

Chapter 15, *Supervision in Communications Analytic Therapy* by Ernst G. Beier and David M. Young, presents the use of examining communications of patients and therapists as ways of understanding the client, effecting client change, knowing the therapist's own impact, and using the impact to selectively engage the patient toward therapeutic ends.

CHAPTER 10

Supervision and the Bipersonal Field

ROBERT J. LANGS

INTRODUCTION

The present paper offers an adaptational-interactional model of the supervision of psychoanalytic psychotherapy (and psychoanalysis proper).[1] It is further designed to empirically explore a number of relatively neglected issues pertinent to present-day supervisory practices, and will stress the utilization of the patient's unconscious supervisory efforts within the treatment experience.

Accepting the premise that a supervisor's theory and practice of supervision is founded on his conceptualization of the therapeutic situation, I will begin with a brief resumé of the bipersonal field concept of treatment. Proceeding in outline form, I will then briefly explore (a) the structure of the supervisory bipersonal field and its influence on the supervisory process, (b) a basic model of supervision which stresses prediction and validation, and (c) the issue of the supervisor's countertransferences and the means through which a supervisee can validate the work of his mentor. A brief clinical excerpt will conclude the paper.

THE BIPERSONAL FIELD CONCEPT OF THE TREATMENT SITUATION

Psychotherapy (and psychoanalysis) can be characterized as taking place within a bipersonal field defined by its ground rules (framework), within which a communicative interaction occurs between patient and therapist. Within the field, every experience has, in varying proportions, vectors from both patient and therapist. The therapeutic work takes place along a communicative interface determined by the assets and pathology of both participants, and in the ideal situation, the major pathological inputs derive from the patient. The goal of therapy may be stated as providing the patient with adaptive, inner structural change through insight and inherent positive introjective identifications through

---

[1] I will not attempt here to distinguish between psychoanalytic psychotherapy and psychoanalysis, since the basic principles and issues related to supervision under discussion here are essentially comparable. An investigation of possible distinctions, although of some importance, is beyond the scope of this paper. I will therefore focus on the supervision of insight psychotherapy.

which he adaptively modifies and resolves his neurosis (a term used here in its broadest sense to allude to all forms and types of psychopathology; for details see Langs, 1975a, b, 1976a, b, 1978b, c, d.)

The essential nature of the communicative interaction between patient and therapist is determined, first, by the establishment of a relationship and sets of goals; second, by the delineation and maintenance of the ground rules and framework of the bipersonal field; and third, by the nature and functions of the free associations and behaviors of the patient on the one hand, and on the other, by the nature and function of the therapist's interventions and behaviors. In considering the material from the patient, the therapist makes use of the listening process in all of its dimensions (Langs, 1978c), and this includes affective, intuitive, empathic, cognitive, and interactional sensitivities. The full understanding of the patient's communications derive from organizing them around sequential *adaptive contexts,* all ultimately related to the therapeutic interaction, and which are defined as the reality precipitants or intrapsychically significant events (day residues) or stimuli for the patient's conscious, and especially unconscious, evocations and responses. Similarly, the therapist's interventions are viewed as therapeutically designed adaptive reactions to the interactional stimuli from the patient, and studied for both their conscious and unconscious communicative qualities. For both patient and therapist, each communication is seen as a mixture of reality and fantasy, valid and distorted response, appropriate and inappropriate reaction—that is, a mixture of both transference and nontransference, countertransference and noncountertransference (Langs, 1976a, b, 1978c, d).

An evaluation of the material from the patient shows three levels of meaning and function: *manifest content,* which alludes to the surface of the material; *Type One derivatives,* which are immediate inferences developed by the therapist; and *Type Two derivatives,* which are organized around specific adaptive contexts, thereby yielding currently active, definitive, and dynamic latent meanings and functions, usually in terms of the ongoing therapeutic interaction.

This classification also leads to the delineation of three communicative styles in patients and therapists, and of three types of communicative fields produced by their interaction: *Type A,* in which the use of symbolism, illusion, and a play space prevails; *Type B,* in which projective identification and action-discharge is basic; and *Type C,* in which falsification and impervious intrapsychic and interpersonal barriers prevail (see especially Langs, 1978b).

In sum, then, a conception of the bipersonal field indicates that valid therapeutic work takes place on a number of levels. Most basic are issues related to the ground rules or framework, since the status of the frame determines the nature and implications of all other communications between patient and therapist. Therefore, both management responses and interpretations related to the ground rules are a first-order arena for therapeutic work. Next, there are the patient's responses to the therapist's interventions, which themselves may be essentially valid or erroneous, and often contain mixtures of truth and distortion. The patient's unconscious perceptions of, and reactions to, correct and erroneous interventions, as well as his subsequent pathological elaboration of the valid cores within his responses, are essential areas for therapeutic work. Such endeavors must, however, maintain a sensitivity to the sectors of the patient's valid functioning, as well as to the expressions of his neurosis.

The third level of therapeutic work involves the exploration of resistances expressed through the patient's associations and behaviors as they impinge upon the treatment situation and the ground rules. Often, such resistances receive unconscious contributions from the therapist and are best termed *interactional resistances* (Langs, 1976a), as a means of characterizing their interpersonal and intrapsychic elements. Unconscious collusive resistances may be termed sectors of *therapeutic misalliance*— joint efforts by patient and therapist to achieve symptom relief through some means other than insightful therapeutic work (Langs, 1975a)—and the rectification and interpretation of these unconsciously founded actualities takes precedence over work with the patient's essentially intrapsychic resistances, and core pathological fantasies and introjects. Analytic work in this latter sphere—the so-called analysis of contents—constitutes still another crucial level of therapeutic work.

In all, then, it is evident that the therapist's work (and the efforts of his supervisor) is by no means simply focused on interpretations of the patient's associations in terms of their unconscious contents, meanings, and functions. In principle, actuality must take precedence over fantasy, and difficulties to which the therapist has contributed must be both rectified and interpreted before dealing with the patient's own pathological contributions. Essential to this approach is one final observation: that every communication from the patient on some level alludes to the therapeutic interaction, and that virtually all of the meaningful therapeutic work will occur in this particular sphere.

THE BASIC MODEL OF SUPERVISION

In several recent books (Langs, 1976a, 1978c, d, in press), I have presented my own supervisory work, including the supervision of two supervisory situations. I will therefore summarize here a set of basic supervisory principles, and leave to the interested reader the opportunity to study through those separate contributions my own interpretation of the application of these principles (see also below).

The supervisory bipersonal field is defined by a framework that is far more flexible in many respects than that of psychotherapy, though it nonetheless should have as well a degree of basic structure. Thus, supervision may occur in groups or individually (here, I will concentrate on individual supervision) and should unfold primarily on a once-weekly basis, at a set time, and with a defined duration —all factors open to variation. The fee too can be a matter of flexibility. However, total confidentiality should prevail, since this offers the best hold, support, and sense of security available to the supervisee. The primary commitment of the supervisor should be directed toward the patient, in keeping with the principle that once a physicianly responsibility is established on any level, it takes precedence over all else. This aspect of the structure of supervision has many ramifications, and it should be explicated with due consideration for tact and sensitivity in regard to the supervisee's needs. However, it contributes to a very fundamental dimension of the supervisory experience, in that it dictates that the supervisory work be directed primarily toward the therapeutic needs of the patient, and that the supervisor's interventions include all that is essential for the cure of the patient. Clearly, this may lead to discussions of issues that will be somewhat disturbing to the supervisee, but which, nonetheless, cannot be avoided because of the requirements of the patient. Within that framework, the learning needs of the supervisee are addressed with utmost concern, empathy, and sympathy.

As a counterpart to the fundamental rule of free association in the therapeutic situation, it is essential that the main focus of the supervisory work unfold from the *sequential direct presentation* of process notes describing each individual session, written by the supervisee as soon as possible *after* each hour. In order to make feasible the predictive and validating supervisory approach to be described below, such a detailed presentation is vital, and must be carried out in the order in which the actual therapeutic session unfolded. This also permits the supervisor an opportunity to empathize with both patient and therapist as to their unfolding interactional experiences, and to sense on some level the anxieties, moments of relief, periods of confusion or understanding—and whatever—that they shared or felt separately.

For his part, the supervisor should base virtually all of his interventions on the clinical material presented by the supervisee. All extraneous comments should be linked in some way to this body of data, although the supervisor's personal feelings, alterations of anonymity, and nonneutral interventions (see below) may all have a *small* place in the supervisory interaction. Such human comments may help develop an atmosphere of trust and cordiality, and even a positive identification with the supervisor; however, these remarks also contain strong potential for countertransference-based inputs that lead to disruptive and pathological unconscious identifications that are often outside of the awareness of both supervisor and supervisee.

In the main, then, the supervisor should concentrate his interventions on his evaluation of the material from the patient and the therapist's interventions. While he must certainly be free to use this basic format as a takeoff point for the discussion of broader relevant issues, and to introduce pertinent literature and opinions, so long as he makes use of the material from the therapeutic interaction as a basis for his formulations, he is in a sound position to validate his hypotheses, or if necessary, to revise them. Although from time to time, especially at times of crisis (see below), the supervisor may discuss a question or problem with the supervisee that is not immediately pertinent to the material at hand, such interludes should be rare; they also should be recognized for their relatively loose quality and for the impossibility of sound validation. It is in this context that we may note that the supervisory situation is not designed for the free associations of the supervisee, and therefore cannot be the arena for any direct form of psychotherapy on his behalf.

In general, at a point of culmination or coalescence of meaning as reflected in the patient's associations, or at a juncture where the supervisee has intervened, it is incumbent on the supervisor to offer his own formulation of the material to that moment and, wherever possible, to indicate how he himself would have intervened—or remained silent—under these conditions. As a further step, in principle, it is essential that the supervisor evaluate the supervisee's intervention in terms of its formal qualities, and especially in terms of its unconscious communicative properties. It is in this realm that most supervisory work has been severely limited, especially with trainees, and it is here that the use of prediction proves vital (see Langs, 1976a, 1978c, d, in press).

The predictive model stresses the delineation by the supervisor of specific hypotheses related to the material from the patient, and to the unconscious nature of the therapist's interventions. It relies on the validating process (Langs, 1976b, 1978a, c), through which psychoanalytically founded verification of all proposed formulations becomes a consistent quality of the supervisory experience. Not only should the supervisor himself consistently apply the validating process, but the details of its application should be part of his basic teaching to the supervisee.

The validation of a supervisor's formulation related to a sequence of associations from the patient takes the form of the appearance of subsequent material which illuminates in a unique and unexpected manner the thesis offered by the supervisor. Under ideal conditions, the ultimate form of validation would take place if the supervisee had intervened in his session with the patient in a manner in keeping with the proposed hypothesis. Under those conditions, confirmation should take the form of Type Two derivatives organized around the adaptive context of the therapist's intervention, through which a truly new and unexpected revelation emerges in indirect (derivative) form. In Bion's (1962) terms, this constitutes the appearance of a *selected fact* which organizes already known data in an unanticipated form that gives meaning beyond that which is already known. In addition to this cognitive form of validation, indications of a positive unconscious introjective identification with the therapist who has intervened correctly constitutes the interactional level of validation.

A second application of the validating process occurs after the supervisee has actually intervened. Here, the supervisor attempts to formulate the nature of the supervisee's unconscious communications to the patient. Included is not so much an evaluation as to whether an intervention is correct or incorrect, based on the material from the patient or not, truly interpretive or not, or deviant in one of many possible ways (Langs, 1975b, 1976a, 1978c, d, in press), but an attempt to understand the unconscious meanings and functions of a particular intervention. To the extent that it does not constitute a valid rectification of the framework or interpretation to the patient, or falls outside of the six basic interventions that I have recently defined (Langs, 1978e: silence, management of the framework, interpretations-reconstructions, the playback of selected derivatives around a hidden adaptive context, the interpretive processing of a projective identification, and the interpretation of metaphors of the Type C field), an evaluation must be made of the countertransference-based unconscious communications emanating from the therapist. This commentary then serves as a prediction of the material that will follow from the patient who, as a rule, will resond with Type Two derivatives organized around the adaptive context of the therapist's interventions, largely in terms of the pathological inputs involved. It is at this point that the patient will unconsciously attempt to exploit the expressions of the supervisee's countertransferences, but will in addition attempt to help the supervisee correct his errors—in essence, become the unconscious supervisor of the supervisee, and embark upon unconsciously curative efforts (see below; see also Searles, 1965, 1975; Langs, 1975a, 1976a, 1978d).

While extraneous comments from the supervisee and the sudden recollection on his part of additional unreported material constitute a second-order level of validation of the supervisor's hypotheses, it is to be stressed that the first line of validation must always derive from the continued therapeutic interaction—from the further associations of the patient and the additional interventions of the therapist. The supervisor must, however, be open to nonvalidating responses, and to the possibility of the introduction of his own countertransference-based biases. These require self-analytic understanding and rectification (see below).

In all, then, within a somewhat structured—though relatively loose—framework, in which an essential requisite is the sequential presentation of process notes, the supervisor's functions unfold in response to the material from the patient and the interventions of the therapist. While it is conceivable that in a given supervisory session, the supervisor will have little or nothing to say, in the main, it is his responsibility to develop repeated formulations of the material from the patient and the comments of the therapist, and to consistently explore the communicative interaction with which he is faced.

In principle, and prepared to modify his overall plan in keeping with the immediate needs of the patient and supervisee, the supervisor should follow a teaching sequence. In general, he should concentrate his initial efforts on the listening process, which is the therapist's (and supervisor's) fundamental tool (Langs, 1978c). He should move next to the ground rules—the basic framework for the therapeutic interaction. A study of the therapeutic relationship itself should follow, and finally, a delineation of how to intervene. While there will be overlap and interruptions in this sequence of teaching, it will serve as a useful guide.

The supervisor's ear must also be attuned to a hierarchy of therapeutic issues —an order of precedence established from the patient's vantage point. This begins with attention to the framework and a sensitivity to all possible deviations and their implications within the ongoing therapeutic interaction. Next, he must determine the communicative style of the supervisee and patient; and the nature of their shared communicative bipersonal field. Listening, relating, and intervening (and supervising) are distinctive in each communicative field. Other tasks relate to the issues derived from the model of psychotherapy described above. In principle, the supervisor should move from a study of the conscious and unconscious ramifications of realities (ground rules, technical errors, valid interventions, and the like) to the implications of fantasies-memories, and introjects.

Contributions from the therapist (and supervisor) are to be considered before (and in interaction with) those from the patient, as should communicative style and resistances before contents.

Overall, with a flexible use of the principles described here, the supervisor should be capable of gentle but candid work which sensitively acquaints the supervisee not only with the nature of his main difficulties as a therapist, but with his unrecognized assets as well.

With this as the basic model, I will now consider a number of specific supervisory issues.

THE SUPERVISORY COMMUNICATIVE INTERACTION; COUNTERTRANSFERENCES IN THE SUPERVISOR

In keeping with the classification offered above, the supervisory situation may take place in any one of the three types of communicative fields. A Type A field requires a supervisee capable of presenting sequential process notes and of understanding the representational communications of the supervisor, who himself must be capable of symbolic expression in his supervisory work. A Type B field may develop with a supervisee who generates often intense comments extraneous to the clinical presentation, designed unconsciously for the riddance of his own inner tension and disturbing inner contents and mechanisms, which he unconsciously endeavors to place into the supervisor—either as a means of evoking proxies (Wangh, 1962) or of unconsciously burdening and attacking the supervisor. Sometimes, such efforts are reflected in the way in which the process notes are prepared so that there are inexplicable gaps and other confusing qualities.

The supervisor too may unwittingly use the supervisory situation as a scene of action-discharge and pathological projective identification, unconsciously making use of his comments to the supervisee for countertransference-based expressions. (Here, I use the term "countertransference" to apply to any expression of pathology in a therapist or supervisor as it pertains to psychotherapeutic work.) It is my impression that this is a not uncommon occurrence, and that it is a significant blind spot in certain supervisors.

The detection of countertransference-based difficulties in the supervisor is a difficult matter, and it must rely, first, on self-evaluations that follow nonvalidated hypotheses, and second, on the experience of interactional pressures and tensions within the supervisory relationship that direct the supervisor to a similar form of self-examination and self-analysis. Extraneous and critical comments from the supervisee should be investigated for grains of truth when they touch upon possible areas of disturbances within a supervisor, and the latter should make consistent efforts to identify clues of the presence of countertransference factors in his supervisory work.

The detection of countertransference expressions in the direct supervisory interaction itself, from either the supervisor or supervisee, is a difficult matter. It relies on a reflection process in both participants. For the supervisor, it calls for an openness to examining his possible contribution to any source of tension between himself and the supervisee, and to any moment of acute disturbance or stalemate in the supervised treatment situation.

A Type C supervisory field may eventuate from relatively barren and uninformative presentations by the supervisee, and from relatively terse, general, clichéd interventions on the part of the supervisor. Since these barriers serve to defend against inner turmoil and catastrophe (usually, an underlying psychotic disturbance or part of the personality), they are strongly maintained and difficult to modify in the supervisory situation. A Type C supervisor will either make no use of the validating process or accept the most vague and general forms of confirmation of his own formulations, and he will tend to accept similarly ill-defined formulations and interventions in his supervisee.

In general, then, there is an important interaction between the communicative style of the supervisor and that of the supervisee. It may serve the growth of both participants, or the defensive needs of each, and every effort must be made to establish a Type A field in order to truly foster the education and technical development of the supervisee. Because here too the nature of the communicative interaction determines the implications, meanings, and functions of the supervisor's interventions, and the responses of the supervisee, the development of a Type A supervisory field is a first-order essential for truly growth-promoting supervision. Such work requires the tolerance of some degree of regression and anxiety in both supervisor and supervisee, and will especially require painful confrontations and self-realizations on the part of the supervisee who truly cannot learn without periods of regression, disorganization, chaos, and—it is hoped—subsequent reconstitution at a higher level of functioning.

One final note regarding communicative styles: every supervisor will have his preference for a particular communicative mode of his own, and will tend to focus his efforts on one of the three basic areas of unconscious communication between the patient and the therapist: the cognitive, the object relational, and the projective identificatory—the last two being essentially interactional (Langs, 1978c). It is important for an unbiased experience that the supervisor be aware of his own propensities, and that he attempt to maintain a balanced approach to both the cognitive and interactional spheres in his supervisory work, despite the presence of biases. Similarly, he must be prepared equally to deal with frame issues, interactional problems, and essential intrapsychic contents within the patient, rather than tending to favor one or another particular focus. Any tendency to narrow the supervisory field should ultimately be experienced by the supervisor as an expression of an unresolved countertransference difficulty—which then becomes his private responsibility to analyze and rectify.

THE COUNTERTRANSFERENCES OF THE SUPERVISEE: THE PATIENT AS SUPERVISOR

Among the issues most perplexing to those who have written on supervision is the problem of how to deal with the supervisee's countertransference prob-

lems. Suggestions have included the use of the supervisee's therapist or analyst as a supervisor, and the adoption of a directly therapeutic role by an independent supervisor when countertransference manifestations emerge. In
contrast, many feel that the supervisory situation cannot ever permit the supervisor to function in a directly therapeutic way for the supervisee, and that
at best, signs of countertransference difficulties in the supervisee should be
identified, and then left for him to work through in his own therapy or
through self-analysis.

In keeping with my proposal that the nature and implications of the transactions between the supervisor and the supervisee are determined by the conditions
of the supervisory bipersonal field, and that these conditions do not, indeed, lend
themselves to the therapy of the supervisee, it is my contention that the relevant
basic principle should be stated as follows: The supervisor should make use of the
patient's unconscious perceptions and introjections of the expressions of the
supervisee's countertransference difficulties, as reflected in his ongoing associations and behaviors, as a means of identifying, clarifying, and helping to resolve
the supervisee's countertransference difficulties. This principle can be stated in
another, clearly noncontroversial manner: The supervisor should be working with
what concerns the patient and with the disturbances within the bipersonal field
that require rectifying and interpretive interventions. If, at a given juncture, the
patient is unconsciously mainly working over a pathological input from the
therapist-in-training, the supervisor has no choice but to address this particular
problem: it is the central adaptive context, meaning, and function for the patient's
communicative response.

There is considerable evidence that, in the presence of countertransference-
based inputs by the therapist, the patient will respond in a characteristic manner:
in part, he will conceal his own pathology within that of the therapist, while
unconsciously introjecting and working over the communicated unconscious
conflicts and fantasies, introjects, anxieties, role and image evocations, barriers,
and projective identifications conveyed by the therapist's interventions or inappropriate failures to intervene (Langs, 1976a, 1978c, d, e). Much of these efforts
can be characterized as *unconscious supervision* for the therapist: they include
endeavors to indirectly call the therapist's error to his attention; associations
unconsciously designed to guide him back on the right path by rectifying the
situation; and *unconscious interpretations* designed to cure the therapist of aspects
of his countertransference problem—whatever additional unconscious exploitation and pathological responses develop in the patient.

In derivative form, unconsciously the patient will consistently respond with
what can be characterized as general supervisory efforts in response to technical
errors by the therapist—either in the realm of the management of the framework
or the verbal-interpretive sphere. Such a conception implies that on some unconscious level the patient knows something of his therapeutic needs, that he makes
use of his own validating process (Langs, 1976b), and that whatever his resistances and need to preclude cure, he makes significant efforts unconsciously to
guide the therapist toward insightfully curative interventions. The patient's neurosis is maintained primarily because these insights exist on an unconscious level

and he is incapable of the relevant conscious understanding and mastery (Langs, 1976a, 1978c); he is in a position, therefore, only to unconsciously guide the therapist who has the responsibility to make such insights and understanding conscious for the patient in return. In fact, as Searles (1975) so sensitively noted, perhaps the most destructive response that the therapist can make to his patient is a failure to implicitly detect and utilize the patient's unconscious curative-supervisory efforts. Such failures lead to profound disorganization and depression in the patient (Langs, 1976a, 1978c), and in therapeutic situations where this level of interaction is ignored, there are many such interludes which are either erroneously formulated or entirely misunderstood.

In supervision, then, in dealing with the expressions of the supervisee's countertransference difficulties in his work with his patient, it is important to establish a predictive approach. The supervisor should formulate moments when the supervisee has failed to intervene, or define when and how an actual intervention is in error and therefore countertransference-based. The supervisor has the further responsibility of identifying the communicative unconscious nature of the error, in terms of its cognitive and interactional qualities. Having made his assessment and predictions, he can then turn to the patient's responsive material—his *commentary* on the therapist's intervention (Langs, 1978c)—for the patient's own supervisory-curative responses.

In principle, the supervisor's formulation and the patient's reactions, considered as Type Two derivatives in the adaptive context of the therapist's interventions or inappropriate failure to intervene, should correspond significantly: the supervisor's commentary should state on a manifest level what the patient communicates on a latent (derivative) level. And while this agreement serves then to validate the supervisor's work, the supervisee should also be reminded that the implication of this material is that the patient is, indeed, unconsciously working over and attempting to correct his therapist's error.

On those occasions when the supervisor has missed a point that required a supervisory intervention, he may take his cue directly from the patient's unconscious commentaries on the supervisee's interventions, recognizing their valid elements as well as any possible distortions. In this way, he too makes use of the patient's unconscious communications in terms of their supervisory functions. It is to be remembered, however, that such a formulation must be then subjected to subsequent validation from the material from the patient and therapist.

In concluding this part of the discussion, we may note that the therapeutic bipersonal field is not created or designed for the resolution of the therapist's pathology. This does not preclude therapeutic benefit on his part, but it does remind us that such gains should be coincidental to the main work of therapy and that they carry with them many risks for the insightful cure of the patient. Finally, it is to be noted that the patient's unconscious supervisory responses are not confined to the therapist's errors; valid interventions will evoke positive and complimentary derivative reactions as well.

THE SUPERVISEE'S VALIDATION OF THE SUPERVISOR'S WORK

In keeping with the relative neglect of the supervisor's countertransferences, and with a tendency toward either overidealization or hostile attacks by a supervisee upon a given supervisor, little has been written regarding the more rational means through which a supervisee can evaluate the work of his mentor. There are, however, a number of avenues available to him for such an assessment. First, he should consider whether the supervisor utilizes a predictive model and a sophisticated application of the validating process—in their absence, virtually anything can be stated and since there is no criteria of proof, falsely maintained. Next, there is the extent to which the material from the patient and the supervisee's own subsequent interventions truly validate the formulations of his supervisor in indirect, derivative form. The supervisee can also study the extent to which the supervisor's formulations and comments coalesce to provide him with a sensible, workable approach to psychotherapy, and the degree to which they help him to recognize both his countertransference difficulties and his valid therapeutic efforts. However, the dangers of defensiveness and distortion in this regard are considerable; the supervisee should strive to develop a special form of the validating process for his assessment of his supervisory experiences.

The supervisee should be especially wary of a supervisor who consistently praises his therapeutic endeavors and fails to detect expressions of his countertransferences. There are well-founded tenets that no one ever entirely resolves his countertransferences, and that a therapist who has not been analyzed or treated in intensive psychotherapy is especially vulnerable in this regard. This should lead a supervisee to expect consistent countertransference-based inputs to his work with his patients, and create a tolerance for a supervisor who can detect and discuss these problems within the limitations imposed by the conditions of the supervisory bipersonal field. This type of experience should move the supervisee toward a private working over of the underlying countertransference fantasies and introjects, efforts that require an ability to recognize and accept valid criticism.

In the main, then, validation through the generation of selected facts identifiable in the material being presented should be the basic criterion through which the supervisee judges the value of a supervisor's work. In this respect, the supervisee must soon become acquainted with his own anxieties and resistances to doing insight psychotherapy, his fear of the patient's and his own inner mental world, and his struggle against a perceptive supervisor (Langs, 1976c). Such anxieties can be one factor in expressions of countertransference in the supervisee's direct relationship with his teacher (and in his work with the supervised patient), and they can, of course, interfere with an unprejudiced evaluation of the supervisor's efforts. In all, it is the consistent use of the predictive model and the in depth validating process in the supervisory bipersonal field that must serve as the main guarantor against idiosyncratic and pathological disturbances in the supervisory experience derived from the pathology of either participant.

SUPERVISORY CRISES

There are two main sources of crises in supervision: an urgent situation in the supervised treatment and an unresolved conflict between the supervisor and supervisee. In principle, there is no need for the supervisor to modify his teaching techniques in the first situation, since the most effective means of resolution lies in a careful study of the material from the patient and therapist. Often, as is well known, countertransference-based inputs from the therapist play a crucial role in such interludes, but this should not be a matter of assumption and should be determined from the process note material.

However, the possible contributions of the supervisor to a crisis situation in the supervised therapy must not be overlooked. It is here that the supervisor has the responsibility of monitoring the material from the patient as an unconscious commentary on his (usually and preferably unknown to the patient) supervisory efforts with the therapist. As I have indicated elsewhere (Langs, in press), the patient may be unconsciously aware of the influence of what I have termed the *supervisory introject* on the treating therapist: the sometimes inadequately metabolized and poorly integrated supervisory communications which create special pressures on the supervisee in his work with the patient (in addition to their possible constructive qualities). Often, in clinics and other teaching centers, the patient is consciously or unconsciously quite cognizant that his therapy and therapist are being supervised, although this does *not* constitute a basis for the deliberate modification of the framework by the therapist through the self-revelation of the presence of a supervisor (see Langs, 1973). His presence should, instead, be a matter of silent realization, one that the supervisee is prepared to explore interpretively with the patient should it arise, based entirely on the patient's conscious and unconscious perceptions and fantasies—though in actuality, this generally proves to be an extremely difficult issue for trainees.

It is essential then that the supervisor accept the material from the patient and therapist as a commentary on his supervision—and as therefore containing both conscious and unconscious perceptiveness, as well as possible distortions. The supervisor should treat these commentaries as essentially valid until proven otherwise, and as the patient's unconscious efforts to supervise him in addition to the therapist. It is therefore the supervisor's responsibility to explore his possible contributions to a treatment crisis and, of course, to discuss and rectify these influences with the supervisee. As always, the validating process should be applied to the formulations of the supervisor's role in the crisis; if sound, they should be borne out in the material from the continuing therapeutic interaction.

The second and related crisis occurs directly between the supervisor and the supervisee, and may be initiated by either participant, though it usually has contributions from both. It is here that the supervisor is on most treacherous ground, since he has no analyzable and interpretable material to formulate, and no clear-cut methodology and means of validation on which to rely. He must therefore be as straightforward as possible, base his critique as much as possible on his observations of the therapist's work with his patient, and introduce as few extraneous comments as feasible. He should make no attempt to explore in a therapeutic way the contributing factors from the supervisee, but should confine himself to a sophisticated, perceptive, and yet sensitive and cautious direct discussion. He must consistently be prepared to recognize his own contribution to the crisis, however small, and he should take special cautions against projectively identifying—placing through interactional means—these influences into the supervisee, blaming him entirely for the critical situation. His capacity to recognize and directly acknowledge some of his own difficulties as they have contributed to the problem at hand is extremely helpful under these conditions.

There are many factors within both supervisor and supervisee that can generate a disruptive crisis within supervision. On the part of the supervisor, there may be envy of his usually younger supervisee, antagonism because of the supervisee's basic attitude toward his therapeutic work when it is at variance with that of his own, unresolved competitive and other conflicts, disruptive responses to supervisory resistances in the supervisee, heterosexual or homosexual anxieties and issues related to aggression, and threatening impingements based on the material from the case under consideration—to name but a few of the main possibilities. The supervisee may generate a crisis because of his own envy of the supervisor, his fear of the supervisor's knowledge and perceptiveness, his dread of regression and anxiety in the face of threats to his pathological defenses and modes of gratification, a particular fear of exposing himself and his mistakes, a dread of the more psychotic part of his own personality and that of the patient, a fundamental anxiety related to his own and the patient's inner mental world, and a variety of sexual and aggressive conflicts directly related to the supervisory experience. In addition, should the supervisor, supervisee, or both be in therapy or analysis, there is the ever-present danger of the displacement of conflicts and issues centered within their own therapeutic experience, shifted to, and enacted within, the supervisory relationship.

In dealing with such crises, all but general interpretations should be avoided, and attempts at dynamic formulation kept to a minimum, if used at all. Instead, direct efforts to resolve the conflict, to return the focus to the teaching needs of the supervisee and the therapeutic needs of the patient, and to resolve the immediate obstacles are to be preferred. Inappropriate interventions will tend to promote negative supervisory introjects which then serve to further intensify the crisis at hand.

A CLINICAL ILLUSTRATION

A brief vignette will serve to illustrate some of the concepts and issues discussed in this paper. Mr. A was a young man in therapy with Dr. B for periods of depression and confusion; he was being seen once weekly in the therapist's office which was located in the outpatient section of a large hospital. Therapy was on a private basis and, without the knowledge of the patient, Dr. B was presenting this therapeutic experience to me in supervision.

In the session prior to the one on which I will focus, the patient spoke about being upset about not being able to get a date. His friends were unavailable. One of his co-workers had behaved in a crazy way, and it had interfered with the patient's job. He had tried to pick up a girl who was walking with several other people, and he was afraid that they thought he was homosexual. He felt frightened in the midst of crowds.

The therapist intervened, alluding to the crazy situation at work, to Mr. A's feelings of being stared at and being thought of as homosexual, and his anxiety in crowds—noting that these were themes that seemed to be prominent in the last few sessions. The patient then spoke of his great sensitivity to being observed and to crowds, and stated that he had been nervous in the clinic waiting room ever since he had begun therapy a year ago. He tried to pretend that he was well, and that everyone else was sick. He wanted to possess the therapist, and this was disturbed by the presence of the other patients in the waiting room. The therapist intervened again, noting the patient's feelings of anxiety, his concerns about homosexual feelings, and his fear of closeness with the therapist, and he suggested that this was related to being seen in the medical center.

The patient then elaborated on his anxieties about sitting in the waiting room and spoke of his need for his own "turf"—a place to belong. He then alluded to his recent decision to take full financial responsibility for his treatment, although he had recently taken a few dollars from his father. After referring to the patient's efforts to break his ties to his parents, the therapist suddenly asked the patient if he had actually seen anyone that he knew in the waiting room. Mr. A responded in amazement: How did you know? Two weeks earlier he had met a close friend there, and hadn't known what to say; were they both sick, or what? He ended the hour by saying that he envied the therapist and felt that it would be nice to be an analyst.

Without detailing much of the supervisory process related to this session, this therapist had been making recent efforts to rectify the framework of this treatment, and had, indeed, interpretively helped the patient to take full responsibility for his fee. With this step secured, the patient soon became frightened of the closeness to the therapist, and the underlying homosexual and primitive fantasies that were impinging upon him. The material had shifted to themes of crowds and exposure, and it became evident that the patient was quite concerned about another aspect of the frame: the lack of privacy in the waiting room and the therapist's use of an office in a hospital where it was evident that he had a high-level position.

The material in this particular session seems to validate the hypothesis that the patient was, in part, attempting to work over these issues. However, the therapist's initial interventions were somewhat biased and incomplete. They were unable to explain why Mr. A, in the presence of other patients in the waiting room (who could serve as protectors), should feel so terrified of his conscious and unconscious homosexual fantasies. A more likely hypothesis was proposed in supervision, to the effect that for the moment this material unconsciously alluded to the patient's fantasies and beliefs regarding the *therapist's* (unconscious?)

homosexual anxieties and his need to defend against them by having his office in a relatively public place, rather than in a private setting. (In addition to considerable supportive evidence from earlier material, this formulation can be arrived at by monitoring this material as Type Two derivatives around the adaptive context of the location of the therapist's office, applying the me/not-me interface, which states that every communication from the patient alludes on some level to both himself and the therapist, and then attempting to assess the validity and distortion involved; see Langs, 1978c.) Partly on the basis, then, of an unconsciously perceived dread within the therapist of his underlying residuals of homosexual countertransference, the patient was having difficulty in managing his own homosexual anxieties and in exploring them in this particular communicative field.

The therapist's final intervention, however, was discussed at some length in supervision because of its striking noninterpretive qualities and omniscient cast. Dr. B acknowledged a sense of anxiety and impatience in dealing with this area, and indicated an intense need to know whether something specific had aroused this patient's anxiety in the waiting room. In keeping with the principle that the patient should create each session and put the fragments needed for an integrated intervention into the therapist, it was suggested, based on the process notes and formulations already described, that unconsciously this particular intervention could serve as a defense against the patient's unconscious perceptions of the therapist's homosexual countertransference, while at the same time it might well intensify these perceptions and introjects because of the therapist's need to be powerful, all-knowing, and seductive. It was predicted that this particular intervention would serve as a major adaptive context filled with unconscious meaning for the following hour; it would be a central reality stimulus for the organization of the patient's associations as Type Two derivatives that were bound to contain powerful commentaries—mixtures of perceptiveness and distortion—on this particular intervention and the underlying basis for it within the therapist. (It is essential in offering such supervisory predictions to maintain an open mind, and to be prepared for nonvalidation and for the possibility of an entirely different locus for the patient's working over. The supervisor must maintain a delicate balance between efforts at prediction and an openness for unexpected communicative threads.)

Mr. A began the next hour by stating that he had been with a young man who worked as an aide in a state hospital. The friend had spoken in detail about many of his patients and about different forms of therapy. He mentioned the Freudian analyst who sees a patient five times a week and says nothing, who is a blank. In response, Mr. A was very upset and wondered how crazy he himself was; he thought of asking the therapist, but knew he would not get an answer.

He had had a dream. It was prompted when a former girl friend whom he had dated in his home town had broken a tentative date with him. He had responded with a fantasy of commandeering a one-man submarine (he worked in a related industry) and taking it to the bottom of the ocean—but he really wasn't that depressed.

In the dream he was at a large university and was trying to get to class. He opened the door to a huge lecture room that was crowded, but he found a seat and then had to take an exam. He didn't know anything, and he leaned over to copy from the guy in front of him who had hair that looked greasy, but wasn't really greasy. He couldn't see this other guy's paper.

Mr. A went on to recall feeling anxious on his way to the session and wondered if it didn't have to do with the prior hour. He remembered the therapist having said in that hour that he was beginning to break his ties with his parents, and he felt that that was good, but it frightened him—he felt better, but alone. He wanted to ask the therapist how sick he was, but didn't expect an answer; actually, it was better that way. He knew that he was struggling with something and that he was upset after he left the last session.

In the supervisory situation, it is often valuable to organize the listening process around the report of a dream which, while it should be treated in a manner comparable to all of the associations of the patient, nonetheless usually signals a special communicative need on his part (Langs, 1978f). It is important, however, to always begin with the day residue or adaptive context, and to then attempt to organize the material as Type Two derivatives around that context. Lacking an identifiable context, much of the discussion will center on Type One derivatives monitored around the therapeutic relationship, along the me/not-me interface, for both unconscious perceptions and unconscious fantasies that pertain to both the patient and the therapist—and to their interaction.

In this supervisory session, we did indeed attempt to organize this material as described, both after the report of the dream and at the moment that the supervisee announced that he had intervened in the hour. In principle, the supervisor should ask the supervisee to formulate first. While the central teaching effort should be based on the supervisee's actual interventions in the hour, additional teaching needs are expressed in the supervisee's formulations which may help to specify aspects of his listening process, with its perceptive areas and blind spots, that are not entirely conveyed in his interventions.

In this instance, the supervisee was quite convinced that the adaptive context for this material was his interventions in the previous session. He remembered that there had been some discussion related to treatment in that hour, but initially, he was unable to recall his specific intervention. This amnesia highlights another aspect of supervision: in keeping with the principles that the therapist should enter each session without desire, memory, or understanding (Bion, 1970; Langs, 1978c), and that he should allow each session to be its own creation (Langs, 1978c), supervision should also unfold with these two basic qualities by turning directly to fresh process notes without a summary of the prior hour or the prior supervisory session. In this way, both supervisor and supervisee have an opportunity for a new beginning, and for the discovery of material, themes, conflicts, fantasies, and the like which have been previously unrecognized. In addition, as illustrated here, in this way, the supervisor has an opportunity to discover the gaps in his own recollection of the previous supervisory session (the material presented and the supervisory experience), as well as any blocks in the recall of the supervisee. These often provide crucial clues for underlying counter-transferences in either member of the supervisory dyad.

Returning to this supervisory experience, the supervisee was allowed to develop his formulation and to struggle to modify his repressive defenses. He soon remembered his interventions, especially his final question. He then suggested that the patient was unconsciously attempting to offer a model of a sound therapist to him (the relatively silent analyst), and that Mr. A was talking about good and bad therapy, and the craziness of some therapeutic situations. He felt too that the patient was responding to his need as a therapist to repeat certain interventions and to the self-revelations so contained. He linked the dream to the hospital and to the crowded waiting room, and made note of the theme of cheating, but was unclear as to its implications.

The supervisee then described his intervention in the session at hand: he noted that the patient was alluding to the previous hour, to psychiatric centers and to crazy people, and that he had referred to analytic blankness. The dream had to do with a crowded room and conveyed a quality of wanting to find something out and not being able to, of wanting something to be revealed and yet not revealed.

At this point in the supervisory hour, I undertook some additional clarification. I suggested that the adaptive context was, indeed, the therapist's interventions in the previous hour, and especially his question about whether the patient had met anyone he knew in the waiting room. Through a series of questions, I brought out the hypothesis that, in addition, a second and related context was the therapist's continued use of an office in the medical center—an actuality regarding which Dr. B was having a great deal of conflict. After all, the patient's material was suggesting that there were many inappropriate qualities to the location of his office, and that it was interfering with the therapeutic work. This was a difficult confrontation for Dr. B to handle.

Much of the initial part of this session, then, can be viewed as an unconscious effort by the patient at supervision: a working over of the two main adaptive contexts in a form designed to help the therapist become aware of some of his major difficulties, and to assist him in rectifying them and understanding their basis—undoubtedly as a prelude to the necessary therapeutic work with the patient's own related problems.

To document this thesis: the patient begins with a reference to the aide who revealed information about his patients. This is an allusion to the frame, to a modification in confidentiality. As a Type Two derivative organized around the adaptive context of the therapist's last intervention, it suggests the unconscious fantasy and belief that there had been an alteration in confidentiality to which the therapist was a party—be it someone else's treatment or the patient's own therapy. It suggests as a strong "silent hypothesis" (Langs, 1978c) the patient's hunch that another patient had told the therapist that he had seen Mr. A in the waiting room (which was not, in actuality, true), and that it was on this basis that the therapist had made his intervention—that is, Dr. B had used confidential material from another patient in intervening. In a more general way, the patient is conveying something of the implicit destructiveness in modifying the framework, and this must allude too on some level both to the nonneutral aspects of the therapist's intervention and to the location of his office.

The patient then speaks about different forms of therapy, and how it should best be done, and then refers to a girl friend who broke a commitment—a date. In the adaptive contexts already identified, this alludes in derivative form to the therapist's implied unconscious sexualization of the treatment situation (and undoubtedly the patient's, as well), and to the violation of a commitment—to provide total confidentiality and privacy, and interpretive interventions. The patient then describes his sense of depression under these conditions, as well as his specific wish for privacy. On another level, these associations suggest an unconscious interpretation to the therapist that underlying his need to intervene omnisciently and to have his office in the medical center is a sense of depression which is being guarded against through manic defenses (see Little, 1951; Langs, 1976a, 1978b).

Developing these threads as silent hypotheses as the material was being presented, the dream, in derivative form, makes it unmistakable that the adaptive context of this session relates to the clinic waiting room and related issues. The reference to things seeming to be one way, but actually being different, is a rather compelling image of the uncertainties regarding the communicative properties of a bipersonal field whose frame is compromised, and of the inconsistent therapist who is party to such a situation. The patient wishes to cheat, and to see something that he cannot see; on a latent level, this may well allude to the therapist's seeming dishonesty in knowing something about the patient from another source (here, this is indeed an unconscious fantasy, misperception, or false belief, but one based on a powerful stimulus from the therapist), and the material alludes also to the difficulties that the therapist is having in seeing the relevant issues.

The reference to the therapist's prior intervention regarding the patient's breaking his ties with his parents is another unconscious interpretation in which the patient offers himself as a model to the therapist: break your ties with the parent-hospital center and become independent; don't be frightened of being alone; it is growth promoting in the long run. On another level, this material manifestly refers to one aspect of the prior hour, when the central issue that the patient is unconsciously working over is a quite different—latent—aspect of that particular session. The question of how sick the patient is also alludes to his doubts about the therapist, while his expectations that the therapist won't answer (which the patient said is good) is another model of maintaining the frame and not responding noninterpretively to the patient.

The therapist's intervention touched upon some of the intrapsychic and interactional conflicts with which the patient was dealing, but omitted the allusion to cheating. Here, the patient probably was attempting to evoke an image in the therapist, derived from his own interventions, that was in all likelihood incompatible with Dr. B's picture of himself; this led to avoidance and blocking. Further, an accurate appreciation of the supervisory efforts by this patient would confront the therapist not only with the countertransferences related to his premature interventions, but more importantly to the issue of the location of his office—one which he was unable to resolve at the time (i.e., the location is a form of cheating).

It is of considerable value in supervision, when a definitive adaptive context is available, to apply the full exercise of the listening process to the details of the patient's associations (Langs, 1978c). It not only fosters the development of this process in the supervisee, but it also permits the specific delineation of underlying psychopathology in both the patient and therapist. It generates a formulation that can then be compared with the therapist's actual intervention, and which, in addition, permits a clearer recognition of the deviant unconscious communications in that intervention. It also fosters a precise use of the validating process.

Returning to the session at hand, the patient responded to the therapist's comments by saying that his friend had spoken repeatedly of sick patients and had laughed at them, poking fun. He had revealed too much. Sometimes, Mr. A felt that the therapist was talking to others about him, but he didn't really think so—still, he sometimes felt that Dr. B was telling everyone about him. The crowd in the dream did indeed remind him of the discussion about the waiting room, and all week, he was wondering why the therapist had asked that question. It blew his mind and he felt like a little kid—why had the therapist done it? He wanted to tell the therapist that he could handle the situation, that he hadn't been upset at seeing the friend in the waiting room, but he was afraid that the therapist would see him as too arrogant and as a know-it-all.

Here, the therapist suggested that the patient had seen his own comments as arrogant and hurtful, as reflecting a view of Mr. A as weak, and that the patient seemed to wonder why the therapist had such "chutzpah." The patient responded that he was very happy that the therapist remembered his own comments and that he felt better now. He went on to say how interested he was in what the therapist thought, and why he had said what he had said; he too would like to return to college and become a therapist.

Having established a series of initial hypotheses, and having suggested certain gaps in the therapist's intervention based on unresolved countertransferences, we can see how the patient himself responded to the intervention by attempting to call to the therapist's attention the missing elements—further supervisory efforts. In this situation, the patient does so almost directly—a finding that is rather unusual, since as a rule, such efforts are undertaken in far more disguised and derivative form. The patient reveals that the therapist's last intervention, and the office location, led to a sense of mistrust and suspiciousness, or at the very least, to a struggle in this area. This material indicates how modifications in the framework can drive patients crazy (Searles, 1959) and evoke iatrogenic paranoid syndromes (Langs, 1973).

Partly because of the patient's own sensitivities, and based too on a probable underlying paranoid core, the patient continues his supervisory efforts on an almost conscious level, raising the specific question as to why the therapist had intervened in a way that infantilized him and implied an incapacity to deal with the waiting room situation—an incapacity that is actualized for the moment more in the therapist's interventions than in the patient's associations and behaviors.

Using a typical introjective identification, the patient referred to the arrogance and omniscience involved, and the therapist picked this up, although he did so without referring to the specific adaptive context involved, and he further contaminated his interventions by the use of a Yiddish (Jewish) word, meaning "nerve." This seems to reflect the therapist's continued, unresolved, seductive homosexual countertransferences, his need for undue closeness with the patient, and it seems to confirm the hypothesis that the office location serves as a defense against these unresolved pathological needs, while his question was an inappropriate attempt to draw the patient closer to him.

In brief, the patient's response to this particular intervention seems to suggest the gratification of a type of manic fusion with the therapist who has used a special word, and who in addition has understood some aspects of the previous hurtful interventions. Still, the patient's wishes to return to school and to become a therapist reflect an unconscious recognition on his part that he still has much therapeutic and supervisory work to do with this particular therapist—as does the therapist himself.

In demonstrating the patient's unconscious and conscious, supervisory and curative efforts, it is to be understood, as noted above, that psychotherapy is not designed for the treatment of the therapist, that it should focus on the pathology of the patient, and that ideally, such interludes and gains for the therapist should occur only occasionally and should remain as a kind of incidental benefit that may accrue to him. However, in situations in which the therapist's inputs are distinctly countertransference-based, the patient will introject the disruptive interventions and some of their latent implications, and will inevitably work over the pathological introject—as a means of curing both the therapist and himself. It is at such times that the patient may rather dramatically, and usually in unconscious, derivative ways, take over the functions of therapist and supervisor.

In terms of the principles of supervision being developed here, I have attempted to stress the extent to which prediction and validation should be a cornerstone, and how the patient can, indeed, provide the fragments of material for the supervisor's interventions. The latter's main task, then, is to organize these fragments into a meaningful whole by identifying the most pertinent adaptive context and shaping the material as Type Two derivatives—fantasies and perceptions—around that context. He is in a position to state his formulations, and to then search for additional validation through Type Two derivatives. In this instance, my remarks in supervision were virtually restated by the patient, providing an unusual form of validation—as a rule, such echoing occurs, as I said, in a more disguised way.

CONCLUDING COMMENTS

It is more than evident that supervisory insight depends in a major way on the supervisor's understanding and conception of the therapeutic process, interaction, and relationship. As a supervisor becomes sensitized to the intense and extensive unconscious communicative interaction between patient and therapist, the main problem in supervision becomes one of modulating his supervisory interventions so that they can be maintained at a level that is constructive to the supervisee, and neither overwhelming for him nor neglectful of the patient's needs. This is an extremely delicate and difficult balance to maintain, though every effort must be made to do so.

In the vignette offered here, the supervisee was an advanced student, and had reached a point where very direct and candid evaluations could be made for him to work over. This particular supervisee was not, to my knowledge, in therapy or analysis at the time, and the difficulties that he was having in mastering his homosexual countertransferences in particular may serve as a reminder of the limitations of supervision. As Freud (1910) rightfully stated in his first pronouncements regarding countertransference, no therapist can take a treatment situation beyond the level of his own resistances. Similarly, it is unrealistic for a supervisor to expect that an intellectual working over of countertransferences will have anything but a minimal effect on their underlying basis within the supervisee. At best, these efforts can help the supervisee to develop a conviction regarding his own need for therapy or analysis.

These are areas very much in need of further investigation; they touch upon the realm of what I have termed "the rock bottom" or limiting factors of supervision. The supervisor may spell out in careful detail from the material of the patient and therapist definitive evidence of countertransference difficulties, but he is then faced with the limitations of the supervisee's self-awareness, self-knowledge, and self-analytic capacity. The supervisor must be prepared to tolerate these limitations, and to patiently rework these issues as they reemerge in subsequent presentations.

Little is said of the gratifications of supervisory work. Aside from the evident prestige of being on the faculty of a medical school or other teaching institution, the supervisor has the additional satisfaction of assisting in the growth of new therapists who are entering the field. In addition, however, by virtue of the added distance between himself and the patient, and because his responsibilities are quite different in supervision as compared to therapy (they are not entirely and immediately devoted to the therapeutic needs of the patient and may take a wider scope), supervisors have a special opportunity for creativity and growth. It is, I believe, no coincidence to realize that it seems likely that Freud's discovery of transference was greatly facilitated by his supervisory-like role in observing the therapeutic work of Breuer (Breuer and Freud, 1893–1895). Speaking personally, much of my own creative work and discoveries has been derived from the supervisory situation. It is a setting rich in potential for research and insight that deserves far more extensive utilization.

In concluding, it is well to turn to the much-neglected subject of self-supervision. Ultimately, every supervisee should not only carry out supervisory work of his own, but also should take over full responsibility for the never-ending task of the self-supervision of his own work with patients. Essential to this requisite is a *self-supervisory attitude,* the consistent use of the predictive-validating methodology described in this paper, and the inevitable though restricted utilization of the patient's unconscious supervisory efforts. In a way, these principles remind us that our countertransferences are never entirely resolved, that they are an element, however small, in every intervention (Langs, 1978e), and that both self-analysis and self-supervision (different approaches to the same problem) are the major correctives to our best, though never perfect therapeutic efforts.

REFERENCES

Bion, W. Learning from Experience. In W. Bion, *Seven Servants.* New York: Jason Aronson, 1977.

Bion, W. Attention and Interpretation. In W. Bion, *Seven Servants.* New York: Jason Aronson, 1977.

Breuer, J., and Freud, S. (1893–1895). Studies on hysteria. *Standard Edition* 2:1–335.

Freud, S. 1910. The future prospects for psycho-analytic therapy. *Standard Edition* 11:- 141–151.

Langs, R. *The Technique of Psychoanalytic Psychotherapy,* Vol. 1. New York: Aronson, 1973.

Langs, R. Therapeutic misalliances. *International Journal of Psychoanalytic Psychotherapy,* 1975, *4,* 77–105. (a)

Langs, R. The therapeutic relationship and deviations in technique. *International Journal of Psychoanalytic Psychotherapy,* 1975, *4,* 106–141. (b)

Langs, R. *The bipersonal field.* New York: Aronson, 1976. (a)

Langs, R. *The therapeutic interaction* (Vols. 1 and 2). New York: Jason Aronson, 1976. (b)

Langs, R. On becoming a therapist: discussion of "Empathy and intuition on becoming a psychiatrist," by Ronald J. Blank. *International Journal of Psychoanalytic Psychotherapy,* 1976, 5:255–279.(c)

Langs, R. Validation and the framework of the therapeutic situation. *Contemporary Psychoanalysis,* 1978, *14,* 98–124. (a)

Langs, R. Some communicative properties of the bipersonal field. *International Journal of Psychoanalytic Psychotherapy,* 1978, *7:* 89–136.

Langs, R. *The listening process.* New York: Jason Aronson, 1978. (c)

Langs, R. *Technique in transition.* New York: Jason Aronson, 1978. (d)

Langs, R. Interventions in the bipersonal field. In R. Langs, *Technique in Transition.* New York: Jason Aronson, 1978. (e)

Langs, R. Dreams in the bipersonal field. In R. Langs, *Technique in transition.* New York: Jason Aronson, 1978. (f)

Langs, R. *The supervisory experience.* New York: Jason Aronson, in press.

Little, M. Counter-transference and the patient's response to it. *International Journal of Psycho-Analysis,* 1951, *32,* 32–40.

Searles, H. The effort to drive the other person crazy–an element in the aetiology and psychotherapy of schizophrenia. *British Journal of Medical Psychology,* 1959, *32,* 1–18.

Searles, H. *Collected papers on schizophrenia and related subjects.* New York: International Universities Press, 1965.

Searles, H. The patient as therapist to his analyst. In P. Giovacchini (Ed.), *Tactics and techniques of psychoanalytic therapy, Vol. II Countertransference.* New York: Jason Aronson, 1975

Wangh, M. The "evocation of a proxy": A psychological manuever, its use as a defense, its purpose and genesis. *The Psychoanalytic Study of the Child,* 1962, *17,* 451–469.

CHAPTER 11

Psychoanalytic Psychotherapy Supervision

STANLEY MOLDAWSKY

Teaching psychotherapy to clinical graduate students or professional school students is not the same as teaching candidates from a psychoanalytic institute. The candidates expect to fulfill the tripartite training model, namely the training analysis, the control analysis (supervision), and course work. The course work consists of the basic theory of psychoanalysis plus seminars in technique and problems of therapy. The candidate in an analytic institute has begun the self-exploration and the resolution of conflicts so necessary to becoming an effective therapist. The necessity is based on the observation that anxiety in the patient induces anxiety in the therapist, and unless the therapist is open to the experience, he/she will defend against the anxiety by characterological or symptomatic defenses and will unconsciously encourage repression in the patient, rather than exposure (or a variety of other defenses such as acting-out or intellectualization).

The analytic candidate is at a different point in his career when he undertakes training. The basic professional education has been completed (either psychiatry, psychology, or social work) and he is practicing a profession while learning psychoanalysis. The graduate student, on the other hand, is in a student status, is less experienced, and the evaluation function of the supervisor takes on a more formidable aspect. The student is also less likely to have begun an analysis and arrives in graduate school with a generally negative attitude towards psychoanalysis. The typical exposure to psychoanalytic thought has been in undergraduate psychology courses, taught by nonanalysts, thus the learning begins in an apprehensive skeptical atmosphere. Nevertheless, with these obstacles facing us, we introduce the student to the dynamic principles of psychoanalysis, encourage personal therapy (analysis later), assign a case for therapy, and provide a supervisor. One more word of introduction is in order: the "Analytic Attitude" on the part of the therapist is a fundamental part of the "analyzing instrument" and needs instruction, affirmation, and reinforcement. It is an attitude that seems contrary to general notions of how a healer behaves. It is an attitude hard to maintain in brief therapy, and is difficult for therapists whose personal life style is to be active. In essence, the attitude is one of listening to the patient with respect for his/her autonomy. They came, hoping for a change in their symptoms, or hoping for change in their spouses or family members, and are not aware of the need to change anything within themselves in order to relate differently to the important people in their lives. To gain their support for the therapeutic work, which is truly a collaborative effort, requires an educational stance in the therapist. An "I will show you the way to a better life," does not reflect a proper therapeutic stance; rather "we will discover what is inhibiting you or preventing you from achieving your goals so that you can do something about it," reflects a respectful attitude. Thus, we don't know in advance what is producing the difficulties in the patient's life, but we will try to find out what it is. In this orientation, there is an awareness that unconscious processes are at work which need to be discovered. This cannot take place in an unempathic, cold intellectual atmosphere. So that along with (1) the respect for the patient's autonomy, and (2) the discovering, rather than the knowing in advance, there must be (3) a genuine interest in the patient and an accepting, warm feeling in the therapist. In addition, there must be (4) a respect for the powerful resistances in the patient to really experience that which they so mightily defend against, and a recognition that these resistances will appear again and again. When a patient suddenly improves markedly, there will be as much interest in that phenomenon as any other. (5) The therapist must be careful not to take sides in the patient's conflicts and to remain empathic—but yet neutral. This is an ingredient of the analytic attitude that has to be learned by the student. (6) If the therapist is not too active, but allows the direction for the therapy to flow from the patient (maintains a neutral, interested, respectful attitude), soon the relationship (transference) will begin to reflect all the inner conflicts of the patient. Then the focus of the treatment will move to examining the transference which in turn will elicit the memories and feelings for which the transference has been a replacement.

The adoption of this analytic attitude is the first task of the student, and the first task of the supervisor is to teach it! If the student is in analysis, his own experience will teach him the analytic attitude. The supervisor must reflect this same attitude towards the student—respectful, interested, and empathic. The supervisor may be an advanced senior professional with whom the student can identify. It is likely that the supervisor is also feared, and the evaluative function induces some anxiety in the student (perhaps in the supervisor as well). Despite this, they must form a *learning alliance* (Fleming and Benedek, 1966), just as the therapist and patient must have a working alliance. The working alliance (Greenson, 1967) is fostered by statements from the therapist such as "we will try to understand," and the like, and the therapist must convey the we-ness genuinely. To form a working alliance, the patient must have achieved a developmental level in which the "other" is related to as a separate human being. In schizophrenic pathology, for example, the object is not seen as separate, and therefore no working alliance develops.

This does not rule out treating schizophrenics psychoanalytically. It requires a more flexible use of the therapist's personality with careful attention paid to the countertransference reactions (Boyer and Giovacchini, 1967, and Searles, 1965).

PURPOSE AND FUNCTION OF SUPERVISION

The supervisory situation is very complicated and it can be made overly burden-some if the setting is not supportive of the psychotherapy endeavor. (See Ekstein and Wallerstein, 1958 for an excellent discussion of these matters.)

The administrative setting and the supervision itself provide two sources of potential support or problem to the therapist. Administrative support for the psychotherapy program can vary from enthusiastic interest to minimal tolerance. In graduate training it is optimal when the clinic facilities are available to the student, where there is administrative support and encouragement for the learn-ing of this skill and for the full utilization of the clinic, and for the availability of experienced supervisors who are eager to provide their services. In our setting, at Rutgers University Graduate School of Applied and Professional Psychology, the patients are seen in our clinic with the full support of the administration. The supervisors work either at the school or in their private offices. Their time is offered with a token remuneration by the school for the privileges of affiliation.

DeBell (1962) has emphasized the two functions of the supervisory process: teaching and testing. These two can inhibit each other so that fear of the supervi-sor's evaluation can interfere with learning from the supervisor. How best to reduce the impact of the testing function? Mueller and Kell (1972) suggest that "anxiety approachers" make good therapists as well as good supervisors. That is, the anxiety approacher is aware of his anxiety, able to label it and admit it, and to begin to search inside self and outside for its cause. Putting a therapist and supervisor together who share this tendency can lead to an open-consultative relationship as they search and wonder. The student learns that the supervisor is not omnipotent—all-knowing—but rather willing to explore and learn and face the anxiety. This serves to reduce some of the anxiety in the testing aspect of the relationship. The supervisor must convey a constant respect for the student so as not to encourage dependency. The learning alliance does have support built in and the supervisor offers information and advice regarding form and timing of interpretations, but must be careful to protect the student's autonomy. As a student reports about his patient I often respond with associations from my own experience. This encourages a collaborative atmosphere in the supervision. It reduces awe; it provides another modeling for the student. The student says, "This is the way my supervisor works; he associates, he explores his own feelings, he is involved with his patient."

For many students, having the patient involved in a sexualized transference can be disturbing. I recall a student who wanted to see his patient and her husband and another couple in a couples group. The suggestion had been the patient's, particularly after she learned the therapist had been involved in a marital-prob-lems workshop. The timing of the suggestion, plus the therapist's interest in engaging in this study made the supervisor suspicious. As the supervisor and therapist explored together how this would be useful, what emerged was the therapist's discomfort with the patient's sexual interest and his own wish to deflect it back to the husband—to have them confront each other, so to speak.

The supervisor encouraged the student to tolerate the erotic transference and allow it space. He gave an example from his practice as to how the sexual transference could be managed. This approach is, of course, based on the conviction that to experience the feelings and the conflict in the transference makes it a truly alive experience and permits the past to be used reconstructively *only* as it relates to the here and now. The therapist uses himself experientially, not as an interpreter of the past but as an *exposer* of the present. The patient will make the appropriate interpretations of the past. For the student to allow the patient to experience him in whatever way is emerging requires patience, courage, willingness to face anxiety in himself, and interest or curiosity. The student can be helped to learn this courage, not only through facing his own anxiety in his own analysis, but by observing patience and courage in the supervisor.

There have been articles written on whether supervision is teaching or therapy (Arlow, 1963; Wagner, 1957; Solnit, 1970; Windholz, 1970; Lebovici, 1970; Fleming and Benedek, 1966). It is the general consensus that the purpose of supervision is teaching, not therapy. It is true that the analytic process with free association, and transference analysis can free the therapist to "be with" his patient fully, and this has been taken as a paradigm for freeing the therapist to be with his patient. The argument, on the other hand, is that there are many technical interventions and approaches to the process of therapy in the realm of information-giving, diagnostic sharpening, support, encouragement to be genuine, exploration of meaning in the patient's association and behavior, readings to broaden the knowledge, and so on, which are best given by the supervisor. It would change the nature of the analytic transference if the analyst adopted such a teaching role. Today, most analytic institutes do not request any information from the analyst about the student other than number of hours of analysis. In years gone by, the analyst determined how his analyzand would progress in his training and had the power to recommend passage through the program. This could only burden the transferences with a reality too powerful to resist. That is, one had to "win" approval from one's analyst. This practice has been discontinued, but one wonders about the effect on those analysts who went through those passage rites.

It is generally agreed that the counter-transference of the therapist is a given and must be elucidated if the therapy is to progress. Is this the function of the supervisor? I am in agreement with Windholz, when he points out to the therapist that he failed to interpret specific material. This is as far as I go. From here the therapist can explore his unconscious motivation in analysis. As in the example cited above, I could speculate about why the erotic transference was uncomfortable and the therapist had a desire to deflect it, but that would overstep the bounds of supervision as I see it.

Racher (1957) described supervision with an analytic candidate in which a number of the analyst's patients were suddenly getting divorced. He discovered that the marital problems of the analyst were stimulating him to subtly encourage his patients to act out (seek divorces) for him. It was brought to his attention that he was encouraging this behavior. From this point on the therapist used his judgement as to ways of correcting it.

There are different needs of supervision by therapists at different stages in their own development of skill. Thus, beginners have a need based on their inexperience, their lack of knowledge, their anxiety related to adapting a new professional role. More experienced therapists often reach an impasse with a patient because of their own anxiety that has been stimulated by the patient. I recall an experience from my practice, when an attractive woman was sending me signals that she was very interested in a sexual affair with me. Before I actually "read" the signals, I only became aware that I was anxious in my work with her. One Sunday morning, I called a colleague, who consented to talk with me. We poured some coffee and I began a case presentation. I reviewed the case and we discussed the patient's hopes and desires related to me. I became aware of erotic fantasies about her. This time, in my friend's presence, I let the fantasies flow over me, and as I contemplated them I relaxed. My anxiety was clearly that I would act on them, fulfill forbidden wishes (and all that that meant to me personally), and destroy my professional role. The patient's therapy would be over! Returning with renewed awareness and interest, I was able to make comments which helped to expose my patient's wishes. As we discussed them, she offered many memories, associations, and feelings, both related to me and her beloved father. My anxiety had caused me to not want to know what I already knew and to keep the material from being there between us.

This example comes under the heading of countertransference. It is a frequent reason for problems that arise in the therapy relationship. In an experienced therapist, it is often easier to arrive at, because the problems of inexperience are not involved. Rather, the therapist has to be aware of his anxiety—has to expose (associate) his feelings and ideas—and this confrontation should lead to movement. The expectation that this can happen by self-analysis when in fact the therapist is defending against exposure I find questionable.

Many authors have implied that self-analysis can overcome the impasse. There is a joke that is known to most therapists: "Self-analysis doesn't work because of the countertransference." I believe this! I find that presenting the case to a trusted colleague clears the air. It allows for verbalization and associations which may produce insight or free up some blocked feelings. The therapist who tends to rationalize the impasse as the patient's problem overlooks the interactive process—how the transference affects the therapist and how the therapist responds to the transference demands.

The problem in analyzing countertransference in supervision is that defenses will be evoked that are the same in treatment. The supervisor does not have a working alliance with the student; therefore, resistance will increase. The supervisor can confront the student—to observe something in the patient, or to note that something is omitted or that the therapist is not intervening. This should be sufficient to encourage the student to work it through himself. This kind of countertransference in the therapist is taken for granted and does not interfere with the therapist's capacity to analyze the patient (Arlow, 1963).

A student called me for advice following a forgotten appointment. She was out jogging when she suddenly realized that she had missed her patient by one hour, that the appointment had slipped her mind. She jogged home and called me. We discussed the forgetting and I wondered aloud whether something had occurred in the last session to make her anxious and not want to see her patient. The patient had begun to get angry about pending termination—due to the therapist's leaving —and as well had become frightened of emerging angry feelings towards her mother. The therapist, by forgetting the appointment, was making a statement that she was afraid of the anger. It was also a defense against her own anger toward the patient. In preparing herself for the pending termination, the patient was negating the impact of the therapist: "You haven't helped me—therapy has not done very much. I don't know what I'm getting out of this," and so on. This was making the therapist angry, and rather than face this work with anger she repressed it and forgot the appointment.

My confrontation broke through her defensiveness; she discovered her feelings and could recognize the patient's anger. I made no efforts to find the roots of the student's fear of her anger. We discussed the question of whether to call the patient. I advised her to call the patient in order to make another appointment, apologize for the forgetting, and, if necessary, discuss the event and be ready to admit her error and the reasons. But a strange thing had occurred. The patient arrived an hour late for the appointment, found that the therapist wasn't there, and assumed she had waited but finally left. So, when the phone call came, the patient did not know the therapist had forgotten, and apologized for being an hour late. Nonetheless, the therapist also admitted her error. We both looked forward to the next appointment with interest and eagerness. The exposure which followed led to open expressions of anger from the patient toward the therapist. Only then did the therapist feel ready to accept the feelings and not have to protect herself from them.

In a subsequent conversation about this event, after the therapy had terminated, the student recalled feeling supported by the supervisor. The confrontation had the effect of removing a defense. The student did not feel attacked; rather she developed some insight into her own handling of anger.

The supervisory process described here is a combination of patient-centered and therapist-centered. There is a full awareness of the counter-transference; however, it is my conviction that the countertransference issue is settled elsewhere. Support for this mode of operating can be found in the writings of Grotjahn (1955), Searles (1955), and Eisenbud (1978).

It seems to be a well-known phenomenon that therapists often behave in supervision in the same way the patient behaves in therapy. Thus, if a patient is experiencing a sense of helplessness and "leans" on the therapist, the same sense of helplessness will be reflected in the therapist as he "leans" on the supervisor. This is a transient identification with the patient and it is acted out in the supervisory situation. Arlow (1963) gives another example of this when he observed the hypomanic state of the therapist in supervision. It was a reflection of the patient's behavior, but without any awareness on the part of the therapist.

This has also been called "Parallel Processes" in supervision and psychotherapy. Mayman, in a forward to a doctoral dissertation on this subject by Doehrmann (1976), states that "parallel processing" is a universal phenomenon in treatment.

Doehrman investigated the parallel process by clinical interviews of patients, therapists, and supervisors over a period of time. She concluded that the usual understanding (mentioned above as *reflection* of patient-therapist behavior in therapist-supervisor interaction) goes only half the way. Rather, the supervisor stirs the therapist, who then acts out with his patients. Thus, parallel process is not reflection alone—it works in both directions. This discovery has just begun to find its way into supervisors' work. It speaks to the complexity of the patient-therapist-supervisor interactions and encourages a humbleness in supervisors. Just as the therapist may identify with the patient and act out the patient's problem with the supervisor, so the supervisor can stir the therapist so that the therapist "plays supervisor" with his/her patients.

A student was assigned a supervisor and began with a patient who was ambivalent about being in therapy. As the patient continued her ambivalence, the student became aware of resentment towards the supervisor. The student had had considerable experience as a therapist and resented the process of presenting his work for the scrutiny of the supervisor. The student confronted the supervisor with his resentment and they discussed it openly. The supervisor was empathic and offered his own experiences for the student. He reduced the power differential by pointing out that a third party listening to the therapy process unfolding can see what the therapist cannot see. The distance provides greater objectivity. For therapy to be alive and meaningful, the therapist must be involved. To be involved clouds one's objectivity.

The supervisor was attempting to reduce his power so that the student would feel less resentful. The parallel process was operating so that the student confronted the patient with her resentment. The patient subsequently discontinued therapy. The supervisor felt that the patient was on the verge of leaving even in the first session and that the therapist was not responsible for therapy being discontinued.

SUPERVISORY CASES

Finding suitable patients for psychotherapy by beginning students is difficult. The setting often determines the cases selected (see Weiner and Kaplan's Chapter 4). A university clinic tends to get students as patients; a hospital or alcohol or drug unit gets more regressed patients, however, student therapists rotate through such units and may even start seeing the most difficult cases imaginable. Supervision in these cases often requires emotional support for the therapist who is struck by the difference between the patients and him or herself. As psychology students, eager to grow, they entered therapy well-motivated. Their patients, on the other hand, are poorly motivated and eager for secondary gain. A 20-year-old woman who had left home at the age of 13, who had been addicted to heroin for 6 years, and had earned money prostituting, came to a methadone-maintenance unit of a city hospital and was assigned a student therapist. The welcome to the world of psychotherapy for the student was frightening. How to form a relationship with someone who acts out; how to develop confidence in oneself as a therapist when faced with the problems this woman presented—the situation seemed hopeless. Yet the therapist was willing to form a relationship, and the *act of verbalizing* all of her concerns to the supervisor was sufficient to reduce her anxiety and help her to continue to try to reach this patient. The supervisor discovered that the therapist had a number of personal concerns, such as:

1. If this first patient assigned leaves me, this will be seen as failure, and therefore perhaps I am unsuited for psychotherapy.

2. If a failure results, my continuation in the training program may be jeopardized.

3. The patient is demanding and intimidating. What do I do? She makes me angry and helpless. What do I do with those feelings?

These concerns became the focus of the supervisory hour. Some were handled by information giving *(teaching),* some by *modelling* (supervisor giving clinical examples from his own practice: how he handled them and how he felt), some by *support* (understanding the extreme nature of the case, recognizing the difficulties for any therapist under the circumstances, reinforcing the therapist's opinions and interventions when appropriate, and offering reassurance), and finally, some concerns by clinical judgment and advice. These four areas, teaching, modelling, support, and judgment were seen as critical dimensions of the initial supervisory experience for beginning psychiatric residents (Tischler, 1968). The problems for the supervision were the same, even though the patient was difficult to treat. However, the student therapist was able to learn important facts, such as the ingredients of supportive psychotherapy and how it differs from intensive analytic therapy. Writing a report on supportive therapy was a useful adjunct to the supervisory experience.

In cases such as this addictive personality or a borderline personality structure, it is still important to maintain an analytic attitude as much as possible. Parameters are introduced because the patient is unable to tolerate abstinence. How much is a real need on the patient's part, and how much is the therapist needing to give and nurture has to be teased apart, and the supervisor can be helpful in discovering whose needs are dominating. Again, this can be discussed in supervision without having it becoming therapy for the student (see Eissler 1953 for a discussion of parameters).

Once a relationship has begun, the therapist discovers that the learned analytic attitude is not adequate to the task. He/she has to bend the approach to fit the needs of the patient. As this naturally occurs, the student begins to anticipate criticism from the supervisor. Varying defenses in the student will emerge— self-depreciation, depression, counter-phobic defense, and the like. It is important for the supervisor to be sensitive to this and discuss how the basic analytic model can be modified for the patient. The problem of the student therapist feeling that he or she simply isn't applying the proper technique, and feeling guilty if he or she "gratifies" any of the patient's demands can be worked out in the supportive atmosphere of supervision. Abstinence, for Freud, means that you analyze the wishes (whatever they are) rather than gratify them. With character disorders, borderline patients, and those who have the defense of acting out, it is intolerable for the patient to bear the abstinence. There is built-in dependent support by the consistency and regularity of the therapist's presence—however, this proves not enough for many patients. Maintaining an optimal balance between gratifying and analyzing is an act of clinical judgment by the therapist. The supervisor has to instruct in the ways the parameters are introduced and help the student therapist with the development of his/her own "professional superego." Students feel (particularly after reading early Freud) that they should not permit telephone calls, should never offer advice, should never see other members of the family, and so on. These kinds of activities have to be judged on their own merits, and the use of parameters can be flexibly adapted with the support of the supervisor.

The pleasure in supervision is (in addition to the new learning of resistances) the gratification that any other teacher or parent receives as the student grows and identifies with the supervisor. This feels good! The supervisor has to be careful that the student is always a free agent. Original, creative ideas in the student can be encouraged, even enjoyed. The need in the supervisor to see his mirror image as he gazes at his student had best be tempered.

Supervision is still the cornerstone of clinical training. Efforts must be made to keep it free of the difficulties inherent in a relationship with differential power.

REFERENCES

Arlow, J. The supervisory situation. *Journal of the American Psychoanalytic Association.* 1963 *11,* 576–594.

Boyer, L.B., & Giovacchini, P. *Psychoanalytic treatment of characterological & schizophrenic disorders.* New York: Science House, 1967.

DeBell, D. E. A critical digest of the literature on psychoanalytic supervision. *Journal of the American Psychoanalytic Association, 11,* 546–575, 1963.

Doehrman, M. J.G. Parallel processes in supervision and psychotherapy. *Bulletin of the Menninger Clinic,* 1976, *40*(1).

Eisenbud, R. J. *Countertransference—the therapist's turn on the couch: Psychoanalytic Psychotherapy.* Addison-Wesley Series in Clinical and Professional Psychology, Reading, Mass.: Addison-Wesley 72–91, 1978.

Eissler, K. The effect of the structure of the ego in psychoanalytic technique *Journal of the American Psychoanalytic Association,* 1953, *1,* 109–143.

Ekstein, R., and Wallerstein, R. *The teaching and learning of psychotherapy.* New York: Basic Books, 1958.

Fleming J., and Benedek T. *Psychoanalytic supervision.* New York: Grune and Stratton, 1966.

Frijling-Schreuder, E.C.M. On individual supervision. *International Journal of Psychoanalysis,* 1970, *51,* 359.

Greenson, R. *The technique of psychoanalysis* (Vol. 1). New York: International Universities Press, 1967.

Grotjahn, M. Problems and Techniques of Supervision. *Psychiatry,* 1955, *18,* 9–15.

Lebovici, S. Technical remarks on the supervision of psychoanalytic treatment. *International Journal of Psychoanalysis,* 1970, *51,* 385.

Mayman, M. Foreward to Parallel processes in supervision and psychotherapy. *Bulletin of the Menninger Clinic, 40* (1), 1976.

Mueller, W. J., and Kell, B.L. *Coping with conflict,* Appleton-Century-Crofts, New York, 1972.

Racher, H. The meaning and uses of countertransference. *Psychoanalytic Quarterly,* 1957, *26,* 303–357.

Schuster, D. B., Sandt, J. J., and Thraler, O. F. *Clinical supervision of the psychiatric resident* New York: Brunner/Mazel, 1972.

Searles, H.F. The informational value of the supervisor's emotional experiences *Psychiatry,* 1955, 18, 135–146.

Searles, H.F. *Collected papers on schizophrenia and related subjects.* New York: International Universities Press, 1965.

Solnit, A. Learning from psychoanalytic supervision. *International Journal of Psychoanalysis,* 1970, *51,* 359.

Tischler, G. L. The learning resident and supervisor *Archives of General Psychiatry* 1968, *19,* 418–422.

Wagner, Frederick F. Supervision of psychotherapy *Association of Psychotherapy* 1957, *11,* 759–768.

Windholz, E. The theory of supervision in psychoanalytic education. *International Journal of Psychoanalysis,* 1970, *51,* 393.

CHAPTER 12

A Client-Centered Approach to the Supervision of Psychotherapy

LAURA N. RICE

It seems entirely appropriate that one of the earliest detailed statements on the supervision of psychotherapists was written by Carl Rogers (1957a). The question of how one "learns" to be therapeutic has concerned Rogers and his colleagues in client-centered therapy almost from the beginning. Much of this concern has not appeared in the literature, but is part of the folklore, handed down from supervisor to apprentice therapist. Thus it comes as a surprise when one enters a multidisciplinary setting to see how very different client-centered supervision is from most other approaches.

As a framework for examining the supervision process in detail, one can point to two themes that run through the thinking of Rogers and other client-centered theorists. These themes are often overlapping, sometimes seemingly in opposition, but always in a relationship of creative tension with each other. In the first place client-centered theory is a *theory of process.* This is beautifully brought out by Rogers (1975) as he writes of the experiences he and his students had in the early 1940s of listening for the first time to tape-recorded interviews.

> I cannot exaggerate the excitement of our learning as we clustered about the machine which enabled us to listen to ourselves, playing over and over some puzzling point at which the interview clearly went wrong, or those moments in which the client moved significantly forward. (Rogers, 1975, p.3)

Rogers and his students began to realize that they could identify points at which the therapist's response seemed to be decisively related, for good or ill, to the level of self-exploration achieved by the client. Clearly this was to be the pattern for client-centered supervision; tape recordings of interviews would be a central part of the supervisory process (Rogers, 1942). One would be asking *process* questions, focusing on the client's process of self-exploration and how it could be facilitated by the therapist's style of participation.

Although the enormous complexity of the interaction was recognized, there was a faith that it could be studied, demystified, and even become a focus for research. Even the eager clustering around the machine to listen and learn, that Rogers describes, reflects the spirit of good client-centered supervision today. In a sense the interview can be placed "out there" to be listened to freshly and almost impersonally, a source of interesting process hypotheses for apprentice-therapist and supervisor alike.

136

But Rogers (1975) goes on to describe his own swing toward emphasizing the second theme in client-centered theory, the *theory of relationship.* He began to feel that the focus on trying to understand the process was leading to an over-emphasis on technique. It seemed as if a kind of passive, mechanical "carica-ture" was being widely mistaken for the real thing. Thus he began to swing toward stressing the basic attitudes of the therapist that he considered necessary for building a therapeutic climate in which a client could grow. For many years this became the central focus for Rogers himself and for many other client-centered therapists. The therapist as a genuine person entering a *real,* though of necessity limited, relationship with the client is a central ingredient in client-centered therapy. This relationship with a genuine, caring therapist is consid-ered to be in itself growth-producing, and of course it is considered to be one of the necessary preconditions for a client to engage in an optimal process of self-exploration.

This fear of losing the genuine relationship in a calculated focus on technique has led, in my opinion, to a pervasive ambivalence toward dealing with technique in supervision. On the one hand process research, including the examination of the moment-by-moment interactions of client and therapist, is a strong focus in client-centered therapy. But on the other hand client-centered supervision often focuses more on the apprentice therapist's own feelings and attitudes in relation-ship to the client than it does on examination of the therapist's actual responses and their probable effects. Therefore, although both aspects will be discussed in the present paper, the focus will be more on the theory of process and the style of participation of the therapist.

Before moving into discussing the implications for supervision of these two trends, it seems appropriate to point out briefly what client-centered theory is *not.* It is not a theory of personal contents. The client-centered therapist is not concerned with forming hypotheses about "core conflicts" or "primary defenses". The therapist and the supervisor do not map out content areas that *must* be dealt with if change is to take place. Diagnosis is important only in relation to adminis-trative or situational constraints, such as the presence or absence of a protected environment, or the need for medical referral. This is probably the greatest difference from supervision in dynamically oriented therapies. This position, of course, stems from some basic client-centered assumptions about the nature of human-ness, and about the mechanisms of change. Since people are assumed to be fundamentally motivated toward growth and differentiation, it is further as-sumed that they will explore unknown, anxiety-producing areas of self *if* condi-tions of safety and facilitation are established. If inter-personal anxiety is kept to a minimum, the person will be able to tolerate the intra-personal anxiety of self-exploration. Furthermore, it is assumed that the individual *can* get in touch with his/her own experience in an accurate and differentiated fashion, without interpretation from outside. And finally, focusing on this inner awareness will yield new data, leading to reorganization of the client's concept of self-in-the-world. Thus the "treatment plan" is simply to establish a therapeutic relationship and, within that relationship, to facilitate the client's self-directed exploration of inner experience.

SUPERVISION AND THE CLIENT-CENTERED RELATIONSHIP

The two basic ingredients here are, in Rogers' terms, "unconditional positive regard" and "congruence" (Rogers, 1959). Although unconditional positive regard has a precisely defined meaning in Rogers' theory statements, it is a somewhat daunting term suggesting, as it seems to, an unlimited caring. Many of us prefer the term "prizing" (as contrasted with appraising), a term originally used by Dewey and suggested for use in the therapy context by Butler (1952). In essence, it means valuing people not because of what they do or don't do, but just because they *are*. The second ingredient, congruence, refers to the therapist's wholeness during the hour. What one expresses to the client, what one is aware of in oneself, and one's own internal processes are all consistent. Thus one is not sending mixed messages either to oneself or to one's clients. Together these ingredients make up the essence of the client-centered climate, enabling the client to experience feeling truly prized by another human being, not by a bland, detached, perpetually accepting robot, but by a real, spontaneous human being.

From my perspective as a supervisor, there seem to be two groups of attitudes that enable the therapist to implement the basic client-centered conditions that can be worked with more directly in supervision. These can be roughly divided into: (1) attitudes about human nature and the mechanisms of change, and (2) attitudes toward self.

Attitudes Toward Human Nature and Change

In the first place there is the belief in the basic growth motivation, a push toward differentiation, autonomy, and new experience. Related to this is the confidence of the therapist that if the client-centered process of self-exploration can be facilitated, the client will move in positive directions. One of the most difficult things for a novice therapist to overcome is the feeling that he/she must *do* something *for* the client, that he/she must solve the problem. Sometimes this leads to "taking over" or, more commonly among client-centered trainees, to a sense of being immobilized, feeling unable even to listen fully. It can also lead to what I call "smuggling," that is, including under the guise of a "reflection" ideas or connections that one thinks the client should be aware of but isn't. For instance, earlier in the hour a client was discussing his deep resentment about his father's arbitrary decisions. Now, later in the hour, he is expressing puzzlement about his inability to work smoothly with his academic advisor. Although the client has not expressed resentment toward the advisor nor made any connection between these two topics, the therapist responds "So I guess you're saying this is one more example of an arbitrary guy telling you what to do." In this case the therapist is maintaining the client-centered reflective form but *not* the basic noninterpretive attitude. It is important for the supervisor and trainee to hear this discrepancy. Most of us would suggest at this point that if such a connection is very much on the therapist's mind, it would be better to take responsibility for it as his/her own idea and pose it to the client as a tentative hypothesis, thus maintaining the clarity and honesty of the relationship.

Another related attitude is that of viewing the client as a colleague in the search, with a different but equally important kind of expertise. The therapist is an expert on process. The client is an expert on him or herself, the one who is the arbiter of the accuracy of reflections, the one who makes decisions and tries out new ways of being. This attitude is conveyed in all sorts of subtle ways and is, I think, decisive in the nature of the therapeutic alliance that develops. I think that one of the ways that this can be fostered is to encourage the apprentice therapist to answer very honestly and fully any questions the client has about the process and about what each participant is doing, and even be willing to discuss one's own views on how change takes place. From doing this I think the therapist learns that clients can indeed be treated like colleagues and that therapy need not be surrounded with mystique or "one-upmanship" in order to be effective.

A further point to mention here is the nondiagnostic attitude toward the client that is maintained by the client-centered therapist. This is much broader than simply not making a formal diagnosis. It is a focus on the relationship and on the therapist, but not a labeling of the presumed personality dynamics of the client. For instance, supervisors in some other orientations would point to a client's "manipulativeness" and warn the supervisee to be prepared to counter this. The client-centered supervisor, on the other hand, would be more likely to emphasize the importance of the therapist's becoming aware of his/her own limits, and being able to be clear and open with both self and client about these limits. An example may clarify this approach. One apprentice therapist complained that her client often got panicked in the early morning and called her up at home. These early morning calls became mini-therapy sessions, and afterwards the therapist could not get back to sleep before it was time to get up and start the day. The crowning annoyance was that the client then sometimes canceled a regular appointment later in the day. The therapist wondered if she should confront the client with her "manipulative and exploitative behavior". My suggestion to the therapist was to tell the client in the next session about her *own* limits, that she didn't *like* to be awakened in the early morning, and that it disrupted her night's sleep, although she would, of course, be willing to be called in occasional emergencies. When she later told the client this, it certainly didn't bring about an immediate solution. The client became angry, and accused her of putting her own comfort first. But this led to a number of explicit discussions of the relationship, and a fuller awareness of the rights and feelings of each of the two participants, which in itself seemed to be therapeutic.

Many trainees are attracted to the client-centered orientation because it seems to be compatible with their personal beliefs. Others develop these attitudes as they experience—both as clients and as therapists—the therapeutic effects of these attitudes. With some trainees these attitudes probably cannot be developed. If it is administratively possible, the student and potential supervisor should have a pre-supervision interview to discuss such basic attitudes. I have found that simply identifying my general orientation as client-centered is inadequate. The more I can convey the actual flavor of my focus in supervision, the better the match is likely to be. To some students the basic faith in a growth motivation seems like an absurdity; clients must be pushed and shaped from the outside. In a sense, of course, this basic faith is always a kind of working hypothesis, one that is challenged in each new difficult situation. And yet I think one must have enough confidence in this hypothesis to be able to relate to clients in a way that will enable one to see for oneself that clients *are* able to discover new feelings and connections, and *are* able to use these new data to find constructive solutions to their own problems. Without this provisional commitment to growth motivation the apprentice attempting to do client-centered therapy is likely to relate to the client in ways that are ineffectual or inconsistent, with results that more or less confirm the expectation of no client change. One way that the hypothesis can be strengthened is to devote a session or two to functioning as client and therapist for each other, not role-playing but working on real issues. The experience of emerging newness, of feeling something shifting in oneself, is a very compelling one for the novice therapist who is functioning as client.

But it is not just the attitude toward growth motivation that may cause a mismatch. With some students the belief in a dynamic unconscious is so much a part of their thinking that any approach not involving interpretation, especially interpretation of the transference, is unthinkable. With other students there seems to be a kind of basic need to feel active and in control. Even an intensely active empathic process is not fully satisfying to them. In some cases these differences can be worked through. In others a change of supervisor seems preferable if it can be arranged. After all, there exist such a variety of therapeutic orientations from which to choose, and there is so little hard evidence concerning their differential effectiveness, it seems pointless to push trainees into some mold that they sense to be inappropriate for them. Also I think it is important for supervisors to have a clear feel for their own limits regarding the therapeutic approaches they are competent to supervise and comfortable in doing so. To operate beyond these limits for the sake of being "flexible" seems to me to be a disservice to everyone, especially the client.

Self-Attitudes

One obvious point that seems to me to be often overlooked concerns the self-attitudes of the therapist. A basic client-centered assumption is that it is difficult to be truly accepting of others if one cannot accept oneself (Rogers, 1959). This seems true in a very specific sense in the therapy hour. Anxiety about one's own competence as a therapist disrupts the ability to listen. Even more destructive is the therapist who obliquely expresses his own insecurity by being subtly punitive toward a client who is not "working" well in therapy. A delicate balance must be maintained here. Some therapy orientations tend to be extrapunitive, viewing inadequacies in the process as stemming mostly from client defensiveness. Client-centered therapists tend to be more intropunitive, blaming their own inability to facilitate the client. It seems to me that the constructive use of tape-recordings can help to establish an impunitive focus in supervisory sessions. The therapist and supervisor can join in listening for clues to process, letting the tape speak for itself. One can focus on points at which the therapist's response seems to have been especially facilitative, scrutinizing it to see what is so very good about it. Even in poorly handled sections, the focus can be on spotting the point at which the process started to go wrong, and discussing how it might have been handled.

Working with the therapist's particular conflicts and blind spots is probably less central in client-centered supervision than in some other orientations (cf. Mueller and Kell, 1972). They do emerge and are worked with, but as one would expect in the client-centered framework, they would not be diagnosed or interpreted by the supervisor. They would be recognized by the therapist as he/she listens to interview sections in which he/she simply wasn't hearing the client. The discrepancy between his/her reflections and what was being said would become obvious. If the climate of the supervisory session was sufficiently prizing, the therapist would begin to deal with some of these things and the supervisor would move into an empathic listening mode. At that point supervision would resemble therapy for longer or shorter intervals, depending on the needs of the apprentice therapist and the availability of personal therapy.

Before concluding this section a word about evaluation is in order. When one has agreed to take on the supervisory role, one makes a deep commitment to the apprentice therapist as a person and as a colleague. Although there is typically more teaching and explicit feedback in supervision than in therapy, the climate of prizing and congruence is fairly similar. Some appraisal may well be required by the training center, and there will on occasion be a question of the student's fitness to continue in the field. These realities have to be discussed openly with the student. However, in my opinion, the optimal climate for the therapist's growth is a great deal of moment-to-moment feedback based on listening to tapes, and a minimum of evaluation as a person.

SUPERVISION AND THERAPIST PROCESS

The most basic ingredient in the process dimension is considered to be the therapist's engagement in an empathic process, attempting to stay in the client's internal frame of reference and to sense the client's immediate awareness as if it were one's own, without ever losing sight of the "as if" (Rogers, 1959). Although there are many possible vehicles for expressing empathy, the "reflective response" is the one most commonly found in client-centered therapy. This consists of reflecting back to the client as accurately and sensitively as possible the awareness that he/she is trying to express, and asking, implicitly or explicitly, for the client to check this against his/her own experience. These reflections probably serve several functions. They indicate to the client that he/she is truly heard and received. There is also the safety of knowing that whatever is encountered inside, the client will be the first to see it. And perhaps most important of all, clients start to listen to themselves and begin to trust their own experience. Gendlin (1974) expresses particularly clearly the view that the therapist will use a variety of other modes of responding to the client, and yet the reflecting response will be the base from which one starts and a point to which one always returns. "[It] should be the baseline, the single precondition on which all other kinds of responding should be built" (Gendlin, 1974, p.116).

A number of client-centered theorists have suggested that in addition to its function of conveying accurate understanding, a reflective response can serve a crucial stimulating function. Butler and Rice (1963) postulated a basic need for new experience and suggested that stimulating therapist reflections generate more new self-experiences in the client, thus helping to make the therapy process itself an exciting and intrinsically satisfying one. It was pointed out that a variety of therapist reflections to a given client statement may be equally accurate in picking up the client's feelings, and yet have very different stimulus value for the client. Wexler (1974), conceptualizing client-centered therapy in the framework of cognitive, information processing theory, pointed out ways in which the therapist, functioning as a kind of surrogate information processor, could in his responding, stimulate a richer substrate for processing on the part of the client. In another paper, also in a cognitive, information-processing framework, the present writer described in some detail the "evocative function" of the therapist in enabling clients to reexperience and reprocess problematic areas of experience, and thus to reorganize basic cognitive-affective structures (Rice, 1974). The present discussion of supervision draws heavily on this line of thinking.

Now let us get back to problems of supervision. If it is administratively possible, it seems desirable to have novice therapists first engage in some kind of group training program in which they learn attending behavior, learn to distinguish the internal frame of reference (the client's view of self and the world) from an external frame of reference (either the therapist's view or some view of external "reality"), learn to focus on a "feeling" level, and learn to express in their own words what is heard. Such training programs have been designed by Truax and Carkhuff (1967), and by Ivey and his colleagues (Ivey et al., 1968). Although a number of studies have attempted to determine optimal combinations of components in such training programs, it is not yet clear what the most effective combination would be (Birk, 1972; Hansen and Warner, 1971; Pierce and Schauble, 1970; Toukmanian and Rennie, 1975). My own preference is toward inclusion of practice dyads, in which one student as the client talks about a real, though not necessarily central problem, while the other student functions as the therapist. A central value of this kind of procedure is for each participant to learn what it feels like to be vulnerable as a client with different therapists, to experience safety or frustration depending upon the nature of the therapist's responses.

However it has been accomplished, let us assume that our beginning therapist has learned to stay in the internal frame of reference, attending to feelings, and reflecting them back to the client with reasonable accuracy. Further, let us assume that he/she has some of the basic attitudes described above, and has developed, at least tentatively, enough faith in the efficacy of the process to be simply engaged in it, not to be driven to *do* things for the client. At this stage it seems to me the supervisor can be tremendously helpful in enabling the therapist to move to a more deeply empathic and evocative mode of functioning.

In the first place the supervisor can help the novice therapist to learn how to listen. The client-centered hypothesis is that if the client can get in touch with whatever feels live and poignant inside and explore it, whatever differentiated experiencing is thus generated is likely to lead to valuable reorganization. In other words this "all roads lead to Rome" hypothesis assumes that the best guide to what is important to explore is usually the level of liveness at which it is being experienced rather than the particular content.[1] The suggested strategy, then, is to learn to listen for whatever is live or poignant for the client at that moment and to reflect that. Some clients are extraordinarily well able to do this for themselves. Others are so out of touch with themselves that a moment of liveness gets drowned in a sea of deflections to new topics or in the recounting of other related examples which lead them further and further from the point of liveness.

One of the most useful indicators of liveness or poignancy is the voice quality of the client (Rice and Wagstaff, 1967). There is a kind of voice quality that seems to indicate an inner focus on something that is being seen or felt freshly. Sometimes in the midst of a long client discussion expressed in a highly externalizing voice quality one hears just a small blip of focused voice. The voice slows, softens without losing energy, pauses, and loses the "premonitored" quality of the externalizing voice. This should be an indicator to the therapist that this part *must* be heard and responded to. There is a liveness here that might flower into a whole new moment of experiencing. For instance, a client is recounting in great detail in an externalizing voice a trying day at the office. Suddenly he describes an interaction with the office manager over the misplacement of a file, and his voice becomes momentarily focused, then he swings back to the recounting. The apprentice therapist hears this, waits until the client stops for breath, and then reflects as vividly as possible to the client that moment in the file room. The incident comes alive and unfolds and the client gets into the feelings of being wrongly judged, of feeling helpless anger in the face of authority. And the apprentice therapist has learned an effective and nonpunitive method of intervening at a time when he/she was feeling drowned by the verbal output of the client.

Another indicator of liveness is the presence of highly sensory or idiosyncratic words, or combinations of words. For instance, the client is talking about approaching social situations with trepidation, and reports feeling "cringy," or talks about a "stretched" smile on his face. The content area discussed may be less than exciting, or it may have been talked into the ground in session after session, but if the apprentice therapist can hear and respond freshly to this bit of liveness, he/she may learn that if "old" material can be freshly heard, new and differentiated personal meanings may emerge.

A third thing that the therapist can learn to listen for is a point at which he/she truly doesn't understand the client. At such points a client-centered therapist could usually respond with some glib surface understanding that would satisfy the client. And the novice therapist usually has all too much of an investment

---

[1]Some indirect support for this hypothesis is provided by research showing that the client's level of functioning on such stylistic process measures as Experiencing (Klein et al., 1970) and Client Voice Quality (Rice and Wagstaff, 1967) in sampled interviews predicts the eventual outcome of the therapy.

in being able to reflect at the drop of a sentence. But if one can stop and realize that there is something here that one can't get a real feel for, and can tell the client this in a way that doesn't seem to carry blame, then the client will often respond with, "Yes, I guess I don't understand that either.", or with a further unfolding of something that has been highly condensed. The apprentice therapist learns that truly empathic nonunderstanding can often be more helpful than surface understanding.

A fourth kind of listening can be approached and practiced almost as a game in supervision sessions. The essence of the approach is that almost any client statement can be turned "outside-in." The client says: "It got on my nerves to hear that puppy. It sounded so lonely." An accurate, but externally descriptive, response would be: "It really bothered you that the puppy was lonely," maybe adding something like, "Something about loneliness bothers you." An inside response on the other hand would be: "The puppy's sad little bark gave you a sense of desolation, 'where have they all gone?'." Although there is some artistry involved in phrasing the responses, there seems to be a kind of "inside listening" that can be consciously developed. I'm talking here about an extremely active listening process in which one listens and tries to experience what it would be like to *be* the client just at that moment. It is almost as if one were running a movie as the client talks, but it isn't primarily visual, but rather auditory, kinesthetic, and above all attuned to inner experiencing.

Now turning from listening to responding, there are several points to be made concerning the therapist's right to be active in the process. For instance a superficial acquaintance with client-centered therapy seems to leave the impression that therapists must passively wait for clients to finish a "turn" before they are free to make a response. For instance, a novice therapist played a tape in which the client galloped from topic to topic with hardly a pause for breath. Even when the client did pause the therapist was unable to muster an adequate response. The tape was stopped and the following dialogue took place:

Supervisor: What were you feeling at this point?

Therapist: Just overwhelmed. I couldn't get hold of *anything* to respond to.

Supervisor: Kind of a frantic feeling, I guess, really off balance.

Therapist: Yes, kind of helpless, but angry too.

Supervisor: I realize that you're trying hard to stay with the client, but I think *you* have some rights, too.

Therapist: Maybe I should be tougher and more confrontive.

Supervisor: I don't think you need to be. I think you can assert your right to a pace at which you can function comfortably. You can break in and create space for yourself. You can tell the client you're getting lost and would like to check your understanding of what he is saying. Let's try listening to the tape some more, and whenever you have some feel for something the client is expressing, stop the tape and try reflecting what you have heard.

(Later in the session)

Supervisor: How do you feel toward the client now?

Therapist: Not so angry and not so overwhelmed. I think next time I can break in if necessary and slow us both down, and leave enough space for myself to be able to function.

One further point to be made about therapist activity is that one need not passively follow the client into whatever content is being talked about. The therapist's job is to help the client to follow his/her *own* trail. Often clients deflect themselves with elaborations, associations, justifications, and so forth. The therapist can, by means of his/her reflection, refocus the client at the last point that was live. If the therapist gets a vivid feel for something live, but is unable to focus on it at that moment, he/she can take the client back to it explicitly a few minutes later, even though some other content has intervened. Students have sometimes commented that this seems to them to be terribly directive. The answer I give is that I try to be "nondirective" as to content, but I am shamelessly "directive" as to process.

There is much that could be said here about forming responses in such a way as to leave an open edge for exploration, about using evocative, high imagery language, etc. However, I question whether this should be taught directly. When approached directly, metaphor has a way of becoming sterile analogy or a flowery distraction, satisfying to the therapist, but baffling to the client. It seems more productive to help apprentice therapists learn the kinds of inner listening just described, and to help them learn to respond directly *from* that listening, and to learn to trust what comes out. The therapist can learn that a response at the right level doesn't have to be "right on." Some of the most productive moments come when the client can say; "Well, no, I wasn't really 'terrified', more 'intimidated'."

Therapists learn that they can do this inner listening *only* if they are not using up part of their attentional capacity in forming hypotheses *about* the client. Therapists learn that if, instead of interpreting a meaning or connection *for* the client, they simply help the client to explore his/her *own* experience, the new meanings, when they come, will be much richer and more satisfying to both the participants, than the contemplated interpretation. One apprentice therapist put this process very vividly, saying that when he was listening and responding in this way, it felt as if he had put himself into a whole different gear. He didn't know quite how he changed gears, and he couldn't always do it, but he knew what it felt like and found himself achieving it oftener and oftener. If this begins to happen, I am well satisfied with the supervision process.

CONCLUSION

The creative tension between psychotherapy as a very genuine and spontaneous human relationship, and psychotherapy as an interaction process that can be learned, perfected, and even incorporated into research designs, will probably always characterize client-centered thinking. The supervision process should probably represent some balance between the two aspects, depending upon the needs and the learning styles of the supervisees and the style of the supervisor. In really successful supervision the two seem to mesh and interact. Although the kind of listening and responding we are talking about can be studied explicitly, and even translated into "techniques," it can never become an empty push-button device, because it requires the therapist's whole processing capacity, the whole self. It cannot be learned perfunctorily; it cannot be faked. And it is partly this intensive, empathic process that makes prizing so easy and spontaneous. When one has seen clients coming to trust their own experience, discovering their own meanings, and making creative choices, it becomes natural to trust the human potential for actualization.

REFERENCES

Birk, J. M. Effects of counseling supervision method and preference on empathic understanding. *Journal of Counseling Psychology,* 1972, *19,* 542–546.

Butler, J. M. The interaction of client and therapist. *Journal of Abnormal and Social Psychology,* 1952, *47,* 366–378.

Butler, J. M., and Rice, L. N. Adience, self-actualization and drive theory. In J. M. Wepman and R. W. Heine (Eds.), *Concepts of Personality.* Chicago: Aldine, 1963.

Gendlin, E. T. Client-centered and experiential psychotherapy. In D. A. Wexler and L. N. Rice (Eds.), *Innovations in client-centered therapy.* New York: Wiley, 1974.

Hansen, C. J., and Warner, R. W. Review of research on practicum supervision. *Counselor Education and Supervision,* 1971, *10,* 261–272.

Ivey, A. E., Normington, C. J., Miller, D. C., Merrill, W. H., and Haase, R. F. Microcounseling and attending behavior: An approach to prepracticum counselor training. *Journal of Counseling Psychology,* 1968, *15* (Monogr. Suppl. 5).

Klein, M. H., Mathieu, P. L., Kiesler, D. J., and Gendlin, E. T. *The Experiencing Scale: A research and training manual.* Madison: University of Wisconsin, Bureau of Audio-Visual Instruction, 1970.

Moreland, J. R., Ivey, A. E., and Phillips, J. S. An evaluation of microcounseling as an interviewer training tool. *Journal of Consulting and Clinical Psychology,* 1973, *41,* 294–300.

Mueller, W. J., and Kell, B. L. *Coping with conflict: Supervising counselors and psychotherapists.* New York: Appleton-Century-Crofts, 1972.

Pierce, R. M., and Schauble, P. G. Graduate training of facilitative counselors. *Journal of Counseling Psychology,* 1970, *17,* 210–215.

Rice, L. N. The evocative function of the therapist. In D. A. Wexler and L. N. Rice (Eds.), *Innovations in client-centered therapy.* New York: Wiley, 1974.

Rice, L. N., and Wagstaff, A. K. Client voice quality and expressive style as indexes of productive psychotherapy. *Journal of Consulting Psychology,* 1967, *31,* 557–563.

Rogers, C. R. The use of electrically recorded interviews in improving psychotherapeutic techniques. *American Journal of Orthopsychiatry,* 1942, *12,* 429–434.

Rogers, C. R. Training individuals to engage in the therapeutic process. In C. R. Strother (Ed.), *Psychology and Mental Health.* Washington, D. C.: American Psychological Association, 1957, 76–92.(a)

Rogers, C. R. The necessary and sufficient conditions of therapeutic personality change. *Journal of Consulting Psychology,* 1957, *21,* 95–103.(b)

Rogers, C. R. A theory of therapy, personality, and interpersonal relations as developed in the client-centered framework. In S. Koch (Ed.), *Psychology: A study of a science* (Vol. 3). New York: McGraw-Hill, 1959.

Rogers, C. R. Empathic: An unappreciated way of being. *The Counseling Psychologist,* 1975, *5,* 2–9.

Toukmanian, S., and Rennie, D. L. Microcounseling vs. human relations training: relative effectiveness with undergraduate trainees. *Journal of Counseling Psychology,* 1975, *22,* 345–352.

Truax, C. B., and Carkhuff, R. R. *Toward effective counseling and psychotherapy: Training and practice.* Chicago: Aldine, 1967.

Wexler, D. A. A cognitive theory of experiencing, self-actualization, and therapeutic process. In D. A. Wexler and L. N. Rice (Eds.), *Innovations in client-centered therapy.* New York: Wiley, 1974.

CHAPTER 13

Supervision of Behavior Therapy

MARSHA M. LINEHAN

The training and supervision of behavior therapists is a topic not often dealt with in the behavioral literature. Although substantial research has been conducted on the training of paraprofessionals (e.g. Pomerleau, Bobrove, and Smith, 1973), teachers (Kazdin and Moyer, 1976), and parents (Gardner, 1976) in the use of behavior modification, little empirical work has been done on the training of the professional behavior therapist. Similarly there has been little effort to systematically apply psychological, especially learning, theories to the professional training of behavior therapists, even though historically behaviorists have exerted a great deal of energy delineating the relationship of these same theories to the professional practice of behavior therapy (e.g., Feldman and Broadhust, 1976; Kanfer and Phillips, 1970). This apparent paradox is nicely summarized by Loeber and Weisman (1975) who note that although behavior modifiers usually put a heavy emphasis on environmental variables, "remarkably enough, little attention has been paid to the analysis and control of that class of environmental variables comprising the responses emitted by therapists and trainers" (p. 660). Matarazzo (1971), commenting on the sparsity of well-formulated specifications of techniques for training behavior therapists in the early 1970s, suggested that the reason might be "because the methods are seen as simple and easily learned by non-professionals" (p. 918). Research on training of non-professionals, however, suggests that a wide range of issues must be attended to if training is to be successful (Gardner, 1976; Kazdin and Moyer, 1976). At the very least, one would surmise that the issues involved in teaching the professional are as complex as those encountered when teaching the non-professional. Even if the aim of training is to teach the professional to design and supervise therapeutic procedures, rather than to actually implement them (Ullmann, 1967), a specification of methods for training a behavioral engineer is needed.

This neglect of training issues in the behavioral literature does not represent an absence of programs designed to train behavior therapists. The *Directory of Training Programs in Behavior Modification* (Association for the Advancement of Behavior Therapy, 1978), for example, lists over 200 departments of psychology and social work claiming to offer at least some training in behavior therapy. In addition, there are countless medical training programs, internships, and post-doctoral training seminars which offer behavior therapy training. In an effort to offer at least some supervised training in behavior therapy, several psychology departments in recent years have started their own therapy training clinics (e.g., SUNY at Stony Brook) or arranged for their own faculty to supervise therapy conducted in community clinics (e.g., West Virginia University). In this way, the students are assured of an opportunity to obtain clinical supervision of behavior therapy. Clearly, therefore, the need to offer specific training in behavior therapy, including clinical supervision, is recognized by many behavior therapists.

The basic goals of therapy supervision, regardless of therapeutic orientation, are to assist the therapist both to do effective therapy in the present and to achieve the capability to carry out effective therapy independent of the supervisor. In essence, at least within professional training programs, supervision is aimed at helping a person learn to do therapy (or a particular type of therapy) by utilizing the person's clients and case material. Although few would disagree with these general goals of supervision, both the methods employed to attain these goals and the models of supervision which guide the supervisory process vary considerably. To a large extent the development of methods of psychotherapy supervision has been closely tied to models of therapy. For example, Wolberg (1977) points out that traditional methods for supervising psychoanalytic therapy rest on the assumption that "teaching-learning is similar to psychoanalytic process, requiring diagnosis, interpretation, and the working through of resistance by both student and teacher" (p. 949). Arbuckle (1963) stresses that since the task of the therapist is to engage the client in an interpersonal process, the goals of the supervision should be engagement in both interpersonal and intrapersonal processes. From his point of view, the model of both therapy and supervision rests on the premise that personal change can best be brought about through examination of the interpersonal process which occurs between the learner (client, trainee) and teacher (therapist, supervisor). In contrast, Levine and Tilker (1974) note that a behavioral orientation to supervision, as with a behavioral approach to therapy, focuses on the direct modification of specified response patterns in the learner. Lloyd and Whitehead (1976) describe a training program for behavior therapists which systematically applies the same behavioral principles used in therapy to . student practicum supervision.

In theory, it is possible to distinguish the approach one takes to supervision from the approach one takes to therapy. For example, one could conceivably employ behavioral supervision procedures to supervise a trainee's attempts to do psychoanalytic therapy; one could supervise behavior therapy by means of client-centered processes. In practice, however, it is more likely that supervisors will employ a model of supervision similar to their own model of therapy. The primary focus of this chapter is on describing a behavioral model of psychotherapy supervision.[2] Although much of the learning of behavior therapy occurs in classroom

[2]Since behavior therapy can be viewed as a type of psychotherapy, the terms are used interchangeably throughout the chapter. If a particular type of psychotherapy is to be differentiated from behavior therapy, a qualifying adjective is used to note the distinction. In addition, although some authors differentiate behavior modification from behavior therapy, no distinction is made here.

settings, group meetings, and various other settings, the primary focus of this chapter is on issues involved in individual clinical supervision. A behavioral model of supervision could be utilized to teach nonbehavioral psychotherapy; this chapter, however, is primarily concerned with the supervision of behavior therapy. Since a behavioral model of supervision is based on a behavioral approach to therapy, what follows is first an overview of the general definition and characteristics of behavior therapy. Next is a summary of the behavioral models of supervision which have so far been suggested in the behavioral literature. A broadband approach to behavioral supervision, based on a three-dimensional model of behavioral functioning, is then proposed and described. Finally, issues relating to assessment, supervision contracting, and pragmatic problems which arise in the course of behavioral supervision are discussed.

CHARACTERISTICS OF BEHAVIOR THERAPY

No single agreed-upon definition of behavior therapy exists. Definitions offered in the behavioral literature have generally been constructed according to one or more of at least three different criteria: the *content* of behavior therapy; the *focus* of the therapeutic intervention; or the *methodological* approach of the behavior therapist (Kazdin, 1978). Most definitions of behavior therapy encompass to varying degrees each of the criteria. However, the weight given to any one factor, as being critical in differentiating behavior therapists from nonbehavior therapists or behavior therapy from nonbehavioral psychotherapy, differs among particular definitions.

Content

Content-based definitions refer either to the theoretical base from which therapeutic techniques are derived or to a specific enumeration of the techniques themselves. Early definitions of behavior therapy were tied to the specific theoretical content area of learning theory (Wolpe and Lazarus, 1966; Eysenck, 1972). Indeed, until recently, the definition of behavior therapy was so closely tied to the application of behavioristic learning theory that several heated debates arose in the literature about whether or not behavior therapy is "really" based on learning theory (e.g., Breger and McGaugh, 1965, 1966; Rachman and Eysenck, 1966; Waters and McCallum, 1973). More current definitions of behavior therapy have expanded the content area used to define the term (Feldman and Broadhurst, 1976). Common to all current definitions is an emphasis on the role of basic psychological research and experimental findings in generating therapeutic procedures. What appears to be developing is a consensus that any area of research which yields empirical data about variables related to the maintenance and change of behavior can be fruitfully used in the development of behavior therapy techniques.

Definitions which stress the procedural, rather than theoretical, content of behavior therapy include varying lists of procedures which are defined as behavioral (e.g., systematic desensitization, token economies, response rehearsal). Reference to procedural content in defining behavior therapy is sometimes made in order to exclude particular methods from the domain of the behavior therapists. O'Leary and Wilson (1975), for example, suggest that "behavior therapy cannot be defined so broadly as to include *anything* that is reportedly effective, e.g., lobotomies, dream analysis, or primal screams" (p. 15). Stolz and Associates (1978) state: "Professionals in this field agree that behavior modification does not include psychosurgery, electroconvulsive therapy, or the noncontingent administration of drugs—that is, the administration of drugs independent of any specific behavior of the person receiving the medication" (p. 5). Thus, even though the behavior therapist might be encouraged to use any procedure of proven effectiveness, the fact of their use by a behavior therapist does not necessarily imply that the procedure should be labeled behavior therapy. In a similar vein, although a hallmark of the behavioral approach is the systematic, empirical evaluation of treatment effectiveness, the very fact of proven effectiveness does not, of itself, define a procedure as behavioral. Contrary to what some behavior therapists may have implied in past controversies, if it's good, it isn't necessarily behavior therapy.

The content of behavior therapy has important implications for behavioral supervision and training. First, with respect to the goals of supervision, one might question whether training should be limited to procedures labeled as "behavioral". This becomes especially important when other treatments might be more effective, either alone or in combination with behavioral procedures. There might be some virtue in teaching the novice a behavioral approach when nonbehavioral procedures are equal in proven effectiveness for a given problem; this virtue is lost (at least from the client's point of view), however, when other approaches might be more effective in helping the client. Although nonbehavioral psychotherapy has not, to date, been demonstrated superior to behavior therapy within any given problem area, the available data does suggest that, at times, pharmacotherapy, either alone or in combination with behavior therapy, might be superior to behavior therapy alone in specific kinds of cases (Bergin and Lambert, 1978; Hollon and Beck, 1978). In these instances, a responsible supervisor must be open to either teaching these procedures or helping the student obtain competent consultation. The content of behavior therapy is related to behavioral supervision in a second way, in that the procedures used by the supervisor to teach the novice therapist are very often identical to the procedures used in therapy. Thus one might find a behavioral supervisor using response rehearsal, systematic feedback, reinforcement, shaping of responses, and even relaxation or systematic desensitization if warranted.

Therapeutic Focus

Definitions which rely on specification of therapeutic focus are generally offered as a means of distinguishing behavior therapy from nonbehavioral psychotherapy (e.g., Kazdin, 1978; Ledwidge, 1978; Goldfried and Davison, 1976). These definitions stress that the focus of behavior therapy is on the direct modification of the problematic behaviors which brought the client into therapy. This is in contrast to the therapeutic focus of more traditional psychotherapies which might focus on underlying psychodynamic processes that are presumed to mediate the problematic behavior. In actuality, the great diversity among behavior therapists with respect to views about which variables control behavior and the relative influence of such variables has led to little theoretical agreement on the most suitable focus of treatment with a given problem. An analysis of some of the major divisions within the field of behavior therapy suggests that differences among various groups are often related to differences about the locus of variables most important in the modification and control of behavior. For example, a large subarea of behavior therapy, applied behavioral analysis, emphasizes the application of the findings and the methodology of operant conditioning to clinical problems. The environmental consequences of behavior are emphasized as critical in controlling behavior; therapy is usually an application of the principles of reinforcement punishment, extinction, or their combinations. In contrast, another subarea, cognitive-behavior therapy, emphasizes the role of cognitive processes in controlling overt behavior. Even when the clinical problem is stated in terms of overt behavior, the focus of treatment is often on cognitive behaviors which are presumed to be functionally related to the problem behavior. Common across schools of behavior therapy, however, is a tendency to define the client's problems in behavioral terms, stressing the importance of current, as opposed to historical, controlling variables, and measuring treatment outcome by changes in overt behavior. These tendencies are a direct outgrowth of an emphasis on the objective and reliable measurement of the client's problem, the variables associated with the problem, and treatment outcome.

This therapeutic emphasis on the direct modification of the client's problematic behaviors and the relative avoidance of underlying psychodynamic processes is similar to the focus in behavioral supervision. Instead of identifying and resolving general interpersonal and intrapersonal problems of the individual trainee, supervision is more likely to focus on identifying and changing specific responses which the therapist emits or fails to emit during the therapeutic sessions. Thus, the goals of supervision are likely to be the modification or strengthening of specified behavioral patterns which the trainee engages in, with little emphasis on more general changes or "growth" in the trainee.

Methodological Approach

Cutting across almost all definitions of behavior therapy, including those which stress a content and/or therapeutic focus, is the contention that behavior therapy represents an experimental approach to clinical treatment. For example, Yates (1970) states that ". . . behavior therapy is fundamentally distinguishable from other therapeutic efforts by . . . the application of the experimental method to the understanding and modification of abnormalities of behavior" (p. 18). Goldfried and Davison (1976) contend that "behavior therapy is more appropriately construed as reflecting a general orientation to clinical work that aligns itself philosophically with an experimental approach to the study of human behavior" (p. 4). O'Leary and Wilson (1975) suggest that "Behavior modification is an individually-oriented approach in which therapy is an experiment of $N = 1$" (p. 17). Kazdin (1978) has perhaps best captured the essence of current definitions by stating: "With the emphasis upon experimental evaluation and diversity of approaches, contemporary behavior modification is more an advocation of a scientific approach toward treatment and clinical practice rather than a particular conceptual stance" (p. 375).

The emphasis on an idiographic, empirical approach cannot be overemphasized in describing the behavioral model of therapy. Thus, the determination of the specific variables influencing a given client's problematic behavior is itself a scientific process. This process, the behavioral assessment, determines the type of therapeutic intervention strategy employed. As noted by Linehan (1977), clinical assessment in behavior therapy can be characterized as a cyclic process of hypothesis generating and hypothesis testing. Although as noted earlier, behavior therapists vary in terms of the theories guiding the generation of their hypotheses (e.g., cognitive behavior therapists usually generate cognitive hypotheses and operant therapists often generate hypotheses suggesting the environment is controlling the problem), it is this emphasis on applying a scientific method of hypothesis testing that best characterizes behavior therapy. The emphasis in behavioral assessment and therapy on specifying client problems in terms of behavioral referents and on collecting observable data about the problem, either via direct observation by the therapist or self-observation and recording by the client, is a direct outgrowth of the application of scientific methodology to the clinical situation. It should be noted here that this ideal does not necessarily describe every instance of behavior therapy. Certainly, the behavior therapist is not immune to theoretical biases which might, at times, be more influential than actual data in selecting and evaluating a particular intervention. The assertion trainer is prone to assuming assertion deficits are critical in every case; the applied behavior analyst is apt to ignore the influence of a particular client's interpretation of a given environmental event; the biofeedback advocate is likely to view physiological responses as influential even when the evidence is slight. Overall, however, the emphasis on both the public evaluation of particular treatment procedures for given problems and the idiographic evaluation of the efficacy of that procedure in the clinical situation, is characteristic of the behavioral model.

The emphasis on experimental methodology often becomes a critical issue in behavioral supervision. Idiosyncratic personality theories, attitudes, biases, and innumerable other factors can lead to prejudging the client and failing to respond sensitively to both the client and the data at hand. It takes an astute supervisor both to pinpoint these biases and to help the trainee become more empirical in dealing with the client. From the point of view of the behaviorally oriented supervision process itself, it is equally important that the supervisor be willing to collect data on the effectiveness of the supervisory procedures being used. It is essential that the supervisory process be open to modification such that the most effective procedures with each individual trainee will be used. In addition, this openness to empirical data can result in modifications of the procedures which the supervisor may direct the trainee to employ in a given clinical case. For example, when treatment plans of the supervisor and trainee clash, the conflict might be resolved by collecting data on the efficacy of each approach.

To summarize, current definitions of behavior therapy generally include the following criteria: 1) The contents—that is, the procedures—are based on psychological or behavioral principles derived from a wide variety of psychological experimentation. 2) The focus of therapeutic intervention is generally on the direct modification of behavior with both the presenting problem(s) and outcome criteria specified in behavioral terms. 3) The methodology of behavioral assessment and therapy involves the application of an experimental method with each individual client to determine the variables controlling the client's problematic behavior as well as to evaluate the effectiveness of the intervention. In a similar vein, behavioral supervisors frequently rely on supervision procedures which are adaptations of the procedures used in behavior therapy; the trainee's current clinical behaviors, rather than historical determinants or underlying psychodynamics, are usually the focus of supervision; and an experimental process is used to guide the supervisor's responses both to the trainee and, indirectly, to the client.

BEHAVIORAL MODELS OF TRAINING AND SUPERVISION

For the most part, discussions of professional training of behavior therapists have focused on training within psychology graduate programs. Given that the content of behavior therapy characteristically involves the application of psychological theories and research methodology, this orientation is not surprising. Until recently, most of the emphasis in these discussions of graduate training has been on describing, in rather broad outlines, the curriculum or type of experiences which students should be exposed to. Considerable attention has also been given to an analysis of the behavioral psychologist's role as opposed to the role of the traditional clinical psychologist. Thus, attention has been given to specifying the content and goals of behavioral training programs. Historically, little attention has been given to specifying methods of clinical supervision or practicum training. This lack of attention was probably somewhat due to the emphasis by many of the early pioneers in behavior therapy on the role of the behavior therapist as a program consultant or social planner (Krasner, 1969, Ullmann, 1967). For example, Gardner (1976) suggests strongly that the behavior modifier should act as a consultant to the persons who are in daily contact with the client and that individual sessions between the client and the psychologists should be limited. Although primarily directed to professionals engaged in the treatment of the retarded individual, Gardner's comment suggests that persons in the client's environment can, with professional guidance, effectively carry out behavior therapy procedures. From this point of view, training the clinician in the individual application of behavior therapy would not be stressed.

A second reason for the de-emphasis on practicum training is perhaps best reflected by a statement by Ullmann and Krasner (1965).

Even though we take a stand that behavior therapy is easily taught, we do not think that it is a mechanical procedure devoid of either skill or personal warmth. In fact, there are two major aspects to the teaching of behavior therapy. The first includes the specifics of current techniques. But the second, and more important aspect, is the teaching of a way of viewing clinical problems so that the ingenuity of the student can come into play in moving on to even more useful techniques. We believe that any progress in the matter of training people to modify behavior effeciently rests with scientific procedure, particularly adherence to operationally defined concepts (p.44).

What Ullmann and Krasner are suggesting here is that the most important aspect of training behavior therapists is the teaching of a scientific, behaviorally oriented conceptual approach to the client. If this is the aim of training, it can perhaps be as easily accomplished in didactic seminars as in supervised practicum training. Thus, while the need for skill training in techniques, which usually occurs in supervised practicum training, is not ignored, it is not seen as a very difficult or complex task. This early emphasis on the ease of teaching how to implement a behavioral procedure (as opposed to designing the treatment plan) is further highlighted by the conclusion of Davison (1965) that "highly motivated students can be trained in a very short time to execute a behavior-control program" (p. 146). Davison gave inexperienced undergraduates four didactic sessions covering social learning principles, followed by practice sessions with the autistic child clients. After one practice session, Davison concluded that the students were competent to carry on the program.

Models of behavioral training which stress the consultative role of the behavior therapist generally are a blend of didactic and experiential training. For example, Krasner (1969) suggests a training program which would consist of two years of course experience followed by a one-year internship during which diagnosis and therapy would be given only a minor role. The emphasis of the internship would be on seminars, and experiential and written assignments related to four areas of investigation: the patient, the installation, the community, and the psychologist. Krasner further suggests that the intern meet with a supervisor at least once a week to help integrate the experiences into a meaningful pattern. He does not, however, specify how the supervision should proceed so that this integration would be successful. Although Krasner suggests that the student take a postdoctoral internship in order to become skilled with the evaluation and modification of behavior, he does not specify how this skill training should be carried out.

Lloyd and Whitehead (1976) have developed a behaviorally taught practicum for training students in a wide range of both consultation and treatment skills. The students' practicum responsibilities were first broken down into their component skills. These skills were then arranged such that they were taught in sequence over three semesters. Supervision was accomplished in team meetings where advanced students supervised less advanced students. Students were observed in their contact with clients and also in team meetings, and points were given contingent on the presence of required behaviors. Although Lloyd and Whitehead did not give many details about the conduct of the supervisory meetings, they did provide a supervisor rating sheet. Relevant supervisor attributes are listed, and include behaviors which might be categorized as nonauthoritarianism, sensitivity, feedback, modeling, and reinforcement. In addition, supervisors are rated specifically on how well they use behavioral processes in teaching professional behaviors.

Thoresen (1972) describes a behavioral systems approach developed to train students as behavioral counselors. The approach, combining systems and behavioral techniques, is characterized as follows:

1. Behavioral objectives are stated in terms of observable trainee performances.

2. Social learning principles and hypotheses are the basis of specific counseling techniques.

3. Empirical and experimental methods are used to produce data to make training decisions about what to change, how much, and for how long.

4. Analysis and synthesis methods are used in examining existing systems and in devising new systems.

5. Cybernetic concepts and procedures such as control and feedback are employed.

6. Contemporary physical and social environments ("here and now") which control client and trainee behavior are analyzed. (p. 52)

Consistent with a behavioral approach, the training is competency based with students moving through various subsystems, including practicum, at their own rate. Use of such behavioral techniques as modeling, guided practice, immediated feedback, and positive reinforcement are emphasized as training procedures throughout the entire system. The activities of the practicum supervisor, however, are described as listening to tapes, reading and discussing write-ups and consulting with the trainee on particular tasks. Thus, although the program as a whole is behaviorally based, there does not appear to be a detailed description of how behavioral principles should be implemented in the supervisory process itself. Instead, supervision seems to be more concerned with "checking" the students' progress, with actual skill training occuring in classroom settings.

Jakubowski-Spector, Dustin, and George (1971) have also proposed a model for training the behavioral counselor. The model, based on a behavioral model for counselor education suggested by Krumboltz (1966), stresses a behavioral perspective on student behavior (e.g., viewing behavior as situational as opposed to an indicant of personality traits) and enumerates the activities of the behavioral counselor as follows: specifying goals in behavioral terms, systematically planning for transfer of training effects by giving students practicum experience in settings similar to those in which they will eventually work, serving as a model, and acting as a reinforcing agent. The model is intended to apply to graduate training of behavior counselors as a whole and thus is not explicitly directed at specifying the activities of the supervisor of behavioral counseling. Hector, Elson, and Yager (1977) have recently proposed a model for teaching counseling skill which relies on behavioral self-management procedures. The procedures are utilized within the context of prepracticum and practicum courses with the instructor supervising the student's progress. The supervisor within this framework would presumably function as a behavioral consultant, although Hector et al. did not explicitly discuss the role of the instructor-supervisor.

The above behavioral models are helpful in delineating what behavioral supervision involves; however, none address in depth the issue of supervising behavior therapy. A model of therapy training proposed by Levine and Tilker (1974), therefore, is somewhat unique in that it is the only model which deals directly with one-to-one supervision of the clinical trainee. Their approach emphasizes techniques of modeling, direct feedback, and use of audio-visual equipment to develop a response repertoire for the trainee and is based on the belief that gradual exposure to clinical practice and fading of external direction produces the best learning. After first learning academic principles of behavioral assessment and therapy, the students observe experienced therapists in clinical interaction with clients and then practice clinical responses by role-playing with the supervisor. Once the trainee has developed a reasonable repertoire of responses, he or she is brought into direct contact with the client by sitting in with the supervisor. Over time the trainee is expected to take increasing responsibility for conducting the therapy. As the trainee becomes increasingly active in the therapy, the activities of the supervisor decrease and eventually the supervisor moves out of the room and observes the trainee through a one-way vision screen. This method of sitting in with the supervisor is quite similar to a cotherapy method of behavioral training, proposed by Leventhal and Pumroy (1969), for use with experienced nonbehavior therapists. Once the supervisor is out of the therapy session, Levine and Tilker recommend the use—at least initially—of a small radio receiver, which fits into the trainee's ear, to give any needed feedback or advice. The supervisor then fades out the audio instruction and eventually conducts supervision by going over audio and visual tapes. Finally, the supervisor functions as a consultant, going over only those areas of therapy in which the trainee feels in need of help. To date, this model of supervision is the most comprehensive approach to applying behavioral principles to individual supervision of behavior therapy. The model which is proposed in the next section is based on many of the same principles which guided Levine and Tilker and in some respects is an extension and broadening of their approach.

THREE-DIMENSIONAL MODEL OF BEHAVIORAL SUPERVISION: GOALS, PROCEDURES, AND UNIVERSES OF GENERALIZATION

Issues in psychotherapy training and supervision can be usefully analyzed from at least three different points of view or dimensions: the goals of supervision, the methods and procedures used to achieve these goals, and the universes (e.g., settings, client types, therapeutic modalities) across which one wishes these goals to generalize. Figure 1 illustrates the relationship among these three dimensions. The grid presented here is an adaptation of the grid presented by Linehan (1979) to illustrate these same dimensions within the context of assertion training. The similarity between the assertion training and supervision grids is due to the fact that both activities are aimed at teaching a set of skills which can be utilized by the client-trainee across a variety of settings. What follows is first a brief description of a more general model of behavioral functioning on which the supervision model is based followed by a more detailed analysis of each of the supervisory dimensions.

Either explicitly or implicitly, models of both therapy and supervision are based on more general models of human functioning. The model of supervision proposed here is based on a tripartite theory of personality and behavioral functioning. The essence of this approach is the belief that human functioning can be fruitfully conceptualized as occuring in one or more of three separate, although interrelated, systems: the cognitive response system; the physiological/affective response system and the overt motor response system. In less technical terms, this approach suggests that behavior can be thought of as involving thinking (the cognitive system), feeling (the physiological/affective system), and acting (the overt motor system). Lines between the systems are not always clear; at many points there may be overlap among the systems, and complex responses often contain elements from each of the systems. It is useful, however, to discuss each of the systems separately. For example, affective responses are usually a complex interaction between the cognitive and physiological systems. But, since affect

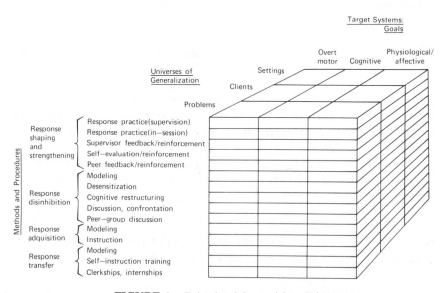

FIGURE 1. Behavioral Supervision Grid

always involves some bodily or physiological response, it is designated as part of the physiological response system. This tripartite model is based on the social behavioral approach to personality proposed by Staats and Staats (1963), and Staats (1975). A similar view has been proposed by Lang (1971) and was recently reiterated by Wolpe (1978). Although the notion that cognitions should be considered as behaviors is controversial (Ledwidge, 1978), the model has served as a useful organizing principle for conceptualizing issues in both behavioral assessment (e.g., Cone, 1977) and therapy (e.g., Linehan, 1979; Rachman and Hodgson, 1974).

The relative weight given to responses within each of the three systems is perhaps one of the distinguishing factors among different schools of supervision and therapy. For example, training programs for behavior therapists have been accused of attending to the cognitive and motor systems to the relative neglect of the physiological/affective system. Teaching behavioral techniques and ways of conceptualizing clinical problems has often been stressed to the exclusion of other factors which might be important. In contrast, more traditional psychodynamic approaches to teaching and supervision have emphasized the physiological/affective system, giving much less attention to the motor system, that is, *what* the therapist does within the session. For example, a major emphasis in psychodynamic approaches to supervision is on transference and countertransference issues. The behavioral approach suggested here would indicate that not only must the trainee respond appropriately across all three systems (thinking, feeling, acting) but also that the relative influence of each system on responses in the other systems (e.g., thinking on feelings, actions on thinking, feelings on action, etc.) and thus the attention needed, may vary across trainees. From this point of view, the variables controlling the trainee's therapeutic behavior must be discovered empirically for each individual and within individuals for each setting. An example of the latter point might be a trainee whose effectiveness was interfered with in one case by inappropriate anger towards a client who did not improve as fast as desired and in another case by a faulty conceptualization due to insufficient knowledge of the variables influencing that client's problem. In the first instance the supervisor needed to attend to the physiological/affective system (i.e., the anger responses) and in the second instance to the conceptualization of the case which is a cognitive response.

Goals of Supervision: Target Systems and Skills

With respect to issues in supervision, the tripartite behavioral model is most applicable to delineating the goals or objectives of supervision. To the extent that the goals can be conceptualized as involving an increase in therapeutic skills, broadly conceived, the needed skills can be classified as belonging primarily to one or more of the behavioral systems. From this perspective, the supervisor must be concerned with how the trainee thinks, feels, and acts insofar as these responses are relevant to treatment of clients.

One of the first questions that the supervisor should ask a trainee is what he or she expects from supervision. Two issues need to be discussed and carefully distinguished from each other: the skills or target behaviors which the trainee would like to develop and the methods and procedures which will be used to arrive at these goals. For example, discussion of feelings and attitudes about therapy is a supervisory procedure which might conceivably be useful in the attainment of a variety of goals. It is a method or procedure of supervision, however, not a goal in itself. From this point of view, goals of supervision refer to the "end-product," the target skills which the trainee wishes to develop, the capabilities which the trainee would like to have at the end of supervision.

The frequent assumptions that the supervisor knows best and therefore should be the sole arbiter of goals, or that the goals are so obvious as to need little discussion can lead to confusion, mismanagement of both supervision and the client, subsequent anger or hurt feelings, and a host of other problems. Although almost anyone would agree that a principle goal of supervision is to help the trainee become more effective in his or her clinical work, the specific skills needed in order to be effective are not always clear. At times the trainee and supervisor may disagree on the relative importance of various treatment procedures and skills. Conflicts are especially likely to arise when the trainee and supervisor disagree on the breadth of the goals. For example, a supervisor who believes the most important aspect of being an effective therapist is knowing and understanding oneself (e.g., Bergantino, 1978) is likely to focus on broader objectives than desired by a trainee who views the goals of supervision as learning a narrow range of specified treatment techniques. The trainee who wants to learn both a full range of effective procedures, and skills of selecting, implementing, and evaluating treatments, is likely to have trouble with the supervisor who is intent on teaching only procedures that have been identified in the literature as behavioral in nature.

Although a characteristic of behavior therapy is the setting of precise behavioral goals, there has not been a corresponding effort among behavior therapists to either identify behavioral goals for supervision or specify procedures for arriving at such goals. A major reason for this is probably that neither behavior therapists in particular, nor psychotherapists in general, have arrived at a clear notion of precisely what are the critical skills. Behavior therapists have stressed the importance of identifying the specific operations involved in effective behavior therapy procedures; however, the simple learning of these procedures is not sufficient. Certainly, the successful behavior therapist must have a wide range of assessment, interpersonal, and conceptual skills to effectively utilize the behavioral procedures. Little research has been carried out to determine just what skills are necessary to successfully implement a behavioral program.

There have been attempts to designate the skills which should be taught in training the applied behavior analyst. Lloyd and Whitehead (1976) identified fifty behavioral skills by asking faculty to list every relevant aspect of student practicum performance. The skills were then divided into four separate categories: personal management skills (e.g., coming to meetings on time), applied skills (e.g., writing treatment programs), social-professional skills, (e.g., dealing with parents tactfully), and academic skills (e.g., being familiar with the applied behavioral literature). Sulzer-Axaroff, Thaw, and Thomas (1975) generated a list of response capabilities which they thought were either necessary or desirable for behavior modifiers. Eleven response categories were identified: (1) knowledge of the behavior modification model (e.g., ability to list the essential steps in designing and conducting a behavior modification program), (2) assessment, goal formulation, and targeting capabilities, (3) familiarity and application of ethics, law, and philosophy, (4) behavioral observation skills, (5) measurement skills, (6) design skills, (7) skills with behavioral procedures, (8) communication skills (oral, written, and audio-video), (9) training and consulting in behavior modification skills, (10) administration skills, and (11) research skills. The conditions and specific practitioner responses for each category were described together with criteria for assessing achievement. The list of responses was sent to a sample of behavior analysts. With the exception of the audio-visual communication skills, a majority of respondents indicated that the skills listed were necessary or desirable for a behavior analyst. Thoresen (1972), in describing a behavioral model of counselor training, lists several performance areas in which counseling trainees are evaluated. Some of these areas seem to represent specific behavioral responses which trainees must learn (e.g., listening accuracies), whereas others seem to involve general tasks, with little specification of which specific skills or responses are needed by the trainee (e.g., lead and assess counseling group).

What follows is a more detailed analysis of at least some of the skills needed by the effective behavior therapist. Before discussing these skills specifically, however, a few words should be said about the concept of skills in general. The term is used here in its broadest sense to include not only specific motor actions (e.g., reflections of feelings) or procedures (e.g., desensitization), but also the cognitive capabilities (e.g., accurate perception and coding of the situation, knowledge of outcomes) needed to decide when and how to engage in the action (cf. Welford, 1976), as well as the arousal management capability needed to maintain physiological and affective responses at an optimum level. This wider approach to a therapy skills definition is based on the tripartite model of personality and behavioral functioning presented above. From this point of view, therapeutic skills can be looked at as involving all three behavioral systems; trainees must develop cognitive, overt motor, and physiological/affective capabilities or skills. This broadband approach to skill definition is in contrast to the more common organization of training approaches where skill training refers almost exclusively to teaching specific overt motor activities (e.g., Mahon and Altmann, 1977).

The division of skills into each of the three response systems is somewhat arbitrary. For example, the skills having to do with trainees' affective response —that is, their feelings, their emotional reactions to their clients, and their capability of dealing with their own emotions—are all included under the physiological system. However, research data suggest that emotional responses are more appropriately conceptualized as a complex response involving aspects of two or perhaps all three of the behavioral systems (Shachter, 1966; Lazarus, Averill, and Opton, 1970).

Cognitive skills

Krasner (1969) suggests that the role of the behavior therapist is that of "basic scientist and professional applier of science" (p. 545). Krasner is here identifying behavior therapy with both the content and the methodological approach of science. This point of view is similar to the current definitions of behavior therapy referred to earlier and has direct implications for the cognitive capabilities which the novice therapist must develop. The cognitive capabilities necessary for the behavior therapist include knowledge across several content areas as well as the cognitive abilities to utilize the acquired knowledge effectively in the therapeutic situation. Content areas where mastery is needed include scientific methodology, theoretical and empirical literatures relevant to problematic behaviors and treatment, basic psychological principles, and ethical and legal issues. In addition to these four content capabilities, the novice behavior therapist must develop capabilities to organize and integrate information gained from experience, to conceptualize a case and identify the problem, that is, to assess the client, to plan effective treatments, to make good clinical judgments, and to be aware of the influence of one's own values, beliefs, and characteristic expectations in the treatment setting. These content areas and capabilities are meant to be suggestive rather than inclusive; what follows is a brief discussion of these capabilities, highlighting their relevance to behavior therapy.

The behavioral emphasis on a scientific approach in all phases of clinical work suggests that the novice therapist must have a firm grounding in *scientific methodology,* especially $N = 1$ designs and methods of determining reliability and validity of measurement. This point is congruent with the Boulder model of clinical psychology training (Raimy, 1950) which endorses training of the scientist-practitioner and has had broad acceptance within psychology, regardless of psychotherapy orientation. A major purpose of teaching research methodology within the Boulder model, however, is to train the clinician to be a sophisticated and critical *user* of clinical research. Clinical practice and clinical research are clearly differentiated. In contrast, from a behavioral perspective the clinical practitioner needs to know research methodology in order to *do* research within the clinical setting. Within the clinical setting, this emphasis on scientific rigor is most apparent in the attention given to objective methods of assessment, both initially to identify the problem and the variables influencing it, and throughout therapy to monitor the efficacy of the intervention. Contrary to what the novice behavior therapist often fears, scientific methodology within the clinical setting does not necessarily mean the application of multiple baseline and/or reversal single-subject research designs. It cannot be overstressed that the emphasis on scientific rigor in behavior therapy is intended to benefit the individual client. Thus, although it may be critical to objectively measure the client's problematic behaviors, their surrounding events, and whether or not change has occurred, there are many instances where a rigorous determination of the specific variables which actually influenced a given client's change are neither necessary nor in the best interest of the client. In addition, although *what* changes should occur as a result of therapy is primarily a values issue (Strupp and Hadley, 1977), *whether* change has in fact occurred in a given client is an empirical question.

If the behavior therapist is going to select empirically validated treatments, familiarity with the *theoretical and empirical literatures relevant to problematic behaviors and treatment* is also necessary. In general, the emphasis here is on first trying interventions which have the best research evidence for effectiveness with a particular type of client and problem area. Since very little research has been conducted to determine the interaction effects of client characteristics (other than the identified problematic behavior) and therapist characteristics on treatment effectiveness, the therapist often must choose simply on the basis of the demonstrated effectiveness of an intervention procedure in a specific problem area.

Unfortunately, the state of psychotherapy research is such that the therapist is often faced with either a clinical problem for which there is no demonstrably effective treatment or a client with whom empirically validated treatments, for one reason or another, are not applicable. In these instances the therapist is faced with the task of developing or modifying a treatment suited to the individual client. Although at times a certain amount of almost random trial and error and "seat-of-the-pants" theorizing occurs in these situations, knowledge of *fundamental principles of behavioral functioning and behavior influence* is critical if the therapist is to be both efficient and effective. This emphasis on broad psychological knowledge is a direct result of one of the basic assumptions underlying behavior therapy: behavior, including problematic behavior seen in clinical settings, is best understood in light of principles of behavior derived from basic psychological experimentation (Goldfried and Davison, 1976). Thus, to the extent that the behavior therapist is a professional applier of behavioral science, knowledge of the principles and method of that science is essential. Generally, this will include a basic competence in an array of research areas covering aspects of learning, physiology, personality, social and cognitive psychology, as well as basic research on deviant behavior.

A final content area requiring competence is that of *ethical and legal* issues. In general, ethical issues relevant to behavior therapy are the same as those important in considering any human service, including nonbehaviorally-oriented therapies. Legal knowledge is needed about those areas covering professional practice of psychotherapy and relevant state laws on client rights, acceptable interventions (a concern in some institutional settings), hospital committment procedures, and so on.

The emphasis on applying general psychological knowledge should not negate the importance of knowledge gained from experience, both in general living and in clinical settings. Self-knowledge about what types of interventions and clients one is usually successful with as well as general knowledge about how one can most effectively interact interpersonally can be extremely useful. To the extent that the therapist can *organize and integrate information gained from experience,* important information can be gained as to which procedures and therapeutic methods will be successful, at least when utilized by that particular therapist. Although, as noted previously, little research has been done on the interaction of therapeutic methods with therapist variables, it is likely that this is an important dimension which needs to be considered in selecting treatments.

Familiarity with research methodology and relevant empirical findings in the abstract, however necessary, is not sufficient. Lazarus (1969) in discussing his experience in training behavior therapists, noted that "intellectual and theoretical brilliance failed to prevent many individuals from committing serious clinical blunders" (p. 189). A primary task in supervision is to help the novice therapist learn to apply the methodology and findings of psychological research in clinical settings. The trainee needs a workable conceptual model of human functioning and must be able to apply this model in the individual case. It would seem that the most critical skill, here, is the ability to *conceptualize a case and identify the problem, that is, assessment.* Assessment activities of the behavioral therapist involve information gathering and hypotheses testing in the following five areas: "(1) identification of problem behaviors and specification of behavioral objectives (target identification); (2) identification of current and potential controlling variables; (3) identification of client (i.e. person) variables which may interact with the treatments under consideration; (4) identification of environmental variables which may enhance or interfere with the treatments selected; and (5) evaluation of the treatment" (Linehan, 1977, p. 32). Although gathering the data on which to identify and evaluate these variables requires a range of skills besides cognitive capabilities (e.g., interpersonal skills, behavioral observation skills), the combining of the data to answer important assessment questions is a complex cognitive task. This emphasis on assessment skills is similar to that of Lazarus (1968), who suggested that the two most important skills to teach novice behavior therapists are problem identification and selection of appropriate techniques. A similar point is made by O'Leary and Wilson (1975).

The ability to *plan effective treatments* is stressed by Ullmann and Krasner (1965). This skill is most needed when the therapy research literature does not immediately suggest which treatment procedure would be helpful in a given case. Effective treatment planning is contingent on adequate assessment; to a large extent many treatment failures which have been blamed on ineffective intervention strategies are instead the result of faulty identification of either the critical problem or the variables controlling the problem. In addition, effective treatment planning requires the therapist to integrate and apply diverse behavioral principles in the individual case and to creatively modify and combine treatment components from a variety of more general procedures.

The successful application of these interventions requires an ability to *make good clinical judgments.* Included here are the abilities to judge when to institute a treatment, when to change treatments and sometimes goals, and when to drop a treatment plan—even if only temporarily—to deal with other issues which might arise. Observations of novice therapists suggest that even when procedures, methods, and assessment and treatment planning skills are well learned, the requisite clinical judgment capability is rarely present. Although what judgment capability does exist is most likely to be interfered with—at least initially—by anxiety or inaccurate beliefs about supervisors' expectations, a prime task of supervision is helping the trainee develop the needed judgment and timing skills.

A final cognitive capability has to do with an ability *to be aware of the influence of one's own values, beliefs, and characteristic expectations in the treatment setting.* Ullmann and Krasner, perhaps more than anyone else, have discussed the critical role of values in the clinical process (Ullmann and Krasner, 1965; Krasner, 1969; Krasner and Ullmann, 1973) and point out the importance of both accepting the inevitability of the value decisions of the therapist and of training the therapist to accept this social responsibility. Supervision, therefore, must be concerned with teaching the novice how to continually examine the consequences and value implications of behavior changes both for the individual client and for the society. This is in direct contrast to the notion of some behavior therapists that, somehow, behavior therapy is value free. This belief in the absence of intrinsic values in behavioral approaches is most probably based on the refusal of behavior therapists to label certain behavior patterns as either pathological or healthy—a label which, in the absence of biological data, is necessarily based on value judgments. Individuals, both clients and therapists, are necessarily valuing organisms. Even if one states that all behavior is equally valuable and that the client's values will determine the goal of therapy, one is taking a stand based on a belief system which values the individual. This would be in contrast to behavioral approaches which view adaptation to the social system of which one is a part as most valuable. The pull between the values of the client, of society, and of the individual therapist involved (and, during training, of the supervisor), which often arises when setting treatment goals, and less frequently when deciding on the specific treatment procedure, must be dealt with in supervision. The point to be made here is that values cannot be avoided either in therapy or in supervision. Permutations of the dilemma are endless. For example, the client and therapist might agree with each other but disagree with the supervisor. A case example would be when a male therapist and a female client both agree that the goals of treatment should be to help her be less assertive (labeled "aggressive") with her dominant husband. If the supervisor would advocate desensitizing the client to the husband's criticism and training in more effective assertive techniques, not only must the value problem be discussed but the supervisor must also decide on a course of action. If discussion and clarification of the issues does not result in a modification of the therapist's goals, the supervisor has a number of options. The therapist could be ordered to change the treatment goals; the supervisor could use his or her greater power and sophistication to indirectly cause the therapist to view the original goal as simplistic or due to faulty assessment; the supervisor could go along with supervising a treatment contrary to his or her own values, or the trainee could be switched to another supervisor. Rarely, however, are such value dilemmas as clear-cut as this. Often it is the client and therapist whose values are in conflict (e.g., the client who wants abortion counseling with an anti-abortion therapist). In these instances, the supervisor can only highlight the conflict and help the trainee think through the consequences of various courses of action.

A critical evaluation of one's own values is especially important in personally relevant areas where the therapist must be able to accurately assess the probabilities of various events occurring at all, as well as the consequences of events when they do occur. New therapists in training are subject to a host of faulty, and sometimes irrational, beliefs and expectations. For example, beliefs and expectations that clients will either "fall apart" or terminate treatment if confronted verbally by the therapist, that not liking one's own client means that there is something wrong with you, or that supervisors and other classmates will think you are incompetent if a client terminates therapy are but three of a long list of interfering beliefs and expectations which are common among novice therapists. This attention to cognitive variables in behavioral supervision is similar to that in cognitive-behavioral approaches to behavior therapy (Mahoney, 1974; Meichenbaum, 1977).

Overt motor skills

Overt motor skills include the entire repertoire of overt behavioral responses which the therapist might engage in during clinical work. It includes simple as well complex behavioral skills, brief responses as well as those integrated patterns which occur over a period of time. This response system can be distinguished from the cognitive and physiological/affective systems in that responses in the latter are not directly observable. For example, although knowledge of a treatment procedure (a cognitive capability) is necessary in order to describe it, the actual describing of the procedure is an instance of overt motor behavior. Thus, the ability to describe treatment plans to clients in ways that they can understand would be considered an overt motor skill. In a similar manner, although feelings of warmth or liking toward clients may be a physiological/affective response, the actual communication of warmth in therapeutic sessions requires overt motor behaviors. The overt motor skills needed by the behavior therapist can be roughly categorized into five behavioral classes: (1) procedural skills, (2) interpersonal-clinical skills, (3) behavioral-clinical skills, (4) professional skills, and (5) self-development skills. What follows is not meant to be an exhaustive list of the overt behavioral skills needed by the behavior therapist. A representative sample from each category, however, is discussed.

Procedural skill refers to the capability of the therapist to carry out needed assessment and treatment techniques. If procedures with demonstrated utility and effectiveness are to be useful in the individual clinical case, the novice therapist must be able to perform or emit the relevant behavioral response patterns. The ability to describe a particular procedure in the abstract is very different from the ability to actually employ that procedure in a therapy session. As Gitterman and Miller (1977) aptly note, "knowing that" is different from "knowing how". The specific procedural repertoire which the successful behavior therapist needs is ever changing as a function of a developing research literature. Thus, a list of required procedures would be quickly obsolete. Some more standard procedures, with substantial empirical support, however, will probably remain important for the forseeable future. For example, the assessment procedures of naturalistic observation, structured behavioral role-play tests, and behavioral interviewing and the treatment procedures of response rehearsal (including role-playing) and relaxation training (with or without desensitization), are not likely to be discarded soon. Although the novice therapist may learn the rudiments of these procedures outside of actual clinical cases, the behavioral supervisor will usually be involved in helping the trainee apply the procedures with individual clients. In the individual supervisory relationship, the needs of the particular clients whom the trainee is seeing will most likely be decisive in determining which procedures will be taught in supervision.

Contrary to popular opinion and even some professional views, most, if not all, behavior therapists would agree that *interpersonal-clinical skills* are critical for successful therapy. In fact, research by Sloan, Staples, Cristol, Yorkston and Whipple (1975) suggests that, while conducting therapy, behavior therapists, as contrasted with more traditional psychotherapists, show higher levels of interpersonal contact, accurate empathy, and therapist self-congruence. Behavior therapists and nonbehaviorally oriented psychotherapists were equal on the degree of warmth and unconditional positive regard shown toward the client. A major factor in creating the belief that behavior therapists do not value interpersonal skills is probably the apparent neglect of therapist interpersonal behaviors in the behavioral research literature. What is not generally noted, however, is that the attention placebo groups in most behavioral studies, where subjects meet with and are involved in an interpersonal relationship with the therapist, would not be included if these same interpersonal processes were not deemed likely to be therapeutic. The research attention given to more specific techniques and procedures, however, suggests that behaviorists do not consider clinical interpersonal skills as sufficient for effective therapy, even if they are necessary. Even the most rigorus proponents of behavior therapy as technique (Lazarus, 1967) or as applied science (Krasner, 1969; O'Leary and Wilson, 1975) discuss at the same time the necessity of general clinical and interpersonal skills. If the therapist cannot communicate warmth and caring for the client and if adequate sensitivity to the client's direct and indirect communications is not demonstrated, it is likely that the client may stop therapy, not follow directions of the therapist, or simply stop communicating important information to the therapist. The most powerful behavior change techniques would thereby be rendered useless.

A second important area of interpersonal-clinical skill for the behavior therapist, that of keeping structure, has been suggested by Phillips (1977). Phillips lists a number of specific response capabilities which the behavioral supervisor must help the new therapist develop:

1. Asking questions of the patient if you do not know what he or she means by a given statement. . . .

2. Responding often enough to the patient's remarks to leave the impression with the patient that you (the therapist) understand, follow, or perhaps even concur in what the patient is saying. . . .

3. Relating what the patient has previously said—or what you may think has been said . . . to the present context, that is, tying loose ends together. . . .

4. Introducing topics if this seems to be of some value in the course of the therapeutic discussion. . . .

5. Pointing out an inconsistency or contradiction in what the patient has said. . . .

6. Encouraging the patient to talk more about a given topic or to continue to express feelings. . . .

7. Holding to an agenda (if one is used or if one has been agreed upon). . . .

8. Offering hypotheses or conjectures—openly identified as such to the patient. . . .

9. Suggesting that the patient try this or that activity in order to clarify a problem, . . .

10. Asking the patient to react to what you have said; . . .

11. As a therapist you may be able to say anything to a patient if you say it in the 'correct' way. . . .

12. No topic is too tender, too pat, or too trivial to be reacted to by the therapist if the latter thinks the topic (or some related comment) can be of value in the therapy" (pp. 110–112).

In addition to more general clinical skills, the behavior therapist must also have an array of more specific *behavioral-clinical skills*. These skills include the abilities to adequately explain behavioral treatment and assessment rationales to clients, to identify and solve ahead of time at least some of the problems which may interfere with carrying out the treatment procedures, and to trouble-shoot when a treatment strategy is not working as well as expected. The therapist must also be able to use a wide range of psychological principles to elicit and maintain the client's participation in the treatment process. Although one could conceivably modify institutionalized persons' or small childrens' behavior without their voluntary cooperation, it is essential in most instances of behavior therapy to get the client to actively participate in implementing the treatment. Novice therapists frequently blame treatment failures on characteristics of the client when in reality the problem may have been an inadequate behavioral plan for teaching the client the requisite therapy behaviors. For example, the behavior therapist must be adept at enhancing motivational variables necessary to maintain the clients engagement in activities crucial for therapeutic progress. Shaping skills are equally important. In other instances, especially when self-control strategies are used, the therapist may function as a behavioral consultant, advising the client on procedures which could be implemented between sessions to change problematic behaviors. In these cases, the therapist must be able to not only elicit the client's cooperation, but also to teach behavioral principles to the client.

Professional skills include the abilities to engage in professional consultations with members of the therapist's own or other disciplines; report and progress note writing skills; developing graphs and charts which will communicate progress to both the client and other professionals; self-management behaviors involved in starting and ending therapy sessions on time, completing reports when due, and following relevant administrative procedures; cooperating with peers and other professionals when needed; collecting fees and discussing finances with clients; and adhering to relevant ethical standards. Most of these areas are given scant attention in academic behavioral training programs. Thus, the responsibility for teaching professional skills is often left to the supervisor.

Self-development skills are those behaviors which put the trainee into learning environments other than supervision (Hayes and Hawkins, 1976). Students abilities to manage their own learning environments will be critical once they have left the formal training situation and, thus, are an important area of concern in supervision. Some behaviors which might be included in this category are the trainee's reading, attendance at conventions, colloquia, and lectures, and membership in professional organizations relevant to behavior therapy. In addition, for some trainees, participation in individual, personal therapy, or experiential groups could be considered an activity likely to result in the self-development of interpersonal skills important in behavior therapy. It should be noted here, also, that personal therapy is often critical in helping a trainee identify and change cognitive values and beliefs which might interfere with effective treatment.

Physiological/Affective skills

The physiological/affective system is one of the most neglected areas in discussions of behavioral training. This is in marked contrast to accounts of training in more traditional psychotherapy methods where attention to the affective responses of the therapist, both in therapy and in supervision, are considered paramount. For example, Altucher (1967) suggests that "learning to be a counselor is both an emotional and an intellectual experience, and of the two, the emotional is the most crucial" (p. 165). This lesser attention to therapist emotional responses in the behavioral literature, however, does not reflect a total lack of interest. Several studies attempting to apply behavioral procedures to the reduction of therapist anxiety are based on a recognition of the probable interfering effects of fear and anxiety in the therapeutic process (Monke, 1971; Carter and Pappas, 1975). Ullmann and Krasner (1965) suggest that active concern for the welfare of the client is necessary for the behavior therapist. Although they do not equate this concern with an emotional response, it does seem that care and concern would be more likely to occur in the presence of a positive affective response to the client and in the absense of excessive anger or dislike.

In general, behavior therapists must learn to cope with the same range of affective responses as do nonbehavior therapists. Physiological variables can interfere with cognitive activities, such as optimum perceptual coding of client behavior, retrieval of information, and combining of clinical data. Indeed, the central task for many novice therapists during their first few clinical sessions is to keep arousal low enough such that any cognitive activity at all can take place. For some trainees, it may be several months before they can manage their arousal levels well enough to process and integrate new information while actually conducting a therapy session. Thereafter, any number of affective responses may interfere with appropriate clinical behaviors. For example, fears that clients will terminate therapy may inhibit confronting them or bringing up sensitive topics; anxiety about client disapproval and dislike may lead to therapeutic approval and praise following any client behaviors, even self-destructive ones; sexual arousal stimulated by the client may lead to inadvertent sexual advances or avoidance of important topics. Other negative affective responses can be equally detrimental. Anger may lead to excessive confrontations and, if extreme, is likely to interfere with cognitive processing. Dislike of the client may result in blaming the client for any lack of therapeutic progress. Any experienced supervisor can list dozens of other examples. The critical issue here is that skills in labeling and controlling the problematic affective responses which frequently occur in clinical settings must be learned by the novice. Since emotional responses always involve a physiological component, these skills will also include attending to and managing physiological arousal levels.

A second area of physiological/affective responding important in supervision has to do with the trainee's reactions to the supervisor. Evaluation apprehension, for example, especially with respect to supervisory evaluations, can be especially detrimental, both to trainees in general and to their overall clinical effectiveness. The tendency of many novice therapists to equate their clinical skills with their general interpersonal capabilities and, often, their clinical effectiveness with their worth as a person, can create serious obstacles in the training process if the supervisor is not sensitive in dealing with the student. A generally nonevaluative response set seems needed here, and praise—as opposed to criticism—should be the norm. Anxiety and/or anger, sometimes generated by supervisory requests to change characteristic behavior patterns or styles of dealing with clients, can interfere with the trainee's ability to try out new behaviors which might be more helpful to the client.

In dealing with the trainee's physiological/affective responses, both to the client and to the supervisor, it is important that the supervisor maintain the same empirical openness required of the trainee. Thus, rather than assume that a trainee is having a particular affective response congruent with a particular overt response, the supervisor needs to carefully assess the actual determinants of the trainee behavior in question. Although the trainee who is chronically late for therapy sessions may indeed be angry with his or her client, it is also possible that a self-management skill deficit or an over-scheduled course load are in fact the controlling variables.

Behavioral Methods of Supervision: Procedures and Techniques

The general method in any clinical supervision is to use the trainee's own case material to teach therapy skills. At a minimum, this will generally require verbal, audio, video, or observational communication to the supervisor of important events which occur in the process of therapy followed by a discussion of these events and any ideas about what might be done in future therapy sessions. How these discussions should be carried out and the appropriate focus of concern are topics which have generated considerable debate. The use of alternative procedures, in addition to case discussion, varies considerably across supervisors.

A behavioral approach to supervision will generally involve the utilization of a range of procedures which have been shown to be effective in teaching cognitive, overt-motor, and physiological/affective arousal management skills across a range of behavioral content areas. The focus of concern will most often be directly on the behavioral skills outlined in the previous section. As with the selection of target goals, however, it is essential that the trainee and supervisor agree on which supervisory techniques will be used. The supervisee who wants to discuss emotional responses and the role of the clinician in general will most likely encounter serious problems with a supervisor who is only interested in rehearsing novel treatment procedures during supervision sessions. Little research has been done to establish which procedures are most effective in developing skilled behavioral clinicians. In the absence of empirical guidelines, both parties must work out procedures suited to the trainee's needs and desires as well as the talents and style of the supervisor.

There are a large number of skill training techniques to select from. For the most part the procedures discussed here have been developed by behavior therapists to teach interpersonal skills (Linehan, 1979; Bellack and Hersen, 1979); cognitive skills (Meichenbaum, 1977) and physiological-arousal management skills (Goldfried, 1977). Skill training procedures can be classified in terms of their functional operations (Rich and Schroeder, 1976) and broken into four catagories: (1) response shaping and strengthening procedures, (2) response disinhibition procedures, (3) response acquisition procedures, and (4) response transfer procedures (Linehan, 1979). The procedures and associated categories are listed in Figure 1. Response inhibition or suppression procedures are not included for several reasons. First, inappropriate responses made by the trainee must be replaced by more useful responses; rather than punishing the old response, the supervisor can just as easily suggest or otherwise teach new responses to take the place of the old behaviors. The superiority of reinforcement over punishment techniques in teaching behavioral skills is well documented (Feldman and Broadhurst, 1976). Secondly, a side effect of punishment is to make the person delivering the punishment less potent as a source of future reinforcement. Thus, if punishment is used in supervision, interpersonal distance occurs between supervisor and trainee. This distance and decreased potency as a reinforcer has a range of negative effects, including decreasing the effectiveness of the supervisor as a teacher. Third, punishment is aversive and frequently increases trainee anxiety. What the novice therapist frequently needs, as much as anything else, is support, praise, and encouragement. Although division of procedures into the categories is, at times, arbitrary, it is useful to discuss each category separately. What follows is a brief summary of some of the procedures which might be used in behavioral supervision.

Detailed instructions on how to carry out each of the procedures are beyond the scope of this chapter. Descriptions of the procedures, however, can be found in many textbooks on behavior therapy (e.g., Rimm and Masters, 1974), cognitive-behavior therapy (e.g., Meichenbaum, 1977; Kendall and Hollon, 1979) and skill training (Bellack and Hersen, 1979). In general, the procedures included here are independent of the target skill system to which they can be applied. In theory, at least, each procedure listed could be used to teach cognitive skills, overt-motor skills, and physiological-arousal management skills.

Response shaping and strengthing procedures refer to those techniques designed to reinforce interpersonal and therapy skills which the trainee already has in his or her behavioral repertoire. These procedures are especially relevant for the trained therapist, skilled in other approaches to therapy, who is learning behavioral methods of therapy as an additional skill. It should be recognized, however, that most beginning therapists, at least if they have a more or less ordinary social history, also have in their repertoire many of the communication and interpersonal skills necessary to help individuals in trouble. Since many trainees have also received extensive academic training in general and clinical psychology before they see their first client, considerable cognitive and conceptual skills probably also exist. Response shaping and strengthing procedures include (1) response practice within the supervision session itself (role-playing), (2) response practice in actual clinical settings, including carrying clients (practicum experience), (3) supervisor feedback, coaching, and response reinforcement, and (4) self-evaluation and self-regulated reinforcement. If supervision is conducted in groups, peer feedback, coaching, and reinforcement can also be used. Feedback can be based on direct or indirect observation. In direct observation the supervisor observes the therapist's behavior, both in supervision (e.g., treatment planning, role-playing) and in therapy sessions via sitting in, observing through a one-way mirror, or using audio- or videotapes. Indirect observation usually involves listening to the therapist's description of the therapy session. Unfortunately all of the problems of verbal report as a method of assessment (Linehan, 1977; Bellack and Hersen, 1977) are also present in indirect methods of therapy observation. It should be noted here, that an important task of supervision is to teach the novice therapist to use client feedback and progress as the primary response strengthening and shaping mechanism. Ultimately, it is the client, more than the supervisor, who must direct the therapist's behavior.

Respone disinhibition procedures are designed to reduce or modify those variables which might be inhibiting the therapist from utilizing skills which have been previously learned. As noted in the discussion of the physiological/affective skills in the previous section, negative emotional responses can inhibit behaviors which would be helpful to the client. In addition, as noted in discussing cognitive skills, unrealistic expectations and beliefs, or faulty application of values to the clinical situation, can lead to the supression of various clinically useful responses which the therapist would otherwise be able to engage in. The therapist who believes that clients will "fall apart" if verbally confronted is not likely to give critical feedback during sessions. Therapists who evaluate persons with problematic behavior patterns as "sick," pathological, manipulators, or other value-laden and pejorative terms are not likely to either respect their client or assess and utilize the client's strengths. A therapist who believes that if a therapist cannot do effective therapy he or she is not a good person (or must have difficulty relating to people, or can never help anyone) is likely to have excessive evaluative apprehension such that it interferes with clear thinking during sessions. A therapist who expects to never dislike clients, never feel angry, never feel sexually aroused or attracted to a client, never feel threatened by a client, never feel nervous, and so on, is likely to mislabel such feelings and thus not utilize them when they might be informative in the treatment sessions.

Procedures which might be used in response disinhibition include (1) modeling of the inhibited responses, (2) desensitization for possibly interfering anxiety responses, (3) cognitive restructuring procedures, and (4) continuing discussion with the supervisor about the therapist's own values, beliefs, and goals. On occasion, as noted by Levine and Tilker (1974), the supervisor may need to use verbal confrontation as a procedure for helping the trainee attain more realistic labeling of his or her own values and beliefs and possible consequent effects on their own clinical behavior. An often helpful procedure is peer-group discussion of clinical experiences. Often the very sharing of fears and concerns is useful in alleviating them.

No matter how skilled the novice therapist, supervision will almost always involve the use of *response acquisition* procedures designed to teach the trainee novel responses as well as new ways of patterning already existing repertoires. Response acquisition procedures include modeling of relevant skills and instructions. Modeling can be accomplished in a variety of ways. The supervisor can model directly by conducting therapy and engaging in other clinical activities which the trainee observes via one-way mirror, tape, or by nonparticipatory sitting in with the supervisor. In addition, supervisors can provide symbolic modeling by describing clinical methods used in their own practice and how they accomplish other clinical activities, and by sharing their own values, beliefs, and conceptual models. Instructions can be given in any number of ways. Trainees can be given books and articles to read, alternate methods of treatment can be suggested and discussed during supervision, the supervisor can teach some skills didactically, and, on occasion, the therapist can be given direct instructions about how to proceed with a given case. While actively practicing their therapy skills, trainees can be given suggestions through a bug-in-the-ear device such that only they, and not the other person, can hear the supervisor. Although Levine and Tilker (1974) suggest the use of this procedure in actual therapy settings, it seems more appropriate in structured role-play training. On occasion, if important decisions must be made immediately, the therapist can be instructed to leave the client to consult with the supervisor before concluding the session. No matter what procedures are used, once the trainee has acquired new responses, response shaping and strengthening procedures must be implemented to insure the development and stability of the new skills.

Response transfer procedures are primarily intended to help the trainee utilize the newly acquired clinical skills in a variety of settings other than those encountered during the initial acquisition. Procedures involve: (1) modeling, either symbolically (e.g. case conferences, reading) or behaviorally, of the application of diverse methods across a wide range of clinical problems; (2) self-instruction training where the therapist is taught to identify and label the principles underlying the effectiveness of techniques used in individual cases so that the fundamental principles can be applied again in novel settings; and (3) clerkships and internships such that trainees carry many different types of clients across diverse settings.

Certainly, all of the procedures included here will not be useful or necessary in every case. The supervisor and trainee need to select those procedures which seem most appropriate for specific purposes. Nor should these supervisory procedures be viewed in isolation from the supervisory clinical skills which the supervisor must have if the application of the procedures is to be successful. Effective behavioral supervisors must be able to apply to supervision the same cognitive, overt motor, and physiological/affective skills described above as necessary in conducting behavior therapy.

Universes of Generalization

Universes of generalization relevant to behavioral supervision refer to settings, client types, and therapeutic modalities across which trainee skills are expected to generalize. The situational specificity of many behavioral patterns (cf. Mischel, 1968) suggests that generalizability cannot be taken for granted. Thus a diversity of training opportunities together with planning for transferability of skills is needed. A second implication of the absence of a generalizability assumption has to do with how the trainee's behavior in general, outside the therapeutic milieu, is conceptualized. Although the presence of adequate social behaviors—for example, accurate reflection and listening behaviors—may indicate the *presence* of these skills in the trainee's behavioral reportoire, their absence in nontherapy social settings does not necessarily indicate a corresponding *absence* of these skills in the trainee's reportoire. It is possible that an individual might exhibit adequate clinical skills within therapeutic settings while, at the same time, failing to demonstrate these skills in other settings observed by the supervisor. Once again, the issue is an empirical question which can only be resolved by the supervisor observing the trainee actually conduct therapy sessions. Observations of trainees in nontherapy settings, including supervision sessions, may be an important source of hypotheses about the student's behavior; these observations, however, do not justify conclusions about the trainee's behavior in other settings.

EVALUATING CLINICAL SKILL

An important question in supervision has to do with how one knows when a therapist is competent; that is, how does one evaluate therapeutic behaviors and general clinical skills. To the extent that one can specify the behavioral responses which constitute good clinical behavior, the problem is easily solved. One simply puts the trainee in a situation where the behaviors are required and notes whether the requisite responses are emitted. The diversity of therapeutic approaches, even within the behavioral field, together with the novel, or at least idiosyncratic, requirements of each case make such a solution improbable. In addition, the tenuous empirical link between specific interpersonal skills and therapeutic effectiveness, and the virtual absence of any specification of what, in the abstract, constitutes adequate assessment skills suggests that evaluation of the clinician in the absence of data on clinical effectiveness is tenuous at best. An alternate strategy would be to assume that trainees who demonstrate the capabilities of helping clients achieve their goals, that is, those who do successful therapy, must thereby have whatever skills are necessary. This approach is summarized, if somewhat polemically, by Wolpe (1973).

One consequence of the realization that neurotic behavior is learned is that it places the responsibility for the patient's recovery unequivocally in the hands of the therapist—in contrast to the view that emanates from the psychoanalytic mystique that the patient is responsible for failures of his treatment (the presumption being that the therapist would not fail but for the patient's invidious resistance!). The fact is that if a patient fails to improve despite his diligent cooperation in the treatment programs that have been applied to him there must be technical reasons for this. There may have been a faulty stimulus-response analysis of his case, or the techniques may have been inappropriately applied, or the techniques that are available may simply not be adequate to his particular problem" (p. 10).

A major objection to relying on clinical effectiveness as a criterion for clinical competence is the contention that it is not the therapist's responsibility if the client does not achieve the goals set at the beginning of therapy. Recalcitrant problems for which no effective treatments exist, unmotivated and/or resistant clients, environmental events and a host of other variables besides the clinician's skill are held responsible for lack of improvement. (In fairness to advocates of this approach, it should be noted that they also do not necessarily attribute therapeutic progress to therapist skill.) Certainly there are times when non-controllable events result in ineffective treatment. A behavioral point of view on this issue, however, would suggest also that it is precisely in identifying variables which might interfere with or preclude progress and either changing goals or developing treatment plans to solve the problems, that the skill of the individual behavior therapists is most evident. Although certainly clients should be free to change their opinions about the desirability of targeted behavioral changes without being labeled a therapeutic failure, often clients wish to change in the targeted direction but simply lack self-management skills or reinforcement contingencies needed to follow through on therapeutic suggestions. A critical clinical skill in applying effective treatments is shaping clients to participate actively in their own treatment.

If clinical effectiveness is ever used to evaluate a person's general clinical competence, an adequate sample of cases would need to be observed. Even the most competent behavior therapist has a share of therapeutic failures. Difficulties in obtaining large and representative samples, differentiating supervisory from therapeutic input, and even, at times, in measuring clinical effectiveness preclude the sole use of this variable in general evaluation. However, in the individual case an emphasis on therapeutic results is often useful in that decisions which the trainee makes, and procedures and response patterns tried can be evaluated in the light of the effectiveness in helping the individual client achieve his or her goals. In the final analysis, clinical data is the best source of evaluative information about how well the therapist is doing. Teaching trainees to look to their clients' behavior instead of to the supervisor or clinical theory for validation of their skills is perhaps one of the most important things a supervisor can teach if trainees are to maintain and develop their clinical skills throughout their careers.

SUMMARY

This chapter has presented an overview of definitions of behavior therapy, behavioral models of supervision, and a three-dimensional model of behavioral supervision based on a tripartite model of personality and behavioral functioning. Behavior therapy can be defined according to three criteria: (1) the content which is usually based on general research and experimental findings in psychology, (2) the therapeutic focus which is usually on the direct modification of the problematic behaviors which brought the client into therapy, and (3) the application of an idiographic experimental methodology to the understanding and modification of behavioral problems.

Behavioral models of psychotherapy training originally focused on training in scientific procedure as applied to the individual case and the consultative role of the behavior therapist. More recent attempts to develop behavioral training models have emphasized behavioral specification of psychotherapy competencies, and some attention has been given to applying behavior therapy procedures to training the novice behavior therapist.

The three-dimensional model proposed here rests on a tripartite model of human functioning which suggests that behavior can be fruitfully conceptualized as occurring in one or more of three response systems: the cognitive system (thinking), the overt motor system (actions), and the physiological/affective system (feelings). This behavioral model is most applicable to the goals of supervision. Skills needed by the behavior therapist can be divided into cognitive skills, overt motor skills, and physiological/affective skills. The trainee must respond appropriately across all three systems. Methods used to accomplish these goals represent a second dimension and can be differentiated from the goals themselves. Procedures which might be used were categorized as (1) response shaping and strengthening, (2) response disinhibition, (3) response acquisition, and (4) response transfer. The third dimension of the supervision model focuses on the universes to which the novice therapists skills generalize.

Finally, the evaluation of supervision was discussed. It was suggested that the therapist is primarily responsible for what occurs in behavior therapy and the advisability of using therapist effectiveness as a criterion of competency was analyzed. It was concluded that one of the most important tasks of supervision is teaching trainees to look to their clients' behavior instead of to the supervisor or clinical theory for validation of their skill.

REFERENCES

Association for the Advancement of Behavior Therapy. *Directory of training programs in behavior modification.* New York 1978.

Altucher, N. Constructive use of the supervisory relationship. *Journal of Counseling Psychology,* 1967, *14,* 165–170.

Arbuckle, D.S. The learning of counseling: Process not product. *Journal of Counseling Psychology,* 1963, *10,* 163–168.

Bellack, A.S., and Hersen, M. The use of self report inventories in behavior assessment. In J.C. Cone and R.P. Hawkins (Eds.), *Behavioral assessment: New directions in clinical psychology.* New York: Brunner/Mazel, 1977.

Bellack, A.S., and Hersen, M. *Research and practice in social skills training.* New York: Plenum, 1979.

Bergantino, L. A theory of imperfection. *Counselor Education and Supervision,* 1978, *17,* 286–292.

Bergin, A.E., and Lambert, M.J. The evaluation of therapeutic outcomes. In S.L. Garfield and A.E. Bergin (Eds.), *Handbook of psychotherapy and behavior change: An empirical analysis* (2nd ed.). New York: Wiley, 1978.

Breger, L., and McGaugh, J.L. Critique and reformulation of "learning-theory" approaches to psychotherapy and neurosis. *Psychological Bulletin,* 1965, *63,* 338–358.

Breger, L., and McGaugh, J.L. Learning theory and behavior therapy: A reply to Rachman and Eysenck. *Psychological Bulletin,* 1966, *65,* 170–173.

Carter, D.K., and Pappas, J.P. Systematic desensitization and awareness treatment for reducing counselor anxiety. *Journal of Counseling Psychology,* 1975, *22,* 147–151.

Cone, J.D. The relevance of reliability and validity for behavior assessment. *Behavior Therapy,* 1977, *8,* 411–426.

Davison, G.C. The training of undergraduates as social reinforcers for autistic children. In L.P. Ullman and L. Krasner (Eds.), *Case studies in behavior modification.* New York: Holt, Rinehart, and Winston, 1965.

Eysenck, H.J. Behavior therapy is behavioristic. *Behavior Therapy,* 1972, *3,* 609–613.

Feldman, M.P., and Broadhurst, A. (Eds.), *Theoretical and experimental bases of the behavior therapies.* London: Wiley, 1976.

Fix, A.J., and Haffke, E.A. *Basic psychological therapies: Comparative effectiveness.* New York: Human Sciences, 1976.

Gardner, J.M. Training parents as behavior modifiers. In A. Yen and R.W. McIntire (Eds.), *Teaching behavior modification.* Kalamazoo, Mich.: Behaviordelia, 1976.

Gitterman, A., and Miller, I. Supervisors as educators. In F.W. Kaslow and Associates, *Supervision, consultation, and staff training in the helping professions.* San Francisco: Jossey-Bass, 1977.

Goldfried, M.R. The use of relaxation and cognitive relabeling as coping skills. In R.B. Stuart (Ed.), *Behavioral Self Management.* New York: Brunner/Mazel, 1977.

Goldfried, M.R., and Davison, G.C. *Clinical behavior therapy.* New York: Holt, Rinehart, and Winston, 1976.

Hayes, S.C. and Hawkins, R.P. Behavioral administration of analytic training programs: A beginning. In S. Yen and R. McIntire (Eds.) *Teaching Behavior Modification.* Kalamazoo, Mich: Behaviordelia, 1976.

Hector, M.S., Elson, S.E., and Yager, G.G. Teaching counseling skills through self-management procedures. *Counselor Education and Supervision,* 1977, *17,* 12–22.

Hollon, S., and Beck, A.T. Psychotherapy and drug therapy: Comparisons and combinations. In S.L. Garfield and A.E. Bergin (Eds.), *Handbook of Psychotherapy and behavior change: An empirical analysis* (2nd ed.). New York: Wiley, 1978.

Jakubowski-Spector, P.J., Dustin, R., and George, R.L. Toward developing a behavioral counselor education model. *Counselor, Education, and Supervision,* 1971, *10,* 242–250.

Kanfer, F.H., and Phillips, J.S. *Learning foundations of behavior therapy.* New York: Wiley, 1970.

Kazdin, A.E. *History of behavior modification: Experimental foundations of contemporary research.* Baltimore: University Park Press, 1978.

Kazdin, A.E., and Moyer, W. Training teachers to use behavior modification. In S. Yen and R.W. McIntire (Eds.), *Teaching behavior modification.* Kalamazoo, Mich.: Behaviordelia, 1976.

Kendall, P.C., and Hollon, S.P. (Eds.), *Cognitive-behavioral interventions: Theory, research, and procedures.* New York: Academic, 1979.

Krasner, L. Behavior modification—values and training: The perspective of a psychologist. In C.M. Franks (Ed.), *Behavior therapy: Appraisal and status.* New York: McGraw-Hill, 1969.

Krasner, L., and Ullman, L.P. *Behavior influence and personality: The social matrix of human action.* New York: Holt, Rinehart, and Winston, 1973.

Krumboltz, J.D. (Ed.), *Revolution in counseling.* Boston: Houghton Mifflin, 1966.

Lang, P.J. The application of psychophysiological methods to the study of psychotherapy and behavior modification. In A.E. Bergin and S.L. Garfield (Eds.), *Handbook of Psychotherapy and Behavior Change.* New York: Wiley, 1971.

Lazarus, A.A. In support of technical eclecticism. *Psychological Reports,* 1967, *21,* 415–416.

Lazarus, A.A. The content of behavior-therapy training. In R.D. Rubin and C.M. Franks (Eds.), *Advances in behavior therapy, 1968.* New York: Academic, 1969.

Lazarus, R., Averill, J., and Opton, E. Towards a cognitive theory of emotion. In M. Arnold (Ed.), *Feelings and emotions.* New York: Academic, 1970.

Ledwidge, B. Cognitive behavior modification: A step in the wrong direction? *Psychological Bulletin,* 1978, *85,* 353–375.

Leventhal, A.M., and Pumroy, D.K. Training in behavior therapy: A case study. *Journal of College Student Personnel,* 1969, *10,* 296–302.

Levine, F.M., and Tilker, H.A. A behavior modification approach to supervision of psychotherapy. *Psychotherapy: Theory, Research and Practice,* Summer 1974, *11* (2), 182–188.

Linehan, M.M. Issues in behavioral interviewing. In J.D. Cone and R.P. Hawkins (Eds.), *Behavioral assessment: New directions in clinical psychology.* New York: Brunner-Mazel, 1977.

Linehan, M.M. Structured cognitive-behavioral treatment of assertion problems. In P.D. Kendall and S.P. Hollen (Eds.), *Cognitive-behavioral interventions: Theory, research, and procedures.* New York: Academic, 1979.

Lloyd, M.E., and Whitehead, J.S. Development and evaluation of behaviorally taught practica. In S. Yen and R.W. McIntire (Eds.), *Teaching behavior modification.* Kalamazoo, Mich.: Behaviordelia, 1976.

Locke, E.A. Is "behavior therapy" behavioristic? (An analysis of Wolpe's psychotherapeutic methods). *Psychological Bulletin,* 1971, *76,* 318–327.

Loeber, R., and Weisman, R.G. Contingencies of therapist and trainer performance: A review. *Psychological Bulletin,* 1975, *82,* 660–688.

Mahon, B.R., and Altmann, H.A. Skill training: Cautions and recommendations. *Counselor, Education, and Supervision,* 1977, *17,* 42–49.

Mahoney, M.J. *Cognition and behavior modification.* Cambridge, Mass.: Ballinger, 1974.

Matarazzo, R.G. Research on the teaching and learning of psychotherapeutic skills. In A.E. Bergin and S.L. Garfield (Eds.), *Handbook of psychotherapy and behavior change.* New York: Wiley, 1971.

Meichenbaum, D.H. *Cognitive behavior modification.* New York: Plenum, 1977.

Mischel, W. Toward a cognitive social learning reconceptualization of personality. *Psychological Review,* 1973, *80,* 50–83.

Mischel, W. *Personality and assessment.* New York: Wiley, 1968.

Monke, R.H. Effect of systematic desensitization on the training of counselors. *Journal of Counseling Psychology,* 1971, *18,* 320–328.

O'Leary, K.D., and Wilson, G.T. *Behavior therapy: Application and outcome.* Englewood Cliffs, N.J.: Prentice Hall, 1975.

Phillips, E.L. *Counseling and psychotherapy: A behavioral approach.* New York: Wiley, 1977.

Pomerleau, O.F., Bobrove, P.H., and Smith, R.H. Rewarding psychiatric aides for the behavioral improvement of assigned patients. *Journal of Applied Behavior Analysis,* 1973, *6,* 383–390.

Rachman, S., and Eysenck, H.J. Reply to a "critique and reformulation" of behavior therapy. *Psychological Bulletin,* 1966, *65,* 165–169.

Rachman, S., and Hodgson, R.I. Synchrony and desynchrony in fear and avoidance. *Behavior Research and Therapy,* 1974, *12,* 311–318.

Rich, A.R., and Schroeder, H.E. Research issues in assertiveness training. *Psychological Bulletin,* 1976, *83,* 1081–1096.

Rimm, D.C., and Masters, J.C. *Behavior therapy: Techniques and empirical findings.* New York: Academic, 1974.

Schacter, S. The interaction of cognitive and physiological determinants of emotional state. In C. Spielberger (Ed.), *Anxiety and behavior.* New York: Academic, 1966.

Sloane, R.B., Staples, F.R., Cristol, A.A., Yorkston, N.J., and Whipple, K. *Psychotherapy versus behavior therapy.* Cambridge, Mass.: Harvard University Press, 1975.

Staats, Arthur W. *Social Behaviorism.* Homewood, Illinois: Dorsey, 1975.

Staats, W., and Staats, C.K. *Complex human behavior.* New York: Holt, Rinehart and Winston, 1963.

Stolz, S.B. and Associates. *Ethical issues in behavior modification.* San Francisco: Jossey-Bass, 1978.

Strupp, H.H., and Hadley, S.W. A tripartite model of mental health and therapeutic outcomes: With special reference to negative effects in psychotherapy. *American Psychologist,* 1977, *32,* 187–196.

Sulzer-Axaroff, B., Thaw, J., and Thomas, C. Behavioral Competencies for the evaluation of behavior modifiers. In W.S. Wood (Ed.), *Issues in evaluating behavior modification.* Champaign, Ill.: Research Press, 1975.

Thoresen, C.E. Training behavioral counselors. In F.W. Clark, D.R. Evans, and L.A. Hamerlynck (Eds.), *Implementing behavioral programs for schools and clinics.* Champaign, Ill.: Research Press, 1972.

Ullmann, L. The major concepts taught to behavior therapy trainees. Paper presented at the meeting of the American Psychological Association, Washington, D.C., 1967.

Ullmann, L.P., and Krasner, L. (Eds.), *Case studies in behavior modification.* New York: Holt, Rinehart and Winston, 1965.

Waters, W.F., and McCallum, R.N. The basis of behavior therapy, mentalistic or behavioristic? A reply to E.A. Locke. *Behavior Research and Therapy,* 1973, *11,* 157–163.

Welford, A.T. *Skilled performance: Perceptual and motor skills.* Glenville, Illinois: Scott Foresman, 1976.

Wiest, W.M. Some recent criticisms of behaviorism and learning theory: With special reference to Breger and McGaugh and to Chomsky. *Psychological Bulletin,* 1967, *67,* 214–225.

Wolberg, L.R. *The technique of psychotherapy, Part two.* New York: Grune and Stratton, 1977.

Wolpe, J. Cognition and causation in human behavior and its therapy. *American Psychologist,* 1978, *33,* 437–446.

Wolpe, J. *The practice of behavior therapy* (2nd Ed.). New York: Pergamon, 1973.

Wolpe, J., and Lazarus, A.A. *Behavior therapy techniques: A guide to the treatment of neuroses.* New York: Pergamon, 1966.

Yates, A.J. *Behavior therapy.* New York: Wiley, 1970.

CHAPTER 14

Supervision in Rational-Emotive Therapy

RICHARD L. WESSLER AND ALBERT ELLIS

The term supervision, as used in this article, refers to the teaching of psycho-therapeutic skills and not to the taking of responsibility for the work of another person. Hence, most of our discussion will be about the teaching of rational-emotive therapy (RET) skills and about the supervisory practices employed at the Institute for Rational-Emotive Therapy. These practices are designed to enable professionals to master RET approaches to psychotherapy and counseling.

Our first objective in training is to prepare professionals thoroughly in the principles of RET, as these are outlined in various writings (Ellis, 1962, 1971, 1973, 1978 and 1979; Ellis and Grieger, 1977; Ellis and Harper, 1975). While this point may seem obvious, the fact is that one of the most frequent mistakes made by beginners is their failure to grasp fundamental principles of RET. Rational-emotive therapy concentrates on the detection and correction of self-disturbing philosophies. But this knowledge does not, in itself, assure the supervisee that he/she will be able to identify a self-disturbing idea held by a client; nor that he/she will have the skills to challenge such an idea and to show how it leads to disturbances and how it can be changed. Consequently, close supervision is highly desirable for the effective training of an RET practitioner. We do not expect one to learn RET skills simply by reading theory any more than we would expect someone to learn to play a musical instrument by reading books on musicology.

At the Institute for Rational-Emotive Therapy, we introduce people to RET through workshops conducted by professionals. These workshops include lectures on the fundamentals of RET, as well as demonstrations of RET procedures, usually employing one or more volunteers from the workshop participants who bring up their own problems. We also recommend books and articles, as well as tape recordings of lectures and of therapy sessions from the Institute's professional library.

These introductory workshops, which acquaint participants with the basics of RET, usually summarize its well-known ABC theory of personality disturbance and treatment. *A* stands for an Activating event or experience—any action or happening that leads to a disturbed emotional Consequence, *C*. *B* stands for the Beliefs or ideas that people use to interpret and evaluate what is happening to them at *A*. The main theory or contention of RET is that people's Consequences (both emotional and behavioral) do not directly stem from their Activating experiences alone but from their interpretive and evaluative Beliefs *about* these experiences. RET shares this assumption with several other cognitive-behavioral approaches to human disturbances—such as those of Beck (1976), Goldfried and Davison (1976), Greenwald (1974), Lazarus (1976), Mahoney (1974, 1977), Maultsby (1975), and Raimy (1975).

Rational Beliefs (rBs), according to RET, lead to appropriate emotional Consequences—that is, Consequences appropriate to one's goals of survival and happiness. Irrational Beliefs (iBs) lead to inappropriate emotional Consequences—that is, self-defeating anger, anxiety, depression, guilt, and shame. Rational thinking is based on personal preferences, values, wishes, and wants, expressed (especially to oneself) in nondogmatic, nonabsolutistic ways. Irrational thinking, on the other hand, consists of such dogmatic and absolutistic demands as "I *must* get what I want!" "You *must* give me what I desire!" and "Things *must* be the way I prefer them to be!"

To demonstrate to professionals in training how strong evaluative thinking frequently leads to emotional disturbances, we often put the basic ABCs of RET in this form:

Irrational demand: "I *must* not get seriously blocked in the fulfillment of any of my basic desires."

Activating experience: "Someone has deprived me of something that I very much want."

Irrational conclusions: "Therefore, (1) I find it *awful* and *horrible* that this state of affairs has come about. (2) I can't stand it! It's unbearable! (3) My life is utterly miserable! and (4) I'm a worthless person because I need what I want to prove my worth as an individual!"

The emotional Consequences that closely follow these irrational conclusions: anxiety, depression, and rage at oneself or others.

The task of the therapist or counselor is to help clients change their unreasonable demands and irrational conclusions and thereby change their disturbed or self-defeating conclusions to those that are are more goal-promoting. The task of the RET supervisor is to teach the therapist or counselor how to elicit and identify clients' irrational thoughts and inappropriate feelings and to change irrational Beliefs (iBs) producing these self-defeating thoughts and feelings. Therapists' challenging or Disputing (at point D) clients' irrational Beliefs usually involves a persuasive dialogue, without which the therapy sessions may prove little more than a lecture to the client of RET principles.

Therapists or counselors who work effectively within an RET framework structure the therapy sessions with the content provided by the client. Therefore, RET therapists are unusually active: asking questions, offering comments, pointing out self-disturbing evaluations, and Disputing irrational Beliefs. While RET therapists direct sessions with active interventions, they do not direct clients—do not tell clients how to live their lives.

The structure provided by the therapist is based on the ABC model of human disturbance. Typically, a session begins with C, the disturbed emotional Consequence. It then focuses briefly on A, the Activating experience. Then the therapist is shown how to focus on B—the client's rational (rBs) and irrational Beliefs (iBs). Starting with this CAB sequence, the session then usually moves to D—the Disputing or challenging of the irrational Beliefs (iBs).

D (or Disputing) is perhaps the most characteristic part of RET—and the the most difficult part for therapists to learn. While many therapists and counselors are quite willing to think of therapy as a learning process and willing to employ an educational model, some are hesitant to think about it as a persuasive process. RET involves both: clients are taught how they disturb themselves with irrational Beliefs and how to spot future instances of self-disturbance; and are also challenged to rethink their personal philosophies. The RET therapist actively helps clients to give up dogmatic, absolutistic, *must*urbatory aspects of living.

Unfortunately, because of their training in somewhat passive systems of psychotherapy, many therapists and counselors have had little experience in helping people to change their thinking, and in fact may not understand what it takes to show disturbed individuals how to modify their attitudes. Thus, they may have an adequate understanding of clients' irrationalities but can think of nothing better than to tell these clients, over and over again, that their beliefs are irrational. At this point, supervision is especially helpful if the RET supervisor models intervention approaches and teaches the supervisee some effective persuasive methods.

RET theory particularly states that people interactionally and transactionally make themselves disturbed: that their "emotions" include thoughts and actions, their "actions" include thoughts and feelings, and their "thoughts" include feelings and behaviors (Ellis, 1962; Ellis and Harper, 1961). Consequently, when RET clients are helped by their therapists to change their "philosophy of life," they are concomitantly shown how to significantly change their feelings and their actions. Even the most helpful "philosophy" of living is of little benefit unless one acts upon it, and RET clients therefore are frequently given in vivo homework assignments during each session. Ideal assignments are those in which clients figure out and self-assign *doing* something differently—for example, deliberately doing something that they are neurotically afraid of, or deliberately disciplining themselves in some way that they are irrationally avoiding. When clients do not make their own assignments, RET therapists can encourage or coach them to do so. RET supervisors often check on the nature of the assignments encouraged by supervisees to see whether they are appropriate and effective and whether better alternatives are available for use by clients.

We have been describing RET practice during a typical session, because the work of the supervisor cannot easily be grasped without knowing what kinds of behaviors the supervisor's efforts are attempting to influence. We shall now discuss the basic clinical and/or counseling skills used by almost any therapist who takes an active-directive approach.

GENERAL CLINICAL AND COUNSELING SKILLS

In our experience, professionals who most quickly and effectively learn RET are those who already have sound basic clinical and counseling skills. They have had experience in interviewing and discussing problems with clients. They know how to ask provoking, open-ended questions and how to deal with a wide variety of people both personally and professionally. They can read nonverbal cues (without making a fetish of every little gesture and movement) and pick up significant vocal inflections (Kaslow, 1977).

Effective therapists know how to form clinical and counseling judgments, including diagnosing clients' problems and assessing current behavioral functioning. They can spot and describe defensive attitudes and hypothesize about how defenses will work against clients' trying new behaviors and implementing insights into self-disturbing Beliefs.

Experienced counselors are able to empathize with clients, not merely in the sense of sensing what these clients are thinking and feeling in their communications to the therapist but also to sense what basic philosophies (and particularly self-sabotaging philosophies) lie behind their communications. RET-oriented empathy, therefore, is "deeper" and more "knowledgeable" than some other kinds of therapist-instituted empathy.

Experienced therapists can monitor relevant aspects of the interaction between therapist and client. While RET practitioners do not view their "relationship" with clients as especially "curative," they do realize that relationship factors can add to the therapist's credibility and thereby enhance his/her effectiveness. On the other hand, an intense therapist-client relationship can also be iatrogenic in several ways: (1) It can interfere with therapy if the therapist is fearful about confronting the client because it might "harm the relationship." (2) It may encourage the client to develop intense feelings about the therapist and focus on these rather than on uncovering and disputing irrational Beliefs about the client's *outside* relationships and affairs. (3) It can provide so much reassurance and direct advice-giving that the client becomes dependent on the therapist and thereby increases his/her disturbed needs for love and approval.

Experienced therapists know that patterns of interaction emerge whenever two (or more) people engage in a voluntary relationship over a period of time, and that this goes for therapeutic as well as for social relationships. Such patterns can either help or hinder psychotherapy and counseling; and effective RET (and other) therapists therefore acknowledge them, analyze them, and sometimes use them to show clients how they are disturbing themselves in the therapeutic relationship itself and what they can do to understand and minimize their irrationalities in this connection.

General therapeutic skills include disclosing relevant facts or feelings about oneself, modeling more appropriate behaviors, and the therapist's thinking rationally and emoting appropriately. They include the therapist's working flexibly with clients, rather than taking the same rigid approach with everyone and assuming that there are no significant individual differences among people (Kaslow, 1977).

Experienced clinicians tend to possess skills in structuring sessions, in confronting clients with their defensiveness and misperceptions, and in acting expressively and emotively rather than stiffly (as though they were therapy machines rather than people responding to other people's thinking, emoting, and behaving). They also are acquainted with many theories of personality and psychopathology, as well as with a broad general knowledge of psychology and other behavioral sciences. Because of their formal and informal knowledge, they can better understand the larger social context whence their clients come, as well as their ethnic, religious, and regional backgrounds, and the irrational and rational customs and beliefs they are likely to have partially picked up from these backgrounds.

Clinical experience and training, therefore, help professionals understand and work successfully with RET supervisors. At the same time, however, some of their experience and training may interfere with the new learning they are likely to encounter in RET supervision; and some of their old and inefficient therapeutic habits may die hard.

Thus, therapists who are skilled at nondirective listening may find it difficult to adopt a more active-directive approach. Professionals with a strong background in "pure" behavior therapy may continue to want to do extensive behavioral assessments and to focus on environmental factors and underrate mediating cognitive tendencies. Or they may overemphasize providing symptomatic relief to their clients (e.g., through relaxation training) and not strive for the more fundamental philosophic change that is a goal of RET. Social skill trainers and specialists in assertiveness training may teach clients these skills—which, however valuable they may be, may often help sidetrack such clients (and their therapists) from the RET task of uncovering and helping people to change their irrational belief system.

Let us be clear about this! We are not opposed to therapists using previously learned skills, including those mentioned in the above paragraph. As long as a basic RET framework is used, almost any kind of effective therapeutic technique may be used within this framework; and, in this respect, RET is perhaps the most eclectic of any system of therapy and is notably multimodal (Ellis, 1977a, 1978, 1979; Ellis and Grieger, 1977). However, we caution against the use of various behavioral and skill training techniques *instead of* (rather than *in addition to*) the therapist's showing clients how to actively Dispute their irrational Beliefs (iBs) (Ellis, 1977b). The RET supervisor, therefore, guards against letting experienced professionals *only* or *mainly* use their already well-learned skills so that they can thereby avoid trying out unfamiliar RET-disputing skills. Because virtually all individuals seem to easily stick with the familiar and the "tried and true," RET supervisors had better remain alert to their supervisees' "copping out" and refusing to employ RET active-directive skills.

RATIONAL-EMOTIVE SKILLS

We have just listed some general clinical and counseling skills that the new RET practitioner acquires in the course of his/her training and experience. How about unique RET-oriented skills that this practitioner had better possess? What, in other words, do we specifically seek to accomplish in RET supervision?

RET practitioners, as we have noted above, require skills in actively listening, probing, and evoking clients' statements of what they are telling themselves: of their rational and irrational Beliefs. Without having a considerable degree of these skills, it is virtually impossible to do effective RET.

A second skill of the RET practitioner is that of showing clients the connections between thinking and emoting—between B (Belief system) and C (emotional and behavioral Consequence) in the ABC model. If therapists do not have this skill, clients may perceive them as merely carping about supposed irrationalities. Remember that the goal in RET is not simply to help people change their irrational Beliefs; it is, more importantly, to help them change their philosophy of living—in order for them to achieve a greater degree of enjoyment.

RET practitioners had better acquire skills in Disputing (D) or challenging irrational Beliefs (iBs) and in giving follow-through homework assignments to aid the achievement and maintenance of the corrected misperceptions. The supervisor therefore encourages them to use a sizable number of Disputing techniques, including debating, paradoxical intention, rational-emotive imagery (Maultsby, 1975; Maultsby and Ellis, 1974), and in vivo behavioral approaches to help clients confront their fears and act against them. No matter how adept an RET therapist may be at the most common form of Disputing or cognitive restructuring, the supervisor tries to see that he/she also has other challenging methods at his or her disposal—such as Disputing Irrational Beliefs (DIBs) (Ellis, 1974), semantic analysis, and the teaching of the logico-empirical method of science (Ellis, 1977a, 1979; Ellis and Grieger, 1977).

THE RET MODEL OF SUPERVISION

The model of supervision that is mainly employed at the Institute for Rational-Emotive Therapy includes a master-apprenticeship relation. In all Institute training programs, starting with training for the Primary Certificate and through to the Associate Fellowship and Fellowship Programs, supervised therapists bring in tape recordings of their sessions with clients and present these to small groups of supervisees working with one or more supervisors. By actually listening to the clients and the therapist, the supervisor can give accurate feedback and can immediately teach the therapist new skills. A supervisor who can effectively critique sessions, offer suggestions, and listen for progress helps promote successful and improved performance.

Supervision in small groups of four to eight therapists offers several advantages: (1) Participants learn from each other as well as from their supervisor. (2) The group can easily convert itself into a group therapy session, for the benefit of several of the participants; and it can also turn into a seminar to consider theoretical and research issues. (3) New techniques and suggestions can be tried out, with the presenting therapist role-playing with another therapist or with the supervisor. (4) New skills can be developed as the supervisor models alternate styles of intervention.

While supervision focuses upon the patient and his or her problems and the RET approach to solving them it is advisable at times to shift the focus in supervision to the therapist. The therapist may become the subject of RET therapy when it becomes apparent to the supervisor or to other members of the supervision group, or perhaps to the therapist him/herself that he or she has a significant problem that is interfering with the progress of therapy. Since the supervisor is in charge of the supervision session, ultimately it is his or her decision to decide to shift the focus from the patient's problems to the therapist's problems. This shift would not be done very often for it is advisable to have provisions for therapists to receive their own psychotherapy in a setting other than supervision. Thus, if a therapist's problem were frequently interfering with his or her work, group supervision time would not normally be taken, but the therapist would be referred for intensive work on his or her problem. In other words, the main concern of supervision is the improvement of therapists' skills. Only when therapists' personal problems interfere with such improvement does the supervision group become converted by the supervisor into a therapy group for a brief period of time.

One of the most effective ways to introduce professionals to RET is an approach that we call "peer counseling." Participating therapists in our practica are paired off to interview one another, each in turn presenting a personal problem (and *not* role-playing someone else's problem). The other acts as counselor and attempts to use RET principles and practices to solve the presenting problem. Later, the first counselor acts as a client and the initial client acts as a counselor.

Tape recordings of these peer counseling sessions are then presented to a supervisor and a supervision group, and are thoroughly analyzed and discussed by the group. Of the several hundred people who have now participated in peer counseling of this sort at the Institute's primary certificate programs, a large majority report that they have found this approach exceptionally valuable in solving their personal problems as well as in learning how to do effective RET. They report getting significant help with their personal problems because they not only receive special attention from their peer partner in regard to such problems but also receive help when the supervisor and the other members of the supervision group join in the uncovering of their irrational Beliefs and in helping them actively Dispute such Beliefs.

In supervision groups at more advanced levels (practica where therapists are prepared for the Associate Fellowship and Fellowship certificates of the Institute), supervisors and other supervisees also readily explore therapists' personal problems, especially when these seem to interfere with the effectiveness of their therapy. Because RET supervisors show the same kind of acceptance toward their supervisees as they would like these supervisees to show toward their own clients, a climate of free exchange usually prevails. This fact, plus the emphasis that supervision is a learning experience and not an evaluation of the therapist as a person, reduces the number of "games" that occur during supervision (Kadushin, 1968; Kaslow, 1977).

RET supervisors try to remain especially alert to times when supervised therapists agree with their clients' irrational Beliefs; when they thereby become co-sufferers; and when they help their clients avoid rather than work on their disturbances. While it is not necessary (or possible!) for therapists to be perfect in this respect, it is important that they do not reinforce their clients' irrational thinking.

One of our main objectives in working with therapists and counselors is to teach them to identify and to confront and challenge irrational Beliefs (iBs). Some of the main areas of human irrationality include "demandingness" (or *must*-urbation), "awfulizing," self-rating, and low frustration tolerance. We want our supervisees to keep these in mind and to develop sensitivity to what clients say and do, thereby revealing their personal versions of irrational thoughts.

We also encourage therapists in RET training to present tape recordings of good *and* bad sessions with their clients. Many therapists, in our experience, seek help only for problems and situations that they think they handle badly, and fail to recognize errors they make with their "good" cases. Other therapists present only the "good" sessions, in order to impress their supervisors and supervision groups.

We use several formal supervision techniques. Most of these are not original, and in most instances we do not know who first suggested them:

1. *Round robin.* This is done in group supervision, with each therapist taking a turn working with the supervisor (and with the other supervision group members as well). By the same token, if possible each therapist brings up personal problems and then acts as a therapist with each of the other members of the supervision group. This is a good technique for identifying individual therapist styles and for different kinds of modeling. It also promotes problem analysis and fast thinking.

2. *Selective listening.* Each group member is given a different aspect of a therapeutic interview to listen for. One person may listen for therapist's affect, another for client's affect, another for irrational Beliefs, and so on. This is especially good for unraveling subtle features of the client-therapist interaction and for keeping all members of the supervision group actively involved in the supervisory process.

3. *Feedback tape.* The supervisor assigns the presenting therapist the task of returning the following week with a tape-recorded sample that demonstrates the effects of the suggestions made by the supervisor and the other supervisees. The purpose is to check whether the supervisee is actually trying out new approaches suggested during supervision and whether he/she is doing so adequately. This kind of feedback tape enables the supervisor to monitor

the supervisee's performance and to see whether suggestions made to the supervisee had as much merit as the supervisor thought they had when the group made them. Thus, the tape tends to give valuable information about the supervisee's performance as well as about the suggestions made by the supervision group.

4. *Feedback on cases.* Although this may seem obvious, we stress the importance of the supervisor's obtaining feedback on the progress of the cases being supervised. While this practice stems from our concept of supervision as "taking responsibility for the work of another professional," it has important learning implications in its own right.

5. *Therapeutic couplet.* To help therapists prepare for "next time," when their clients say something that the therapists did not respond to well, we often have every supervisee propose an alternate response with the supervision group. Each response is discussed and evaluated. As a result, everyone in the group, including the supervisor, has an idea of what may be done "next time."

6. *Videotape of supervision group.* This can be a useful form of feedback to therapists, especially when they seem unaware of some of their habits—for example, appearing flat, dull, and uninteresting. Videotaping can provide growth-promoting information.

7. *Taping supervisory comments.* Many supervisees forget what the group discusses with them or become so involved with writing down supervisory comments that they get an abridged or distorted message. We therefore encourage them to tape record their individual and/or group supervision, so that they can help themselves learn.

8. *Peer supervision within group.* One of the members of the supervision group may be designated as "the supervisor," while the "real" supervisor acts as an observer. This is a good way to learn to do supervision, and it can reveal some sound data about the supervisee's approach to problem solving. Peer supervision can also be done outside the supervision sessions by having participants exchange tapes with each other and give each other written comments about these tapes. A copy of the written comments goes to the supervisor for monitoring and for the supervisor's later comments to the therapist who conducted the peer supervision exercise.

9. *On using tape recordings.* Although tape recordings can be so useful for teaching counseling and psychotherapy that we wonder how anyone ever learned before their invention, their use can present some problems. We usually supervise short segments of tape—about seven minutes at a time—to prevent attention from wandering. We ask that supervisees have their tapes cued to the portion of the therapy session they desire to present, and that they tell the supervisor and supervision group what they want listened for and what they want special help with. Occasionally, we listen to whole tapes—but not during group supervision, since it wastes time. We listen to them when we are alone; or we assign supervisees to listen to each other's whole tapes in peer supervision.

10. *Self-supervision.* One goal of all our efforts as supervisers in RET is to help therapists learn to supervise themselves. With the help of a tape-recorded session and a checklist of things to listen for, experienced therapists can give themselves regular supervisory checkups. Some items for such a checklist include: (a) How was the session actively structured? (b) What specific statements of the client's thoughts and feelings were elicited? (c) What major irrational Beliefs were identified? (d) How were these challenged? (e) What were the results of this challenging? (f) What activity or cognitive homework assignments were given? (g) How were they completed? (h) Did the therapist help sidetrack the client (i.e., shift the focus of the therapeutic discussion)—especially the long-term client—at some points? (i) Is the therapist-client relationship developing into a patterned, stylistic interaction in which the client is allowed to avoid the therapist's interventions? (j) Does the therapist offer any practical advice that is sound and appropriate? (k) What kind of problem-solving was done and how effective was it?

By encouraging our supervisees in RET to keep steadily supervising themselves with this kind of checklist, we try to get over to them the idea that therapy supervision is a continual process, and that we hope that they will not let themselves down in persisting to work at it. By themselves, and from time to time with a trained RET supervisor, they can continue this process for the rest of their professional career. And we hope that they do.

REFERENCES

Beck, A. T. *Cognitive therapy and the emotional disorders.* New York: International Universities Press, 1976.

Ellis, A. *Reason and emotion in psychotherapy.* New York: Lyle Stuart, 1962. Paperback ed.: New York: Citadel Press, 1977.

Ellis, A. *Growth through reason.* Palo Alto: Science and Behavior Books, 1971; Hollywood: Wilshie Books, 1971.

Ellis, A. *Humanistic psychotherapy: the rational-emotive approach.* New York: Julian Press and McGraw-Hill Paperbacks, 1973.

Ellis, A. *The technique of Disputing Irrational Beliefs (DIBS).* New York: Institute for Rational Living, 1974.

Ellis, A. *How to live with—and without—anger.* New York: Reader's Digest Press, 1977. (a)

Ellis, A. Skill training in counselling and psychotherapy. *Canadian Counsellor,* 1977, *12* (1), 30–35. (b)

Ellis, A. Rational-emotive therapy. In R. J. Corsini (Ed.), *Current psychotherapies* (2nd ed.). Itasca, Ill.: Peacock, 1978.

Ellis, A. *Theoretical and empirical foundations of rational-emotive therapy.* Monterey, Calif.: Brooks/Cole, 1979.

Ellis, A., and Grieger, R. *Handbook of rational-emotive therapy.* New York: Springer, 1977.

Ellis, A., and Harper, R. A. *A guide to rational living.* Englewood Cliffs, N.J.: Prentice-Hall, 1961.

Ellis, A., and Harper, R. A. *A new guide to rational living.* Englewood Cliffs, N.J.: Prentice-Hall, and Hollywood: Wilshire Books, 1975.

Goldfried, M. R., and Davison, G. C. *Clinical behavior therapy.* New York: Holt, Rinehart and Winston, 1976.

Greenwald, H. *Direct decision therapy.* San Diego: Edits, 1974.

Kadushin, A. Games people play in supervision. *Social Work, 13*(3) July 1968, 23–32.

Kaslow, F. W., and associates. *Supervision, consultation, and staff training in the helping professions.* San Francisco; Jossey-Bass, 1977.

Lazarus, A. A. *Multimodal behavior therapy.* New York: Springer, 1976.

Mahoney, M. J. *Cognition and behavior modification.* Cambridge, Mass.: Ballinger, 1974.

Mahoney, M. J. Reflections on the cognitive-learning trend in psychotherapy. *American Psychologist,* 1977, *32,* 5–13.

Maultsby, M. C., Jr. *Help yourself to happiness.* New York: Institute for Rational Living, 1975.

Maultsby, M. C., Jr., and Ellis, A. *Technique of rational-emotive imagery (REI).* New York: Institute for Rational Living, 1974.

Raimy, V. *Misunderstandings of the self.* San Francisco: Jossey-Bass, 1975.

CHAPTER 15

Supervision in Communications Analytic Therapy

ERNST G. BEIER AND DAVID M. YOUNG

ON HAVING A POINT OF VIEW

In order to conduct effective psychotherapy it seems important that the therapist work from a particular theoretical orientation or point of view. Haley (1969) agrees, and proposed that nothing but failure could result if we were to avoid working from *any* theoretical posture. Supervisors of psychotherapists first of all should state clearly their own view of the psychotherapy process. We are not suggesting that supervisors maintain an authoritarian stance over the clinical thinking of their students, but we do suggest that students, while in supervision, should be exposed to the competency that the supervisor has to offer for his model of psychotherapy. This is most likely to enhance the learning of a specific model, and it will also permit the student to evaluate the supervisor's beliefs and biases about the therapeutic process. If the student has a model he will know more clearly how to evaluate the supervision itself. In line with this thinking, several critical assumptions of communications analytic therapy (CAT.) are presented below.

THEORY OF COMMUNICATIONS ANALYTIC THERAPY

There are several theories basing their definitions of psychological distress on a careful analysis of the patient-therapy communication pattern (Beier, 1964; Haley, 1977; Kiesler, 1973; Mahl, 1971; Ruesch, 1961; Ruesch and Bateson, 1951; Sullivan, 1953, 1954; Watzlawick, Beavin & Jackson, 1965; Watzlawick, Weakland, and Fisch, 1974). The ideas expressed here are based on the work of these researchers. Communications Analytic Therapy has developed a theoretical position based on a number of assumptions. One of our assumptions is that the patient is in psychological distress because he feels that he cannot accept full responsibility for his conduct. We argue that the psychological distress of the patient is based on the Rankian conflict between two mutually exclusive motivations: the desire for his individual freedom and integrity on one hand, and the need to socialize, to accept controls, and to adopt undesirable values on the other. The patient will find a compromise between expressing his particular sense of freedom and adopting foreign values, and he will cling to this compromise. The distress, the pain experienced is a message to self and others, and the patient will accept this pain to show that he is not responsible for the "undesirable" compound of the compromise. Mahl (1971) calls it the "adaptive compromise." A "symptom" is such a compromise. For example, when a patient is depressed, the patient communicates to another person (and to himself) that he suffers. This communication is likely to convince self and others that he is *not* responsible for another, more hidden message with which he conveys just "how" he is depressed. This second message is sent in the service of his sense of freedom, and it has to be subtle because he has learned that he must not express it openly. He will subtly arouse sympathy, a sense of helplessness, anger, always without feeling responsible for doing so. (We do not deny physiological factors in depression, but see them merely as a disposition.) Here we center on the patient's style of communication, and its meaning to others. The deep distress permits the patient to convince himself and others that he would not voluntarily engage in such a manipulative behavior, and the patient can deny responsibility for the expression of his forbidden emotions and the control he exercises with them upon others. The patient has considerable skill in "engaging" others through verbal and nonverbal information, thus engagements amount to creating an "emotional climate" in the other person favorable to the patient's own expectations. The "emotional climate" will serve the patient by avoiding the respondent's reasoned judgment; it will emotionally involve the respondent to act in an area which the patient feels competent to handle. A depressed patient might greatly frustrate her husband and make him very angry, but she can always deny that she desired such unpleasant results with her conduct.

Another of our assumptions is that the patient will attempt to control interpersonal behavior by actively seeking out situations which will enhance the possibility of experiencing the symptoms—that is, the compromise described above. For example, a patient feels vulnerable to accept responsibility for closeness to a person of the opposite sex. In line with our assumption, he will now seek out a situation where his compromise, "getting close" (culturally demanded) and "not getting close" (to stay free of encumbrance) is likely to occur. The "not getting close" of course must occur in such a way that he is not left with a sense of responsibility for his selfish wish. He might go out and woo a woman and, just when the woman is likely to count on him, he will break the implicit promise by some action for which he cannot be held responsible. For example, he might transfer to another city, get into trouble with the police, or engage in a behavior ("unable to help himself") which the woman despises. All these are just some of the many ingenious ways the patient can choose to maintain a state of distance without being held responsible for having avoided commitment.

From the Communications Analytic Therapy point of view, the patient seeks to accomplish this adaptive compromise by sending messages through overt as well as covert channels of communication. With the covert part of the message, based on such cues as voice, facial expression, and posture, the patient is able to subtly constrict his own and/or the respondent's awareness as to his "unacceptable" motivation. In this manner he can create feelings (the emotional climate) and consequent responses in the respondent without being held responsible for them. This "adaptive compromise" is achieved through what we have called "interpersonal repression" (Beier, 1964, p. 92). This method permits the patient to mislead self and others as to the nature of his conduct. The more vulnerable he feels about expressing his "forbidden" motivation, the more skillful he will have to be in the act of interpersonal repression. Actually, this "adaptive compromise" is not only seen in patients, but in many ways occurs in the everyday life of anyone. The husband of a "frigid" wife collects his injustice in the form of sexual rejection. He propositions his wife nightly with a commanding, "Honey, tonight is the night!" He knows full well that this display is certain to prompt coolness. He wants to appear as a virile person to himself and to his wife, but does *not* want to be tested whether or not he is virile. His freedom here is freedom from sex! Consequently, through his covert message—lexically asking for love but in fact creating coolness—the husband can blame his wife for not being able to show whether or not he is virile; and, in addition, with this skillful message, he is contributing to an unhappy marriage. By sending covert messages without awareness, all of us obtain predictable and partially satisfying responses (Beier, 1966). This pattern enables people to "have their cake and eat it," to engage in a certain act and at the same time deny that they have done so. While all people appear to engage in such shifts of responsibility, the people we call "patients" appear to make such shifts more compulsively, and they do so predominantly in the most significant areas of their lives. They are caught and constantly engage in this "adaptive compromise." They make choices automatically and without awareness in these vulnerable and sensitive areas. By engaging repeatedly in these preferred behavior patterns, people avoid making choices for which they could be held responsible. They have reaped the benefit of being able to rationalize their behavior, and they have lost the ability to use their heads (See also Carson, 1969).

In Communications Analytic Therapy we assume that the patient's characteristic style of behaving occurs inevitably within the therapeutic hour. Here appear almost immediately the "engagement" patterns the patient is typically using for achieving the adaptive compromise. We assume that the patient will attempt to constrict the awareness of the therapist as he constricts awareness of others on the outside. Very soon the familiar engagement patterns of the patient emerge. When engagement succeeds with the therapist and the pattern is not recognized, the patient can mark up another success with his adaptive compromise, and the *status quo* can be maintained. When the therapist succeeds in recognizing the engagement patterns of the patient and responds to them adequately, the patient will be challenged to experiment with new choices.

New students of the Communications Analytic Therapy model are often distressed when supervisors point out (often after listening to the first few minutes of the treatment hour) exactly how their patients are succeeding in engaging them. But there is no reason to be frustrated upon such a discovery; the art of therapy is not in avoiding engagement, but in recognizing engagement and accomplishing disengagement. Students learn that in order to disengage and provide the patient with a sense of uncertainty about his unfortunate "adaptive compromise," the therapist must first listen carefully and fully understand the communication style of the patient. The therapist must specifically discover *how* the patient succeeds in constricting his own awareness of the conflicting motivations which he "appeases" with his adaptive compromise. This task becomes especially difficult because the patient not only limits his own awareness of such material, but has learned to communicate his compromise in a way that does not make this information easily available to the respondent either—which means that the therapist also is to stay unaware. In other words, the therapist faces the dual task of learning how the patient conceals his covert manipulations from self-awareness and from the awareness of others. Here the student needs most help. We typically ask the budding therapist: "What did the patient *say and do* so that you feel the way you do?" The student not only needs to learn that he got engaged, but he must discover what behaviors were responsible for engaging him. Students learn that patients are very skillful at the subtle art of engagement. The student can appreciate that the patient survives psychologically through the skill of using the adaptive compromises. The patient will make a great effort to cling to this compromise, which leads him to behaviors he can deal with, and not to accept uncertainty. Patients struggle against this sense of uncertainty until they start trusting the therapist because they are convinced that the therapist is caring. Once this is established, disengagement by the therapist from the emotional climate set by the patient interrupts the patient's routine. New options become possible and even necessary. The student in psychotherapy has to learn to show caring for the patient and to disengage from the social engagement patterns, in order to have the patient tolerate uncertainty.

Supervision is not merely an assistance to the beginning therapist; it is absolutely necessary, because the strength of the engagement patterns would reduce any therapeutic effort. For the untrained it is extremely difficult *not* to respond to the patient's communications in an expected or social fashion. This is even true in petty everyday communication. The untrained person is likely to respond with a conventional "thank you" to a patient's friendly gift, but the supervised therapist learns to disengage, to "metacommunicate," about the covert messages the client is sending (Kiesler, 1978). By responding to a gift with something like, "You need to show me that you care for me with something you bought for me," the therapist tries to give the patient the new experience that a gift is just another therapeutic event, and he passes the responsibility for the statement back to the person: He says to the patient, "Must you really express caring with spending money?" Responding asocially to the patient's message is the major vehicle for having the patient consider new options (Beier, 1966; Watzlawick, Weakland, and Fisch, 1974, p. 133). We believe that asocial, unexpected, or paradoxical responses (Beier, 1975, p. 27; Haley, 1977; Watzlawick, Beavin, and Jackson, 1965) will enable the patient to experience what we have called *"beneficial uncertainty."* The patient becomes *uncertain* because customary styles of communicating no longer produce expected responses. The uncertainty aroused can be *beneficial* because the asocial response comes from a caring person and occurs within the safe and empathic environment of the consulting room. The sting of uncertainty is cushioned by the special nature of the therapeutic alliance. When the patient is encouraged by such unexpected responses to try new ways to communicate interpersonally, the patient can do so because the protective setting of psychotherapy resembles a *play* situation: One can try out new things without the dire consequences one expects in "real" life.

Students are trained to learn to identify and respond to the patient's style of engagement; they are warned not to develop behaviorally oriented treatment goals. We believe that the therapist who invests interest in specific goals of the patient is necessarily increasing the propensity for engagement; he would not "hover evenly over all ideas," as Freud (1949 ed.) said. By definition, to aim for a specific goal must impede the patient's search for new options. The only goal acceptable to Communications Analytic Therapy is the concept that the patient is helped to search for new and ethical options in life and to accept responsibility for such options. While this goal does not seem to differ from those of many other models, an actual analysis of statements of other models shows other implied goals beyond the one stated here. This is not the place to go into detail, but briefly, psychoanalysis employs a health model, with health—rather than options—as its goal for humans; behavior modification uses a specified goal or target model; Rogerian psychotherapy centers on a growth model in which the patient is expected to go beyond the adaptive compromise; and in Gestalt therapy the model is one of "sophisticated" health, in which the patient's potential is to be developed as in self-actualization. In Communications Analytic Therapy, however, psychotherapeutic value is placed largely in the act of exploration itself, and the goal is to help the patient to question and vary his routines and accept the uncertainty which is a by-product of interpersonal exploration. Creativity, or the ability to make effective personal changes, can be seen as starting with this freedom to explore.

KNOW THY OUTPUT

In the Communication Analytic Therapy model, the budding therapist under supervision is evaluated on how well he understands the patient's communication, but even before that, he has to learn to understand the information he gives to the patient. The importance of therapists coming to an understanding of their own "communication" characteristic impact on the patient is seen as the first task of the supervisory meeting. The therapist's "output"—his own communications directed at the patient—influences the content and the style of the patient's messages. Just as the patient is responsible for eliciting desired behaviors from the therapist, the therapist is actively shaping the patient's content and style of communication.

Two forms of therapist output are usually examined in the supervision sessions. The first and most readable type of information is related to the identity of the therapist. Simple demographic or observable features such as the age, sex, race, and general appearance of the therapist often influence the patient's in-therapy behavior. The titled middle-aged gentleman who displays a silvering goatee and Viennese accent is bound to evoke different emotional climates (and responses) than a young black woman taking her first practicum course. Because therapists do not look or act alike (as some models actually assume), students should at least become aware of their impact on others. Students of psychotherapy can ill afford to neglect the lessons learned in research on person-perception (e.g., Cline, 1966).

The second type of therapist output monitored in Communication Analytic Therapy supervision is related to the typical engagement patterns of the therapist. This is *not* countertransference, that is, related to deep-seated problems of the therapist. It is what we have called "social countertransference" (Beier, 1966), or how to get caught in the social-manipulative skills of the patient. The issue is that therapists have a bias, an emotional attitude which is subject to easy engagement. Some therapists' output is clearly designed, albeit covertly, to get their patients to show them love or respect. Others have a "therapeutic urge" and want to heal the patient—as fast as possible. Others yet are cold and distant with an intellectual focus. Some others cannot conceive that they themselves may be a love object to the patient. All these characteristics, among many others, serve to give the patient the needed information to engage him at the most vulnerable place. When a therapist who likes to be liked is told that he *is* liked, this is likely to immobilize him and blind him to patient activities which are less flattering. Therapists ought to be aware of the weaknesses they have regarding social countertransference and the impact such a weakness has on the behavior of patients. We are all children of our culture, and we are likely to be affected by social information—and we can be sure that the patient, with a specifically directed communication pattern, will scan the therapist well enough to use his knowledge for his own protection, that is, to maintain his "adaptive compromises." If trainees were robots who issued behavioral orders, as some models have it, there would be no need to explore their proclivities for social countertransference. However, most human beings are equipped with personal needs and a response system to social information which is open to engagement.

We employ three general methods in helping students discover the impact of their output. They are: discussion of observed engagement pattern during the student's presentation of patient material; special Communication Analytic Therapy group marathon sessions; and finally (where we observe lasting engagement or "true countertransference") referral to therapy. It should be stressed that the goal of teaching students to understand their output is not an attempt to do psychotherapy, it is an attempt to alert students to disengage from social cues which have caught their attention too heavily. A referral to treatment is made only when the student is governed so heavily by problems that he no longer understands the patient properly. The therapist is the only instrument present in the therapeutic hour, and he cannot afford to be dull.

In reviewing a therapy tape, the supervisor has the dual task of exploring the engagement pattern of the therapist as well as the patient's messages that evoke engagement. In a typical session we would listen for a few minutes, pay special attention to the feelings the patient arouses in the therapist, the way in which it is done, and then analyze each response of the therapist which deals with these feelings.

A student saw a patient who apparently had made him angry. The supervisor asked him what had made him so angry. The student began to describe the constant barrage of depreciation the patient had fired at him. The supervisor suggested that this patient's constant negative output was probably the one which not only caused the therapist's engagement, but got the patient into trouble in the first place. From this stylistic pattern of the patient one does not yet learn *why* a patient gets into trouble, but one can get some convincing information on *how* he does it. His communications were directed at the student's inexperience, lack of skill, and nerve to set himself up as a helper ("Oh, I am your first case?"). The supervisor then asked the student what he should do to get the patient out of that preferred routine. It was clear that the student could not afford to be angry, because this would reinforce the patient's style—it was clearly the socially expected response. By disengaging from anger and responding with concern, the therapist might, however, help the patient to bring into doubt the expected consequences of depreciating behavior. Most students can "re-label" their relationship enough to overcome their socially aroused feelings and disengage, once they have been alerted to their engagement.

We have found Communication Analytic Therapy marathon groups to be one of the efficient vehicles by which students can learn about their own output. The supervisor usually calls for a marathon group of practicum students at an early time in the semester. It generally lasts for some six hours and serves to explore the students' own output. Intimate statements and catharsis are not encouraged. When students are in the protective environment of the class, all students in this Communication Analytic Therapy group become respondents to the target person. By avoiding intimate disclosure the target person can tune into his or her own characteristic styles of relating to others. The extended time is *not* designed to strip away defenses and get to core problems of each student. The marathon lasts until all students make the rounds and explore their impact on the other group members. The students are not seen as patients, and the analysis of their communication has no therapeutic intent to find out what he or she is "really like"; its only purpose is to help the student understand how he is *perceived* by others.

We have mentioned that referral to therapy helps certain students who especially need to become aware of and need to learn how to control their own output. Such referrals are the exception rather than the rule, yet we should also state that while we do not require it, we generally favor having students experience the other side of the therapeutic alliance, as we believe that the experience generally has beneficial effects on their own performance as therapists.

LEARNING TO LISTEN

A second major skill area that we attempt to teach in Communication Analytic Therapy is how to listen and what to listen for. The first hurdle—already discussed above—is for the students to learn to listen to their own emotional responses to the patient. Here we shall be looking at the dyad's interaction: the patient's messages as a stimulus, the therapist's internal response to these stimuli, and the formulation of his response message. It is essential that students learn to answer the phenomenological question "How does the patient make me feel?" We have noted that with beginning therapists patients often bring out a sense of helplessness in the therapist, in line with their resistance to disclose themselves. Consequently, we alert the students to their own "therapeutic urge" to heal fast. We teach our students to listen carefully for patients' use of "word cages," the communication equivalent of patients' resistance. Faulty labeling, blaming (shifting responsibility), and tautological thought processes are often apparent when the patients present their problems. They all serve resistance, and actually are the tools with which the patient gets himself into trouble. Another form of resistance is the patient's insistance on a nonresponse ("I couldn't face him!" or "I am just lazy"). We train students to recognize the no-response and to inquire just what the patient does instead: "I can't read my textbook"; "What do you do when you don't read your textbook?"; "I go skiing." We try to teach our students to be careful listeners—listening is the major tool of helping the therapist understand the patient's view of the world, and additionally, empathic listening is by itself a very important message to the patient: it conveys caring. The training of these listening skills will be discussed further.

We assume that patients communicate in ways that will emotionally engage others. In order to understand the patient, the therapist first needs to discover the emotional climate evoked in himself. The experienced therapist is able to identify *what* emotional climate the patient fashions through his style often without actually getting "engaged," but the new therapist will feel first and think later; he has to use himself as the measuring instrument. He or she will experience the patient through the patient's engagement patterns, and it is this experience which gives the therapist the information "where the patient hurts." It reveals to the therapist the part of the patient's personality which is likely to be in need of change. The simplest device of using one's self as a measuring instrument is to ask the question, "What does this patient want from me with his messages—and what sort of feeling is he trying to arouse in me to get it?"

In order to disengage from the patient's unconscious manipulations, the therapist—not the patient—must have insight into the nature of the patient's conflicts; the therapist must learn about the *how* and the *why* of the patient's style. When we ask students how the patient made them feel, we expect them to be able to talk about the "how," to give us a detailed description of the patient's stylistic output. The more precisely the student can describe the patient's most preferred automatic responses, the more adequate he will be to introduce uncertainty into the preferred pattern—not to destroy it, but merely to help the patient develop new options. *Why* the patient has adopted a certain style is more difficult to decode. We have two sources of information as to the why: One comes from the exploration of the style itself. The angry patient who has no friends possibly has a desire to see himself as a "loner" and may have learned early that commitment has too many strings attached. Often one gets support for the "why" from a content analysis of the patient's statements. A second source is contained in the sequential choices a patient makes once his routine is interrupted. The formerly angry patient may find his first friend after the intervention but be extremely sensitive to obligations to his new friends.

We have found the supervisory group to be an effective vehicle for training students in our model. Although students alternate in presenting cases, all of the group members are encouraged to share feedback about the case. Students with varying levels of experience are "mixed" in the supervisory group. When a patient is "presented" to the supervisory group, and the student talks about the case for a few minutes before playing a tape, the student often tips his emotional hand—and we are able to learn, indirectly, about the patient's conflicts and interpersonal style. In these short descriptions, the patient's emotional impact on the therapist becomes evident. During a recent supervisory session, a seemingly puzzled student was describing his first hour with a patient: "Well, I should get lots of practice with this guy. He told me he's stayed in every 'psych' ward in town and has run through three therapists at a mental health center. He says he is depressed, suicidal, and not too talkative. I really want you to hear him because I'm not sure what to do." The student's introductory remarks give the supervisor information about the patient's style of subtle influence, at least enough to form some preliminary hypotheses. Selecting from all the information provided by the patient in the initial hour, the student in his presenting the case centered on the patient's history of hospitalization and poor track record with several therapists. The student also made reference to his own lack of skill and need for practice and advice. We can reason at least hypothetically that the patient succeeded in engaging the student by presenting himself as a very challenging, experienced patient who has difficult and somewhat frightening problems, but who—once cured—would add immeasurably to the glory of the therapist. The total effect of this great challenge is to intimidate ("I am not sure what to do," the student confides), and we can begin by looking at the patient as one who intimidates others by oversized expectations. We encourage students to hypothesize but then flexibly look for support or rejection of the hypothesis in the patient's behavior. We find that the students' early hypotheses often are correctly reflecting the patient's style: The patient will bring all his skills into the confrontation with the stranger. The above patient has lost both his marriage as well as his relationship with his son as a result of his intimidating behavior.

It is easy for even the most experienced therapist to become intellectually and emotionally engaged by a patient's difficult past, socioeconomic constraints, or physical problems. Often the therapist obtains this information from the patient himself and develops a bias, an opinion on the patient. We teach students that they are not detectives, they cannot find out the truth of the many statements made, and they should not even try: They must center their attention on the data at hand, the *how* and the *why* of the patient's behavior.

Students often ask us whether we should not account for our own contributions to our feelings in the therapeutic hour rather than "blaming" it all on the patient. For example, when a student feels angry, perhaps he had a bad morning. We point out to the student that in order for the patient to manipulate the therapist the therapist must indeed have feelings of his own. One can only intimidate a person who has a propensity for intimidation, and the patient "plays" the therapist just where the therapist is perceived as vulnerable. This is another reason why the student should indeed know his own typical preferred behaviors: If he is generally intimidated by anger, he must learn to discount some of the patient's doing. This very possibility makes it important that the therapist know his own output and preferred behaviors.

LEARNING TO BE ASOCIAL

From our earlier analysis of the patient's distress, it follows that therapeutic messages must: (1) be disengaged from the emotional climate provided by the patient, and (2) must arouse uncertainty. This latter condition is actually the basis for most models of psychotherapy—at least from a communication theory point of view. We assume that the active ingredient in therapeutic gain is that the therapist behaves in an "asocial" or unexpected way in response to the patient's usual interaction style—in a setting that is reasonably free from threat and conveys a caring attitude.

The patient's statement "I hate my mother!" typically gets censorship ("How can you say that!) or agreement ("I hate mine too") in a social setting. A possible analytic response, "You are really afraid of your father," a Rogerian response "You feel very deeply about this," a Gestalt response "One of many feelings," or a paradigmatic Communication Analytic Therapy response, "The way you are saying it, I almost feel sorry for her," all have in common that: (1) they are "asocial," they are unexpected and arouse uncertainty, and (2) the responses bounce the "ball" back to the patient, they are conveying to the patient "You must deal with these feelings—I, the therapist, refuse to be your conscience." At first glance, the analytic, Rogerian, and Gestalt responses may not appear to be as asocial or unexpected as the communication-analytic response. However, they are asocial to the extent that they differ from a conventional or predictable reply.

There are good reasons why disengagement skills are difficult for students to master. As social human beings, we are all trained to respond in a conventional manner to the words and feelings of others. We usually respond gently to tears, obediently to authority, and with horror at violence. These response patterns are deeply ingrained and difficult to change. To make the training situation more immediate and like the therapy situation, we often train students in disengagement by analyzing responses to a hypothetical situation. We would ask all supervisory students to work together on this; one student would be instructed to make the critical statement, and all other students would find responses, first a social response, then a professional response from other schools, and then a Communication Analytic Therapy response. The class evaluates each response separately. The student playing a patient says: "I think my boss is unfair." First there is a round of expected social responses. A student simulating a friend says, "Amen, I sure know how that goes." One simulating a loyal supporter of the boss puts up a strong argument for the fairness of the boss. The group then discusses other varieties of social responses, and then goes to professional responses, all asocial. This task is designed to give the student a chance to show and defend his familiarity with other models. A student in a psychoanalytic vein offers the interpretation, "He reminds you of your father," and explains his choice of responses. A Rogerian simulation brought in by another student is "You are angry." A student interested in behavior therapy talks about constructing a program to reward only noncomplaining statements. The communications analytic therapist responds with a relationship comment: "You would like me to know that you are a victim to incompetent authority." All these statements are discussed for their disengagement value, and the degree of uncertainty they arouse.

Engagement is the patient's great expertise. Patients have had a lifetime of practice at their particular style of covert manipulation. Thus, at first encounter, patients are always more skillful than their therapists. We teach our students, then, that old covert manipulation patterns are not easily removed. When an attempt is made to extinguish the patient's response repertoire, it often follows the laws of learning theory: the response so singled out is likely to temporarily increase in frequency. But, as the patient does not get his familiar rewards, new ways of relating will be explored.

In prepracticum we often ask students to practice giving unexpected (friendly) responses. A student with a serious undertaker's face is encouraged to smile at people; a nondemonstrative girl to hotly embrace her friend; a stern mother given to saying no to most of the demands of her daughter, to surprise her daughter with an unexpected yes. Students enjoy these "games" because they often get to know the other person more intimately—they obtain responses to the novel behavior which they, too, would not have expected. The "no" mother said yes to a rock concert request of her daughter after a whole year of no's, and the daughter was so upset about the yes that she insisted that her mother would have to come along. The mother learned that she had become her daughter's conscience.

Students are not encouraged to imitate the supervisor. In Communication Analytic Therapy there is no response which all students should use at a given time. Instead, the student is encouraged to use his own best strength, his own style to bring across disengagement. He is trained to distinguish the emotional climate in which disengagement takes place. Disengagement can be injurious if it is not presented in a caring climate and it will fail to arouse beneficial uncertainty. A patient saying: "You must help me, I am in a terrible suicidal dilemma" is responded to with an accurate but cold and confrontive "ANOTHER ONE OF YOUR GAMES?"—a statement which can be easily understood as sarcastic and which does not express caring properly. The student has to learn to use himself as an instrument for conveying to the patient both disengagement and caring. There is a sense of challenge produced from the confronting qualities of disengagement. Yet, when coupled with caring, this challenge is thought to enhance the patient's readiness to accept uncertainty and hence the patient's readiness to make new choices. Some students couple confrontation and caring by a serious demeanor, some by laughing, some use a little more intellectualizing than others, and others are even moderately seductive or angry or bland. Within limits all students are trained to use the sort of "output" they are most familiar with (we do not encourage cloning) as long as they know what it is and as long as they can reasonably assess the impact they have on the patient. We teach that errors (faulty impact) are unavoidable ("The patient said I criticized him") and that the art of a good therapist is to listen—and to understand why a patient would feel criticized by an ambiguous cue. Just as the therapist wants the patient to ask the question "How did I contribute to my problem," so the therapist has to ask himself what he did to the relationship where a patient selects a cue to complain about being criticized.

In the Communication Analytic Therapy model the therapist can change the topic of discussion under two conditions: when he gets too anxious, or when he gets bored—that is, when he thinks he understands the patient's communication. These excuses are legitimate (though we would want to pay special attention to students who become too often anxious or bored), as the therapist is the major instrument present in the therapeutic hour, and there cannot be much help for the patient when the therapist is diverted in attention.

PUTTING IT ALL TOGETHER

When the student of Communication Analytic Therapy has developed listening and disengagement skills, the model will have several important consequences on his future conduct. The student will learn that there is no specific end point at which the therapist stops offering services. Even when the patient reports "progress," as in coming to a difficult decision, the therapist will maintain a consistent questioning attitude ("Must you do what you are doing?"). The therapist who chooses to congratulate the patient on a given choice teaches the patient only how to win praise from the therapist. In other words, there is no reward to be given for good behavior, no punishment for bad. There is no "health model" where the patient is declared well and healthy, no "skill model" where the patient has acquired new skills, not even an insight model where the patient knows himself better. All such models lend themselves too easily to engagement. Unless the patient is judged disoriented, dangerous to himself or others, he must arrive at the decision to let go of this help himself. Termination can only occur when the patient takes responsibility for his own behavior, including the exit from therapy. The patient then has learned to make his own choices and acts accordingly.

In order to present a variety of choices for limiting or ending the contact the patient can choose whether he wants to terminate or reduce the contact; he can choose biweekly, monthly, bimonthly, or even yearly contacts. In Communication Analytic Therapy we believe that the hypnotic quality of sharing responsibility for problems with the therapist several times a week can easily be a hindrance to recovery and that looser contacts should be explored. In fact we have experience with several patients whom we only see once a year, and THE HOUR is of great importance to them. When contact is merely reduced, we also allow for an extra hour now and then, as the need arises.

We feel that in Communication Analytic Therapy we get almost immediately to the heart of the patient's skill of creating his problems. By analyzing a patient's stylistic communication we recognize after a very few hours the distress as well as the pleasure of the patient's adaptive compromise which then permits the therapist to provide beneficial uncertainty through disengagement. The patient experientially, often *without* insight, begins to explore new choices. This form of therapy does not carry the unnecessary superimposed theoretical burden imposed by the Insight Model, Health Model, Skill Model, or even the Behavioral Model, and the patient can engage in exploration without first learning a new therapeutic language. Several of us practicing this form of psychotherapy believe it can significantly reduce the number of required contact hours for successful treatment.

Finally, we try to impress students with the need for continued supervision or control monitoring. Just as therapists should keep abreast of research developments in their field, we feel it is important that therapists be actively interested in the more personal experience of continued supervision. We have noted that all therapists experienced and otherwise become engaged by the social, manipulative, covert messages of their patients. Frequently, the patient is so skillful and the nature of this engagement is so subtle that it escapes the eye of even the most experienced therapist who works with a patient. Engagement creates misreading of communication and makes for faulty assessments. We teach our students, then, that even an experienced therapist who spends one hour a month with a competent professional can learn more quickly how to escape therapeutic quagmires.

To some extent Communication Analytic Therapy is vying for the status of a general theory (Beier, 1977). By relying on an analysis of communication we are looking at the simplest common denominator of all models, and this line of thinking would serve to eliminate some of the differences among models, particularly those which confuse *theories of change* with the more obtuse theories for achieving *mental health*. The simplest denominator for explaining therapeutic gain is in the principle of promoting exploration. When we teach Communication Analytic Therapy, we believe that we teach something akin to a basic model, which can stand on its own or may be the point of departure for those who wish to follow other orientations.

REFERENCES

Beier, E. G. On supervision in psychotherapy. *Psychotherapy: Theory, Research and Practice,* 1964, *1,* 91–95.

Beier, E. G. *The silent language of psychotherapy: Social reinforcement of unconscious processes.* Chicago: Aldine, 1966.

Beier, E. G. *People Reading.* New York: Stein and Day, 1975.

Beier, E. G. Toward a theory of nonverbal behavior. *New York Academy of Science, Psychology Section* Publications, (in press).

Carson, R. C. *Interaction concepts of personality.* Chicago: Aldine, 1969.

Cline, V. B. Interpersonal perception. In B. A. Maher (Ed.), *Progress in experimental personality research* (Vol. 1). New York: Academic, 1966.

Freud, S. *Collected papers* (Vol. 2), London: Hogarth Press, 1949.

Haley, J. *The power tactics of Jesus Christ and other essays.* New York: Grossman Publishers, 1969.

Haley, J. *Problem-solving therapy: New Strategies for effective family therapy.* San Francisco: Jossey-Bass, 1977.

Kiesler, D. J. *The process of psychotherapy: Empirical foundations and systems of analysis.* Chicago: Aldine, 1973.

Kiesler, D. J. A communication analysis of relationship in psychotherapy. Paper presented at the University of Minnesota Conference on Psychotherapy and Behavioral Intervention, Minneapolis, Minnesota, April, 1978.

Mahl, G. F. *Psychological conflict and defense.* New York: Harcourt Brace Jovanovich, 1971.

Ruesch, J. *Therapeutic communication.* New York: Norton, 1961.

Ruesch, J., and Bateson, G. *Communication: The social matrix of psychiatry.* New York: Norton, 1951.

Sullivan, H. S. *The interpersonal theory of psychiatry.* New York: Norton, 1953.

Sullivan, H. S. *The psychiatric interview.* New York: Norton, 1954.

Watzlawick, P., Beavin, J. H., and Jackson, D. *Pragmatics of human communication: A study of interactional patterns, pathologies, and paradoxes.* New York: Norton, 1967.

Watzlawick, P., Weakland, J. H., and Fisch, R. *Change: Principles of problem formation and problem resolution.* New York: Norton, 1974.

PART FOUR

Teaching Formats

Part IV, "Teaching Formats," describes four technologies of skill acquisition. Certainly several other chapters address issues of teaching technologies, but their focus dictated their placement in other parts of the book. Notably Rioch, who discusses group supervision, and Dies, who discusses group and cotherapy supervision, are pertinent. However, these four chapters provide techniques and structures for psychotherapy supervision. The four chapters are written by authors who are active in conducting training programs based on the models they describe. Each is committed to refining the models by way of research programs.

Chapter 16, *The Use of Role-Play and Simulation Techniques in the Training of Psychotherapy* by T. John Akamatsu, reviews the various simulation procedures, from role play to computer models, and the empirical foundations for their deployment. Chapter 17, *Vertical Supervision* by David S. Glenwick and Elizabeth Stevens, describes the structured use of more experienced peers to supervise those at a lower rung of the training ladder. Some of the advantages and drawbacks are discussed particularly as they apply in a university-based community-clinical training program. Chapter 18, *Microcounseling: An Approach to Differential Supervision,* by Douglas R. Forsyth and Allen E. Ivey, describes a comprehensive schema of the essential skills of counseling, and a coordinated system of training. Research that has been accumulated is summarized, and a system of analyzing major psychotherapy orientations into their component skills is presented. Chapter 19, *Influencing Human Interaction—Eighteen Years with IPR,* by Norman Kagan, describes a major training program in counselor education. The considerable research across cultures and client groups is presented.

CHAPTER 16

The Use of Role-Play and Simulation Techniques in the Training of

Psychotherapy

T. JOHN AKAMATSU

Role-play and simulation techniques have been utilized in the training of psychotherapy for over 20 years, but for a number of reasons they have not received the
attention which such a history of use might suggest. Although the beginnings of
their use in training can be traced back to Rogers' (1957) suggestion that beginning therapists should be eased into doing therapy through a series of graded steps
which gradually approximate therapy with real clients, and to Strupp's use of
filmed clients to study therapist effects in treatment (e.g. Strupp and Jenkins,
1963; Strupp and Wallach, 1965), the bulk of the current writing appears in the
counseling and paraprofessional training literature. In addition, most of the
empirical studies which have been carried out focus on the acquisition of basic
listening and communication skills. Psychotherapy trainers vary in the extent to
which they feel such skills are important in the practice of psychotherapy, hence
much of the literature may have been ignored. Both factors may be responsible
for the lack of attention afforded such techniques.

For the purposes of this chapter, however, a wide range of data sources have
been considered in an attempt to familiarize the reader with the varied simulation
approaches which have been utilized. Also to this end, reference will be made to
both descriptive and empirical studies. This approach will enable the reader to
select elements of various programs which might be applicable to his or her
unique needs and interests. In the present chapter in addition to literature review,
the program utilized at Kent State University will be described as an example of
the ways in which such techniques can be integrated into a clinical training
program.

A REVIEW OF THE LITERATURE

An overview of the literature on role-play and simulation techniques in psychotherapy training supports Flower's (1975) contention that the distinctions between these terms are not clear cut. Authors in the literature not only vary in their
definitions but also often utilize role-play, simulation, and modeling procedures

within the same training program. For these reasons, all three types of approach have been reviewed. In addition, computer simulations and multistage-integrated training programs will also be considered.

Descriptive Material

The earliest accounts of the use of role-playing as a training technique discuss its application in the training of counselors (Schwebel, 1953) and guidance counselors (Stripling, 1954). These authors and other more recent writers (e.g. Baldwin, 1973; Cody, 1974) suggest that role-playing is an effective method of training because it allows students to come face to face with "clients" with a much reduced risk of doing them harm. It allows for efficient use of time, develops involvement in the training process, allows trainees to experience the client role (hopefully with increased empathy), and can serve as an evaluative measure of competency. These benefits have been reiterated in a number of other descriptions of training programs which utilize role-play and simulation techniques.

Fleming and Hamburg (1958) describe the use of the "Dynamimetic Interview" in training psychiatric residents to do psychotherapy. In this approach, the supervisor plays the role of a patient with whom he is familiar and is interviewed by a resident in training. Observation of the interview by other trainees and subsequent discussion provide a rich training experience resulting in benefits beyond those gained in more traditional supervision.

Delaney (1969) and Spivack (1973) report the use of videotaped client behaviors in training counselors. Delaney utilizes such simulations to teach basic therapist behaviors such as working with a nontalkative client, or shaping the client to produce more affectively laden responses. Trainees interact with the videotaped clients and they are given feedback and further practice. Spivack focuses on utilizing simulations of "critical incidents" (e.g. manipulative, dependent, or hostile client behaviors). Rather than interacting with the simulated client, trainees recall and discuss their reactions to the tape and various ways of responding in the situation.

Still other modifications have been presented in the literature. Finney (1968) describes a semester-long role-playing program in which therapist and client meet biweekly for hour long role-played therapy sessions. Verbatim transcripts of each session are reviewed by the supervisor and feedback is provided. Boyarsky and Vance (1970) also describe a semester-long program which utilizes role-playing in conjunction with observation of ongoing therapy sessions. After one student observes the other, they discuss and role-play particular events which occurred in the actual session, thus providing feedback and practice in terms of elucidation of therapist's feelings, hypotheses concerning patient dynamics, and discovery and remediation of problems in therapist communication and technique.

Another variation of the use of role-play (Clements, 1976) involves the use of multiple therapists who, as a group, interact with a single client. The role-play is audiotaped and played back to the group. Feedback is provided to the trainees and opportunities to alter or refine responses are provided. Such an approach reduces anxiety associated with role-playing and allows for maximal learning, since a variety of therapist responses can be generated. Process considerations (e.g. reluctance to respond, dissatisfaction with responses) can be discussed.

Dillon (1976) and Zweben and Miller (1968) discuss role-play and simulation techniques in the training of family therapists. Dillon (1976) describes the training program utilized at the Family Therapy Institute of Marin, San Rafael, California. Simulated families with trainees playing roles of family members are utilized to familiarize trainees with the supervision process, to allow modeling of various therapeutic techniques, and to aid trainees in dealing with family issues. Zweben and Miller (1968) discuss the use of role-playing the four modes of communication based on Satir's formulation of family interaction. Each mode involves the use of a different set of rules of interaction. Such role-playing can be used as a training technique, for didactic purposes, and as a therapeutic intervention with families.

In addition, role-play and simulation have been utilized in training of other professional though nonpsychotherapeutic behaviors, such as a counselor involvement in PTA or teachers' meetings (Gysberg and Moore, 1970) or the clinician's role as a consultant in a community mental health center (Signell, 1974). Scheffler (1973) has used role-playing to sharpen students' assessment skills by assigning a diagnostic category to each student, who then researches and develops a role for a client from that category. The role is played out in an interview with a counselor in the presence of the whole class. Subsequent discussion focuses on issues relevant to the behaviors displayed and on treatment issues appropriate for the diagnostic category in question. Rose, Cayner, and Edelson (1977) report the development of a Behavioral Role-Play Assessment technique to measure interpersonal competence among social work students. Similar in nature to the device utilized in the assessment of assertiveness, trainees role-play various situations in which particular professional interpersonal behaviors (e.g. giving or seeking clarification, using appropriate affect) are required. Responses are rated by trained observers and scores can be derived both for general professional competence and competence in particular situations. Situations, client responses, and the scoring system were developed empirically. Medical students (Molnar, Kent, and Houser, 1973) and child abuse hot-line counselors (Kokes, 1976) have also been trained utilizing role-play and simulation. Lastly, Fitch (1975) reports on the development of a package of simulation materials to be utilized for the training of supervisors of counselors. Trainees, in this case, play the role of a supervisor with a videotaped supervisee.

Thus, a variety of behaviors, trainee populations, and variations in procedures have been presented in the literature. These articles have been descriptive in nature and no formal evaluation measures have been reported.

Empirical Studies

Perhaps the earliest investigation in which evaluative data on the effects of role-playing as a psychotherapy training device is presented is that of Thompson and Bradway (1950). To teach students to become more aware of nonverbal affective components in the interview situation, the authors had students role-play interviews without using words. Several affectively laden situations were acted out in this manner. Two experienced psychotherapists were able to correctly match interview recordings with affectively laden situations. Although no data is presented regarding the effectiveness of the technique as a training device, the authors report that students found the approach enlightening and did pay greater attention to expressed feelings in subsequent training experiences.

A number of studies in the literature have compared the effectiveness of role-playing training approaches with other methods of instruction. Pancrazio and Cody (1967) and Balinsky and Dispenzieri (1961) compared role-playing with lecture/discussion methods in the training of counselors. In the former study, role-playing was found to have no incremental effect in measures of knowledge or on performance on a task in which subjects were to choose the most appropriate response to brief excerpts of counseling sessions. In the latter study, students exposed to role-playing showed increased frequency of reflection and fewer probes, statements of reassurance, and ego-defensiveness in response to a tape-recorded simulated client than students exposed only to lectures and discussion. Because subjects exposed to role-playing had also received lecture and discussion treatments, the effectiveness of role-playing per se cannot be evaluated independent of the cumulative effects of all components in the student's experience.

In other studies with more adequate controls, the effects of role-playing are somewhat easier to identify. Panther (1971) found that school psychology students who had undergone a role-playing procedure were able to produce better recommendations in a subsequent test situation than were students who had undergone only the regular training program. Similarly, Peter (1973) found role-playing to be more effective in increasing ratings of response effectiveness and empathic understanding in the interview behavior of military science cadets compared with subjects who were exposed to normal training procedures. Newton (1974) found that residence hall paraprofessionals exposed to a role-play based training program displayed greater empathetic understanding, respect, and communicative understanding in a role-played test interview.

Goldstein and Goedhart (1973) employed a structured training program with modeling and role-playing components, and found that paraprofessionals' empathy scores improved significantly with training and that the increase was maintained after a one-month followup. Ferree (1975) reported that role-play training resulted in greater facilitation of communication skills and self-confidence as a counselor than did an identical training procedure which utilized problem discussion instead of role-playing. The training population in this case was a group of nursing students.

In contrast to the results of the aforementioned studies, Howard (1975) reported no differences in effectiveness of role-playing, discussion, or control groups in terms of rated empathy, respect, or genuineness among nursing students undergoing training to work with dying patients. Ratings were made on the nurses' responses to simulated patient statements. Similarly, Wells (1976) compared procedures which involved role-playing versus discussion of real life problems of trainees (social work students) and found no differences in rated empathy displayed in response to simulated client statements.

Lastly, Saltmarsh (1973) reported the effective use of a programmed instruction package which utilizes both written and tape-recorded material to train empathy. Subjects exposed to this package displayed greater empathy as measured by the Michigan Affective Sensitivity Scale.

Other empirical studies in role-playing as a training technique have examined some of the parameters of the procedure. Morrison (1974), for example, found that providing focused feedback on video-taped role-plays enhanced the levels of accuracy of empathy, genuineness, and unconditional warmth shown by counseling students in subsequent role-plays. Increases were noted in both verbal and nonverbal behaviors, and the effect was enhanced by continued feedback. Mader (1973) found that feedback provided to the subject during the role-play was more effective in enhancing reflective behavior than was delayed feedback. Both feedback conditions were superior to control conditions.

Flanagan (1973) compared student counselors trained with actual clients who were paid for participation versus role-played clients over a nine-week pre-practicum experience. No differences in rated accuracy of empathy, warmth, or genuineness were found for trainees exposed to the different types of clients. Approaching the issue of simulation versus real life clients from a somewhat different direction, Sigal, Lasry, Guttman, Chayoga, and Pilon (1977) compared therapist behaviors with real versus simulated (video-taped) families. They found that noncontent measures of therapist behaviors, such as average length and number of speeches, remained fairly constant across the simulated and real situations. However, content measures such as statements which stimulate interaction, ask for information, or provide an interpretation did not correlate across situations. These differences were attributed to the lack of feedback to the therapist when simulated families were used.

In an investigation designed to examine systematic bias in the rating of responses to simulated clients, Trotzky (1977) found that judges (trained advanced graduate students) gave higher ratings to responses of female counselor trainees, and that ratings for same-sex stimulus sequences were higher than opposite-sex responses. These findings warrant replication and have implications for research in the area since ratings of responses to simulated clients are a frequent dependent measure in much of the research in psychotherapy training.

In summary, the empirical studies on the utility of role-play are generally positive in their findings. Trainees of various sorts are able to learn basic listening and communication skills by role-playing, and feedback appears to facilitate the process. It would appear that the utility of role-playing procedures is most evident in situations involving measures based on interview behavior as opposed to situations in which discrete responses to simulated clients are evaluated. In somewhat artificial conditions in the single response simulation situation (e.g. lack of client feedback, discontinuity of the interaction) the types of skills learned in the role-play training may not have a chance to manifest themselves. In a similar way, the more realistic the role-play situation the greater is the transfer to therapy behavior.

Modeling Studies

As was mentioned before, modeling research is intimately tied in with the role-play and simulation literature. Modeling can be viewed as a simulation technique, and many of the studies to be discussed in this section utilized role-play and simulation as part of their treatments and/or to assess the outcome of training procedures. The literature can be divided into two categories: those studies which have investigated parameters of the modeling effect and those studies which have compared modeling with other training procedures.

In a series of studies (Payne and Gralinski, 1968; Payne, Weiss, and Kapp, 1972; Payne, Winter, and Bell, 1972) the effectiveness of audiotaped modeling of empathetic responses has been demonstrated. Subjects exposed to modeling consistently demonstrated greater rated empathy in response to simulated client statements than subjects who experienced no modeling.

A number of authors have designed studies to investigate the effects of the fidelity (i.e. degree to which the actual situation is approximated) of modeling techniques. Stone (1975) compared the effectiveness of a written manual, audiotape, videotape, or in-vivo modeling in increasing the production of counselor tacting response leads (CTRL). The CTRL is defined as any response which helps the client discuss abstract concepts in more concrete terms (Stone, 1975) and is thought to be a basic counseling skill. In this study, the effects of fidelity of practice conditions and mode of assessment (written or oral) were also assessed. The results suggested that subjects exposed to the high fidelity composite treatment made the most CTRLs. Interactions suggested that main effects for fidelity of model and fidelity of practice resulted from the overall poor performance of subjects exposed to the low fidelity composite treatment. Other treatment combinations were equally effective. The author interpreted these results as an indication that fidelity of model is not an important factor in the effectiveness of training and that less expensive audiotaped procedures could be utilized as effectively as video or in-vivo techniques. A similar conclusion was reached by Pratt (1974) who also investigated fidelity effects on the acquisition of CTRLs.

In contrast to these findings, Shepell (1974) found videotaped models to be more effective than audiotaped or written modeling procedures in the acquisition of reflection of feeling responses. These divergent findings might be explained in terms of the nature of the therapist response under investigation. The importance of fidelity of modeling treatment may vary as a function of factors such as frequency that target responses might occur in a therapy session, or the level of abstraction required to understand or utilize the response.

Among other studies of modeling parameters, Eskedal (1975) found that subjects exposed to a 30-minute videotaped interview, whose attention was directed towards desireable therapist behaviors learned more than subjects exposed to the tape without such cues. Both modeling groups performed better than control groups. The dependent measure in this case was the score received by the trainee on an objective true-false examination designed to assess integration of appropriate verbal and nonverbal therapist behaviors. Since the exam was closely related to the therapist behaviors depicted in the tape, the effectiveness of modeling treatments is not surprising; however, the additional benefit provided by focused attention is highlighted in the data. Goldstein, Cohen, Blake, and Walsh (1971) investigated the effects of the model's level of attraction towards the client on the acquisition of therapeutic behaviors among nursing personnel. They found that a high level of attraction resulted in greater warmth but not empathy in trainees' responses to simulated interviews. In another study of model/therapist attributes, Cook (1974) compared the effectiveness of initially apprehensive but ultimately successful peer models versus models who appeared calm and competent throughout the session. He found no differences in level of counselor performance as rated in a role-play interview; however, greater variability in performance was shown by subjects who had observed the expert model. Interestingly, these subjects also showed greater variability in rated level of anxiety in the interview session.

Lastly, Wilson (1975) designed a training strategy in which the trainee served as his or her own model. Selected portions of counseling sessions were shown to trainees prior to subsequent interviews. Not surprisingly, when these segments were systematically selected, greater improvement in skills such as reflection of affect and focusing on client statements occurred than when randomly selected segments were shown or when no self-modeling was experienced.

Other authors in the modeling literature have compared the effectiveness of modeling with other instructional techniques. The rationale in many of these studies has been to try to tease out the effects of various components of integrated training programs (to be discussed later in this chapter) in an attempt to identify the relative contribution of each component.

Modeling of effective therapeutic behavior has been compared with direct feedback in training therapist behaviors such as CTRLs in response to simulated client statements (Eisenberg and Delaney, 1970), and rated empathy in a simulated interview (Ronnestad, 1977; Gulanick and Schmeck, 1977). In each study, modeling was found to be more effective than feedback in facilitating acquisition of the desired behavior. Frankel (1971) compared single presentations of modeling or feedback, a combined modeling-feedback condition, and a reading control group. Within groups, modeling was found to be more effective than feedback alone, in terms of rated counselor effectiveness; however, when initial differences were taken into account modeling, feedback, and combined conditions were all found to be more effective than the control procedure. When modeling preceded feedback in the combined condition, the greatest behavior change was found.

Modeling and instructions have also been compared. Perry (1975) found that ministers exposed to high empathy modeling displayed more empathy in responding to a simulated (taped) client than subjects exposed to low empathy models or no model. Instructions had no effect on empathy. In a generalization test involving a role-played interview, neither modeling nor instructions resulted in increases in empathy. Uhlemann, Lea, and Stone (1976) found that instructions and instructions plus modeling were more effective than modeling alone or a control condition in determining the proportion of reflection of feeling responses made by trainees in a role-play interview measure. In terms of rated empathy scores, the combined instruction-modeling groups performed better than either approach by itself. Kuna (1975) studied the effects of lecture, reading, and modeling on the acquisition of the restatement response which involves verbatim repetition of the client's words without interpretation. The design of the study (four treatment conditions: control, lecture alone, lecture plus reading, and lecture, reading, modeling) does not allow the effectiveness of each component to be assessed individually. As might be expected, he found the lecture alone group made more restatement responses to simulated client statements than controls, and that lecture-reading subjects produced more restatements than lecture alone subjects. The addition of modeling did not increase production of restatements. The efficacy of modeling in this study cannot be directly evaluated since no modeling alone condition was utilized. It is likely that a simple response such as restatement could more easily be acquired through instructions, while a more complex response like an empathetic one might be best learned through a modeling approach.

Finally, the effects of modeling and role-playing techniques in the training of therapeutic behaviors have been assessed. Shaw (1975) found that a combined modeling role-play procedure was effective in increasing reflections of feelings as measured by scores on the Counselor Effectiveness Rating Scale. No effects were noted in regard to other types of verbal responses (e.g. attending, verbal following, paraphrasing).

The effect of modeling, feedback, and role-playing on performance in a simulated interview situation were examined by Bailey, Deardorff, and Nay (1977). Modeling was found to be the most effective training procedure, with feedback second and role-playing third. The authors indicated that role-playing alone had almost no effect on interview behaviors. Instructions, modeling and role-playing with feedback, and the various combinations thereof were compared by Stone and Vance (1976). On a written measure all treatment groups improved in empathy from pre-to post-test with the exception of the no treatment control. Post-hoc analyses revealed that the presence or absence of the instructions component was the critical determinant of empathy. For empathy ratings based on verbal responses to simulated clients it was found that combined treatments performed better than those treatments involving only one kind of training procedure. In this case, post-hoc tests revealed that modeling was the most critical determinant of empathy scores.

In summary, it appears quite evident that modeling approaches to training are effective in teaching basic therapy skills. The utility of modeling approaches seems most evident in cases in which the behavior to be acquired is complex as opposed to simple (e.g. empathy versus restatement), and in those cases in which the response measure more closely approximates actual interview behavior (e.g. role-play interviews versus written responses to client statements or true false exams).

The importance of modeling component prior to role-play training and the value of focused feedback is also highlighted in the results of the studies which have been reviewed.

Computer Simulations

Advances in computer technology have enabled the development of computer simulations of psychodiagnostic and therapy interviews. Computer programs have been developed so that trainees may interact with the machine in a fairly realistic manner, as therapist or client. Basic programming consists of a sequential or adaptive multistage decision process (Bellman, Friend and Kurland, 1966) in which responses of the computer are determined by responses made by trainees in accordance with rules established by the program. Trainee and computer thus interact with each other in a dynamic process which approximates actual interviewing.

Starkweather, Kamp, and Monto (1967) describe the simulation of both client and interviewer roles in psychiatric diagnostic interview situation, and Hummel, Lichtenberg, and Schaffer (1975) describe a program which simulates an initial counseling interview. Helge (1972) compared reactions of both inexperienced and experienced therapists to live versus computer simulated clients. He reported that subjects found the computer simulation to be realistic; however, consistency in style of response to live versus computerized clients was shown only by experienced therapists.

Computer simulations thus provide useful training experiences in both diagnostic and therapy situations. Starkweather, et al. (1967) reiterate the utility of trainees' playing client roles as was the case with role-plays in terms of empathetic gains. Hummel, et al. (1975) indicate that the explicitness and consistency in computer simulation provide benefits beyond regular role-playing since interventions may be repeated over and over again, or alternate responses can be attempted with consistent outcome. Because of the controlled nature of the simulated environment it also can be utilized productively as a research device. Precise records of the therapy interaction can be obtained and therapy process can be critically examined. In fact, the development of new computer programs itself can be a potent teaching device since a knowledge of the theory and pragmatics of personality and psychotherapy is required for the development of realistic programs.

Integrated Training Programs

A number of integrated programs which utilize role-playing as one component in the training package are currently available. Two of the most popular programs, those of Kagan and Ivey, are discussed in other chapters of the present volume.

The other leading training program is that of Carkhuff and his colleagues (e.g., Truax and Carkhuff, 1967; Carkhuff, 1969). The "didactic-experiential" approach to training effective therapist behaviors (empathy, nonpossessive warmth, and genuineness) employs role-playing in several stages of training. After listening to therapy tapes of experienced therapists, students practice making responses to audiotaped client statements. Feedback is provided regarding correctness of content, voice quality, and so on. In later stages of training extended interactions are used, culminating in the role-playing of an entire session. Throughout feedback, modeling by the trainer and group discussion are utilized. This procedure has been extended to use in training paraprofessionals (Carkhuff, 1971) and educators (Gazda, 1973).

Similar training programs have been developed by other authors who have developed further innovations in the use of role-play. Danish and Hauer (1973), for example, include modeling and practice of low level skills along with subsequent high level modeling and practice. Brammer (1973) describes a procedure he calls "round robin trio helping" in which triads rotate playing therapist, client, and observer, such that all participants play each role. Process discussion follows each of the three role plays. Another variation involves a group procedure in which three trainees leave the room while the rest of the group develops a client role. Trainees are brought in individually to play the role of therapist. This procedure allows comparison of therapist styles as well as feedback from the group "client."

Thus, role-playing is an integral part of many of the packaged training programs which have been developed. Because it is only one component in the package it is difficult to determine the unique effectiveness of role-playing itself.

THE KENT STATE PROGRAM

The purpose of the present section is to provide an example of how role-playing techniques can be integrated onto an on-going clinical training program. While the role-playing components are utilized in other programs (Brown, 1978; Carson, 1978), descriptions in the literature are lacking. The Kent State program is still evolving but the lessons we have learned may be helpful to the reader.

Among the reasons for the adoption of role-playing in our training program was the underlying assumption that basic listening and communication skills were important regardless of the theoretical orientation that one might hold. These skills are seen as necessary but not sufficient for effective psychotherapy. At the same time, students who are just beginning to conduct psychotherapy experience a great deal of anxiety about their performance. In an attempt to reduce this anxiety, role-playing and simulation techniques were instituted. Students at this level are very positive about structured kinds of experiences which at least initially give them some sense of what to do.

Our practicum is carried out through a departmental psychological clinic which serves both students and community clients. Thus, service delivery needs also influenced the adoption of these techniques. It was felt that beginning therapists with at least basic skills would be more effective and less potentially harmful than students without them.

In the first year of graduate school students are involved in a pre-practicum experience which consists primarily of Ivey's (1971) microcounseling program with the addition of one or two microlab sessions in which students' concerns about becoming therapists are discussed. Students also learn to process role-plays utilizing Kagan's IPR procedure (Kagan, Schauble, Resnikoff, Danish, and Krathwohl, 1969). Training objectives in this portion of the program are the acquisition of basic listening and communication skills, practice in interpersonal process recall, and familiarization with basic procedures involved with the Psychological Clinic.

Beginning in the summer between their first and second years, students become involved in the practicum and begin to see clients through the departmental training clinic. In addition to seeing clients under supervision, the training program is continued on a biweekly basis. The focus of these sessions is on learning specific skills which are often needed in dealing with clients who are seen through the clinic. Topics include: determination of suicidal risk in a severely depressed client, dealing with an acutely psychotic client, dealing with an acute anxiety reaction, and dealing with demanding, seductive, manipulative, and aggressive clients.

In each session a didactic presentation covering basic treatment issues relevant to the topic is made. Videotaped modeling sequences of appropriate therapist behaviors are shown and discussed. Then students break up into triads to role-play and process the problem situation. The group meets as whole following the role-playing and processing to discuss general issues (e.g. common problems, innovative interventions).

It should be noted that this program is viewed as supplementary to the ongoing training process which is more traditional in nature, (supervision, faculty presentations, case conferences), and is obviously not a substitute for it. As such, it has been accepted without much controversy by members of the clinical faculty as an integral part of the clinical training program. Student reaction has been quite enthusiastic, although we have found that introduction of role-playing early in graduate training is an important factor. When introduced later, reactions are somewhat less positive—perhaps because students feel more threatened after some training has already occurred and some level of competence is expected.

Even among less enthusiastic individuals, subsequent situations requiring skills that had been role-played were found to be far less anxiety provoking. A number of such reports have reinforced our positive feelings about the utility of the training procedure. We are currently in the process of collecting data on the efficacy of the training program. Preliminary results indicate significant improvement in discriminative skills following the pre-practicum experience as compared to a traditional academic control group (Aronson, 1978). Other data, including supervisor ratings of effectiveness, treatment outcome measures, and so on, are still in the process of being analyzed.

CONCLUSIONS

It is thought that the foregoing discussion is generally indicative of the utility of role-playing and other simulation techniques in the teaching of psychotherapy. Such techniques have been utilized in a wide variety of ways to provide a safe learning situation which can be designed to approximate real life therapy situations. Both basic and more complex therapist behaviors can be acquired and practiced; and client behaviors, feelings, and reactions can be experienced and thus be more fully understood. Modeling of appropriate behaviors and provision of feedback through observation by the supervisor or through a processing procedure are important components in the learning experience. As Schwebel (1953) pointed out, such techniques bring the student face to face with reality; intellectualization or only partial description of what went on in the session are eliminated as blocks to the supervision process.

More general benefits are also apparent. Baldwin (1973) indicates that the use of role-play and simulation can enhance commitment and involvement of students in their training program. Practice in the giving and receiving of feedback facilitates the flow of information regarding interpersonal behaviors which can be invaluable not only in therapy training, but in other aspects of graduate training. Our experiences support this contention. Our students appear less defensive and more open to suggestions and support from both faculty and peers.

Some cautions in the use of such techniques are also warranted. Role-playing can be an anxiety producing situation so it must be introduced in a nonthreatening way, and early in training before students have a chance to become defensive about their effectiveness as therapists. If not carefully introduced, planned out, and integrated into an ongoing program, role-playing can become very superfical. Trainers must model not only appropriate therapy behaviors, but also nonthreatening giving of feedback and supportive behaviors. Trainers should also guard against overconfidence among their trainees, and must be sure that inappropriate therapy behaviors are not reinforced (e.g. overintellectualized therapist responses or lack of response to affective material).

The literature suggests that role-playing approaches are most effective in teaching behaviors which are assessed in more realistic situations as opposed to less realistic simulated situations. Since the goal of training is therapist behavior change in real life psychotherapy, the added benefits provided by role-playing over instructions or modeling procedures alone seem to warrant its use. Combined (didactic, modeling, and role-play) training programs appear to be most effective, and role-playing alone is not sufficient for learning of effective therapeutic behaviors.

Several issues remain for future research. Foremost among these is the question of the utility of training basic therapist skills, as so often has been done in the role-play/simulation literature. In a recent review article, Lambert, DeJulio, and Stein (1978) have concluded that the utility of such training has not yet been adequately demonstrated in the literature. Clearly, more research is required in this regard.

Moreover, the bulk of the role-play/simulation literature to date focuses on therapist behaviors derived from the client centered model of treatment. Investigation of the use of role-play/simulation in the training of theoretically divergent and more complex therapist behaviors should be carried out. While a few attempts in this direction have been reported above, many other potential applications remain untested.

Another question which has received only minimal attention in the literature is that of generalization of training effects to actual therapy behaviors. Effectiveness of training has been assessed in role-play interviews, at best. Observation of actual therapy interviews, feedback from clients, and evaluation by subsequent supervisors are suggested as more appropriate dependent measures.

Lastly, the effectiveness of role-play/simulation training in therapy outcome has not yet been adequately demonstrated. This situation, of course, is not unique to the role-play/simulation literature. Problems inherent in psychotherapy outcome research are multiplied when evaluation of training is attempted. Successful attempts in the evaluation of training are few, and further progress awaits the ingenuity and inventiveness of future investigators.

REFERENCES

Aronson, D. *A beginning evaluation of the Psychology Department's practicum training program.* Unpublished manuscript, 1978.

Bailey, K. G., Deardoff, P., and Nay, W. R. Students play therapist: Relative effects of role-playing, videotape feedback, and modeling in a simulated interview. *Journal of Consulting and Clinical Psychology,* 1977, *45,* 257–260.

Baldwin, B. A. A developmental training strategy for use with role-playing techniques. *Journal of College Student Personnel,* 1973, *14,* 477–482.

Balinsky, B., and Dispenzieri, A. An evaluation of the lecture and role-playing methods in the development of interviewing skills. *Personnel and Guidance Journal,* 1961, *9,* 583–585.

Bellman, R., Friend, M., and Kurland L. Simulation of the initial psychiatric interview. *Behavioral Science,* 1966, *11,* 389–399.

Brammer, L. M. *The helping relationship: process and skills.* Englewood Cliffs, N.J.: Prentice Hall, 1973.

Boyarsky, R. E., and Vance, T. G. The use of role-play in psychotherapy training. *Group Psychotherapy and Psychodrama,* 1970, *23,* 35–40.

Brown, O. H. Personal communication, October 1977.

Carkhuff, R. R. *Helping and human relations: A primer for lay and professional helpers* (2 vols.) New York: Holt, Rinehart and Winston, 1969.

Carkhuff, R. R. *The development of human resources.* New York: Holt, Rinehart and Winston, 1971.

Carson, R. C. Personal communication, November, 1977.

Clements, C. J. Group helper: A training technique. *Counselor Education and Supervision,* 1976, *16,* 66–68.

Cody, J. J. Role-playing with stimulated recall. In G. F. Farwell, N.R. Gamsky, and F. Mathiew-Coughlan, (Eds.). *The counselor's handbook,* New York: Intext, 1974.

Cook, D. W. The effects of differential modeling strategies on counselor performance, anxiety, and tolerance of ambiguity (Doctoral dissertation, University of Missouri— Columbia, 1974). *Dissertation Abstracts International,* 1975, *36,* 127A. (University Microfilms No. 75-15, 979)

Danish, S., and Hauer, A. *Helping skills: A basic training program.* New York: Behavioral Publications, 1973.

Delaney, D. J. Simulation techniques in counselor education: A proposed unique approach. *Counselor Education and Supervision,* 1969, *8,* 183–189.

Dillon, I. L. Teaching models for graduate training in psychotherapy. *Family Therapy,* 1976, *3,* 151–162.

Eisenberg, S., and Delaney D. J. Using video simulation of counseling for training counselors. *Journal of Counseling Psychology,* 1970, *17,* 15–19.

Eskedal, G. A. Symbolic role modeling and cognitive learning in the training of counselors. *Journal of Counseling Psychology,* 1975, *22,* 152–155.

Ferree, E. H. The effects of using contrived role-plays and real life experiences in practice trials of human relations training (Doctoral dissertation, The American University, 1975). *Dissertation Abstracts International,* 1976, *36,* 3599B. (University Microfilms No. 76,815).

Finney, B. C. Some techniques and procedures for teaching psychotherapy. *Psychotherapy: Theory, Research and Practice,* 1968, *5,* 115–119.

Fitch, J. M. The development of simulation materials for the training of counseling supervisor's awareness in issues of supervision (Doctoral dissertation, University of Pittsburgh, 1975). *Dissertation Abstracts International,* 1976, *36,* 5820A–5821A. (University Microfilms No. 76-5437)

Flanagan, W. M. An examination of the effects of the use of paid and role-played clients in a full-time day Masters pre-practicum (Doctoral dissertation, University of Pittsburgh, 1973). *Dissertation Abstracts International,* 1974, *34,* 4738A–4739A. (University Microfilms No. 74-1548)

Fleming, J., and Hamburg, D. Analysis of teaching psychotherapy with description of a new approach. *Archives of Neurology and Psychiatry,* 1958, *79,* 179–200.

Flowers, J. V. Simulation and role-playing methods. In F. H. Kanfer and A. P. Goldstein (Eds.), *Helping people to change.* New York: Pergamon, 1975.

Frankel, M. Effects of videotape, modeling, and self confrontation techniques on microcounseling behavior. *Journal of Counseling Psychology,* 1971, *18,* 465–471.

Gazda, G. M. *Human relations development: A manual for educators.* Boston: Allyn and Bacon, 1973.

Goldstein, A. P., and Goedhart, A. The use of structured learning for empathy enhancement in paraprofessional psychotherapy training. *Journal of Community Psychology,* 1973, *1* 168–173.

Goldstein, A. P., Cohen, R., Blake, G., and Walsh, W. The effects of modeling and social class structuring on paraprofessional psychotherapist training. *Journal of Nervous and Mental Disease,* 1971, *153,* 47–56.

Gulanick, N., and Schmeck, R. R. Modeling, praise, and criticism in teaching empathic responding. *Counselor Education and Supervision,* 1977, *16,* 284–290.

Gysberg, N. C., and Moore, E. J. Using simulation techniques in the counseling practicum, *Counselor Education and Supervision,* 1970, *9,* 277–284.

Helge, A. S. Computer simulation of counseling interviews as a means of comparing diverse styles of dyadic interaction (Doctoral dissertation, University of Texas at Austin, 1972). *Dissertation Abstracts International,* 1973, *33,* 3383A. (University Microfilms No. 73-453)

Howard, M. S. The effectiveness of action training model (using role-playing, doubling, and role reversal) in improving the facilitative interpersonal functioning (empathy, respect, and genuineness) of nursing students with dying patients (Doctoral dissertation, University of Maryland, 1975). *Dissertation Abstracts International,* 1975, *36,* 3005B–3006B (University Microfilms No. 75-28,744)

Hummel, T. J., Lichtenberg, J. W., and Shaffer, W. F. Client 1: A computer program which simulates client behavior in an initial interview. *Journal of Counseling Psychology,* 1975, *22,* 164–169.

Ivey, A. *Microcounseling: Innovations in interview training.* Springfield, Ill.: Charles C. Thomas, 1971.

Kagan, N., Schauble, P., Resnikoff, A., Danish, S. J., and Krathwohl, D. R. Interpersonal process recall. *Journal of Nervous and Mental Disease,* 1969, *148,* 365–374.

Kokes, J. H. Simulated calls on a crisis hotline (Doctoral dissertation, Northwestern University, 1976). *Dissertation Abstracts International,* 1977, *37,* 6952A–6953A. (University Microfilms No. 77-10,051).

Kuna, D. J. Lecturing, reading, and modeling in counselor restatement training. *Journal of Counseling Psychology,* 1975, *22,* 542–546.

Lambert, M. J., DeJulio, S. S., and Stein, D. Therapist interpersonal skills: Process, outcome, methodological considerations and recommendations for future research. *Psychological Bulletin,* 1978, *85,* 467–489.

Mader, P. E. Differential effects of immediate and delayed feedback in role-playing counseling sessions (Doctoral dissertation, University of Southern Mississippi, 1973). *Dissertation Abstracts International,* 1974, *34,* 3878A–3879A. (University Microfilms No. 73-32,014).

Molnar, E. T., Kent, J. T., and Houser, A. C. Role-playing in preparing junior medical students for psychiatric interviewing. *Small Group Behavior,* 1973, *4,* 157–162.

Morrison, J. L. The effects of videotape focused feedback on levels of facilitative conditions (Doctoral dissertation, University of North Dakota, 1974). *Dissertation Abstracts International,* 1975, *36,* 712A. (University Microfilms No. 75-18,018)

Newton, F. B. The effects of systematic communication skills training on residence hall para-professionals. *Journal of College Student Personnel,* 1974, *15,* 366–369.

Pancrazio, J. J., and Cody, J. J. A comparison of role-playing and lecture-discussion instructional methods in a beginning course in counseling theory. *Counselor Education and Supervision,* 1967, *7,* 60–65.

Panther, E. E. Simulated consulting experiences in counselor preparation. *Counselor Education and Supervision,* 1971, *11,* 17–23.

Payne, P. A., and Gralinski, D. M. Effects of supervisor style and empathy upon counselor learning. *Journal of Counseling Psychology,* 1968, *15,* 517–521.

Payne, P. A., Weiss, S. D., and Kapp, A. Didactic, experiential, and modeling factors in the learning of empathy. *Journal of Counseling Psychology,* 1972, *19,* 425–429.

Payne, P. A., Winter, D. E., and Bell, G. E. Effects of supervisor style on the learning of empathy in a supervision analogue. *Counselor Education and Supervision,* 1972, *11,* 262–269.

Perry, M. A. Modeling and instructions in training for counselor empathy. *Journal of Counseling Psychology,* 1975, *22,* 173–179.

Peter, M. H. A short-term program to teach facilitative communication skills to military science cadets. (Doctoral dissertation, Michigan State University, 1973). *Dissertation Abstracts International,* 1973, *34,* 3068A. (University Microfilms No. 73-29,761)

Pratt, G. W. The effects of high and low fidelity simulation on counselor training as measured in high and low fidelity performance situations. (Doctoral dissertation, University of Virginia, 1974). *Dissertation Abstracts International,* 1975, *35,* 4166A-4167A. (University Microfilms No. 74-29,202)

Rogers, C. Training individuals in the therapeutic process. In C. Strother (Ed.), *Psychology and Mental Health,* Washington, D.C.: American Psychological Association, 1957.

Ronnestad, M. H. The effects of modeling, feedback, and experiential methods on counselor empathy. *Counselor Education and Supervision,* 1977, *16,* 194–201.

Rose, J. D., Cayner, J. J., and Edelson, J. L. Measuring interpersonal competence. *Social Work,* 1977, *22,* 125–129.

Saltmarsh, R. E. Development of empathetic interviewing skills through programmed instruction. *Journal of Counseling Psychology,* 1973, *20,* 375–377.

Scheffler, L. W. Helping counselors understand emotional disturbance through role-playing. *Counselor Education and Supervision,* 1973, *13,* 72–75.

Schwebel, M. Role-playing in counselor training. *Personnel and Guidance Journal,* 1953, *32,* 196–201.

Shaw, M. W. The effects of automated group desensitization and symbolic modeling plus role-rehearsal on beginning counselor-trainees' state anxiety. (Doctoral dissertation, Washington State University, 1975). *Dissertation Abstracts International,* 1976, *36,* 5060A. (University Microfilms No. 76-4381)

Shepell, W. E. Encouraging reflection of feeling through modeling as a function of communication mode in counselor preparation. (Doctoral dissertation, University of Pennsylvania, 1974). *Dissertation Abstracts International,* 1975, *35,* 4153B. (University Microfilms No. 75-2776)

Sigal, J. J., Lasry, J. C., Guttman, H., Chayoga, L., and Pilon, R. Some stable characteristics of family therapists interventions in real and simulated therapy sessions. *Journal of Consulting and Clinical Psychology,* 1977, *45,* 23–26.

Signell, K. A. An interaction method of teaching consultation: Role-playing. *Community Mental Health Journal,* 1974, *10,* 205–215.

Spivack, J. D. Critical incidents in counseling: Simulated video experiences for training counselors. *Counselor Education and Supervision,* 1973, *12,* 263–270.

Starkweather J., Kamp, M., and Monto, A. Psychiatric interview simulation by computer. *Methods of Information in Medicine,* 1967, *6,* 15–23.

Stone, G. L. Effect of simulation on counselor training. *Counselor Education and Supervision,* 1975, *14,* 199–203.

Stone, G. L., and Vance, A. Instructions, modeling, and rehearsal: Implications for training. *Journal of Counseling Psychology,* 1976, *23,* 272–279.

Stripling, R. O. Role-playing in guidance training programs. *Teacher's College Record.* 1954, *55,* 425–429.

Strupp, H. H., and Jenkins, J. The development of six sound motion pictures simulating psychotherapeutic situations. *Journal of Nervous and Mental Disease,* 1963, *136,* 317–328.

Strupp, H. H., and Wallach, M. S. A further study of psychiatrists' responses in quasi-therapy situations. *Behavioral Science,* 1965, *10,* 113–134.

Thompson, C. W., and Bradway, K. The teaching of psychotherapy through content free interview. *Journal of Consulting Psychology,* 1950, *14,* 321–323.

Trotzky, A. S. An investigation to determine the existence of sex bias in counselor-trainee responses to a video-based simulation. (Doctoral dissertation, Oregon State University, 1977). *Dissertation Abstracts International,* 1977, *37,* 6962A (University Microfilms No. 77-10,450)

Truax, C. B., and Carkhuff, R. R. *Towards effective counseling and psychotherapy.* Chicago: Aldine, 1967.

Uhlemann, M. R., Lea, G. W., and Stone, G. L. Effects of instructions and modeling on trainees low in interpersonal-communication skills. *Journal of Counseling Psychology,* 1976, *23,* 509–513.

Wells, R. A. A comparison of role-play and "own problem" procedures in systematic facilitative training. *Psychotherapy: Theory, Research and Practice,* 1976, *13,* 280–281.

Wilson, S. H. Determining the effects of two differential self-modeling techniques on the acquisition of appropriate counseling behaviors of counselor trainees. (Doctoral dissertation, University of Tennessee, 1975). *Dissertation Abstracts International,* 1976, 5066A–5067A. (University Microfilms No. 76-1996)

Zweben, J. E., and Miller, R. L. The systems games: Teaching, training, psychotherapy. *Psychotherapy: Theory, Research and Practice,* 1968, *5,* 73–76.

CHAPTER 17

Vertical Supervision

DAVID S. GLENWICK AND ELIZABETH STEVENS

The vertical supervision model is perhaps the most well-known and popular of the several alternatives that have arisen as an outgrowth of criticisms of the traditional models of supervision and mental health services delivery. After a brief overview of the most commonly perceived shortcomings of the conventional supervision format and of some proposed alternatives to this format, the present chapter will attempt to define vertical supervision, emphasizing the concepts and components that appear to be integral to the approach. The potential advantages and dangers—competency-related, affective, and organizational—of such a hierarchical supervision arrangement will then be discussed, followed by examination of the complex relationships of vertical supervision to community psychology. The chapter will conclude by highlighting the special problems involved in interdisciplinary vertical supervision and by suggesting some directions that research on vertical supervision might take.

SOME SHORTCOMINGS OF THE TRADITIONAL SUPERVISORY STRUCTURE

Since the advent of the psychodynamic therapies, the modal format for psychotherapy supervision has involved a professional (usually certified or licensed) supervisor meeting individually with a trainee for an hour per week to discuss the trainee's cases. While such a format would appear to serve the purposes of supervision well, the extent to which it may actually hinder learning, decrease a trainee's sense of self-esteem and importance, and lead to affective problems can be raised as legitimate concerns. One ostensible function of supervision, for example, is to provide the trainee the opportunity to express feelings regarding clients, the trainee's lack of self-confidence, and other concerns. This can prove to be a difficult task for the trainee who finds him/herself in an evaluative setting with a professional, causing supervision to become a secretive, stilted ordeal that precludes accurate reporting of therapy sessions or trainee emotions. As Barnat (1973) noted in reflecting upon his own experience, the supervisor may appear as guarded as the trainee, creating a mutually tense encounter between the two. Such an emotional climate, in combination with the demand characteristics of the situation, is unlikely to produce the ideal learning environment.

Of equal importance is the effect that an authoritarian relationship may have upon the supervisor's ability to deal directly with any personal problems of the trainee that interfere with therapy (Gaoni and Neumann, 1974). Such a relationship, in fact, can itself result in iatrogenic negative effects, with deterioration of the trainee's self-concept and self-esteem being an inherent risk in this evaluative setting. Abramowitz, Weitz, and James (1974), for instance, followed 18 trainees during three months with supervisors who exhibited deviancies in their own self-concepts. While the trainees began the program with less deviant self-concepts than their supervisors'; as measured by the Tennessee Self-Concept Scale, all trainees increased in their degree of psychological disturbance over the three-month period.

In addition to the clinically-oriented concerns that have been raised regarding the traditional supervisory format, one-to-one supervision can be questioned on organizational, cost efficiency grounds. In individual supervision, the time demands on the professional mount rapidly if he/she assumes supervisory responsibility for more than one student. With community mental health facilities typically discovering the demand for services to be greater than the availability of service providers, individual supervision of interns can represent an inefficient use of personnel.

ALTERNATIVES TO THE CONVENTIONAL SUPERVISION FORMAT

Given the above perceived shortcomings of the conventional approach, several alternative mechanisms of supervision have been offered. A popular alternative is for the professional to meet with two or three trainees at the same time (McGee, 1974). Sometimes two of the trainees who are jointly running a therapy group may prepare a summary of each group therapy session to present in supervision. Bloch, Brown, Davis, and Dishotsky (1975) have suggested that a three-to-seven page written summary of the group be sent to all of the therapy group members to provide additional feedback for trainees and clients. This may reduce both the time spent by, and the emphasis placed upon, the professional supervisor.

Peterson, Peterson, and Cameron (1975) have suggested that "pyramid groups" may offer trainees more immediate feedback and specific structure than supervision typically allows. Pyramid group therapy is led by both trainees and the supervisor who, along with group members, choose topics for subgroups to discuss. Each subgroup of clients is then led by a trainee, with the supervisor in attendance for a short period at each group, followed by the total group convening to discuss their topics. While this system permits the supervisor a more accurate assessment of students' performance than does traditional supervision, it entails a greater time commitment on the part of the professional.

A model that decreases professional time to a minimum has been proposed by Winstead, Bonovitz, Gale, and Evans (1974). Supervision under this model is performed by trainees of approximately equal levels of experience in a therapeut-ic-like supportive group composed solely of trainees. However, Winstead et al. report that such exclusive peer supervision may be too supportive or advice-giving and that trainee care may take precedence over client care. For client-related teaching to be retained in supervision, some form of hierarchy may need to exist to maintain the distance and objectivity of the supervisor. This brings us to the next alternative format, vertical supervision, upon which we shall focus in the remainder of this chapter.

VERTICAL SUPERVISION: DEFINITION AND CONCEPTS

Vertical (also referred to as umbrella or hierarchical) supervision has proven to be a popular supervision model in many clinical facilities. While the operational specifics of the model often vary, salient hallmarks of this approach appear to be the following:

1. A minimum of three hierarchical levels of personnel. These levels may consist of professionals possessing a variety of degrees and experience, graduate students at diverse levels of training, and undergraduates and other paraprofessionals.

2. A supervision format in which a person at each level (except the top) (a) receives supervision, on at least part of his/her caseload, from someone on a higher level, and (b) in turn provides supervision to a lower level worker.

3. A professional with formal responsibility for the activities carried out by all those beneath him/her on the hierarchy.

While this description may suggest a somewhat static quality, vertical supervi-sion should be viewed as a fluid, dynamic system in which the levels of the hierarchy are connected in a manner similar to the rungs of a ladder rather than suspended in midair. Thus as a worker gains in experience, degree, and/or certification, there should be the opportunity to advance to a higher rung. (In theory this should be a bidirectional process; however, one rarely hears of some-one falling from grace to a lower level based on displayed incompetence.)

Though the above three characteristics are generally found in nearly all facili-ties utilizing this model, the details of implementation may vary considerably both across and within settings. Thus, in the agencies and institutions with which the present authors have been associated, several variations on the theme have existed, including:

1. A Ph.D. psychologist supervised a senior intern's entire caseload and a portion of a junior intern's load, with the senior intern supervising the junior on the remainder of the latter's cases.[1]

---

[1] Senior interns and trainees are arbitrarily defined for present purposes as advanced students who are in at least their third (and usually their fourth or fifth) year of graduate school and who possess their

2. A Ph.D. psychologist supervised a postdoctoral fellow who, in turn, supervised five undergraduate premedical students functioning as paraprofessionals in a school for the multiply handicapped.

3. A Ph.D. psychologist supervised a senior intern who supervised a community volunteer serving as a Big Sister to one of the intern's clients.

4. A child psychiatrist supervised (a) a senior intern leading a group for the mothers of hyperactive youngsters and (b) a junior intern running a simultaneous group for the children themselves. The junior intern then had supervisory responsibility for his undergraduate co-leader of the children's group.

5. A Ph.D. psychologist supervised a senior trainee who instructed parents and teachers in cognitive behavior modification techniques to employ with their impulsive children.

6. A Ph.D. psychologist supervised a senior trainee who taught undergraduates assertiveness procedures and client-centered counseling skills to utilize with emotionally and physically disordered rehabilitation center clients (Glenwick and LaGana Arata, in press).

These examples are illustrative of the flexibility inherent in the vertical supervision approach. A multitude of types of personnel, activities (e.g., clinic- and/or community-oriented), and supervision setups (e.g., individual, dyadic, groups) are possible, limited only by available resources and administrative creativity. There is, however, one supervisory arrangement which, though frequently described as falling under the vertical supervision rubric, is more appropriately classified under the heading of traditional supervision. This is the vertical supervision team approach often employed in agencies having a strong training component, such as university counseling centers and psychology department clinics. The "vertical quality" of such teams derives from the fact that (a) each is usually composed of a senior staff person or faculty member plus a group of graduate students differing in their level of experience and year in program, and (b) tasks are assigned on the basis of that differential experience (e.g., less advanced students perform intakes and assessments or serve as co-therapists, while more advanced trainees are delegated greater case responsibility). Clinical *supervision* in these teams, however, tends to be conducted in conventional formats, such as having (a) the entire team meet for a single block of time each week, with the senior person or faculty member being the dominant influence (i.e., a "listen to the guru" approach) and/or (b) each team member meet separately with the senior staff person for individual supervision. Thus, in determining whether a given supervision system is indeed vertical, one should examine the actual operation of that system rather than rely upon often obfuscatory labels.

M.A. degree. Junior interns and trainees and practicum students are normally in their first three years of graduate school and typically have not yet completed the M.A. portion of their program.

ADVANTAGES OF VERTICAL SUPERVISION

The advantages of the vertical supervision approach may be categorized in three areas—competency building, affective advantages, and organizational advantages. In discussing the pluses and minuses of vertical psychotherapy supervision, we shall focus on the most common structure, that involving a professional supervisor, senior trainee, and junior trainee.

Competency Building

Perhaps the most noteworthy benefit of vertical supervision is that it offers an excellent opportunity for a trainee to obtain exposure to diverse viewpoints and techniques. This is particularly true if the hierarchy is arranged such that the trainee's caseload is distributed among several supervisors. It has been our experience that supervision carried out by advanced peers (e.g., senior trainees) tends to be more case-related and have a more pragmatic orientation than that conducted by professionals; that is, it may be easier for the former to stick to the material at hand and to refrain from didactic lecturing.

At times professional supervisors may attempt to seem unbiased and hence do not overtly espouse their own viewpoint. This apparent absence of a point of view for the trainee to accept or respond to may be of limited usefulness and, in fact, may be more subversive because the point of view is hidden and subtle. Trainees desire direction and, within suitable limits (i.e., that do not cramp their "natural" style), ought to be provided it. Advanced peers may be more adept at recognizing this wish in their less experienced supervisees and in fulfilling the need.

Another way in which competency building is fostered by vertical supervision is that an in vivo shaping and modeling process occurs. As trainees progress in their clinical duties (e.g., from intake interviewers to co-therapist to therapist), they can also advance in their supervisory responsibilities, hopefully utilizing some of the procedures and orientations acquired from their own supervisors. By receiving supervision on supervision, trainees may be able to avert the sense of inadequacy that many novice supervisors often feel when, like a new parent, they are thrust into a role for which they have received no training and in which they are expected to be adept.

Finally, a multiple supervisor, vertical supervision format may be close to ideal for conveying a maximum amount of supervision in a short period of time. Illustrative is the 10-week summer internship provided by a community mental health center with which we have been associated for (a) Kent State University (KSU) clinical students completing their first year of graduate school and (b) third-year KSU undergraduates enrolled in a six-year B.S./M.D. program. By having the advanced interns (e.g., postdoctoral fellows, third, fourth, and fifth year graduate students), as well as the professional staff, involved in the supervision of these fairly untrained groups, a surprising breadth of experience can be acquired in 2½ months.

Affective Advantages

In addition to skill training, participating in a vertical ladder simultaneously as supervisor and supervisee creates empathy for both positions and, it is hoped, enhances one's performance in each role. This point is illustrated by the following vignette from the first author's experience. An advanced intern who had been somewhat "resistant" to supervision complained to his professional supervisor about the recalcitrance and irresponsibility of a Big Brother he was supervising. In reply, the supervisor remarked that "it sure is frustrating when someone you're supervising doesn't seem to be listening to you, isn't it?" The intern was quick to realize that this comment was applicable not only to the intern/Big Brother relationship but also to the supervisor/intern one.

Secondly, being supervised by an advanced peer gives the trainee a person with whom to talk about both personal and professional experiences related to clinical activities, a person with whom he/she might feel more comfortable and less pressured to appear competent and wear a mask of (unfelt) sophistication. Having as one's supervisor someone who has not long forgotten his/her own graduate school and early clinical training experiences (i.e., an advanced peer often coming from the same background and program as the supervisee) may allow for a freer exchange than can occur with a more experienced therapist perceived as an authority figure. Consequently the trainee can more readily self-disclose and discuss him/herself as "person/therapist"—his/her weaknesses, fears, and concerns about being inexperienced—which may be a valuable "therapeutic" experience. For instance, sessions between trainees and advanced peer supervisors at agencies with which the present authors have been associated have included fairly open discussion of beginning therapists' discomfort with professional supervision, as well as their negative feelings about particular clients and concerns about their own competency.

A third affective benefit is that trainees can develop a sense of their importance that is often absent in the traditional clinical environment, where they may believe (often accurately) that they are delegated the tasks that others do not enjoy or feel to be beneath them. Functioning as both supervisor and supervisee may increase trainees' *awareness* of the competencies they do possess and of the situations when it is appropriate for them to rely upon themselves. This enhancement of self-esteem is further fostered by the greater amount and frequency of positive reinforcement that advanced peers may give, compared to that of professional supervisors. Doctoral level supervisors, especially those not currently engaged in the delivery of direct services (e.g., many faculty or administrators), may tend to dispense reinforcement on a relatively thin schedule, as they forget the difficulties faced by the novice therapist. In short, regular meetings with advanced peers to analyze cases may be an opportunity—all too often absent in graduate school—for students to provide one another with mutual support, as well as mutual learning.

Organizational Advantages

Two potential gains from employing vertical supervision in a mental health center are that it can (a) add to staff cohesiveness and morale and (b) free professionals from much of their traditional duties so as to create a more effective use and distribution of personpower. With respect to the first-mentioned gain, the increased contact generated by vertical supervision among colleagues at a center can lessen the sense of isolation that many workers feel and can enhance identification with the staff as a whole and with the organization's goals, as well as the development of a sense of community within the agency. Furthermore, each staff member becomes viewed as a worker with particular areas of interest and competencies and as a full-bodied person, rather than as an unknown quantity encountered only in passing in the hallway or at weekly staff meetings.

With regard to its second potential organizational advantage, introducing vertical supervision into a system permits the members of that system to perform more varied tasks than might otherwise be possible. Instead of having a major portion of their time taken up by direct supervision of staff beneath them, the "higher level" professionals are able to devote more of their energies to such alternative activities as (a) consultation to community agencies and natural caregivers, (b) program development, (c) evaluation of organizational functioning, and (d) direct service. Additionally, with the freeing up of time created by vertical supervision, a greater number of trainees can perhaps be entered into the system.

DISADVANTAGES AND DANGERS OF VERTICAL SUPERVISION

The disadvantages and dangers of vertical supervision are the flip side of the benefits outlined in the previous section, in that each potential benefit contains the seeds of harmful and counterproductive outcomes if vertical supervision is not implemented with reflection and good judgment. Thus the dangers can be similarly subsumed under the three headings of competency destroying, affective and personality problems, and organizational difficulties.

Competency Destroying

Receiving supervision from more than one person (either concurrently or sequentially over a short span of time) can create fragmentation and confusion for trainees by overwhelming them with too much diverse input. Although some degree of confusion is probably helpful in forcing trainees to examine their assumptions and therapeutic behaviors and in arriving at their own synthesis, excessive uncertainty may cause the novice therapist to feel adrift at sea when faced with an actual client. The professional supervisor (as opposed to one's advanced peer supervisors) can be helpful here in assisting trainees in integrating the different perspectives and techniques to which they are exposed.

For this reason, a trainee should probably not be receiving all of his/her supervision at any one time solely from advanced peers. An additional argument for always providing a trainee with some higher level professional supervision is that supervision by advanced peers is provided by persons with less clinical experience (compared to professionals) on which to base their judgment. [Some, we suppose, would assert that such a situation is not necessarily deleterious in that the increased experience of veteran therapists, compared to younger therapists or paraprofessionals, may cause them to be more rigid in their approach and expectancies and less open to new experiences and perspectives (Zax and Cowen, 1972)].

Affective and Personality Problems

Some trainees may complain that they are being offered second-rate treatment by receiving supervision from advanced peers. A nondefensive, low-keyed approach on the part of the advanced peer, in which he/she is willing to acknowledge and discuss the trainee's feelings, is a helpful first step in handling this situation. Over time, assuming that the advanced peer is able to demonstrate and share his/her competencies, any resentfulness will often dissipate as the trainee comes to appreciate that (a) the advanced peer does possess skills worth acquiring and (b) the advanced peer supervisor/trainee relationship has unique advantages of its own.

Additionally, vertical supervision requires trainees (both as supervisors and supervisees) to develop greater autonomy and handle more responsibility than they otherwise would. Faced with this challenge, some trainees may balk at having to decrease their dependency. While perhaps painful and somewhat taxing for the trainee in the short run, this can be a "growth experience" if handled sensitively and successfully. Being supportive of supervisees' difficulties in assuming greater independence and allowing their autonomy to develop gradually (i.e., a shaping process) are ways that such development can be facilitated.

Due to status similarity and related factors, a trainee, feeling more at ease with an advanced peer supervisor, may evidence a reduced willingness to share material (both personal and professional) with his/her professional supervisor, preferring instead to expose him/herself to the advanced peer. Though in many cases this does not lead to problems, there may be circumstances in which, for the good of clients or the trainee him/herself, the professional should know information that the trainee may be choosing to divulge only to the advanced peer. In such cases, the advanced peer is faced with the decision of when and how to reveal, or aid the trainee in revealing, this material to the higher level professional supervisor.

The personality of the advanced peer supervisor appears crucial in determining the outcome of vertical supervision. Because of his/her own sense of inadequacy, the advanced peer may act in an authoritarian manner or, on the other hand, lack confidence in either making suggestions to the supervisee or in saying "I don't know." While each of these behaviors may be appropriate in particular circumstances, a habitual style of supervision in one of the above modes (e.g., authoritarian, passive) can result in frustration for the supervisee (Cherniss and Egnatios,

1977), leading him/her to circumvent the advanced peer and go directly to the professional supervisor for assistance. As this is immediately reinforcing for the trainee, it may lead to a pattern in which the advanced peer supervisor is avoided by the trainee except for mundane issues. Such behavior should be discouraged in that its continuation can result in dents in the advanced peer's self-esteem. (The professional ought, though, to help the advanced peer in recognizing and working through the difficulties causing the latter's ineffectiveness as a supervisor.)

Organizational Difficulties

Establishing a vertical supervision system does not reduce the demands made on the professional supervisor; it does, though, produce different types of demands. An effective, smooth-running hierarchy of supervision requires coordination of the entire operation from the top—a function that the professional supervisor needs to assume. In addition, he/she is ultimately responsible for monitoring the quality of service to clients delivered by all trainees beneath him/her. When one is several steps removed from the actual client-trainee interaction, thorough monitoring may be difficult to conduct.

Other potential organizational problems stem from the relationship among the supervisee, advanced peer supervisor, and professional supervisor. Because the advanced peer may possess little formal authority, his/her suggestions may be ignored by the supervisee. In our experience this has been particularly true during the beginning stages of the advanced peer supervisor/trainee relationship, when the trainee may be somewhat doubting of the peer supervisor's competence.

Additionally, the vertical system can be an inefficient one if the advanced peer him/herself needs too much supervision regarding the supervisee. While the professional should be available to assist the advanced peer with issues concerning supervision in general and/or a particular supervisee (e.g., dress, inappropriate self-disclosure by supervisee to clients), excessive reliance by the advanced peer on the professional for input creates a time lag and a repetition of information which may result in a more cumbersome operation than the conventional supervision approach.

VERTICAL SUPERVISION, COMMUNITY PSYCHOLOGY, AND PROFESSIONAL REGULATIONS

Vertical supervision fits comfortably within, and may be seen as deriving from, a community psychology model of training and service delivery (see Aponte's Chapter 25). Ideally, according to a community psychology conceptualization, programs should arise from a needs assessment of a given population and environment, rather than from preconceptions regarding needs (Rappaport, 1977). It is our impression that vertical supervision, though presented in this chapter as a well-defined model, is in fact usually introduced into particular settings because of the perceived training and service demands of that setting, instead of on a priori theoretical grounds. On the other hand, it can be argued that someone with a community psychology orientation will utilize a needs assessment of almost any setting to justify implementation of vertical supervision. That is, the professional duties inherent in vertical supervision are frequently regarded (together with consultation, applied research, and evaluation) as primary functions of a community-oriented psychologist. In an effort to shift the role of the psychologist away from a medical model-type provider of direct clinical services to "patients" or "clients," community psychology has emphasized the role of the professional as supervisor and trainer of, and consultant to, subprofessionals and paraprofessionals (Rappaport, 1977; Zax and Specter, 1974). Vertical supervision offers one method of systematizing such duties in order to broaden the scope of services offered to a community. Thus Cowen (1973) has advocated "mental health quarterbacking," and Seidman and Rappaport (1974) the "educational pyramid"— systems in which a professional trains (or supervises several graduate students who themselves train) a number of paraprofessionals (e.g., undergraduates, retirees, and high school students) to work with high risk populations.

While consonant with innovative provision of community mental health services, vertical supervision may conflict with some states' licensing requirements and regulations for psychologists. In Ohio, for instance, persons are exempted from the licensing requirements for professional practice only if they are supervised directly by a licensed psychologist (Ohio Revised Code, 1972). These regulations are further circumscribed by the following guidelines of the Ohio State Board of Psychology: "Psychological interventions requiring training at the graduate level and involving the use of professional judgment, knowledge of psychopathology, and potentially having significant effects on the lives of clients may not be performed, even under direct supervision, by a psychological technician . . . who has not had graduate course work in the specific techniques" (Ohio State Board of Psychology, 1977a). Among the psychological procedures included by the Ohio Board under these guidelines are "psychological psychotherapy, behavior therapy, group psychotherapy, family therapy, and biofeedback therapy." The upshot of the above regulations and guidelines is that psychological interventions, to be considered legally performed, may be conducted only by persons who have received graduate training in the appropriate techniques and who are directly supervised by a licensed psychologist.

Thus, if interpreted strictly, vertical supervision and such other "psychological interventions" as crisis counseling as currently practiced would in most cases probably be considered illegal activities in Ohio. While some forms of vertically supervised graduate training might pass muster under such regulations, other forms (as well as most of those utilizing undergraduates and other paraprofessionals) would likely not be approved. As the Ohio Board noted, "The 'umbrella' of a Psychologist's . . . license does not extend beyond his/her own supervision of an unlicensed person. That is, the license protects the supervised activities of the supervisee but *not* the activities of yet another unlicensed person who is being supervised by the unlicensed supervisee" (Ohio State Board of Psychology, 1977b). One might expect that much psychological counseling or therapy occurs outside, or on the periphery, of approved work. This is indeed the case, as the Ohio Board's survey of supervision practices "found evidence of abuse of the protection offered by licensees' 'umbrella' of supervision" (Webster, 1977).

Although, due to the present authors' familiarity with them, Ohio regulations have been discussed here at some length, in all states the same conflict exists to some extent between the training of psychologists for professional practice and the organizing of mental health services for a community. As a recent president of the Ohio Board has noted, "there may indeed be differences between ideals for licensure and ideals for delivery of community mental health services via a community psychology model" (McPherson, 1978). Those involved in professional psychology who are opposed to umbrella or vertical supervision have claimed that such supervision is "probably not beneficial to the profession or its consumers" (Summary of State Board of Psychology Activities, 1977, p. 68), thereby focusing on quality of client care and professionalism as the major relevant issues. [One might also suggest the existence of some (often appropriate) guild interests and financial motives, as well, such as ensuring reimbursement by third-party payers for services delivered.] It should be noted, however, that some psychologists concerned with professionalism and professional training have (a) granted that "hierarchical training of sub-doctoral personnel . . . does seem to be consistent with one point of view about professional training recently espoused at . . . [the] Vail Conference" (McNamara, 1977, p. 10), and/or (b) argued for the validity of the vertical model on the grounds of cost effectiveness, that is, "the most cost effective models of care are the ones with greatest survival value in the long run" (Fox, 1977, p. 45).

Given the centrality of cost-benefit analyses and client welfare to the present discussion, a brief overview of the outcome literature on the use of subdoctoral persons and paraprofessionals in helping roles may be warranted. To the extent that such persons are found to produce results at least equivalent to those of licensed professionals or registered supervisees, then one would question the necessity of having all therapy and supervision conducted exclusively and directly by and for the latter groups. That is, are the skills needed for the successful practice of counseling and therapy ones which only licensed psychologists can perform and pass on (and pass on only to registered psychology graduate student supervisees)? A survey of the literature uncovers encouraging evidence (e.g., Bleach and Claiborn, 1974; Cowen, Trost, Lorion, Dorr, Izzo, and Isaacson, 1975; Durlak, 1979; Katkin, Ginsburg, Rifkin, and Scott, 1971) that paraprofessionals from a wide range of backgrounds and experiences (e.g., homemakers, the elderly, students at various levels) can be successfully utilized in diverse settings (e.g., hospitals, schools, crisis centers) (see Burkhart's Chapter 26). In an early report, for example, Appleby (1963) found that nonprofessional ward aides, psychiatrists, and treatment teams (composed of a mixture of professional and nonprofessional mental health workers) were of approximately equal effectiveness in working with chronic schizophrenics. Poser (1966), in fact, discovered that undergraduate paraprofessionals were more effective than professionals in running in-patient therapy groups (success being measured by psychomotor, perceptual, verbal, and adjustment patient indices). Surveys (e.g., McGee, 1974) have indicated that crisis intervention teams, which typically employ primarily non-professionals, may often achieve greater community visibility and broader population contact than do community mental health centers. It appears, in short, that paraprofessionals may possess the ability to reach target populations more frequently and in a different way than do professionals (Rappaport, 1977).

Additionally, data reveal (e.g., Cowen, Zax, and Laird, 1966; Gruver, 1971) that those (e.g., college students, hospitalized patients) functioning in the role of nonprofessional counselors or companions do themselves demonstrate improved adjustment, problem-solving ability, and self-esteem. Such support for Riessman's (1965) "helper" therapy principle—that is, that people providing services to others in need often reap rich emotional rewards themselves—suggests that capitalizing upon high-risk populations in the "helper," as well as "helpee," role might be both an economical and effective approach to community service delivery. As has been noted (Durlak, 1979; Gruver, 1971; Karlsruher, 1974; Rappaport, 1977), further empirical studies in this area are needed to investigate in a methodologically rigorous manner (e.g., employing multi-outcome, objective, and follow-up treatment measures) such issues as the process of paraprofessional intervention; the interaction between client factors and paraprofessional therapist factors; and selection, training, and supervision procedures. Research to date, however, would seem to indicate, using client welfare and cost-benefit effectiveness as criteria, at least equal success for the vertical or pyramidal model and the use of subdoctoral and paraprofessional supervisors and supervisees compared to that of professionals as therapeutic agents.

CROSS-DISCIPLINARY VERTICAL SUPERVISION

While this chapter has been written from the perspective of psychology (due to the authors' experiences and the focus of the current volume), in some facilities vertical supervision may incorporate several disciplines. For instance, in a hospital or community mental health center a psychiatrist may supervise a social worker who, in turn, supervises a psychology intern. Though our preceding remarks should be generally applicable to most vertical supervision situations, cross-disciplinary vertical supervision does pose some unique problems. Three of the most noteworthy of these potential problems are:

1. Ascribed (either by self or others) status differences among the various mental health professions. Such status differences (real or perceived) may produce an adverse effect on the supervisor-supervisee relationship, mainly through their impact upon the affective qualities of the relationship as discussed above.

2. Language problems among the various professions. Psychiatry, psychology, and social work may all possess different terminology for the same phenomena. Insistence upon using a particular jargon, in conjunction with

the belief that it describes activities unique to a given discipline (e.g., the terms "casework" in social work or "child study" in school psychology), can both hinder supervisor-supervisee communication and lead to an over-valuation of disciplinary uniqueness.

3. Differences between a supervisor from one discipline and a supervisee from another discipline in what they think the supervisee should learn. Based upon a belief in the superiority of his/her own profession or upon a precon-ception of the functions of the supervisee's profession, the supervisor may arrive at a supervisee's role definition that differs from predominant practice and thought within the supervisee's profession. Thus, depending upon the supervisor's belief system, the supervisee's duties can be restricted to, or come to incorporate, tasks which either truncate or inappropriately expand his/her role definition. (For a variety of reasons the supervisee may collude in this process.) A psychiatrist may, for example, regard a psychologist as one who tests, and consequently may limit a psychology supervisee's activi-ties to assessments. Similarly, a social work intern may be consigned to interagency coordination duties because his/her psychologist supervisor is of the opinion that "psychotherapy" should not be carried out by social workers.

One viable solution to, and means of avoiding, these problems centers upon the concepts of *contracting* and *competencies.* Specifically, the possessed competen-cies of the supervisor and the desired competencies of the supervisee can form the basis for the supervision agreement, or contract, between them. Supervision, then, can be based upon what the supervisor has to offer (within the boundaries of professional ethics). With respect to psychotherapy, a supervisee may seek out a specific supervisor (who may be of a different profession or discipline) because of the latter's reputation as a good therapist in general or as expert in a particular orientation (e.g., psychoanalytic, behavioral, gestalt) or modality (e.g., marital, family, group). At times (particularly with special populations, such as delin-quents or the handicapped), the on-line workers may possess knowledge greater than (or complementary to) that of the professionals in that setting. In such cases, a trainee could benefit from informal peer (horizontal) supervision and consulta-tion, similar to peer tutoring. Of course, involvement with cross-disciplinary supervisors or nonprofessional peer consultants brings one face to face again with the licensing and regulatory dilemmas noted above, as experiences with such supervisors or consultants will frequently not be credited by licensing boards as part of the trainee's supervised experience.

SUGGESTIONS FOR FUTURE RESEARCH

Discussions such as the present one often conclude with the exhortation that "more research is certainly needed." Concerning vertical supervision, the state-ment that "any good pertinent research is needed" would be more appropriate, because (with the exception of some of the studies on the use of paraprofessionals) research on vertical supervision as such is almost totally lacking. Thus much of this chapter has consisted of anecdotal report, personal opinion, and the authors' own Proustian "remembrance of things past" (and present). While we are obviously biased towards a vertical supervision model for some portion of therapy training and service delivery, research is desirable to investigate whether in fact the supposed advantages (i.e., competency building, affective, and organizational) of the model as detailed here are more real than apparent.

Client outcome under vertical supervision could be studied for those cases in which trainees are supervised by advanced peers (senior interns), compared to those in which supervision is conducted by professionals. A similar research project could examine whether trainees who supervise others do better with their own clients than do trainees who do not engage in supervision. [One might derive such a hypothesis from the assumption that being a supervisor provides a senior intern with an opportunity to achieve greater objectivity (or at least more disciplined subjectivity) regarding client problems, a skill which the intern can then carry over to his/her own therapeutic activities.] Cost-benefit analyses of vertical supervision could aid in determining whether the model when actually implemented is indeed more efficient than the conventional approach. Does the hierarchical model, for instance, truly free up more time for the professional supervisor who, in order to perform responsibly, will still need to devote considerable attention to (a) coordinating the vertical ladder, (b) monitoring trainee activities, and (c) ensuring client welfare?

Research of this nature might well discover that, rather than being either universally called for or totally contraindicated, vertical supervision is appropriate for certain types of trainees utilizing certain types of therapies with certain types of clients in certain types of settings, thereby providing another dent in the already well-battered armor of the uniformity myths of psychotherapy (Kiesler, 1971). Such findings would then, it is hoped, be utilized as part of the data base for the formulation of regulations and guidelines concerning professional practice.

Additionally, research could profitably address the supervision of advanced students who are functioning as supervisors. What is the best method, or combination of methods, for supervising such novice supervisors? Didactic/consultative verbal instruction, audio- and videotapes, in vivo modeling, and role playing come to mind as approaches worthy of consideration in the training of supervisors. Related to a comparison of these various instructional modalities would be process research (analogous to that of therapist-client sessions) on the interactions occurring during supervision between the professional supervisor and the senior intern/advanced student supervisor, as well as those between the advanced student supervisor and the junior trainee. Such process investigation could both (a) uncover any reciprocal effects produced by the participants in these interactions, and (b) explore the relationship, if any, between these interactions and client and therapist outcome data.

REFERENCES

Abramowitz, S. I., Weitz, L. J., and James, C. R. Supervisor self-concept and self-concept deterioration among psychotherapy trainees. *Journal of Clinical Psychology*, 1974, *30*, 300–302.

Appleby, L. Evaluation of treatment methods for chronic schizophrenics. *Archives of General Psychiatry*, 1963, *8*, 8–21.

Barnat, M. R. Student reactions to supervision: Quests for a contract. *Professional Psychology*, 1973, *4*, 17–22.

Bleach, G., and Claiborn, W. L. Initial evaluation of hotline telephone crisis centers. *Community Mental Health Journal*, 1974, *10*, 387–394.

Bloch, S., Brown, S., Davis, K., and Dishotsky, N. The use of a written summary in group psychotherapy supervision. *American Journal of Psychiatry*, 1975, *132*, 1055–1057.

Cherniss, C., and Egnatios, E. Styles of clinical supervision in community mental health programs, *Journal of Consulting and Clinical Psychology*, 1977, *45*, 1195–1196.

Cowen, E. L. Social and community interventions. *Annual Review of Psychology*, 1973, *24*, 423–472.

Cowen, E. L., Trost, M. A., Lorion, R. P., Dorr, D., Izzo, L. D., and Isaacson, R. U. *New ways in school mental health: Early detection and prevention of school maladaption.* New York: Human Sciences, 1975.

Cowen, E.L., Zax, M., and Laird J. D. A college student volunteer program in the elementary school setting. *Community Mental Health Journal*, 1966, *2*, 319–328.

Durlak, J.A. Comparative effectiveness of paraprofessional and professional helpers. *Psychological Bulletin*, 1979, *86*, 80–92.

Fox, R. E. For the professional school: A reply to McNamara or play it again, Sam. *Ohio Psychologist*, 1977, *23*, 11; 43; 45; 47; 49.

Gaoni, B., and Neumann, M. Supervision from the point of view of the supervisee. *American Journal of Psychotherapy*, 1974, *28*, 108–114.

Glenwick, D. S., and LaGana Arata, C. Assertiveness training in a college companion program: Effects on student volunteers and rehabilitation center clients. *Rehabilitation Psychology*, in press.

Gruver, G. G. College students as therapeutic agents. *Psychological Bulletin*, 1971, *76*, 111–127.

Karlsruher, A. E. The nonprofessional as a psychotherapeutic agent: A review of the empirical evidence pertaining to his effectiveness. *American Journal of Community Psychology*, 1974, *2*, 61–77.

Katkin, S., Ginsburg, M., Rifkin, M. J., and Scott, J. T. Effectiveness of female volunteers in the treatment of out-patients. *Journal of Counseling Psychology*, 1971, *18*, 97–100.

Kiesler, D. J. Experimental designs in psychotherapy research. In A. E. Bergin and S. L. Garfield (Eds.), *Handbook of psychotherapy and behavior change.* New York: Wiley, 1971.

McGee, R. K. *Crisis intervention in the community.* Baltimore, Md.: University Park Press, 1974.

McGee, T. F. The triadic approach to supervision in group psychotherapy. *International Journal of Group Psychotherapy*, 1974, *24*, 471–476.

McNamara, J. R. Against the professional school: A critique of the "proposal for the creation of a school of professional psychology in Ohio." *Ohio Psychologist,* 1977, *23,* 10; 42; 44; 46; 48.

McPherson, S. Personal communication, April 17, 1978.

Ohio Revised Code (Amended Substitute Senate Bill No. 176). Columbus, Ohio: Ohio Legislative Service Commission, June 1972.

Ohio State Board of Psychology. *Guidelines for activities of a non-psychologist under direct supervision of a psychologist.* Columbus, Ohio: State Board of Psychology, 1977a.

Ohio State Board of Psychology. *Letter to interested professional groups.* Columbus, Ohio: State Board of Psychology, 1977b.

Peterson, C. E., Peterson, B. M., and Cameron, C. Pyramid groups: A new model for therapy and intern training. *Professional Psychology,* 1977, *4,* 214–221.

Poser, E. G. The effect of therapist training on group therapeutic outcome. *Journal of Consulting Psychology,* 1966, *30,* 283–289.

Rappaport, J. *Community psychology: Values, research, and action.* New York: Holt, Rinehart and Winston, 1977.

Riessman, F. The "helper" therapy principle. *Social Work,* 1965, *10,* 27–32.

Seidman, E., and Rappaport, J. The educational pyramid: A paradigm for research, training and manpower utilization in community psychology. *American Journal of Community Psychology,* 1974, *2,* 119–130.

Summary of state board of psychology activities. *Ohio Psychologist,* 1977, *23,* 67–69.

Webster, W.C. II. Personal communication, August 15, 1977.

Winstead, D. K., Bonovitz, J. S., Gale, M. S., and Evans, J. W. Resident peer supervision of psychotherapy. *American Journal of Psychiatry,* 1974, *131,* 318–321.

Zax, M., and Cowen, E. L. *Abnormal psychology: Changing conceptions.* New York: Holt, Rinehart and Winston, 1972.

Zax, M., and Specter, G. A. *An introduction to community psychology.* New York: Wiley, 1974.

CHAPTER 18

Microtraining: An Approach To Differential Supervision

DOUGLAS R. FORSYTH AND ALLEN E. IVEY

Since its inception (Ivey, Normington, Miller, Morrill, and Haase, 1968) microtraining and microcounseling have been concerned with the education of helpers. Originally developed as a method to train beginning counselors, microcounseling has grown to become much more. This chapter will briefly describe the microcounseling model of helper training and examine the process of supervision as it relates to the learning of helping skills. We will also explain how the microcounseling process can be used to teach and learn increasingly complex helping skills from several theoretical perspectives. Finally, we will explore the future of microtraining with specific focus on the cultural-environmental-contextual (C-E-C) implications of helping as well as the process of appropriately matching helpee needs with helper interventions.

Microcounseling is a detailed and specific approach to counselor training that has as its major goal the development of competent culturally effective helpers who can assist people to become culturally effective in their own environment. A culturally effective individual, either helper or helpee, is defined as one who is able to:

1. Generate a maximum number of verbal and non-verbal sentences to communicate with self and others within the culture.

2. Generate a maximum number of sentences to communicate with a variety of *diverse groups* within the culture—and, where possible, with diverse groups in other cultures.

3. Formulate plans and act on the many possibilities which exist in a culture and reflect on these actions (Ivey and Authier, 1978, p. 15).

The concept of the *generative* culturally competent individual is particularly important as it sets the stage for the examination of the type of sentences a counselor or therapist generates (cf. Chomsky, 1965, 1968 Ivey, 1980). Microcounseling is concerned with assisting beginning and experienced counselors to increase their response capability. As counseling and therapy are verbal processes, the consideration of the array of sentences used by any helper is particularly important. The sentences generated by a Gestalt therapist, for example, are vastly different in style and content than those generated by Rogerian or Freudian counselors. Similarly, sentences generated by the clients of these differing orientations vary according to their experience in the interview. This point will be illustrated in more detail in a later section.

MICROTRAINING: A TECHNOLOGY AND A CONCEPTUAL FRAMEWORK

To achieve competence as a culturally effective helper one must look to the two major components of microcounseling: its technology and its conceptual framework. The technology of microcounseling is the systematic format for teaching and learning an infinite variety of single helping skills. This is normally done by using videotape, precise training manuals, and self/other observation with individuals or groups.

The step-by-step techniques of microtraining require the following:

1. *Commitment to teach only one skill at a time.* This will avoid overteaching and underlearning on the part of the client.

2. *Presentation.* A video model of the skill is presented coupled with brief written manuals describing the skill (cf. Ivey and Gluckstern, 1974a and b; 1976a and b).

3. *Practice.* Trainees practice with video or audiotape until the skill is mastered. *Self-observation* is particularly important and may be used on a pre-post basis.

4. *Mastery.* Trainees practice the skill until they attain specific levels of mastery (e.g., "in your five minute interview, demonstrate a minimum of five open and three closed questions"). Students can move through the systematic framework individually or in small groups until full mastery occurs.

The conceptual framework is concerned with providing a mechanism for the detailed examination, from a variety of theoretical perspectives, of what happens in the helping process. It provides a structure through which what happens between a counselor and client can be analyzed, taught, and learned as single helping units that are gradually integrated into meaningful therapeutic constructs (see Figure 1).

A. *Basic attending and self-expression skills.* Underlying all attending and influencing skills are culturally appropriate patterns of eye contact, body language, and verbal following behavior. Vocal tone, speech loudness and rate, and proxemic variables are also important but are not stressed in beginning phases of helper training.

B. *The microtraining skills.* Different helpers use different helping leads. The single skills of microcounseling categorize helper behaviors into teachable units divided into attending and influencing skills.

Attending skills:

Closed questions. Most often begin with "do," "is," and can be answered by the helpee with only a few words.

Open questions. Typically begin with "what," "how," "why," or "could" and allow the helpee more room for self-exploration.

Minimal encourage. Selective attention to and repetition back to the helpee of exact words or phrases. May also be represented by "Tell me more . . ." or "Uh-huh."

Paraphrase. Gives back to the helpee the essence of past verbal statements. Selective attention to key *content* of helpee verbalizations.

Reflection of feeling. Selective attention to key affective or emotional aspects of helpee behavior.

Summarization. Similar to paraphrase and reflection of feeling but represents a longer time period and gives back to client several strands of thinking.

Influencing skills:

Directions: Telling the helpee or helpees what to do.

Expression of content: Giving advice, sharing information, making suggestions, giving opinions, providing reassurance, sharing honest feedback, etc. Several categories of expression of content exist, but the prime emphasis is on the broader skill to avoid overemphasis on counselor/therapist talk.

Expression of feeling. Sharing personal or other people's affective state in the interview.

Influencing summary. Stating the main themes of the helper's statements over a period of time.

Interpretation. Renaming or relabeling the helpee's behaviors or verbalizations with new words from a new frame of reference.

C. *Focus dimensions.* The main theme or subject of the helpee's or helper's sentence often determines what either individual will speak on next.

Client. The helper's statement focuses on the client. May be demonstrated by the helper using the client's name or the personal pronoun "you". In the case of the helpee, this focus is generally manifested by an "I" statement.

Counselor or therapist. The helper makes an "I" statement, or the helpee may focus on the helper through "you" or the helper's name.

Dyad (Group). The predominant theme is an "I-you" focus with both helper and helpee ideas or their own relationship being examined. In group counseling, the words "group" or "we" will appear.

Others. The subject of the sentence is some other individual not present.

Topic. The subject of the sentence is a special topic or problem such as job search, tests, and abortion.

Cultural-environmental context. The subject of main theme of statements focus on the surrounding culture or environment. "This is a situational problem" or "Women often have this concern."

D. *Qualitative dimensions.* It is also possible to rate helper (and helpee) statements for the quality of response. Microtraining has attempted to provide single skill units for several underlying facilitative dimensions of helping.

Concreteness. The statement may be vague and inconclusive or concrete and specific.

Immediacy. Statements may be rated for tense—past, present, or future.

Respect. Enhancing statements about the self or others are considered to represent respect, while negative statements or "put-downs" indicate an absence of this dimension.

Warmth. Transmitted primarily through nonverbal/or paraverbal means (smiles, touching, vocal tone), warmth is a more subjective factor whose definition often depends on client reception of counselor messages.

Confrontation. Discrepancies in the self or between self and others are noted.

Genuineness. There is an absence of mixed verbal and nonverbal messages. In particularly effective communication, verbal and nonverbal movement synchrony between helper and helpee may be noted.

Positive regard. Selective attention to positive aspects of self or others and/or demonstrated belief that people can change and manage their own lives.

FIGURE 1.   The Taxonomy of Microtraining—Quantitative and Qualitative Skills.

MICROCOUNSELING AND SUPERVISION

The single skill units of Figure 1 are useful in a variety of ways. First, beginning helpers can learn the interviewing process systematically in a step-by-step fashion. As they become more expert, they are able to analyze their skills and qualities on video and audiotape and their impact on the client. A typical student assignment in a microcounseling course is the development of a typescript in which each counselor and client response is scored according to the taxonomy of skills and qualities. As students develop, they find themselves able to define what they are doing in the interview rather precisely. The vocabulary of microtraining is also convenient for the supervision. Rather than saying, "That was an ineffective response" and threatening the beginning helper, supervisors may say, "You used a closed question there. What happened? What were some other alternatives?" Further, students often find themselves more able to discuss their interviewing process with one another. A "self-supervision" program often evolves wherein trainees start developing and generating their own unique conceptions of themselves and how they relate to the counseling process.

As one becomes more expert, it is possible to start to analyze client generation of sentences. It has been found, for example, that clients in the early phases of the interview often generate sentences which tend to fall in the expression of content category; that they avoid expression of feeling, and tend to be vague rather than concrete, nonimmediate, and lack self-respect. If the helping process has been successful, this pattern of client responding changes. The microskills taxonomy is useful not only for teaching about the therapeutic process, but also for evaluating and researching process and outcome variables in the interview. For example, it has been found that beginning counselors tend to topic jump frequently and to have great difficulty in focusing on clients. More often they talk about the problems or topic than the individual before them in the interview. They tend to ask closed questions and very rapidly tend to give advice and suggestions (expression of content). After training in microcounseling skills, students have a more complete response repertoire and ask more open questions, reflect more feelings, and demonstrate higher levels of qualitative conditions (cf. Ivey and Authier, 1978).

Finally, as the developing counselor or therapist becomes more expert, he or she can start to examine the patterns of response of alternative orientations to helping. Microskills analysis makes it possible to determine rather precisely what it is that a rational-emotive therapist does, or a family therapist, or an individual adhering to any of a variety of theoretical orientations. New units in microskills are being developed (Ivey, 1980) to teach via microskills many widely differing counseling approaches. Although developed as a general frame for helping, it has now been found that microskills can be used to develop systematic training in many settings for many differing types of people.

Supervising the Beginning Counselor

Microcounseling is based on the assumption that helpers learn best if the helping process is organized into discrete, well-defined skills that can be objectively observed, evaluated, and practiced. By learning one skill at a time, the confusion and frustration often felt by beginning counselors is avoided and their effectiveness with clients is enhanced. The effectiveness of microtraining for teaching attending and influencing skills and the focus dimension to beginning counselors is well documented (Gluckstern, 1972, 1973; Guttman and Haase, 1972; Haase and DiMattia, 1970; Haase, DiMattia and Guttman, 1972; Ivey and Authier, 1978; Ivey, et al., 1968; Moreland, Phillips, Ivey, and Lockhart, 1970; Kerrebrock, 1971; Savicki, 1975; Spooner and Stone, 1977).

However, the qualitative dimensions of helping are recent additions to the microcounseling model (Ivey and Gluckstern, 1976b). They were included in recognition of the importance of the "core facilitative conditions" of counseling that enhance the effectiveness of the helping process. They also provide a qualitative balance to the quantitative and behavioral, yet effective (Dunn, 1975; Hearn 1976, Moreland, Ivey, and Philips, 1973; Toukmanian & Rennie, 1975), approach of the early microcounseling model. The qualitative dimensions (i.e. concreteness, immediacy, respect, genuineness and confrontation) are subjective constructs that become behaviorally described through the usual microcounseling process of precise definitions, modeling, practicing, and learning the skill in question. It is important that beginning counselors become adept at using all the skills of microcounseling. However, the qualitative skills are particularly important for the beginning counselor and supervisor, in that they represent the previously intangible but highly influential dimensions of helping that are most difficult to define and learn. The following are the qualitative skills of microcounseling:

Concreteness: A common complaint about beginning helpers is that they are vague and inconclusive while counseling. How often have we said to a beginning therapist, "this session certainly was superficial"? Often this results from the client being unable to state, clearly and specifically, what is troubling him/her, and the counselor "follows" the person through this nonspecific, abstract maze. This, too, happens during supervision. What is required is more specificity. Several authors (Bandler and Grinder, 1975; Carkhuff, 1969; Egan, 1975) have indicated that it is very important that the counselor and client give concrete and detailed attention to the specifics of client comments for the interview to be considered an effective helping session. To do this the beginning counselor must help the client learn to become more and more specific and concrete about his/her concerns. This can be easily done by using the microcounseling skills of questioning and/or directions (e.g. "could you be more specific?" or "tell me some more about that"). It should be noted that while concreteness of expression is basic to the helping process the definition of concreteness depends on the theoretical perspective of the helper.

Immediacy: This concept relates to the time dimension of counseling as reflected by the tense of the sentence structure used by the therapist. It has been reported that present tense counselor statements are more immediate and impactful than either past or future tense statements (Ivey and McGowan, 1977). Thus the most effective way to teach beginning counselors this concept is through emphasizing the present tense. The supervision process can model this by focusing on here and now reactions of the trainee. As beginning helpers become more experienced and have a clearer sense of their theoretical orientation they will begin to manipulate and integrate verb tenses for more effective helping.

Confrontation: Fundamental to teaching and learning the skill of confrontation is an understanding and an ability to identify incongruent or discrepant client messages. Most often the client is unaware that he/she has simultaneously expressed two messages that are in conflict. The therapist must be sensitive to messages such as "I love my wife but she really makes me mad" (two incongruent verbal messages); or "I love my wife" with a simultaneous crossing of the legs and arms (verbal message discrepant from nonverbal message). Confrontation is a skill that is useful to help the client resolve incongruities within themselves. Some authors (Authier and Gustafson, 1973; Grinder and Bandler, 1976) feel that the resolution of incongruities through confrontation is the most basic and important purpose of counseling. Ivey and Gluckstern (1976b, p. 46) define confrontation as "the pointing out of discrepancies between or among attitudes, thoughts or behaviors. In a confrontation individuals are faced directly with the fact that they may be saying other than that which they mean, or doing other than that which they say." To be effective the therapist must attend to, recognize, and confront these discrepancies. It must be emphasized that confrontation is *not* a separate skill in the microtraining frame. Rather, it is an area of emphasis. A reflection of feeling or other microskill lead may or may not contain a confrontation element. Confrontation appears in a supervisor lead when he or she reflects back to the beginning counselor "You say you enjoy and believe in the Rogerian mode of helping, but as I examine your interview, I see only one reflection of feeling in a half hour. How do you put that together?" Confrontation—the pointing out of discrepancies—can be most useful in bringing espoused theory and theory of practice into harmony.

Respect: Ivey and Gluckstern (1976b) defined respect as listening, honoring, and appreciating different perceptions of the same event. It is an effort to operationalize Rogers' (1961) constructs of respect and warmth. In microcounseling, respect is communicated through enhancing and appreciation of differences statements. Enhancing statements reflect a positive valuing of the clients' experience (e.g., "you worked hard at achieving that insight"). Appreciation of difference statements communicate that you respect the helpee's opinions and feelings even though they are not congruent with the therapist's (e.g. "I can understand how you arrived at the conclusion even though I would have seen it differently.") Negative "put downs", on the other hand, indicate an absence of respect. Regardless of theoretical orientation beginning helpers must communicate their real felt respect for the person if they are to be helpful. If respect is missing from the relationship one can expect, at best, no change in the person and at most, severe damage to client. This is also true for the supervisory relationship. Effective learning of the helping process demands sincere respect between supervisor and helper. Warmth is a dimension of helping. Warmth is a subjective inner dimension of helping that is communicated primarily by nonverbal behavor. The vocal tone, the degree of trunk lean, the gestures used, the facial expression, the touch are all nonverbal behaviors that communicate warmth. Bayes (1973) has noted that "smiling is the best single predictor of warmth. When coupled with respect, warmth allows for a deeper communication with the helper." It is important that the communication of warmth and respect be synchronous for it to be considered genuine.

Genuineness: Rogers (1957) once listed this concept as the "third condition" of therapeutic personality change. He defined genuineness as the therapist being "a congruent and integrated person." (Rogers, 1957, p. 97) One who, within the therapeutic relationship, can be herself and accurately represent her actual experience without knowingly or unknowingly resorting to defenses and facades. Ivey (Ivey and Gluckstern, 1976b) defines genuineness from its opposite—falseness. Genuineness, then, is not being closed, professional, evasive or defensive. It is being open, spontaneous, attentive, and expressing congruent verbal and nonverbal messages. Ivey and Gluckstern (1976b) define two types of genuineness. The first is genuineness in relationship to self. This means that the helper knows himself well and is congruent in every aspect of his behavior. He does not send mixed and discrepant messages either to himself or the client. The second type of genuineness exists in relationship to another person. When this condition exists there is a synchrony between the helper and helpee at both the verbal and nonverbal levels. A helper may also be genuine if she identifies an incongruity between she and the client and openly discusses this with the client. The goal in microcounseling is to help the counselor learn how to create a positive synchronous movement between helper and helpee. This is often best done by positive and consistent modeling by the supervisor.

Positive regard: Ivey and Gluckstern (1976b) define this concept as the selective attention to the positive aspects of helpee verbalizations. It was derived by analyzing Rogerian interviews and observing that the counselor maintained a constant emphasis on the positive aspects of the client. The Rogerian philosophy, that people are basically self motivated and growth-centered, provided the conceptual structure for this construct.

Microcounseling and Group Supervision

The teaching of specific microcounseling skills involves important supervisory-counseling skills. In addition to modeling the skills to be taught, the supervisor must reward any amount of improvement and not judge the overall level of effectiveness of the response. In this way, a genuinely supportive relationship between the trainee and the supervisor is established. It is clear that these skills and attitudes are most easily exhibited through a one-to-one trainee-supervisor relationship.

There are several other methods of supervision that can be effectively used with beginning counselors. It has been demonstrated (Gluckstern, 1973; Hearn, 1976; Scroggins and Ivey, 1976) that group instruction can be as effective as individual supervision if detailed attention is paid to the instructional process and ample skill practice is allowed. The following steps are usually followed when using a group approach:

1. *Create the learning environment.* It is important to know the class and the unique needs of the participants. It is also important that they know one another. Most crucial is establishing a sense of trust and well-being within the group. This is often done by modeling good group facilitator skills and rewarding improvement while ignoring errors.

2. *Training.* The specific skill to be taught is presented using the standard microcounseling procedure (lecture, manual, observation of positive and negative models).

3. *Practice.* In this step, trainees demonstrate and practice what has been presented in step 2. This is usually done by creating small groups of four trainees each with a specific role. One of the participants is designated as trainer, a second as co-trainer and the other two as helper and helpee. The co-trainers are responsible for coaching the helper through the skill until competence is achieved. At this point, the roles shift and the training procedure is repeated. This process continues until all participants achieve competence in the skill. The supervisor moves from group to group to answer questions and assist in whatever way necessary.

4. *Extensions.* It is clear that microcounseling skills will soon be lost unless specific attention is paid to extending the learning beyond the workshop to actual interview situations (Gluckstern, Ivey, and Forsyth, 1978). Behavioral contracting for using the workshop learned skills helps reinforce the learning and makes generalizations to actual helping sessions possible.

5. *Evaluation.* At the end of the workshop each small group meets with the supervisor to determine if each person has achieved competence and if the behavioral contract is appropriate.

Using this general workshop format, trainees in groups of four to 100 have been taught the entire microcounseling conceptual framework.

Individual and group approaches to supervision are particularly effective with beginning helpers. As trainees become more skilled and experienced, individual supervision, co-supervision, and self-supervision become the norm.

Microcounseling and the Experienced Counselor

Microcounseling is used with experienced helpers to extend and refine the skills the counselor has already learned. This approach requires that previous criterion levels of acceptable skill performance be adjusted upwards and that the counselor and supervisor focus primarily on the integration of microcounseling skills into sophisticated and effective approaches to helping. The supervisor and trainee may also be interested in introducing or learning the more broadly based concepts of self-disclosure, direct-mutual communication and refocus on the cultural, environmental, contextual implications of helping.

Self-disclosure is based on the constructs of expression of content, expression of feeling, and summarization, and is built upon the theoretical work of Jourard (1971a and b), Jackins (1965), Laing (1967), McCarthy and Betz (1978), and Rogers (1970). Their work stresses that interpersonal openness between helper and helpee is necessary for growth to occur. Self-disclosure, in the microcounseling approach, has four key elements:

1. A self-disclosure must be from an "I" reference by the helper. The direct or implied use of personal pronouns, ("my," "mine," "I'm") are required for a statement to be considered a self-disclosure.

2. Expression of content and expression of feeling are disclosing statements if stated from an "I" reference. Self-disclosure of feeling statements appear to be more impactful, exposing the helper to an open but vulnerable position —much like that of the clients.

3. The object of the sentence should be about the helper's own experience (I've been there too) or one's personal experience of the client's experience ("My experience of your experience is . . ." Laing, 1967).

4. While self-disclosure statements may be in any tense, past tense is the safest for the helper and present tense disclosures are most powerful.

The use of self-disclosure in helping remains a controversial professional issue. The theoretical orientation of the supervisor will determine if the skill is taught or not.

Direct-mutual communication is a synthesis of many micro-counseling skills plus several of the qualitative dimensions. Direct-mutual communication is defined by Higgins, Ivey, and Uhlemann (1970) as:

> The skill(s) focused on in this study is one in which two individuals attempt to focus on their interaction as they perceive and feel it, and attempt to share with each other their experience of the other. Rather than talk about politics, their liking of certain movies, books, classes, etc. (the content of most typical conversations), they are to react to the experiences they have (or have had) with each other. They are to share personal feelings

with each other and to respond to these shared feelings with new and past reactions to these feelings (p. 21).

This skill was modeled on the behavior taught in sensitivity, encounter, and T-group sessions. From a psychoanalytic point of view it may be considered a frank and mutual exploration of the transference relationship. A behaviorist would use this skill to develop mutual reinforcement modalities while existentialists would gain a fuller understanding of themselves in relationship to the person they are working with. The concept of direct-mutual communication will be of special interest, and assistance, to those helpers who are interested in using modeling and studying interpersonal openness as a means of promoting individual growth.

Only recently has microcounseling, and the profession for that matter, recognized that cultural, environmental, and contextual issues heavily influence the course of therapy (Ivey and Gluckstern 1976a and b). Fundamentally, Cultural-Environmental-Contextual is a focus dimension concerned with understanding individual behavior from a systems perspective. It builds on the early work of community psychologists and family therapists and their attempts to broaden the perspectives of helpers from predominant "I-Thou" attempts at therapy to systems approaches to helping. It is a recognition of the socio-economic, political, and cultural issues underlying the practice of helping. A focus on cultural-environmental and contextual issues means direct cross-cultural training to facilitate understanding and helping across cultures. It is also designed to highlight the necessity for consciousness raising for the supervisor, helper, and person being helped about the impact of racism, sexism, and other forms of human oppression on the behavior of the victim (Ryan, 1971) and helpers.

Some in our profession consider counseling without a full understanding of the social, cultural, and contextual dimension to be nothing more than pacification and political indoctrination programs (Halleck, 1971; Szasz, 1961; Steiner, 1975). The Pedersen (1973) cross-cultural triad model is an effective method to conduct this training. This model has as its major objective the transcending of cultural and language barriers. This is attempted by using a modification of the microcounseling paradigm in which the helper is matched with a client and an anti-helper. The client and anti-helper are from a culture different from the helper. The client portrays the usual client role while the anti-helper fights for survival against the whole helping process using the anti-helper's cultural similarity with the client. As the weapon of survival through this process, the helper learns about his authenticity through feedback from the "client". If the counselor is authentic, the client will move toward the helper; if not, toward the anti-helper. This model presupposes that in a cross-cultural setting three sets of forces are operating at once. They are (1) the experiential world of the client, (2) the experiential world of the helper and (3) years of largely unconscious socio-cultural socialization. This is a powerful method for assisting potential helpers to confront their own cultural prejudices in the struggle to be effective and useful to *all* people. For supervision to be effective, the supervisor must continuously confront her own cultural prejudices and model appropriate helping behavior and understanding of the cultural-environmental and contextual focus. However, Ivey and Authier (1978) suggest that counselors should have a firm grasp of basic microcounseling skills before engaging in cross-cultural training. It is clear that for helping to be effective we must know and appreciate the culture and environmental context the helpee must live within. Cross-cultural training is one way for counselors and therapists to begin to explore their own feelings and values as they relate to sexism, racism, socioeconomic discrimination or any other formal oppression or blocks to growth.

The supervisor may also use the microcounseling model as a diagnostic procedure to facilitate the learning process of more experienced therapists. This often takes the form of having the therapist and supervisor view and independently score a videotape of a particular therapeutic session. The ratings are compared and discussed thus enhancing learning. The fundamental focus for both the supervisor and helper is on the helper's behavior and its impact on the client. Second, they should be sensitive to breaks in eye contact and rapid or unusual changes in body language by either the counselor or client. These are usually indications of uncomfortable topics for either or both parties. Third, one would expect the degree of verbal and nonverbal synchrony of the counselor and client to be high. Occasions when the sessions are "out of synch" are important to explore and analyze in depth. Fundamentally the supervisor and therapist are searching for signs of trouble; spots where the therapist has deviated from her/his usual effective style.

As the trainee becomes more experienced as a helper, the nature of supervision can shift from the control of one-to-one to self and co-supervision. Individuals trained through microcounseling procedures can use the methodology to supervise themselves. This is done by taping a session with a client creating a typescript and carefully scoring it with the microcounseling taxonomy. The detailed analysis of the type-script of a particularly troublesome session often reveals the source of difficulty and allows for correction and improvement.

Co-supervision is the use of colleagues, who are also familiar with microtraining skills and procedures, to provide feedback to each other. This may be done in many ways, from direct observation with behavioral counts of the skills used, to detailed analysis of video tapes using the taxonomy. Co-supervision is an effective method, particularly when other resources are not immediately available.

Theory Specific Skills

The work of Sherrard (1973) and Chadbourne (1975) has demonstrated that therapists of differing theoretical orientations use varying combinations of microcounseling leads in their work with clients. Thus we can differentiate between therapists by the combinations of skills they use and teach a standard combination of skills that are reflective or a particular theoretical orientation. Or, the precise skills of that theory may be defined and taught. Most of the work done to date has been concentrated on the former effort. Ivey (1980) and his colleagues (Ivey and Gluckstern, 1976b; Ivey and McGowan, 1977) have reported that Gestalt therapists predominantly use influencing skills (directions, expressions of content and feeling and interpretations) whereas Rogerian helpers primarily use attending skills (minimal encouragers, paraphrases, reflections of feelings and summarizations). Analytically oriented therapists also use attending skills (paraphrase, reflection of feeling, and summarization) and have almost exclusive use of the influencing skill of interpretation. Behaviorists, on the other hand, use the more directive attending and influencing skills (open and closed questions, minimal encouragers, directions, expression of content, and influencing summary).

In addition to differences between the attending and influencing skills used by helpers of various theories of counseling, there are also differences in the focus and qualitative dimensions. While all theories of helping have a central focus on the client they differ in what additional dimensions of focus are appropriately included in the therapeutic process. For example, nondirective and Gestalt oriented helpers have an almost exclusive focus on the helper. Analytically oriented therapists will focus on the dyad (i.e., transference) and other people. Behaviorists will usually include other people, topic, and the cultural-environmental-context (C-E-C) as appropriate focal points. The clearest example of how the qualitative dimensions of the microcounseling model are defined differently by various theories occurs with the concept of immediacy. As indicated earlier, this concept is concerned with the tense of the language used by the client and counselor. Behaviorists are most interested in present and future behavior and their language contains a predominance of present and future verb tenses. Analytically oriented therapists are most interested in the impact of past experiences on present behavior and their sentence structure reflects this through a heavy use of the past tenses.

With a solid understanding of the skills and qualities of the microtraining framework, it then becomes possible to analyze the sentences generated by clients of therapists of differing theoretical persuasions. While no systematic research has yet been done, we have found that psychodynamic clients tend to generate sentences in the past tense, Gestalt in the present tense, and behavioral clients may emphasize the future more often. Psychodynamic clients tend to use more interpretation, Rogerian clients talk more about feelings (expression of feeling), and clients of vocational counselors tend to give more expression of content (information, planning) responses. At this point, the possibilities for analyzing process in the therapy and counseling interview become immense; but for the first time, they appear "do-able". The microtraining framework does provide a system whereby the complexity of the interview is broken down and single skill units and their impact on *both* client and counselor may be examined. It may be anticipated that a major direction of future development in counseling and therapy supervision is the precise teaching of microskills so that clients can be predicted to generate new and more useful types of sentences. It is at this point, of course, that the concepts of the linguists (cf. Chomsky 1965, 1968; Bandler and Grinder, 1975) may come to the fore. Counseling is about the generation of sentences, and formal analysis of sentences will ultimately move to include the study of grammar, syntax, and other systematic verbalizations of the client. Micro-counseling itself may be considered a form of generative grammar, but the emphasis is on skill building and the generation of a larger response repertoire.

Figure 2 presents examples of microcounseling leads used in different theoretical orientations.

By identifying the constellation of microcounseling skills that relate to a particular theory, the supervisor can directly teach these skills to therapists through the procedures outlined in this chapter. There is, however, increasing interest in matching client needs with an appropriate counseling approach. How can we determine which theoretical approach is most effective and appropriate with which individual at what time? While research on this fundamental issue is just beginning to emerge (Hunt, 1974), clinical experience suggests that helpers must be culturally competent in several theoretical approaches (i.e., existential, analytic, behavioral) if they are to match what the client expects and needs. At the very least, the helper must be able to recognize that her/his approach to helping is inappropriate and refer the client elsewhere. Most often, however, this is impossible or not done. Microcounseling is a method that can effectively teach the skills of several theoretical approaches. After a counselor reaches minimum criterion performance levels for one set of theoretical skills he/she would then learn a new and different constellation of skills that would reflect another theoretical position. In this way we would assist therapists to become more flexible and, perhaps, more effective helpers.

Research: Microcounseling and Supervision

Since 1968, the microcounseling model has been the subject of over 150 data-based studies. This volume of research clearly indicates that it is a paradigm, precise enough for experimental rigor yet practical enough to be useful in applied settings. This research has fallen into five general categories. The major trends of the research and its implications are presented below. [The reader is referred to Ivey (1980) and Ivey and Authier (1978), for a complete analysis.]

1. Identifying behavioral skills. Many helping skills have been identified, refined and investigated. New skills, specific to a particular theoretical orientation are being explored (Gluckstern, 1972, 1973; Sherrard, 1973). Particular combinations of skills and their effectiveness with new populations are also being investigated (Nuttall and Ivey, 1979).

2. Effectiveness of the Microtraining Program. The early studies of Ivey et al. (1968) have demonstrated the power and efficiency of the model to teach and learn helping skills. Since that time, additional works have also demonstrated its efficacy (i.e., Moreland, Phillips, Ivey, and Lockhart, 1970; Kerrebrock, 1971). Current research in this area is focused on investigating how long and under which conditions microcounseling skills are retained (Haase and DiMattia, 1970; Haase, DiMattia and Guttman, 1972; Scroggins and Ivey, 1976; Gluckstern, Ivey, and Forsyth, 1978). This research suggests

FIGURE 2. Twelve counseling and psychotherapy theories: their use of quantitative, qualitative, and focus skills.

Theory	Closed question	Open question	Min. encourage	Paraphrase	Reflect. feeling	Summarization	Directive	Express. content	Express. feeling	Inf. summarization	Interpretation	Helpee	Others	Topic	Helper	Mutual	Cultural–envir.	Primary empathy	Additive regard	Positive regard	Respect	Warmth	Concreteness	Immediacy	Confrontation	Genuineness
	Microskills: Quantitative Dimensions											Focus						Empathy: Qualitative Dimensions								
Psychodynamic	X	X	X			X					XX	XX	X					X	XX	X	X		X	P	X	
Behavioral	XX	XX	X	X	X	X	XX	XX		X		XX	X	XX			X	X	XX	X	X		XX	F	X	
Nondirective			X	XX	XX	X						XX						XX		XX	XX	XX	XX	H	X	X
Modern Rogerian			X	XX	XX	X		X				XX			X	XX		XX	X	XX	XX	XX	XX	H	X	XX
Exist.–humanist.		X		X	X	X		X				XX	XX		X	X	X	X	X		X	XX	X	H	XX	X
Gestalt	X	X					XX	X				XX	XX					XX	X				X	H	XX	X
Transpersonal	X	X	X	X	X	X	XX	X	X	X	XX	XX	X	X	X	X	XX	X	XX	XX	X	X		F	X	XX
Trait and factor E	X	XX	X	X	X	X	X		X	XX	X	XX		XX			X	X	X	X	X	X	XX	F	X	X
Rational–emot.	X	X					X	XX			X	XX	XX		XX			X	X	XX	X	X	X	P/H	X	
Trans. analysis		X	X	X	X	X	X	XX		X		XX	XX	XX	XX			X	XX	X			X	P/H	XX	
Reality therapy	X	X	X	X	X	X	X	XX	X	X	X	XX	X	XX	X	X	XX	X	X	XX	X	X	X	P/F	X	XX
Strategic	X	X					XX					X	XX		X			X	XX	X			XX	P/H	XX	

LEGEND

- XX Most frequently used dimension.
- X Frequently used dimension.
- ☐ Dimension may be used, but is not a central aspect of theory.
- P Primary emphasis on past tense immediacy
- H Primary emphasis on present tense immediacy.
- F Primary emphasis on future tense immediacy.

that generalization to work setting and retention will occur if it is planned for through training to pre-established criterion levels, follow-up and refresher training, and reinforcement in the work setting.

3. Comparing Microtraining with other training formats. A few studies have compared microtraining with other training formats with generally favorable reports (Moreland, Ivey, and Phillips, 1973; Dunn, 1975; Toukmanian and Rennie, 1975; Gustafson, 1976). The work done by Fletcher (1972), Boyd (1973), and Welch (1976) suggest that the combination of microtraining and Interpersonal Process Recall (Kagan, 1975) is a particularly effective method of training. Clearly the question before us now is: Which training systems are most effective with what type of individual under what conditions?

4. Client Outcomes. A new area of research has recently emerged and is concerned with how changes in helper behavior directly influence the verbal and nonverbal behavior of the client. Studies completed to date indicate that client verbalization is, in large part, determined by helper behavior, and patterns of client behavior are expected while working with helpers of a particular theoretical orientation (Ivey and Authier, 1978).

5. Studies of the components of the model. The model components, supervision, modeling, feedback, and self-observation have generated the most research. In general, these studies have indicated that if all of the components are used, the most learning occurs.

The importance of supervision in teaching counseling skills using microcounseling has been the subject of several investigations with conflicting results reported. For example, Hutchcraft (1970) as well as McDonald and Allen (1967) found supervision to be one of the most important elements for learning microcounseling skills. Goldberg (1970) and Frankel (1971) however, found supervision unnecessary for accurate reflection of feeling to be learned. In a series of two studies, Authier and Gustafson (1976a, 1976b) found that neither the supervised or the unsupervised groups improved their skills after microcounseling training. In the second study the opposite results were obtained. That is, they found significant improvement in skills for people trained under the microcounseling procedure, with and without supervision.

Several studies suggest that when supervision specifically focuses on the techniques of counseling, higher levels of skills acquisition are reported when compared to experiential or process supervision (Forge, 1973; Payne, Weiss, and Kapp, 1972; Payne, Winter, and Bell, 1972).

While the results of these studies are inconclusive, they do point out that those studies that specify clearly the dependent and independent measures in precise, rather than global, terms achieve significance. For example Scroggins and Ivey (1976) found that when trainees' scores on overall evaluations were examined after 6 months, no changes had occurred. When the specific skill measures were evaluated, it was found that some subjects improved on some skills but had diminished functioning on other skills, indicating that global measures may mask actual trainee performance changes.

While the results of the studies investigating the importance of supervision in teaching helping skills are mixed, it is reasonable to expect that supervision as a major method of teaching will remain.

THE NECESSARY AND SUFFICIENT CONDITIONS OF MICROTRAINING

Each individual is unique and responds differently to the several parts of the microtraining paradigm. While many find self-observation of their videotape performance to be the most important aspects of the experience, others find videotape models illustrating how the skill is demonstrated most valuable. Still others consider the written manual defining one specific skill or the assistance of an effective, warm supervisor the most important dimension of their learning interviewing techniques.

Clinical experience has revealed that there is no one way in which microtraining is most effective. Rather, evidence suggests that individuals respond to different aspects of the training paradigm. Some appear to need the support of the written word, others the relationship with an understanding supervisor, while still others apparently could change simply by watching themselves perform without benefit of external influence. As people do indeed differ the multimedia approach of microtraining appears to be one way in which unique differences can be recognized and utilized for each individual's growth. In the same vein, it may be anticipated that microtraining itself may be an inappropriate vehicle for teaching some individuals interviewing skills. In such cases, alternatives may be considered, ranging from traditional training techniques to in-depth supervisor-trainee relationships such as those proposed by Kell and Mueller (1966) or Wideman (1970). An additional possibility is the combination of microtraining with other systematic approaches to helper training.

As noted earlier, McDonald and Allen (1967) in their research noted that different trainees responded most favorably to different parts of microtraining. The same observations were made by Higgins, Ivey, and Uhlemann (1970) examining media therapy. It is suggested that there are no necessary and sufficient conditions for successful microtraining. The question seems to be not which method is best, but *which method, with what individual, under what conditions is best?* *

REFERENCES

Authier, J., and Gustafson, K. Enriching intimacy: A behavioral approach. Unpublished training manual, Omaha: University of Nebraska Medical Center, 1973.

Authier, J., and Gustafson, K. Application of supervised and non-supervised microcounseling paradigms in the training of paraprofessionals. *Journal of Counseling Psychology,* 1975a, *22,* 74–78.

Authier, J., and Gustafson, K. Developing relationship skills in medical educators. *Biomedical Communications,* 1975b, *3,* 18, 29, 35, 38.

Authier, J., and Gustafson, K. Step group therapy-training: A theoretical ideal. Unpublished paper, Omaha: University of Nebraska Medical Center, 1976a.

Authier, J., and Gustafson, K. The application of supervised and non-supervised microcounseling paradigms in the training of registered and licensed practical nurses. *Journal of Consulting and Clinical Psychology,* 1976b, *44,* 704–709.

*From Ivey and Authier's, *Microcounseling: Innovations in interviewing, counseling, psychotherapy, and psychoeducation.* 1978. Reprinted by permission, C. C. Thomas, publisher.

Bandler, J., and Grinder, R. *The structure of magic I.* Palo Alto, Calif.: Science and Behavior Books, 1975.

Bayes, M. Behavioral cues of interpersonal warmth. *Journal of Counseling Psychology,* 1972, *39,* 333–339.

Boyd, J. Microcounseling for a counseling-like verbal response set: Differential effects of two micromodels and two methods of counseling supervision. *Journal of Counseling Psychology,* 1973, *20,* 97–98.

Brammer, L. *The Helping Relationship.* Englewood Cliffs, N.J. Prentice-Hall, 1973.

Blocksma, D., and Porter, E. A short-term training program in client-centered counseling. *Journal of Consulting Psychology,* 1947, *11,* 55–60.

Carkhuff, R. The counselor's contribution to facilitative processes. Mimeographed manuscript, Buffalo: State University of New York, 1968. Cited in Carkhuff, R. *Helping and Human Relations.* New York: Holt, 1969.

Chadbourne, J. *The efficacy of the Ivey Taxonomy of group leader behavior for use with classroom teachers.* Unpublished doctoral dissertation, University of Massachusetts, 1975.

Chomsky, N. *Aspects of the theory of syntax.* Cambridge: MIT Press, 1965.

Chomsky, N.: *Language and mind.* New York: Harcourt Brace Jovanovich, 1968.

Dunn, R. Comparative effects of three counselor training techniques on reflection of feeling. Paper presented to the Canadian Psychological Association Annual Meeting, Quebec City, June 1975.

Egan, G. *The Skiller Helper.* Monterey: Brooks/Cole, 1975.

Ekstein, R., and Wallerstein, R.: *The teaching and learning of psychotherapy.* New York: Basic Books, 1958.

Fletcher, J. *Increasing skills of offering acceptance.* Unpublished doctoral dissertation, University of Washington, 1972.

Forge, H.: *Comparison of three variations of microtraining in teaching basic interviewing skills to counselor trainees.* Unpublished doctoral dissertation, University of Missouri, Kansas City, 1973.

Frankel, M. Effects of videotape modeling and self-confrontation techniques on microcounseling behavior. *Journal of Counseling Psychology,* 1971, *18*(5), 465–471.

Gluckstern, N. *Parents as lay counselors: The development of a systematic parent program for drug counseling.* Unpublished doctoral dissertation, University of Massachusetts, 1972.

Gluckstern, N. Training parents as drug counselors in the community. *Personnel and Guidance Journal,* 1973, *51,* 676–680.

Gluckstern, N., Ivey, A., and Forsyth, D. Patterns of Acquisition and Differential Retention of Helping Skills and their effect on client verbal behavior. *Canadian Counsellor,* 1978 13(1), 37–39.

Goldberg, E. *Effects of models and instructions on verbal behavior: An analysis of two factors of the microcounseling paradigm.* Unpublished doctoral dissertation, Temple University, 1970.

Grinder, R., and Bandler, J. *The structure of magic II.* Palo Alto, Calif.: Science and Behavior Books, 1976.

Gustafson, K. *An evaluation of enriching intimacy—a behavioral approach to the training of empathy, respect-warmth, and genuineness.* Unpublished doctoral dissertation, University of Massachusetts, 1975.

Guttman, M., and Haase, R. The generalization of microcounseling skills from training period to actual counseling setting. *Counselor Education and Supervision,* 1972, 12, 98–107.

Haase, R., and DiMattia, D. The application of the microcounseling paradigm to the training of support personnel in counseling. *Counselor Education and Supervision,* 1970, *10,* 16–22.

Haase, R., DiMattia, D., and Guttman, M. Training of support personnel in three human relations skills: A systematic one-year follow-up. *Counselor Education and Supervision,* 1972, *11,* 194–199.

Haase, R., Forsyth, D., Julius, M., and Lee, R. Client training prior to counseling: An extension of the microcounseling paradigm. *Canadian Counselor,* 1971, *5,* 9–15.

Haase, R., and Tepper, D. Nonverbal components of empathic communication. *Journal of Counseling Psychology,* 1972, *19,* 417–424.

Halleck, S. *The politics of therapy.* New York: Science House, 1971.

Hearn, M. Three modes of training counsellors: A comparative study. Unpublished doctoral dissertation, University of Western Ontario, 1976.

Higgins, W., Ivey, A., and Uhlemann, M. Media therapy: A programmed approach to teaching behavioral skills. *Journal of Counseling Psychology,* 1970, *17,* 20–26.

Hunt, D.E.: Matching Counseling Approach to clients. Paper presented at Ontario School Counselors' Association, Toronto, Ontario, 1974.

Hutchcraft, G. *The effects of perceptual modeling techniques in the manipulation of counselor trainee interview behavior.* Unpublished doctoral dissertation, University of Indiana, 1970.

Ivey, A. *Microcounseling: Innovations in interviewing training.* Springfield, Ill. Thomas, 1971.

Ivey, A. *Counseling and psychotherapy: Skills, theories, and practice.* Englewood Cliffs, N.J.: Prentice-Hall, 1980.

Ivey, A., and Authier, J. *Microcounseling: Innovations in interviewing, counseling, psychotherapy, and psychoeducation.* Springfield, Ill.: Thomas, 1978.

Ivey, A., and Gluckstern, N. *Basic attending skills: Leader manual.* Amherst, Mass.: Microtraining, 1974(a).

Ivey, A., and Gluckstern, N. *Basic attending skills: Participants manual.* Amherst, Mass.: Microtraining, 1974(b).

Ivey, A., and Gluckstern, N. *Basic influencing skills, leader and participant manuals.* North Amherst: Microtraining, 1976(a and b).

Ivey, A., and McGowan, S.S. Microcounseling: A systematic approach for improving helping skills and teaching them to others. *Focus on Guidance,* 1977, *9,* 1–10.

Ivey, A., Moreland, J., Phillips, J., and Lockhart, J. Paraphrasing. Unpublished manual. Amherst, University of Massachusetts, 1969.

Ivey, A., Normington, C., Miller, C., Morrill, W., and Haase, R. Microcounseling and attending behavior: An approach to pre-practicum counselor training. *Journal of Counseling Psychology,* 1968, *15:* Part II (Monograph Separate) 1–12.

Jackins, H. *The Human Side of Human Beings: The Theory of Re-evaluation Counseling.* Seattle: Rational Island, 1965.

Jourard, S. *Self-Disclosure.* New York: Wiley, 1971a.

Jourard, S. *The Transparent Self.* New York: Van Nostrand, 1971b.

Kagan, N. *Influencing Human Interaction.* Washington, D.C.: American Personnel and Guidance Association, 1975.

Kell, B., and Mueller, W. *Impact and Change: A Study of Counseling Relationships.* New York: Appleton-Century-Crofts, 1966.

Kelley, J.: The use of reinforcement in microcounseling. *Journal of Counseling Psychology* (in press).

Kerrebrock, R. Application of the microcounseling method using videotape recordings to the training of teachers in basic counseling techniques (Doctoral dissertation, University of Southern California, 1971). *Dissertation Abstracts International,* 1971, *32,* 740A. (University Microfilms No. 71-21, 470)

Laing, R. *The Politics of Experience.* New York: Ballantine, 1967.

Levy, L. *Psychological Interpretation.* New York: Holt, 1963.

McCarthy, P.R., and Betz, N.E. Differential effects of self-disclosing versus self-involving counselor statements. *Journal of Counseling Psychology,* 1978, *25*(4), 251–256.

McDonald, F., and Allen, D. Training effects of feedback and modeling procedures on teaching performance. Unpublished report. Stanford, Stanford University, 1967.

Matarazzo, R., Phillips, J., Wiens, A., and Saslow, G. Learning the art of interviewing: A study of what beginning students do and their patterns of change. *Psychotherapy: Theory, Research and Practice,* 1965, *2,* 49–60.

Mehrabian, A.: *Nonverbal communication.* New York: Aldine-Atherton, 1972.

Moreland, J., and Ivey, A. Interpretation. Unpublished manual. Amherst: University of Massachusetts, 1969.

Moreland, J., Ivey, A., and Phillips, J. An evaluation of microcounseling as an interviewer training tool. *Journal of Clinical and Consulting Psychology,* 1973, *41,* 294–300.

Moreland, J., Phillips, J., Ivey, A., and Lockhart, J. A study of the microtraining paradigm with beginning clinical psychologists. Unpublished paper. Amherst, University of Massachusetts, 1970.

Nuttall, E., and Ivey, A. Research for action: The tradition and its implementation. In Goldman, L. (Ed.), *Research and the Counselor.* New York: Wiley, 1979.

Payne, P., Weiss, S., and Kapp, R. Didactic, experiential, and modeling factors in the learning of empathy. *Journal of Counseling Psychology,* 1972, *19,* 425–429.

Payne, P., Winter, D., and Bell, G. Effects of supervisor style on the learning of empathy in a supervision analogue. *Counselor Education and Supervision,* 1972, *11,* 262–269.

Pedersen, P. A cross-cultural coalition training model for educating mental health professionals to function in multicultural populations. Paper presented to the IXth International Congress of Ethnological and Anthropological Sciences, Chicago, September, 1973.

Phillips, J., and Matarazzo, R. Content measures of novices' interview techniques. *International Mental Health Research Newsletter,* 1962, *4,* 11–12.

Phillips, J., Lockhart, J., and Moreland, J. Minimal encouragers to talk. Unpublished manual. Amherst: University of Massachusetts, 1969(a).

Phillips, J., Lockhart, J., and Moreland, J.: Open invitation to talk. Unpublished manual. Amherst: University of Massachusetts, 1969(b).

Rogers, C. *Client-Centered Therapy.* Boston: Houghton-Mifflin, 1951.

Rogers, C. The necessary and sufficient conditions of therapeutic personality change. *Journal of Consulting Psychology,* 1957, *21,* 95–103.

Rogers, C. *On becoming a person.* Boston: Houghton-Mifflin, 1961.

Rogers, C. *Carl Rogers on encounter groups.* New York: Harper and Row, 1970.

Rogers, C.: Empathic: An unappreciated way of being. *The Counseling Psychologist,* 1975, *5,* 2–10.

Ryan, W. *Blaming the Victim.* New York: Vintage, 1971.

Savicki, V. Some data and speculations concerning maintenance of basic interviewing skills for experienced interviewers. Unpublished paper. Eugene, Oregon College of Education, 1975.

Scroggins, W., and Ivey, A. An evaluation of microcounseling as a model to train resident staff. Unpublished manuscript. University of Alabama, 1976.

Sherrard, P.: *Predicting group leader/member interaction: The efficacy of the Ivey Taxonomy.* Unpublished doctoral dissertation, University of Massachusetts, 1973.

Spooner, S., and Stone, S. Maintenance of specific counseling skills over time. *Journal of Counseling Psychology,* 1977, *24,* 66–71.

Steiner, C. (Ed.). *Readings in radical psychiatry.* New York: Grove, 1975.

Szasz, T. *The Myth of mental illness.* New York: Dell, 1961.

Toukmanian, S., and Rennie, D. Microcounseling vs. human relations training: Relative effectiveness with undergraduate trainees. *Journal of Counseling Psychology,* 1975, *22,* 345–352.

Truax, C., and Carkhuff, R. *Toward effective counseling and psychotherapy: Training and practice.* Chicago: Aldine, 1967.

Welch, C. *Counsellor training in interviewing skills: Interpersonal Process Recall in a microcounseling model.* Unpublished doctoral dissertation, McGill University, 1976.

Wideman, J.: *Growth and development in counselor education.* Unpublished doctoral dissertation, Harvard University, 1970.

CHAPTER 19

Influencing Human Interaction—Eighteen Years with IPR *

NORMAN KAGAN

ORIGIN

In 1962 my colleagues and I first observed and later described (Kagan, Krathwohl, and Miller, 1963) a phenomenon which seemed to have utility for effecting knowledge and improvements in human interaction. We named the basic method IPR (Interpersonal Process Recall). It took five years of controlled studies (Kagan and Krathwohl, 1967) to discover when and how the phenomenon could be useful, and ten more years of research and development to produce and validate a film "package" (Mason Media, n.d.) so that instructors in medicine and a variety of mental health programs could be trained to offer an IPR course to their students.

What we observed, in 1962, was that if a person is videorecorded while he or she is relating to another and is then shown the recording immediately after the interaction, the person is able to recall thoughts and feelings in amazing detail and in depth. Usually there was some self-evaluation as well as a detailed narrative of the impact on the person of the "other" he or she had been relating with. If a remote control stop-start switch was given to the people so that they could stop and start the playback at will, usually a wealth of understanding about some of their underlying motives, thoughts, and feelings during the interpersonal transaction could be verbalized by them. We also found, in these initial experiences, that the phenomenon could be counted on to work more reliably, and more information about underlying feelings could be elicited if the person viewed the videotape with the help of someone especially trained in how to encourage the viewer to verbalize and elaborate on that which is recalled during the viewing.

We found that the person who facilitated the recall was most effective when he or she actively encouraged the person, usually a student, to describe *underlying thoughts and feelings* rather than encouraging critique or encouraging self-confrontation. The facilitator's role required that he or she ask such questions as, "Can you tell me what you felt at that point?" "Can you recall more of the details of your feelings . . . where did you feel these things, what parts of your body responded?" and, "What else do you think (the other) thought about you at that

---

*This paper is a summary of research and development in IPR. The basic processes, descriptions of early developments and research reports on IPR have appeared in journals, books and monographs. This summary thus includes some material which has been reported elsewhere.

point?" The catalyst's role is that of an active, *inquiring colleague.* The word "inquirer" was finally chosen to describe the facilitative person in an IPR session. The basic discovery then was not just of the value of videoplayback alone but of this unique combination of human role and technology.

IPR proved in time to be a method by which mental health workers and a myriad of other professional and paraprofessional groups could learn and improve their ability to interview, communicate with, or help other people. It also proved to be a useful vehicle for developing affective sensitivity scales (Campbell, Kagan, and Krathwohl, 1971; Danish and Kagan, 1971) for formulating theory about human interaction (Kagan, 1975) and for the study of medical inquiry (Elstein, et al. 1972). Its potential for accelerating client growth in therapy is still under study (Schauble, 1970; Hartson and Kunce, 1973; Van Noord and Kagan, 1976; Tomory, 1979).

The IPR Model—A Method for Influencing Human Interaction

Analysis of our early failures led us to the development of the concept of interpersonal "developmental" tasks a neophyte would have to accomplish in order to obtain knowledge and skill at influencing human interaction. We then sequenced these tasks so that learning progressed from the least threatening to the most threatening phases.

Elements of Facilitating Communication—Expanding One's Repertoire of Response Modes

The first phase in the revised model grew out of our early attempts to develop a behavioral counseling rating scale. We had developed the scale items by analyzing videotapes of counselors whose skills usually led to positive client comments on recall and comparing these with videotapes of counselors who seemed ineffective to their clients as well as to experts who reviewed the tapes. In addition we consulted the literature. Our conclusion was that, among other undefined characteristics, the successful counselors: (1) focus much of their attention on client's affect, (2) listen carefully and try to understand fully the client's communication while conveying to the client that they are trying to understand, (3) could be extremely frank and honest (but gentle) rather than manipulative or evasive in responding to the client, and (4) respond so as to encourage the client to explore further and to assume an active role in the counseling process. These four behaviors were then used as a basis for rating of the trainee-client interviews. The first stage in the revised training system is to share these four concepts with the neophyte by means of a 52-minute color film in which a narrator presents examples and then simulation exercises for student practice.

Counselor Recall—Studying Oneself in Action

The next phase of the emerging system was designed to help counselors overcome two dynamics which often interfere with the counselor's ability to understand the client or to communicate that understanding. We had repeatedly observed in IPR sessions that people perceive and understand much more of their communication with each other than one would suspect as one observes the interaction. It appears that people "read" one another's most subtle communications fairly well, but as socialized beings they often pretend that they read only the surface phenomena, the "official" message. Beginning counselors acted as if they did not perceive or understand the meaning behind many of their client's statements, but during recall indicated that indeed they did understand but were unable to act on their perceptions. In IPR sessions in which the counselor alone is the focus of the recall process, the "feigning of clinical naïveté" becomes clear. "I knew she [the client] was very unhappy underneath that put-on smile, but—and I know this is stupid —I was afraid she might cry if I told her I knew she was 'hurting', and then I would feel that I had made her cry.", or, "I knew [the client] was lying but I didn't 'call' him on it . . . I was afraid he wouldn't come back for a next session if I was honest with him . . . he might even get up and walk right out of the room. . . . I guess I would feel hurt if he did these things, and yet I know he probably wouldn't, but I couldn't risk it, I guess." The second dynamic which we hoped to influence in this phase of the system is the dynamic of "tuning out," of actually not seeing or hearing the other person for periods of time during the session. This usually occurred when the students were especially concerned about the impression they hoped to make on the client. For instance, during IPR sessions medical students often heard their patient for the first time say things of importance which they had not heard during the interview! The most frequent explanation by the medical students was, "I kept worrying about how to say things in such a way that I would appear to be older and more experienced than I am. I kept thinking about how I should look and how I should phrase my statements at those times. Even though I look as if I'm listening I really haven't heard a thing the patient said." Teachers often missed important cues about their students. The young teachers, not really comfortable with their subject matter, so often were "rehearsing" the material to themselves that they were simply not open to attending to external stimuli.

After recall sessions these two dynamics (feigning clinical naïveté and tuning out) were exhibited less often by students. The second phase in the revised supervisory system, then, was to set up a counseling session and do little or no recall with the client, but rather to conduct a recall session of the student. Typically, through this procedure, students learn to recognize where and how they failed to hear or to deal with client messages. Students also usually became more sensitive to their own feelings in human interaction.

Inquirer Training—Peer Supervision

The next phase is learning the inquirer role. The specific questions one asks in the inquirer role and—even more important—the learning-by-discovery philosophy of the recall process are very useful skills and attitudes for students to have within their repertoire. In learning the inquirer role most students also learn that assertive behavior is not necessarily hostile behavior. The inquirer role, though relatively nonjudgemental, is nonetheless confronting and assertive. It requires that one ask such questions as, "How did you want that other person to perceive you?" "Were there any other thoughts going through your mind?" "Were those feelings located physically in some part of your body?" The safety of reviewing a video or audiotape recording of behavior (rather than face-to-face interaction where the next moment in time is unknown), and the clearly structured cues to be used in the inquirer role, usually enable students in the inquirer role to use and become more comfortable with assertive, nonhostile behaviors. As students proceed through a series of structured exercises in which they learn and practice the inquirer role they learn not only to conduct recall sessions for each other without reliance on the instructor but also develop important new and useful human interaction skills. From the instructor's point of view, of course, an extremely time-consuming process can now be assumed by students for each other. From an administrator's point of view an expensive supervisory process is replaced by one of modest cost.

Client Recall—Feedback from the Consumer

Awareness of and sensitivity to their own feelings and often inappropriate behaviors seemed to help students do a better job with their next clients or patients but awareness of self was often not enough. Typically the students still needed additional help to become more involved with their clients. It also seemed to us that by the time the second phase was completed the student was now also ready to learn more about client dynamics through feedback. An IPR tool was fashioned both to provide client feedback and afford the student additional experience using exploratory probes, the primary mode used in recall. In this phase, the students themselves are required to perform the function of inquirer with another student's client. Thus, the counselor has an opportunity to try out new behavior (the exploratory probes basic to the inquirer role) with the support of the videotape and the realization that the counselors are working with their peer's client, not their own. When the students later switch roles, the counselor's partner then does recall with one of the counselor's clients. The students may agree to exchange notes later, to listen to audio recordings of their partner's recall or may even agree to observe the session through a one-way mirror and so learn about the client's recalled reaction to the session. Thus both students learn—the one in the counselor role and the one in the inquirer role. By this phase students are ready for such feedback and are not overwhelmed by it (especially since it is a peer, not the supervisor, who is the client's inquirer). The instructor or a staff member is available to be of assistance with any technical problems and to discuss with students their reactions to the role of inquirer and to the feedback they got from their clients. Students usually learn, often to their amazement, that they can be both confrontive and supportive, that questions or comments raised by the interviewer which might be embarrassing or bold in most social settings are appropriate and productive in a counseling or medical interview when accompanied by communication of concern or interest. Students learn, too, how clients react to them and which of their behaviors clients found helpful and which they did not.

Most often students are also amazed to learn of the extent to which clients are deeply concerned about the counselor's feelings about them. No matter how remote in space and time from the counselor-client interaction the content of the session appeared to be, they learn that a large part of the client's attention is focused on the here-and-now interaction between themselves and their counselor. This awareness creates in students a readiness for the next phase of the system.

Mutual Recall—The Relationship as Content

It is one thing for students to learn experientially that an important part of client's concern involves the counselor and especially the client's anticipations but it is quite another thing for students to *learn to use the relationship itself* as a case in point to help clients understand their usual interpersonal behavior and feelings and to learn to relate in new ways. Again, with the developmental task defined and awareness of the probable readiness of the student for new learning an IPR experience was fashioned to help achieve the goal.

Counselor and client are videotaped as before. During the recall session *both* counselor and client remain in the same room and are joined by an inquirer. During the recall session both counselor and client are encouraged to recall their thoughts, feelings, and especially how they perceived each other and what meanings they ascribed to each other's behaviors. A situation is thus created in which two people, a client and a student, are helped to talk about each other to each other. Such *mutual recall* sessions typically enable students to become better able to communicate with clients about the here-and-now of their interaction. Students become more involved, more concerned, more assertive, and more honest with their clients and use the ongoing counselor-client relationship as a case-in-point to help clients understand their relationships with others in their life.

EVALUATION OF THE EARLY MODEL

Did the system which was developed to that point work? This early version of the model was used in conjunction with a graduate practicum (Kagan and Krathwohl, 1967). A study, directed by Alan D. Goldberg, which was the first clear-cut evidence to support our hunches that the methodology could be used to implement an effective counselor training model is reported here in greater detail than those studies which followed it.

A pre-post and between-treatment design, replicated with three different samples in each of the three academic quarters, was used which permitted an analysis of the effectiveness of IPR-based supervision and of intensive traditional supervision. The design also permitted a comparison between the outcomes of IPR and traditional supervision. The pre-testing served not only as a base for determining the amounts of change for each group, it also enabled the matching of students on the basis of initial skill and the assignment to a treatment group. At the beginning of each program both IPR and traditional groups were given a common framework about the goals of the program and were given experience rating prerecorded tapes using the same instruments which would later be used to rate them at the end of training. The traditional supervision was one in which a student's supervisor observed each interview through a one-way mirror and then immediately spent an hour reviewing the session with the student, using an audiotape of the interview whenever the supervisor or the student chose to. Supervisors were either faculty members or advanced doctoral students. Each ascribed importance—if not centrality—to "relationship factors" in promoting client change. Although all supervisors had themselves been trained by traditional methods and had had considerably more practice with such methods, several hours of IPR training were considered adequate for assignment of supervisors to both groups. The IPR model did not include the affect simulation films which at the time had not been adequately experimented with. Each treatment was limited to a total of only ten hours during an eight-week period. Eight students participated during the first eight-week period and 14 students during each of the next two academic quarters.

The students' pre- and post-tests were of an initial interview with tenth grade high school girls who had requested counseling. Tapes were randomly ordered and assigned to independent judges. The rating scale used, the Counselor Verbal Response Scale (Kagan and Krathwohl, 1967), is a procedure which required that each of 20 consecutive counselor responses taken from the middle portion of an interview be rated on five dichotomized dimensions—affective/cognitive, understanding/nonunderstanding, specific/nonspecific, exploratory/nonexploratory, effective/ineffective.* A t test for paired observatiosn was computed for each of the five dimensions of the Counselor Verbal Response Scale for both the IPR supervised and the traditionally supervised groups.

Although ten hours of training are hardly an adequate program to achieve competence, there were statistically significant pre- to post-gains. Apparently, both supervisory approaches were effective in bringing about changes in a counselor's interview behavior. An examination of the differences within groups by academic quarters on each dimension indicated a consistent pattern of change in each quarter.

A t test for paired observations was computed across all 18 pairs of counselors to evaluate the relative effectiveness of each of the treatments.

There were statistically significant differences in counseling skills as rated on a double-blind basis by independent judges between the groups. Differences were found to be in favor of the IPR treatment on counselor behaviors in the categories of "affective," "understanding," "specific," "exploratory," and "effective." Again, an inspection of mean between-group differences by academic quarter indicated consistency of differences favoring the IPR model. On the WROS, a rating of 4 indicates a willingness on the part of the client to talk about personal

---

*We have since then dropped the category "effective/ineffective" and changed the titles of two of the dimensions so that they more adequately describe the behaviors rated.

Table 1.   Comparison of Pre- and Post-Treatment Means on Each Dimension of the CVRS for the IPR-Supervised Group

Dimension	N	Pre-Mean	Post-Mean	t	p
Affective	18	3.30	7.74	6.42	.001
Understanding	18	6.00	13.05	8.81	.001
Specific	18	3.35	9.33	7.57	.001
Exploratory	18	5.81	12.18	7.68	.001
Effective	18	4.06	10.57	9.97	.001

Necessary: t .05 = 1.74 for 17 df.
Necessary: t .01 = 2.57 for 17 df.

Table 2.   Comparison of Pre- and Post-Treatment Means on Each Dimension of the CVRS for the Traditionally Supervised Group

Dimension	N	Pre-Mean	Post-Mean	t	p
Affective	18	3.13	5.37	5.46	.001
Understanding	18	5.76	8.48	6.97	.001
Specific	18	3.24	5.85	5.02	.001
Exploratory	18	5.57	8.76	6.78	.001
Effective	18	4.18	7.50	7.36	.001

Necessary: t .05 = 1.74 for 17 df
Necessary: t .01 = 2.57 for 17 df

concerns while a rating of 3 is a willingness to talk to the counselor only about factual matters such as educational and vocational concerns and some of the personal meanings associated with these. As with the CVRS, a quarter-by-quarter analysis showed consistent differences between groups.

Using even fewer sessions (hardly ideal!) Kingdon found that clients of counselors given IPR supervision made greater gains than clients of counselors supervised by other means (Kingdon, 1975).

Table 3.   Comparison of Post-Interview Scores on Each Dimension of the CVRS Between Pairs of IPR-Supervised and Traditionally Supervised Counselors

Dimension	IPR Mean	Trad. Mean	Se[a] Diff.	t	p
Affective	7.74	5.37	.93	2.94	.005
Understanding	13.05	8.48	1.00	4.57	.0025
Specific	9.33	5.85	1.05	3.31	.005
Exploratory	12.18	8.76	1.12	3.05	.005
Effective	10.57	7.50	1.07	2.95	.005

Necessary: t .05 = 1.74 for 17 df
Necessary: t .01 = 2.57 for 17 df

MEDICAL EDUCATION AND OTHER APPLICATIONS

Although originally designed for use with counselors, psychiatrists, and other mental health workers, the IPR model had an immediate appeal in undergraduate medical education. Most students enter medical school with an interest in human health and disease, and because of the extensive knowledge they need before they can be of any help to patients they are usually not permitted to interview patients for some time. Certainly it would be helpful if they were able to have experience at interviewing early in medical school. IPR seemed to offer a solution, but modifications in the model were necessary. Under the direction of Jason (Jason, et al. 1971) IPR was adapted for use with medical students. Amateur and professional actors and actresses were recruited. The actors were trained to play the part of patients in specified conditions of health or illness, friendly and unfriendly, communicative and uncommunicative, forthright and deceptive. The "concerns" which were to have brought each patient to seek medical care were always related to areas of study which the medical students had been through or else required no specific knowledge of disease entities, and so the students were potentially able to be of some help to the patient. It was hoped that talking with live people about their problems would help the students integrate their academic medical knowledge. After some pilot experiences it became apparent that the "tool" could help students to understand better their behavior with patients and to become more skillful at medical interviewing, both at eliciting information and at the counseling functions. Often practicing physicians from the community could be recruited and, after themselves going through the various IPR formats, served as inquirers for the freshman medical students. Incidentally, these practicing physicians often volunteered that their own behavior with patients had improved in their practice.

The actors played their parts well. Although students were told their patients were actors, the interviews were considered to be very real and meaningful by the students. Evaluations of the program (Resnikoff, 1968; Werner and Schneider, 1974) indicated that medical students made statistically significant gains in interviewing skills and in sensitivity to interpersonal messages. A very similar approach was later used in medical inquiry studies to demystify the diagnostic processes used by highly competent medical specialists (Elstein, et al., 1972).

Transfer of learning from the classroom or workshop setting where students counsel with each other or with coached clients for practice, to the actual work setting with real patients and clients can be a very difficult transition for some students. To aid in the transfer of skills to other settings students can be required later to use the various recall formats (counselor recall, client recall, and mutual recall) in the clinic setting with real clients or patients. Where video recording is impractical (i.e. on rounds), simple audio cassette recorders have been used effectively. In clinics, internists gained significantly over controls (Robbins et. al., 1979).

To facilitate transfer-of-learning to the students' own personal "support system," IPR courses have been given for couples. The student and a significant other in his/her life take the course together. Several of the lab sessions are devoted to the couple's individually or mutually reviewing tapes of their interaction. Joe and Fran Kertesz have offered such couples IPR course at Michigan State University.

AFFECT SIMULATION–COPING WITH INTERPERSONAL NIGHTMARES

After the studies cited above validated the revised system, affect simulation or "stimulus" vignettes were added to the model (Kagan and Schauble, 1969; Danish and Brodsky, 1970). The idea for such vignettes came from the experience of conducting hundreds of recall sessions. In numerous IPR sessions we observed that people often feared from each other behaviors which in all likelihood they would never be subjected to. Clients often feared, for instance, that if they told their counselor or psychotherapist "the truth" about themselves, the counselor would walk out of the room in disgust, abandoning the client. Teachers often fantasized that if they gave up "too much" control in the classroom chaos and destruction would follow. Medical students often feared being discredited or even mocked by patients because of their age or fallibility. In general, the fears could be categorized under four general rubrics: fear of the other's hostility toward the student; the student's fear of loss of control of his/her own aggressive impulses; fear that the other would become too intimate, too seductive; and fear by the student of his/her own potential for seductiveness. These "interpersonal nightmares" were often elicited and examined during recall sessions if the student was introspective enough and if the real or simulated encounter in the videotaped interview had stimulated the nightmare sufficiently, but it seemed to us that it might be possible to create a more reliable way of helping people face their interpersonal fears. It occurred to us that if we filmed actors looking directly at the camera lens (so that the resultant image then looks directly at the viewer) and if the content of the filmed sequence portrayed one or another of the more universal nightmares, that it might be possible to help students discuss and come to understand better their interpersonal behaviors. A series of filmed vignettes were made. These were meant to be used for a wide range of subjects and so actors were instructed to portray the various types of affect with varying degrees of intensity, but to avoid words which would ascribe a role to them or which would define too specific a story, (e.g. in one vignette an actor looks at the viewer for a few seconds, tears appear in his eyes and between sobs he asks, "Why did you do that—I did nothing to you"). In another vignette a woman slowly licks her lips and tells the viewer that, "If you don't come over here and touch me I'm going to go out of my mind." Students are told to imagine that the actor is talking privately to them. Students are then asked such questions as, "Did the vignette have any impact on you? What did you feel? What did you think? Has anything close to that kind of situation ever actually happened to you? How do you usually respond? How do you wish you could bring yourself to respond? What did the person on the screen really want of you?." Most students have little difficulty in getting involved in the process.

After our initial experiences with the filmed simulation of general or universal interpersonal threat, we turned to creating vignettes of the kind of threat which might influence performance in a specific occupation. A series of films were made especially for teachers and instructors based on some of the fears teachers typically have. Similarly vignettes were made for physicians and medical students (e.g. "We've been to so many doctors who were just awful! But we're sure *you'll* be able to help us.") The vignettes are used with students in small groups. Other formats have also been used. In one, students and the image on the screen are videotaped using two cameras and a split-screen technique as the student watches the film. At the conclusion of the simulated experience students are then engaged in a video recall of the tape. In another format, each student's heart rate, skin conductance, respiration, and other physiological processes are also recorded and included on the videotape so that during the recall a student not only can see how he/she looked during the playing of each vignette but also how his or her physiological processes were responding.

MORE EVALUATION

Did the model which was now expanded to include affect simulation work? Controlled studies indicated that the model reliably enables students to make significantly greater gains than control students who received more didactic training (Spivack and Kagan, 1972). It was also found that the model was effective in other cultures (Kagan and Byers, 1973, 1975). It has been in use in Australia, New Guinea, Hong Kong, Germany, Holland, Denmark, Sweden, Holland, England, Israel, and with native groups in Alaska. Especially exciting for mental health workers was the finding that the IPR model could be used to help paraprofessionals learn basic counseling skills. Dendy (1971) provided a 50-hour program to undergraduate bachelor degree candidates. Among his findings were significant improvement in interviewing skills, significant growth on an affective sensitivity scale, and no loss of skills during a three month no-training period. Most exciting of all, before the program was undertaken, independent judges rated the undergraduates' interview skills and also rated tapes of Ph.D. level supervising counselors employed at the university's counseling center. Both groups interviewed clients from the same client pool. Before the 50-hour program, there were large differences favoring the Ph.D's (fortunately!) but, after training, independent judges found no significant differences between the groups on scales of empathy and other basic communication skills.

Archer and Kagan (1973) then found that these same undergraduates could, in turn, train other undergraduates so that the peer-instructed students scored significantly higher than other students who experienced an encounter group of similar duration. They also scored higher than a comparable no-treatment group, not only on measures of affective sensitivity and self-actualization, but also on scales given to roommates and other peers not in the study. When given lists of all participants, dormitory residents selected the

IPR trained students as the ones they "would be willing to talk to about a personal problem," significantly more frequently than they rated either the encounter trained student or the control group member. Apparently, then, dormitory residents were able to identify the increased therapeutic skills of those peer instructed students in the IPR group.

It must be pointed out, however, that the undergraduates used in both the Dendy and the Archer studies were carefully selected and were highly motivated. Heiserman (1971) applied a 16-hour variation of the model to a population of court caseworkers who did not seem to perceive their role as requiring or including counseling skills. No significant gains were found. The learning potential of IPR is not irresistible! Nor have we yet achieved measurable success in rehabilitating alcoholics (Munoz, 1971) with IPR.

The majority of IPR validation studies have been pre-post evaluations of the impact of all or major segments of the model. There have been relatively few intra-model studies to examine the impact of *each* of the major elements. Some evidence was obtained by making physiological recordings of a person as he/she watched stimulus vignettes (Archer, et al., 1972), and then also recording physiological behaviors during a video playback to the person of him/herself watching each vignette. Major shifts in recorded pattern during the initial viewing of the films were too often repeated during the videotape review for such repetition of pattern to have been a chance occurrence. This strictly "clinical" observation has not been quantified but certainly is convincing evidence that the recall process is a reexperiencing rather than a fabricated story to explain one's previous behavior. Recently Katz and Resnikoff (1977) found a more systematic, controlled way to test the validity of the basic recall process. Persons are trained by them to provide an ongoing account of the intensity of their feelings on an event recorder as they interact with another person and then again during a videotape recall of the recorded interaction. Significant correlates between ongoing affect and recalled affect were found in all four of their experimental groups. In another intramodel study, evidence to support the basic premise that the affect simulation vignettes do indeed have an impact on people was found by Grossman (1975). Vignettes were produced of an actor looking at the viewer and presenting five antagonistic messages to the viewer. The same actor was also filmed presenting noninflammatory information to the viewer. The antagonistic vignettes were then presented to two groups of 10 men and women and the informational scenes were presented to two other groups each of 10 people. Limb tremors were measured with an accelerometer in an object the size of an infant which each viewer was asked to cradle in his/her arms. There was significantly greater change in magnitude of limb tremor for the groups receiving the antagonistic message than for the groups receiving the informational message. If we are to believe the data obtained in studies using IPR to examine covert processes (i.e. to demystify medical inquiry) then more such studies of the validity of basic IPR processes need to be encouraged.

ADDING A FRAME OF REFERENCE–AN INTERPERSONAL THEORY FOR EVERYDAY COMMUNICATORS

Rowe (1972) found that if in addition to the experiential processes of the model, students were also taught theoretical constructs, their skill development was significantly augmented. Based on her findings, theoretical constructs about interpersonal communication were added to the IPR model.

An overview of the theory is presented here. Students are cautioned that acceptance or rejection of the theory is not crucial to learning from the IPR model. Instructors are encouraged to modify or substitute their own theoretical constructs.

Basic Elements

People need each other. One of people's most basic interpersonal drives is for some optimum level and frequency of sensory stimulation. This need is basic and life-giving and without it pain and death result. We propose that people are the best, the most complete potential source of sensory stimulation for other people. People can be the greatest source of joy for each other—more interesting, more stimulating, and more satisfying than any other single source of satisfaction in the environment.

But, *people learn to fear each other.* Just as people can be the most potent source of satisfaction for each other, people can also be the most potent source of horror for each other. People have the ability to inflict great pain on each other. Because one's earliest, most impressionable, imprinted experiences are as a very small being in a large person's world, vague feelings of fear and helplessness may, to a greater or lesser extent, persist throughout one's life.

This is why so many of the "gut-level" feelings that we repeatedly hear people eventually admit in the course of IPR sessions appear very infantile—living vestiges of early fears. We hear such things as, "I don't know why I feel he's going to hurt me, but it almost feels like any minute I'm going to be picked up as if I were very small and beaten or thrown away," or, "It feels as if, if I'm not careful he'll get up and walk out; he'll leave me and I just know that I won't be able to survive on my own. I'll die."

Fear of people usually clusters around four basic themes: (1) "the other person will hurt me," or (2) "the other person will incorporate or seduce me." Similarly, we learn to fear our own potential to: (3) strike out, or to (4) incorporate others. These fears are usually vague and seem irrational to us because we cannot adequately ascribe them to a reasonable source. They are usually unlabeled, unstated, and so are inaccessible to the logic of language. Such feelings are denied or not recognized and the source is not subject to cognitive scrutiny. The "enemy" remains unknown.

Manifestations

The basically opposed states, the need for people and the fear of people, manifest themselves in a variety of behaviors.

People are unable to give up attempts to achieve interpersonal intimacy, despite their fears of such contact. This approach-avoidance behavior seems to characterize most human interactions. People appear to both approach and retreat from direct, simple intimacy with others. The approach-avoidance syndrome appears to be a cyclical process—intimacy followed by relative isolation, followed by new bids for intimacy.

The movement toward-and-away-from people appears to establish a specific range of psychologically "safe" distance unique for each individual. People "settle in" at a psychological distance at which they are more or less intimate with each other and yet able to feel tolerably safe from the potential dangers which they sense in the situation. They seek and establish relationships with people who will accept their particular kind of "contract."

The individual's movement toward and away from others may be summarized as an attempt to find a balance between the pain of boredom and deprivation when contact is too distant and the experience of anxiety when the interpersonal contact is too close. Because the need for interpersonal contact is so strong, people continuously seek what they can from an interpersonal relationship yet carefully constrain themselves at a distance by the imagined frightening potential of the relationship.

The greater the fear, the further is the distance one establishes. The further the psychological distance one's approach-avoidance syndrome places one from another, the more rigidly the individual holds to that position. Those who gain most easily from psychological "growth" experiences are those who already are able to be close with others. Those who are most resistive are those who are most frightened. The principle of regression-toward-the-mean does not apply here; rather, the rich most easily get richer.

The further the distance one establishes, the greater the likelihood that substitutes for human contact will be sought.

The less frightened people are of each other, the better is their ability to achieve sustained intimate contact, the more flexible, the more effective, and the healthier a person is likely to be.

The fears people have of each other usually become translated into an interpersonal mythology and expectation, a "slogan" which enables one to avoid the frightening interpersonal nightmares—that is, "People have always perceived me in X ways and ultimately react to me accordingly, and they always will."

These anticipated reactions by others foster a self-fulfilling prophecy in which people make their nightmares happen. They expect others to react to them in certain ways, and so they search for and create evidence that indeed the others do react to them in the ways expected and feared. It's as if one paints a picture and then puts oneself in it. According to Horney (1945) the effect of a neurosis is its purpose. The position one finds oneself in interpersonally is the position one has carefully maneuvered into, sometimes with much difficulty and cunning.

One of the manifestations of this approach-avoidance dynamic is in the way in which people send and receive messages. Much of "direct" communication is not acknowledged by the sender and is not acknowledged by the receiver. As people interact they sense each other on many levels, but they label or acknowledge only a very limited range of what they send or perceive. An example of this process is illustrated in this old slogan:

A DIPLOMAT

A diplomat is a gentleman who can tell a lie in such a way to another gentleman (who is also a diplomat) that the second gentleman is compelled to let on that he really believes the first gentleman, although he knows that the first gentleman is a liar, who knows that the second gentleman does not believe him. Both let on that each believes the other, while both know that both are liars.

What I am suggesting is that to a greater or lesser extent *people behave diplomatically.*

People have an almost uncanny ability to hear each other's most subtle messages although they acknowledge and label only a small part of what they perceive and of what they do actually react to. I see this "feigning of clinical naïveté" as an almost universal characteristic. Feigning is sometimes justified by participants as fear that the other may cry or become angry and rejecting. More often, however, the reluctance to label messages honestly is based on an unwillingness to become *that* involved with the other.

However, sometimes even very obvious messages are not seen or heard despite what looks like attentiveness by the other. This complete tuning-out usually occurs at times when neophyte teachers, counselors, or medical students are deeply immersed in their own thought processes, anxiously belaboring their next moves. *Extensive covert analysis, especially when accompanied by anxiety, limits one's ability to attend to the other.* Extremely anxious teachers literally do not see many of the behaviors they are actually looking at.

Another manifestation of the approach-avoidance dynamic is in *life-style,* the basic interpersonal patterns which people characteristically rely on to survive in a world they need but perceive as dangerous. Here a two-stage model helps organize the observations. People have typical response styles in the immediacy of their interactions (one stage), but they also have long-term interpersonal postures (the second stage of the model).

The first stage's first two "styles" are similar to a typology first proposed by Horney (1945). The basic styles are "attack"—a continuum of aggressive behaviors ranging from assertiveness to attacking; "withdraw"—ranging from mildness to withdrawal; and "conform"—ranging from cooperation to conformity.

The long-term life-style *may* be different from what the immediate response style implies. That is, a person who relies primarily on aggressive behaviors may behave in ways which invite others to engage him/her in active, lively interaction;

but the same behavior style may be so enacted as to achieve a long-term withdrawal posture. The second stage of the model consists of six such "interpersonal postures". First, a person's immediate response to other people may be along an aggressive continuum with attack at one extreme. He/she may tend to rely on attack as an adaptive technique. This is exemplified by the nasty person, the grouch, the person who has a short fuse and who prominently displays that characteristic but whose interpersonal posture or long-term life-style is one of relative isolation. The surface attacks keep them isolated and distant from other people as a basic way of life. Here the response mode is to *attack* and the long-term pattern is one of *withdrawal*. The extreme of this mode achieves the long-term position of distance or withdrawal from human interaction.

Other people attack and achieve a life-style not of withdrawal, but of a degree of conformity to a particular group or a set of norms. Such people *attack* to *conform*. Their theme seems to be, "Don't tread on me, don't disturb the things that I want to believe and the people I want to obey or believe in." Again, this serves as a way of maintaining a degree of safety, a behavioral pattern which, however imperfect, is relied on and clung to, often tenaciously, because it is perceived as having permitted one to survive in a hostile environment.

Another response has as an extreme to *withdraw* under immediate interpersonal threat or encounter, to pull back, to escape. This may achieve for one an interpersonal posture of *attack* as an overall life pattern. In this category is the traditional passive-aggressive personality.

One may also *withdraw* in order to *conform*—to remain loyal to a group or to an unchallenged set of standards or beliefs. The surface behavior lies on a continuum of withdrawal, and the long-term posture is one of conformity.

Finally in the typology is the person whose immediate interpersonal response is relative *conformity*—in the extreme, a person whose immediate reaction is very chameleon-like. The overall postures which may accompany a conformity response are *attack* or *withdraw*. Social manipulators fit these categories. 4.1. Rather than think in terms of each of the above behaviors as discreet entities, each of the behaviors should be considered a continuum; that is, *attack* refers to a range of behaviors from assertive to aggressive hostility. Thus the behaviors are not necessarily negative or maladaptive.

Less effective people tend to rely on a particular interpersonal pattern and posture. One of the characteristics of more effectively functioning people is not only their ability to establish and maintain interpersonal intimacy, but their flexibility in being able to use a variety of response modes, depending upon the situations and their goals within the situations (Mischel, 1968). But less effectively functioning people—people who generally are unable to establish and maintain interpersonal intimacy—tend to rely on a single response mode and are quite inflexible in their ability to deviate from it. Their behavioral repertoire is very limited. They experiment in very limited ways and with much fear.

The above concepts are among those which are now included in the IPR materials. Again, the ideas are *offered* to the student as a set of constructs or cognitive roadmaps. Students and instructors are encouraged to use these concepts as stimuli for their own theory building. As a point of departure for discussion, students may reject all or any part which does not make sense to them and to substitute other constructs which are more compatible with their beliefs or experiences.

DISSEMINATION

Since our first publication reliable replication of the model by others has been a primary concern to us. The inquirer role, so basic to the process, is very difficult to communicate in writing. Even the filmed stimulus vignettes could easily be used in ways which would not encourage productive learning by students. This concern has led us to experiment with "packaging" the entire model so as to greatly simplify the task of the instructor and to make the model reliably replicable without the need for "outside" consultants. Our first attempt was limited to a black and white film and videotape series containing illustrations, instructions, demonstrations, and didactic presentations but aimed primarily at mental health workers. The package was obtained by more than 40 universities, schools, and social agencies, most of which reported satisfactory experiences. A controlled evaluation by one of them (New York University) indicated that counseling students taught by instructors using the package made significantly greater gains than a control group receiving an equivalent amount of other curriculum offerings (Boltuch, 1975). Recently, the package' entitled, "Influencing Human Interaction" was revised and expanded so that it now consists of color films or color videotapes (Mason Media, n.d.) and contains illustrations from a wide variety of disciplines including medicine, teaching, and family therapy. The new series also contains scenes which can be used by instructors to stimulate discussions of sexism and racism. An extensive instructor's manual and student handouts were also prepared. The new package is currently in use in medical, pharmacy, and law schools, hospitals, secondary schools, agencies, and prison personnel programs in the United States, Canada, Australia, Sweden, Denmark, Norway, Germany, Puerto Rico, Israel, and elsewhere.

NEW APPLICATIONS AND THE "SELF-CONTAINED" FORMAT

The most recent modifications in the model grew out of an interest my colleagues* and I have had for some time in the possibilities of influencing the productivity and happiness of entire communities of people by offering IPR training to large numbers of people who would then be expected to use the skills and knowledge, not so much as counselors for others but as a way of relating more directly and being capable themselves of more intense involvement with those they live and work with. For instance, prison inmates who received IPR training at the prison reception center prior to assignment to the prison they would serve their "time" in were later rated by guards as more approachable than a control group of inmates (Singleton, 1975). Teachers were rated by junior high school students as

*During the past five years J. Bruce Burke has directed or co-directed many of the IPR research and development projects.

being more human and more likeable after the teachers received training (Burke and Kagan, 1976). In the IPR formats discussed above the instructor or a trained cadre of instructor-aides had to conduct the first recall sessions for the students (prior to the students learning the inquirer role and then conducting client and mutual recall sessions for each other). The number of students enrolled in such a course then would have to be limited to the number of inquirers the instructor could recruit or the number of recall sessions the instructor could reasonably conduct. Would it be possible to teach the inquirer role to students *prior* to the first IPR session so that their first interview is then followed by a recall session conducted not by the instructor or instructor-surrogate but by one of the student's peers? In other words, is it possible to teach students to supervise each other in this model right from the start? A controlled comparison of the model using "outside" inquirers and a "self-contained" version indicated that very little was actually sacrificed for the increased efficiency.

It is therefore now possible for one or two people to have a positive influence on an entire school community (note 4). Based on class groups of 25, it has been possible, for instance, for each IPR instructor at Michigan State University to offer to 100 students every 10 weeks the kind of individualized experiential learning which had previously been reserved for medical students or for graduate students pursuing mental health careers.

Such courses are now also offered on a regular basis at MSU and elsewhere to nutritionists, nurses, prison personnel, and a wide range of students majoring in chemistry, business administration, and to persons who want to improve their ability to relate with others in professional or personal interactions.

WHY DOES IT WORK?

Why is IPR an effective learning program? Undoubtedly there are several vocabularies which could be applied and more than one learning theory. I prefer to explain it in the following ways:

1. Intimate interpersonal encounter is not a dominant theme of life in our society. Most people simply have never had opportunities to develop adequate skills that enable and facilitate such involvement. The program confronts this problem by beginning with exercises in skill definition and skill practice. Also such activities probably offer the least threatening type of interpersonal activity and are the least likely to raise excess student anxiety.

2. Skills are not enough. If people are frightened of each other, then simply teaching them ways to get closer may have limited utility. People need to be helped to come face-to-face with their most feared interpersonal nightmares. If these can be experienced from a position of maximum safety and security, it is possible for people to learn to deal with and overcome such fears. Film simulation seems to offer this security by permitting people to talk about and gradually come to both experience and *label* the kinds of

stress that ordinarily would evoke too much anxiety to permit acknowledgement, awareness, and understanding. Simulation enables people to enter what would otherwise be overwhelming experiences without being overwhelmed. A great deal of control and mastery can come through such experience followed by labeling and cognitive analysis. Finding words for what had been vague feelings is often described by students as "freeing." It is as if the ferocious wolf, on close examination, is found to be old and toothless. Videotape feedback of one's reactivity to experienced simulated threat seems to give people an opportunity to look at some of the most frightening of interpersonal potentials, but from a secure position, so that the "nightmare" can be experienced and also examined and understood. Whenever physiological feedback has been included, the potential for learning has been further increased. As anxiety is reduced new behaviors can be considered, learned, and used.

3. Meeting in small groups with others to describe reactions to simulated situations affords people an opportunity to learn about other people's covert life. This not only helps students expand their repertoire of descriptive words and phrases for covert behaviors, but offers one an experience of intimacy and sharing with others. One also learns that others may share some of their nightmares, thus reducing feelings of aloneness and shame.

4. In the IPR interviewer recall format, one is encouraged to make explicit one's perceptions and aspirations, thoughts, and feelings about an actual recorded dyadic session. This leads to increased awareness of the way in which people frequently "put their right hand in their left pocket" or frustrate the achievement of their own goals. The examination of an actual behavioral sample gives one an opportunity to recognize the daily expression of one's own ways of interpersonal distancing. Also of benefit, the recall process is in itself a *practice of new behavior.* One says the things one perceived or was tempted to say during the recall process and hears the not unpleasant sounds of these statements. For instance, "What I was really trying to ask throughout this entire section was, 'there are times when your behavior completely confuses me,' but I couldn't find a good way to ask it . . . I guess I could have said it the way I just said it now. . . ."

Again, the careful management of anxiety level is a basic consideration. Student and inquirer are to be alone together during the initial recall sessions. If the inquirer is supportive and respectfully inquires of the student about the student's experience, then the student is likely to be free to acknowledge and "own up to" much of the covert experience. If the inquirer enacts the function well, the student has little to defend against except the student's own self perceptions. If the inquirer is supportive, the student is encouraged to participate in an exciting learning-by-discovery experience rather than in an analysis of the extent to which "appropriate" goals were or were not achieved.

Given this support, and the more than abundant feedback available from the videotape recorder, it's intriguing to hear neophytes describe complex dynamics which even astute supervisors had not been aware of. Truly people are the best authority on their own dynamics and the best interpreter of their own experience. Ronchi's (1973) formulations further clarify why the inquirer role works. In a sense, the inquirer is an active agent in fostering perceptions of personal intention and personal control. "Peripheral awareness of the procedure as an attempt by an outside agent to modify behavior may preclude an interpretation of personal intention. Recent work has provided insight into the way that external attempts to control behavior serve to undermine what might be called 'intrinsic' motivation to perform the behavior in question" (pp. 7–8).

5. Skill at assisting human beings to work out their own concerns, assisting others to explore and struggle through complexities in their own lives requires skills which most people do not "naturally" possess. Learning and practicing the inquirer role does more than make the model more efficient, it provides people with skill at assisting another to learn by discovery.

6. People ordinarily associate assertive behavior with hostile behavior. Practicing the inquirer role helps people learn assertive but nonpunitive, nonhostile relationship skills. It is here as well as elsewhere in the program that what might be thought of as "interpersonal courage" is nutured.

7. I have already described the phenomenon of "feigning of clinical naivete." If one does not have to teach people to develop a "third ear", but rather one has primarily to free people of their fears so that they are willing to risk labeling messages that they already perceive, then the simulation films and the interviewer recall should have helped students recognize and understand and be less controlled by their fears of others. The response-skill training and inquirer-training phases should have given students specific skills with which to implement their new readiness for involvement.

   In the client-recall phase of IPR, students learn about interpersonal communication and the nature of helping directly from the client. The student's previously unverbalized hunches are confirmed or denied. The student learns to recognize how the client's life-style is enacted in the here-and-now of the client's relationships. Students learn that as clients talk with counselors, teachers, and others about concerns outside the immediate dyadic relationship, much of their energy is focused on the ways in which they feel about the person they are with and the ways they want the other to feel about them.

8. It is one thing for students to recognize and understand the importance of the here-and-now of an interaction, but it is another thing for them to actually incorporate this understanding into their behavior, to learn to respond to others in new ways, and especially to risk being more direct with others in the immediacy of the interaction. The mutual recall IPR format helps people reduce their fears and shorten the interpersonal distancing that blocks this kind of interaction. In the presence of the third person seated between them and with the *here-and-then* of the videotape playback, people are usually able to risk describing, in each other's presence, what their perceptions had been of each other and the aspirations they had had for themself and wanted of the other. This here-and-then situation enables two people to practice relating in a new way with each other. Typically, in the

early minutes of the mutual recall, each participant addresses the inquirer and talks about the other on the videotape as "him" or "her." As the session progresses, the inquirer is usually bypassed as each participant finds the courage to address the other directly and to talk about "you" and "me," our fears about each other, our impressions, aspirations, and strategies.

9. Typically students go through these training sessions being clients for each other. At the end of the series, whenever possible, students then engage in interviewer, client, and mutual recall sessions with people from the actual populations they are to influence. For instance, teachers are videotaped in their classrooms and conduct a teacher recall session with a colleague as inquirer. At another time, the colleague conducts a recall session of the students in the classroom without the original teacher's presence. Finally, a teacher is videotaped in her classroom and a fellow teacher conducts a mutual recall in which both teacher and students are encouraged to describe their reactions and covert behaviors to each other. This facilitates transfer of learning beyond the IPR seminar and lab rooms. Trainees are also encouraged to use the methods in their daily work rather than to think of the experience as a "one-shot" learning sequence or course. For instance, medical students are encouraged to use the methods during their clinical experiences and to focus on both affect and cognitive inquiry processes during recall.

It is difficult to identify all of the factors responsible for the apparent success of the learning program. The above constructs are my best approximation at this time. As we continue to use and test the model these ideas may well change.

WHAT NEXT?

The ongoing developmental process of IPR is opening up new ways to assist people who wish to grow in their interpersonal understanding and skills. Offering the IPR program to any interested person on campus with absolutely no course prerequisites has proved a huge success. There are currently seven sections with 30 students in each section and these are fully enrolled well in advance of each term. In addition to the students who take IPR as a requirement in the medical schools, more than 800 people a year now go through the IPR program—a series of experiences once considered too expensive to offer to other than medical students or graduate students in counseling. What impact this might have on the lives of these people and on the quality of life at the university are probably researchable questions.

The model itself could be intensified. I am particularly optimistic about the possibilities of including self-study of one's own physiological reactions to interpersonal messages. The methods for this do now exist, we have only to find a practical, economical procedure to allow large-scale implementation.

Ultimately the film series itself will be expanded. Vignettes and illustrations have been added which inevitably stimulate discussion of sexism and racism.

Additional material on loss and grieving, on aging, and on problems associated with being a single parent could be included. Much remains to be done.

REFERENCES

Archer, J., Jr., Feister, T., Kagan, N., Rate, R., Spierling, T., and Van Noord, R. A new methodology for education, treatment and research in human interaction. *Journal of Counseling Psychology,* 1972, *19,* 275–281.

Archer, J., Jr., and Kagan, N. Teaching interpersonal relationship skills on campus: A pyramid approach. *Journal of Counseling Psychology,* 1973, *20,* 535–541.

Boltuch, B. S. *The effects of a pre-practicum skill training program; Influencing Human Interaction: On developing counselor effectiveness in a Master's level practicum.* Unpublished doctoral dissertation, New York University, 1975.

Burke, J. B., and Kagan, N. *Influencing human interaction in urban schools,* NIMH Grant #1+21MH13526-02, Final report, 1976.

Campbell, R. J., Kagan, N., and Krathwohl, D. R. The development and validation of a scale to measure affective sensitivity (empathy). *Journal of Counseling Psychology,* 1971, *18,* 407–412.

Danish, S. J., and Brodsky, S. L. Training of policemen in emotional control and awareness. *Psychology in Action,* 1970, *25,* 368–369.

Danish, S. J., and Kagan, N. Measurement of affective sensitivity: Toward a valid measure of interpersonal perception. *Journal of Counseling Psychology,* 1971, *18,* 51–54.

Dendy, R. F. *A model for the training of undergraduate residence hall assistants as paraprofessional counselors using videotape techniques and Interpersonal Process Recall (IPR).* Unpublished doctoral dissertation, Michigan State University, 1971.

Elstein, A. S., Kagan, N., Shulman, L., Jason, H., and Loupe, M. J. Methods and theory in the study of medical inquiry. *Journal of Medical Education,* 1972, *47,* 85–92.

Grossman, R. W. *Limb tremor responses to antagonistic and informational communication.* Unpublished doctoral dissertation, Michigan State University, 1975.

Hartson, D. J., and Kunce, J. T. Videotape replay and recall in group work. *Journal of Counseling Psychology,* 1973, *20,* 437–441.

Heiserman, Mary Sue. *The effect of experiential-videotape training procedures compared to cognitive-classroom teaching methods on the interpersonal communication skills of juvenile court caseworkers.* Unpublished doctoral dissertation, Michigan State University, 1971.

Horney, *Our inner conflicts: A constructive theory of neurosis.* New York: W. W. Norton, 1945.

Jason, H., Kagan, N., Werner, A., Elstein, A., and Thomas, J. B. New approaches to teaching basic interview skills to medical students. *American Journal of Psychiatry,* 1971, *127,* 1404–1407.

Kagan, N. Influencing human interaction—Eleven years with IPR. *The Canadian Counselor,* 1975, *9,* 74–97.

Kagan, N., and Byers, J. IPR Workshops conducted for the United Nations World Health Organization in New Guinea and Australia. World Health Organization, Manila, 1973 and 1975.

Kagan, N., and Krathwohl, D. R. *Studies in human interaction: Interpersonal Process Recall stimulated by videotape.* East Lansing, Mich.: Michigan State University, 1967.

Kagan, N., Krathwohl, D. R., and Miller, R. Stimulated recall in therapy using videotape —a case study. *Journal of Counseling Psychology,* 1963, *10,* 237–243.

Kagan, N., and Schauble, P. G. Affect simulation in Interpersonal Process Recall. *Journal of Counseling Psychology,* 1969, *16,* 309–313.

Katz, D. and Resnikoff, A. Televised self-confrontation and recalled affect: A new look at videotape recall. *Journal of Counseling Psychology,* 1977, *24,* 150–152.

Kingdon, M. A. A cost/benefit analysis of the Interpersonal Process Recall technique. *Journal of Counseling Psychology,* 1975, *22,* 353–357.

Mason Media, Inc. Influencing human interaction. Mason, Mich.: Mason Media, Inc.

Mischel, W. *Personality and assessment.* New York: Wiley, 1968.

Munoz, Daniel G. *The effects of simulated affect films and videotape feedback in group psychotherapy with alcoholics.* Unpublished doctoral dissertation, Michigan State University, 1971.

Resnikoff, A. *The relationship of counselor behavior to client response and an analysis of a medical interview training procedure involved simulated patients.* Unpublished doctoral dissertation, Michigan State University, 1968.

Robbins, A. S., Kaus, D. R., Heinrich, R., Abrass, I., Dreyer, J., and Clyman, B. Interpersonal skills: Evaluation in an internal medicine residency. *Journal of Medical Education,* 1979, *54,* 885–894.

Ronchi, D. Attribution theory and video playback: A social psychological view. Paper presented at the Annual Meeting of the American Educational Research Association, New Orleans, 1973.

Rowe, K. K. *A 50-hour intensified IPR training program for counselor.* Unpublished doctoral dissertation, Michigan State University, 1972.

Schauble, P. G. *The acceleration of client progress in counseling and psychotherapy through Interpersonal Process Recall (IPR).* Unpublished doctoral dissertation, Michigan State University, 1970.

Singleton, N. *Training incarcerated felons in communication skills using an integrated IPR (Interpersonal Process Recall) videotape feedback/affect simulation training model.* Unpublished doctoral dissertation, Michigan State University, 1975.

Spivack, J. S., and Kagan, N. Laboratory to classroom—the practical application of IPR in a masters level pre-practicum counselor education program. *Counselor Education and Supervision,* September 1972, 3–15.

Tomory, R. E. *The acceleration and continuation of client growth in counseling and psychotherapy: A comparison of Interpersonal Process Recall (IPR) with traditional counseling methods.* Manuscript in preparation, 1979.

Van Noord, R. W., and Kagan, N. Stimulated recall and affect simulation in counseling: Client growth reexamined. *Journal of Counseling Psychology,* 1976, *23,* 28–33.

Werner, A., and Schneider, J. M. Teaching medical students interactional skills. *New England Journal of Medicine,* 1974, *290,* 1232–1237.

PART FIVE

Developmental Perspectives

Part V focuses on psychotherapy from a developmental perspective. Specifically, particular problems in psychotherapy with special client groups can lead to particular supervisory issues. Chapter 20, *Child Psychotherapy* by John M. Reisman, considers qualities of the psychotherapist, the nature of child psychotherapy and the impact of these two areas on the tasks of the supervisor. Chapter 21, *Supervision of Psychotherapy with Adolescents* by Kathryn A. Hess and Allen K. Hess, describes the developmentally specific issues that arise in psychotherapy with this age group. Often the supervisor faces the task of clarifying value-laden issues for the psychotherapist to enable the work of allowing client decision making to occur.

Chapter 22, *Geropsychotherapy: Training and Supervision* by Charles V. Lair, reports about the educative and supportive needs of the student psychotherapist when he or she works with elderly clients.

CHAPTER 20

Child Psychotherapy

JOHN M. REISMAN

Clinical psychology began as an endeavor both to provide psychological services to children and to provide psychologists with a specific form of instruction and supervision. From its inception in 1896, when Lightner Witmer at the University of Pennsylvania responded to the challenge of a local school teacher to apply psychology to the problems of children by founding the first psychoeducational clinic—really the first child guidance clinic—in the world, issues of training were addressed. Witmer conceived of clinical psychology as a novel application of the clinical method (Witmer, 1907), a time-honored procedure for doing *in vivo* research and training. The clinician tests hypotheses and theoretical predictions in every individual case, since even a single exception to a universal generalization is sufficient to require its modification. Further, the clinician trains and instructs through personal demonstrations and supervised practice with actual clients, which is the essence of the clinical method of education.

Two important facets about the early work of clinicians with children should be noted. First, a careful assessment was considered essential in developing a treatment plan. This assessment included not only the contributions of psychologists, but also physicians, teachers, social workers, and all other relevant professionals. Significantly, perhaps the first case—a child with spelling problems—was treated and helped by having glasses prescribed! This emphasis upon assessment has endured as an attribute of sound practice.

Second, the children were viewed as having educational problems and deficits. This does not mean that treatment was restricted to children with what today would be called learning disabilities. Rather, it means that every conceivable problem of children was regarded as a problem in education or training. The aggressive or delinquent child of today was conceived of as a moral defective, as someone whose moral training was lacking; the aim was to train the child in proper behavior (Witmer, 1908–1909). The autistic child of today was seen as a case of arrested development, false feeble-mindedness and strong will, whose attention needed to be seized and directed toward growth (Witmer, 1919–1922). This conceptualization, aside from its modern ring, is noted to serve as a reminder that the structure and content of supervision are very much dependent upon the theoretical understanding of the supervisor.

For almost 40 years clinical psychology was essentially clinical child psychology (Reisman, 1976). World War II, the Wechsler-Bellevue, the Rorschach, the Thematic Apperception Test, the Veteran's Administration, and a rapid increase in training programs and new psychologists changed all that. Clinical child psychology was so buried by the stampede that it was 20 years before it was picked up, dusted off, and "rediscovered" as a specialty subarea of the field. Also forgotten, almost mercifully, were the attitudes of some authorities toward the treatment of children.

Seemingly the size of the client was equated with the seriousness of the problem and the difficulty of treatment. Children, since they were smaller than adults, were thought to have smaller problems which could be more easily solved. Accordingly, the extent of professional training could be somewhat less for those who worked with children. Alfred Adler, a physician, encouraged the training of teachers and parents to deal with the psychological problems of youngsters. And when in 1925–29 there was turmoil within analytic circles about the need for analysts to be medically trained, it was temporarily resolved when the New York Psychoanalytic Society conceded that lay analysts were appropriate for children, but not for adults (Jones, 1957; Reisman, 1976, p. 185).

To some extent those attitudes persist. Although no one seriously doubts the child is a precursor to the adult, the study of the adult is regarded as a broad, general field within psychology and clinical psychology, while the study of the child is categorized as a narrow field of specialization. Skepticism is expressed about the validity of children's problems (Lapouse and Monk, 1964), and the conclusion is soberly advanced that not much needs to be done about them because most of them go away by themselves. A thoughtful discussion of the issue of "spontaneous remission" and the factors that may account for a child's resolution of psychological difficulties without therapeutic intervention is provided by Anna Freud (1971, pp. 94–99), but all too frequently it is assumed that remissions in childhood are entirely felicitous and without any long-range consequences. To the extent that these attitudes do persist among professionals and students, they may be expected to impede and have a bearing upon the supervisory process in child psychotherapy.

This introduction is also meant to convey that treatment for children has been both a persistent and perplexing problem for psychologists. On the one hand there have been the demands of distressed parents, teachers, and responsible adults to do something to help troublesome, if not troubled, children. On the other hand there has been the subtle, and sometimes not-so-subtle, communication that the therapy of children is not especially taxing of professional skills or even necessary. Obviously, to the extent that this last communication is valid, then the training of therapists to work with children can be relatively brief and simple.

To confess my biases at the outset, I believe professional work with children is challenging, that it requires an understanding of human development, both child and adult, and that it compels an integration of what is valuable into a coherent approach that is of benefit to the individual client. In order to make clear this position, an *integrative* psychotherapy (Reisman, 1973), and its implications for supervision and training, let us begin by a consideration of what psychotherapy means.

THE MEANINGS OF PSYCHOTHERAPY

Some years ago I attended a symposium during which a teacher presented the outcomes of a day treatment program with children (Gold and Reisman, 1970). Modestly, the teacher attributed the favorable results of the school to the training and educational efforts of the faculty and nonprofessional staff. Immediately he was challenged. It was argued that the results had been obtained through psychotherapy, and this argument was difficult to settle because there was confusion about the meaning of the term.

One result of that meeting was my attempt to consider the meanings of psychotherapy and to develop a definition that would be operational, recognizable, and divorced from its intended effects and professional stipulations (Reisman, 1971a, b). A review of a large number of definitions of psychotherapy was undertaken, which disclosed that the term is used in several ways. First, psychotherapy can mean any procedure, including drugs and psychosurgery, employed in the treatment of mental disorders. Second, psychotherapy has been used to mean more or less vaguely specified psychological procedures and techniques intended to alleviate disorders. Third, psychotherapy has been defined to mean certain processes, such as a special learning process or a process of growth; or it has been defined in terms of the intended outcomes or effects, that is, it is described as a procedure which aims to provide an improved adjustment or to arouse emotional experiences. Fourth, psychotherapy has been defined as a professionally provided service, with broad or narrow specifications of those professions qualified to render it.

There is merit and utility in each of those definitions, but each has certain deficiencies from a scientific point of view. The term may be so broadly defined that anything could be called psychotherapy if someone says its aim is to treat a mental disorder or if it is performed by a member of a designated profession. When defined by its effects, it admits of no failure, since by definition the effects must be produced for the treatment to have been said to be administered. This is a singular state of affairs for any treatment, although some therapists have argued for it; that is, they have contended that if the client has not improved, a therapeutic relationship has not been produced and there has been no psychotherapy.

A definition of psychotherapy was proposed to counter the above deficiencies which stated: "An analysis of what has been presented suggests three common elements in communications that appear to be psychotherapy: one, there is a wish to be of help to the client; two, in each, respect for the client is implied; and three, in each there is communication of understanding of what the client has said or done, or of what the client might do to improve his condition or behavior. It is the presence of these three elements that distinguishes psychotherapy from other forms of communication. Tentatively, the communication of person-related understanding, respect, and a wish to be of help defines psychotherapy" (Reisman, 1971a, p. 66).

This definition provides a basis for supervision, for understanding the therapeutic role, and for determining when psychotherapy is being performed, regardless of who is doing it or under what circumstances it may occur. Although it seems a simple definition, it is not. Eight forms of communication are described that may possibly fall under person-related understanding, with research called for to determine the appropriateness of their inclusion. Briefly, they are empathic, responsive, expository, interrogative, interpretative, suggestions, evaluations, and self-disclosure (Reisman and Yamokoski, 1974).

Moreover, it is also recognized that psychotherapy may be legally defined for statutory purposes as a professionally offered service. It is in these two senses—as a specific form of communication of understanding, respect, and a wish to be of help, and as a professionally offered service—that the term psychotherapy will be used. Broadly speaking, child psychotherapy is a professionally offered service of psychological assistance to children and the adults who may appropriately be involved with them. Speaking narrowly and precisely, child psychotherapy is the communication to the child of understanding, respect, and a wish to be of help. Conceivably, a child psychotherapist may see a child for psychotherapy over a course of many sessions and never provide psychotherapy as it has been precisely defined. The same may be true for an adult psychotherapist with adult clients.

For example, the author had occasion to observe a student see a child in play therapy. During the entire session the child ran about the room strewing toys in every direction, spilling paint, scribbling on walls, ripping papers, and creating one enormous mess. Meanwhile the student sat in a corner of the room out of the line of destruction, smiling benignly. Throughout the entire meeting the student said only two words. They were, "Time's up." This was not child psychotherapy, neither according to the precise definition proposed nor perhaps according to the understanding of most professionals about this service.

Similarly, the definition may help us to clarify other issues. Is the setting of limits psychotherapy? Is toilet-training a child psychotherapy? Is paper-training a dog psychotherapy? Is teaching an autistic child to speak psychotherapy? Is teaching a parrot to speak psychotherapy? Is playing with a child psychotherapy? Is child psychotherapy composed of doll play, painting, and other cathartic, constructive, and expressive activities? These are not idle questions. How psychotherapy is defined, or whether it is defined at all, has a bearing upon what child psychotherapists are trained to do, how they perform, and what is determined about the effectiveness of this service.

THE MEANINGS OF CHILD PSYCHOTHERAPY

According to English law an infant is anyone below the age of 21 years. In the United States the legal definition of a child varies from state to state. A child, for legal purposes, may be anyone below the age of 21 years or 18 years or 16 years or 13 years. What we mean by child psychotherapy has a similar arbitrariness and nonsensical quality when considered by the range of what may be done.

In actual practice a child psychotherapist may see a child in one or more of any of these treatment modes: play therapy, individual psychotherapy, family therapy, activity group therapy, group therapy, behavior modification or therapy, milieu therapy, and specific training programs. The treatment always involves cooperation with, or at least taking into account, other adults who are responsible for the child or intimately associated with the child's upbringing: parents, teachers, social workers, foster parents, pediatricians, and so on.

Unlike the situation described in many books about child therapy, a child ordinarily does not appear on his or her own initiative in treatment and undertake the service with touching gratitude and appreciation for the service. Children almost always are brought to the therapist by some adult. It cannot be assumed by the trainee that these clients know why they are being seen, that they feel a need for help, or that the reasons for their being referred are valid. Nor can the trainee assume that because the child and therapist agree that help is needed, the parents or adults responsible will allow it to be provided. When working with children the supervisor must instill in the trainee that almost nothing can be assumed and almost everything has to be investigated, negotiated, and worked out.

Halpern and Kissel (1976) discuss these issues in their *Helping Resources for Troubled Children:*

> What are some questions that the clinician faces in deciding on intervention techniques when confronted by the child in need of his services—no matter whether the child's problems are within himself, in the matrix of the family relationships, at school, or among peers? Is the child to be treated alone or in a group? Should the family be seen collaterally or as a unit? Is quick symptom removal preferred or should more extensive relationship therapy be tried? What are the indications for environmental maneuvers? For pharmacotherapy? What conditions make parent education primary? When do school programs become treatment modalities in their own right? (p. 13).

Children in the typical clinic or agency are persons ranging in age from shortly after birth to 18 years. Therefore, child psychotherapy as it is actually practiced means the provision of a number of therapeutic modalities to preschoolers, children, and adolescents, and their families. In this book for the purposes of this chapter child psychotherapy has a more restricted meaning; it refers to individual psychotherapy with a youngster who has not attained puberty, usually in a play therapy or play setting. This narrow meaning spares us the consideration of many of the questions that are raised in the actual practice of child psychotherapy and the implications that those questions have for supervision and training. Nevertheless, it should be remembered that our task has been limited for the purposes of convenience and that in the real world those concerns and more compel our attention.

Even within the narrow meaning of this chapter, there may be disagreements about what should or should not be included. How many different approaches to play therapy should be discussed? There are, to mention a few, psychoanalytic (Freudian), psychoanalytic (neo-Freudian, Kleinian, ego-analytic), Rogerian or client-centered, existential, Gestalt, Adlerian, primal, integrative or eclectic, Rankian, and Jungian. Should behavior therapy and behavior modification with children be here? Fortunately, the definition of psychotherapy provides a guide. Every system of psychotherapy communicates understanding. They differ in the content of what is communicated and understood, but for each, there is a framework of understanding and the task of conveying it. The structural problems are the same for all. Therefore, that is what will be emphasized in this chapter, the structural issues involved in training and supervision of psychotherapy with children.

QUALIFICATIONS OF THE CHILD THERAPIST

There are legal and parochial considerations which state the qualifications required for licensure and practice as a psychotherapist. The professional must have an advanced—usually a doctoral—degree from a recognized university. Certain courses in appropriate areas must have been taken, and a period, usually one or two years, of supervised experience must have been obtained. The professional must be of good moral character, aware of ethical guides and restrictions, and conscientious in maintaining proper behavior.

From the above we can infer that the supervisor of child therapy must be alert to corresponding qualifications and deficiencies of students. Such students should have taken courses—developmental psychology, child psychopathology, child treatment—and/or gained experiences that provide a theoretical and practical framework for understanding human behavior and how children can be helped. The student must be dedicated, conscientious, responsible, somewhat fond of children, and interested in being of help to them.

Some years ago Carl Rogers (1939) gave his attention to the qualifications for trainees in clinical psychology. He recommended that these students be selected for their ability to enter into warm human relationships and to accept intimacies. They must be sincerely interested in people, mature in their functioning, and persons of integrity. Moreover, he suggested, these qualities might be promoted and developed if the students themselves were helped to gain understanding of their own behaviors through their training experiences.

There is surprisingly little disagreement about the qualifications of the professional child therapist. While there may be theoretical differences about how much professional training is actually needed to produce a competent child therapist, the issue has often been settled by licensing and certification requirements and regulations. Less settled is the issue of personal therapy or analysis for the developing clinician; students are usually aware of this as a requirement in psychoanalytically oriented programs, with other programs less likely to make this demand.

In general, the training required does not differ too much from what was described by Moustakas (1959, pp. 307–311). The student is encouraged to acquire a theoretical orientation for the understanding of children and their treatment, a familiarity with other approaches, and a grounding in research methodology and literature. Observations of professional therapists seeing a number of children of different ages and problems should be provided. These observation experiences may be live, on audio tape, transcriptions on video tape, or in varying combinations of the preceding. Discussions with an experienced child therapist help to clarify issues and misunderstandings encountered by the student.

Of most importance, the student begins to see children in play therapy under supervision. The supervisor bears a responsibility to select for the student children who afford instructive, constructive, and encouraging experiences; clients who can reasonably be expected to be helped and to complete the course of treatment in the time the student has available.

Moustakas felt that normal children might well provide the early training for fledgling students. This recommendation was made at a time and within circumstances that made child therapy appear only beneficial and never harmful. Times change, and a number of possible hazards have been identified that make child therapy desirable only for those who definitely are in need of it: (1) the child may be encouraged to act out or engage in socially unacceptable impulses, (2) the child may be encouraged in fantasy production, weakening contacts with reality, (3) being seen in therapy may threaten the child's self-esteem, (4) the child may be labeled and ostracized by peers, (5) the time for the therapy may disrupt the child's schooling and create friction within the family, (6) the child may be isolated and exposed to deviant models of behavior, and (7) the therapist could be harmful if unskilled or unresponsive to the child's needs (Kessler, 1966, p. 399; McCord, 1978).

The risks of harm are sufficient to make it seem inadvisable, if not unethical, to see normal children in play therapy, although a helpful background can be acquired through playground and school observations and psychological evaluations of children. Experiences are, therefore, best gained with children who appear to be in need of the service. It is primarily through actual contacts with children in play therapy and discussions with the professinal therapist supervising the case that the student acquires the background, comfort, and confidence that are significant qualifications in the performance of the therapeutic task.

We have mentioned a number of personal qualifications—good moral character, conscientiousness, and so on. Some of these are legally mandated by licensure or certification laws. In practice they are indicated by keeping appointments, attention to reports, notification of clients about scheduling changes, and so on. However, some—warmth, unconditional positive regard, genuineness—are important attributes of a particular theoretical orientation, though how essential they are for therapists of every kind remains to be determined. It would seem most prudent, as I have contended elsewhere (Reisman, 1975), to guide fledgling therapists into programs that are compatible with their characteristics, rather than to assume that a deficiency in some personal attribute only valued by a particular system disqualifies them from practice.

THE WORK OF THE CHILD THERAPIST

Every method of treatment recognizes that there is just so much a student can be taught, and that a certain amount of individual expression and spontaneity contribute to the effectiveness of the therapist, if not the therapy. This suggests some restriction upon how specific, detailed, and controlling the supervisor should be. Nevertheless, there are extremes in the latitude tolerated. Moustakas (1959), who has described his method as existential play therapy, asserted:

> Instruction, caution, and direction inhibit the student, make him uncertain, and contribute to rigid and static preconceptions. The training is not aimed at teaching the student what to say and what to do or how to approach and relate to children in therapy. The preliminary experiences are offered as background to the central purpose which is the evolvement of a significant therapeutic relationship with a child. The actual experience cannot be alive unless the student is free to approach the child in his own way and to develop skill through his own insights and errors (p. 308).

On the other hand, the freedom of the therapist-student may be severely curtailed by the supervisor of another orientation in an attempt to afford freedom for the child. Limits upon the child may be kept to a minimum, but limits upon what the student-therapist can do may be harsh and artificial (Reisman and Yamokoski, 1974). To illustrate, L. Guerney (1978), in discussing a training program for graduate students in client centered play therapy, described it as follows: "This means that they may not offer advice, suggestions, directions, judgments or evaluations (even of a positive nature), or ask questions (except to have something not heard repeated). On the positive side, they are checked for their ability to respond empathically to the child's expression of feeling, to structure adequately, to impose and enforce limits, and to respond appropriately to content, indicating interest and involvement with the child."

Obviously, the supervisor of students being trained in one system of psychotherapy will expect trainees to perform somewhat differently than the supervisor in another. An analytic approach seeks to encourage its practitioners to foster a positive transference, or a highly favorable impression of the therapist by the child, as soon as possible. To this end, Anna Freud (1971) recommended doing favors for the child, giving little presents, demonstrating the therapist's strength and power, and, if necessary, going so far as to promise a cure—a step that today would probably be judged unethical.

A client-centered or Rogerian approach to supervision has a quite different immediate and continuous objective, which is to develop therapists who believe in the capacity for change and growth, who assist the child to be independent of the therapist, and who foster in clients a sense of personal responsibility for their freedom. "A therapist is not ready to go into the playroom with a child until she has developed self-discipline, restraint, and a deep respect for the personality of the child. There is no discipline so severe as the one which demands that each individual be given the right and the opportunity to stand on his own two feet and to make his own decisions" (Axline, 1969, p. 64).

To further their end, Rogerian supervisors try to have trainees implement their confidence in the strengths of the child, rather than to promote the child's confidence in the strength and power of the therapist. Although virtually every system of psychotherapy talks about the importance of the therapist-client relationship, clearly the specific nature of this relationship and the tactics employed to achieve it and maintain it may be quite different. One system may approve the giving of food, birthday presents, and words of encouragement and praise to the child in order to foster a dependent relationship; another system may strongly discourage these tactics precisely because it does not seek dependency at any stage of the treatment process.

These differences have a strong bearing upon training and supervision, especially when one considers that in a behavioral system rewards and punishments are at the heart of the treatment. What should a student do or say when a child who has been underachieving in school comes into his play therapy session carrying his latest report card with markedly improved grades? Almost anything might be right, according to one system or another, which is why eclectic approaches are the despair of those who favor a consistent point of view.

From the narrow view of a particular theoretical system, a supervisor can narrowly specify the work of the child therapist. Axline (1969) listed eight principles to guide the Rogerian child therapist: (1) develop a warm, friendly relationship as soon as possible, (2) accept the child for what he is, (3) promote a feeling of permissiveness and freedom of expression, (4) recognize the child's feelings and reflect them back, (5) respect the child's ability to solve personal problems and maintain the responsibility for those choices and decisions with the child, (6) in no way attempt to direct the child's actions or conversation, (7) in no way attempt to limit or expedite the process of therapy, and (8) maintain limits to a minimum.

The psychoanalytic position is usually not so explicitly stated. However an amalgamation of Freud (1971) and Weiner (1975) leads to these guides for the supervision of the analytic child therapist: (1) During the initial phase of the therapy, the therapist should assess the circumstances, enlist the cooperation of parents, evaluate the child, and determine how the child's needs can be met by treatment. (2) Efforts should be made to insure and to foster a positive impression of the therapist. (3) A treatment contract should be formed. (4) During the middle phase of treatment, the therapist should interpret resistances and play activities, work through feelings and transference reactions, and be alert to any countertransference attitudes. (5) In the final phase of treatment, when there is termination of contacts, there should be a working through of the problems and feelings associated with termination.

Note that in the psychoanalytic position the supervisor is concerned about assessment and evaluation, a treatment contract, transference and countertransference reactions, resistances, and termination. These issues are almost nonexistent for the Rogerian supervisor, for whom transference, countertransference, and resistance exist only as theoretical terms, while evaluation, treatment contracts or goals, and termination depend upon the wishes and initiatives of the client.

Supervision in psychoanalytic child therapy involves almost the same concerns as the treatment. The supervisor is alert to countertransference attitudes toward the student and to resistances and transference attitudes of the supervisee toward the supervisor. Similarly, other methods structure the supervisor-supervisee relationship according to their theories of treatment. The supervisor of the student Rogerian child therapist strives for a feeling of freedom and exploration in their relationship, while respecting the sensitivity, understanding, and decisions of the trainee. At one extreme, supervision may be a highly complex and worrisome business. At the other extreme, "supervision" may not rightly be regarded to exist.

Surveys suggest that the majority of therapists regard themselves as integrative or eclectic (Garfield and Kurtz, 1976). Reisman (1973) formulated a set of seven principles that seem to guide the work of this large body of child therapists: (1) the therapist assesses the child as a precondition to psychotherapy and as an integral part of the process of psychotherapy; (2) the therapist listens to the child and allows ample opportunity for the expression of feelings and beliefs; (3) the therapist communicates understanding of the child, respect, and a wish to be of help; (4) the therapist negotiates with the child a purpose or goal for their meetings; (5) the therapist makes clear what is unusual or inconsistent in the child's behavior, feelings, and beliefs; (6) when dealing with behaviors that are supported within a given system, the therapist may modify the behaviors by negotiation within the system; and (7) the therapist negotiates termination with the child when it seems more advantageous to terminate than to continue.

These principles have clear implications for supervision and emphasize that the child therapist bears a continuing responsibility to determine the appropriateness of treatment, to obtain the child's informed consent and cooperation in the therapeutic enterprise, to make explicit the contradictions and inconsistencies in the child, to effect changes through environmental manipulations and consultations with parents and other adults, and to terminate the service when there is little point in its continuance. The use of negotiations in these principles is deliberate; it seeks to stress the importance of cooperation and mutual respect between therapist and child in decision-making.

In actual practice the situation becomes more complex and the trainee has to be mindful of these complexities. Decisions about treatment often cannot be made by therapist and child alone. The parents, referral sources, and other responsible adults may have to be consulted. It is not uncommon for the child and the parents to profess ignorance about any need for help and to lay the responsibility for their seeking treatment upon some referring adult or agency, frequently the school or court. Therefore, the trainee may have to be prepared to undertake a somewhat lengthy and involved process to determine if treatment should be offered, to negotiate a purpose or goal, or at some later stage to explore termination. It does happen that the child and the therapist may be ready to terminate, but the parents may not, or vice versa. The checking and rechecking and consulting may seem foreign, tedious, and needless to the trainee, and supervision may have to deal repeatedly with the importance of verification and communication among all the parties concerned. This dependence of child upon adult upon referral source is a cardinal fact that must be grasped by the trainee in child psychotherapy.

The principles of psychotherapy specify what the trainee should do in a given session and some of what should be accomplished over the course of contacts with a child. Supervision would aim at the student's awareness of these principles and their implementation, and, as with other systems, the principles provide a guide for the structuring of the supervisor-supervisee relationship.

LIMITS

Although the setting of limits is often a problem with adults, it is a common problem with children and may be the major focus of treatment. Bixler (1949) argued that, "limits are therapy." From the definitions discussed earlier in this chapter, we might say that limits can be psychotherapeutic, but they are not psychotherapy. Essentially, limit-setting is a form of training. To the extent that a clinician must spend time setting limits, psychotherapy in the form of the communication of understanding is probably not being conducted and one might well question the need for a professional child therapist.

Particularly with play materials around, children may do things that are never encountered with adults. They may pick up a block and throw it at the therapist or out the window. They may lap paint, suck chalk, and chew crayons. They may suddenly smash expensive toys or dash out of the room to get a drink of water. They may throw a terrific tantrum because they can't have something they want.

Every system of play therapy agrees there are certain limits, certain things the child is not allowed to do. Destructiveness and physical aggression directed against the therapist are not permitted (Dorfman, 1951). Almost everyone wants appointments to begin and end on time, and the child to remain in the playroom for the duration of the meeting. After that, there are differences of opinion about what should be tolerated and how limits should be enforced.

Questionable limits, which some therapists feel are important and some do not, are: joining the child in play, giving or accepting gifts (Ginott, 1961), social contacts outside the therapy session (Singer, 1965), allowing the child to do homework or listen to the radio during the meeting.

Similarly, there is general agreement about how the limits should initially be imposed. If the child threatens to break a limit, the therapist says something to the effect that the child would like to do such-and-such, but it is not permitted. If the infraction occurs and it is an isolated incident, the therapist responds in the past tense, that is, you wanted to do such-and-such, but it isn't permitted.

Accounts usually end with the child responding positively to an empathic statement and an admonition. However, there are children who repeatedly break limits. This issue has been discussed at length (Reisman, 1973, pp. 89–95), along with the differences among therapists in how they recommend dealing with it. A reasonable procedure would seem to be that if the limits broken are serious and intolerable and continuously occurring, the session should be terminated with the hope that the child may be in better control the next time. Should the therapist suspect that the limits are being broken so the sessions may be terminated, the therapist should explore with the child and the parent some change in the treatment arrangement, possibly with the parent and child being seen together. In such an arrangement, the temporary focus of the therapy might be on the parent's means for dealing with the child's violation of limits.

The supervision of child therapists—or any kind of therapist for that matter —often involves the setting of limits. Generally, a supervisor is concerned that a trainee not unduly restrict the freedom of the child, that prohibited behaviors not be tolerated in the session because the trainee is reluctant to impose limits or because the trainee gains some vicarious satisfaction from seeing them expressed, that supervisory appointments begin and end on time, that reports are turned in promptly, that progress notes are kept, that required forms are completed, that the playroom is kept clean, and that treatment recommendations are followed, or at least considered.

A failure to bring the trainee's breaking of limits to attention presumably leads to the same harmful consequences that could occur if the therapist neglected to deal with the child's infractions. The supervisor might experience mounting anger toward the trainee, which could be expressed in an unconstructive outburst that both parties might regret. The trainee could experience mounting anxiety about the ambiguity of limits in the training session and guilt about the unpunished "crimes." Here, too, supposedly the mere mentioning of what is troubling corrects the problem, and everyone can be relieved and effective again. For example, most trainees respond appropriately to an explanation about why the playroom should be restored to order that emphasizes the importance of modeling acceptable behaviors, cooperation between child and therapist, and its therapeutic value.

There can be no argument that promptly discussing what is troublesome reduces the supervisor's anxiety and perhaps the trainee's as well, and demonstrates the effectiveness of the supervisor in the performance of that job. However, again, as with clients, there may be the problem of what to do should the trainee's breaking of limits persist. Berlin (1967) discussed his handling of a resident in child psychiatry who, for 2½ years, was late for work, meetings, appointments with patients, and handing in reports. These infractions were repeatedly pointed out to the resident, but they nevertheless continued. That this behavior was tolerated for 2½ years is, in itself, a matter for some reflection in weighing how effectively supervisors deal with their supervisees. After resolving his own feelings of "impotent anger," Berlin, ". . . was able to do with firmness and conviction what I had previously done rather tentatively. I outlined the consequences of the continued dereliction of duties in terms of a hearing before the Hospital Superintendent and pointed out the possibility that the resident might lose his residency status."

Incidentally, Berlin stated that the reason individual psychotherapy was not recommended for the above resident was that he was already in it and was using it as an excuse to fend off the setting of limits with him—that is, "I'm working on it in my analysis." Although 2½ years may be more time than some supervisors have available to wait for change, the step-by-step approach discussed by Berlin in dealing with supervisees seems generally accepted. One, the supervisor, in a calm, patient, friendly manner, brings the violation to the student's attention, with the supervisor maintaining respect for the supervisee's capacity to deal with the issue reasonably and to change in her or his handling of the matter constructively. Two, the supervisor should psychologically be prepared to go through the same procedure, with perhaps a little more intensity and concern, again and again. Three, if the problem persists, the supervisor should outline or present the harmful consequences that the student may bring upon himself or herself by continued violations. Finally, if ultimately necessary, the supervisor should see that those harmful consequences have the opportunity to be invoked.

Implicit in what has been said are limits upon making the supervision into personal treatment. Szurek and Berlin (1967) have suggested this may be done if it is not coerced and is done by mutual consent. However, many professionals would probably agree with Caplan (1970), who in his views on consultation urged that the relationship not become that of therapist-patient and that treatment, if needed, be provided elsewhere.

PARENTS

There are four ways in which parents may be involved in the treatment of their child. One, they may give their permission for their child being seen in therapy, but refuse or be unable to take advantage of any services for themselves. Rather than condemn or endorse such an arrangement, it is preferable to consider the circumstances when it may be appropriate. There may be situations when the parents are genuinely unable to adapt their schedules to mesh with the times that professionals have available to see them, and their child can profitably be seen without them. The child's problem may not involve the parents, or the need of the child may be to disengage or create psychological distance from the parents. Under these conditions the parents may be no more involved than a referral source, that is, they may be informed about the beginning and termination of therapy, and there may be more or less periodic exchanges of information about progress.

Two, the child may not be seen in therapy, but the parents may be counseled and guided on how to help their child. There may be training of the parents to themselves provide child therapy, as in filial therapy (Guerney, 1964), or to provide suitable methods of training and handling (Schopler and Reichler, 1971). The therapist may meet with the parents to provide counseling or therapy or consultation or training so that their concerns may be alleviated and their effectiveness as parents increased. This may be a treatment of choice if the child's problems seem transitory, if the parents are misinformed and unduly anxious about their child's behavior, if some minor modification in parental behavior can readily be acquired, or if the child is too young or too deficient in functioning to be seen in child therapy.

Three, the parents and the child may receive psychological services from different therapists or be seen at different times. This may be called conjoint or collaborative therapy, and it is a form followed in many child guidance clinics. It is particularly indicated when there are issues that may be damaging to the integrity of the family should they be aired in the company of all members—for example, sexual problems between the parents, contemplation of divorce or infidelity, intense and unrealistic hostility of one member toward another.

Four, the parents and the child may be seen together by the same therapist in family therapy. This approach is particularly indicated when the child is capable of participation, when the family members are desirous of more harmonious relationships, and when problems center on misunderstandings and communication.

Regardless of how the parents are involved, the therapist with the child is expected to maintain a professional attitude toward them. This professional attitude means that the child therapist does not blame the parents for the child's problems, nor is there any dwelling on past mistakes or on what is currently wrong. Instead, the therapist attempts to enlist the cooperation of the parents in being of help to their child and gives advice only with patience and caution.

Some years ago I had the good fortune to attend a talk given to parents by Sol Gordon. In response to requests for direct advice, Gordon said something like the following: "I'll give you advice, but I'd like you to promise me something— if you're not able to do it, think about why you're not." That's good advice. If you do give suggestions to parents—and you shouldn't until you've found out how they have already dealt with the problem and whether they really want your advice—do so with the wisdom and understanding that can accept that advice being rejected or not followed.

From what I have been saying, it is clear that child therapists do not routinely put the parents in the role of the true patient, nor are they so sanguine that they have complete trust in every parent obediently doing what some professional says is in their child's best interests. This balanced attitude towards parents, which presumes neither innocence nor guilt, obstructionism nor ready compliance, in connection with their child's problem, is probably the one that ideally should be communicated by the supervisor to the supervisee.

Supervision of child therapists promotes their balanced, reasonable attitudes and deals with their attitudes toward parents that interfere with the effectiveness of treatment and the development of a cooperative relationship. The trainee may regard the parents with hostility, accepting the child's perceptions as gospel or being incensed by behaviors of the parents that appear counter-productive or damaging. There may be an identification with the child against the parents and against the professionals who are working with the parents. The trainee's difficulties in dealing with authority and authority figures may result in similar tactics to frustrate staff members and resentments in supervision about implementing the supervisor's recommendations. These problems, when pointed out, may be rationalized by supervisees as concerns about confidentiality and protecting the rights of the client.

The trainee, for example, may refuse to speak with the parents, justifying this action on the grounds that the child may fear a breech of confidentiality or see the adults in a conspiratorial alliance. Forgotten is the idea that all concerned should be in a cooperative undertaking. An unfortunate consequence is often the resentment of parents toward the service and an abrupt termination of treatment.

A trainee walked out with a little girl after a successful session of play therapy. However, the mother of the child was distressed because the girl had become soaked in water play. She asked that this form of play not be permitted because the girl might catch cold. The trainee responded the child was free to play as she wished and he would not limit her use of water. Neither mother nor child was seen at that agency again. The trainee had made his point, had emphasized his integrity and initiative, had defied parental interference and authority, and had lost his client.

A mother asked a trainee if she could observe her child in play therapy. The trainee thought the request reasonable but did not know what to say. In supervision it was decided he would ask the mother why she had made the request. What eventually developed was that the mother was concerned about how she handled the child, and with the child's consent and at a time aside from the play therapy hour, the trainee observed the mother and son in interaction and offered helpful comments.

A father refused to participate in the treatment of his child. However, after a few play therapy sessions, he asked to sit in the meetings with his wife so he could find out what was going on. The trainee, thinking this might signify the beginning of paternal involvement, permitted this to occur. His curiosity satisfied, as well as his dominance, the father refused additional appointments. Several weeks later the mother reported her husband's renewed interest in coming in with her for one of her appointments. The trainee wondered if he should be firm with the father and/or give him one more chance.

When ordinary supervision does not produce the behaviors desired, consultation and consideration of treatment for the supervisee or supervisor may be indicated. Particularly among psychoanalytically oriented child therapists, questions are raised about unconscious motivations for entering this line of work (Szurek, 1967). It takes no great stretch of the imagination to see budding child therapists drawn to this area by an attempt to work through again and again their unmet needs as children and their conflicts with their parents. Moreover, even assuming a satisfactory degree of resolution, it is quite possible that the experiences in child therapy elicit memories and feelings for supervisor or supervisee that had been thought long dormant. This reawakening of conflict may affect a professional attitude with one's clients, with one's colleagues, with one's supervisor, and with one's supervisee.

Szurek (1967) spoke of two major sources of anxiety: those anxieties arising from current problems and difficulties and those feelings of apprehension brought on by conflicts and troubles from the past. Within the supervisory session both sources of anxiety may be triggered, especially as they relate to the trainee's parental attitudes. In work with children and parents, one's own childhood relations tend to be stimulated and brought to mind. In work with the supervisor (supervisee), the trainee (supervisor) is often confronted by someone who has many parental (child-like and youthful) characteristics: superior knowledge and experience (innocence, enthusiasm, vigor), superior status (aspirations to get ahead), authority to be rewarding or punitive, demanding of certain standards of performance and behavior.

While Ekstein and Wallerstein (1958) have argued that it is best to regard supervisor-supervisee problems as problems in learning, it cannot be denied that any relationship based on unequal status and dominance-submission is going to have its difficulties. To an extent, those difficulties can be minimized by reducing the inequality of status and emphasizing the cooperation so essential to the success of supervision, which in effect is similar to the attitude of understanding, respect, and helpfulness that the therapist seeks to communicate with clients.

RESEARCH

The Spring 1978 issue of the *Journal of Clinical Child Psychology* was devoted to the subject of training. Most of those articles had to do with the desirability of training in specific areas of consultation, and none dealt exclusively, or even primarily, with supervision. One of the few mentions of supervision was made by Schwartz and Tuma (1978), who surveyed graduate training in consultation and surmised that the amount of supervision was probably greater in APA-approved programs than it was in non-APA-approved programs.

There are a number of questions about supervision that would seem to be important to the field and that could have implications for other close helping relationships, such as individual psychotherapy. Indeed, considering the difficulties in generalizing from analogue research in psychotherapy, the study of supervision might have certain advantages over analogue studies, in that the former is not contrived and does deal with a meaningful, helping relationship that does aim at growth.

Some of the questions that have been raised are basic to the field as a whole and have pertinence to what should be taught in supervision. Is child therapy an effective form of treatment? Is one form of child therapy more effective than another in treating a certain disorder? Which disorders do not respond well to child therapy and are better treated by some other approach? What frequency of child therapy sessions is optimal for what disorders? What amount of time per individual session? What duration of treatment? How much psychotherapy, as it has been precisely defined, is actually practiced in different forms of child therapy? Is the quantity of psychotherapy, as it has been precisely defined, correlated with differences in outcome?

Some of the questions raised are more specific and have to do with selection of child therapists and their training. What personality characteristics and skills are associated with an effective child therapist? What characteristics would contraindicate suitability for this work? It has been suggested (Szurek, 1967) that child therapists cannot hope to help their clients progress beyond their own level of fixation with regard to the conflict in need of treatment; is that so? Do therapists who have undergone personal treatment perform more effectively than those who have not? Do certain disorders and certain clients respond better to certain therapists than others?

There has been very little research published about supervision in child psychotherapy and what little there is has not advanced knowledge much beyond the chapter "The Training of Counselors and Therapists" in *Client-centered therapy* (Rogers, 1951). In that chapter we learn that people can learn some therapeutic skills in as little as two weeks, and, more convincingly, in as little as six weeks; that not all trainees welcome personal therapy when it is offered, but those who take advantage of it regard it as a helpful and significant aspect of their training; and that supervision is "of crucial importance."

A subsequent study by Linnell (1977) investigated the effectiveness of having graduate students themselves play in a playroom for an hour a week for seven weeks. There were four graduate students in this experimental group, which met as a group with an experienced child therapist. When compared with four control group graduate students, there was no significant difference between the two groups in performance as play therapists nor in effectiveness with children. Nevertheless, the students in the experimental group reported they had found the experience valuable, and the small numbers of participants ($N = 4$) increased the probability of a Type II error (accepting the null hypothesis when it is false) so the value of this training experience may merit further investigation.

Similar results were found by Arnold (1976) in an investigation of the effectiveness of microcounseling techniques for the training of child therapists. Microcounseling focuses upon the acquisition of perhaps one or two definite skills in an intense training experience: the trainee receives materials, manuals, and tapes which discuss and model the skill; the trainee interviews a client and attempts to implement the skill; and there is "immediate feedback from a warm, supportive supervisor" concerning the trainee's success in performing the skill. These procedures were employed with graduate students to promote skill acquisition in limit setting and reflection of feelings in play therapy. Although there was a statistically significant difference in the performance of the experimentally trained group over that of the control immediately after training, this difference was no longer found after a lapse of two weeks.

Much of the material brought to bear upon matters of supervision is drawn from personal experiences, clinical anecdotes, and testimonials of proponents of a specific method. Traditionally, such material has been regarded as of the greatest value. It presents dearly bought clinical wisdom and the rich complexities of supervision. Still, it is to be hoped that continued progress in this field will be augmented by the sometimes discouraging, sometimes painful, but always enlightening process of research that directly tests the issues and impressions raised in child psychotherapy supervision.

REFERENCES

Arnold, J. S. Effectiveness of microcounseling procedures in the training of play therapists. *Dissertation Abstracts,* 1976, *37,* 3408–3409.

Axline, V. M. *Play therapy.* New York: Ballantine, 1969.

Berlin, I. N. Some implications of ego psychology for the supervisory process. In S. A. Szurek and I. N. Berlin (Eds.), *Training in therapeutic work with children.* Palo Alto: Science and Behavior Books, 1967.

Bixler, R. H. Limits are therapy. *Journal of Consulting Psychology,* 1949, *13,* 1–11.

Caplan, G. *The theory and practice of mental health consultation.* New York: Basic Books, 1970.

Dorfman, E. Play therapy. In C. Rogers (Ed.), *Client-centered therapy.* Boston: Houghton Mifflin, 1951.

Ekstein, R. and Wallerstein, R. S. *The teaching and learning of psychotherapy.* New York: Basic Books, 1958.

Freud, A. *The psychoanalytical treatment of children.* New York: Shocken, 1971.

Garfield, S. L., and Kurtz, R. Clinical psychologists in the 1970s. *American Psychologist,* 1976, *31,* 1–9.

Ginott, H. G. *Group psychotherapy with children.* New York: McGraw-Hill, 1961.

Gold, J. and Reisman, J. M. An outcome study of a day treatment unit school in a community mental health center. Paper presented at American Orthopsychiatric Association Convention, San Francisco, 1970.

Guerney, B., Jr. Filial therapy: description and rationale. *Journal of Consulting Psychology,* 1964, *28,* 304–310.

Guerney, B., Jr. Evaluation of consultation-supervision in training conjugal therapists. *Professional Psychology,* 1978, *9,* 203–209.

Guerney, L. Training and evaluation of students as consultants in an adult-child relationship enhancement program. *Professional Psychology,* 1978, *9,* 193–197.

Halpern, W. I. & Kissel, S. *Human resources for troubled children.* New York: Wiley-Interscience, 1976.

Jones, E. *The life and work of Sigmund Freud* (Vol. 3). New York: Basic Books, 1957.

Kessler, J. W. *Psychopathology of childhood.* Englewood Cliffs, N.J.; Prentice-Hall, 1966.

Lapouse, R. and Monk, M. Behavior deviations in a representative sample of children. *American Journal of Orthopsychiatry,* 1964, *34,* 436–446.

Linnell, A. T. The effects of adult play therapy on therapist skill development and client change. *Dissertation Abstracts,* 1977, *37,* 5834–5835.

McCord, J. A thirty-year follow-up of treatment effects. *American Psychologist,* 1978, *33,* 284–289.

Moustakas, C. E. *Psychotherapy with children.* New York: Harper and Row, 1959.

Reisman, J. M. *Toward the integration of psychotherapy.* New York: Wiley-Interscience, 1971, (a).

Reisman, J. M. The definitions of psychotherapy. *Mental Hygiene,* 1971, *55,* 413–417. (b)

Reisman, J. M. *Principles of psychotherapy with children.* New York: Wiley-Interscience, 1973.

Reisman, J. M. Trends in training in treatment. *Professional Psychology,* 1975, *6,* 187–192.

Reisman, J. M. *A history of clinical psychology.* New York: Irvington-Halsted, 1976.

Reisman, J. M., and Yamokoski, T. Psychotherapy and friendship: an analysis of the communications of friends. *Journal of Counseling Psychology,* 1974, *21,* 269–273.

Rogers, C. R. Needed emphases in the training of clinical psychologists. *Journal of Consulting Psychology,* 1939, *3,* 141–143.

Rogers, C. R. *Client-centered therapy.* Boston: Houghton Mifflin, 1951.

Schopler, E., and Reichler, R. J. Parents as cotherapists in the treatment of psychotic children. *Journal of Autism and Childhood Schizophrenia,* 1971, 1, 87–102.

Schwartz, S., and Tuma, J. M. Graduate training in consultation and liaison. *Journal of Clinical Child Psychology,* 1978, *7,* 47–49.

Singer, E. *Key concepts in psychotherapy.* New York: Random House, 1965.

Szurek, S. A. Remarks on training for psychotherapy. In S. A. Szurek and I. N. Berlin (Eds.), *Training in therapeutic work with children.* Palo Alto: Science and Behavior Books, 1967.

Szurek, S. A. and Berlin, I. N. The question of therapy for the trainee in the psychiatric training program. In S. A. Szurek and I. N. Berlin (Eds.), *Training in therapeutic work with children.* Palo Alto: Science and Behavior Books, 1967.

Weiner, I. B. *Principles of psychotherapy.* New York: Wiley-Interscience, 1975.

Witmer, L. Clinical psychology. *Psychological Clinic,* 1907, *1,* 1–9.

Witmer, L. The treatment and cure of a case of mental and moral deficiency. *Psychological Clinic,* 1908–09, *2,* 153–179.

Witmer, L. Orthogenic cases, XIV—Don: a curable case of arrested development due to a fear psychosis the result of shock in a three-year-old infant. *Psychological Clinic,* 1919–22, *13,* 97–111.

CHAPTER 21

Supervision of Psychotherapy with Adolescents

KATHRYN A. HESS AND ALLEN K. HESS

Psychotherapy with adolescents presents a variety of issues that merit particular attention. While many issues in conducting psychotherapy with adolescents are shared with adult psychotherapy (e.g., dealing with depression) and child psychotherapy (e.g., third party problems with confidentiality), adolescent treatment involves both particular variations on the problems, and problems unique to adolescents. This chapter will discuss (a) the definitions of adolescence, (b) concerns focused around adolescence per se, (c) technical issues in psychotherapy and in supervision, and (d) issues regarding the involvement of third parties.

DEFINITIONS OF ADOLESCENCE

Adolescence has been defined in two principal ways: psychophysiologically and psychosocially. A number of theorists describe various stages of adolescence, but Muuss (1969) observes, "No exact agreement exists among the various stage theories as to the number, characteristics, and psychological meaning of each of the stages" (p. 189). Most theories see adolescence beginning between 10 to 14 years of age, at about the time pubescence or physical and sexual maturity are achieved. Psychosocial tasks change as the child progresses into adolescence, as will be described below. The termination of adolescence is less well demarcated. The indicators more often are social, psychological, and vocational in nature. Thus, when the tasks of adolescence change or are completed, adulthood begins. Problems can develop when the less definite fading into adulthood is not accomplished, or when the mature adult who decides on career shifts is then placed in adolescent roles. For example, a twenty-seven-year-old assistant professor was heard talking about his "kids in class." At least one-third of the "kids" were thirty years or older. Thus, severe conflicts can occur when age-role definitions collide. A physically and sexually mature seventeen-year-old, who has caused a child's birth, will have adult tasks thrust upon him or her. The confusion that results from not resolving developmental tasks of late adolescence, added to the conflicting expectations for being an adult and an adolescent simultaneously, can be severe. Similarly, the lieutenant with peach fuzz on his cheeks commanding a veteran combat platoon will face tremendous cross pressures.

The supervisor and psychotherapist of adolescents are well advised to become familiar with conceptualizations of adolescence such as Sullivan's (1953) descriptions of the change from childhood to the juvenile era, pre-adolescence, early and late adolescence. Erikson (1959) has been popular in terms of his psychosocial stages: IV (industry versus inferiority), V (identity and repudiation versus identity diffusion), and VI (intimacy and solidarity versus isolation). Stage VII (generativity versus self-absorption) is implicated in the transition to young adulthood. Gesell, Ilg, and Ames (1956) describe the traits and issues of each year between ten and sixteen. Havighurst (1951) specifies nine tasks of the twelve- to eighteen-year-old:

1. Accepting one's physique and a sex role.

2. New relations with agemates of both sexes.

3. Emotional independence of parents and other adults.

4. Achieving assurance of economic independence.

5. Selecting and preparing for an occupation.

6. Developing intellectual skills and concepts necessary for civic competence.

7. Desiring and achieving socially responsible behavior.

8. Preparing for marriage and family life.

9. Building conscious values in harmony with an adequate scientific world picture.

Some familiarity with these and other theories (cf. Muuss, 1969) are essential for working with youth.

CONCERNS OF ADOLESCENCE

Anyone working with adolescents must have an accurate sense of the issues contemporary youth face in order to approach an effective working relationship. Reliance on the fact that the therapist (and supervisor) was at one time an adolescent and thus has direct experience of the adolescent's position fails to recognize the different environmental conditions and stressors the adult therapist, supervisor, and parent faced compared to the client's world. Many texts (Ausubel, Montemayor, and Svajian, 1977; Caplan and Lebovici, 1969; Coleman et al., 1974; Conger, 1977; Dragastin and Elder, 1975; Havighurst and Dreyer, 1975; McCandless and Coop, 1979; Muuss, 1975; and Yankelovich, 1974) and journals *(Adolescence, American Journal of Orthopsychiatry, Developmental Psychology,* and the *Journal of Youth and Adolescence)* provide a review of enduring issues of adolescence, such as biological changes, as well as exploring how these issues are shaped or channeled by current forces in our society. Of course, this source of knowledge necessarily must be complemented by spending time with adolescents to attain a sense of the contemporary scene from their view. The functioning of normal and deviant youth should be observed so the therapist can gain a feel for acceptable limits of behavior within the peer culture to balance his or her adult view of adolescent behavior. Also, a feel for issues which the therapist may have experienced some time ago, and issues which are novel—such as newer educational methods—might be best gained in vivo.

Among the important characteristics of adolescents is an *orientation to action.* While parents wonder how hour upon hour can be spent on the telephone or in a favorite hangout, this passivity is contrasted by sudden and seemingly impulsive acts. Projects may be the object of endless and idle speculation or of long bursts of all consuming activity. "Youth is wholly experimental," said Robert Louis Stevenson. The commitment to the activity and trying out one's resolve is as important as the nature of the project. The intense need to be taken seriously can result in the youth's use of *ultimatums.* This is too often countered (or sometimes provoked) by the parent's use of ultimatums. Adolescents, in the course of learning about how the society should function ideally, often try to put these ideas into effect. The joining of idealism with the action orientation and the need to attain competence (White, 1963) creates in the youth a situation in which he or she takes an action or a position, perhaps precipitously, which is then defended with a sense of desperation plus moral superiority. Turgeniev said youth has "that air of superiority to the rest of the world that usually disappears once the twenties has passed."

Both the brittleness of idealism and the grave self doubts give rise to despair and depression. Only recently has the number of youthful suicides and life threatening behavior been recognized. Mears and Gatchel (1979) report that the last twenty years has seen adolescent suicide increase by almost 250%. The therapist should have an awareness of the dynamics and forms that life threatening behavior to self and others may have in adolescents.

Psychotherapy with adolescents requires knowledge of the profound *physical and hormonal changes* (Carroll, 1968), plus the more subtle intellectual shifts that are occurring at this age. Schoenfeld (1969a) discusses four aspects of body images: (a) the subject perception of appearance and of ability to function, (b) internalized psychological factors, (c) sociological factors, which are most immediately seen in parent and peer expectations, and (d) an ideal body image. Essentially, rapid and qualitative changes such as facial, axillary, and pubic hair growth, menses and seminal emissions, and changes in muscle and bodily contour occur. When they occur in a person whose childhood did not result in a stable and positive image of him or herself, the changes may stimulate a variety of reactions in the adolescent. Knowledge of the changes is important, and may prove essential when the client requires factual information which the therapist may be in the best position to provide.

The cognitive changes (Osterrieth, 1969), characterized by Piaget as a transition from concrete to formal operations, open a whole world to the adolescent's eyes. The adolescent can begin to conceptualize the world in other than egocentric and concrete terms, and to see relationships between parts and the whole (Muuss, 1969). Interestingly, Piaget (Inhelder and Piaget, 1958) describes a burst of egocentrism at the transition between the concrete and formal stages. Muuss (1969, p. 156) says "This high level egocentrism takes the form of a naive but exuberant idealism with unrealistic proposals for educational, political, and social reforms, attempts at reshaping reality, and disregard for actual obstacles." The moral issues (Kohlberg, 1975) raised by considering the nature of the world and trying to find one's place in it are paralleled by the growing sensitivity to the needs and motivations of others.

Complicating the whole process are the changing demands placed upon the adolescent. While physically able to have sex, one faces legal and moral (and parental) sanctions; while able to reason about moral issues, one must defer to the "final decision" of adult teachers and parents; while having the ability to elude adult supervision and have great mobility, one can be "grounded" summarily. These conflicting issues can be troublesome for the parent, the teacher, and the therapist as well. Problems occur both when the adult necessarily sets some limits, and when there are issues in the adult's own adolescence that may not have been resolved satisfactorily. Regarding the therapist, such issues must be encountered in supervision, as noted below in the third part of this chapter.

Vocational choices must be made in adolescence. While the authors believe most people see the choice as critical and irrevocable, vocational choice in adolescence is in fact one in a series of experiments or choices. As life spans increase, more people are embarking on second and third careers. However, the work habits and attitudes formed in adolescence serve as templates upon which future employment situations may be structured. Additionally, the academic, professional, or vocational training one attains will affect dramatically the next two decades of one's life, which will determine the youth's capability to support a family of his or her own. The recent demands upon adolescent women to choose between the career path of a research biologist *or* a housewife, for example, will mean they can focus on one career or the other, but only with difficulty on both. Decisions reached in adolescence have profound effects on young adulthood. The view expressed here, though, is that the valuing and decision process must be an ongoing one. The changes in decisions do have real costs (and benefits), as in the case where a mother of three decides to return to school. Psychotherapy can provide an atmosphere defused of intense emotion and investment on the part of the adult where the adolescent can review options without admonishment.

As critical as any other issue is the *separation, differentiation, or individuation from family.* As mentioned earlier, adolescence bridges about a chronological decade and has several substages within it. Different skills change at varying rates. Some skills seem to surge forward, then fall back. Confusing as this may be for the youth, the parents can find it intolerable. The parent may have needs to continue seeing the youth as a dependent child, validating the mother or father's worth as a parent, or the parent may find it easier to see the child with the constancy of behavior that the pre-adolescent period provided. Osterrieth (1969) reports a fourteen-year-old as saying, "What's wrong with parents is that they knew us when we were little." The prime issues crystallize as interpersonal misperception and control. The therapist can provide a meeting ground for parents and youth to recognize needs in the other and come to agreements that resolve conflict. Contingency contracting (Bandura, 1969; Homme, Csanyi, Gonzales, and Rechs, 1969; Patterson, 1977; Stuart, 1971, Stuart and Lott, 1972; Stumphauzer, 1973; and Weathers and Liberman, 1975a, b), social and communication skills training (Brownstone and Dye, 1979; and Gnagey, 1979), and conflict resolution training (Kifer, Lewis, Green, and Phillips, 1974) are effective behavioral tools for parent and youth to come to terms with each other. Similarly, both the parent and youth can receive specific help from therapy. The parent may come to learn what to expect from the normative contemporary adolescent—to find out about the peer climate as well as developmentally important issues about adolescence from the therapist. The youth can gain a sense of effectance from being able to behave in specified ways that will result in particular payoffs from adults who previously may have seemed impervious to the youth's attempts at achieving certain ends. The needs for the youth to have the support and structure of the family while attaining independence and self-sufficiency without the structure of the family stultifying the growth are paramount.

The issue of *identity formation,* particularly negative identity formation, is addressed sensitively by Erikson (1959) and Sullivan (1953). Facing identity diffusion the youth says in effect, "I'd rather be somebody with an effect even if it involves being horrid, rather than being fragmented, or—even worse—being ignored." Erikson quotes a young woman saying, "At least in the gutter I'm a genius," and he quotes a young man as saying, "I would rather be quite insecure than a little secure" (p. 132). Sullivan (1953) discusses the child who discovers his or her needs for tenderness can either go unmet or be actively rebuffed. He or she learns to turn away from tenderness to "that something else, the basic malevolent attitude, the attitude that one lives among enemies," resulting in "the juvenile [who] makes it practically impossible for anyone to feel tenderly toward him or to treat him kindly." A gravitation toward a "bad me" rather than a "not me" self-concept or dynamism forms. The youth may depend on two sources for estimates of his or her own selfhood. One is a peer group guided by the vagaries of mass media and each other's conjectures about life. The second source is the parents, who can paradoxically provide the negative identity which is "perversely based on all those identifications and roles which, at critical stages of development, had been presented to the individual as most undesirable and dangerous, and yet also as most real" (Erikson, 1959, p. 131). The involvement of sex (including homosexuality), drugs, fighting, running away, and suicide as forms of expression of anguish about identity partially or negatively formed is epidemic, and requires the understanding of the therapist. One teenage client of ours, whose father was racially bigoted, selected a black male as her accomplice in running away from the hospital and living in a "crash pad" in a seamier part of the city. She perspicuously pushed his most sensitive button, provoking him (a person of considerable political influence) to initiate a state police search for her (abortive), leaving him enraged and frustrated. When she decided to return, she confronted his rage with an air of innocence and moral righteousness that race made little difference to her, exposing his bigotry further, but also escalating the conflict which caused him to continue to act punitively.

In summary, this section outlined some of the critical content areas important to anyone who intends to engage adolescents in psychotherapy or to supervise adolescent psychotherapy.

TECHNICAL CONSIDERATIONS IN PSYCHOTHERAPY SUPERVISION

This section considers the management of adolescent psychotherapy with particular reference to the contributions of supervision.

The supervisor may be confronted by one of several immediate tasks. Too often supervision comes about under a state of emergency when the adolescent, parent, therapist, administrator, or a combination of the four call upon the supervisor for help. The supervisor must be clear about who is the client—that is, to whom are which kind of lines of responsibility extended. Ekstein and Wallerstein's (1972; Ekstein, 1964) rhombus outlining the relationship between the supervisor and the agency, client, and therapist is complicated here by the additional parental parties. If the supervisor accepts the supervisory relationship at the behest of the therapist, the chief client is the therapist. Since it is at the therapist's option and request, the supervisor must work with those motivations which brought about the request. This variant of the collegial-peer model (see Hess' Chapter 2) usually involves areas in which the therapist feels less secure or knowledgeable. The self-exposure this entails needs to be recognized by the supervisor, requiring confidentiality and sheltering of the supervisee-therapist. Only in cases where ethical problems or misfeasance occurs ought the supervisor violate this. In some cases the supervisee will have some feelings that what was occurring in therapy was not quite right, and the gentle guidance of the supervisor will be sufficient to enable the therapist to correct the therapy process. Other times the errors will catch the supervisee by surprise. Then, the supervisor would be well advised to present the new view or information and allow the supervisee to think about the issues and, perhaps in the next session, speak about the problems as the supervisee sees them. Often new information has strong drive properties of its own which will stimulate the therapist to change, or at least to explore areas previously unknown to him or her. The greater the latitude the therapist feels, the more likely the resolution of the problem will be internalized and felt to be his or her own solution. Paradoxically, the supervisee will feel more freedom of movement or expression in supervision and grow both independent in thought and comfortable in expression of self-doubt, conflict, and emotion in supervision.

Assessment of the supervisee's knowledge base is necessary. In an ongoing case, readings may be suggested to the therapist. If supervision develops on a more planful basis, perhaps on an agency basis where a trainee or a novice therapist is assigned or selects a supervisor, readings, in-service workshops, case conferences, and observational learning can precede the supervisee's involvement in therapy. The selection of appropriate cases can be accomplished (see Weiner and Kaplan's Chapter 4), as well as preparation of the therapist regarding questions or doubts he or she may have. The norm is for the supervisee to have many grave self-doubts (see Chapters 4, 5, 7, 8, and 9 in this book). These require the supervisor's attention in selecting an appropriate beginning case if possible, and in meeting with the supervisee before any therapy is enjoined. Considerations regarding the therapist's expectations of him or herself and of the patient from available case records merit exploration. Questions such as what to do if the adolescent, perhaps brought by parents, resentfully decides not to talk, and how to distinguish this from an adolescent beginning a schizophrenic withdrawal pattern may arise after one or several sessions.

Often adolescents can be acutely candid. The uncertainty about what therapy consists of can provoke direct questions of the therapist, including direct personal questions. Holmes (1964) suggests *self-disclosure* on the therapist's part because (a) he cannot hide his personality and attitudes anyway, and (b) there is no good reason not to self-disclose. Lynch (1974), Schoenfeld (1969b), and Freudenberger (1971) advise the sharing of personal experiences with the adolescent within reasonable limits. Questions occur such as "Are you seeing me only because I was assigned to you?", "Jim saw you at the lake with a little girl when he was on pass last weekend. Are you married? How many children do you have? Do you like kids? Do you really ski on one ski?" Certainly, evasiveness on the therapist's part is a poor role model; it fails to develop a therapeutic atmosphere and fails to make good use of the client's involvement. The therapist and supervisor might assess the functional value of self-disclosure. The client's feelings of being acknowledged as a person worthy of self-revelation and of mutual engagement is facilitative. If the questions serve a defensive function, the disclosure may disarm some of the anxiety stimulating the defense. When enough trust is established, the defense can be encountered, "You seem to want to talk about me," or when enough data are gathered for an interpretation the therapist may respond, "Might you be wondering whether I am interested in you and care for you?" The way the therapist uses the adolescent's personal inquiries is quite fruitful to discuss in supervision. The technical error of disclosure in order to be a "good guy" or a friend, with little regard for the therapeutic strategy, is ill advised. More serious is the error of the therapist who takes the inquiry as an opportunity to launch upon a narcissistic account of his waterskiing, or of his daughter's exploits. For these reasons we do not advocate unmindful answers to personal questions, but do advocate honest disclosure that serves the therapeutic purposes or strategy. Further, we suggest that the *way* the therapist chooses to self-disclose may be examined for the light it sheds on the therapist and how he or she chooses to use his or her self in therapy. Care must be taken, since sharing one's more intimate aspects of self could result in a loss of professional objectivity and an increased vulnerability. As with any potent technique, the way disclosure is used determines its efficacy.

The proclivity of adolescents toward issuing ultimatums, mentioned in the previous section, is certainly not excluded from showing itself in psychotherapy.

"I won't attend typing class no matter what you or anyone else says," "If you back up my parents on their curfew, I'll run away," "If you don't talk to my P.O. for me, I won't come in anymore," "I can have sex with any guy in the street and you or no one else can do anything about it" are some difficult postures to encounter. First, one must assess whether any elements of moralizing or telling the youth what to do are implicit in the therapist's statements or attitude. Could the adolescent be responding to a real restraint or moral agent? Secondly, the intensity of the statement can be dealt with. For example, "When you present your view like that, you leave little room for discussion. I suppose you feel like you have no room either, when people give you threats." Thirdly, pointing out how this may be a pattern of behavior with effects on the environment is useful procedure.

Related to the ultimatum, or perhaps a motoric representation of it, is the problem of *acting out.* Adolescents are often brought to psychotherapy because parents are at "their rope's end." The therapist may likely have been portrayed explicitly or implicitly by parents as "fixing the youth's wagon" or "straightening out" the client. How the therapy is structured or presented initially, as well as the confidentiality issue, needs careful attention by the therapist and supervisor. It is natural for the youth to test the therapist. The general role of the therapist is to assist the client to assume responsibility for his or her own actions and, in doing so, therapists typically shrink away from disciplining or curbing the client's actions. Freidman (1974), on the other hand, sees value in the therapist assuming limit setting roles, particularly where parents have abandoned their responsibilities. Rotman and Goldburg (1976) feel the aim of psychotherapy with adolescents is to tell the patient to "grow up." But in doing so the therapist, they contend, will confront areas in which he or she has not grown up, resulting in countertransference problems. It is essential that the therapist's necessary setting of limits be subject to careful supervision.

The therapist's failure to intervene or the therapist's setting of limits both are likely to tap conflicts the therapist brings to the setting. Similarly the supervisor needs to be aware of failing to review the setting of limits issue or of taking a particular adamant stand in response to the therapist's pondering. The alternatives might well indicate issues the supervisor needs to explore. Interestingly, the supervisor may find the supervisee's "acting out" in supervision to be most difficult (Ekstein and Wallerstein, 1972; Semrad and Van Buskirk, 1969) and a cause to seek consultation. This will usually co-occur when the therapist is having a most difficult time with the client's behavior.

Some of the acting out or motoric definition of one's psychological space and its boundaries may take the form of manipulation and argumentation. The adolescent may question whether the therapist really is concerned. The scenario may proceed thusly, "If you cared for how I did in school, you would see how I need my parent's car so I could go to the library to study," or on an inpatient basis, "You and the staff say I need to be better socially, so if you talked to the staff about lifting restrictions I could go on the trip to the amusement park and get more social." If the therapist accedes to this bargaining for quick behavioral gain, the promise of which will seldom ever be paid or realized, it will lead to an erosion of the perception of the therapist as a source of unequivocal guidelines. What will be learned is that manipulation and psychological blackmail are the ways to get what one wants. The supervisor will face a supervisee who will not acknowledge what occured until the youth is found not to either have gone to the library or behaved well on the outing (you can be sure the youth will, with excruciating clarity, make this known to the therapist), at which point the rage, or depression, of being defeated will be clear in supervision. The task of supervision then is to process these reactions and help the supervisee regain a therapeutic perspective using the manipulation as grist for the therapeutic mill.

The adolescent client "is emotionally ungrammatical in that he so often uses an exclamation point where a question mark is called for" (Holmes, 1964, p. 110). A detached response to argumentation fails to acknowledge both the youth and what might be quite valid problems. Through arguing, the youth may develop a more refined view of the issue. Holmes (1964) writes of the positive value of arguing. However, the opportunity for the therapist to become authoritarian or to lose perspective of the therapeutic end of having the client explicate his or her conflict is increased. Again, supervision is most helpful in managing this issue.

A more subtle problem is that of *resistance.* Marshall (1972) defines resistance simply as lengthy silence, stereotyped or repetitive talking, and objection and refusal to attend sessions. To this one can add distraction mechanisms that lead the therapist away from a topic. He recommends a variety of techniques for working with resistance. These can be termed "joining techniques" which acknowledge and directly manipulate the resistance. One example, hypervaluation, would, with an excessive talker, have the therapist say "Some people are not able to talk as much as you can when you wish not to hear me talk about certain things. I think that is a good way for you to indicate to me when you want not to talk about a sensitive topic." Most often the recognition of the client's sensitivity will help the client face the conflict, as seen in the following vignette from one of the authors' cases:

Louise, a 16-year-old who had not been attending school for the past four years, had a long history of family dysfunction and appeared very much in need of separation from her family in order to allow her to learn to function as an adolescent. She had made several superficial suicidal acts during the past seven years, which each time resulted in her receiving outpatient counseling and then being removed from counseling when the therapist recommended a return to school or Louise began showing independent behaviors. On this occasion she had been referred for an overdose consisting of 6 aspirin, 2 multi-purpose vitamins, and 3 cold tablets. When the therapist began discussing residential placement, the client's parents began crying and Louise loudly began insisting that she really would succeed in killing herself if she were to go anywhere but home. The therapist reported that she felt that Louise had less chance to do that in the residential setting than at home but that *the decision would be left up to Louise and her parents* (as legally the therapist could not force her to go into the residential program). Louise quickly took control of the situation and not only convinced her parents that it would indeed be too dangerous for her to stay at home and that they should file for commitment for her, but also explained her need for hospitalization quite clearly to the judge at the time of her commitment hearing.

The use of *youthful argot, attire, and adornments* is one issue on which theorists differ. Freudenberger (1971) suggests reading underground newspapers, listening to current music, attending rock concerts, and hanging around areas where adolescents congregate. Schoenfeld (1969b) advises against the use of argot. While some therapists may feel they are closer to the client or gaining trust and building rapport, there is something less than authentic in the appearance of a 32 or 48-year-old therapist in the guise of a "guru" or "earth mother." Certainly a therapist may consider less formal language and clothing than when he or she interviews for a job, but since the therapist is not an adolescent, to mimic one is not productive. The therapist and supervisor would be doing a second-rate job if they did not learn the street jargon, drug names and effects, fashions, rumors and myths, and the other elements that go into being an adolescent in the contemporary sense, as Freudenberger suggests. This will help in understanding the client, and will be appreciated by the client, but mutual respect and therapeutic progress are best served by the therapist and client meeting each other with full respect for who one is and who the other is. It is through this process that negative valuing or identity can be shed since the client can see a person who operates congruently yet within the frame of a traditional (or in many cases, a not too traditional or staid) role in society. Moreover, the need systems that are operating to impel the therapist toward the (re)enactment of adolescence and the loss of perspective entailed in being an adolescent should be subject to supervisory discussion. We recall our child at the age of three, in response to an adult who used "baby talk" with her, saying "How come that person talks like a baby?" No doubt many of these efforts are sincere ones based on an attempt to relate better with the client. Supervisory patience and guidance are called for then, while the therapist learns about adolescents without repeating his or her own adolescence.

Another set of technical considerations involves the planning of the psychological intervention. The *sex of the therapist and client (and supervisor)* is a critical issue in the assignment of cases. The ability of a female adolescent to present seductive behavior which a naive male therapist overlooks seems to be a common experience. Sex role child development literature indicates a differential threshold of the opposite sexed parent to the peccadilloes of his or her youngster. Specifically, Rothbart and Maccoby (1966) found mothers to be more permissive to supplications for dependency by boys and fathers to girls. The same authors find fathers to be more severe to boys' aggression while mothers will accept more anger from boys than girls [also cf. Block (1973) and Lambert, Yackley, and Hein (1971)]. Fathers seem to elicit behavior from their daughters that conforms to the fathers' image of a sexually attractive woman (Maccoby and Jacklin, 1974). It seems, then, that the parent may be—or feels he or she is—more aware of the same sexed youngster's motivations or needs. ("I know what you're thinking because when I was your age I did the same thing.") Given this, there is considerable merit in the supervisor being female and the therapist being male, when the client is a female who is seductively involving the therapist. This is not to say the therapist ought to be a male, or that a male supervisor would not pick up the seduction. But certain issues may become salient or lie dormant depending on the gender of the parties. In fact, there is merit in every therapist receiving both male and female supervision for the experience of one's own ways of interacting with the perspectives that the different supervisors provide. In an analogous fashion, a male consultant was called upon when a female supervisor and female therapist were confronted with what they perceived to be an actively violence prone client. Examination of Rorschach and other test materials allowed the consultant, supervisor, and therapist to conclude that this 19-year-old client was not at all violence prone [being neither an under- nor over-controlled type (Megargee, 1966)] but was reacting in a positively assertive fashion to a demanding mother seeing her son about to leave the nest. The consultant left the supervisor and supervisee the (unspoken) choice as to whether or how they wished to deal with their expectation of male violence. Many issues discussed earlier will be sex role dependent (e.g., limit setting, handling ultimatums, how to present what kind of information) and require attention.

Often *individual and long-term psychotherapy* are entered into when alternatives that have not been considered would be much better. Most adolescent needs can be met with a briefer form of intervention. In fact, the stigmatization process or creation of a career client is a real cost to be considered when setting the length of psychotherapy. The need of the client for long-term psychotherapy may be present, but too often this need may be overestimated. One does not want the identity of the client to be coalesced around psychotherapy. When long-term treatment is the treatment of choice, the therapist may find support necessary in dealing with long periods of time that appear nonproductive. This may be due to the appearance of repetitive behavior, resistance, negativism, or the grave characterological nature of the problem. In this case the monitoring or reviewing of routine adjustments of adolescence may not be seen by the therapist as either "psychotherapy" or as "interesting" by the supervisor. Our view is, if it involves the therapist as an influence agent, the supervisor as one who can provide learning for the therapist, and helps the client, it is a clinical intervention, and hence psychotherapy broadly construed.

Group treatment can provide a situation with greater change possibilities than individual treatment modalities. Since adolescents are particularly responsive to group pressure, more rapid change can be attained in groups. The supervisor and therapists need to consider the variety of issues common to group therapy. These include the degree of pathology, sex and age of clients, the size of the group, and the way in which clients are added. Friedman, Schlise, and Seligman (1975) and Brandes (1971) discuss group treatment and supervisory issues in the treatment process.

In group the client may feel less intimidation inasmuch as there are many peers with but one or two adults, as opposed to facing an adult and the responsibility of producing verbal material for 50 minutes in traditional individual therapy. The presence of peers allows more experimentation by the client. The therapist can see the behavior in vivo that previously was available only through secondary, distorting sources. The client can learn vicariously what he or she is not ready to try experientially. In both sexed groups, the forum to learn about the other sex is invaluable. Learning that one is not alone in experiencing rebuff from other youth, or in feeling conflict or neglect from parents, can be a revelation. The realization that an adult can be more understanding than a peer can be instructive and make positive identifications that otherwise would not have developed.

One final concern that will serve to introduce the final section is that of *third parties,* especially parents or guardians. Laing (1971) exquisitely depicts the enmeshment of the parents in the genesis and maintenance of many adolescent psychopathologies. Similarly, Carson (1969) and Berne (1964) discuss illegitimate interpersonal strategies that can ensnare the therapist.

The younger or the more pathological the client is, the more essential is the establishment of a working alliance with the parent. One schizophrenic client's father "could not get the car started" for sessions the week after the father suggested an intervention for the therapist to use with the client that the therapist did not relay to the client. In the course of conversation the week following the missed sessions, enough information was given by the father and client for the therapist to conclude that the functioning of the ignition system was correlated strongly with the affective state of the father toward the therapist. The frustration and anger engendered in the therapist, plus the range of alternatives available, need to be discussed in supervision. The supervision can entail ventilation, information gathering, support, and even legal consultation regarding client rights and therapist liability if he or she performs in ways that approach abridgment of parental rights. The model of supervision can range from peer consultation to administrative support for an action on behalf of a clinic.

Quite clearly, too, the issue of confidentiality becomes critical with third parties. The issues of a third (payer) party's right to know [cf. *The Clinical Psychologist,* 1979 (Spring), *32,* (3)], whether the party is an insurance company or a parent, can (and usually does) directly conflict with the client's right to unbroached privacy in treatment. Can the youth who was sexually abused by a parent feel the unqualified trust of the therapist to allow for the revealing of this secret! A testing of the therapist on lesser issues may indicate to the client whether the therapy is safe and the therapist able to tolerate the awesome weight of the secret. The supervision can help monitor the ambience of the therapy to guide the therapist who may be too close to assess it.

The supervisor would be well advised to go over with the therapist what he or she will tell the client and parent about the parameters of treatment. Often this is best done with the client and parent both present, and before therapy begins. While this need not be ponderous, it should be clear and brief. It also can involve inculcation of what problems are to be addressed in treatment and how treatment is to proceed. This type of session can clarify client and parent expectations, and help the therapist avoid siding with the parent to discipline what in the parents' report may be a horrendous fiend, or siding with the youth to dethrone the despicable despot that the client may perceive the parent to be.

Supervision must be sensitively attuned to the therapist adopting one or the other party's metaphors with its attendant narrowing of focus and alienation of the other party. While there may be cause for sympathy with the parents about their endless suffering at the hands of their psychopathic son, or for an adolescent's outrage at a sexually abusive father, the supervisor can help the therapist realize that anyone can feel the sympathy or outrage. It is precisely because a therapist *can* respond in a nonstereotypic and asocial fashion—a fashion that allows for exploration of the needs, behaviors, contingencies, conflicts, or whatever one's theoretical persuasion causes one to explore—that the therapist occupies an unusual (and exalted) position. The asocial position allows the client the possibility to experience and behave in new ways. The many facets of the parent-therapist-client-(supervisor) interrelationships are woefully underrepresented (if represented at all) in the literature. The supervisor and therapist are well advised not to underestimate its importance and, instead, to spend time examining the interrelationships.

ADOLESCENT CONSENT AND RIGHT TO TREATMENT

The last issue to be considered in this chapter, though possibly of prime importance, is that of the role of the adolescent in consent and right to treatment.

Adolescents can enter treatment voluntarily, through the authority of the parent, or through the authority of an agency in loco parentis (e.g., the court or department of child welfare). Many states are currently exploring their laws regarding consent of minors where the latter two paths are followed. Schowalter (1978) reports that, as of 1976, five states (Alabama, Arkansas, Kentucky, Maryland, and Minnesota) allowed medical treatment of minors with the treating professional's judgment as the determining factor. Perr (1976) notes that generally a minor may assume the responsibility for treatment and give consent if he or she can understand the nature of the problem and the role of treatment. Thus an adolescent of 14 to 16 might consent to treatment without the parents' consent.*

Specific laws tend to cover specific problem areas, as in the case of venereal disease, drug usage, and problems related to pregnancy, where separate statutes allow for the minor's consent, without granting blanket consent to minors. Perr reported that generally emancipated and semi-emancipated minors (e.g., college students) have already been granted consent for psychotherapy or counseling.

*The report of the National Commission for the Protection of Human Subjects of Biomedical and Behavioral Research (1977) concludes that informed consent must be obtained from children from the age of seven or older for their participation in research. The area of consent, and client rights generally, is changing so rapidly that the practitioner is advised to be aware of current rulings in his or her own state.

Problems occur in situations where it is felt the parent must be notified to help arrange the most appropriate treatment, as in hospitalization or residential care, either because of the state's commitment procedures, or due to the agency's payment policy. Although there is little legal clarification available, most professionals are reluctant to force treatment of a nondangerous adolescent who, following evaluation, choses not to cooperate. Similarly, many professionals in private practice are also reluctant to treat minors who desire treatment without parental knowledge or consent. Schowalter (1978) suggests that their reasons for this may include: the belief that the treatment is not possible without parental involvement, the fear of a parent's anger, a fear of malpractice litigation or of nonpayment by the minor, and, since the parent was uninvolved in contracting the service, nonpayment from the parent.

Additionally, some states are currently changing the laws by which the parents can voluntarily commit an adolescent either by not allowing "voluntary" commitment of adolescents over the age of 13 by their parents (Massachusetts and Tennessee) or by allowing the adolescent to seek and obtain their release without parental consent [Illinois (age 13 to 17) and Connecticut (16 and over)] even though they have been committed by their parents. The same issues arise when one considers governmental agencies acting in place of parents.

In considering the rights of adolescents to confidentiality, the supervisee may well have difficulty providing the parents (bill payers) sufficient information without breaking the confidentiality of the client, as parents often are quite insistent in their demands for specific information. One mother called following each session for the alleged purpose of determining when the next appointment had been scheduled, and to ask if the therapist felt her daughter was going to follow her instructions from now on. Again, as mentioned above, supervision should explore the strategic handling of this situation, including the possibility of a session with the parents to explore their needs, and to provide corrective information regarding the general treatment goals. In this case, the mother's goals for the daughter, the nature of confidentiality, and the therapist's working style were discussed. Assessment of the mother's uncertainty of her effect on the daughter and her fears or perceptions of the daughter's "misbehaviors" were explored beneficially.

Psychotherapists and supervisors must be aware of state statutes and local customs or mores in working with adolescents.

SUMMARY

This chapter reviewed definitions of adolescence, discussed general adolescent issues that the psychotherapist and supervisor must be concerned with, presented technical issues the supervisor must attend to, and considered the adolescent's right to treatment and consent.

REFERENCES

American Psychological Association, Division 12. *The Clinical Psychologist,* 1979, *32*(3), Washington, D.C.: Author.

Ausubel, D. P., Montemayor, R., and Svajian, P. *Theory and problems of adolescent development* (2nd ed.). New York: Grune and Stratton, 1977.

Bandura, A. *Principles of behavior modification.* New York: Holt, Rinehart and Winston, 1969.

Block, J. H. Conceptions of sex role: Some cross-cultural and longitudinal perspectives. *American Psychologist,* 1973, *28,* 512–526.

Brandes, N. S. Group psychotherapy for the adolescent. *Current Psychiatric Therapies,* 1971, *11,* 18–26.

Brownstone, J. E., and Dye, C. J. *Communication workshop for parents of adolescents.* Champaign, Ill.: Research Press, 1979.

Berne, E. *Games people play.* New York: Grove Press, 1964.

Caplan, G., and Lebovici, S. (Eds.). *Adolescence: Psychosocial perspectives.* New York: Basic Books, 1969.

Carroll, J. F. Understanding adolescent needs. *Adolescence,* 1968, *3,* 381–394.

Carson, R. C. *Interaction concepts of personality.* Chicago: Aldine, 1969.

Coleman, J. S. et al. *Youth: Transition to adulthood—Report of Panel on Youth of the President's Scientific Advisory Committee.* Chicago: University of Chicago Press, 1974.

Conger, J. J. *Adolescence and youth* (2nd ed.). New York: Harper and Row, 1977.

Dragastin, S. E., and Elder, G. H., Jr. (Eds.). *Adolescence in the life cycle: Psychological and social context.* New York: Wiley, 1975.

Ekstein, R. Supervision of psychotherapy: Is it teaching? Is is administration? Or is it therapy? *Psychotherapy: Theory, Research and Practice,* 1964, *1,* 137–138.

Ekstein, R., and Wallerstein, R. S. *The teaching and learning of psychotherapy* (Rev. ed.). New York: Basic Books, 1972.

Erikson, E. *Identity and the life cycle: Psychological issues.* New York: International Universities Press, 1959.

Frank, J. *Persuasion and healing.* Baltimore: Johns Hopkins Press, 1961.

Freudenberger, H. J. New psychotherapy approaches with teenagers in a new world. *Psychotherapy: Theory, Research and Practice,* 1971, *8*(1), 38–43.

Friedman, H. J. New considerations in the treatment of certain adolescent patients. *Adolescence,* 1974, *9,* 155–168.

Friedman, R., Schlise, S., and Seligman, S. Issues involved in the treatment of an adolescent group. *Adolescence,* 1975, *39,* 357–368.

Gesell, A., Ilg, F. L., and Ames, L. B. *Youth: The years from ten to sixteen.* New York: Harper, 1956.

Gnagey, T. D. *How to put up with parents.* Champaign, Ill.: Research Press, 1979.

Havighurst, R. J. *Developmental tasks and education.* New York: Longmans, Green, 1951.

Havighurst, R. J., and Dreyer, P. M. (Eds.). *Youth: The twenty-fourth yearbook of the National Society for the Study of Education.* Chicago: NSSE, 1975.

Holmes, D. J. *The adolescent in psychotherapy.* Boston: Little, Brown, 1964.

Homme, L., Csanyi, A. P., Gonzales, M. A., and Rechs, J. R. *How to use contingency contracting in the classroom.* Champaign, Ill.: Research Press, 1969.

Inhelder, B., and Piaget, J. *The growth of logical thinking* (A. Parsons and S. Milgram, Trans.). New York: Basic Books, 1958.

Kifer, R. E., Lewis, M. A., Green, D. R., and Phillips, E. L. Training pre-delinquent youths and their parents to negotiate conflict situations. *Journal of Applied Behavior Analysis,* 1974, *7,* 357–364.

Kohlberg, L. Moral stages and moralization: The cognitive-developmental approach. In T. Lickona (Ed.), *Moral developmental and behavior.* New York: Holt, Rinehart and Winston, 1975, pp. 31–53.

Laing, R. D. *The politics of the family and other essays.* New York: Pantheon Books, 1971.

Lambert, W. E., Yackley, A., and Hein, R. N. Child training values of English Canadian and French Canadian parents. *Canadian Journal of Behavioral Science,* 1971, *3,* 217–236.

Lynch, C. Psychotherapy with adolescents: Some suggestions. *Family Therapy,* 1974, *1* (1), 98–104.

Maccoby, E. E., and Jacklin, C. N. *The psychology of sex differences.* Stanford, Calif.: Stanford University Press, 1974.

Marshall, R. J. The treatment of resistances in psychotherapy of children and adolescents. *Psychotherapy: Theory, Research and Practice,* 1972, *9,* 143–148.

McCandless, B. R., and Coop, R. H. *Adolescents: Behavior and development* (2nd ed.). New York: Holt, Rinehart and Winston, 1979.

Mears, F., and Gatchel, R. F. *Fundamentals of abnormal psychology.* New York: Rand McNally, 1979.

Megargee, E. I. Undercontrolled and overcontrolled personality types in extreme antisocial aggression. *Psychological Monographs,* 1966, *80*(Whole No. 611).

Muuss, R. *Theories of adolescence* (2nd ed.). New York: Random House, 1969.

Muuss, R. *Theories of adolescence* (3rd ed.). New York: Random House, 1975.

National Commission for the Protection of Human Subjects of Biomedical and Behavioral Research. *Research involving children: Report and recommendations.* Washington, D.C.: Author, 1977.

Osterrieth, P. A. Adolescence: Some psychological aspects. In G. Caplan and S. Lebovici (Eds.), *Adolescence: Psychosocial perspectives.* New York: Basic Books, 1969, pp. 11–21.

Patterson, G. R. *Families: Application of social learning to family life* (Rev. ed.). Champaign, Ill.: Research Press, 1977.

Perr, I. N. Confidentiality and consent in psychiatric treatment of minors. *The Journal of Legal Medicine,* 1976, *4*(6), 9–13.

Rothbart, M. I., and Maccoby, E. E. Parents' differential reactions to sons and daughters. *Journal of Personality and Social Psychology,* 1966, *4,* 237–243.

Rotman, C. B., and Goldburg, S. J. The psychotherapist's feelings about the adolescent patient (countertransference). *Adolescence,* 1976, *9,* 155–168.

Schoenfeld, W. A. The body and body image in adolescents. In G. Caplan and S. Lebovici (Eds.), *Adolescence: Psychosocial perspectives.* New York: Basic Books, 1969, pp. 27–53. (a)

Schoenfeld, W. A. Trends in adolescent psychiatry. *Current Psychiatric Therapies,* 1969, *9,* 52–62. (b)

Schowalter, J. E. The minor's role in consent for mental health treatment. *American Academy of Child Psychiatry,* 1978, *17,* 505–513.

Semrad, E. V., and Van Buskirk, D. (Eds.). *Teaching psychotherapy of psychotic patients: Supervision of beginning residents in the "clinical approach."* New York: Grune and Stratton, 1969.

Stuart, R. B. Behavioral contracting within the families of delinquents. *Journal of Behavioral Therapy and Experimental Psychiatry,* 1971, *2,* 1–11.

Stuart, R. B., and Lott, L. A. Behavioral contracting with delinquents: A cautionary note. *Journal of Behavioral Therapy and Experimental Psychiatry,* 1972, *3,* 161–169.

Stumphauzer, J. S. *Behavioral therapy with delinquents.* Springfield, Ill.: C. C. Thomas, 1973.

Sullivan, H. S. *The interpersonal theory of psychiatry.* New York: Norton, 1953.

Weathers, L., and Liberman, R. P. Contingency and contracting with families of delinquent youth. *Behavior Therapy,* 1975, *6,* 356–366. (a)

Weathers, L., and Liberman, R. P. The family contracting exercise. *Journal of Behavior Therapy and Experimental Psychiatry,* 1975, *6,* 208–214. (b)

White, R. W. Ego and reality in psychoanalytic theory. *Psychological Issues,* 1963, *3*(3), Monograph 11.

Yankelovich, D. *The new morality: A profile of American youth in the 70's.* New York: McGraw-Hill, 1974.

CHAPTER 22

Geropsychotherapy: Training and Supervision

CHARLES V. LAIR

Can psychotherapy be used to treat the emotional problems of old age? Just a few years ago, the answer would have been at least a probable no. Freud (1924, p. 258) expressed doubt that people over 50 were flexible enough to change, and his point of view certainly reflected general beliefs in his time about the course of aging. Historically, age has been a topic of ambivalent interest to philosophers, scientists, and the lay public (Bromsley, 1974, pp. 33–75). Even in modern times, real concern for the problems of aging has emerged only since World War II (Riegel, 1977). Typically, negative attitudes about old people are still prominent (McTavish, 1971), and even professional therapists are, as a group, inclined to focus on young rather than old (Dye, 1978).

Current population trends suggest the very real possibility that the number of individuals over 65 will equal or exceed the population below age 30 by the year 2000. At the same time that the proportion of aging people is increasing, the number who are receiving appropriate support from the mental health system appears to have been dropping off (Kahn, 1975). Fortunately, education in gerontology seems to be expanding (Gerontology Education in the United States, 1978) which may portend a brighter future for services to the elderly. So, too, has attention to psychotherapy with the elderly increased in recent years with evidence that age is no barrier to a positive outcome (Krasner, 1977). This chapter addresses some basic issues associated with training in psychotherapy with the aged: (a) definitions of aging, (b) preparation of the potential therapist, (c) pathology of aging, (d) assessment and evaluation, (e) therapy, and (f) issues in supervision.

DEFINING AGING

Krasner (1977) points out that success or failure of psychotherapy is not related to age. This is understandable since age is not a clearly defined concept, as Birren has stated (1964). Individuals should be evaluated in terms of personal resources for adaptation (psychological age), the roles they play in society (social age), or the condition of their bodies (biological age), and none of these is necessarily equivalent to chronological age. Factors which affect psychotherapy of older people may be lifelong personality patterns of adjustment, expectancies, attributions to self and the elder role, physical health, and various demographic variables such as education, financial security, and even basic nutrition. The central issue is that chronological aging is relatively less influential on the course of psychotherapy than are other far more compelling factors.

PREPARING THE POTENTIAL THERAPIST

In training a prospective student psychotherapist for the aging, it is essential that he or she receive a substantial background in life-span psychology. There are normal developmental crises as the individual grows older; for example, retirement, children moving away from home, and deaths among family and friends (Datan and Ginsberg, 1975). Also, the student should understand the import of failing senses, response slowing, and decreased risk taking on the behavior of the aged. There are an increasing number of good texts and reference books in the area of adult and aging psychology by such authors or editors as Botwinick (1973), Kimmell (1974), Elias, Elias, and Elias (1977), and Birren and Schaie (1977). It is also essential that a solid background in behavior pathology, treatment techniques, and resources for the aged be gained. There are now several fine texts with which the student should be familiar; for example, Butler and Lewis (1977), Busse and Pfeiffer (1977), Howells (1975), Storandt, Siegler, and Elias (1978), and Verwoerdt (1976). Among the more important journals to which the student should refer are the *Journal of the American Geriatric Society, International Journal of Aging and Human Development, Geriatric Psychiatry, The Gerontologist,* and the *Journal of Gerontology.*

To assist students in gaining experience with the elderly, they should be given ample opportunity to mix with normal aging as well as those who have pathology (Davis and Klopfer, 1977). Initial clinical experiences can be gained in nursing homes and hospitals, but even better is placement in an adult day care center or in the aging unit of a community mental health center. Students should see the elderly not only in the institutional framework, but they should visit the elders in their homes to gain better insight into their style of life and areas of family stress, or even to evaluate physical barriers to the client's welfare. Although more young students are manifesting interest in working with the aged, their knowledge may go no deeper than occasional contacts with a grandparent for whom there is fondness and/or concern; therefore, provision of a broadening experience with both normal and abnormal elderly is essential preparation.

In the early stages of pathology of the aging, it is difficult to discriminate what is organic and what is functional in origin (Donnelly, 1954; Wolff, 1963). Even in advanced stages, a severely retarded depression can be confused with senile deterioration. The eagerness of beginning psychotherapists can lead them to the unhappy conclusion that every disorder is functional and that all the ills of the aged can be reversed with psychotherapy. For this reason, the next important step in shaping the behavior of the therapist is to teach the absolute necessity of adequate diagnosis. The interrelationships of organic and functional symptoms should be clearly delineated. Even where the functional symptom is secondary to a more serious organic problem, psychotherapy may increase the comfort of the client at the least.

An example of how an accurate assessment of a client helped sustain a student's interest and provided direction to his behavior is as follows. An advanced graduate student had been seeing an elderly woman in therapy for a short time when she took a sudden turn for the worse. The client was hospitalized in the psychiatric unit of a local hospital where she was given a hasty diagnosis of organic deterioration and sent to the state hospital. The graduate student who had made a thorough evaluation of his client was upset but helpless within the situation. He was given supervisory support and advised to be patient. As expected, the client was discharged from the state hospital within about two weeks. The graduate student, who was convinced that the client had been suffering a depressive episode, felt vindicated and continued to provide psychotherapy to the client until she was discharged from his care in a fair state of remission. Two factors are revealed in this example important to the student's education. First, he received reassuring feedback as to the accuracy of his diagnostic skill. Second, when the client returned home, he was prepared to continue therapy without great modification of his own goals.

PATHOLOGY OF AGING

The single most important etiological factor in the aged is loss: loss of occupation, loss of status, loss of money, loss of friends, or loss of family (Karpf, 1977; Krasner, 1977). When such catastrophic crises occur at a stage in life where time and opportunity to recoup barely exist, it is little wonder that the elderly are overwhelmed and helpless. The problems of the elderly have been classified in various ways. A particularly useful framework for the student is the one that follows. Ingebretsen (1977) has grouped the disorders into (a) organic brain syndromes, (b) problems that stem from earlier years, (c) special crises, and (d) existential tasks. While the organic brain syndrome is a source of difficulty for many old people, other aspects of physical decline can be equally stressful. Deterioration of vision and hearing may not only reduce mobility by preventing these persons from driving their cars, they may be left vulnerable, withdrawn, and suspicious because of their inability to participate in normal interpersonal interactions. Student therapists too frequently write off these people, as in the instance of one novice who routinely referred older clients to the clinic psychiatrist for medication. He reasoned that such old people could only be there because they could receive free medication. He did not believe it worthwhile to take time to complete a diagnostic examination, presuming nothing further could be done.

Organic Disorders

As Gottesman, Quarterman, and Cohn (1973) have stated, all of the individual's life, he or she tend to perform below his or her basic biologic capacity. With the aged, though, there is an increasing tendency to perform near or at this theoretical ceiling. Thus, when some major disorder strikes, such as organic brain syndrome, diabetes, or arthritis, it places a damaging stress on the psychological functioning as well. Such people can be treated, and they can show improvement (Goldfarb, 1971). An older patient who repeatedly returned to the hospital for treatment became known to the medical staff as a dependent, inadequate personality. He was seen in psychotherapy. In a discussion of arthritis, its etiology, and its treatment, this patient expressed surprise that there was no "cure." None of the medical staff had taken time to tell him the nature of his disorder so he had been returning periodically to the hospital in belief that this was expected of him. In discovering the true picture, he stated that he could control his symptoms at home, and he would not be returning to the hospital for his arthritis. The point of this example is to show the necessity of being open, objective, honest, and genuine with the older patient. This may take a good deal of time, but it is time well spent for the gains that can be made.

Early Life Personality Patterns

The ways one adjusts to the problems of old age are largely determined by the personality developed in earlier years (Krasner, 1977). Those who have survived on a neurotic life style may find the stresses of late age beyond their level of mastery. Treatment in such cases largely is a continuation of those techniques and methods begun in early life.

Special Crises

Life crises are amost inevitable when one lives long enough. As previously outlined, these are such factors which often suddenly and critically alter lifestyle—retirement, death of a spouse, and unexpected financial losses—the consequences of these being guilt, self-degradation, depression, and a sense of helplessness. It should be noted that each and every one of these kinds of problems probably lies outside the first-hand experience of the typical student therapist. A not unusual concern with the novice therapist is his inability to totally empathize when confronted with these kinds of issues. For example, an elderly man was referred to treatment for depression. Part of the difficulty was his refusal to cash his retirement compensation. The graduate student, who was harried by his own heavy load of studies and financial hardships, really fantasized the day when he could shed the whole thing, and thus he failed to fully understand how this elderly man could feel guilt because he felt he had not earned his money. The student had to be made to understand how an individual conditioned for many years in the "Puritan ethic" could not readily accept a socially imposed retirement and the attendant new value system.

Existential Crises

These are themes which emerge in almost every instance of psychotherapy of adults and the aged. Two issues stand out: (a) coming to terms with death and one's own demise, and (b) evaluating individual worth both to others and to one's self. Because these are such important characteristics in therapy with the aged, familiarization with the literature on death and dying is essential. Especially recommended are books by Becker (1973), Feifel (1977), Kastenbaum and Aisenberg (1972), and Kubler-Ross (1969).

ASSESSMENT AND EVALUATION

Gilbert (1977) has stressed the need to have elderly patients medically evaluated as a first step. If the client has not had a recent physical examination, a referral should be made. Second, a complete history and inquiry into the life situation must be completed. Very possibly the problem of the old person can be better solved by a welfare agency than by a psychotherapist. When the issue is the threat of loss of house, or inadequate nutrition due to lack of finances, then the therapist must be flexible enough to recognize his/her own limitations. Sometimes the conflict is with a family member, in which case the counseling should be done with them and not the older client. The problem may be in the incongruency between a family expectancy and the expectancy of the elder as to role or disposition of property. In each of these instances, the elder client may need some help, but the student needs to recognize that psychotherapy is not the treatment of choice.

Instrumentation

Students should next be familiarized with both rating scales and appropriate tests. Various chapters in Storandt et al. (1978) discuss these. Students working with the elderly might be expected to have especially strong skills in assessing organic brain impairment. Finally, in the experience of the author, students are too often poorly trained in recognizing what alternative therapeutic modalities are available or have to offer. An important aspect of assessment is formulation of a treatment plan. Making an intelligent plan is impossible when one is unfamiliar with the functions of occupational therapy, recreational therapy, vocational rehabilitation services, public welfare, daycare or day treatment centers, and other agencies, any or all of which have something to offer or are actively engaged in the life of the client at the time of psychotherapy.

THERAPY WITH THE AGED

Today, there is general agreement that older people can benefit from psychotherapy, and that psychotherapy should be problem oriented (Gagliano, Gianturco, and Ramm, 1975; Kastenbaum, 1978). There are several points that any student therapist should be acutely aware of: (a) techniques, (b) therapist characteristics, (c) countertransference and transference problems, (d) special modifications, and (e) issues in supervision.

Techniques

There was a time when there was prestige in "restructuring" a personality whereas "support" was relegated to the lesser skills of the so-called paraprofessionals. With some students, there may yet be some such attitudes lurking in the background. There is no question that it is neither economical nor practical for most older people to be subjected to prolonged analysis even though for some years now there have been those who recognized that the elderly could benefit from traditional psychoanalytic techniques (Abraham, 1978; Grotjahn, 1940). There are three aspects of therapy technique that need to be addressed: (a) flexibility of approach, (b) appropriate matching of technique to problem, and (c) modifications of technique to meet the needs of the elderly. First, a student should be provided with a variety of therapeutic skills. There is no "geriatric" therapy as such, and there is every reason to believe that the elderly can benefit from established therapeutic procedures (Kastenbaum, 1978). Second, Gottesman et al. (1973) have provided a useful framework for the youthful therapist in deciding what technique is appropriate. These writers have divided approaches into four areas: biological capacities, societal demands, expectancies from significant others (family), and self-expectations. Similarly, Ingebretsen (1977) has specific therapeutic techniques to be applied. For example, organically disordered people (many of whom are institutionalized) can benefit most from modest goals such as greater comfort within a restricted environment. Often group work is to be preferred to individual; the focus is typically didactic, supportive, and oriented toward socialization. Such recommendations are well in line with much of the literature on group psychotherapy with the aged as reviewed by Goldfarb (1971). In treating those aged who are still grappling with neuroses and similar signs of ego weakness, the ideal treatment is directed toward symptom relief and provision of psychological support. In some instances, environmental change might be considered, especially where the neurotic demands of the client come into conflict with significant others. In instances of grief, loss, and depression, the initial act is to provide crisis intervention which may mean brief hospitalization, medication, or simply listening through the anguish of the client. Ultimately, clients must work through their feelings. The therapist must provide the love, the support, and the authority to sustain the client until these can be transferred more appropriately to family, friends, and to a restored self. Finally, the problems of death anxiety, issues of personal worth, and the questions of meaning of existence, all can be approached through the life review (Butler and Lewis, 1977, pp. 268–269). The tendencies of the elderly to reminisce about past life experiences are too often viewed by the young therapist as "resistance" to dealing with the real dynamics when in fact this life review is the therapy, the effort to organize one's life, and to search for one's place in the overall scheme of existence. All too often the student therapist has a preferred approach to therapy which is applied with abandon. Such schemas as those of Gottesman et al. (1973) or Ingebretsen (1977) can assist in discriminating techniques as related to problem areas.

Regardless of techniques, certain modifications of therapy have been suggested by several writers [e.g., Busse and Pfeiffer (1977), Gilbert (1977), Whanger and Busse (1976)]. In summary, these modifications are (a) more directive and exploratory activity on the part of the therapist, (b) greater emphasis on current problem-solving, (c) setting rather concrete, limited goals, (d) using more information giving, (e) encouraging environmental manipulation when useful, and (f) readiness to modify length and frequency of therapy sessions contingent on adjustment level of the client. Again, these modifications should be viewed by the beginning therapist as a basis for pragmatically modeling the therapeutic approach to the client rather than forcing the client into a situation he or she disapproves. An example of this situation occurred some years ago when an elderly man with satyriasis was referred for psychotherapy. This gentleman had been working in the office of a religious institution, and he felt that he literally had been forced into retirement since the daily contact with young females was a constant source of stimulation and consequent embarrassment in the office. This seemed to the inexperienced therapist an ideal case for behavior modification. The elderly client consented to go along with this approach although he let it be known that this was not his idea of "psychoanalysis." After two sessions, the client wrote a letter to the therapist discontinuing treatment. Efforts to re-engage him were to no avail. It was obvious to the therapist that even though he may have been correct in his selection of techniques, it conflicted with the expectancies of the client. If there is a moral to this anecdote, it is that sometimes in therapy, it is less right to be correct than it is to keep the client in treatment when alternative and more acceptable techniques are available.

Therapist Characteristics

Not a great deal has been written on this problem. However, Verwoerdt (1976, pp. 132–146) has addressed some of these issues as related to physicians in training. Incorporating these characteristics with other factors necessary for therapeutic training with the aged, the following considerations should be made. First, beginning therapists have not had the experiences of older people. Especially a young person cannot fully appreciate the effects of the Great Depression, World War II, or even the advent of television on the perceptions of the older person. These kinds of differences can make both understanding and empathy more difficult. Second, culture-wide bias and half-truths about the aged may be accepted as truths by those inexperienced in working with the aged (for example, the idea that because one is old, he or she does not need to have as much money to meet his or her needs; or that memory losses are inevitable with age). Third, young therapists sometimes fail to discriminate at upper age levels between the young-old and the old-old (Neugarten, 1978, p. 635). Fourth, there is a failure to recognize that young people may talk down to their elders, and that the young tend to view the elderly as less competent (Rubin and Brown, 1975). Fifth, there are erroneous sexual expectations in dealing with the aged. In fact, there is often failure to take into account that the elderly still are capable of sexuality (Botwinick, 1973, pp. 35–49), and there is a failure in assessing the effect of both age and sex of therapist and client. Mitchell (1978) has presented interesting evidence that elderly men and women do respond differentially to younger men and women. In summary, it is important that both the supervisor and the novice therapist spend substantial time in therapy exploring their attitudes toward the elderly, which leads into the next major consideration in which these factors are involved—transference and countertransference.

Transference and Countertransference

Both the client and the therapist approach the treatment situation with certain expectations. Sank and Prout (1978) discuss the problems of countertransference in the student therapist, while Goodstein (1962) addresses the special issues of transference as related to aging. First, there is the problem that the student is confronting a person who represents what he may be 30 or 40 years in the future. This arouses fear of becoming ill, old, and facing death. Anxiety created by this preview of one's future can seriously impede therapy because of the tendencies to deny, avoid, and repress important feelings in oneself. A second area of difficulty lies in residuals of early emotional conflicts with parents which are reactivated in working with older clients. Thus unconsciously, the therapist begins to reenact a childhood relationship because of the identification of the older client with his or her parents. A third factor rests in the frustration of working with older persons who often seem rigid, slow to learn, poorly motivated, and who have no future to work toward. Such reasoning is heard often in the clinic or hospital when staff as well as student therapists state that since they have more work than they can do anyhow, why not spend their time with the young who can benefit most. It should be mentioned that on the reverse side, older persons find themselves resisting projection of authority and expertise onto a fledgling therapist. In fact, a novice therapist may well have to become comfortable working within the framework as the projected son/daughter or even grandchild. Among all these issues, there is opportunity for the novice therapist to experience unexpected feelings and emotions that must be worked through in supervision (or in some cases personal therapy). Therapists who have not confronted their own attitudes and conflicts on age and death are not likely to be wholly effective in the role of a behavior changer.

Special Modifications

Precisely how much modification of therapeutic techniques is necessary in application with the aging is highly dependent on whether the client is still active in the community, a resident of a nursing home, or a patient in a mental hospital. Regardless of setting, a novice therapist may run into situations not normally anticipated in adult psychotherapy. These may range from the proprietary attitudes of the social welfare worker to the overprotectiveness of the family. Examples of how these problems are met by students are plentiful. An especially interesting illustration was one where the student had been assigned to get a social history on an older client. This client had been under the care of a local mental health center and also a social welfare agency. A daughter discovered that her mother had been seen, and suspected that her mother had been revealing all the family secrets. Following this, the daughter initiated numerous phone calls to the student, the supervisor, and the mental health center, with threats of lawsuits and sundry punishments. Although the client had been in a mental hospital at one time, she was not legally incompetent and therefore could decide for herself to whom she could talk. The student responded to the threats with anxiety, and he did considerable self-searching over his own role. With supervisory support, he took appropriate action and resolved the situation successfully. He furthermore had to deal with the social welfare agency which also had presumed some responsibility for making decisions for the client. It was an ideal, though not necessarily pleasant, opportunity for the student to learn to handle a sticky interpersonal situation, all stemming from a presumption on the part of the family and a welfare agency that the client was no longer capable of her own decision making.

Whether to conduct individual or group psychotherapy (Krasner, 1977), to opt for environmental manipulation, consultation with family, or to leave well enough alone are all special considerations in training a new therapist. He or she should be impressed with the fact that good clinicians may at times do more good as a consultant and as coordinator than as a direct service giver. The name of the game with the elderly is, as stated previously, to accurately assess, prepare a treatment plan, and remain flexible in meeting the needs of the client within his social and economic context.

ISSUES IN SUPERVISION

Cherniss and Egnatios (1978) propose some models for supervision in psychotherapy. Probably what they describe as "close" supervision is more effective at some times whereas "professional" supervision is more effective at other times. Given a psychotherapist who has worked with professionals in a geriatric center, and who has observed the behavior and heard the problems of elderly clientele, initial assignments of clients should probably be those that offer a fair certainty of positive outcome. Individual and group therapy experiences both in the community and in the institution should be provided.

In working with the student in supervision of individual therapy, he or she should be given opportunity to structure his or her treatment plan with assistance only as needed. As supervision is ongoing, the student should be encouraged to describe in detail the process of the session and to reveal both his feelings and his interpretations of what is happening with the client. Tape recordings used as an adjunctive tool can serve as a reality check.

Group therapy typically should be co-therapy. The co-therapist may also be the supervisor, but there is much to be said for a peer co-therapist with the supervisor maintaining better and more objective perspective outside the actual therapeutic situation.

At all times, the student should have ready access to a supervisor. Frequently, problems will not wait until the next supervisory session; on the other hand, the student needs to be encouraged to make independent decisions. Finally, the student should be provided evaluative feedback preferably on the basis of ratings of objective performance factors. These should be discussed in the context of supervision and provision should be made for modification where weaknesses are revealed.

SUMMARY

Training and supervision of psychotherapy with the aging begins with a knowledge base in the basic research on life-span development, with special emphasis on the adult years. This should be followed by guided experiences in working with the elderly in a variety of settings. An opportunity to learn about various therapy modalities, pathology of the aged, assessment procedures, and a variety of therapeutic techniques should precede supervised therapy experiences with the aged. Supervision should provide the opportunity both to explore self-attitudes and feelings about the elderly, as well as to confront such basic existential issues as fear of death and the meaning of one's being, the final training goal being the development of technical skills for behavior change.

REFERENCES

Abraham, K. The applicability of psychoanalytic treatment to patients at an advanced age (1919). Reprinted in S. Steury and M. L. Blank (Eds.), *Readings in psychotherapy with older people.* Rockville, Md.: National Institute of Mental Health, 1978, pp. 18–20.

Becker, E. *The denial of death.* New York: The Free Press, 1973.

Birren, J. E. *The psychology of aging.* Englewood Cliffs, N.J.: Prentice-Hall, 1974.

Birren, J. E., and Schaie, K. W. (Eds.). *Handbook of the psychology of aging.* New York: Van Nostrand Rheinhold, 1977.

Botwinick, J. *Aging and behavior.* New York: Springer, 1973.

Bromley, D. B. *The psychology of human ageing* (2nd ed.). Hammondsworth, England: Penguin, 1974.

Busse, E. W., and Pfeiffer, E. (Eds.). *Behavior and adaptation in late life* (2nd ed.). Boston: Little, Brown, 1977.

Butler, R. N., and Lewis, M. I. *Aging and mental health* (2nd ed.). St. Louis: C. V. Mosby, 1977.

Cherniss, C., and Egnatios, E. Clinical supervision in community mental health. *Social Work,* 1978, *23,* 219–223.

Datan, N., and Ginsberg, L. H. *Life span developmental psychology: Normative life crises.* New York: Academic, 1975.

Davis, R. W., and Klopfer, W. G. Issues in psychotherapy with the aged. *Psychotherapy: Theory, Research and Practice,* 1977, *14,* 343–348.

Donnelly, J. Psychiatric therapy in the geriatric patient. *Journal of the American Geriatric Society,* 1954, *2,* 655–661.

Dye, C. J. Psychologists' role in the provision of mental health care for the elderly. *Professional Psychology,* 1978, *9,* 38–49.

Elias, M. F., Elias, P. K., and Elias, J. W. *Basic processes in adult developmental psychology.* St. Louis: C. V. Mosby, 1977.

Feifel, H. (Ed.). *New meanings of death.* New York: McGraw-Hill, 1977.

Freud, S. On psychotherapy. In *Collected papers* (Vol. 1). London: Hogarth, 1924, pp. 249–263.

Gagliano, L., Gianturco, D., and Ramm, D. Treatment goals in geropsychiatry. *Journal of the American Geriatric Society,* 1975, *23,* 460–464.

Gerontology education in the United States. (C. R. Bolton, project coordinator.) Omaha: University of Nebraska, 1978.

Gilbert, J. G. Psychotherapy with the aged. *Psychotherapy: Theory, Research and Practice,* 1977, *14,* 394–402.

Goldfarb, A. I. Group therapy with the old and aged. In H. I. Kaplan and B. J. Sadock (Eds.), *Comprehensive group psychotherapy.* Baltimore: Williams and Wilkins, 1971, pp. 623–642.

Goodstein, L. D. Problems in counseling older disabled persons. *Journal of Rehabilitation,* 1962, *28,* 24–25.

Gottesman, L. E., Quarterman, C. E., and Cohn, G. M. Psychosocial treatment of the aged. In C. Eisdorfer and M. P. Lawton (Eds.), *The psychology of adult development and aging.* Washington, D.C.: American Psychological Association, 1973, pp. 378–427.

Grotjahn, M. Psychoanalytic investigation of a seventy-one-year-old man. In S. Steury and M. L. Blank (Eds.), *Readings in psychotherapy with older people.* Rockville, Md.: National Institute of Mental Health, 1978, pp. 94–101.

Howells, J. G. *Modern perspectives in the psychiatry of old age.* New York: Brunner/Mazel, 1975.

Ingebretsen, R. Psychotherapy with the aged. *Psychotherapy: Theory, Research and Practice,* 1977, *14,* 319–332.

Kahn, R. L. The mental health system and the future aged. *The Gerontologist,* 1975, *15* (Pt. 2), 24–31.

Karpf, R. J. The psychotherapy of depression. *Psychotherapy: Theory, Research and Practice,* 1977, *14,* 349–353.

Kastenbaum, R. Personality theory, therapeutic approaches, and the elderly client. In M. Storandt, I. C. Siegler, and M. C. Elias (Eds.), *The clinical psychology of aging.* New York: Plenum, 1978, pp. 199–224.

Kastenbaum, R., and Aisenberg, R. *The psychology of death.* New York: Springer, 1972.

Kimmel, D. C. *Adulthood and aging.* New York: Wiley, 1974.

Krasner, J. D. Loss of dignity—courtesy of modern science. *Psychotherapy: Theory, Research and Practice,* 1977, *14,* 309–318.

Kubler-Ross, E. *On death and dying.* New York: Macmillan, 1969.

McTavish, D. G. Perceptions of older people: A review of the research methodologies and findings. *The Gerontologist,* 1971, *11,* 90–102.

Mitchell, H. D. *Preferences of older versus younger counselors among a group of elderly persons.* Unpublished doctoral dissertation, Auburn University, 1978.

Neugarten, B. Personality and aging. In J. E. Birren and K. W. Schaie (Eds.), *Handbook of the psychology of aging.* New York: Van Nostrand Reinhold, 1977, pp. 626–649.

Riegel, K. F. History of psychological gerontology. In J. E. Birren and K. W. Schaie (Eds.), *Handbook of the psychology of aging.* New York: Van Nostrand Reinhold, 1977, pp. 70–102.

Rubin, K. H., and Brown, I. D. R. A life span look at person perspective and its relation to communicative interaction. *Journal of Gerontology,* 1975, *30,* 461–468.

Sank, L. I., and Prout, M. F. Critical issues for the fledgling therapist. *Professional Psychology,* 1978, *8,* 638–645.

Storandt, M., Siegler, I. C., and Elias, M. F. (Eds.). *The clinical psychology of aging.* New York: Plenum, 1978.

Verwoerdt, A. *Clinical geropsychiatry.* Baltimore: Williams and Wilkins, 1976.

Whanger, A. D., and Busse, E. W. Geriatrics. In B. Wolman (Ed.), *The therapist's handbook.* New York: Van Nostrand Reinhold, 1976, pp. 287–324.

Wolff, K. *Geriatric psychiatry.* Springfield, Ill.: Charles C. Thomas, 1963, pp. 13–23.

PART SIX

Special Modalities

Part VI, "Special Modalities," presents a set of chapters which describe training of people making psychological interventions in ways that were viewed as exceptional and tradition breaking a short time ago.

Chapter 23, *Group Psychotherapy: Supervision and Training* by Robert R. Dies, reviews the major training strategies employed in group psychotherapy. Each area that is reviewed is accompanied by instrumentation that allows the involved reader to assess change.

Chapter 24, *Supervision of Marriage and Family Therapy* by Craig Everett, surveys training approaches and the development of professional standards in the area of marital and family therapy. He includes a training model he employs in an integrative training approach.

Chapter 25, *Supervision in Community Settings: Concepts, Methods, and Issues* by Joseph F. Aponte and Michael J. Lyons, describes the development of various conceptualizations of community psychology and change that can be brought about in community settings. They focus on the nature and types of supervision useful for community psychologists.

Chapter 26, *Training and Supervision of Crisis Workers* by Barry R. Burkhart, discusses the concept of crisis and reviews the elements that comprise the successful crisis worker. Using the police as a prototypic crisis worker, he suggests that the supervisor pay attention to the worker's metaphors and understanding of the client, and work to attain the crisis agent's alliance.

CHAPTER 23

Group Psychotherapy: Training and Supervision *

ROBERT R. DIES

More than 200 articles on the training and supervision of group psychotherapists have been published during the past decade. This literature is often confusing and contradictory as authors debate the relative merits and limitations of a wide variety of training programs and specific training methodologies. Fortunately, several excellent reviews have appeared recently which bring some coherence to this growing body of literature (Berman, 1975; Coché, 1977; Lakin, Lieberman, and Whitaker, 1969). The existence of these reviews, however, leaves the present writer reluctant to add still another survey of this literature for it would seem unnecessarily redundant at this time. Therefore, this chapter simply highlights the more important points addressed in these reviews, and then focuses upon an elaboration of relatively unexplored topics and on recommendations for improvement of current training practices. This choice of emphasis was influenced by an earlier observation that many group psychotherapy practitioners are generally dissatisfied with the quality of training they have received (Dies, 1974).

This chapter is written from a general point of view for the mental health professional who is interested in group psychotherapy. Concern for the special problems in the training of paraprofessional group leaders and prescriptions for training in particular theoretical models are avoided. Some readers may question the need for a separate chapter devoted to training in group psychotherapy. Indeed, many might argue that the skills required of any therapist (e.g., knowledge of psychodynamics, empathic ability, intervention skills), are highly similar despite wide variations in treatment format—individual, couples, families, or groups. Lakin et al. (1969), however, in their informative review of training issues, have demonstrated convincingly that the intensive group experience represents a unique medium for therapy, and consequently demands specialized skills and training procedures uniquely suited to the group context. From the viewpoint of group members, participation in a developing social microcosm, interpersonal feedback, consensual validation, and reciprocal functioning as helper and helpee are uniquely group phenomena (Kaul and Bednar, 1978), and it is essential for the aspiring group leader to understand the dynamics of these and other group

*The author is grateful to Ms. Merrie Jensen for her assistance in the preparation of this chapter. The help of Alice Benmaman, Thomas Hittinger, Michael Robin, and Patricia Teleska, who served as telephone interviewers for our survey, is also appreciated.

parameters. Moreover, familiarity with these variables is probably best acquired through participation in training programs designed to incorporate direct group participation as an important vehicle for training. Lakin et al. discuss a number of specific training procedures including participant learning; didactic instruction; vicarious exposure to groups through tapes, films, transcripts, or observation of live groups; role plays and exercises; and, apprenticeship learning. Berman (1975), Stein (1975), and most recently Coché (1977) have also offered integrations of these training methods in their reviews of the literature.

In addition, numerous published descriptions of specific training programs can be found. Thus, Sadock and Kaplan (1971), Horwitz (1971), and Roman and Porter (1978) describe two- or three-year group therapy programs for psychiatric residents. Their respective papers address issues in each phase of the training program and detail the coordination of various educational techniques. Appley and Winder (1973) have two chapters devoted to training in their book, one concerned with group psychotherapy and the other focused upon training in laboratory or T-group methods. Berman (1975) and Shapiro (1978) discuss the special problems of training group psychotherapists in an academic setting. Each of these papers is an excellent source for ideas about designing group training programs. While there are many variations in the programs discussed, most of them generally endorse the guidelines established by the American Group Psychotherapy Association:

1. Seminars in the theory and technique of group psychotherapy for a minimum of 45 hours per year for two years.

2. Experience in conducting a psychotherapy group as the responsible therapist or co-therapist for 120 hours, in one to three groups, but with at least one of the groups extending for 60 or more hours in an outpatient setting. The group experiences should be accompanied by at least 75 hours of individual supervision by a qualified supervisor.[1]

3. Participation in a continuous conference on groups for a minimum of 45 hours.

4. Participation as a patient in group therapy and/or as a participant in a group process experience for a minimum of 120 hours.

5. Completion of 1200 hours in the direct treatment of patients in individual psychotherapy with a minimum of 50 hours of qualified supervision, plus the 120 hours as a group therapist as stated in point two above.

The American Group Psychotherapy Association has nearly two dozen local and regional affiliate societies, and almost a dozen international affiliate associations, who offer training in group psychotherapy generally following the guidelines of the parent organization. Scores of related training programs, with equally

---

[1] At the time of this writing, members of the American Group Psychotherapy Association are voting on this last sentence to eliminate the exclusive emphasis on "individual" supervision.

exacting standards for leadership training, are scattered throughout the country in residency programs, graduate schools, postgraduate centers, and so on. Group leader training programs are also offered by a number of organizations which cater more to proponents of encounter, personal growth, and T-group methodologies. Unfortunately, only a handful of these programs have adopted rigorous standards of training. In fact, we recently conducted a survey of 110 "major growth centers in the United States," listed in Lewis and Streitfeld (1970, p. 273), to inquire about their group leader training programs. The Centers were initially contacted via mail, and then in a follow-up by dialing the appropriate long-distance operator for a telephone listing. We found that almost 60% of the Centers could no longer be located, and of those who did respond to our inquiry, only a few described formal training programs in group leadership.

Despite the broad diversity of training programs and techniques found in the literature, there is agreement that they can be subsumed under four general categories consisting of an academic component, an observation component, an experiential component, and supervision (Shapiro, 1978; Tauber, 1978; Yalom, 1975). This chapter is organized around these four components. They are discussed separately, although it is clearly recognized that they are dynamically interrelated factors. Didactic and experiential aspects of training inevitably overlap and merge, and what begins as classroom instruction may become a highly personal experience (e.g., when a role play generates personal feedback), and conversely what starts as a highly personal experience may become quite didactic (e.g., when the processing of an experiential group becomes specifically educational). Thus the distinctions among the four training components are seldom clear-cut.

SURVEY OF GROUP PSYCHOTHERAPY SUPERVISORS

The author recently surveyed experienced group psychotherapy supervisors to sample their opinions about several aspects of training relevant to this chapter. The sample consisted of 100 professionals from various mental health fields who averaged 17½ years experience as group psychotherapists and nearly 12 years experience in the supervision of others in group leadership. Almost one-third of the sample were psychiatrists, close to one-half were psychologists, and the rest were primarily social workers; males outnumbered females 63 to 37. The professionals were drawn from the membership of the American Group Psychotherapy Association ($N = 50$) and from a variety of leadership training programs across the country; 26 different states, the District of Columbia, and Canada were represented. Most of the professionals had multiple affiliations in a variety of training contexts. Theoretical orientations spanned the entire spectrum: psychoanalytic (28), existential-humanistic (15), eclectic (15), psychodynamic (12), interpersonal (8), social learning (8), group-as-a-whole (7), TA/Gestalt (5), and neo-analytic (2), although most of the professionals espoused some combination of theoretical perspectives.

In order to insure a high rate of cooperation, these professionals were contacted by telephone; only two people refused to cooperate. In these interviews, the professionals were asked to recommend specific readings, training techniques, and specialized feedback procedures for beginning group leaders; to indicate the most common mistakes made by neophyte group leaders; and to offer guidelines for the proper combination of academic, observation, experiential, and supervisory components in a training program.

Considerable diversity of opinion was evident among the professionals regarding the appropriate balance of training components, but the averages were as follows: academic (20.1%), observation (18.2%), experiential (27.5%), and supervision (34.2%). That the more active experiential components were preferred is not surprising, and the findings are consistent with prior research. Several years ago the author (Dies, 1974) found that experienced group therapists ranked twelve different training experiences from most to least helpful as follows:

1. Co-therapy experience with a qualified therapist.

2. Discussion of your own therapy tapes with a supervisor.

3. Supervised experience in individual therapy.

4. Co-therapy experience with a peer, followed by sessions with a supervisor.

5. Attendance at group psychotherapy workshops.

6. Attendance at T-group training workshops.

7. Participation as a patient in a therapy group.

8. Discussion of films or videotapes produced by experts.

9. Careful analysis and discussion of audiotapes produced by experts.

10. Serving as a recorder-observer in a group.

11. Didactic seminars (theory, research, case study).

12. Learning by doing, self-taught (practice, reading).

The first four items relate to supervision, the next three to experiential learning, the next three to observation, and the last two to didactic instruction.

From our most recent survey, we found that the preferred sequence of training activities starts in the classroom context and then moves progressively closer toward the actual experience of conducting a group under supervision. This chapter is organized according to this progressive development of the beginning group therapist.

ACADEMIC COMPONENT

Anyone who has ever received formal training in group psychotherapy probably has an extensive reading list filed away somewhere in a folder labeled, "for future reference." Just as certainly as these bibliographies exist, so too does the fact that most of us have failed to follow-through on our intentions to read the recommended references. Setting our busy schedules aside for the moment, reading and didactic instruction is just not as interesting or involving as the experiential aspects of training. Confirmation of this observation is reflected in results of recent research studies (Dies, 1974; Ruiz and Burgess, 1968), in our survey of 100 experienced group supervisors, and in the fact that very few published reading lists appear in the literature. Moreover, reviewers of the training literature devote proportionally little attention to didactic issues (e.g., Berman, 1975, Lakin et al., 1969).

Lakin et al. suggest three questions that arise concerning the use of didactic instruction in group psychotherapy training. The first question relates to the selection of articles, books, or topics: "Is a single, internally consistent approach to group therapy to be presented? Does the instruction present a limited number of conceptual approaches, different but compatible in outlook and emphasis? Or does it present the full range of views and theory, exposing the student to all the unresolved contradictions and controversies?" (pp. 316–317). Undoubtedly, the particular readings selected by various training institutions will vary as a function of professional affiliation, theoretical perspective, experience levels, therapeutic needs, and so forth. Nevertheless, we recently explored the possibility that there might be some consensus among group trainers on a set of standard readings for the beginning group leader. In our telephone survey, we asked each of the clinicians to identify three to five basic texts or journal articles they would recommend; Table 1 lists the readings most widely endorsed.

Table 1 Suggested Readings for Beginning Group Psychotherapists: Replies from 100 Supervisors

Recommendation[a]	% Endorsement
1. Yalom (1975). *The Theory and Practice of Group Psychotherapy.*	76%
2. Bion (1959). *Experiences in Groups.*	29%
3. *International Journal of Group Psychotherapy.*	16%
4. Whitaker and Lieberman (1970). *Psychotherapy Through the Group Process.*	14%
5. Lieberman, Yalom and Miles (1973). *Encounter Groups: First Facts.*	12%
6. Durkin (1964). *The Group in Depth.*	11%
7. Kaplan and Sadock (1971). *Comprehensive Group Psychotherapy.*	10%
8. Sager and Kaplan (1973). *Progress in Group and Family Therapy.*	10%
9. Mullan and Rosenbaum (1962). *Group Psychotherapy: Theory and Practice.*	8%
10. Foulkes and Anthony (1965). *Group Psychotherapy: The Psychoanalytic Approach.*	6%
11. Rosenbaum and Berger (1975). *Group Psychotherapy and Group Function.*	6%
12. Slavson (1964). *A Textbook in Analytic Group Psychotherapy.*	5%
13. Parloff (1968). "Analytic Group Psychotherapy."	5%
14. Rioch (1970). "The Work of Wilfred Bion on Groups."	5%

[a]Readings suggested by five or more people.

Our results show that only one text received widespread endorsement. Only eleven books, one journal, and two articles were cited by 5% or more of the sample. The group supervisors offered 352 suggestions for readings which included references to 90 different books, 43 specific articles, and numerous allusions to general topic areas, and 4 journals. The overwhelming majority of these readings reflected a highly individualized approach to training. Although there was some consistency among clinicians espousing similar conceptual models, the readings they suggested were related more to their own personal style. Very few of the readings allowed for a comparative analysis of differing theoretical models of group leadership or group function. The largest proportion of the readings were technique oriented (e.g., dealing with resistance, transference, structuring, patient types), a smaller percentage were theoretical, and only a handful were research oriented. These findings are quite consistent with results of a prior survey (Dies, 1974) in which group therapists indicated that didactic seminars should focus primarily on case study and technique-oriented discussions (40%), and less on theory (25%), research (20%), or other topics (15%).

The second question raised by Lakin et al. relates to the issue of the timing of didactic instruction: "Should a trainee be exposed to conceptual ideas about groups before or after he has had personal experience as a patient, as an observer, as a therapist?" (p. 317). The results of our telephone survey indicate that most group trainers attempt a continuing integration of didactic materials with the experiential components of training, and this corresponds with other reports in the literature (Lerner, Horwitz, and Burstein, 1978; Roman and Porter, 1978). There is some general agreement that didactic instruction should precede the actual experience of conducting a group, but the particular format and extent of such instruction varies tremendously. Most training programs package their group leadership training in terms of the sequence being followed in this chapter: academic seminars, observation of groups, experience as a participant, and then supervision of practice. The trainee is gradually introduced to the experience of actually conducting a group. The particulars of the didactic-experiential integration change throughout this sequential development, but there is a tendency among group supervisors to prefer a coherent model to facilitate the organization of these experiences. Bascue (1978), for example, has proposed a model for conceptualizing group therapy which attempts to promote the integration of factual and theoretical information into actual practice. The author describes several dimensions for comparing and contrasting theoretical orientations, and then illustrates how a wide variety of models would rank along these continua, for example, temporal (past to future orientation), spatial (here-and-now versus there-and-then), volitional (cognitive-affective focus), and systemic (individual-interpersonal-group focus). Bascue's model is interesting and informative. Unfortunately, there are relatively few papers in the literature which discuss the details of how to integrate didactic and experiential material. Hopefully, the remainder of this chapter will contribute to understanding how some of this integration might be accomplished.

The third question posed by Lakin et al. (1969) concerns the use of didactic teaching in conjunction with other methods. "Should the material which is read or heard then be discussed in seminars? Can a theory best be tested and assimilated by applying to groups what has been observed or conducted? Can exercises be devised to help the trainee compare and evaluate different theoretical approaches?" (p. 317). The most fundamental question in all of this is how to make didactic instruction more than an empty academic gesture, so that reading in conceptual, methodological, and research topics can facilitate the skill development of beginning group leaders. The question goes beyond the issue of how to coordinate readings with experiential learning—it also includes concerns about how to create an instructional environment which is not characterized by the passive-receptive student orientation so common in the classroom context. Three methods have been mentioned in the literature: audiovisual techniques, role-plays, and instrumentation.

Audiovisual Aids

Several reviewers of the training literature have discussed the use of tapes and films in didactic seminars. Appley and Winder (1973) and Lakin et al. (1969) indicate that the major advantage of audiovisual techniques is that they can simulate the actual group experience and thereby heighten student involvement. These procedures are especially useful when trainees are instructed to assume a leadership role and to intervene as they might in the actual group therapy setting. By stopping the film periodically, members of the seminar can discuss the implications of various therapeutic interventions. Since the situation is simulated, there is little pressure about leadership responsibility for the group, and considerably less concern about making the "right" response. The "group" will "wait" until the leaders have had a chance to discuss different leadership techniques, and there can even be an instant replay of the process. The principal disadvantage of the various audiovisual approaches, of course, is that "the material is 'cold', the trainee does not experience the situation in the same way that he would if he were actually in the real situation" (Lakin et al., 1969, p. 319).

Professionally produced tapes and films are available from a variety of sources. The American Academy of Psychotherapists, and Behavioral Sciences Tape Library, for example, furnish catalogs of audiotapes of group therapy sessions, whereas the American Group Psychotherapy Association and the American Personnel and Guidance Association have annotated bibliographies of films. A wide assortment of theoretical orientations and treatment issues are recorded. Many training programs have also produced their own audio and videotapes. In general, as an initial exposure to group process and diverse leadership models, tapes and films can be valuable adjuncts to any training program. Audiovisual aids represent a relatively inexpensive and nonthreatening instructional approach which can significantly enhance the impact of didactic material.

Role-Play Techniques

Surveys of the training literature have generally cited role-play procedures as another method for improving didactic instruction in group psychotherapy. Berman (1975), for example, concludes that role-playing exercises are a more affectively involving variation of the didactic seminar, and are especially useful when other more experiential forms of teaching are unavailable and the traditional lecture format fails to convey the feeling component of group issues. Appley and Winder (1973, p. 151) state that role-plays give the trainee "the opportunity to see a situation as another would see it and to assume the responsibility for behaving as the other person would behave." Coché (1977) suggests that the practice sessions give the trainee a chance to try out varying responses in a safe setting, and with supervisory feedback to improve upon intervention skills to become better prepared for the actual therapeutic experience. Lakin et al. (1969) indicate that a wide range of role-playing situations can be designed to fit particular training needs. The technique is indeed extremely flexible and valuable for beginning and advanced trainees alike.

Other writers have also discussed the merits of role-play techniques to improve learning. The presentations range from brief accounts of particular structured exercises (MacLennan, 1971), to relatively thorough descriptions of didactic-experiential courses following a role-playing model (Roman and Porter, 1978). A recent book by Cohen and Smith (1976) outlines a wide variety of "critical incidents" that can be role-played by beginning group therapists. The possibilities, of course, are almost endless. Perhaps this is why the approach proves to be so popular. Nearly half of the 100 experienced group trainers we recently surveyed mentioned role-play techniques as helpful in the training of novice group leaders.

A word of caution should be added, however. Lakin et al. (1969) note that role-playing techniques can become nonconstructive if an "atmosphere of mutual trust and acceptance has not been established within the group of trainees, and if unresolved problems are still present having to do with competitiveness, resentment of the training staff and the program, etc." (p. 321).

Instrumentation

Another means of increasing the involvement of students in the formal aspects of training is to introduce a variety of research and training instruments which focus on leadership issues. Unfortunately, only a few instruments have been specifically designed for leadership training, but with a little resourcefulness many research instruments can be adapted to suit training purposes. The following list has been drawn from the author's own experience. These are all self-report instruments which can be used without any prior group experience.

1. *Fundamental Interpersonal Relations Orientation—Behavior,* (Schutz, 1967).

A measure of a person's characteristic behavior toward other people in the areas of inclusion, control and affection. It is designed not only to measure individual characteristics but also to assess relationships between people, such as compatibility (FIRO-B).

2. *Fundamental Interpersonal Relations Orientation—Feelings,* (Schutz, 1967).
   This measure is meant to parallel FIRO-B but focuses on feelings rather than on behavior. FIRO-F assesses feelings in the areas of significance, competence, and lovability, the feelings presumed to be behind inclusion, control, and affection, respectively.

3. *Group Leader Self-Disclosure Scale,* (Dies, 1977a).
   Designed to assess attitudes toward group therapist transparency, the questionnaire incorporates statements varying along a self-disclosure dimension. Content ranges from relatively innocuous self-revelations to more intimate disclosures; items are written to include external past and present issues and here-and-now attitudes and feelings of the leader toward self, individual group members, or the group as a whole.

4. *Group Leadership Functions Scale,* (Conyne, 1975).
   Based on the research of Lieberman, Yalom, and Miles (1973), the scale is designed to explore four basic leadership functions: emotional stimulation, caring, meaning attribution, and executive function.

5. *Group Leadership Questionnaire,* (Wile, 1972).
   This instrument presents brief descriptions of 21 group situations, and asks trainees to select from 19 possible responses those they might make as the group leader: directive versus nondirective, individual versus group focus, reassurance versus confrontation, asking questions versus making interpretations versus remaining silent, and so on.

6. *Hill Interaction Matrix-B,* (Hill, 1977).
   The scale measures interpersonal behavior in terms of a matrix consisting of two dimensions. The first dimension, Content, contains four categories of increasing growth potential: topic, group, personal, and relationship. The second dimension, style, contains four categories in ascending order of willingness to take a facilitative role and risk interpersonal threat: conventional, assertive, speculative, and confrontive.

7. *Interpersonal Relationship Rating Scale,* (Hipple, 1976).
   This scale consists of 24 seven-point numerical rating scales which attempt to measure attitudes and/or behaviors in the individual's relationships with others and how he/she views self. For example: ability to listen, tolerance of differences, reaction to expression of warmth, reaction to conflict.

8. *Reactions to Group Situations,* (Thelen, 1976).
   A measure of preferences for certain kinds of behavior in group settings: inquiry, fight, pairing, tendency, flight. It is a way of introducing trainees to Bion's influential theory of basic assumptions of people in therapy groups.

9. *Strength Deployment Inventory,* (Porter, 1976).

The inventory assesses a person's motivation and orientation for seeking interactions with others when things are going well and when faced with conflict and opposition: altruistic-nurturing, assertive-directing, and analytic-autonomizing.

10. *Understanding Your Leadership Behavior,* (Johnson and Johnson, 1975). This instrument attempts to evaluate approaches to leadership in terms of a task-maintenance grid. Task functions include information and opinion giver, starter, direction giver, summarizer and other behaviors intended to keep a group goal-oriented. Maintenance functions include encourager of participation, harmonizer, communication helper, trust builder and other relationship-oriented behaviors.

Page limitations prevent the discussion of these and other instruments which can be used to increase personal involvement in the didactic portions of leadership training. It is clear, however, that a variety of instruments can be incorporated, and that these instruments have the potential of contributing considerably to an understanding of a wide range of theoretical, methodological, practical, and personal issues. The instruments can be oriented toward group leadership technique (e.g., Wile, 1972), focus more upon personal aspects of leadership (e.g., Dies, 1977a), or accent a variety of personality attributes relating to one's interactional style (e.g., Schutz, 1967). In addition to facilitating insight into leadership and group issues, these methods may provide feedback of a much more personal nature. To this end, a variety of personality inventories might also be built into the didactic segment of the training program.

Finally, the utilization of instruments in a training program might well furnish trainees with a greater appreciation of group psychotherapy research, and increase their willingness to explore research issues in their own training. Readings which evaluate leadership research (e.g., Dies, 1977b and c) and outcome of group treatments based upon many of these instruments (e.g., Bednar and Kaul, 1978; Parloff and Dies, 1977) can be incorporated into the didactic assignments. Moreover these articles can serve as a source of information about additional instruments.

OBSERVATION COMPONENT

This aspect of training in group leadership has received very little attention in the literature, and it appears to be the least popular of the four training components. The respondents to our telephone survey gave observation the lowest priority, even lower than the academic component. It is the only component of training not formally endorsed in the guidelines published by the American Group Psychotherapy Association. The relative unpopularity of this training technique is probably due to the position of passivity the observer frequently assumes while watching an ongoing group. Lakin et al. (1969, p. 320) state: "If he is in the same room with the group, he cannot discuss events as they proceed, and he must to some extent control his nonverbal reactions so as not to distract the group. If he is watching from behind a one-way screen, he can comment as the group moves along, although again he cannot stop the action."

These authors also note that observing, especially through one-way mirrors, tends to reduce empathic responses to individual patients. Berman (1975) mentions the potentially detrimental effects of observation on the patients and group process, and these concerns are discussed in greater detail by Cottle (1968) and Mackie and Wood (1968). These adverse reactions include defensiveness, resentment toward the therapist for permitting observers, concerns about confidentiality, scapegoating, and so on. A parallel concern for Berman and others is the potentially inhibiting effect of the presence of observers upon the group therapists, particularly if they are relatively inexperienced. Mackie and Wood (1968) point to the likelihood that observers may be perceived as hostile critics, whereas Fielding, Guy, Harry, and Hook (1971) cite the leaders' fears of revealing their own pathology, and exhibitionistic tendencies as potentially intrusive factors.

Fortunately, most of these authors discuss procedures for working through these pitfalls and problems, and list several distinct advantages of observational techniques. Shapiro (1978) comments that imitation learning can be a valuable source of training: "Watching a professional group leader is a golden opportunity for a trainee to get a realistic picture of the true nature of group leadership. Observing such a therapist, the trainee can view both successes and failures, can begin to discover weaknesses in his own developing skills, and can see the results of specific therapeutic interventions in specific situations" (p. 151). Mackie and Wood (1968) identify several advantages of using observation in training. Most of these relate to the post-session feedback observers can provide the group leader: reporting data missed by the therapist, illuminating the interpretive comments, and reflection of hidden agendas and emotional reactions within the patient group. Yalom (1975) regards the post-meeting discussion as "an absolute training necessity" and says that there "is no better time for the group leader to meet with his student observers than immediately following the group" (p. 505).

Podnos and Robinson (1967) suggest that observation encourages trainees to become more perceptive of group process, apparently because they have more freedom to engage in diagnostic speculation. Mackie and Wood (1968) suggest that observation may even facilitate an awareness of research issues as the trainees struggle to reach a shared understanding of the group process.

The remainder of this section focuses on procedures for improving the value of observation as a training tool. Three general issues are discussed briefly: Integration of Didactic and Observational Learning, Instrumentation, and Post-Group Processing.

Integration of Didactic and Observational Learning

Observation, in and of itself, is probably of limited value unless the trainees have the opportunity to evaluate the accuracy of their observations and to discuss alternative perspectives on group process. The presence of several observers behind the one-way glass allows for this possibility, since the trainees can discuss the group while it is in progress. If one of the observers is also an experienced group leader and/or supervisor the value of the one-way mirror can be significantly enhanced. Podnos and Robinson (1967) describe an approach to training in which the supervisor and two or more trainees observe a therapy group being conducted by another pair of trainees. While the group is in progress, the session is recorded on one track of a stereo tape recorder, while comments of the supervisor and the viewing trainees are recorded concurrently on the other track. Immediately after the group session, the observers and co-leaders convene to discuss the meeting. This method can accommodate several groups so that trainees have the opportunity to serve as both leaders and observers of different groups within the same training program. The learning potential of this model can be enhanced by observing more than one group, which allows one to comparatively analyze leadership styles, the influence of group composition, and so forth.

There are two important sources of learning for trainees within this observational model: (1) the information acquired about leadership and group process as the observers discuss the ongoing group from their vantage point behind the one-way mirror, and (2) the feedback observers provide to their fellow trainees who are serving as co-leaders in the therapy group. If the trainees are observing an experienced group leader, they benefit from their post-group discussion of the group with their supervisor (Yalom, 1975). The use of the post-session wrap-up will be evaluated subsequently. This section emphasizes the learning experience behind the one-way mirror.

While the therapy group is in progress, the supervisor and trainees have the opportunity to comment on the session from a variety of methodological and theoretical perspectives, and the particular focus can be designed to fit the training needs that are prevalent at the time. A didactic framework can be conceptualized to parallel the events transpiring within the group therapy sessions. Initial didactic material can focus on leadership strategies in beginning groups (e.g., contracting, dealing with dependency, structuring); later the emphasis can shift to issues of control (e.g., resistance, conflict resolution), and still later issues of intimacy and affection can be accentuated. The assigned readings can thus complement the experiential facets of the groups. The supervisor and co-observers can evaluate the group from a variety of theoretical perspectives, and the supervisor could provide different readings to each trainee to allow for some diversity in the theoretical commentary. Readings on leadership, individual and group dynamics, phases of group development, termination, and so on can be incorporated into the discussions of the events occurring within the group being observed.

Formal methods of evaluating group process might also be integrated into the observation period. Trainees can first do the recommended reading and then come prepared to process the group using a systematic rating scheme.

Instrumentation

A variety of research and training instruments are available for recording the events of ongoing groups. Use of these instruments can substantially enhance the trainees' learning by sharpening their observational skills and familiarizing them with novel conceptual frameworks, while at the same time introducing them to systematic procedures for researching group process. The particular instruments selected will depend, of course, on the unique goals of the training program; instruments may focus on leadership and/or group process issues. The following list is based upon the author's own experiences. The instruments vary from relatively simple techniques (e.g., Who Speaks to Whom), to more intricate rating schemes (e.g., HIM—G). Even if the scales are not formally applied to the groups, they can be discussed in the didactic-observation integration of the material.

Scales Focused on Leadership:

1. *Checklist of Leader Behavior* (Lieberman, Yalom, and Miles, 1973).
   This scale contains 28 items divided into five general categories: (1) evocative behavior, e.g., questioning, challenging, calling on; (2) coherence making and cognitive learning, e.g., explaining, summarizing, interpreting; (3) support; (4) management, e.g., starting, stopping, pacing; and, (5) use of self.

2. *Facilitator Behavior Index* (Long and Bosshart, 1974).
   The instrument emphasizes three main attributes presumed to relate to leadership effectiveness: generalized interpersonal sensitivity, ability to express spontaneously a full range of emotions and feelings, and nondirective leadership style.

3. *Hill Interaction Matrix-G* (Hill, 1977).
   The two-dimensional framework, Content versus Style, was discussed above in the list of instruments under the academic component; HIM-G parallels HIM-B. Leader "sponsoring" and "maintaining" behaviors are scored within each cell of the matrix. It is possible to derive separate scores for each cell in the grid and to assess overall activity level of the therapist.

4. *Reinforcement—Prompt Code* (Liberman, 1970).
   This procedure was developed to measure the frequency with which the therapist reinforces (acknowledges) and prompts (elicits) the verbal behavior of group members in certain content areas.

5. *Trainer Behavior Factors* (Bolman, 1971).
   Several items measure each of the seven primary dimensions of group leadership: congruence-empathy; conceptual input; conditionality; perceptiveness; openness; affection; and dominance.

Scales Focused on Group Process:

1. *Group Atmosphere Scale* (Silbergeld, Koenig, Manderscheid, Meeker, & Hornung, 1975).
   This scale was developed to measure systematically the psychological environment of therapy groups. Twelve content subscales, each containing ten

true-false items, assess the consensual psychosocial environment. Several of these serve as indicators of group cohesion and conformity.

2. *Group Rating Schedule* (Cooper, 1977).
   This scale measures 21 different aspects of group process organized into five internally consistent factors: process orientation, social atmosphere, trainer involvement, relationship between trainer and participant, and participant emotional cohesiveness.

3. *Interaction Process Analysis* (Bales, 1950; Mills, 1974).
   This technique evaluates group behaviors in terms of two areas, task and socio-emotional. Subcategories relate to problems of orientation, evaluation, control, decision, tension management, and integration. The first three are further divided into "questions" and "attempted answers," while the other three are separated into "positive" and "negative" reactions, thus yielding twelve distinct categories.

4. *Moss Behavioral Rating of Disclosure* (Moss and Harren, 1978).
   This scale contains ten scales to rate leader and member self-disclosure: frequency, duration, stimulus, desirability, distance, concreteness, affect of the message, congruity, vocal intensity, and topic.

5. *Who Speaks to Whom*
   This is a simple method of tallying verbal behavior in groups. The names of all the group members are listed down the left margin, and across the top of the page (plus a column for group). A simple tally of who speaks with whom is tabulated.

Post-Group Processing

Unquestionably, the information conveyed by the observers to the co-leaders can be of considerable value to the leaders' own development as group therapists. The feedback, whether it is based upon spontaneous reactions or conceptualized within the framework of various instruments, can furnish valuable insights to the group leader. Comments on this aspect of the post-group processing, however, are reserved for the fourth major segment of this chapter, under the Supervisory Component. The emphasis here is on the merits of the post-session meeting to the observers.

The observers, by providing their perspectives on the group process, are in actuality serving as part of the supervisory team. In that capacity they learn quickly that to provide effective feedback they must be able to conceptualize their observations clearly and concretely, and to offer their evaluative commentary in a constructive fashion so as not to precipitate defensiveness and hostility in the co-leaders. Then, too, they learn that their feedback is appreciated more if they can get beyond the "this is what you did wrong" orientation and recommend alternative intervention strategies, and to comment on the positive aspects of leadership they noted through the one-way mirror. By tuning into the reactions of the co-leaders, the observers develop greater awareness of their own supervisory and interpersonal styles. If the roles are ever reversed in the training program, so that students play both the leader and observer roles, they can more readily appreciate the importance of sensitive, perceptive feedback which is delivered in a supportive manner. In other words, the observers learn through the process of supervising their peers. This is analogous to Reissman's (1965) "helper therapy principle," the recognition that the helper often achieves more through helping than does the client, or in this case the fellow trainee. "The sharing of information, similar experiences, and supervision constitute the most therapeutic and instructive aspects of supervision . . ." (Smith, 1976).

EXPERIENTIAL COMPONENT

It was noted earlier that the American Group Psychotherapy Association considers participation in an experiential group an essential ingredient in leadership training. Our recent survey indicates that there is widespread agreement on the value of this training component. Of the 100 experienced group therapists who were asked, "what specialized training procedures have you found especially helpful for teaching group therapeutic skills?", 90% mentioned process, therapy, or training groups or workshops incorporating a major focus on experiential learning. This is in contrast to the 26% response rate for didactic seminars and readings, and the 21% figure for observation of ongoing groups.

Shapiro (1978) argued that,

In order for trainees to learn about the effects of a group in nonacademic, nonintellectual ways, they must experience a group as a member. . . . Unless a leader can empathize with the intense pressures and fears of membership, his or her understanding of members will be subsequently diminished. Group leaders must understand group phenomena affectively and sensorially as well as intellectually" (p. 151) . . . "opportunity of seeing an experienced group leader in action, concurrent with their own high levels of affect . . . is different from pure observation, in which trainees can view the group action more dispassionately" (p. 152).

Berman (1975), in his review of the training literature, concludes that participation in a group offers experiences not elsewhere available to the trainee, including the experience of the member role, understanding of the group as a powerful social system, and greater appreciation of the leader role through their own identification and unrealistic appraisal of the leader.

A variety of experiential groups have been described in the literature. These experiences range in the amount of time and personal commitment required of the trainee. At one extreme are long-term intensive groups, such as the three-year psychotherapy groups recommended by Sadock and Kaplan (1969; 1971), while on the other end of the continuum are brief workshops such as those offered by the American Group Psychotherapy Association at its annual conferences and institutes.

Process and Therapy Groups

There is some disagreement concerning the most appropriate focus of these experiential groups. Several writers (e.g., Bonney and Gazda, 1966; Sadock and Kaplan, 1971; Woody, 1971) propose that the goal should be explicitly therapeutic. They argue that trainees who plan to include treatment groups in their future practice should first have a personal group psychotherapy experience so as to become sensitized to various group dynamics and to benefit therapeutically. The majority opinion, however, seems to favor the nontherapy process group as the more appropriate training model. Here the focus is more on the acquisition of knowledge about leadership and group function than it is on improved self-understanding (e.g., Garwood, 1967; Horwitz, 1967; Redlich and Astrachan, 1969).

Often, however, the distinction between therapy and education is not a sharp one. "In practice, the effects of these kinds of group experiences overlap: the patient in the therapy group learns something about group processes; the participant in a T-group or study group may recognize and revise maladaptive patterns" (Lakin et al., 1969, p. 317). Berger's (1970a) list of possible advantages of sensitivity groups, laboratory experiences, or basic encounter groups could just as easily have been quoted with reference to psychotherapy groups for training in group leadership:

> To promote awareness and understanding of self and others;
>
> To experience a climate of openness and inquiry . . . ;
>
> For reality testing of behavior and of change in one's behavior;
>
> To increase skills and effectiveness in working with others, even when the task is unclear and accompanied by peaks of anxiety and frustration;
>
> To increase communication skills and to learn how verbal and nonverbal communications are used to establish, maintain, and regulate relationships and self-defeating arrangements with others;
>
> To increase the ability of participants to be innovative;
>
> For greater choice and flexibility of behavior;
>
> To allow one to check out and compare one's values, attitudes, and experiences with others in a spirit of interest, caring, intimacy, concern, understanding, acceptance, trust, and mutuality;
>
> For the further development of one's autonomous interdependency (p. 849).

Many writers have discussed the differences between therapy groups and training groups, but generally conclude that the similarities outweigh the differences. In this latter respect, Lakin et al. (1969) highlight analogous reactions to initial group structuring and suggest comparable membership roles (e.g., scapegoat, isolate), and Ammon and Ament (1967) and Kaplan (1967) discuss parallel phases of group development. The differences between therapy and training groups are more a matter of degree or emphasis. Relative to psychotherapy groups, training groups focus more attention on the "explicit delineation of characteristic group dynamic patterns such as leadership competition, subgrouping, scapegoating pressures under the cloak of 'helping,' pressures for and against intimacy, and pressures hindering and facilitating change and goal achievement among group members" (Garwood, 1967, p. 459). Similarly, Yalom (1975, p. 519) states, "In therapy groups if there is no therapeutic advantage in clarifying group process, I see no reason to do so. In training groups there is always the superordinate goal of education."

Shapiro (1978) has offered three caveats regarding the use of experiential groups in leadership training. One concerns the competitiveness characterizing groups composed of aspiring group leaders: "Because of the competitiveness and desire to practice the therapy role, training group members open up cautiously and slowly, by comparison to members in other groups. They take fewer personal risks, and a large part of the leaders' job is to enhance interpersonal trust, cohesion, and cooperation between members" (p. 153). As a consequence of this pervasive concern about competition and competency (Yalom, 1975), Shapiro's second warning is that the leader of such groups must be selected carefully. Berman (1975) concurs with Shapiro and both recommend that the leader should not be closely tied to the training program administration. This will help to reduce the threat of lack of confidentiality and the identification of the group leader with the program evaluator. Shapiro's third point is political, and relates to the attitudes of other faculty members and staff to the use of experiential groups for training—for example, "forcing psychotherapy onto students" (p. 152). This concern relates to the issue of contract: is participation in a therapy or process group an elective or compulsory training expectation? (Berman, 1975). Horwitz (1971) also addressed these institutional attitudes.

Workshops

The workshop represents another form of experiential group which has considerable merit in the training of group psychotherapists. Although workshops are generally abbreviated learning experiences, some of the same group dynamics can be observed in this context as well. Berger (1967), for example, has remarked on the efforts of many participants to convert these task-oriented groups into specifically therapeutic experiences. For the most part, however, workshops have a more delimited focus in that they are organized around specific themes. The most recent program of the American Group Psychotherapy Association Annual Conference, for example, contains the following titles: "Transference-Countertransference in Group Psychology;" "Resistances in Group;" "The Silent Member in the Group." Each of the workshops incorporates an experiential component. Participants in these types of workshops generally find them to be valuable learning experiences. To illustrate, the "Overall Event Rating" averaged across 100 workshops for the 1978 American Group Psychotherapy Association Conference was almost 82%, where "excellent" was scored as 100% and "good" as 75% on a five-point continuum.

Wile (1973) indicates that, "The professional workshop, consisting of lecture, demonstration, and participatory experience, has become a popular method for training group therapists. Workshops combine the modern-day preference for brief time-limited procedures with the contemporary emphasis upon participatory experience" (p. 185). Research on the outcome of these brief training experiences indicates that they produce a variety of general and specific changes that may be quite long-lasting. "The workshop appears to be an excellent medium through which to teach relatively straightforward, action-oriented, and dramatic approaches to group therapy leadership, particularly those that lend themselves to ingroup demonstration. . . ." (p. 196). Stone and Green (1978) and Selfridge, Weitz, Abramowitz, Calabria, Abramowitz, and Steger (1975) have also demonstrated the impact of workshop experiences on trainees' development of leadership skills. Their findings indicate that the experiential aspects of workshops, more than the didactic portions, are quite influential in the learning process.

Yet, there is also agreement that the experience of being in a group (therapy, process, or workshop) is not sufficient training in itself. "Opportunities to reflect, think over, and study are necessary in order to grasp the complexities of the group situation, the nature of one's own participation and feelings, and the impact of oneself upon others and others upon oneself" (Lakin et al., 1969, p. 310). In his review of the training literature, Coché (1977) observed that the manner in which experiential groups were conducted differed greatly from one training facility to another. In some programs, the emphasis was on didactic information and the group devoted most of its time to discussions of conceptual material; the processes of the group were used only peripherally as they fit into the topics of discussion. At the other extreme were programs in which groups convened for the sole purpose of self-study without the integration of pertinent literature. From his experience, Coché found that an appropriate balance of didactic and group process material was necessary. Groups which devote a large portion of their time to theoretical or clinical material eventually demand a discussion of their processes and experiences. Conversely, groups which spend most of their time in self-study sooner or later request a discussion of relevant literature. The particular format for combining didactic information and group process will depend, of course, on the unique goals of the training institution. Readings, lecture, and demonstrations can be tailored to accommodate the group's needs at the time. Didactic materials can be selected to parallel the experiential group's focus on issues of control or intimacy, structure, phases of group development, termination, and so on.

Instrumentation

One valuable source of learning from experiential groups that has received only scant attention in the literature is the use of instrumentation. Regrettably, too many training programs have failed to capitalize on the rich potential of this approach to training. Only 10% of the clinicians contacted in our telephone survey mentioned specific questionnaires or rating schemes as vehicles for instrumented feedback. An additional 12% referred to the utilization of instruments in a general way without specific identification of an instrument. The list of instruments below is based on the author's own experiences. They represent just a few of the numerous techniques available for providing systematic feedback about one's interpersonal style, leadership potential, and contribution to the group process. Trainees can complete the instruments between experiential sessions. The ratings can be focused on self-assessments or evaluations of fellow group members. Discussion of the ratings within the experiential group can serve to facilitate group process, whereas consideration of the instruments in the didactic portion of training can augment understanding of theoretical and methodological issues.

1. *Contribution to the Normative Structure* (Luke, 1972).
   This scale contains ten statements regarding the perceived norms in an experiential group (e.g., feedback, problem solving, role fixation, process diagnosis, etc.). Members are asked to indicate the degree each participant has contributed to the development and maintenance of the behavioral standards.

2. *Leader Checklist* (Lundgren, 1971).
   This instrument assesses various perceptions of the group leader and/or co-members. Items address perceived helpfulness, activity, involvement, etc.

3. *Personal Description Questionnaire* (Lieberman, Yalom, and Miles, 1973).
   This scale lists 35 bipolar descriptions regarding interpersonal style, and asks for an evaluation of self and other people: enthusiastic-unenthusiastic; relaxed-tense; open-evasive; outspoken-reserved, etc.

4. *Relationship Inventory* (Barrett-Lennard, 1962).
   The instrument consists of four subscales evaluating regard, empathy, unconditionality, and congruence. This is one of the most popular sets of variables in the group literature. Short forms of the scale have been devised (e.g., Cooper, 1969; Frankiel, 1971).

5. *Semantic Differential* (Osgood, Suci, and Tannenbaum, 1957).
   This is a highly flexible technique for evaluating perceptions of group process, member participation, leadership style, etc. Essentially, it consists of multiple bipolar adjectives selected to suit one's own training needs. Participants are instructed to describe the target concept (e.g., co-members) using the bipolar checklist.

SUPERVISION COMPONENT

This facet of training has undoubtedly received the greatest amount of attention in the literature. A wide assortment of supervisory models exist, ranging from more specialized variations such as alternate-therapist observer techniques (Jarvis and Esty, 1968), double reversal group models (Finney, 1968), and bug in the ear approaches (Boyleston and Tuma, 1972), to the more conventional methods:

dyadic, co-therapy, triadic, and group supervisory formats (McGee, 1968). Only these more basic approaches are highlighted in this chapter.

Models

The simplest model of supervision is the *dyadic* approach, in which the trainee reviews his or her group therapy sessions with an experienced supervisor. There are certain advantages of this model; for example, it does not require much effort or preparation by the trainee or supervisor (Coché, 1977) and the teacher-student relationship can be intense and mutually beneficial (Coché, 1977, McGee, 1968). Nevertheless, the general consensus is that the model is less valuable than other procedures. The main objections center on the possible blurring of the distinction between supervision and therapy (Coché, 1977), difficulties for the supervisor in forming a comprehensive and accurate picture of the group (McGee, 1968), and the potential for distortion and resistances (Yalom, 1975). The use of audio and videotape recordings and direct observation by the supervisor might obviate some of the problems, but these compensations do not significantly improve the dyadic model as a strategy for training in group interventions. Methods are needed which are more carefully integrated within the group model of treatment, that is, procedures which emphasize interpersonal processes within group systems. This issue will be examined shortly.

The trainee-supervisor *cotherapy* model is also based on a dyadic relationship (Berman, 1975), but it involves the supervisor in the group therapy in a more direct and intimate fashion. Several writers have examined the merits and drawbacks of this model. The principal advantages are due to the presence of the supervisor in the group which allows for a greater awareness of the trainee's in-therapy style and affords the experienced clinican the opportunity to intervene directly when difficulties arise (Coché, 1977). Under these circumstances, the trainee can observe effective group leadership and thereby learn through modeling the supervisor's behavior. Furthermore, trainee-supervisor co-therapy facilitates the understanding of transference and countertransference phenomena (Anderson, Pine, and Mee-Lee, 1972). Nonetheless, there are numerous disadvantages, and these are related primarily to the stifling effect of the supervisor upon the trainee. Sadock and Kaplan (1971) report that in the apprenticeship model the trainee does not participate as openly or as spontaneously due to feelings of intimidation and anxiety, whereas Berman (1975) describes the trainee's potential inhibitory fear of exposure while in direct view of the "expert." Role differences also adversely influence communication patterns: the trainee's status in the group is lessened (Anderson et al., 1972); the group plays off the student as junior to and less therapeutic than the senior therapist (Berman, 1975); and, there is a dilution of the trainee's responsibility for leadership (Berman, 1975). In addition, the trainee is provided with only one model with whom to identify (McGee, 1968). These difficulties and associated problems are discussed in detail by other authors (Benjamin, 1972; Davis and Lohr, 1971; McGee and Schuman, 1979).

To counteract some of these pitfalls, McGee (1974) has proposed a *triadic* model of supervision in which two trainees are paired as co-leaders with an experienced therapist as a consultant or supervisor. The advantages are that the trainees have more responsibility for the group, there is less chance for distortion even in supervision using retrospective report (Berman, 1975), and the transference feelings between co-leaders become available to the supervisor (McGee, 1968). Disadvantages may also arise due to the co-therapeutic nature of the process; trainees may become affectively involved with each other or become overly competitive and vie for the attention of the supervisor (Coché, 1977). The supervisor must be attuned to these possibilities. The triadic supervisory process evaluates not only the function of the group, then, but also the relationship between the co-therapists, the effects of this relationship upon the group, and the relationship between the supervisor and the trainees. Therefore, this arrangement more closely approximates what transpires in an actual group therapy setting; triadic supervision involves properties of dyadic, co-therapy, and group supervision.

Coché (1977) suggests that co-therapy teams composed of two trainees can also be very supportive, thereby allowing for greater creativity and risk taking, especially if the supervisory relationship is also characterized by nonjudgmental support and encouragement. Podnos and Robinson (1967) share their enthusiasm for this technique and expand the model to incorporate several pairs of trainees who in conjunction with a supervisor share the responsibilities of observation and supervision of their respective groups. The advantages of this model were touched upon earlier in this chapter under observational techniques. The supervisory model has now been broadened to encompass *group supervision,* an approach to training which is uniquely suited to supervision in group treatments: ". . . this approach has the advantage of providing a group context in which the fledgling group therapist can learn about the operation of groups and about his own feelings as a group member. In this sense, it exposes the supervisee directly to the dynamics of groups as a participant rather than as a therapist. It also provides him with a forum in which he can share anxieties and insecurities about becoming a group therapist and, hopefully, learn from the problems and contributions of others undergoing a similar experience" (McGee, 1968, p. 168). Mintz (1978) elaborates on this method for helping trainees cope with the emotional dilemmas they face in their own groups; moreover, she suggests that the approach is helpful in offsetting theoretical biases or personal blind sports the supervisor may possess. Berman (1975) states that group supervision is quite similar in form to the didactic seminar, except now the process, as well as the content, relate to the trainees' experiences in groups. While the trainees may report on their role as therapists, they also experience their role as members of a group.

Several authors have cautioned, however, that group supervision may have certain hazards including the tendency of the trainees and supervisor to conduct a form of "pseudogroup psychotherapy" instead of concentrating on the issue of supervision (Sadock & Kaplan, 1971), and the possibility that problems might develop due to unevenness of experience levels and readiness to undertake group psychotherapy among the trainees (McGee, 1968).

Problems of Beginning Group Therapists

In order to understand the process of preparing group therapists, group educators need to know the types of problems trainees typically encounter (Smith, 1976). Hunter and Stern (1968) have compiled a list of problems they have observed in group supervision among their beginning group leaders: (1) fear of exposure and criticism by peers and the supervisor, (2) threats to self-esteem, (3) sibling rivalry, (4) transference, (5) dependency, (6) destructive impulses, (7) identification with patients, and (8) strong emotional attachments among the trainees. Williams (1966), on the other hand, has presented common "fearful fantasies" characterizing trainees in their initial contact with group patients. He highlights the trainees' fears of (1) encountering unmanageable resistance during early group sessions, (2) losing control of the group, (3) excessive hostility breaking out in their groups, (4) acting out by group members, (5) overwhelming dependency demands on the therapist, and (6) group disintegration. Brody (1966) cleverly illustrates the dynamics of the supervisory relationship in a dyadic model of training through a hypothetical dialogue between a neophyte and his therapy supervisor. He reveals the trainee's feelings of responsibility for the patient group (the need to "make it work"), concerns about being technically adept ("doing the right thing"), and conflicts over therapeutic transparency ("how much should I reveal about myself?").

There is very little information in the literature on the nature of the mistakes made by beginning group therapists in the actual treatment setting. Consequently, we requested the clinicians in our telephone survey to specify the most frequent difficulties they observed in their trainees. Table 2 summarizes the results.

The naming of categories and assignment of the 258 responses was obviously a subjective process. This was accomplished in consultation with a number of other individuals to achieve some objectivity. Although group discussion generally settled differences of opinion, and most of the items were easy to classify, a few of the decisions were more or less arbitrary. The results presented in the Table, however, are quite clear and require little elaboration.

The area of largest agreement among the respondents to our survey was that beginning group leaders experience substantial difficulty with the group therapeutic model. This was expressed as either the trainees' insensitivity to group process or as their failure to utilize the resources of the group effectively: the supervisors saw their students as conducting individual therapy in the group context. This shortcoming is probably related to the fact that many trainees have considerable individual psychotherapy experience before they enter group therapy training. Despite this prior clinical experience, however, supervisors report that the trainees manifest a number of personal fears and anxieties in the group setting (Table 2). They are viewed by their supervisors as being intimidated by the intensity of the group process and feeling unable to manage the situation competently: feelings of anxiety, inadequacy, and defensiveness are common. These findings corroborate the reports of Brody (1966), Hunter and Stern (1968), and Williams (1966). Many trainees are perceived as coping with their anxiety by

Table 2 Difficulties of Beginning Group Psychotherapists: Replies from 100 Supervisors

Category	Frequency
I. *Adequacy of Preparation*	
A. *Background* (*n* = 20)	
1. Inadequate knowledge of theory, technique, or personality.	9
2. Inappropriate "caricature" of the group (e.g., therapy vs. training, different groups for different purposes).	7
3. Overzealous or unrealistic expectations about what can be accomplished in a group.	2
4. Attitude: group as second class therapy; mythology that anyone can do groups.	2
B. *Establishing the Group* (*n* = 12)	
1. Selection of patients, size and composition of group.	7
2. Structuring inadequately in terms of contract, rules, fees, etc.	5
II. *The Leadership Role*	
A. *Difficulties with the Group Model* (*n* = 60)	
1. *Insensitivity to Group Themes or Process* (e.g., "miss common themes, group interpretation and how individuals relate to the theme," "limited ability to process and see things").	33
2. *Individual Therapy in the Group Setting* (e.g., "forget it's a group and do individual work," "not dealing with the group—too specific toward the individual").	27
B. *Technical Aspects of Leadership*	
1. *Technical Errors* (*n* = 16)	
a. Failure to give adequate rationale or follow-through for interventions, or to implement them properly within overall treatment plan.	7
b. Mistakes of content or interpretation, asking too many questions.	4
c. Dealing with resistance to structure.	4
d. Difficulties in adjusting leadership style to fit the group's development.	2
2. *Timing of Interventions* (*n* = 13)	
a. Intervene too quickly (e.g., "too eager to get things going," "jumping into feeling before the group is ready").	11
b. Late in interventions (too delayed).	2
3. *Co-therapy* (*n* = 12)	
a. Communication problems with a peer cotherapist.	6
b. Deference to experienced cotherapists (e.g., "being quiet, not interrupting," "maneuvering into second in command").	4
c. Competition with experienced cotherapist.	2
4. *Special Patient Problems* (e.g., patients who are "monopolists," "uncomfortable," "aggressive," or "argumentative").	4
C. *Role Confusion*	
1. *Activity Level or Structuring* (*n* = 34)	
a. Overstructuring, taking too much responsibility, being too active (often associated with anxiety).	24
b. Extremes of activity or inactivity (directionality not stated).	6
c. Understructuring, too inactive.	4
2. *Impression Management* (*n* = 44)	
a. Need to maintain appearance of "competence," "authority," "power."	20
b. Trying too hard to be "good," "helpful," "supportive," "liked."	13
c. Role conflict: difficulties with self-disclosure, becoming a member.	11
3. *Personal Fears and Anxieties* (*n* = 42)	
a. Specific countertransference issues (e.g., "scapegoating," "personalize early difficulties," "too centered on self," "false dependency on group," "unaware of own needs").	20
b. Intimidated by intensity of groups (e.g., "afraid to confront difficult group issues," "terrified of groups").	12
c. General self-doubts and anxieties (e.g., "feeling inadequate," "lack courage to take risks").	7
d. Poorly adjusted; personal conflicts.	3

becoming too active and adopting artificial therapeutic roles to present themselves as either the "skillful authority" or as the "helpful friend." As a result, they experience considerable conflict in their role (e.g., countertransference, difficulties in self-disclosure, communication problems with a co-leader, etc.).

The pervasiveness of these problems provides important documentation for the need to design training programs to prepare trainees more effectively for the complexity of the group therapeutic situation. To address the trainees' misunderstanding about the differences between group and individual treatments, didactic seminars and observation of ongoing groups might incorporate readings (e.g., Bion, 1959; Rioch, 1970; Whitaker and Lieberman, 1970) and instrumentation (HIM-G, Group Atmosphere Scale, Group Rating Scale) which emphasize group process phenomena. Similarly, participation in experiential groups and supervisory models employing a group process focus should be favored; dyadic models of supervision would only serve to reinforce the trainees' tendency to conduct one-on-one therapy in the group setting. The experiential groups and supervisory models might also focus more systematically on trainees' interpersonal and leadership styles to foster greater self-understanding and to lessen many of their anxieties and uncertainties about their public image, thereby reducing their need for contrived therapeutic roles. The instruments described throughout this chapter can facilitate these outcomes. Instrumentation can also improve the supervisory process as well.

Instrumentation

Tauber (1978) has proposed a training model which provides beginning and intermediate-level supervisees with a framework for organizing and operating within their group sessions. His technique, called Choice Point Analysis, follows a carefully designed rating form which teaches trainees to identify critical points in therapy, to select intervention alternatives to deal with these key points, and to anticipate specific results to be achieved by the interventions. Tauber's article is one of only a few available in the literature which address instrumented supervisory procedures. His method is process oriented and conducted in small supervisory groups. Moreover, it relies heavily on videotape procedures. Use of videotapes in supervision is one approach to instrumentation which is fairly popular (Berger, 1970b). Nearly one-third (30%) of the respondents to our telephone survey indicated that they periodically use the method.

At the end of his article, Tauber suggested that the Choice Point Analysis method could be used for continued self-monitoring when supervision had discontinued or was unavailable. Similarly, Cohen (1973) has recommended a method of self-analysis which relies upon instrumentation. Cohen systematically investigated his own therapeutic interventions by carefully tabulating the frequency and focus of his verbalizations from a tape recording of the group session. He concluded that this and similar methods can give invaluable information about leadership behavior and, therefore, be extremely helpful in one's development as a group therapist.

Another form of self-generated feedback which is available to the clinician is the use of instrumented feedback from group members. Unfortunately, the systematic use of this technique is grossly underutilized. Roback (1976) reviewed the training literature, for example, and concluded:

None of the papers mentions use of *direct* feedback from patients about their group experience in the supervisory process. That few group therapy supervisors apparently attempt to secure this data is surprising in light of the fact that it is widely accepted that a patient's perception of his therapist(s), other group members, the emotional climate in the group, and the potential that the group has in meeting his needs greatly influences his degree of satisfaction with the therapy and the extent to which he is open to the therapeutic possibilities of the group (p. 243).

In his article, Roback presented a 22-item patient satisfaction scale that he finds helpful in supervision. The test covers such topics as feelings of acceptance by co-members, perceived value of the session, reactions to the cotherapists, therapist(s) understanding of the patient's problems, and so on.

Many of the instruments highlighted in the observation and experiential sections of this chapter could be completed by patients to furnish feedback to the trainees and their supervisors. In fact, these instruments might be used to gather multiple perspectives on the group process. Group members, observers, supervisors, and the trainees might complete the same or similar instruments for a comparison of their respective perceptions of leadership style and group process. The *Semantic Differential,* in particular, has this capacity, but other scales such as the *Relationship Inventory* and *Contribution to the Normative Structure* can easily fulfill this purpose.

CONCLUSION

Although we have arbitrarily divided training into four "components," it should be clear at this point that training in group psychotherapy is a multifaceted process. Each component—academic, observation, experiential, and supervision —has both didactic and experiential emphases. They are inseparable. Didactic material, whether it is the study of theory, method, or research, is most exciting and potentially rewarding when it can be experienced totally; affectively, behaviorally, and intellectually. Conversely, experiential learning probably has its greatest impact when it can be assimilated and integrated within a comprehensive conceptual framework. The particular combination of ingredients for a coordinated program in leadership training will vary, of course, from one setting to another, and from one trainee to another. It is important to recognize, however, that training in group therapy is unique, not just because the particular training environments and individual participants are different from one place to another, but also because the group experience is itself unique. The special properties of groups which differentiate this treatment modality from all others must be understood, and training programs must be designed to emphasize this fact. Recommendations have been offered throughout this chapter to facilitate the accomplishment of this goal.

REFERENCES

Ammon, G., and Ament, A. The terminal phase of the dynamic process of a group-dynamic teaching group. *International Journal of Group Psychotherapy,* 1967, *17,* 35–43.

Anderson, B. N., Pine, I., and Mee-Lee, D. Resident training in cotherapy groups. *International Journal of Group Psychotherapy,* 1972, *22,* 192–198.

Appley, D. G., and Winder, A. E. *T-groups and therapy groups in a changing society.* San Francisco: Jossey-Bass, 1973.

Bales, R. F. *Interaction process analysis: A method for the study of small groups.* Reading, Mass.: Addison-Wesley, 1950.

Barrett-Lennard, G. T. Dimensions of therapist response as causal factors in therapeutic change. *Psychological Monographs,* 1962, *76,* 1–33.

Bascue, L. O. A conceptual model for training group therapists. *International Journal of Group Psychotherapy,* 1978, *28,* 445–452.

Bednar, R. L. and Kaul, T. J. Experiential group research: Current perspectives. In S. L. Garfield and A. E. Bergin (Eds.), *Handbook of psychotherapy and behavior change* (2nd ed.). New York: Wiley, 1978.

Benjamin, S. E. Cotherapy: A growth experience for therapists. *International Journal of Group Psychotherapy,* 1972, *22,* 199–209.

Berger, I. L. Group psychotherapy training institutes: Group process, therapy, or resistance to learning? *International Journal of Group Psychotherapy,* 1967, *17,* 505–512.

Berger, M. M. Experiential and didactic aspects of training in therapeutic group approaches. *American Journal of Psychiatry,* 1970, *126,* 845–840. (a)

Berger, M. M. (Ed.). *Videotape techniques in psychiatric training and treatment.* New York: Brunner/Mazel, 1970. (b)

Berman, A. L. Group psychotherapy training. *Small Group Behavior,* 1975, *6,* 325–344.

Bion, W. R. *Experience in groups.* New York: Basic Books, 1959.

Bolman, L. Some effects of trainers on their T-groups. *The Journal of Applied Behavioral Science,* 1971, *7,* 309–325.

Bonney, W. C., and Gazda G. Group counseling experiences: Reactions by counselor candidates. *Counselor Education and Supervision,* 1966, *5,* 205–211.

Boyleston, L., and Tuma, R. Training mental health professionals through the use of the "bug in the ear." *American Journal of Psychiatry,* 1972, *129,* 92–95.

Brody, L. S. Harassed! A dialogue. *International Journal of Group Psychotherapy,* 1966, *16,* 463–500.

Coché, E. Supervision in the training of group therapists. In F. W. Kaslow (Ed.), *Supervision, consultation, and staff training in the helping professions.* San Francisco: Jossey-Bass, 1977.

Cohen, A. I. Group therapy: An effective method of self-supervision. *Small Group Behavior,* 1973, *4,* 69–80.

Cohen, A. M., and Smith, R. D. *The critical incident in growth groups: A manual for group leaders.* LaJolla, Calif.: University Associates, 1976.

Conyne, R. K. Group leadership functions scale. In J. E. Jones and J. W. Pfeiffer (Eds.), *The 1975 Annual Handbook for Group Facilitators.* LaJolla, Calif.: University Associates Publishers, 1975.

Cooper, C. L. The influence of the trainer on participant change in T-groups. *Human Relations,* 1969, *22,* 515–530.

Cooper, C. L. Adverse and growthful effects of experiential learning groups: The role of the trainer, participant, and group characteristics. *Human Relations,* 1977, *30,* 1103–1129.

Cottle, T. J. Facing the patients: Notes on group therapy observation. *Psychotherapy: Theory, Research and Practice,* 1968, *5,* 254–261.

Davis, F. B., and Lohr, N. E. Special problems with the use of cotherapists in group psychotherapy. *International Journal of Group Psychotherapy,* 1971, *21,* 143–158.

Dies, R. R. Attitudes toward the training of group psychotherapists: Some interprofessional and experience-associated differences. *Small Group Behavior,* 1974, *5,* 65–79.

Dies, R. R. Group leader self-disclosure scale. In J. E. Jones and J. W. Pfeiffer (Eds.), *The 1977 Annual Handbook for Group Facilitators.* LaJolla, Calif.: University Associates Publishers, 1977. (a)

Dies, R. R. Group therapist transparency: A critique of theory and research. *International Journal of Group Psychotherapy,* 1977, *27,* 177–200. (b)

Dies, R. R. Pragmatics of leadership in psychotherapy and encounter group research. *Small Group Behavior,* 1977, *8,* 229–248. (c)

Durkin, H. E. *The group in depth.* New York: International Universities Press, 1964.

Fielding, M. B., Guy, L., Harry, M., and Hook, R. H. A therapy group observed by medical students. *International Journal of Group Psychotherapy,* 1971, *21,* 476–488.

Finney, J. C. Double reversal group psychotherapy: A method of teaching and treatment. *International Journal of Group Psychotherapy,* 1968, *28,* 100–103.

Foulkes, S. H. and Anthony, E. J. *Group psychotherapy: The psychoanalytic approach* (2nd ed.). London: Penguin Books, 1965.

Frankiel, H. H. Mutually perceived therapeutic relationships in T-groups: The co-trainer puzzle. *The Journal of Applied Behavioral Science,* 1971, *7,* 449–465.

Garwood, D. S. The significance and dynamics of sensitivity training programs. *International Journal of Group Psychotherapy,* 1967, *17,* 457–472.

Hill, W. F. Hill interaction matrix (HIM): The conceptual framework, derived rating scales, and an updated bibliography. *Small Group Behavior,* 1977, *8,* 251–268.

Hipple, J. L. Interpersonal relationship rating scale. In J. W. Pfeiffer, R. Heslin, and J. E. Jones (Eds.), *Instrumentation in human relations training* (2nd ed.), LaJolla, Calif.: University Associates, Inc., 1976.

Horwitz, L. Training groups for psychiatric residents. *International Journal of Group Psychotherapy,* 1967, *17,* 421–435.

Horwitz, L. Training issues in group psychotherapy. *Bulletin of the Menninger Clinic,* 1971, *35,* 249–261.

Hunter, G. F., and Stern, H. The training of mental health workers. *International Journal of Group Psychotherapy,* 1968, *28,* 104–109.

Jarvis, P. E., and Esty, J. F. The alternate-therapist-observer technique in group therapy training. *International Journal of Group Psychotherapy,* 1968, *28,* 95–99.

Johnson, D. W., and Johnson, F. P. *Joining together: Group theory and group skills.* Englewood Cliffs, N.J.: Prentice-Hall, 1975.

Kaplan, S. R. Therapy groups and training groups: Similarities and differences. *International Journal of Group Psychotherapy,* 1967, *17,* 473–503.

Kaplan, H. I., and Saddock, B. J. (Eds.). *Comprehensive group psychotherapy.* Baltimore: Williams and Wilkins, 1971.

Kaul, T. J., and Bednar, R. L. Conceptualizing group research: A preliminary analysis. *Small Group Behavior,* 1978, *9,* 173–191.

Lakin, M., Lieberman, M. A., and Whitaker, D. S. Issues in the training of group psychotherapists. *International Journal of Group Psychotherapy,* 1969, *19,* 307–325.

Lerner, H. E., Horwitz, L., and Burstein, E. D. Teaching psychoanalytic group psychotherapy: A combined experiential-didactic workshop. *International Journal of Group Psychotherapy,* 1978, *28,* 453–466.

Lewis, H. R., and Streitfeld, H. S. *Growth games.* New York: Harcourt Brace Jovanovich, 1970.

Liberman, R. A behavioral approach to group dynamics: Reinforcement and prompting of cohesiveness in group therapy. *Behavior Therapy,* 1970, *1,* 141–175.

Lieberman, M. A., Yalom, I. D., and Miles, M. B. *Encounter groups: First facts.* New York: Basic Books, 1973.

Long, T. J., and Bosshart, D. The facilitator behavior index. *Psychological Reports,* 1974, *34,* 1059–1068.

Luke, R. A. The internal normative structure of sensitivity training groups. *The Journal of Applied Behavioral Science,* 1972, *8,* 421–437.

Lundgren, D. C. Trainer style and patterns of group development. *The Journal of Applied Behavioral Science,* 1971, *7,* 689–709.

Mackie, R. and Wood, J. Observation on two sides of a one-way screen. *International Journal of Group Psychotherapy,* 1968, *18,* 177–185.

MacLennan, B. W. Simulated situations in group psychotherapy training. *International Journal of Group Psychotherapy,* 1971, *21,* 330–332.

McGee, T. F. Supervision in group psychotherapy: A comparison of four approaches. *International Journal of Group Psychotherapy,* 1968, *28,* 165–176.

McGee, T. F. The triadic approach to supervision in group psychotherapy. *International Journal of Group Psychotherapy,* 1974, *24,* 471–476.

McGee, T. F., and Schuman, B. N. The nature of the co-therapy relationship. *International Journal of Group Psychotherapy,* 1970, *20,* 25–36.

Mills, T. M. Observation. In G. S. Gibbard, J. J. Hartman, and R. D. Mann (Eds.), *Analysis of groups.* San Francisco: Jossey-Bass, 1974.

Mintz, E. E. Group supervision: An experiential approach. *International Journal of Group Psychotherapy,* 1978, *28,* 467–479.

Moss, C. J., and Harren, U. A. Member disclosure in personal growth groups: Effects of leader disclosure. *Small Group Behavior,* 1978, *9,* 64–79.

Mullan, H., and Rosenbaum, M. *Group psychotherapy: Theory and practice.* New York: Free Press of Glencoe, 1962.

Osgood, C. E., Suci, G. J., and Tannenbaum, P. H. *The measurement of meaning.* Urbana: University of Illinois Press, 1957.

Parloff, M. B. Analytic group psychotherapy. In J. Marmor (Ed.), *Modern Psychoanalysis.* New York: Basic Books, 1968.

Parloff, M. B., and Dies, R. R. Group psychotherapy outcome research 1966–1975. *International Journal of Group Psychotherapy,* 1977, *27,* 281–319.

Podnos, B. and Robinson, L. A dynamic approach to supervision of trainees for group psychotherapy. *International Journal of Group Psychotherapy,* 1967, *17,* 257–259.

Porter, E. H. Strength deployment inventory. In J. W. Pfeiffer, R. Heslin, and J. E. Jones (Eds.), *Instrumentation in Human Relations Training* (2nd ed.). LaJolla, Calif.: University Associates, 1976.

Redlich, F. C., and Astrachan, B. Group dynamics training. *American Journal of Psychiatry,* 1969, *125,* 1501–1507.

Reissman, F. The "helper" therapy principle. *Social Work,* 1965, *10,* 27–32.

Rioch, M. J. The work of Wilfred Bion on groups. *Psychiatry,* 1970, *33,* 56–66.

Roback, H. B. Use of patient feedback to improve the quality of group therapy training. *International Journal of Group Psychotherapy,* 1976, *26,* 243–247.

Roman, M., and Porter, K. Combining experiential and didactic aspects in a new group therapy training approach. *International Journal of Group Psychotherapy,* 1978, *28,* 371–387.

Rosenbaum, M., and Berger, M. *Group psychotherapy and group function.* New York: Basic Books, 1975.

Ruiz, R. A., and Burgess, M. M. Group psychotherapy: A preliminary teaching model. *Journal of Medical Education,* 1968, *43,* 455–463.

Sadock, B. J., and Kaplan, H. I. Group psychotherapy with psychiatric residents. *International Journal of Group Psychotherapy,* 1969, *19,* 475–486.

Sadock, B. J., and Kaplan, H. I. Training and standards in group psychotherapy. In H. I. Kaplan and B. J. Sadock (Eds.), *Conprehensive group psychotherapy.* Baltimore: Williams and Wilkins, 1971.

Schutz, W. C. *The FIRO scales.* Palo Alto, Calif.: Consulting Psychologists Press, 1967.

Selfridge, F. F., Weitz, L. J., Abramowitz, S. I., Calabria, F. M., Abramowitz, C. V., and Steger, J. A. Sensitivity-oriented versus didactically oriented in-service counselor training. *Journal of Counseling Psychology,* 1975, *22,* 156–159.

Shapiro, J. E. *Methods of group psychotherapy and encounter.* Itasca, Ill.: F. E. Peacock Publishers, 1978.

Silbergeld, S., Koenig, G. R., Manderscheid, R. W., Meeker, B. F., and Hornung, C. A. Assessment of environment-therapy systems: The group atmosphere scale. *Journal of Consulting and Clinical Psychology,* 1975, *43,* 460–469.

Slavson, S. R. *A textbook in analytic group psychotherapy.* New York: International Universities Press, 1964.

Smith, E. J. Issues and problems in the group supervision of beginning group problems. *Counselor Education and Supervision,* 1976, *16,* 13–24.

Stein, A. The training of the group psychotherapist. In M. Rosenbaum and M. M. Berger (Eds.), *Group psychotherapy and group function* (2nd ed.). New York: Basic Books, 1975.

Stone, W. N., and Green, B. L. Learning during group therapy leadership training. *Small Group Behavior,* 1978, *9,* 373–386.

Tauber, L. E. Choice point analysis-formulation, strategy, intervention, and result in group process therapy and supervision. *International Journal of Group Psychotherapy,* 1978, *28,* 163–184.

Thelen, H. A. Reactions to group situations. In J. W. Pfeiffer, R. Heslin, and J. E. Jones (Eds.), *Instrumentation in human relations training* (2nd ed.). LaJolla, Calif.: University Associates, 1976.

Whitaker, D. S., and Lieberman, M. A. *Psychotherapy through the group process.* New York: Atherton, 1970.

Wile, D. B. Nonresearch uses of the group leadership questionnaire (GTQ-C). In J. E. Jones and J. W. Pfeiffer (Eds.), *The 1972 Annual Handbook for Group Facilitators.* LaJolla, Calif.: University Associates Publishers, 1972.

Wile, D. B. What do trainees learn from a group therapy workshop? *International Journal of Group Psychotherapy,* 1973, *23,* 185–203.

Williams, M. Limitations, fantasies, and security operations of beginning group psychotherapists. *International Journal of Group Psychotherapy,* 1966, *16,* 150–162.

Woody, R. H. Self-understanding seminars: The effects of group psychotherapy in counselor training. *Counselor Education and Supervision,* 1971, *10,* 112–119.

Yalom, I. D. *The theory and practice of group psychotherapy* (2nd ed.). New York: Basic Books, 1975.

CHAPTER 24

Supervision of Marriage and Family Therapy

CRAIG A. EVERETT

The field of marriage and family therapy has grown enormously over the past decade. In many respects, this growth has been prompted by an increasing public need for clinical services in the area. Historical changes over the past century in the sociological character of the American family have been influential. The broad social changes prompted by industrialization have evolved a contemporary family structure which in its diminished size and increased mobility has placed high expectations on spouses and individual members to meet needs of companionship, affection, and support. This increased level of family intensity, along with changes in marital and family roles, educational and employment opportunities, child rearing practices, and sexual expectations have focused growing areas of conflict and contributed to the high rate of marital and family dissolution. The recognition of these needs has been noted not only in the public response to clinical services but in the proliferation of marriage and family practitioners, many of whom are only marginally trained, and in the increasing identification of marital and family treatment components within mental health and psychiatric services.

This growing public response has in many respects outdistanced the professional development of the field. In the early 1960s David Mace, Executive Director of the then American Association of Marriage Counselors (AAMC), wrote a general article on marriage counseling for a popular magazine. The publication of this article brought over 10,000 requests for services to the national office (Leslie, 1968). At that time professional resources were few and issues of supervision and training had not been clearly addressed. Persons practicing in the field represented primarily members of the allied clinical disciplines of psychology, psychiatry and social work who had received some additional training following their terminal degrees.

Two decades ago, with this diversity of professional disciplines represented, the field was only beginning to evolve toward a clearer clinical identity. In 1967, 75% of the membership of the AAMC did not consider themselves as belonging to a new professional discipline (Peterson, 1968). This proportion has changed markedly over the past decade. A recent study of clinical supervisors who are approved by the American Association for Marriage and Family Therapy (AAMFT) reported that while 88% had earned their terminal degrees in the disciplines of Psychology, Social Work, Psychiatry, and Pastoral Counseling, 44% now maintained their professional identity as marital and family therapists (Everett, 1977). Gradually the field has evolved into an identifiable and relatively autonomous clinical discipline. The development of standards for supervision has made available an increasing number of opportunities for clinical training and education. The body of knowledge in the field has grown to new proportions of maturity. Substantive work and resources are available which extend from ego psychology and object relations theory in marital therapy to communications and systems theories in family therapy. Likewise an increasing number of individuals are now seeking terminal graduate clinical degrees specifically in marriage and family therapy. At the same time many practicing clinicians from allied disciplines are seeking supplemental training and supervision to move into this field.

THE FIELD OF MARRIAGE AND FAMILY THERAPY

The practices and models of supervision in marriage and family therapy have evolved clearly within the historical development of the field. The profession itself has emerged rather uniquely through a blending and amalgamation of multiple clinical disciplines and orientations. This has been true both in its applied settings and theoretical origins.

The earliest developments were directed toward treating marital conflicts as a component of the social and economic disorganization following World War I. In the early 1930s only three major clinical centers for marital therapy existed: The Marriage Consultation Center, New York City (Abraham and Hannah Stone); The American Institute of Family Relations, Los Angeles (Paul Popenoe); and the Marriage Council of Philadelphia (Emily Mudd).

Three major clinical approaches emerged at this time. Most prevalent was the extension of traditional individual psychoanalytic treatment with concern for the personality dynamics of each respective spouse. The clients were seen individually, or often concurrently or collaboratively, but rarely together. Individual dynamics were then extrapolated to the understanding and resolution of the marital conflict.

A second approach, which reflected a movement away from the psychoanalytic orientation, intended to treat only the marital relationship. This represented the earliest form of what has become known as conjoint treatment, though here the focus was essentially on conscious material available in the couple's disturbed interactions. The value of the conjoint procedure for marital treatment has been well documented in terms of its ability to focus on the relationship, directly observe the couple's interaction, and identify conflict and distortions (see Leslie, 1964).

The third approach, which is more representative of the field today, involved a concern for assessing and treating both the problematic dynamics of each respective spouse's personality and the resulting patterns of dysfunctional marital interaction (see for example Blanck & Blanck, 1968; Dicks, 1967; Martin, 1976;

Mittleman, 1944; and Sager, 1977). The treatment approaches may involve a variety of combined individual, conjoint, concurrent, or collaborative methods depending on the relative extent of individual psychopathology and its interaction with the marital relationship (see Greene, 1970).

The family therapy field began to evolve in the late 1940s out of a need to extend the traditional individually oriented psychoanalytic approaches to encompass more effective treatment procedures for childhood disorders. Historically the field has integrated the child guidance movement's concern for nonpsychotic children and their family milieu, and the more extensive studies of the family dynamics of hospitalized schizophrenic children. This early work with families was viewed by the traditional disciplines as an affront to the accepted psychoanalytic practices. According to Guerin (1976), the movement finally surfaced nationally when in 1957 John Speigel organized the first presentation of psychiatric family research at the American Orthopsychiatric Association meeting, and in 1958 Nathan Ackerman organized a panel on family issues at the American Psychiatric Association meeting.

The diversity and richness of this field has evolved in part because much of the early work was conducted relatively independently and somewhat covertly by major clinicians and researchers in several distinct settings. In the late 1940s Carl Whitaker, John Warkenton, and Thomas Malone began one-way mirror observations of schizophrenic patients and their families first at Emory University and later privately in Atlanta. Whitaker has moved to the University of Wisconsin and expanded his work with normal families and intergenerational issues (see Napier and Whitaker, 1978). In the early 1950s Gregory Bateson (1972; Bateson et al., 1956) Jay Haley (1963, 1971, 1976), Don Jackson (1968a, b), and John Weakland began their extensive work on communication patterns and the family etiology of schizophrenia at the Palo Alto VA hospital and later at the Mental Research Institute. That work is continued there by Weakland and Paul Watzlawick (1977, 1978). In the 1960s Haley moved to the newly organized Philadelphia Child Guidance Clinic with Salvadore Minuchin (1974, 1978) and Braulio Montalvo. Ivan Boszormenyi-Nagy (1974) was already in Philadelphia at the Eastern Pennsylvania Psychiatric Institute working with the families of schizophrenics in developing his theories of intergenerational loyalties. The later work in family network therapy by Ross Speck and Carolyn Attneave (1973) evolved from this setting.

Murray Bowen (1978) began to invite the mothers of hospitalized schizophrenic children to become involved in his treatment in the early 1950s at the Menninger Foundation in Topeka, Kansas. He later moved his work to the Georgetown University Medical School in Washington, D.C. Nathan Ackerman (1966, 1968), perhaps the most highly respected early theorist in this field, worked with the families of primarily nonpsychotic children during the 1940s and 1950s, and utilized home visits to assess the levels of family dysfunctioning. His work is carried on now by the Ackerman Family Institute in New York City directed by Donald Bloch. (A more thorough history of the family therapy field is available in Guerin, 1976).

These individuals who have pioneered in the respective marital and family treatment methods, have produced the earliest major theoretical and applied literature in the field. However, over the past decade there has developed a gradual convergence in the historically distinct marriage and family movements. As somewhat of a reflection of this convergence, the primary professional association, founded in 1942 as the American Association of Marriage Counselors, changed its name in 1970 to the American Association of Marriage and Family Counselors, and in 1978 to the American Association for Marriage and Family Therapy (AAMFT).

It is apparent from this brief historical overview that concerns for theory and practice took precedence over the development of training standards for the field. The earliest marriage and family practitioners were essentially self-taught and the first several generations of students coming to the field have served essentially apprenticeships with recognized leaders and clinical centers.

It was not until 1971 that the AAMFT formally addressed issues of professional training, and in 1973 the first statement of standards for supervision of marital and family therapy appeared. The movement by the professional association to designate training requirements for Approved Supervisors has grown out of the recognition that the marital and family therapy field now possesses a clear body of knowledge with resultant applied skills and procedures. The concern for supervision is one of professional socialization and development. The student is expected to learn from the experienced supervisor both the knowledge of the field and the manner in which the applied skills evolve from that theory. The marital and family therapy field suffers the hazard of marginally trained individuals who, by attending a patchwork of courses and workshops, have accumulated a variety of clever techniques. What is absent frequently is the integration of theory and practice which is gained typically by a program of ongoing intensive clinical supervision. The AAMFT now requires individuals in training for Clinical Membership to receive 200 hours of approved clinical supervision and candidates for appointment as an Approved Supervisor to have at least nine months of supervision of their own supervision with a minimum of two continuous students. Their training is expected to be with a designated Approved Supervisor and they are required to have several years of supervisory experience with staff or students in a clinical or educational setting (AAMFT, 1976).

The development of supervisory standards have been paralleled by the development of training standards for degree granting programs and clinical training centers. In 1978 the AAMFT Commission on Accreditation received recognition by the Office of Education, HEW, as the accreditation body for degree granting and clinical training programs in marriage and family therapy. Programs offering specialized degrees in this field are still few: Doctoral programs—Brigham Young University, East Texas State University, Purdue University, University of Southern California; Masters programs—Auburn University, Hahnemann Medical College, Loma Linda University, Syracuse University, University of Connecticut, University of Wisconsin-Stout. Major issues involved in the development of degree programs in the field include the organization of adequate foundational resources in areas of personality theory and psychopathology, human development and sexuality, mate selection and marital interaction, family relations and sociology, and professional development. The curricula should be sequenced appropriately to move from this general theory to clinical theory in marriage and family therapy to supervised practice. These academic resources and requirements must be integrated with the supervised clinical practicum in settings which provide students with a case load of at least eight to ten marital and family treatment cases. The general process and structure of graduate clinical education for marriage and family therapy is discussed elsewhere by the author (Everett, 1979).

In addition to these limited degree programs, a number of freestanding clinical training centers and institutes have evolved in the field. Kaslow (1977) identified 40 such programs in 1977. She felt that many of these evolved because of a reluctance among traditional degree programs in medicine, psychology, social work, and theology to add courses or develop specialities in marriage and family therapy. She viewed these as offering a major resource for practicing clinicians to gain postgraduate training in this field. Training centers presently accredited by the AAMFT are: Family Service of Milwaukee, Blanton-Peale Graduate Institute (New York), Marriage Council of Philadelphia, Mental Hygiene Institute (Montreal), and the Onondaga Pastoral Counseling Center (Syracuse). In addition to these, numerous family institutes offer either postgraduate training programs or periodic workshops. Among the better known are the Ackerman Family Institute (New York) and the Family Institutes of Boston, Chicago, Philadelphia, and Washington, D.C.

The development of supervision and training standards must reflect the development of criteria for membership in the professional association. The present AAMFT standards for Clinical Membership are based on a minimum of a Masters degree in marriage and family therapy or other terminal degrees from an allied discipline where the applicant's transcripts demonstrate a course of study including mate selection, marital interaction, and family studies; the theory and practice of marriage and family therapy; human sexuality; personality, psychopathology, and human development; and professional issues. The applicant must complete at least two years of post-Masters clinical practice in marriage and family therapy as well as be in ongoing supervision with an Approved Supervisor. The supervision requirements include 200 hours of supervision of marriage and family therapy practice. Up to one-half of this may be in group supervision, and one-half of the total may be completed during the Master's degree training. This should be completed over a minimum of 1500 hours of actual clinical practice in marriage and family therapy (AAMFT, 1978).

THE PROCESS OF MARRIAGE AND FAMILY THERAPY SUPERVISION

As can be discerned from the previous discussion, the marriage and family therapy field has grown rapidly and reached some maturity in its body of knowledge. Likewise, clear standards for the entrance of practitioners into the field and for training and supervision have been designated. However, significant theories of supervision remain essentially nonexistent. While this may be due in part to the stage of development of the profession, it reflects more so the diversity of historical approaches and clinical orientations. Liddle and Halpin (1978), in a useful and comprehensive comparative review of the training and supervision literature in this field, observed: "Formal theories of supervision and training have not crystallized and hence the reader is faced with the task of abstracting personally useful information from the array of literature" (Liddle and Halpin, 1978 p. 78). They report that most of the literature fails to specify methods or procedures and overall is generally fragmented. They conclude that supervisory and training goals appear to be dependent on the particular theoretical orientations of a supervisor or training center.

It is evident that within this field various seminal personalities and training centers espouse models of supervision which are simply extensions of their own treatment orientations and modalities. While many significant and unique contributions have arisen from this historical milieu, it has become the task of second and third generation marital and family therapists and educators to evolve more consistent and integrated theories of supervision.

For the purposes of this discussion, yet at the risk of oversimplification, it is possible to consider the supervision process and contributions of those clinicians who operate from a generally psychodynamic orientation and those who operate from a structural or systems orientation. The former tend to follow the somewhat classic model of the supervision of psychotherapy outlined by Ekstein and Wallerstein (1972). They view the supervisory experience as often inhibited by intrapsychic conflicts and resistances of the student and occasionally the supervisor. The process of learning and clinical performance is dependent on the supervisor's recognition and management of these issues, as well as concern for the status of the student's client and the administrative structure of the training center. Related to this view is the concern that adjunctive personal psychotherapy is crucial to the overall learning experience of the clinical student. In an early statement, Reiss (1960) addressed the need for the supervising and teaching roles to be separated from the student's adjunctive psychotherapy. He has suggested that the supervisor attempt to identify only those emotional problems of the student that interfere with learning. Nichols (1968) has made a strong case for the coordinated but separate use of psychotherapy with supervision in training marital therapists. This author has discussed elsewhere the importance of psychotherapy in managing personal and developmental issues among young and inexperienced students in graduate clinical programs (Everett, 1979).

An important theoretical concern inherent in this orientation is that marital and family dysfunctions are a product of not simply interactional and communicational problems. They involve however the personal histories and dynamics of the respective partners from their own early families of origin and developmentally through their mate selection process. Thus the concern of the supervision is that the student must become capable of making individual diagnoses and learning to recognize and treat the manner in which these historical dynamics may be projected unto or acted out through the marital relationship and family organization. The importance of advanced training for students in this field in areas of psychopathology, personality theory, and diagnostics was stated early by Albert (1963).

Supervisors from this general orientation tend to rely on the intensity of individual supervision in conjunction with the analysis of the student's clinical role based on extensive intake studies, ongoing process notes, and audio recordings. This is usually supplemented with group supervision in the format of a professional case conference. The student's own personal growth and abilities to implement clinical skills are monitored closely.

Ard (1973) has suggested a two-stage process of supervision for marriage and family therapists which involves initially the supervisor as "mentor" providing preceptorships for novices or beginning students. As the student gains in experience and skill, the supervisory process becomes more of an apprenticeship for the advanced students. Similarly, Nichols (1978) has proposed the use of "close" or intensive supervision in the early stages of a student's training, and then moving more to a consulting role with the advanced student.

The supervisors who represent more of a structural or systems view tend to focus clinically on the reorganization of dysfunctional family interaction or communicational patterns. The literature here is extensive, and their concern for the psychodynamics of individual family members varies, but is essentially secondary to the family dynamics. The recognition of specific marital dysfunctions is viewed generally as either a specific subsystem of the family or as one component among many family dynamics. The implementation of this orientation in supervision and training has allowed for the development of many innovative and unique methodologies.

A major concern is that the student learn to enter a family system while maintaining a therapeutic stance to recognize and manage the dysfunctional components. The extensive use of video resources in supervision is a partial outgrowth of this orientation. This method provides the supervisor with access both to the immediate content of the student's interview, and to the variety of subtle and nonverbal processes, both constructive and resistant, by which the student enters the family. General issues involved in the utilization of videotaping for supervision of psychotherapy are discussed most broadly in Berger's (1970) edited work on psychiatric training, and specifically in works by Chodoff (1972) and Gruenberg et al. (1969). Bodin (1969) has effectively detailed the variety of video methods utilized in the marriage and family therapy field.

From the experience with video resources, this area of the field moved to the development of live supervision. The rationale is similar to the issues regarding video, but here the supervisor not only has direct observational access to the interview but may choose to directly intervene in the direction the student is proceeding with the family. Basically the supervisor, and occasionally the training group, observe a student's work from a one-way mirror. According to differing styles, the supervisor may intervene to offer feedback or suggest new strategies by calling on a telephone to the student therapist in the therapy room, or by calling the student out of the room for consultation; by joining the student in the therapy room, or by taking over for the student and asking the student to observe the family process for a period. This can be a very powerful supervisory resource. The model of live supervision utilizing telephone communication developed at the Philadelphia Child Guidance Clinic has been discussed by Montalvo (1973) with useful case illustrations. The intent of this supervisory observation and communication model is to monitor the process of the student therapist's role with the family and provide an immediate resource for the maintenance of therapeutic control. Kempster and Savitsky (1967) have viewed live supervision as essential to aiding the student in learning to utilize his or her own personal style and interactional resources in the therapeutic process. Similarly, Birchler (1975) values live or video supervision for helping the student to recognize and deal with nonverbal behavior in the therapy session. He has emphasized that the complexity of a student's role in working with couples and families may lead to misperceptions or misrepresentations in the student's reporting of the clinical process. This would then limit both the student's potential interventions and the instructive feedback of the supervisor. Haley (1976) has stressed the value of live supervision in that it offers the supervisor the opportunity to deal with the unit of the family and the student therapist, and not simply one or the other. This focuses the theoretical perspective that the therapist "enters" the family's system and thus the process of the entire unit requires the supervision. Haley emphasizes the need for clarity in the process between the observing supervisor and student. He has suggested a specific contract or agreement with the student whereby calls are to be made reluctantly by the supervisor and only when essential. The calls should be brief, concise and to the point, and the supervisor should make it clear whether the message is a suggestion or a directive. The latter would be utilized only to protect the continuity of the therapy from being jeopardized by a serious student error.

While Haley has advocated "reluctance" in the supervisory feedback process, Russell (1976) has criticized patterns of misuse of live supervision. He is particularly critical of the "bug in the ear" procedure as distracting from the student's involvement with the family, and of supervisors who are excessive in their interventions with the student and the family. Nichols (1975) has identified potentially counterproductive aspects of live supervision in terms of the unnecessary production of anxiety for the student and the additional difficulty of student dependency on the supervisor's immediate availability.

Other related supervisory methods are also in use. Whitaker (Keith and Whitaker, 1977; and Napier and Whitaker, 1978) encourages the role of the supervisor as cotherapist, and Serena and Goldenberg (1975) report the use of group supervision to reenact for the students a pseudo-family milieu with the supervisors as parents and the students as siblings.

Within this general orientation, it should be apparent that the concern for the student's personal growth by means of therapy is somewhat refocused. The basic model is evolved from Bowen's (1978) orientation that the clinical student, as well as the client, must "differentiate" themselves from their own families of origin in order to become effective therapists. In some training centers students are asked to return to the home of their parents to work out unresolved issues. Similarly, Guldner (1978) and Framo (1975) are clear about the value of family therapy and/or marital therapy for the student. Many training programs in this area require their students' participation in this form of adjunctive therapy (see Kaslow, 1977) as others would expect the student to receive personal psychotherapy.

AN INTEGRATIVE MODEL OF SUPERVISION

Despite the apparent diversity and fragmentation of the marital and family therapy field, the clinical supervisor must be responsible for integrating in the training experiexce both the breadth and the depth of the field. One such attempt at a more integrated model of supervision of marriage and family therapy has evolved from the early work of William C. Nichols at Florida State University. This has been extended now in the development of the graduate program at Auburn University. The basic educational philosophy is to provide a training structure which offers an appropriate integration of theory, supervised practice, and professional socialization. The intent is to facilitate the growth of selected students toward becoming competent clinicians. While these are appropriate goals for any graduate program in the clinical disciplines, the relative breadth and complexity of the marriage and family therapy field add additional training dimensions. As indicated previously, the sequencing of didactic material is critical to the student's learning that practice evolves from theory. Thus in the program at Auburn, the graduate students' initial year is strictly sequenced academically, and both comprehensive examinations and clinical faculty reviews are required before a student may be admitted to the second year of supervised clinical practicum. The content of both of these years is sequenced to convey the movement from theory to practice. In the initial year theoretical courses evolve from personality theory and psychopathology to family relations and family sociology. Broad courses in individual and group counseling theories lead to two major courses: Marital and Family Psychopathology, and Marital and Family Therapy. The former course examines all of the major clinical theories underlying the marital and family therapy field, that is, psychodynamic, ego psychology, object relations, communications/interaction, and systems. The latter course operationalizes these theoretical orientations in the variety of treatment practices. Courses in human sexuality and professional development are taught early in the second year to utilize the students' clinical experiences. The second year of supervised clinical practice moves sequentially from a focus on individual diagnosis and marital and family assessment to the integration of prior theoretical resources with the development of clinical strategies, ongoing treatment, and termination issues.

Two graduate programs, for which this author was recently a consultant, identified a problem of apparent ineffectual clinical work by their students and frustration in the teaching roles of their supervisors. In examining their curricula, it was discovered that in one program courses in personality theory and psychopathology could be taken anytime during their clinical year, and in the other program the course in marital therapy was not required until the students had been in their supervised practicums for six months. The supervisors in these programs were overwhelmed by trying to teach critical content material as an aspect of supervision which realistically should have been mastered by students before they interviewed their first clients. Thus, this concern for appropriately sequencing necessary theoretical material can clearly facilitate the process of clinical supervision.

The basis of learning sound clinical skills and of evolving one's professional identity as a competent clinician must take precedence in any integrative model over competing theoretical orientations and techniques. This is particularly critical in this field which recognizes the reciprocal interplay among individual, dyadic, and family system dynamics. Thus, the teaching and supervision of marriage and family therapy may be viewed on a broad clinically developmental continuum. This begins with an in-depth recognition of individual psychodynamics as they have evolved developmentally within the family structure. Here the patterns of childhood family experiences, perhaps even over several generations, become projected in the apparent and latent personal needs which individuals implement in their mate selection process. These patterns may be analyzed individually and conjointly in terms of their extension into the complementary needs of spouses that create an often collusive dyadic bond and into the shifting idealizations that occur throughout the early marriage. The developmental move from marital formation to parenthood may be viewed in terms of the respective psychodynamics of each spouse and the dimensions of the marital history to this point. The addition of each child and his or her normative development not only continues to involve the respective individual and the joint marital dynamics, but also evolves a uniquely collective family system. This system is a culmination and composite of all of the foregoing historical processes, yet with certain predictable structural and interactional patterns.

Recognizing the clinical dimensions of this foregoing developmental continuum defines the task of supervision. The marriage and family therapist must not only understand the theoretical issues behind this continuum but must learn to recognize the patterned dynamics at any point in a given marriage's or family's development. Thus the early stage of supervision involves the student's learning thorough assessment procedures at the intake of a case. The training intake model developed at Auburn defines three initial levels of clinical assessment: (1) diagnostic impressions of all relevant subjects (family members); (2) evaluation of historical and present interpersonal dynamics, that is, marital, parent-child, and intergenerational; (3) the identification of family system dynamics. The resultant supervision of treatment goals and strategies follows this continuum-based clinical assessment and allows the student to recognize the interplay between individual dynamics and structural family patterns. The student can then learn to match appropriately clinical strategies to assessment impressions.

From an integrative approach, the marriage and family therapy student should learn a broad range of potentially effective applied procedures. This involves learning to sort out the extent to which a subject's individual dynamics or psychopathology contribute to marital dysfunction, and also whether those issues need attention before the marital relationship can be treated. Some marital cases may require individual or concurrent psychotherapy prior to direct treatment of the dyad, while others are better treated with an interplay of individual and interactional processes in conjoint therapy. At another level, a schizophrenic member of a family may not tolerate individual treatment, but structural intervention with the entire family may allow the disturbed subject to return to a normal role. Another frequent example is the scapegoated adolescent. Depending on the therapist's assessment of individual developmental needs and of the family organization the adolescent may benefit potentially from either individual or group psychotherapy, family treatment, or marital therapy for the parents (Everett, 1976).

This process of supervision moves the student from the critical marital and family assessment stage to the selection of clinical strategies and then to the learning of ongoing psychotherapy. As has been illustrated, the identification of marital and family clinical theory is utilized in the ongoing assessment and development of clinical strategies with cases. The actual treatment methods are secondary in that they evolve from the theoretical recognition of dysfunctional marital and family patterns. These specific treatment approaches vary widely within the field and may include individual, concurrent, collaborative, or conjoint methods.

The gradual maturing and availability of theory in the marital and family therapy field is defined here as the central component in consolidating a more integrative approach to supervision. The orientations and clinical experiences of supervisors in training centers throughout the country continue to be widely diverse. The extent to which the available integrative knowledge can be utilized to enhance and consolidate procedures of clinical education and supervision remains the central challenge to the field.

CONCLUSION

It should be apparent to even a newcomer to the marriage and family therapy field that the clinical orientations and supervisory models remain somewhat variable and divergent. This paper has attempted to relate crucial historical developments of the field to an explication of the various rationales for training and supervision. As indicated previously, a gradual convergence among the orientations of many of the traditional leaders in marital therapy and family therapy has begun. Over the next decade this should allow for the evolution of more effectively integrated theoretical resources and clearer models of supervision for the discipline.

To the casual observer of the marriage and family therapy field, a sense of fragmentation may be apparent. However, while some oversimplification has been necessary in this brief paper, this author does not wish to convey a sense of incompatibility between psychodynamic and structural/systems orientations. Aside from the dimensions of clinical practice, this issue is particularly crucial in a supervisor's responsibility for the student gaining knowledge and skills representative of the complete field and not simply of one fragmented view or technique. It is from this concern and the broad issues of professional socialization that efforts toward more integrated approaches of training and supervision in the field are necessary.

This field has grown enormously and has reached an increasing level of maturity in its knowledge and applied skills. Professional standards are now clearly designated. The often complex and sometimes fragmented approaches to treatment and education now have available sufficient resources to develop much needed consistent and integrated training and supervisory models.

REFERENCES

Ackerman, N. *Treating the troubled family.* New York: Basic Books, 1966.

Ackerman, N. *Psychodynamics of family life.* New York: Basic Books, 1968.

Albert, G. Advanced psychological training for marriage counselors. *Marriage and Family Living,* 1963, *25,* 181–183.

American Association for Marriage and Family Therapy. *The approved supervisor,* Claremont, Calif.: Author, 1976.

American Association for Marriage and Family Therapy Membership brochure. Claremont, Calif.: Author, 1978.

Ard, B. Providing clinical supervision for marriage counselors: A model for supervisor and supervisee. *Family Coordinator,* 1973, *22,* 91–97.

Bateson, G. *Steps to an ecology of mind.* New York: Ballentine Books, 1972.

Bateson, G., Jackson, D., Haley, J., and Weakland, J. Toward a theory of schizophrenia. *Behavioral Science,* 1956, *1,* 251–264.

Berger, M. (Ed.). *Videotape techniques in psychiatric training and treatment.* New York: Brunner/Mazel, 1970.

Birchler, G.R. Live supervision and instant feedback in marriage and family therapy. *Journal of Marriage and Family Counseling,* 1975, *1,* 331–342.

Blanck, R., and Blanck, G. *Marriage and personal development.* New York: Columbia University Press, 1968.

Bodin, A.M. Video applications in training family therapists. *The Journal of Nervous and Mental Disease,* 1969, *148,* 251–261.

Bowen, M. *Family therapy in clinical practice.* New York: Jason Aronson, 1978.

Boszormenyi-Nagy, I., and Spark, G. *Invisible loyalties.* New York: Harper and Row, 1974.

Chodoff, P. Supervision of psychotherapy with videotape: Pros and cons. *American Journal of Psychiatry,* 1972, *127,* 53–57.

Dicks, H.V. *Marital tensions.* London: Routledge and Kegan, Paul, 1967.

Ekstein, R., and Wallerstein, R. *The teaching and learning of psychotherapy* (2nd ed.). New York: International Universities Press, 1972.

Everett, C. A. Family assessment and intervention for early adolescent problems. *Journal of Marriage and Family Counseling,* 1976, *2,* 155–165.

Everett, C. A. An analysis of AAMFT supervisors: their identities, roles, and resources. *Journal of Marital and Family Therapy,* in press.

Everett, C. A. The masters degree in marriage and family therapy. *Journal of Marital and Family Therapy,* 1979, *5,* 7–13.

Framo, J. Personal reflections of a family therapist. *Journal of Marriage and Family Counseling,* 1975, *1,* 15–28.

Greene, B. L. *A clinical approach to marital problems: Evaluation and management.* Springfield, Ill.: Charles C. Thomas, 1970.

Gruenberg, P.B., Liston, E.H., and Wayne, G.T. Intensive supervision of psychotherapy with videotape recordings. *American Journal of Psychotherapy,* 1969, *23,* 98–105.

Guerin, P. Family therapy: The first twenty-five years. In P. Guerin (Ed.), *Family therapy, theory and practice.* New York: Gardner Press, 1976, pp. 2–22.

Guldner, C. Family therapy for the trainee in family therapy. *Journal of Marriage and Family Counseling,* 1978, *4,* 127–132.

Haley, J. *Strategies of psychotherapy.* New York: Grune and Stratton, 1963.

Haley, J. (Ed.). *Changing families.* New York: Grune and Stratton, 1971.

Haley, J. Problems in training therapists. In J. Haley, *Problem-solving therapy.* San Francisco: Jossey-Bass, 1976, pp. 169–194.

Jackson, D. (Ed.). *Communication, family and marriage.* Palo Alto: Science and Behavior Books, 1968(a).

Jackson, D. (Ed.). *Therapy, communication and change.* Palo Alto: Science and Behavior Books, 1968(b).

Kaslow, F. W. Training of marital and family therapists. In F.W. Kaslow (Ed.), *Supervision, consultation, and staff training in the helping professions.* San Francisco: Jossey-Bass, 1977, pp. 199–234.

Keith, D., and Whitaker, C. The Divorce Labyrinth. In P. Papp (Ed.), *Family therapy: Full length case studies.* New York: Gardner Press, 1977, pp. 117–132.

Kempster, S., and Savitsky, E. Training family therapists through live supervision. In N. Ackerman, F. Beatman, and S. Sherman (Eds.), *Expanding theory and practice in family therapy.* New York: Family Service Association of America, 1967.

Leslie, G. Conjoint therapy in marriage counseling. *Journal of Marriage and the Family,* 1964, *26,* 65–71.

Leslie, G. Changing practices in marriage counseling. In J. Peterson (Ed.), *Marriage and family counseling: Perspective and proposal.* New York: Association Press, 1968.

Liddle, H., and Halpin, R. Family therapy training and supervision literature: A comparative review. *Journal of Marriage and Family Counseling,* 1978, *4,* 77–98.

Martin, P. *A marital therapy manual.* New York: Brunner/Mazel, 1976.

Minuchin, S. *Families and family therapy.* Cambridge: Harvard University Press, 1974.

Minuchin, S., Rosman, B., and Baker L. *Psychosomatic families, anorexia nervosa in context.* Cambridge: Harvard University Press, 1978.

Mittelman, B. Complementary neurotic reactions in intimate relationships. *Psychoanalytic Quarterly,* 1944, *13,* 479–491.

Montalvo, B. Aspects of live supervision. *Family Process,* 1973, *12,* 343–359.

Napier, A., and Whitaker, C. *The family crucible.* New York: Harper and Row, 1978.

Nichols, W.C. Personal psychotherapy for marital therapists. *Family Coordinator,* 1968, *17,* 83–88.

Nichols, W.C. Training and supervision. Audiotape #123, American Association for Marriage and Family Therapy, 225 Yale Avenue, Claremont, Calif., 1975.

Nichols, W.C. Supervision and training in marriage and family therapy. A paper presented to the annual meeting of the Gulf Coast Association for Marriage and Family Therapy, Auburn University, 1978.

Peterson, J. Marriage Counseling: past, present, and future. In J. Peterson (Ed.), *Marriage and family counseling: Perspective and proposal.* New York: Association Press, 1968.

Reiss, B. The selection and supervision of psychotherapists. In N. Dellis and H. Stone (Eds.), *The Training of Psychotherapists.* Baton Rouge, La.: Louisiana State University, 1960.

Russell, A. Contemporary concerns in family therapy. *Journal of Marriage and Family Counseling,* 1976, *2,* 243–250.

Sager, C.J. *Contracts and couple therapy.* New York: Brunner/Mazel, 1977.

Serena, S., and Goldenberg, I. Training issues in family therapy. *Journal of Marriage and Family Counseling,* 1975, *1,* 63–68.

Speck, R., and Attneave, C. *Family networks.* New York: Vintage Books, 1973.

Watzlawick, P. *The language of change.* New York: Basic Books, 1978.

Watzlawick, P., and Weakland, J. (Eds.). *The interactional view.* New York: Norton, 1977.

CHAPTER 25

Supervision in Community Settings: Concepts, Methods, and Issues*

JOSEPH F. APONTE AND MICHAEL J. LYONS

The topic of supervision has received sporadic attention in the psychological, social work, and psychiatric literature over the last two decades. This literature has typically focused on psychotherapy supervision, particularly individual psychotherapy. Until recently, very little attention has been paid to supervision of either students or professionals in community settings, particularly activities other than the traditional forms of psychotherapy. It has not been until the last decade that mental health professionals, especially psychologists and psychiatrists, have begun to move beyond the traditional one-to-one psychotherapy inpatient and outpatient model to providing services in community settings, leading to the emergence of the community psychology and community mental health movements.

There are many reasons for the development of the community psychology and community mental health movements. Some workers were dissatisfied with the traditional forms of psychotherapy, particularly individual therapy and its focus on intrapsychic factors, and the minimal attention to interactional and societal forces. Many of the theories are also inadequate in understanding and addressing societal problems such as poverty, limited educational opportunities, job discrimination, and social conflict. The effectiveness and efficiency of individual psychotherapy has also been seriously questioned, as well as the disproportionate type and amount of services available to people from the lower socioeconomic level and minority groups in our society.

Since the field of community psychology and community mental health is so new, it is understandable that little attention has been directed to supervision in community settings. In order to understand this topic it is useful to make a distinction between two types of supervision in community settings: supervision of trainees or students who are housed in training programs; and supervision of professionals who have completed their formal training and are employed in a community organization or agency. Different issues and problems, as will become evident in this chapter, are raised by supervision of students and professionals in community settings.

*Appreciation is expressed to Dr. Stanley A. Murrell for his helpful comments on this chapter. Particular appreciation is expressed to Ms. Catherine E. Aponte for her help in the conceptualization and clarification of many of the complex problems and issues involved in supervision in community settings.

In order to identify the critical variables in supervising students and professionals in community settings it is necessary to define what is meant by community psychology. The first section of this chapter will consider varying conceptualizations which are based on differing value bases and ideologies. Such varying conceptualizations call for different knowledge and skills which have direct impact on the content, structure, and organization of training programs as well as directly determining the activities of professionals in the field. Traditional activities in community settings dictate certain supervisory models, while innovative activities require different approaches to supervision.

The second section of this chapter will examine the specific roles and functions of community psychologists. These roles and functions will be discussed from a conceptual level—for example, identifying the array of activities that community psychologists can potentially engage in; and from an empirical level—for example, citing the relevant research data in the area. Although the discussion focuses on community psychologists, these roles and functions are applicable to other professional disciplines and speciality areas, such as psychiatry, social work, and public health nursing. The discussion is also applicable to individuals who are trained at other levels including the subbaccalaureate, baccalaureate, masters, post-masters, and postdoctoral.

Included in the third section is a detailed review of supervisory dimensions including supervisory models, supervisor styles, and supervisory formats. Although this review of the psychological, social work, and psychiatric literature focuses primarily on psychotherapy, these models, styles, and formats have applicability to the activities of students and professionals in community settings. Section four identifies the interrelationships between the conceptualization of community psychology, activities of community psychologists, supervisory dimensions, and organizational variables. Finally the last section considers the implications for training programs and the supervision of professionals in community settings.

CONCEPTUALIZATIONS OF COMMUNITY PSYCHOLOGY

A variety of conceptualizations of community psychology currently exist with no clear cut consensus about the meaning of the term (Aponte, 1974). Each author defines his or her particular conceptualization and as Reiff (1977) has pointed out, "After ten years community psychology still does not have a conceptual framework, a value base, or an organizing concept." The ten years that Reiff is referring to is the period from the time of the Boston Conference on the Education of Psychologists for Community Mental Health (Bennett, Anderson, Cooper, Hassol, Klein, and Rosenbaum, 1966). The field of community psychology was differentiated from clinical psychology at that conference.

While there is no consensus regarding a total definition, there are identifiable foci on which community psychology is based. One defining characteristic is an emphasis on identifying community resources and strengths rather than focusing exclusively on community or individual deficits or weaknesses (Rappaport, Davidson, Wilson, and Mitchell, 1975). Iscoe (1974) has stated that community psychology must do more than treat society's casualties. He points out a basic premise of public health: a condition is not prevented by treating its victims. Zwerling (1976) also emphasizes promoting health rather than treating illness, and adds two identifying characteristics: the entire population rather than individuals are the "patients"; and family, community, social class, and cultural factors are all considered.

Several writers have emphasized the interaction between the individual and his or her social environment in their conceptualizations of community psychology. Murrell (1973), for example, has defined community psychology as the area which "*studies* the transaction between social system networks, populations, and individuals; that *develops* and *evaluates* intervention methods which improve person-environment 'fits'; that *designs* and *evaluates* new social systems; and from such knowledge and change seeks to *enhance* the psychosocial opportunities of the individual." Rappaport (1977) also dealt with the concept of "fit": "The defining aspects of the perspective are cultural relativity, diversity, and ecology: the fit between persons and environments."

Goodstein and Sandler (1978) have developed a conceptual matrix for looking at approaches designed to enhance human welfare. Four approaches are discussed: clinical psychology, community mental health, community psychology, and public policy. Each of these approaches is analyzed in terms of the intended target, content of the intervention, process involved in the intervention approach, and the necessary knowledge base for the interventions. The authors conclude from their analysis that community psychology should disengage itself from the community mental health movement. Community psychology would thus be free to devote its time and energies to interfacing with social systems concerned with deviance control, socialization, and support.

In the term "community psychology," as it is used in this chapter, psychology is defined in the generic sense. Thus, psychology is considered to be the study of behavior, both adaptive and maladaptive, and not just the purview of those professionals designated as psychologists. From this perspective it is legitimate to consider the paraprofessional from the community as practicing community psychology as well as to consider the practice of community psychology by those holding the doctoral degree. Public health nurses, social workers, and psychiatrists are other professionals who would also be considered as practicing community psychology.

Community mental health is sometimes used synonymously with community psychology. The community mental health movement is a vital part of community psychology and those individuals involved in providing community mental health services can be practitioners of community psychology. However, community psychology encompasses activities and practitioners not generally associated with community mental health (Aponte, 1977; Goodstein and Sandler, 1978). Demographers, systems scientists, epidemiologists, attorneys, political scientists, urban planners, anthropologists, and others have contributions to make to community psychology. For the purposes of this chapter community mental health will be considered as an important subset within the broad area of community psychology.

The lack of consensus regarding the field of community psychology might be considered an identifying characteristic itself. Perhaps the uncertainty may work to the advantage of community psychology by fostering growth and allowing present formulations to evolve in the future. If we may draw an analogy from physics, community psychology is an attempt to create a unified field theory of human functioning. The goal of reconciling electromagnetic, gravitational, and atomic forces has to date eluded the physicist. Many behavioral scientists may feel that an analoguous effort to incorporate existing knowledge of human behavior is likewise doomed to failure. But just as the lack of success does not prevent physicists from striving toward their goal, students of human behavior continue to attempt to reconcile seemingly disparate areas.

One way to define community psychology is to establish an operational definition. An operational definition gives meaning to a term by describing what operations are performed by the individual carrying out a given task or function. For example, weight is defined as the activity of placing an object on a scale and reading the indicator. Thus, for the purpose of discussing supervision in community settings we may define community psychology by describing various types of activities which are carried out under its rubric. The discussion in the following section is not intended to be exhaustive and activities not discussed should not automatically be excluded from the realm of community psychology.

ROLES AND FUNCTIONS OF COMMUNITY PSYCHOLOGISTS

This section will consider a number of roles and functions associated with community psychology that have implications for supervision. An identification and description of activities that students can be trained for and professionals involved in will first be described followed by data from several studies on the actual activities they are reportedly engaged in. Some of these activities will be typical of the mental health endeavors of clinical psychologists and others will be unique to the field of community psychology. Many skills in the armamentarium of the community psychologist, such as consultation and evaluation research, are not novel. Perhaps the most unique aspect of community psychology is the diversity of combinations and permutations of techniques and settings utilized.

The aspect of community psychology most frequently associated with the traditional services provided by psychology, psychiatry, and social work is intervention. The traditional target of intervention is the individual with a problem who is designated as a patient or client. Intervention at the stage where a person has a recognizable problem requiring treatment is called tertiary intervention. Attempts to identify and remediate problems before they would normally come to the attention of mental health professionals are known as secondary intervention. Primary intervention is an attempt to prevent the development of problems within a segment of the population who may or may not be at risk (Caplan, 1964). Tertiary intervention is the activity which is most like the traditional notion of what psychologists, social workers, and psychiatrists do.

All of these activities share a clinical point of view. Clinic is derived from the word meaning "bedside." As previously mentioned, much of community psychology is moving away from the bedside and hence from traditional clinical orientations. Historically most practitioners of community psychology have emerged from clinical training programs and a clinical orientation. Clinical skills can often provide an entree for the community psychologist into a particular setting. Once the practitioner has legitimized his or her role in an organization, often other, less traditional activities can be undertaken.

Research is an integral part of community psychology. Price and Cherniss (1977) have called for community psychology to dispense with the dichotomy between research and practice. Rather than creating opposing groups of researchers and practitioners they advocate that the topic of research become the very day-to-day activities of the practitioner. Community psychology must adopt the position that research need not be esoteric or complex to be meaningful. Rather, it should emphasize the application of scientific inquiry to the real and pressing problems confronting society. In a time of increasing disenchantment with ineffective approaches to disbursing funds for the solution of social problems it will become increasingly valuable to be able to justify expenditures through objective measurement of need and/or success in meeting a need.

The disenchantment with present services and programs is reflected in a number of areas, including: (1) recent state and federal legislation which mandates needs assessments and evaluation of programs as a prerequisite for funding these programs, (2) the recent emphasis on rational planning of service programs and on service accountability, and (3) the rising tide of consumerism which demands that service providers not only demonstrate the efficacy of their program to their funding sources but also to the populations they purport to serve (Aponte, 1978; Aponte, in press). In general, there is an increasing unwillingness among politicians and administrators to continue to fund programs that are not rationally planned and have no demonstrable results (Mondale, 1972).

Needs assessment, by necessity, has become an important part of community psychology. Needs assessment can be conceptualized as a research and planning activity designed to determine a community's service needs and utilization patterns (Aponte, in press; Warheit, Bell, and Schwab, 1977). A number of needs assessment strategies have been traditionally used, including social indicators, client utilization, field survey, nominal group, and convergent assessment approaches (Aponte, 1976; 1978). The activity of assessing needs is indicative of the difference in perspective between community psychology and more traditional approaches. Conventional service programs are often begun with a priori assumptions about what services are required or needed in the community.

Evaluation research has also become a prominent aspect of community psychology. The original Community Mental Health Act of 1963 called for the evaluation of community mental health programs. According to Weiss (1972), the distinguishing feature of evaluation research is not its method or subject matter, but rather the intent. Evaluation research is carried out in order to make decisions about programs. Over the past decade a number of sophisticated evaluation strategies have been developed such as Goal-Attainment Scaling (Kiresuk and Sherman, 1968), Key Factor Analysis (Rader, 1974), Benefit-Cost Models (Halpern, 1977), and the Denver Community Mental Health Questionnaire (Ciarlo and Reihman, 1977).

Training and supervising students, professionals, and paraprofessionals are important functions carried out by professionals in community settings. There are of course didactic as well as practicum training experiences. The initial didactic training for most personnel will have taken place at a university prior to their arrival at a community setting. Often the trainee is still affiliated with a formal training program even if the practicum training location is not. Heyns (1968) recommends that "students must be geared into the [community] to be sure that they aren't just additional manpower, or given routine assignments; real opportunities for learning must be provided." On campus it may prove difficult to provide the experience necessary to prepare for community psychology but in the community, if reasonable effort is made, such training should easily be arranged.

Consultation is a critical skill in the practice of community psychology. It emphasizes the interactive and proactive nature of a community approach. The environment of any given individual is comprised of a labyrinth of social organizations. A community orientation requires intervention into the environment and consultation with various groups and presents an opportunity for the mental health professional to participate with such groups. Silverman and Fourcher (1975) suggest that consultation provides community psychologists with a skill that legitimizes their right to function within an agency. Consultation provides an opportunity to observe the system, dispense knowledge and to help the service develop and function efficiently.

Carman (1974) has pointed out that mental health consultation is often sought by an agency concerning one particular individual or situation. He maintains that if system change is to be fostered, conceptual and theoretical shifts about the nature of consultation may be necessary. Consultation from a community point of view should address itself to the system and how it might function more effectively, rather than dealing with problems in a piecemeal fashion. Fisher (1976) described the function of a consultant as helping "antagonists analyze and constructively deal with the basic issues in their relationship, rather than mediating negotiated solutions on specific matters."

Administration is a function that community psychology professionals are frequently called upon to carry out. Students are infrequently expected to assume such responsibilities. It is not unusual to find a community psychologist in charge of an agency or a program after graduation from a training program. A community orientation should sensitize an administrator to the ramifications of policy making; the most elegantly designed program is doomed to failure if it is not administered effectively. It behooves practitioners of community psychology to take an active interest in program administration, including the planning and development of service programs, as well as the perhaps more scholarly endeavors of program design and evaluation. Training programs need to incorporate training in administration into their programs.

Thus far, the more conventional roles, functions, and activities within community psychology have been considered. The field is young and to date has successfully evaded any attempts to rigidify its activities. There is no doubt that there is an interest in involvement with social issues but differences exist as to just how involved to become. Some community psychologists advocate taking a rather objective stance when dealing with community problems. Others have recommended that community psychologists become actively engaged in advocacy roles. Rappaport (1977) proposes that, "Community psychology is interested in social change, particularly in those systems of society where psychologists are active participants. Change in society involves relationships among its component parts, encompassing those of individuals to social systems such as schools, hospitals, and courts, as well as to other individuals."

Catalano and Monahan (1975) have called for community psychologists to assume the role of social planner. These authors contend that: "The 'environmental movement' with its broad base of political support, may provide community psychologists the long awaited opportunity to effect environmental change for the psychological well being of the population." The Federal government and several of the states have initiated the policy of collecting data on the environmental impact of a proposed program. This includes impact on the natural environment, human health and safety and the demand for public services. Students and professionals may participate in several steps of this process in social advocacy or urban planning roles.

A number of settings for the training of students and practice of community psychology can be identified in which these various roles can be utilized. These include: community action groups; local citizen councils; welfare rights organizations; church-based groups; self-help organizations (hotlines, drop-in centers, halfway houses; Alcoholics Anonymous); political action and civil rights organizations (Common Cause, Civil Liberties Union); community social, health, and mental health organizations (United Community Services, National Association for Mental Health); governors', mayors', councilmen's, and aldermen's offices; police stations, courts, and prison system for both juveniles and adults; and the public and private primary and secondary school systems (Rosenblum, 1973).

Thus far potential roles and functions which fall under the headings of community psychology have been considered. It would be of interest to know precisely what types of activities are currently being carried out, and to what extent, by individuals who define themselves as practitioners of community psychology. Because of the status of community psychology, that is, its youth, the vague boundaries of the area, and the fact that it crosses the traditional lines between disciplines, it is not possible to investigate its activities with any precision. Acceptable approximations of these activities can be formed by examining some survey data obtained from Division 27 (Community Psychology) members of the American Psychological Association (Andrulis, Barton, and Aponte, 1977; 1978).

According to Andrulis, Barton, and Aponte (1977; 1978), 55% of the 460 respondents (out of approximately 1200 Division 27 members) report their employment to be strongly related to community psychology. The most frequent place of employment is a community mental health center (24%) followed by college or university settings other than a community psychology program (23%), and psychiatric inpatient facilities (10%). In spite of the innovative conceptual stance adopted by community psychology, most practitioners thus find themselves in conventional settings. It is also interesting to note, that although the survey discovered that most are involved in patient care, the majority of the respondents perceived indirect and nonclinical services as at least as important to community psychology as are direct services.

There appears to be a discrepancy between what is reported to be important by individuals calling themselves community psychologists as reported in the Andrulis, Barton, and Aponte (1978) study and reports from psychologists working in the settings where such individuals are most frequently employed. A study by Bloom and Parad (1977) investigating the activities of staff members of community mental health centers offers the best information about how time is actually apportioned in a community setting. Clinical activities occupied the largest single percentage of time—a median value of 17 hours per week. Administrative duties were next with a median of 12.88 hours. The remaining category, community activities, occupied a median of 4.56 hours. The median amount of time spent on research and program evaluation was 18 minutes per week. This certainly suggests a large discrepancy between the focus of a community approach that leaders in the field have advocated and its actual implementation.

METHODS OF SUPERVISION

Most of the literature on supervision is descriptive in nature (Austin, 1952, 1956; Devis, 1965; Feldman, 1950; Fizdale, 1958; Getzel, Goldberg, and Salmon, 1971; Judd, Kohn, and Schulman, 1962; Kadushin, 1968; Leader, 1957, 1964; McGee, 1968; Rosenblatt and Mayer, 1975; Rowley and Faux, 1966; Scherz, 1958; Watson, 1968, 1973). A few surveys have been conducted providing data on attitudes and perceptions about supervision (Cherniss and Egnatius, 1978; Kadushin, 1974; Nelson, 1978). Other studies have examined variables such as reinforcement patterns, type and amount of feedback, supportive and nonsupportive supervisory experiences, and personality differences of supervisees (Davidson and Emmer, 1966; Frankel, 1971; Hegarty, 1974; Reddy, 1969; Rønnestad, 1976).

Very few of these studies have dealt directly with supervision in community settings. Neither have they dealt with the array of activities engaged in by community psychologists. The focus has typically been on individual, family, and group psychotherapy carried out in settings such as outpatient clinics, hospitals, and community agencies. Although the focus has been limited there are a number of issues, problems, and methods that have been identified in this literature that have relevance to supervision in community settings. In order to understand what has been written in this area it is useful to organize this section under the following sub-headings: (1) supervisory goals and purposes, (2) supervisory functions, (3) supervisory models, (4) supervisory styles and behavior, and (5) supervisory media.

Supervisory Goals and Purposes

A number of supervisory goals and purposes for community settings can be identified in the literature including the: (1) transmission of knowledge and skills to students or trainees in a training program, (2) transmission of knowledge and skills to support professional staff in an agency or organization, (3) monitoring of agency and organizational activities in order to maintain standards set by the agency or organization or mandated by state and federal regulations, and (4) improvement of community mental health services to clients by upgrading the skills and functioning of mental health workers. (Fizdale, 1958; Watson, 1973)

Supervisory Functions

Two major supervisory functions have been traditionally identified in the social work literature that have relevance to community psychologists: A *teaching function* and an *administrative function* (Austin, 1956; Feldman, 1950; Watson, 1973). The *teaching function* can occur within the context of a college and university, or a community mental health service agency or organization. *Professional development* often refers to the *teaching function* of supervision when it occurs after an individual has completed his or her formal education. Among the material to be learned under this function are specific knowledge, techniques, and skills in working with service recipients and in delivering services to the community. Included within the *administrative function* are communications, linkages, accountability, evaluation of activities, and assignment of and distribution of work within the agency or organization (Austin, 1956; Watson, 1973).

In order to maximize the *teaching function* Austin (1952) argues that the educational process has to be individualized for the supervisee. There has to be, first of all, an understanding of the needs and capacities of the supervisee. Secondly, the subject matter to be learned must be related to the student's learning. Finally, it is essential that the teaching method used be based on an individualized "educational diagnosis." Such a diagnosis should include an evaluation of the supervisees, person-to-person and group relations, ability to work with individuals with different needs and personalities, ability to translate theory into practice, and the individual's capacity for self-awareness.

Austin (1956) has argued that the assignment of these two major functions— *teaching function* and *administrative function*—tends to concentrate too much power in the supervisor. This dual assignment also places an overly complex burden on the supervisor thus affecting the quality of supervision. She proposes the separating of the teaching and administrative functions of the supervisor and the assigning of these responsibilities to different personnel in an organization.

Devis (1965) argues that such a division of roles already exists for social workers in the U.S. Army and that this practice of social work supervision does not generate the dissatisfaction and staff turnover found in other organization in the community.

Scherz (1958), on the other hand, has argued for a position opposite to that of Austin (1956) and Devis (1965). She argues that both of the major components of supervision—teaching and management—are conceptualized as administrative functions. This argument is based on two assumptions: (1) the core of a supervisor's job is *administrative leadership,* and (2) the supervisee bears the major responsibility for his or her work. An extensive supervisor-supervisee survey conducted by Kadushin (1974) tends to support this position with 74% of supervisors and 57% of supervisees rejecting the idea of any conflict between the *training* and *administrative* functions. However, data are not available on the quality of work provided by these different supervisory functions.

Conceptualizing supervision as essentially an administrative activity as does Scherz (1958) implies that the teaching, management, and evaluative functions cannot be separated from each other, nor can they be assigned to different individuals within an organization as suggested by Austin (1956) and Devis (1965). Scherz conceptualizes the supervisor as a leader and facilitator; the supervisory process places responsibility for the quality of service to the clients and quality of work within the organization on the supervisee's shoulders. Such supervisee responsibilities, within this framework, are different than those about to be presented where supervisee responsibility varies with the supervisory model used.

These various writers do not make a clear distinction between supervision of trainees or students and supervision of professionals who have completed their formal training. For trainees or students the *teaching function* is of critical importance, constituting one of the major supervisory functions. On the other hand the *administrative function* would be less critical, constituting one of the minor supervisory functions since the activities of a trainee or student would be circumscribed in a community setting. For the supervision of professionals the *administrative function* becomes more important than for trainees or students and the *teaching function* typically becomes less important.

Supervisory Models

A number of supervisory models can be identified that have relevance to supervision in community settings, including: (1) *tutorial supervision* (Watson, 1973), (2) *apprenticeship supervision* (Rosenblum, 1973), (3) *case consultation* (Feldman, 1950), (4) *peer group supervision* (Fizdale, 1958; Watson, 1973), (5) *tandem supervision* (Watson, 1973), (6) *team supervision* (Rowley and Faux, 1966), and (7) *group supervision* (Judd, Rohn, and Schulman, 1962). Each of these models has typically focused on individual psychotherapy and has its own distinct advantages and disadvantages. Each of these approaches can be analyzed using a number of dimensions, including: structure and format, nature of the *teaching function,* and the role and nature of the *administrative function.*

The *tutorial supervision* model involves a supervisor and a supervisee in a one to one relationship (Watson, 1973). Supervisory meetings are typically scheduled regularly, usually once a week and at times more frequently if the need is present. Such a model is well suited for students and inexperienced professionals who need close monitoring of their activities. However, the *tutorial* model can be used with experienced mental health workers. In such instances, supervision can occur irregularly and infrequently, usually around difficult problems and crisis. The teaching component is important with this model, particularly with the inexperienced supervisees. Responsibility and accountability for decisions tends to rest on the supervisor's rather than the supervisee's shoulders.

Individuals such as Rosenblum (1973) believe that the most effective form of community training occurs by means of the *apprenticeship supervision* model. The *apprenticeship supervision* model involves a person learning an art or trade by working under a skilled master for a period of time. In a community setting, the supervisor would have established an ongoing relationship with a community group. The apprentice or supervisee, in contrast to tutorial supervision, would accompany the supervisor on his or her community activities, discussing with him or her the contacts and their issues and implications. After a period the apprentice is allowed to go out on his or her own. The teaching function is important in this model and it appears that the supervisor maintains administrative responsibility throughout the process.

Case consultation also typically involves a one-to-one format. Perhaps the best known and most influential consultation model is that of Caplan (1970). According to Caplan mental health consultation is an interactive process between a consultant and consultee. Four different types of consultation are identified by Caplan: (1) client-centered case consultation, (2) consultee-centered case consultations, (3) program-centered administrative consultation, and (4) consultee-centered administrative consultation. *Case consultation* involves discussion of a particular case or group of cases, with the focus on either the clients or the mental health professional. On the other hand, administrative consultation involves the administrator of an agency with the focus either on the program or the administrator.

As Feldman (1950) and Watson (1973) point out, other staff may be present when material on cases is being presented to the consultant. The mental health worker typically presents material to the consultant for consideration. Decisions made on a case are the responsibility of the worker presenting the material on the case. The worker, in contrast to *tutorial* and *apprenticeship* supervisory models, is not bound by the opinions or advice of the consultant. A heavy teaching component is present within this model. A consultant may meet with a consultee on a regular basis or the interaction may be on an as-needed basis. Accountability, evaluation of the worker, and agency linkages are the responsibility of the consultee.

Rowley and Faux (1966) have been particularly critical of supervisory models that involve a one-to-one relationship between the supervisor and supervisee, particularly if the supervisee is a professional. They point out that there are at least three major disadvantages with the traditional one-to-one supervision: (1)

the worker's independence, creativity, and professional growth is often delayed or thwarted; (2) feelings of hostility and dependency often emerge in the relationship; and (3) the method results in waste of supervisor's time and talent that could be more effectively and efficiently utilized with another strategy. Similar criticisms have been identified in a major survey of social workers by Kadushin (1974).

Peer group supervision is one method beginning to address these criticisms. With this method there is no designated supervisor present in the group and the group members participate as equals (Fizdale, 1958; Watson, 1973). The group members, however, need to be mature and at the same general level of competence. In addition, according to Fizdale (1958) the group members have to respect each other professionally and be interested in improving their own skills. As with the consultation model, each member of the group has full responsibility for the case. He or she may choose to ignore the advice of the group. Either a designated person chairs the meetings, or the chair is rotated among the group members.

A variation of the *peer group supervision* model of supervision is *tandem supervision.* This model involves two equally experienced people meeting informally on a case, but with neither individual being designated as the supervisor of the other (Watson, 1973). As with the *peer group supervision* model, teaching is incidential to the discussion of the clients. Any decisions that are made are the responsibility of the therapist working with the client. According to Watson (1973), linkage to the organization resides with the tandem member to whom the case belongs and the designated administrative person within the organization.

Team supervision unlike *peer group supervision,* has varied group membership representing individuals from different administrative levels and professional disciplines (Rowley and Faux, 1966; Watson, 1973). The group meets on a regular basis to discuss cases and arrive at decisions on them. The responsibility for implementing decisions rests with the worker; however, accountability is divided between the group leader and group member. Linkages to the organization are the responsibility of the team leader. Rowley and Faux (1966) argue that the multidisciplinary format of the *team supervision* approach allows for exposure to other orientations, minimizes individual biases and prejudices, and leads to the generation of more creative ideas.

In *group supervision* the supervisor carries primary responsibility for directing the group in focusing on client needs and problems (Judd, Kohn, and Schulman, 1962). The focus of such groups is not exclusively in conveying knowledge, nor in group processes. However, Judd, Kohn, and Schulman (1962) argue that this type of supervision does have a number of advantages including: (1) enlarging the perspective of the worker, (2) strengthening their ability to conceptualize, (3) making the worker more self-reliant, and (4) cutting down on individual supervisory sessions thereby yielding a more economical form of supervision. Getzel, Goldberg, and Salmon (1971) also point out that supervisees draw on each other as resources in group supervision as opposed to more traditional models.

Elaborations of supervisory models have emerged in group psychotherapy which parallel the models already discussed. McGee (1968) identifies four basic group psychotherapy models, including: (1) *dyadic supervision,* where the supervisor meets regularly individually with the group therapist; (2) *group supervision,* in which the supervisor meets regularly with a group of supervisees who are all group therapists; (3) *co-therapy supervision,* where two individuals conduct a therapy group, one of them being a senior co-therapist who assumes the added role of supervising the junior co-therapist who then functions as the supervisee; and (4) *triadic supervision,* where two co-therapists of similar experience levels are supervised by an individual who has more experience in group psychotherapy.

Each method of supervision has its own set of distinct advantages and disadvantages. None of the models can meet all individual or community agency needs. These needs are so diverse and the situational context so variable, that singular adherence to any one model will lead to rigidity that will do damage to the worker, agency, and service recipient. What is needed according to Watson (1973) is *differential supervision* which allows for a range of supervisory methods within an agency or organization. Such a model would maximize the fit between worker and community agency need, leading to the maximum benefit for the client, the most effective delivery of service, and maximum learning for the supervisee.

Supervisory Styles and Behavior

Five basic types of supervisory styles have also been identified in the literature: (1) *laissez-faire,* where the supervisor leaves the supervisee to fend for himself or herself; (2) *authoritative,* in which close monitoring and regulation of the supervisee's activities occur; (3) *didactic-consultative,* in which the supervisor functions as a consultant offering advice, suggestions, and interpretations; (4) *insight-oriented,* where the supervisor asks questions designed to encourage the supervisee to think through and solve problems; and (5) *feelings-oriented,* in which the supervisee is encouraged to question and think about his or her own feelings and emotional responses toward the client in the supervisory process (Cherniss and Egnatios, 1978).

A survey of 164 staff members working in 22 community mental health programs by Cherniss and Egnatios (1978) indicated that the *didactic-consultative, insight-oriented,* and *feelings-oriented* supervisory styles were preferred to the *authoritative* and *laissez-faire* approaches. These findings were similar to those obtained by Kadushin (1974) in his survey of social workers and by Nelson (1978) in his survey of four professional disciplines. However, these staffs perceived a greater emphasis on the *didactic-consultative* approach within their community mental health programs than on the *insight-oriented* or *feeling oriented* styles. The latter two approaches were also found to be more strongly positively correlated with satisfaction with supervision than the other supervisory approaches.

A survey of social work students conducted by Rosenblatt and Mayer (1975) identified four different kinds of supervisor behavior that students considered objectionable. These included: (1) *constructive supervision,* where students felt they were not given enough autonomy in handling their cases; (2) *amorphous supervision,* where instead of offering too much supervision as in the first one, too little supervision is given by the supervisor; (3) *unsupportive supervision,* including supervisors who are cold, aloof, and hostile, and rather than allaying student anxieties, they exacerbate them; and (4) *therapeutic supervision,* where certain attitudes, feelings, and behaviors between the supervisee and client are deemed inappropriate, and are attributed to "deficiencies" in the supervisee's personality and are discussed in the supervisory sessions.

Rosenblatt and Mayer (1975) further discuss a number of coping mechanisms for dealing with objectionable supervisor behaviors. None of the students openly confronted their supervisors despite the existence of norms that exhorted them to be honest and open in supervisory sessions. One reported pattern was that of *spurious compliance,* in which an impression of compliance or willingness to comply is given by the student to the supervisor. Students would also closely monitor the written and oral information they provided, making sure that information that conveyed a particular impression was conveyed to the supervisor. Thus, a number of devices were instituted by the supervisee that protected them in the supervisory relationship from the supervisor.

Supervisory Media

Different media have also been used in the supervisory processes, including: (1) direct observation of supervisees through one-way mirrors; (2) direct observation of individuals in community settings vis-à-vis the apprenticeship model (Rosenblum, 1973); (3) mechanical recording devices, such as audio and video tapes; (4) process notes kept by the supervisee and shared with the supervisor; and (5) written reports from field settings that are sent to both the supervisor and supervisee for review and discussion. As can readily be seen, the type of media used in supervision is only limited by one's imagination and the amount of resources available in particular settings.

As is evident in this extensive review of the supervision literature, there are a number of dimensions and variables that can be identified in the supervisory process. Consideration of supervision in community settings is even more complicated than that of psychotherapy supervision in outpatient clinics, hospitals, and community agencies because of a number of factors inherent in community settings. The next section will focus specifically on supervision in community settings, identifying some of these factors, and the special problems encountered for both the supervisee (either student or professional) and the supervisor.

SUPERVISION IN COMMUNITY SETTINGS

Supervision in community settings presents several unique problems to both the supervisee (trainee or professional) and supervisor. These include the: (1) array of roles available to the individual, (2) variety of services provided and settings in which they are offered, (3) nature and structure of the organizations and agencies in which the activities take place, (4) various types and levels of professionals found in community settings, and (5) nature of the licensure laws and organizational and agency regulations. These factors should all be considered in determining the method of supervision to be used in community settings.

Roles Available to Community Psychologists

The array of potential roles engaged in by community psychologists already listed in this chapter include: (1) psychological intervention (primary, secondary, and tertiary prevention); (2) research, particularly needs assessment and program evaluation; (3) training and supervision of students, paraprofessionals, and professionals; (4) consultation, at the case, organizational, and systems levels; (5) administration; and (6) change-agent, social advocate, and community organizer. Not all community psychologists would, of course, be engaged in all of these activities at the same time. Student supervisees would also not typically be involved in the supervision of other students, paraprofessionals, and professionals. However, the supervisees would typically be involved in several of the activities in the course of a work week.

Supervision of a single activity such as psychotherapy is sufficiently complicated without considering a potential half-dozen other roles. The array of roles and activities available in community settings taxes the supervisory process. It is particularly hard on the supervisor who is expected to provide supervision on these activities. It is possible to have more than one supervisor working with the supervisee on different activities. This is acceptable and feasible for students in training programs, however such a model would be impractical for a professional in a community setting. Multiple supervisors are not cost-effective and not typically available to the professional in community settings.

Although Rosenblum (1973) argues for an *apprenticeship supervision* model for training community psychologists, such a model presupposes the existence of supervisors who are equally experienced and competent across a number of roles and activities. Such renaissance people are difficult to find. Both *team* and *group supervision* would be more reasonable supervisory models than *apprenticeship supervision* for supervising individuals on these multiple roles. *Team supervision,* with its varied group membership, allows for exposure to individuals with different backgrounds, experiences, knowledge, and skills. Similarly, *group supervision* enlarges the perspective of the supervisee by allowing multiple inputs into the supervisory process.

Community Services and Settings

Major types of professional activities such as clinical, community, and administrative activities in community settings call for different types of supervisory models. Clinical activities include: clinical diagnosis and assessment; individual, family, and group treatment; and patient and ward management. These types of activities, particularly for students in training programs, call for *tutorial* and *group supervision.* After an individual has completed his or her professional training these models are still appropriate, but *consultative, team,* and *peer super-*

vision also are appropriate. Both *peer* and *tandem supervision* are appropriate after the individual has acquired extensive clinical experience.

Community service activities, on the other hand, call for different supervisory models. Included in these activities are: aftercare, consultation and education, home visiting, and interagency collaboration (Bloom and Parad, 1977). Other activities such as social advocacy, community organization, and urban planning, although less frequently engaged in, can be considered activities of community psychologists (Rosenblum, 1973). For the beginning student, the *apprenticeship* model appears to be the most viable supervisory model, particularly on activities that do not involve multiple roles. Later, after the student has acquired some experience, the *tutorial* and *group models* may be equally appropriate. As a professional in a community service setting other models such as *peer group* and *tandem* may be equally appropriate.

Research and evaluation, training and supervision, and administration and program development are all grouped by Bloom and Parad (1977) under the general heading of administration. As with community service activities that require delimited roles, the *apprenticeship* model would seem to be the most appropriate for the beginning student. This model would also seem to be the most appropriate for the beginning professional. After the person has acquired some professional experience the *consultation* model appears to be the most workable, since oftentimes staff in community agencies do not have the necessary expertise in this area. The monitoring, evaluative, and accountability responsibilities of supervision would need to be assumed by staff internal to the organization.

As activities change from those classified as community mental health—such as patient treatment and management—to the nonclinical activities of community psychology, the type of supervisory media changes. Video- and audiotaping become difficult and impractical in community settings. Reliance on other approaches such as direct observation, progress notes, and logs are dictated by the situation. For the beginning student the direct observation of his or her activities is important. Direct observation of professionals in community settings is not practical, and thus heavy reliance is placed on the reported activities of the supervisees in these settings. Such reports are subject to distortions and filtering of information by the supervisee.

Nature and Structure of Organizations and Agencies

Little attention has been directed toward the impact of the nature and structure of organizations and agencies on supervision. A number of organizational philosophies can be identified in the literature including the: (1) classical position, which advocates narrow job latitude, close supervision, and an authoritarian tenor; (2) human relations position, which promotes "job enlargement, greater autonomy for workers, wider participation in decisions, less close supervision, closer attention to group characteristics and more trusting attitudes toward the individual worker"; and (3) integrating position, which is less clearly defined than the other two positions, recognizing the interaction between individual and organization and giving more importance to organizational structural properties such as size (Murrell, 1973).

In addition to these organizational philosophies, a number of types of organizational structures can be identified in the literature. For example, two polar types of organizational structures are identified by Murrell (1973): "flat" organizations, and "tall" organizations. "Flat" structures have few hierarchical levels, more people under one supervisor, a wider span of control, and more autonomy in comparison to "tall" organizations. Although these organizational structures can be clearly defined, there is little empirical evidence relating them to job performance and job satisfaction. Other situational factors may be important in influencing job performance and satisfaction.

It can be assumed that certain types of supervisory models would "fit" better with specified organizational philosophies and organizational structures. *Tutorial, team,* and *group supervision,* for example, should be more congruent with a classical organizational philosophy and a "tall" organizational structure. With these supervisory models the lines of administrative responsibility, evaluation, and accountability are clearly articulated. On the other hand, *tandem* and *peer group supervision* should be more congruent with a human relations organizational philosophy and a "flat" organizational structure where the administrative functions are less clearly defined.

Scott (1965) has emphasized the impact of the organizational structure on reactions to supervision. He makes a distinction between *autonomous professional* and *heteronomous professional* organizations. With the former organizational structure considerable autonomy is delegated to professional groups in the organization for setting performance standards and seeing to it that these standards are maintained. On the other hand, professional employees in the latter administrative structure fit in a more rigid administrative structure and are granted very little autonomy. In a study of *heteronomous* organizations Scott (1965) found that workers accepted the supervisory system, although the degree of acceptance varied with the professional orientation of both workers and supervisor.

Types and Levels of Professionals

The types of staff will of course vary, depending upon the agency or organization. Typically within community settings staff from a variety of professional disciplines, such as psychology, social work, and psychiatry will be found. These individuals will vary in theoretical orientation, experience, and type of intervention strategy they utilize in working with people. In addition, different levels of training, including subbaccalaureate, baccalaureate, submasters, masters, Ph.D. and M.D., will be found in these same agencies and organizations. Large numbers of nonprofessionals or paraprofessionals, in particular, have been trained in various types of public service jobs over the last decade (Grosser, Henry, and Kelly, 1969).

Both the types and level of staff will have an important influence on the type of supervisory model used. Although individuals from different disciplines would typically be exposed to different types of supervisory models, particularly *tutorial, apprentice,* and *group supervision,* they would not usually be supervised by people from other disciplines. Within a community setting they may find themselves under the administrative supervision of someone from another professional discipline. Their professional activities, however, may still be supervised by someone from their own profession. If they are supervised by another professional, difficulties may arise in terms of orientation, knowledge and skills, and status.

During a student's training, attitudes and expectations toward supervision, and professional norms about it are taught to the student. Certain professions, such as social work, have a clearly articulated rationale for supervision and an expectation that supervision will continue when they have completed their training and are functioning as professionals in a service setting. For other professionals, the importance of supervision during training is communicated to the student, but its importance as a professional is not clearly articulated. Psychologists and psychiatrists are typically expected to function autonomously upon completion of their professional training with a minimum of supervision of their professional activities.

Licensure Laws and Organizational and Agency Regulations

State laws and regulations often dictate within each of the professions who is required to be supervised, the frequency of the supervision, and how long the individual needs to be supervised. The licensing of community psychologists currently varies from state to state. Such requirements may strongly influence, irrespective of organizational philosophies and organizational structure, the type of supervision that may be conducted in community settings. *Tutorial, group,* and *team supervision,* for example, are more congruent with these regulations than other supervisory forms. The hierarchical supervisory structure where, for example, Ph.D.s are required to supervise M.A. and B.A. level people, places a number of constraints on the supervisory models.

Professional codes of ethics such as those of the American Psychological Association (APA, 1972) and various state licensing laws also limit the practice of professionals to specific areas of competency. Unfortunately these guidelines and regulations are often designed by clinical psychologists and directed toward the practice of clinical psychology, failing to recognize the complexity of roles and activities of community psychologists, the diversity of settings in which they work, and the number of different types of levels of workers with whom they are actively engaged. The guidelines and regulations are consequently either too vague or too narrow and restrictive for individuals in community settings.

Clearly, supervision in community settings presents a number of unique problems not found in other areas. Assuming a broader perspective than that of the direct delivery of clinical services requires the use of multiple supervisory models, methods, and media. Adherence to any one single method will inevitably lead to difficulty in the supervisory process, hampering the functioning of the supervisee and supervisor. As more roles and activities are delineated for psychologists in community settings, supervision will become even more complicated than it presently is. It behooves the supervisee and supervisor to clearly conceptualize and understand those variables and factors that impinge on the supervisory process.

FUTURE IMPLICATIONS

This chapter has attempted to identify the critical concepts, methods, and issues involved in supervision in community settings. In identifying these factors it has become apparent that one has to distinguish between supervision of students and professionals. Too often distinctions between the supervision of these two groups either has not been made or has been confused. The transition from supervision of students in community settings to the activities of professionals in those settings is not often a smooth one. In order to deal with these factors in the future, attention will need to be directed toward the organization and structure of training programs and the conceptualization and utilization of supervisory models.

Organization and Structure of Training Programs

A review of the literature indicates that universities and internships have made substantial gains in establishing community psychology and community mental health experiences as identifiable program components (Barton, Andrulis, Grove, and Aponte, 1976; 1978; Kelly, 1977; Meyer and Gerrard, 1977; Spielberger and Iscoe, 1972). However, these programs and settings continue to define these experiences more in terms of community mental health than in terms of community psychology activities. Such a state of affairs may be a developmental phase in the growth and differentiation of psychology and the present state of the job market for community psychologists.

Although a number of roles for which students can be trained have been identified (Rosenblum, 1973), the most frequently discussed field experience continues to be consultation. A number of goals and mechanisms for training students in consultation have been identified in the literature (Fisher, 1976; Kahn and Schloss, 1975; Silverman and Fourcher, 1975). Future publications in the field should reflect a wider variety of activities particularly since the present state of training indicates that the greatest amount of future development will occur toward the community psychology end of the community mental health-community psychology continuum (Zolik, Sirbu, and Hopkinson, 1976).

A positive trend in training for community psychology is the increasing emphasis on establishing programs in the community rather than exclusive dependence upon clinics within universities (Tyler and Gatz, 1976; Labourdette and Rockland, 1975). Training in clinical psychology has often taken place primarily within a departmental clinic located on campus and serving the college community. The locus of psychiatric residencies is typically in the facility's training hospital. In order to prepare trainees to cope with community issues as well as to increase the relevance of associated didactic material, training in a community setting is highly desirable. To assure the availability of such training settings an increasing number of programs are developing their own. Trainees may gain experience in myriad functions when the training program controls the service facility (Zax and Specter, 1974).

Several training programs include students in the design of curriculum and field experiences (Labourdette and Rockland, 1975; Tyler and Gatz, 1976). Such an organization allows the student to have an impact on the type and amount of supervision he or she receives, and thus begins to place him or her in a collegial role. However, such a training model can only be successful if excellent working relationships and mutual respect and trust exist between students and faculty. Working relations with supervisors from community settings would also have to be excellent. Such a model also presupposes that the supervisors have the skill and flexibility to use several different supervisory models.

Oftentimes it is assumed that community psychologists in community settings have the prerequisite knowledge and skills to utilize different types of supervisory models. Most psychologists in community settings, whether or not they consider themselves community psychologists, come from clinical psychology training programs and backgrounds. Such experiences frequently do not equip them with the necessary knowledge and skills to supervise students in a variety of roles and activities. This is particularly true when they begin to move beyond functions such as consultation that have been emphasized in the past. Thus, a vacuum potentially exists between supervisee needs and supervisor knowledge and skills. The extent of this vacuum is unknown but should be determined.

Another difficulty that has begun to surface in training programs is the professed career interests of students. Two-thirds of the students at the University of Arizona, for example, expressed interest in working in private practice rather than community mental health work (Kahn, McWilliams, Balch, Chang, and Ireland, 1976). Such preferences according to the authors may reflect: (1) student selection process, (2) programatic values which reinforce the scientific approach instead of service in community settings, and (3) feelings of impotence generated by working with disadvantaged and underserved populations. Placement of such students in community settings will inevitably lead to difficulties with the supervisory process in community settings.

Training programs need to continue supporting community psychology values including those advocated by Iscoe (1977). Iscoe argues for moving the focus away from mental illness and onto positive concerns of well being and the enhancement of competencies of both individuals and groups. He also argues for greater emphasis on indirect services implemented at the most effective levels, including groups, institutions, organizations, and communities. Through such an emphasis students will perhaps again begin to see the relevency of such activities and the potentional impact that they can have on all levels of society, including an individual's functioning and well being.

Professionals also need supervision of their activities in community settings. The type and amount of supervision is difficult to specify and can be dictated either by supervisee needs, requirements of professional organizations, legal requirements incorporated in state statutes, or any combination of these factors. Irrespective of whether the supervisee is a student or a professional person, supervisors need to be flexible, admit to their limitations, and provide for other supervisory mechanisms when the roles and activities of the supervisees are beyond either their level or scope of competency. Mechanisms should be established to immediately deal with these issues.

Conceptualizations and Utilization of Supervisory Models

Neither clear conceptualizations of the goals and purposes of supervision nor clear conceptualizations of the different types of models and techniques exist in community psychology. As has been pointed out in this chapter, one has to turn to other disciplines such as social work for a clearly defined rationale and approach to supervision. Neither does there exist a clear articulation of possible stages of supervision that people may progress through as they move from student, to beginning professional, to advanced professional. Again, one has to refer to other disciplines for a discussion of this process; and at best it is a superficial discussion that is of little utility in understanding the complexities of such a process.

Conceptualizations of supervision have to come to grips with the complexities of types and levels of staff in community settings. As Kaslow (1977) has pointed out, the development of community mental health centers ushered in interdisciplinary training and supervision. Similarly, the recent development of approaches such as behavior modification, transactional analysis, and family and group therapies are not the exclusive province of any single professional discipline. Community psychologists either by desire or necessity find themselves being supervised or supervising individuals from other disciplines in a variety of organizations and agencies.

Conceptualizations of supervision in community settings need not wait for clarification of the definition of community psychology. The activities engaged in by community psychologists can be scrutinized and attempts made to conceptualize supervision in terms of these activities. Such an approach will inevitably lead to multiple views of supervision and to multiple supervisory models. This would be more reflective of the field than any single frame of reference. The imposition of a single frame of reference would hamper the future development of community psychology.

Few works, with the exception of Walz, Roeber, Gysbers, and Rønnestad (1974), can be found in the psychological literature that consider supervision from a theoretical point of view. Their discussions of trait and factor, learning, and self theoretical positions, however, only begin to address the complexities of supervision in community settings. Further work in conceptualizing supervision has to include: (1) roles and functions of community psychologists; (2) methods of supervision, including goals and purposes, models, and media; and (3) community settings, including the type, nature and structure of organizations and agencies, types and levels of staff, and laws and regulations.

More empirical research is needed in this area. Most of the literature on supervision is descriptive. The research that can be found in the psychological literature is typically of limited utility (Hansen and Warner, 1971). The research in general indicates that supervisee behavior changes as a result of supervision. However, there is no evidence on the effectiveness of supervision on activities engaged in by the supervisee. Neither is there any research comparing the effectiveness of different supervisory models in community settings. Further empirical research needs to be carried out in order to address these critical questions.

REFERENCES

American Psychological Association, *Ethical standards of psychologists.* Washington, D.C.: Author, 1972.

Andrulis, D. P., Barton, A. K., and Aponte, J. F. Training experiences from the perspective of community psychologists. In I. Iscoe, B. L. Bloom, and C. D. Spielberger (Eds.), *Community psychology in transition.* Washington, D.C.: Hemisphere Publishing, 1977.

Andrulis, D. P., Barton, A. K., and Aponte, J. F. Perspectives on the training experiences and the training needs of community psychologists. *American Journal of Community Psychology,* 1978, *6,* 265–270.

Aponte, J. F. In search of an educational model for community psychology. *Journal of Community Psychology,* 1974, *2,* 301–305.

Aponte, J. F. Implications for the future of needs assessment. In R. A. Bell, M. Sundel, J. F. Aponte, and S. A. Murrell (Eds.), *Needs assessment in health and human services: Proceedings of the Louisville National Conference.* Louisville, Kentucky, 1976.

Aponte, J. F. Clinical community and community mental health models. In I. Iscoe, B. L. Bloom, and C. D. Spielberger (Eds.), *Community psychology in transition.* Washington, D.C.: Hemisphere Publishing, 1977.

Aponte, J. F. A need in search of a theory and an approach. *Journal of Community Psychology,* 1978, *6,* 42–44.

Aponte, J. F. Need assessment: The state of the art and future directions. In R. A. Bell, M. Sundel, J. F. Aponte, and S. A. Murrell (Eds.), *Assessing human service needs: Concepts, methods, and applications.* New York: Human Sciences Press (in press).

Austin, L. N. Basic principles of supervision. *Social Casework.* 1952, *33,* 411–419.

Austin, L. N. An evaluation of supervision. *Social Casework.* 1956, *37,* 375–382.

Barton, A. K., Andrulis, D. P., Grove, W. P., and Aponte, J. F. A look at community psychology training programs in the seventies. *American Journal of Community Psychology,* 1976, *4,* 1–11.

Barton, A. K., Andrulis, D. P., Grove, W. P., and Aponte, J. F. Training programs in the mid-1970's. In I. Iscoe, B. L. Bloom, and C. D. Spielberger (Eds.), *Community psychology in transition.* Washington, D.C.: Hemisphere Publishing, 1977.

Bennett, C., Anderson, L., Cooper, S., Hassol, L. Klein, D., and Rosenblum, G. *Community psychology: A report of the Boston Conference on the Education of Psychologists for Community Mental Health.* Quincy, Mass.: Boston University and South Shore Mental Health Center, 1966.

Bloom, B. L., and Parad, H. J. Professional activities and training needs of community mental health center staff. In I. Iscoe, B. L. Bloom, and C. D. Spielberger (Eds.), *Community psychology in transition.* New York: Hemisphere Publishing, 1977.

Caplan, G. *Principles of preventive psychiatry.* New York: Basic Books, 1964.

Caplan, G. *The theory and practice of mental health consultation.* New York: Basic Books, 1970.

Carman, R. S. Training community consultants for system change. *International Journal of Social Psychiatry,* 1974, *21,* 62–64.

Catalano, R., and Monahan, J. The community psychologist as social planner: Designing optimal environments. *American Journal of Community Psychology,* 1975, *3,* 327–334.

Cherniss, C., and Egnatios, E. Clinical supervision in community mental health. *Social Work,* 1978, *23,* 219–223.

Ciarlo, J., and Reihman, J. The Denver Community Mental Health Questionnaire: Development of a multidimensional program evaluation instrument. In R. D. Coursey, G. A. Specter, S. A. Murrell, and B. Hunt (Eds.), *Program evaluation for mental health: Methods, strategies and participants.* New York: Grune and Stratton, 1977.

Davidson, T. N., and Emmer, E. T. Immediate effect of supportive and nonsupportive supervisor behavior on counselor candidates' focus of concern. *Counselor Education Supervision,* 1966, *11,* 27–31.

Devis, D. A. Teaching and administrative functions in supervision. *Social Work,* 1965, *10,* 83–89.

Feldman, Y. The teaching aspect of case work supervision. *Social Casework,* 1950, *31,* 156–161.

Fisher, J., Third-party consultation. A skill for professional psychologists in community practice. *Professional Psychology,* 1976, *7,* 344–351.

Fizdale, R. Peer-group supervision. *Social Casework.* 1958, *39,* 443–450.

Frankel, M. Effects of videotape modeling and self-confrontation techniques on microcounseling behavior. *Journal of Counseling Psychology,* 1971, *18,* 456–471.

Getzel, G. S., Goldberg, J. R., and Salmon, R. Supervising in groups as a model for today. *Social Casework.* 1971, *52,* 154–163.

Goodstein, L. D., and Sandler, I. Using psychology to promote human welfare: A conceptual analysis of the role of community psychology. *American Psychologist,* 1978, *33,* 882–892.

Grosser, C., Henry, W. E., and Kelly, J. G. *Nonprofessionals in the human services,* San Francisco: Jossey-Bass, 1969.

Halpern, J. Program evaluation, systems theory, and output value analysis: A benefit-/cost model. In R. D. Coursey, G. A. Specter, S. A. Murrell, and B. Hunt

(Eds.), *Program evaluation for mental health: Methods, strategies, and participants.* New York: Grune and Stratton, 1977.

Hansen, J. J., and Warner, R. W. Review of research on practicum supervision. *Counselor Education and Supervision,* 1971, *10,* 216–272.

Hegarty, W. H. Using subordinate ratings to elicit behavioral changes in supervisors. *Journal of Applied Psychology,* 1974, *59,* 764–766.

Heyns, R. W. The university as an instrument of social action. In W. J. Minter and I. M. Thompson (Eds.), *Colleges and universities as agents of social change,* Berkeley, Calif.: Center for Research and Development in Higher Education, 1968.

Iscoe, I. Community psychology and the competent community. *American Psychologist,* 1974, *29,* 607–613.

Iscoe, I. Commonalities in models and approaches to training in community psychology. In I. Iscoe, B. L. Bloom, and C. D. Spielberger (Eds.), *Community psychology in transition.* Washington, D.C.: Hemisphere Publishing, 1977.

Judd, J., Kohn, R. E., and Schulman, G. L. Group supervision: A vehicle for professional development. *Social Work,* 1962, *7,* 96–102.

Kadushin, A. Games people play in supervision. *Social Work,* 1968, *13,* 23–32.

Kadushin, A. Supervisor-supervisee: A survey. *Social Work,* 1974, *19,* 288–297.

Kahn, M. D., and Schloss, J. J. Enhancement of self-concept in beginning clinicians. *Professional Psychology,* 1975, *6,* 425–234.

Kaslow, F. W. Community mental health centers. In F. W. Kaslow (Ed.), *Supervision, consultation, and staff training in the helping professions.* San Francisco: Jossey-Bass Publishers, 1977.

Kelly, J. G. Varied educational settings for community psychology. In I. Iscoe, B. L. Bloom, and C. D. Spielberger (Eds.), *Community psychology in transition,* Washington, D.C.: Hemisphere Publishing, 1977.

Kiresuk, T., and Sherman, R. Goal-attainment scaling: A general method for evaluating comprehensive community mental health programs. *Community Mental Health Journal,* 1968, *4,* 443–453.

Labourdette, I., and Rockland, L. Developing a psychiatric residency program: Focus on the community. *Hospital and Community Psychiatry,* 1975, *26,* 279–281.

Leader, A. New directions in supervision. *Social Casework,* 1957, *38,* 462–468.

Leader, A. L. A new program of case consultation. *Social Casework,* 1964, *45,* 86–90.

McGee, T. F. Supervision in group psychotherapy: A comparison of four approaches. *International Journal of Group Psychotherapy,* 1968, *18,* 165–176.

Meyer, M. L., and Gerrard, M. Graduate training in community psychology. *American Journal of Community Psychology,* 1977, *5,* 155–161.

Mondale, W. Social accounting, evaluation and the future of the human services. *Evaluation,* 1972, *1,* 29–34.

Murrell, A. *Community psychology and social systems.* New York: Behavioral Publications, 1973.

Nelson, G. L. Psychotherapy supervision from the trainee's point of view: A survey of preferences. *Professional Psychology,* 1978, *9,* 539–550.

Price, R., and Cherniss, C. Training for a new profession: Research as social action. *Professional Psychology,* 1977, *8,* 222–231.

Rader, D. The computerized information system as organizational innovation: A case study. In J. Crawford, D. Morgan, and D. Gianturco (Eds.), *Progress in mental health information systems.* Cambridge, Mass.: Ballinger, 1974.

Rappaport, J., Davidson, W. S., Wilson, M., and Mitchell, A. Alternatives to blaming the victim or the environment: Our places to stand have not moved the earth. *American Psychologist,* 1975, *30,* 525–528.

Rappaport, J. *Community psychology values, research, and action.* New York: Holt, Rinehart and Winston, 1977.

Reddy, W. B. The effects of immediate and delayed feedback on the learning of empathy. *Journal of Counseling Psychology,* 1969, *16,* 59–62.

Reiff, R. Ya gotta believe. In I. Iscoe, B. L. Bloom, and C. D. Spielberger (Eds.), *Community psychology in transition,* Washington, D.C.: Hemisphere Publishing, 1977.

Rønnestad, H. Counselor personality and supervisory styles. *Scandinavian Journal of Psychology,* 1976, *17,* 56–60.

Rosenblatt, A., and Mayer, J. E. Objectionable supervisory styles: Students' views. *Social Work,* 1975, *20,* 184–189.

Rosenblum, G. Advanced training in community psychology: The role of training in community systems. *Community Mental Health Journal,* 1973, *9,* 63–67.

Rowley, C. M., and Faux, E. J. The team approach to supervision. *Mental Hygiene,* 1966, *50,* 60–65.

Scherz, F. H. A concept of supervision based on definitions of job responsibility. *Social Casework,* 1958, *39,* 435–442.

Scott, W. R. Reactions to supervision in a heteronomous professional organization. *Administrative Science Quarterly,* 1965, *16,* 65–81.

Silverman, W. H., and Fourcher, L. A. A developmental approach to postdoctoral training in community psychology. *Professional Psychology,* 1975, *6,* 244–249.

Spielberger, C. D., and Iscoe, I. Graduate education in community psychology. In S. E. Golann and C. Eisdorfer (Eds.), *Handbook of community mental health.* New York: Appleton-Century-Crofts, 1972.

Tyler, F. B., and Gatz, M. If community psychology is so great, why don't we try it? *Professional Psychology,* 1976, *6,* 185–194.

Waltz, G. R., Roeber, E. C., Gysbers, N. C., and Rønnestad, M. H. Practicum supervision: An integrated theory of supervision. In G. F. Farwell, N. R. Gamsey, and P. T. Mathieu-Coughlan (Eds.), *The counselor's handbook,* New York: Intext-Chandler, 1974.

Warheit, G. J., Bell, R. A., and Schwab, J. J. *Needs assessment approaches: Concepts and methods.* Rockville, Md.: National Institute of Mental Health, 1977.

Watson, R. The manpower team in a child welfare setting. *Child Welfare* 1968, *47,* 446–454.

Watson, K. W. Differential supervision. *Social Work,* 1973, *18,* 80–88.

Weiss, C. H. *Evaluation research:* Methods of assessing program effectiveness. Englewood Cliffs, N. J.: Prentice-Hall, Inc., 1972.

Zax, M., and Specter, G. A. *An introduction to community psychology.* New York: Wiley, 1974.

Zolik, E., Sirbu, W., and Hopkinson, D. Perspectives of clinical students on training in community mental health and community psychology. *American Journal of Community Psychology,* 1976, *4,* 339–349.

Zwerling, I. The impact of the community mental health movement on psychiatric practice and training. *Hospital and Community Psychiatry,* 1976, *27,* 258–262.

CHAPTER 26

Training and Supervision of Crisis Workers

BARRY R. BURKHART

In reviewing the history of conceptions of mental disorder, two broad trends can be discerned (Rosen, 1968; Zax and Specter, 1974). These are (1) a continuing redefinition of the phenomena of mental disorder, primarily involving a shift from nonrational to naturalistic definitions of behavior pathology, and (2) a consequent broadening of the scope of the field of mental health, such that more and more behavioral phenomena are described as representing legitimate areas of concern for the mental health profession.

The effects of these two processes can be seen in a number of specific changes within the field of mental health. The naturalistic model, the beginning of which can be traced to the Greeks, continues to be elaborated and made more comprehensive. The most recent addition to the fundamental naturalistic model has been the recognition of the power of environmental events in influencing human behavior. This paradigmatic shift has tended to undermine the most prominent model in mental health, the medical model, and bring into focus mental health models which assume a more socio-psychological perspective. As Zax and Cowen (1972) have indicated, this shift has important implications for how behavior pathology is to be understood and eventually how society should respond to mental disorder.

As the naturalistic model gained more and more acceptance, displacing nonrational and moral models of conceptualizing human behavior, concurrent changes occurred in the definition of the scope of the field. Human behavior that previously had been viewed as representing moral failures or the result of divine involvement, came to be seen as problems that were best conceptualized as mental health problems. Historical examples of this process were often striking. Pinel's redefinition of the inmates of Le Bicêtre as mentally ill, instead of morally nonhuman, resulted in massive changes in the care of mentally ill people. Likewise, Freud's conceptualization of hysteria as a psychological rather than neurological phenomenon resulted in an entirely new way of treating neurotic behaviors. More recently, through the work of Anna Freud and Wilhelm Reich, characterological problems, which had been seen simply as moral failings, have been included under the umbrella of the mental health field. The strong interest recently in a psychophysiological understanding of many diseases also is one other manifestation of this broadening process (Schwartz, 1978).

This expansion of the mental health field has resulted in many changes in the service delivery models characterizing mental health practice. Currently, the mental health field has evidenced a marked shift from a medical model toward a community based service model (Zax and Specter, 1974; Rappaport, 1977). The distinctive features of the community mental health model; the emphasis on prevention of behavior disorder through early identification and intervention, utilization of nonprofessional care-givers, reliance on the community for provision of psychosocial resources, and a focus on practice in the community, especially through the development of innovative mental health strategies, seemed to be natural developments generated by the changing Zeitgeist of the mental health field.

Crisis intervention procedures are usually identified as the most articulated and successful of these innovative mental health practices. In this chapter, after reviewing the definitional and theoretical foundations of crisis intervention, selected issues in training and supervising crisis workers will be reviewed. The intent of the chapter is to describe, in broad outlines, the major differences between training and supervision in a traditional psychotherapy context as opposed to a crisis intervention context; and, based on this analysis, to provide a model of effective training and supervision procedures for the development of crisis intervention skills. The focus of the chapter is on the special demands of training and supervising crisis workers. Less attention will be devoted to the actual technology of crisis intervention. There are many useful sources of information about the procedures of intervention; however, there are but few sources designed to help supervisors accomplish the goals of developing and implementing training programs for crisis workers (McGee, 1974).

DEFINITION

Despite the haziness of the construct of *crisis,* Caplan's (1961) original definition seems to represent the consensus of most experts working in this area. According to Caplan, a crisis is a state

> provoked when a person faces an obstacle to important life goals that is, for a time, insurmountable through the utilization of customary methods of problem solving. A period of disorganization ensues, a period of upset, during which many different abortive attempts at solution are made. Eventually, some kind of adaptation is achieved, which may or may not be in the best interest of that person and his fellows (p. 18).

Although, as Korchin (1976) has noted, "crisis intervention is more an orientation and way of thinking than a systematic body of theory, knowledge, and practice" (p. 509), nonetheless, there seems to be a rather substantial agreement about the assumptions necessary to the development of theory and research. Taplin (1971), in an excellent review, identified the major assumptions either implicitly or explicitly made by crisis theorists. These are: (a) human life is inevitably marked by crisis events, (b) each crisis precipitates a characteristic pattern of responding, (c) during a crisis period, people are more susceptible to intervention, (d) the outcome of a crisis can be for the better or the worse, (e) resolving past crises successfully increases the likelihood of successful responding to future crises, (f) during a crisis period, anybody can exert influence, (g) situation variables are critical in sustaining or inhibiting the course of the crisis, and (h) crises usually are precipitated by events, some of which are predictable and thus provide an opportunity for primary preventation procedures.

Auerbach and Kilman (1977), in their major review of the crisis intervention literature, point out that "crisis intervention techniques are loosely organized and cover a wide range of procedures" (p. 1190). Nonetheless, distinctive features distinguishing crisis intervention can be discerned from a review of the literature (Caplan, 1964; McGee, 1974; Getz, Weisen, Sue, and Ayers, 1974; Ewing, 1978). Ewing's (1978) summary of the features characteristic of crisis intervention practice provides a useful descriptive analysis. He asserts that crisis intervention must be readily available in order to reach the wide range of clients who could benefit from crisis services. Furthermore, the techniques used should be reality-based, flexible, and adaptable for use with individuals and their social networks. While the focus is on the client's immediate problem, the intent also should be to aid the client in developing more adaptive coping mechanisms and, in some instances, to prepare the client for further treatment.

Although the evaluation of these assumptions about crisis theory and the practice of crisis intervention is only beginning (Auerbach and Kilman, 1977), their theoretical promise seems to warrant their acceptance as guidelines for the development of crisis intervention services and the training of crisis workers. In fact, most functioning crisis intervention programs do incorporate some or most of these assumptions in their clinical activities. In the rest of this section, the conceptual and practical implications of these assumptions will be delineated, particularly as they relate to issues of training and supervision.

Clearly, one such implication involves the relative importance of training as opposed to supervision. If training is defined as the preparation of a crisis worker prior to service delivery, and supervision is defined as ongoing consultation while the service is being delivered then it is readily seen that, given its very nature, crisis intervention does not lend itself to reflective, on-going supervision. Training, therefore, becomes the critical component. Crisis workers often do not have the opportunity even to meet with a supervisor before their interaction with a client is completed. Consequently, supervision in crisis intervention is more often like a post-mortem than a process evaluation. Nonetheless, crisis supervisors must be available to support their staff. The "burn-out" rate among crisis workers is very high and an effective supervisor should use every opportunity to encourage and remoralize staff.

Another derivative of structuring crisis intervention practice around these guidelines is the opportunity, in fact, necessity, for reliance on nonprofessional care-givers. Although there is a growing respect for crisis intervention procedures among professional care-givers (Ewing, 1978; Butcher and Koss, 1978), from its very beginnings the development of crises intervention programs has depended heavily on the practice of selecting and training nonprofessional workers (McGee,

1974). The term nonprofessional is used to indicate that the primary occupational role of the individual is not in mental health or a primarily mental health context. Generally, this designation includes volunteers, who are interested in serving as helpers for altruistic reasons, and occupational groups whose primary job responsibilities do not include mental health duties, but who, because of the nature of their work, frequently are involved in situations having critical mental health implications. Examples of such groups would include ministers, police officers, teachers, and bartenders, among others.

There are several reasons why these groups offer such potential for crisis intervention services. The demands for immediacy of intervention and availability of service place a premium on sources of support in the natural environment. Therefore, these "natural care-givers" can play a key role, irrespective of professional status. However, a reliance on these nonprofessional care-givers assumes that they will be willing and able to provide the support necessary to the successful resolution of the crisis situation. Clearly, these assumptions often are not met. In order for these requirements to be met, those groups who have the potential to be crisis intervention specialists must be identified, motivated, and trained.

However, this is often an arduous process, much less simple than it might appear at first. Selecting, motivating, and training nonprofessional care-givers is a much different process than the same procedure with professional staff. Unfortunately, these critical differences have not been addressed adequately in the previous literature. Many otherwise well-conceived crisis training programs have been unsuccessful due to their failure to recognize the fundamental differences between training a professional who is conceptually prepared and attitudinally sympathetic, and training a nonprofessional who is neither.

This point introduces the most serious, and yet least understood, issue in training nonprofessionals. That is, often nonprofessionals do not share the trainer's basic conceptual paradigm regarding human behavior. When this occurs the training problem is not simply how to transmit information but how to transmit information in such a way that the conceptually unprepared trainee will understand and accept the knowledge.

For example, police officers are an important resource for crisis intervention work because the police are frequently involved in crisis situations that have clear and extensive implications for human adjustment (Bard and Berkowitz, 1967; Mann, 1973). Although the social stereotype of the occupational responsibilities of police is that they are primarily crime-fighters; in fact, crime-related activities take up the smallest part of their working day (President's Commission on Law Enforcement, 1967). Lefkowitz (1977), in a recent major review, reported that job analyses demonstrated that the greater part of a police officer's job is devoted to interpersonal or social service activities, frequently involving social conflict situations. Additionally, there is clear evidence that police serve as one of the primary gatekeepers for the mental health system (Bittner, 1967; Smith, Pumphrey, and Hall, 1963). Finally, the police are the only social service professionals that maintain their practice in the community; consequently they serve as the resource for many community needs. As one police officer stated, "When you're the only ones who have to make house calls, you learn to expect anything when that door is opened."

This community availability of police, of course, makes them perfect for providing many types of crisis services. In the last few years, an increasing amount of attention has been directed specifically to the general area of family crisis intervention with the police. Beginning with the pioneering work of Morton Bard (Bard and Berkowitz, 1967; Bard, 1969, 1971), several programs have been developed which have attempted to train police in successful family crisis intervention. In addition to the social goals served by reducing or abating family disturbance, additional impetus for these training programs has been provided by the data demonstrating the high incidence of police injuries and fatalities resulting from "family beefs." Additionally, there appears to be solid research support for the effectiveness of these training programs, both in terms of reducing police injuries (Bard and Berkowitz, 1967) and in providing more effective crisis services to disordered families (Driscoll, Meyer, and Schanie, 1973).

Despite this evident importance in mental health related situations, the police culture continues to stress the notion that crime fighting and a "crime-fighters attitude" are the most important attributes of the successful officer (Stotland and Berberich, 1979; Van Maneen, 1975; Burkhart, in press). Because their organizational socialization does not support the self-perception of themselves as mental health workers, police officers tend not to accept a role as social service agents and, thus, represent a particularly difficult group to train. Given this state, there is much that can be learned from the experiences of training police officers about developing training programs for nonprofessionals in general.

Not all nonprofessional groups pose difficulties of this sort. Perhaps the most important distinction in this regard is between selected versus nonselected trainees. Whenever the nature of the crisis intervention program allows for a selection process, such as is the case with most telephone crisis programs, the trainee usually will be much more attitudinally prepared to adopt an appropriate conceptual framework (McGee, 1974). There are several reasons for this. In most of the programs where selection is involved, there is the additional preselection process of volunteering. Volunteers are easier to train both because of their motivation and because of their usual identification with the ideology of the service program. Additionally, the selection process itself allows for the identification of those attributes that are necessary or useful for the task involved. Although there is a growing body of literature on the selection of crisis workers (Chinsky and Rappaport, 1971; Dooley, 1975; Morgan and King, 1975), up to this point the literature offers no specific and compelling data to indicate superiority of any particular selection process. Much like the literature on selection of professional therapists (Parloff, Waskow, and Wolfe, 1978), little is known about the particular attributes and abilities necessary for effective functioning. Nonetheless, most of the experts in the field identify and rely on several general dimensions to select workers (Getz, et al., 1974). Furthermore, despite the evident weakness of the operational definitions of characteristics associated with successful functioning, telephone crisis services that carefully select and train workers do, in fact, seem to provide better service (Genthner, 1974).

BASIC GOALS AND COMPONENTS OF EFFECTIVE TRAINING PROGRAMS

Successful supervision and training programs in crisis intervention must accomplish three basic goals to ensure successful skill acquisition in the training situation and generalization of the skill to the service context. First, the supervision and training program must provide an appropriate cognitive model which defines the problem and specifies the type of intervention. Second, the training and supervision should serve to increase the self-confidence and perception of mastery among the trainees. Finally, the training and supervision must build the basic behavioral skills necessary to accomplish the helping intervention. Because they are difficult to operationalize, these generic goals often are overlooked in the design of training programs. Trainers, however, must address each of these goals as well as the particular goals unique to the specific nature of their training program if the program is to be effective.

The cognitive model provided by the training serves a number of functions. In effect, it serves as the theoretical metaphor for the trainees, just as the assumptions of a particular psychological theory guide the practice of a professional therapist (Lachman, 1960, also see Chapters 1 and 2). Thus, the cognitive model identifies which phenomena are relevant to understanding the basic problem; it provides a mode of representation for these phenomena; and it specifies the quality of the relationships among the variables involved (Price, 1978).

The definitional aspect of the model is critical because by defining what is or is not relevant, the model operates to set the perceptual field for the trainee. For example, in a training program for probation officers based on a behavioral model, the officers were taught that consequences of behavior were the salient feature controlling the behavior of delinquents (Burkhart, Behles, and Stumphauzer, 1974). Following the training program, the juvenile probation officers began to refer to consequences of behavior in their own reports at a higher frequency than before training. Furthermore, their recommendations for treatment more often included programs which involved contingent management of behavior. In short, the probation officers, because of the exposure to the behavioral training model, simply became perceptually oriented to identify and utilize contingent relationships.

In providing a mode of representation, the model serves to "explain" the phenomena by providing a familiar semantic structure. In providing labels that identify and demarcate the boundaries of the different variables, the model also serves to facilitate communication. Finally, by organizing the variables in terms of their interrelationships, the model allows for the conceptual manipulations involved in predicting probable consequences of a particular pattern of behavior, or predicting the outcome of a particular intervention. To continue with the above example, the juvenile probation officers learned to identify consequences as "rein-forcers" or "punishers" and, based on the conceptual relationship implied, to predict the effects of "reinforcing" behaviors.

The net effect of the provision of an assumptive cognitive model is to increase the cognitive complexity of the trainee in reference to the particular focus of the training program. Through this process, the trainee is provided with a therapeutic metaphor which is sufficiently differentiated to allow for appropriate responding to the various combinations and contexts of the problematic behavior. The thera-peutic metaphor thus becomes a conceptual tool through which the trainee selects relevant events, orders their importance, specifies the critical relationships, and effects a propitious intervention.

For example, in training crisis workers to deal with suicide, the concept of suicide as a cry for help (Farberow and Schneidman, 1961) tends to liberate the trainee from the conceptually limiting and inappropriate notion that suicide attempts or threats mean only self-murder. By understanding that the suicidal person is communicating a need for help, trainees can begin to orient themselves toward responding to this request for help rather than being able only to argue with someone that "things are not all that bad."

In addition to increasing the cognitive complexity of the trainee, the assumptive model also should provide a benevolent therapeutic metaphor. That is, the attri-butions and actions toward the client predicated on the basis of the assumptive model should be productive of growth. This point can be illustrated by comparing an assumptive cognitive model which, because of its undifferentiated character and its negative attributional productiveness, is not facilitive of growth with a more benevolent model which could be implemented through a training program. The special significance of this illustration is that, inevitably, trainees enter a training program with an existing cognitive-emotional understanding of the prob-lem and naturally will tend to resist changing their assumptive model. All the skill and power of the trainer is needed to deal successfully with this resistance, for unless this task is accomplished the entire training program will be compromised.

Training police officers brings this issue into bold relief because of the particu-lar assumptive model of human behavior generated by the police culture (Fortier, 1973; Goldsmith and Goldsmith, 1974; Van Maneen, 1975; Burkhart, in press). Police tend to describe problem behavior according to a taxonomic system based on two mutually exclusive dimensions and one process; people are either *bad* or *mad* and determine their behavior through *free choice.* The consequences of this rather impoverished conceptual stance in a helping context are often negative. However, it should be noted that in performing certain job tasks, this stance may be adaptive because it allows for quick, action oriented, controlling responses. Nonetheless, the evaluative, judgmental quality of this conceptual system does not serve well in a helping context and, inevitably, will serve as a resistance to the acquisition of helping skills.

How, then, can a trainer increase the richness and complexity of the trainee's implicit theory? Despite the conceptual sterility of the bad-mad theory, it is supported by the general police culture and, in fact, alternative interpretations are often stigmatized as being bleeding-heart, wishy-washy, overly complex constructions which are not appropriate for "real" police work. If alternative conceptual stances are required, how can they be presented so as to be understandable and acceptable to the trainee?

In order to accomplish this, the relevance of the training has to be established within the *existing* conceptual model of the trainees. For example, it is not very profitable to attempt to persuade police officers to adopt a family crisis intervention model because of the humanitarian values of providing preventative mental health services. Police, generally, are not interested in being seen as "social workers" and tend to resent attempts to push them into such roles. However, one of the most central values in the police culture is officer safety. Stotland and Berberich (1979) identify this value as being exemplified by the comment offered to rookie officers by veterans, "Your job is not to enforce the law, but to make sure I get home tonight (p. 63)." Thus, if the training program is *initially* advertised and presented as "how not to get yourself killed or injured in a family beef," the interest of the officers is assured. Consequently, their initial compliance with the training program is enhanced. The same psychological skills can be taught, but when presented within the sanction of the existing conceptual context, their credibility is more assured.

The importance of such paradigmatic clashes cannot be overemphasized. Too often, well conceived training programs have foundered because the consultants were not sensitive to these conceptual and values differences. In the above example, if the program is built on one of the strongest premises held by police officers, —that is, officer safety—instead of presenting the training program in such a way that it is perceived as antagonistic to this premise, much of the initial resistance of training is turned to the trainer's advantage.

Additionally, in designing training or supervisory programs, it is essential to determine if the trainees are attitudinally prepared or unprepared for the training. Attitudinal preparedness refers to the specific beliefs or evaluations that the trainee possesses about the crisis topic. For example, police officers often believe those social stereotypes of rapes which have been identified as both untrue and potentially damaging to effective responding to the rape victim (Field, 1978). An officer who asserts that "no healthy women can be raped" or, as I have more often heard it put, "a woman can run faster with her skirt up than a man with his pants down," is not likely to be able to provide the necessary emotional support to a victim. In fact, such an officer may increase the guilt and self-recrimination experienced by rape victims. It is the responsibility of the trainer to prevent such an event and to provide the officer with a therapeutically benevolent or, at least, therapeutically benign orientation.

A caveat is in order here for crisis trainers. Often, trainers have a strong degree of professional and, sometimes, emotional commitment to their program. Consequently, when faced with antagonistic or attitudinally unprepared trainees, trainers may respond with anger or discouragement toward the trainees. Training programs can degenerate into debates about various differences in opinion between trainers and trainees or, if the trainer, in an authoritarian manner, puts down a trainee, trainees may simply withdraw or become passive-aggressive participants who effectively undermine the training programs. To prevent this, it is important for trainers to be able to maintain their professional perspective and address the resistance of the trainees in an effective, not emotional, manner.

One way to prevent attitudinal clashes between nonprofessional trainees and professional trainers is, once again, to develop training metaphors which are compatible with some of the more benign attitudes and expectations of trainees. For example, Katherine Ellison (1976), in training police to work with rape victims, stresses the critical importance of the victim as a witness. Because police are strongly committed to the crime-fighting responsibilities of their jobs, she presents her training program as one in which the police officer safeguards the value of the victim as a witness. Police, being well aware of how many rape victims refuse to prosecute or are not effective witnesses, are willing to learn about victim counseling procedures without their usual resistance. In effect, Ellison's procedure, by using a compatible metaphor, sidesteps the potential clashes of the differences in attitudes. It should be stressed that the crisis skills taught to the officers are not compromised by the training metaphor, but are simply rendered more acceptable to them. Additionally, engrossing officers in the training program, having them go through the experiences of learning about the real consequences of rape to victims, and having them counsel victims, even in a role playing context, predisposes them to the additional cognitive and emotional learning which will make them fully aware of their stereotypes. Very frequently, I have had officers who initially participated in a program because it served their interest of preserving the victim as a witness become caught up in the training to the extent that their consciousness was raised considerably about the issue.

Furthermore, by basing the training program on a conceptually familiar rationale, it is easier to accomplish the second goal of all training programs: enhancing the perception of mastery and self-confidence of the trainee. Because the training material assumes relevance to the officer, it is easy to bridge the gap between the new skills being taught and already acquired job skills. This serves, of course, to make the trainee more comfortable with the process of "trying on" the new skills and increases their salience within his or her repertoire. Thus the trainee becomes a better, more complete and accomplished officer.

There are several other ways that the trainer can enhance the self-confidence of trainees. Liberal reinforcement of trainee efforts is, of course, obviously a critical component. However, in order to be effective, the reinforcement source must be credible. Unfortunately, it is often the case that, initially, the mental health professional may not be accepted by nonprofessional trainees as a credible training resource, especially when training is not within a mental health context (Brown, Burkhart, King, and Solomon, 1978). Consequently, trainers have to be able to generate credibility through their personal charisma as well as their professional competence. An effective trainer must possess adequate social stimulus value. It is a fact that an unassertive, socially inept trainer, no matter what his or her professional status, will not be persuasive. Just as the personal qualities of a therapist are critical to successful psychotherapeutic outcome (Parloff, Waskow, and Wolfe, 1978), so are the personal qualities of a trainer important to training outcome. Additionally, trainers have to be aware of the values, ideals, and expectations of the trainees, if they are to be credible and, thus, persuasive. The evaluations of training programs provided by trainees often remark that a particular trainer did or did not "speak our language." In those cases where the trainer was not perceived as being able to communicate effectively, the rest of the training program was to little avail.

Unfortunately, there are little or no direct data regarding the personal characteristics of the effective trainer. Such information is long overdue and, it is hoped, will be developed in the near future. My guess is that the data will be analogous to those characteristics associated with success as a persuader in any other context (e.g., Strong, 1978).

The process of training, itself, should provide confidence as well as competence-enhancing experiences. No better way exists to encourage self-confidence and the perception of self-efficacy than successful task accomplishment. Therefore, whatever the training format, it is essential that it include graduated mastery experiences relevant to the behavioral goals of the training program.

In designing a training format, the concept of the "adult learner" as developed within the adult education literature has important implications for the development of an effective, training process (Miller, 1964). Malcolm Knowles (1970) argues that because much of what is known about learning and teaching has been derived from work with children or animals, we fail to acknowledge the special characteristics of the "adult learner." Based on a presentation and review of the characteristics of the adult learner, Knowles has developed a set of technical guidelines for the development of adult learning programs which appear to be highly relevant to the training of paraprofessionals. He characterizes adult learners as: (a) being less dependent on authority, (b) having more relevant life experience, and (c) being more oriented toward immediate application than nonadult learners. These descriptions are entirely appropriate for the typical trainee involved in a crisis intervention training program.

The technical implications of this analysis of the characteristics of the adult learner are straightforward. To summarize briefly: in order to be most successful, the process of the learning experience must involve a reciprocal exchange between trainee and trainer, the material must be presented so as to emphasize its pragmatic value, and the training techniques must be experiential in nature.

If these guidelines are applied to the development of a crisis intervention training program, the program would be structured around task-relevant activities which are drawn from the real-life experiences of the trainees. Furthermore, the necessary information should be presented within a more informally structured pedagogic style; again, drawing heavily from the life experiences of the trainees. For example, it might be useful to ask the participants to produce a list of problematic situations relevant to the training area, and to structure the presentation around these particular situations.

Having provided trainees with an adequate conceptual paradigm, self-confidence, and skills, the job has only begun. Continued supervisory support is required in order to maintain and expand these newly acquired competencies, especially if the social-organizational milieu does not provide naturally occurring reinforcement for the continued development of the beginning crisis worker. Often group supervision is helpful in this regard. The group supervision can facilitate the development of a supportive network which can provide the necessary encouragement and serve as a resource for problem solving with difficult cases. With this accomplished, the supervisor can alter his or her role to that of a consultant who provides review and staff development opportunities.

SUMMARY

It is evident that human problems are too many and too varied to be addressed adequately through a passive-receptive, medical model of mental health services. Crisis intervention, as a paradigm and set of techniques, offers promise in filling the lacunae evident in existing human services. After reviewing the historical development of a crisis orientation in mental health, the theoretical assumptions of the crisis concept, and the technical features of crisis intervention procedures, the essential components and goals of training programs for crisis workers were identified. Based on this analysis, a training model focused on the particular problems associated with training and supervising conceptually and/or attitudinally unprepared, nonprofessional crisis workers was described.

REFERENCES

Auerbach, S. M., and Kilman, P. R. Crisis intervention: A review of outcome research. *Psychological Bulletin,* 1977, *84,* 1189–1217.

Bard, M. Extending psychology's impact through existing community institutions. *American Psychologist,* 1969, *24,* 610–612.

Bard, M. The role of law enforcement in the helping system. *Community Mental Health Journal,* 1971, *7,* 151–160.

Bard, M., and Berkowitz, B. Training police as specialists in family crisis intervention: A community psychology action program. *Community Mental Health Journal,* 1967, *3,* 315–317.

Bittner, E. Police discretion in emergency apprehension of mentally ill persons. *Social Problems,* 1964, *14,* 278–292.

Brown, S., Burkhart, B. R., King, G. D., and Solomon, R. Roles and expectations for mental health professionals in law enforcement agencies. *American Journal of Community Psychology,* 1977, *45,* 475–482.

Burkhart, B. R. Conceptual issues in the development of police selection procedures. *Professional Psychology,* in press.

Burkhart, B. R., Behles, M., and Stumphauzer, J. S. Training probation officers in behavior modification: Knowledge, attitudes, or behavioral competence. *Behavior Therapy,* 1976, *7,* 47–53.

Butcher, J. N. and Koss, M. P. Research on brief and crisis-oriented therapies. In S. L. Garfield and A. E. Bergin (Eds.) *Handbook of psychotherapy and behavior change* (2nd ed.). New York: Wiley 1978.

Caplan, G. *An approach to community mental health.* New York: Grune and Stratton, 1961.

Caplan, G. *Principles of preventive psychiatry.* New York: Basic Books, 1964.

Chinsky, J. M., and Rappaport, J. Evaluation of a technique for the behavioral assessment of nonprofessionals. *Journal of Clinical Psychology,* 1971, *27,* 400–402.

Dooley, D. Selecting nonprofessional counselor trainees with the Group Assessment of Interpersonal Traits (GAIT). *American Journal of Community Psychology,* 1975, *3,* 371–383.

Driscoll, J. M., Meyer, R. G., and Schanie, C. F. Training in family crisis intervention. *Journal of Applied Behavioral Science,* 1973, *9,* 62–82.

Ellison, K. W. Personal communication, June 1976.

Ewing, C. P. *Crisis intervention as psychotherapy.* New York: Oxford Press, 1978.

Farberow, N. L., and Schneidman, E. S. *The cry for help.* New York: McGraw-Hill, 1961.

Field, H. S. Attitudes toward rape: A comparative analysis of police, rapists, crisis counselors, and citizens. *Journal of Personality and Social Psychology,* 1978, *36,* 156–179.

Fortier, K. The police culture: Its effects on sound police-community relations. *The Police Chief,* 1972, *1,* 33–36.

Genthner, R. W. Evaluating the functioning of community-based hotlines. *Professional Psychologist.* 1974, *5,* 409–414.

Getz, W., Weisen, A. E., Sue, S., and Ayers, A. *Fundamentals of crisis counseling.* Lexington, Mass.: Lexington Books, 1974.

Goldsmith, J., and Goldsmith, S. (Eds.). *The police community.* Pacific Palisades, Calif.: Palisades Publishers, 1974.

Knowles, M. S. *The modern practice of adult education.* New York: Association Press, 1970.

Korchin, S. *Modern clinical psychology: Principles of intervention in the clinic and the community.* New York: Basic Books, 1976.

Lachman, R. The model in theory construction. *Psychological Review,* 1960, *67,* 113–129.

Lefkowitz, J. Industrial-organization psychology and the police. *American Psychologist,* 1977, *32,* 346–364.

Mann, P. *Psychological consultation with the police department.* Springfield, Ill.: Charles C. Thomas, 1973.

McGee, R. K. *Crisis intervention in the community.* Baltimore: University Park Press, 1974.

Miller, H. L. *Teaching and learning in adult education.* New York: Macmillan, 1964.

Morgan, J. P., and King, G. D. The selection and evaluation of volunteer paraprofessional telephone counselors. *American Journal of Community Psychology,* 1975, *3,* 237–249.

Parloff, M. B., Waskow, I. E., and Wolfe, B. E. Research on therapist variables in relation to process and outcome. In S. L. Garfield and A. E. Bergin (Eds.), *Handbook of Psychotherapy and behavior change* (2nd ed.). New York: Wiley, 1978.

President's Commission on Law Enforcement and Administration of Justice. *The challenge of crime in a free society.* Washington, D.C.: U.S. Government Printing Office, 1967.

Price, R. *Abnormal behavior: Perspectives in conflict* (2nd ed.). New York: Holt, Rinehart, and Winston, 1978.

Rappaport, J. *Community psychology: Values, research, and action.* New York: Holt, Rinehart, and Winston, 1977.

Rosen, G. *Madness in society: Chapters in the historical sociology of mental illness.* New York: Harper, 1968.

Schwartz, G. E. Psychobiological foundations of psychotherapy and behavior change. In S. L. Garfield and A. E. Bergin (Eds.), *Handbook of psychotherapy and behavior change* (2nd ed.). New York: Wiley, 1978.

Smith, K., Pumphrey, M. W., and Hall, J. C. The "last straw": The decisive incident resulting in the request for hospitalization in 100 schizophrenic patients. *The American Journal of Psychiatry,* 1963, *120,* 228–233.

Stotland, E., and Berberich, J. The psychology of police. In Hans Toch (Ed.), *Psychology of crime and criminal justice.* New York: Holt, Rinehart, and Winston, 1979.

Strong, S. R. Social psychological approach to psychotherapy research. In S. L. Garfield and A. E. Bergin (Eds.). *Handbook of psychotherapy and behavior change* (2nd ed.). New York: Wiley, 1978.

Taplin, J. R. Crisis theory: Critique and reformulation. *Community Mental Health Journal,* 1971, *7,* 13–23.

Van Maneen, J. Police socialization: A longitudinal examination of job attitudes in an urban police department. *Administrative Science Quarterly,* 1975, *20,* 207–228.

Zax, M., and Cowen, E. L. *Abnormal Psychology: Changing conceptions.* New York: Holt, Rinehart, and Winston, 1972.

Zax, M., and Specter, G. A. *An introduction to community psychology.* New York: Wiley, 1974.

PART SEVEN

Research

Chapter 27, *Research and the Supervisory Process* by Michael J. Lambert, summarizes the empirical foundations of research on supervision. The supervisor can determine which methods have been tested, while the researcher will find direction regarding the large areas of psychotherapy supervision yet to be investigated.

CHAPTER 27

Research and the Supervisory Process

MICHAEL J. LAMBERT

Despite the divergence in systems of psychotherapy, their goals and varied training practices, there is at least one component considered essential to all existing approaches. This component is the supervision of trainees in their work with clients.

Wolberg (1954) defined supervision as "essentially a teaching procedure in which an experienced psychotherapist helps a less experienced individual acquire a body of knowledge aimed at a more dexterious handling of the therapeutic situation." To appreciate this definition and the following discussion some knowledge of the developmental history of supervision is required. Briefly, as Ekstein and Wallerstein (1958) explained it, our present concept of the supervisor grew out of the role of "control" analyst in psychoanalytic training. It seems that the representatives of the Institute of Vienna, in opposition to the European school, thought that the personal analyst should not control (supervise) the first case of the student analyst. The controller (supervisor) was to be strictly a teacher who would explain, correct, and direct. He was to use an entirely didactic approach without touching the affective problems of the beginning analyst. Affective problems were to be considered within the student's personal analysis. Since the movement of psychiatry away from requiring personal analysis or therapy for their trainees (Dellis and Stone, 1960), supervision has become more important in the training of psychiatrists. At the same time its function has been altered.

Supervision has been considered central in the training of allied professionals. The discipline of social work, for example, has emphasized the role of the supervisor in the development of the student's therapeutic skills. Robinson's (1949) book on the subject is exemplary of the voluminous amount written on supervision in this area. The 1964 Greyston Report on the professional preparation of counseling psychologists is an example of an official statement of the necessary and desirable characteristics of the supervisory experience. Hoch, Ross, and Winder (1966), in an *American Psychologist* article on the professional preparation of clinical psychologists, encouraged supervision in psychotherapy as part of the training program. Special workshops involving supervision have been held and the contributions summarized by Dellis and Stone (1960) and Parker (1968).

Gerkin (1969) polled a sample of APA (Division 17) members in regard to their opinion of the attributes necessary for effective training. Of the 156 attributes identified, "Practicum students consult individually with a supervisor at least weekly" was rated highest in its importance to the overall training program. Most of the members, in fact, considered this attribute indispensable.

Supervision of students practicing psychotherapy is a rather unique and exciting aspect of mental health training programs. This important and indispensable activity gives the student an opportunity to develop increased self-awareness. This self-awareness or ability to monitor one's own processes in interaction with others can be enriching professionally, and in a more general sense, may help the student to be more effective in all interactions and relationships.

Supervision is a very personal way of working with neophyte therapists that may have considerable therapeutic effect. It clearly differs from therapy, however, in that the major goal is to help the student to be more effective and useful with clients. Although the goals and activities of supervision can be easily distinguished from those of psychotherapy, there are many parallels in the theories and processes of these two learning procedures. As a result, research on supervision has a great deal in common with research into the effects of psychotherapy.

Despite the prominence given to supervision in training, the earliest studies in this area did not distinguish the effects of supervision from other training experiences (Blocksma and Porter, 1947; Barrington, 1958; Demos and Zuwaylif, 1963; Munger and Johnson, 1960). Later studies, however, have tried to isolate supervision as an independent variable (cf. Demos, 1964; Hansen and Barker, 1964). Waltz and Johnston (1963), for example, had thirty NDEA counselor candidates interview a coached client. An interview check list was marked by supervisors and counselors immediately following the interview. This check list was descriptive of the client-counselor interaction and of the overall relationship. These ratings were not shared. The following day the counselors viewed a videotape recording (VTR) of their interview and rechecked the rating list. The second counselor check lists were more in line with supervisor ratings than the first. The authors concluded that VTR ". . . would seem to change counselor perception without the mediating influence of a supervisor." So even though supervision is considered an indispensable part of training for a variety of professionals, some early research has, in fact, questioned the necessity of the supervisor.

The purpose of this chapter is to review the research which has been conducted on the effects of supervision. In so doing it is hoped that the most salient findings of this research will be presented in such a way as to invite the practitioner to employ them. In addition, it is the purpose of this chapter to facilitate future research on supervision.

WHAT IS SUPERVISION?

Supervision itself, like psychotherapy, runs the risk of being treated with the "uniformity myth" (Kiesler, 1966). It is in reality a heterogeneous set of conditions that are distorted when treated as a unitary variable. Nevertheless, some homogeneity of activities must be assumed if we are to make progress in studying the learning activities subsumed under this word. For the purpose of this review, the term will have several limits. Supervision is that part of the overall training of mental health professionals that deals with modifying their actual in-therapy behaviors. It excludes the parts of training that are primarily didactic, such as classroom teaching, and likewise excludes the parts of training that are purely personal (e.g. experiential groups and the personal therapy experience). It includes training activities, either group or individual, wherein the supervisor arranges experiences that are aimed at helping the student therapist to modify specific behaviors with particular clients. Numerous methods have been used to attain these goals: instruction, supervisor modeling, direct observation, intervention by the supervisor in the actual process (as in co-therapy or with the assistance of mechanical devices), and feedback from direct observations or with audio/-videotape recordings.

TRAINING IN INTERPERSONAL SKILLS

Research in supervision has been limited at least partially by the general status of outcome research. Before we can confidently train therapists it is necessary to specify the actual causal agents in personality or behavior change. The dilemma is well captured in the following quote: "Psychotherapy is an undefined technique applied to unspecified cases with unpredictable results. For this technique, rigorous training is required" (Victor Raimy, cited in London, 1964). This statement, however true at the time, did not reflect the atmosphere of enthusiasm and confidence that was spawned by Carl Rogers and his colleagues.

The client-centered school can be credited with the very active research interest in therapist attitudes that eventually led to an expansion of research and the establishment of training programs that teach a variety of therapist facilitative attitudes or interpersonal skills. Carl Rogers was able to state the conditions that he felt led to constructive personality change with nearly mathematical precision (Rogers, 1959). This early specification of "necessary and sufficient" conditions led to many research reports on the effects of these therapist offered conditions. This research in turn resulted in the growing specification of these variables. Training raters to judge the level of empathy, warmth, congruence, and respect offered by therapists resulted in the application of these same training methods with student therapists themselves.

Truax and Carkhuff (1967) published an influential volume of research related to these dimensions and outlined an experiential/didactic training program. They emphasized the importance of measuring changes in trainee skill subsequent to training. Ivey, Normington, Miller, Merrill, and Haase (1968) also outlined the use of related methods, or "microcounseling" procedures. During the late 1960s, numerous similar methods were developed and applied in counselor education programs, graduate schools of social work and psychology, and medical schools. Matarazzo and her associates (Matarazzo, Phillips, Wiens, and Saslow, 1965) studied such content free variables as length of utterance, reaction time, and frequency of interruptions in an attempt to analyze interviewing "errors." A great deal of research has accumulated regarding the application of methods of teaching therapist interpersonal skills and related concepts.

Much of this research on training methods and models has been summarized by Matarazzo (1978). But even her review overlooks the seemingly limitless number of doctoral dissertations and other published and unpublished reports which examine teaching methods that attempt to alter trainee skills. In addition, her review—in contrast to this one—was not concerned with supervision *per se*. The research on training in interpersonal skills is dealt with here, although most of this training involves pre-supervisory experiences. The skills discussed were once a part of what was taught in early practicum experiences. These skills can no longer be considered a central function of supervision, however, because they are now generally learned prior to the initial counseling experiences that are accompanied by supervision.

In the following figure (Figure 1), we have focused on studies of interpersonal skills *training* with an emphasis on studies that involve supervision. The typical training program involves variants on a general procedure. This procedure includes: (a) focus on a specific skill such as empathic responding, (b) the presentation of a rationale for this skill, (c) audiotape or videotape examples of the presence and absence of the skill in actual therapy interactions, (d) practice at the skill, with (e) feedback about performance. Changes in trainee performance are typically tested in a pretest-posttest experimental design.

Figure 1 lists numerous—but hardly exhaustive—accounts of studies aimed at testing the effects of different forms of supervision and interviewing skills training. They are organized in such a way as to suggest the primary intent of each study. Thus, under the "A" heading are studies which dealt with the question, "Does training (supervision) help?" Later research (summarized under "B") was designed to compare the effects of a traditional method with an innovative method: "Does training paradigm *z* work better than paradigm *x* and *y?*"

Most recently investigators have been more interested in studying the most essential components of an already effective training program. Studies with this goal in mind have been listed under heading "C". These dismantling studies usually ask: Given the effectiveness of training program z, what specific activities are necessary and sufficient to obtain which results?* Additional questions may deal with the differential effects of training on different trainees, and the interaction of the trainee's personality with the supervisor's personality or technique.

In addition, some of the studies under "C" deal with the differential effects of training on specific trainee "types," or the interaction of supervisor personality variables with trainee personality or demographic variables.

Generally, studies comparing training versus a no-training control group have found that training is superior, both in producing greater personal adjustment and in increasing skill development. Studies comparing traditional supervision (usu-

---

*For an excellent discussion of these research questions as applied to psychotherapy, see Gottman and Markman (1978).

FIGURE 1. Studies examining the effects of training and supervision in counseling and psychotherapy.

A	B	C
Studies comparing training with a treatment control group	Studies comparing training vs. traditional supervision or a competing experimental group	Studies dismantling the process of supervision/training
Barrington (1958)	Boyd (1973)	Authier and Gustafson (1975)
Biasco and Redfering (1976)	Cormier, Hackney, and Segrist (1974)	Berenson, Carkhuff, and Myrus (1966)
Blocksma and Porter (1947)	Dalton and Sundblad (1976)	Canada (1973)
Hart (1973)	Deshaies (1974)	Dowling and Franz (1975)
Ivey, et al. (1968)	Dowall (1973)	Forestandi (1973)
	Gormally, Hill, Gulanick, and McGovern (1975)	Forge (1973)
	Kingdon (1975)	Fry (1973)
	Moreland, Ivey, and Phillips (1973)	Kuna (1975)
	Richardson (1974)	Olson (1973)
	Ross (1973)	Perry (1975)
	Silverman (1972)	Peters, Cormier, and Cormier (1978)
	Toukmanian and Rennie (1975)	Ronnestad (1973)
	Vander Kolk (1973)	Rosenthal (1977)
		Stone and Vance (1976)
		Tosi and Eshbaugh (1978)
		Uhleman, Lea, and Stone (1976)
		Wallace, Horan, Baker, and Hudson (1975)

ally facilitated by listening to audiotapes) with systematic training procedures that involved learning specific interpersonal or counseling skills indicate a superiority for the systematic training.

Thus, one can expect trainees who receive no systematic training in such areas as empathic responding, confrontation, attending behaviors, and the like to make much slower progress in developing these skills than the trainees who are involved in a systematic training program. Unfortunately, many of the research designs used to test this hypothesis have methodological weaknesses that favor the experimental group. Still, the research is rather unequivocal. *If a training program values the development of basic interpersonal or interviewing skills this can best be achieved with a program that clearly specifies the skills to be learned and the development of training aimed directly at this goal.*

An example of a study comparing traditional supervision with an innovative approach was published by Moreland, Ivey, and Phillips (1973). Twenty-four second-year medical students were randomly assigned to one of two interview training groups. Twelve were taught with microcounseling techniques which focused on attending behavior, open-ended questions, minimal activity responses, paraphrases, reflection of feelings, and summarization. The twelve control group trainees were observed by faculty members and provided with feedback of a "similar nature" during six group training sessions.

The dependent measures were derived from pre- and post-training interviews with patients at the hospital. Verbal behavior was then categorized and rated with the Attending Behavior Rating Scale (Ivey, 1971) and the Therapist Error Check List (Matarazzo, et al., 1965). Results indicated that both groups of students improved in their skills. Those who received microcounseling improved significantly more on attending behaviors and reflection of feelings and made significantly fewer "errors" on the Therapist Error Check List.

A study showing less positive results was reported by Kingdon (1975), who studied the effects of Interpersonal Process Recall (IPR) compared with "traditional supervision". Thirty-six counselors and 36 clients were assigned randomly to either IPR training or the control group. Six supervisors matched on relevant variables were assigned to either group randomly and trained in the respective technique. In the IPR sessions, videotaping of the counseling interview was followed by a client recall session in which the supervisor and client reviewed the session, with the client commenting on various points. The supervisor facilitated client recall of underlying thoughts and feelings as the trainee observed from outside the room. After the third counseling session, a mutual recall session was conducted with all three participants. The primary purpose of this session was to allow the client and trainee to share their previously unexpressed feelings and attitudes.

In the comparison group, audiotapes of counseling sessions were played during the supervisory hour. The supervisor focused on the counselor-client interaction and attempted to promote self-understanding and a greater appreciation for the dynamics of the interview.

The dependent measures involved three inventories and two process ratings, the Counselor Evaluation Inventory (Lindon, Stone, and Shertzer, 1965), Observation Questionnaire (Gelso, 1972), Counselor Evaluation Rating Scale (Myrick and Kelly, 1971), and ratings of self-exploration and empathy with the Carkhuff scales. The results suggested that the different techniques of supervision did *not* have differential effects on the development of counselor empathy, client satisfaction with counseling, supervisor ratings of counselors' performance or client inhibition. Clients who were being seen by an IPR supervised counselor did show increased self-exploration by the third counseling session. Thus, there was only slight support for the IPR method after three supervisory sessions, and even this conclusion is open to other plausible explanations.

While the types of innovative training procedures vary from study to study, as do the format, time, and measures of improvement, it is generally true that innovative programs involving the training of specific skills show gains in those skills that are superior to those resulting from "traditional" supervision. This conclusion is tempered by some limitations in the data which will be discussed later. First, however, consideration will be given to the results of dismantling studies and the identification of crucial variables within a given training program.

What Are the Crucial Variables in the Training Package?

Those studies listed under section "C" of Figure 1 represent attempts at specifying the most efficient way to achieve the goals of training. All of these studies compare two or more combinations of a treatment procedure. If such a design results in the more clear specification of necessary and sufficient parts of training, then the assumptions underlying the necessity of our established training programs will be questioned.

As an example, microcounseling procedures usually include reading, viewing models, practicing the skill, receiving feedback about performance, and observing others who are receiving similar training. A natural question is: Can one or more of these steps be eliminated without reducing the effectiveness of training? Several representative studies can be described.

Peters, Cormier, and Cormier (1978) analyzed the effects of four training methods on the acquisition of a counseling strategy (a goal development procedure) in 40 beginning counseling students. The comparison methods were adopted from microcounseling procedures and involved four experimental groups: (a) written and videotaped model, (b) written and videotaped model plus practice, (c) written and videotaped model, practice plus feedback, and (d) the procedure used in (c) plus remediation practice following feedback.

The dependent measures included both a written test and a role play interview with a standard client in which trainees were to demonstrate the counseling strategy they had learned. The results showed all students to have improved significantly in their ability to formulate client goals, and these changes were maintained at the two-week follow-up. Differences between the groups were not found to be significant. The authors concluded that there was little evidence to suggest that behavior rehearsal and feedback were necessary for skill acquisition!

Thus, the most efficient training procedure would exclude these components and rely solely on reading and viewing examples of how the skill is to be practiced.

In an earlier study, Uhlemann, Lea, and Stone (1976) compared training offered to undergraduate students composed of either: (a) instructions and guidelines for reflection of feelings, (b) models of poor and good reflective behavior, or (c) a combination of instructions and modeling. A minimal instruction control group was also employed. Dependent measures were derived from a brief role-play interview rated with the Empathic Understanding Scale and the Communication Index (Carkhuff, 1969b). The results were inconsistent across criteria but generally indicated that instruction alone and modeling alone were not as effective as the two combined. It is difficult to generalize from this study because the training was very brief (from 10 to 20 minutes); however, along with several other studies (e.g. Doster, 1972; Payne, Weiss, and Kapp, 1972), it does suggest the importance of modeling and instructions. Some exceptions to this can also be found in the literature. Kuna (1975), for example, found reading a handout sufficient for acquisition of a single skill ("restatement of problem"). And, of course, we know skills can be obtained in the absence of models (cf. Canada, 1973; Wallace, et al., 1975).

Dalton and Sundbald (1976) studied the effects of a videotaped model and of systematic training which included a model as well as feedback on empathic responding. Results showed that empathic responding could be affected by a model and, in fact, trainees in this situation increased their empathy by an over-all level of one scale point on the five-point Carkhuff scale. Trainees did seem to profit more when systematic training was added to the model. The results seemed to suggest that the major increment added by feedback about empathic responding came from a group of trainees who did not originally profit from modeling but did profit from other training procedures. Thus, rather than a slight gain in all trainee scores, it appears that some trainees need feedback while others do not. Unfortunately, the characteristics of these trainees were not specified. This is an excellent example of the type of question which must be answered if the essential ingredients of the training process are to be identified.

One of the most methodologically sound investigations of the components of training was conducted by Perry (1975). She studied the relative contribution of instructions and modeling to the development of accurate empathy responses. A factorial design combined two instructional conditions (instructions versus no instructions) and three modeling conditions (high empathy, low empathy, or no model). The dependent measures included samples of interaction from role-played interviews. The trainees were 66 ministers who participated in brief (unspecified, but probably less than an hour) training sessions. The training group that received the high empathy model condition showed the greatest gain on one of the dependent measures. The addition of written instruction to the modeling procedure did not improve the subject's learning. On the measure of empathy derived from a live interview, there were no differences between treatment groups.

Researchers have also tried to measure the relative contribution of different elements of the didactic-experiential program elaborated upon by Truax and

Carkhuff (1967). These authors, for example, have suggested that effective training should be comprised of (a) highly specific didactic training in interpersonal skills, (b) an experientially based interaction between trainees about personal feelings and reactions to clients and the role of the therapist, and (c) a therapeutic context wherein the supervisor provides high levels of the therapeutic conditions to the trainees.

Several studies have tested this third assumption—that the trainee is affected by the level of facilitative conditions offered by the supervisor. Pierce, Carkhuff, and Berenson (1967), as well as Pierce and Schauble (1970, 1971) tested this hypothesis and found support for the idea that trainees who receive supervision from supervisors who offer high or low levels of the Rogerian conditions move in the direction of their supervisors in their ability to offer these conditions to clients. For example, trainees who are lower than their supervisors in empathy increase in this skill, while those who began at a level higher than their supervisors actually begin to decline as a function of supervision. These researchers, however, did not actually measure the level of empathy, warmth, genuineness, and so on offered to trainees. Instead, they estimated the level of conditions offered to trainees by measuring *supervisor-client* interactions, and assumed that supervisors behave the same with trainees in supervision as they do with clients in therapy.

In a test of this premise—that the interactions between supervisors and clients and between supervisors and trainees do not differ significantly—we had supervisors ($N = 5$) tape record actual therapy sessions (Lambert and Beier, 1974) as well as supervisory interviews with 10 clients and 10 trainees. The interactions from these activities were sampled and rated on empathy, regard, genuineness, and specificity with the Carkhuff scales. In addition, they were categorized with the Hill Interaction Matrix, a group interaction process scale, and frequency counts of therapist verbal behavior were thus obtained. Each therapist statement was rated in terms of the content or *topic* and the implied *relationship* of the supervisor to client or trainee. Statements were classified in one of 16 categories, four of which suggest that therapeutic work is taking place (the Fourth Quadrant). The higher the percentage of supervision statements falling in these four cells, the greater the focus on therapeutic work.

Figure 2 suggests the proportion of therapist behavior that might be classified as therapeutic. Overall, two-thirds of the statements in counseling, but only one-third of the statements in supervision, would be classified as therapy oriented. That is, across therapists, clients, and trainees, there is a clear difference (p = .001) between the two situations. Therapists are much less speculative about trainee dynamics, and the trainee is less likely to accept the "patient role." Therapists are also significantly less confrontive in the supervisory session, at least with regard to topics that concern the trainee's personal problems and the therapist-trainee relationship. Therapists were rated as equally respectful and genuine in the two situations. They were, however, significantly less empathic and specific. In fact, they approached facilitative levels of empathy in counseling but were clearly (as rated with the traditional scales) less than understanding of trainee feelings in their supervisory contacts.

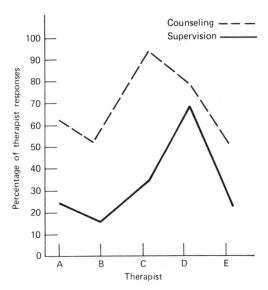

FIGURE 2.   Percentage of each therapist's responses catagorized in the fourth quadrant of the HIM.

Therefore, it does not appear that the facilitative conditions are as high in supervision as in counseling. To what extent a therapeutic climate aids in the acquisition of interpersonal skills is a concern worthy of exploration but, as yet, there is little empirical evidence on this topic.

A related study (Lane, 1974) showed no differential outcome in students as a function of supervisors who were "high" and "low" on the facilitative conditions. And Lennon (1972) showed that differential levels of empathy and respect as offered to trainees in supervision result in different levels of self-exploration, but other hypotheses were not tested. Payne and Gralinsky (1968) tested this hypothesis in an analogue study and found that the learning of empathy was unrelated to supervisor-offered empathy.

Ronnestad (1973) investigated the effects of modeling, feedback, and experiential supervision on the development of trainee empathic communication. In this study, the trainees either watched the supervisor give empathic responses, were given specific feedback about changing their own responding, or participated in a discussion of their feelings in relation to the client. Results suggested that the modeling treatment was more effective than the feedback treatment, which in turn was more effective than the experiential treatment, which was equal to a no-treatment control group.

Grzegorek and Kagan (1974) studied the effects of two training approaches. One emphasized trainee feeling and personal growth; the other emphasized cognitive learning of client dynamics, feelings, and counseling techniques. These different procedures were offered in the context of the Interpersonal Process Recall procedure. The dependent measures included the Affective Sensitivity Scale, Counselor Verbal Response Scale, and tape ratings using the Carkhuff empathy scale. Results showed no significant differences after training between the two training procedures although the affectively oriented training group showed significant increases pre- to post-training on all the criterion measures.

An impression developed in our study (Lambert and Beier, 1974) was that supervisors commonly suggest and model more empathic and otherwise facilitative responses (depending on their own skill as therapists) while behaving in ways that are not perceived as empathic on a moment-by-moment basis. There are, however, serious problems with the typical rating procedures utilized in this area of research, which ignore the basic contract between participants. This contract suggests a degree of trust on the part of the trainee that assumes supervisor understanding. A viable relationship exists but does not require empathy, respect, genuineness, and specificity on a moment-to-moment basis. Learning, therefore, precedes in a relationship that is formed with an implicit contract that the supervisor is understanding and interested in facilitating the growth of the trainee, but the typical rating scales do not capture this implicit contract. While the implicit understanding is important in the formation of a learning contract, it is not necessary for the supervisor to frequently reflect trainee feelings of inadequacy or the like. Nor perhaps is it even desirable for a productive supervisory relationship.

Considerably more research could be carried out in this area. What, for example, is the optimal amount of self exploration, for which trainees, and at what times? If on the average, 33% of a supervisor's responses are "therapeutic," then what are the long- and short-term effects of different supervisory relationships? Can a prescriptive study be undertaken that could clarify the optimal match between trainee and supervisory style?

How Long Lasting Are the Effects of Supervision?

Very few follow-up studies have been reported in the literature, and even when included as part of the research design, follow-up studies are marred by uncontrolled variables. Psychotherapy trainees almost invariably have additional training experiences beyond those included in the research project. Furthermore, follow-up studies have not always applied the same criteria at treatment termination and follow-up. Those studies that have included a follow-up are therefore inconclusive. Pierce and Schauble (1970, 1971), for example, followed trainees who received supervision from either "high" or "low" functioning supervisors (on empathy, regard, genuineness, and concreteness). Those who met with "high" supervisors improved in their skills after supervision. Those trainees who met with low functioning supervisors tended to remain the same or get slightly worse in their interpersonal skills. At a nine month follow-up, 14 counselor-trainees were asked to submit a tape recording of their counseling. The trained judges' ratings of their interactions indicated the continued superiority of the "high" group over the "low" group. The level of conditions trainees offered their clients did not seem to decline during the follow-up period. Unfortunately, the trainees did not appear to be randomly assigned to high and low functioning supervisors.

In contrast to this finding, Spooner and Stone (1977) studied the frequency with which counseling trainees used specifically trained responses in their counseling sessions. The frequency counts were made on the first 30 minutes of actual interviews with clients. These were collected at the end of a pre-practicum experience, during the practicum, and at least three months after training. The response categories included: goal setting; confrontation; reflection/restatement; interpretation/summary; structuring; probing; minimal verbalization; self-disclosure, and information giving. Apparently, training did have an impact on some response tendencies and many of these changes were maintained over time. The use of probing responses, however, increased over time and became the most frequent response used by counselors in actual counseling sessions. On the other hand, confrontation and goal setting were used with decreasing frequency at follow-up.

Gormally, Hill, Gulanick, and McGovern (1975) found that communication skills learned in a 40-hour training group were maintained at the six-month follow-up for their graduate trainees but not for undergraduates. Collingwood (1971) also suggested that while interpersonal skills are learned by undergraduates, they do gradually erode and require retraining.

The results of follow-up studies encourage the view that changes resulting from supervision and training can be maintained without retraining, but many more investigations dealing with the long-term retention and generalization of skills are needed before we will understand the limits of retention.

The General Status of Interpersonal Skills Training Programs

The specification of therapist attitudes and behaviors that contribute to positive personality or behavior change has resulted in some exciting advancements in training and supervision. The amount of research generated on questions related to the development of these attitudes and skills is impressive. The research itself has been a source of additional hypotheses and changes in the requirements and role of supervision in the overall training of therapists.

In my opinion, the importance of these therapist-offered attitudes cannot be underestimated although *research has, at this point, only been able to demonstrate a modestly positive relationship between empathy, regard and genuineness, and psychotherapy outcome* (Lambert, DeJulio, and Stein, 1978; Mitchell, Bozarth, and Krauft, 1977). Another disheartening outcome is the poor results of studies of the more general *therapeutic effects* of training in interpersonal skills.

Carkhuff (1972) has argued that training in relationship skills has a powerful effect on the overall adequacy of trainees. He claims that his model for training (Human Relations Development) has clearly demonstrated positive effects on psychological adjustment and the total functioning of the personality of trainees. In fact, he emphasized that trainee benefits (which supposedly generalize to many life tasks—for example, school performance, work stability, and so on) are the only really significant outcomes of training. To support this contention, he listed 30 studies purported to provide evidence of the strength and efficacy of his helping model. The studies reported by Carkhuff to support this position have been criticized on a number of points (cf. Lambert and DeJulio, 1977). They have failed to specify the nature of treatment and, indeed, its components seem to vary from study to study. Control groups of a comparative type are often missing and, when present, have not been equivalent in expectation, motivation, contact time, and leader skill or enthusiasm. Another major weakness is that the subjects were aware of the criteria for evaluation and, in fact, often trained on the same measures they were later evaluated on. Generally, the studies used to support these training procedures employed criteria that have little or no validity to support their use. It was an infrequent study that used criteria that reflected the real life post-training performance of trainees.

Although training programs—like Carkhuff's—that teach the interpersonal skills derived from Rogers are popular (Aspy, 1972, 1975; Sprinthall, 1972), their impact on therapy outcome is still open to question. Most of the research in this area is so poorly designed, it is no wonder that it has been ignored by major reviews of psychotherapy outcome (Bergin and Suinn, 1975; Luborsky, Singer, and Luborsky, 1975).

Not only is there a growing number of programs that are training people in these interpersonal skills, but Carkhuff (1969a,b) has suggested that there is an increasing number of human relations skills that are important in help-intended communication. He has added several to those already discussed: therapist self-disclosure, concreteness, confrontation, and immediacy. As new interpersonal skills are being specified and taught, there is an ever-widening gap between what is claimed in terms of training program effectiveness, and what has been demonstrated empirically about the efficacy of the facilitative conditions.

The skills training programs mentioned above represent a significant departure from the theory and practice of client-centered psychotherapy as expressed by Rogers. Though Rogers (1975) believed that in the proper environment trainees may become more empathic and genuine, the focus for training has shifted from a somewhat philosophical, existential emphasis on therapist attitudes and beliefs fostered by supervision to a technology for teaching effective and concrete therapist responses.

It is clear that many therapists, especially counselors, are now being trained to use technically sound responses. This, however, seems to be something quite different from the "effective moments of change" alluded to in the following quote from Rogers:

> I feel that when I'm being effective as a therapist, I enter the relationship as a subjective person, not as a scrutinizer, not as a scientist. I feel, too, that when I am most effective, then somehow I am relatively whole in that relationship, or the word that has meaning to me is "transparent." Then I think, too, that in such a relationship I feel a willingness for this other person to be what he is. I call this "acceptance." And then another aspect of it which is important to me is that I think in those moments I am able to sense with a good deal of clarity, the way his experience seems to him. . . . Then in addition to those things on my part, my client or the person with whom I'm working is able to sense something of those attitudes in me, then it seems to me that there is a real, experiential meeting of persons, in which each of us is changed (Buber and Friedman, 1965, pp. 169–170).

ADDITIONAL RESEARCH ON SUPERVISION

Several other research concerns can be identified and provide some interesting results. Hester, Wertz, Anchor, and Roback (1976) studied the relationship of supervisor skillfullness and supervisor-supervisee attitude similarity to attraction of the supervisee to the supervisor. The results indicated that perceived skillfullness had a much stronger impact on supervisee attraction to supervisors than the experimentally manipulated similarity in participants' attitudes.

Silvers (1974) studied changes in trainee empathy, congruence, and client behavior ratings as a function of differential matching on a personality characteristic. Trainees who were considered high, medium, or low on the California Psychological Inventory Dominance Scale were paired with supervisors considered high or low on this scale. No significant results were obtained.

Guttman (1973) studied the defensive behavior of trainees in supervisory sessions. Twenty subjects were randomly assigned to either an experimental or a control group. The experimental trainees were exposed to (a) a manual describing trainee defensive and nondefensive responses to supervisor confrontations, (b) videotaped models of trainee responses to supervisor confrontation demonstrating defensive and nondefensive behaviors; (c) discussion of the models; and (d) viewing of the trainee's own counseling session with feedback from the supervisor and the instruction to try to respond nondefensively.

The control trainees played a videotape of their counseling and received feedback with the instruction to think about the feedback and ways of altering behavior in counselor supervision. The dependent measure was a Lickert-type rating scale of defensive behavior rated by three judges trained in its use. For rating purposes, supervisory sessions were videotaped and the last eight-minute segment was rated. Results suggested that the experimental group was able to significantly reduce their defensive behavior as a result of the training offered. The control subjects did not change their behavior. Unfortunately, no follow-up data is presented, and the results were not shown to generalize beyond the experimental situation. Nevertheless, the study is an example of a creative attempt to make supervision a more productive experience.

Kepecs (1978) elaborated on the use of 10-minute typescripts of therapy interactions in supervisory sessions. These typescripts are coded with a modification of Gottschalk's process scales. The supervisor and therapist then analyze the patient's focal conflict and the meanings they had for therapy interventions. This interesting didactic procedure, founded in psychoanalytic theory and intended to improve the understanding and ultimate performance of the therapist, has not been employed in a research design that clearly states the desired training outcomes.

Several different studies have examined the use of "bug-in-the-ear" devices to provide immediate feedback in actual counseling sessions. McClure and Vriend (1976) provide an interesting example of studies in this area. They studied 84 counseling sessions with counselors using cordless microphone in one ear. They were interested in whether abbreviated or extended clues were most effective, the extent to which trainer formulation of cues made a difference, the importance of cue frequency and the effects of different supervisory styles on the trainees. Overall, the results appeared positive for all the procedures, but differences in procedures could not be identified.

Tentoni and Robb (1977) contrasted outcomes in clients seen by counselors with a "bug-in-the-ear" and those seeing counselors who were not receiving this type of feedback. Clients of counselors in the experimental group rated their counselors on the Counselor Evaluation Rating Scale as being more effective.

Many other isolated studies have been reported and are relevant but fail to provide a coherent picture that can be used to suggest one approach to supervision over another (cf. Silverman and Guinn 1974, who compared immediate feedback, delayed feedback and co-counseling supervision strategies). Often these studies do not build upon the existing literature and contain serious shortcomings (e.g., nonrandom assignment of trainees, lack of a control group, etc.) It is hoped that research on supervision will continue to increase and contribute to, as well as derive from, training practices.

SUPERVISORY AND TRAINING OUTCOME CRITERIA

In order to measure the effects of training and supervision it is necessary to use procedures which reliably reflect the changes that are occurring in the trainee. Clearly, this aspect of research has a powerful effect on the supervisory process in that the measurement of training outcome requires the clear specification of the goals and methods of supervision. Hopefully, the use of meaningful and valid outcome measures will greatly facilitate discovery of the particular teaching procedures which are most valuable.

What Are the Goals of Supervision?

These goals can be classed into two broad categories: personal growth and skill development. Under the heading of personal growth are numerous changes in cognition and feeling. The student becomes more aware of self and of behavioral patterns and tendencies, resolves conflicts, becomes less anxious and more confident, and—one hopes—more knowledgeable. Changes in this domain have normally been assessed with traditional personality inventories. These devices will not be reviewed here. Skill development on the other hand includes the changes mentioned in the above areas, as well as the development of greater competence in making specific interventions with patients.

Measuring devices that have been used to assess changes in skill development in trainees are listed in Figure 3. The measuring devices are categorized by the *source* of the data. This is not only a convenient way to arrange this material, but it is necessary because in outcome and process measurement there is often a failure for measures collected from different sources—such as therapist, patient, clinical judge, significant other, and so on—to agree.

FIGURE 3. Measures of trainee interviewing skills and other training outcomes

Instrument name and primary reference	Primary area of assessment	Source of data	Type of measure
Carkhuff Discrimination Index (Carkhuff, 1969a)	Interpersonal skills	Deviation from expert	Paper-pencil—response provided
Interview Rating Scale (Anderson and Anderson, 1962)	Rapport, ideal relationship	Client	Paper-pencil—response determined
Barrett-Lennard Relationship Inventory (Barrett-Lennard, 1962)	Therapist-client relationship	Client	Paper-pencil report of feelings
Counselor Effectiveness Scale (Ivey, et al., 1968)	Therapist-client relationship	Client	Paper-pencil report of feelings
Counseling Evaluation Inventory (Linden, Stone, and Shertzer, 1965)	Therapist-client relationship	Client	Paper-pencil report of feelings
Truax Relationship Questionnaire (Truax and Carkhuff, 1967)	Therapist-client relationship	Client	Paper-pencil report of feelings
Hogan Empathy Scale (Hogan, 1969)	Therapist personality trait	Trainee	Paper-pencil personality test
Trainee Value of Cues Scale (McClure and Vriend, 1976)	Intervention style	Trainee	Trainee fills out questionnaire
Therapist Orientations Questionnaire (Sundland and Barker, 1962)	Response preference	Trainee	Paper-pencil—response determined
Affective Sensitivity Scale (Kagan, et al., 1967)	Interviewing skills	Judges ratings	Simulation—response provided
Microcounseling Skill Discrimination Scale (Lee, Zingle, Patterson, Ivey, and Haase, 1976)	Interviewing skills	Judges ratings	Simulation—response provided
Psychotherapy Session Report (Orlinsky and Howard, 1975)	Reactions to session	Judges, trainee, and client	Paper-pencil—response provided—response free
Porter Test of Counselor Attitudes (Porter, 1950)	Response preference	Judges ratings	Type script—response provided
Counselor Training Questionnaire (Rosenthal, 1977)	Response preference	Judges ratings	Type script—response provided
Flanders Interaction System (Amidon, 1965)	Verbal behavior	Trained rater	Frequency counts of behavior
Ideal Therapeutic Relationship Scale (Authier and Gustafson, 1975)	Therapist-client relationship	Trained rater	Judgment of quality of relationship

Instrument	Skill type	Rater	Data collection method
Interaction Process Analysis (Bales, 1950)	Verbal behavior	Trained rater	Frequency counts of behavior
Carkhuff Communication Index (Carkhuff, 1969a)	Interpersonal skills	Trained rater	Paper-pencil—response free
Carkhuff Scales of Empathy, Respect, Genuineness, Self Disclosure, Specificity, Confrontation and Immediacy (Carkhuff, 1969b)	Interpersonal skills	Trained rater	Judges ratings—response free
Counseling Strategies Checklist (Hackney and Nye, 1973)	Interviewing skills	Trained rater	Frequency counts of behavior
The Depth of Interpretation Scale (Harway, Dittmann, Raush, Bordin, and Rigler, 1955)	Verbal behavior	Trained rater	Judges ratings—response free
Hill Interaction Matrix (Hill, 1965)	Verbal behavior	Trained rater	Judges ratings—response free
Therapist Activity Level Scales (Howe and Pope, 1961)	Verbal behavior	Trained rater	Judges ratings—response free
Counselor Verbal Response Scale (Kagan, et al., 1967)	Interviewing skills	Trained rater	Simulation—response free, live interviews

As can be seen, the devices that have been typically employed are widely varied and have different purposes. Even when two devices have the same purpose (i.e., assess the same component of trainee change), they differ in (a) the focus of evaluation, such as the trainee or the client; (b) data gathering techniques, such as structured personality tests, or actual interactions with patients who have sought help; (c) the fact that the data provided sometimes comes from the client, sometimes from a supervisor, and frequently from the trainee; and (d) the fact that data is collected at different times, both during and after counseling. All these dissimilarities, plus usual errors of measurement, have the cumulative effect of making it very difficult for agreement to be reached between measures.

The research on empathy is a classic example of the measurement problems in this area. Almost all psychotherapists and behavior therapists agree that the therapist's ability to understand the patient and communicate this understanding to the patient is a very important part of therapy. Even so, there is no single measure of this process which has proven valid. The following studies make this readily apparent: Bozarth and Grace (1970), Caracena and Vicory (1969), Carkhuff and Burstein (1970), Fish (1970), Hansen, Moore, and Carkhuff (1968), Hill (1974), Kurtz and Grummon (1972), McWhirter (1973), Rogers, Gendlin, Kiesler, and Truax (1967), Truax (1966), and Van Der Veen (1970). The results of these studies have been summarized by Lambert, DeJulio, and Stein (1978). They clearly demonstrate the low agreement between measures of empathy.

It is possible that greater agreement could be reached if methodological problems were eliminated. For example, the Relationship Inventory is typically collected after five therapy sessions, whereas the Accurate Empathy Scale is typically applied three times per session to brief three-minute therapist-client interactions. It would probably be a worthwhile endeavor to train clients to discriminate between empathy, warmth, and genuineness. These clients could then rate therapists in units similar to those used with the Truax Scales. This procedure may reduce the tendency of clients to rate therapists in a global way. Thus, the clients' more specific attention to particular therapist attitudes may make their perception of therapy more easy to compare with the ratings of judges. This procedure, or other similar variations in methodology might possibly provide the validity so conspicuously lacking at present in the measurement of therapist effectiveness.

A variety of methods have been used to simplify the measurement of training outcome. The most ambitious designs have involved the measurement of trainee behaviors such as empathy and confrontation during therapy with actual clients. Less ambitious but still rigorous have been designs that measured similar trainee behavior with persons invited to act as patients. These "role play" situations allow for considerable experimental control, but unfortunately they require the assumption that the results in this situation will generalize to situations in which "role playing" is not involved. A step further from actual counseling has been the use of a coached client who plays a designated role. Because of a lack of a personal relationship, the use of a filmed or videotaped client to whom the therapist responds verbally (on tape), by writing out a response, or by picking a response from those provided by the experimenter, is still further from actual counseling.

Another simulation least like counseling has involved the use of a typescript of client expressions. Finally, some researchers have used a questionnaire to ask the therapist to indicate how he or she thinks he or she responds in the therapy situation.

Research on these measurement procedures has been disappointing. Porter's (1950) test—the first actual simulation, and one which reflected obvious pre-post training changes—never was found to correlate with actual counselor behavior. More recent simulations have followed this trend. Butler and Hansen (1973), for example, found no relationship between written and oral performance after training. Perry (1975) also found no carry-over from simulated counseling and a 15-minute live interview. Gormally, et al. (1975) found written responses and interviews with a volunteer client were not significantly correlated. Similar results were reported by Rosenthal (1977).

In general, it can be concluded that *the more distant the criterion measure is from the actual criterion (performance in psychotherapy), the less representative it will be. Stated more strongly, simulated counseling criteria, especially paper-pencil devices, seemingly have little relationship to the phenomena they are supposed to represent.* This appears to be even more true, however, for measures that make no attempt to simulate situational stimuli. The Hogan Empathy Scale, for example, relies on a traditional True-False personality test format (many of the items come directly from the CPI). This scale has shown no relationship with other measures of empathy, nor any relationship to therapy outcome.

The following conclusions seem to be warranted by the current review of training outcome measures:

1. The most useful of these measures focus on the specific behaviors of therapists. They minimize inferences drawn by the raters and concentrate on observable behavior. Specific measures would include, for example, the Counselor Verbal Response Scale, Counseling Strategies Checklist, and Matarazzo Check List of Therapist Behavior. Frequency counts of carefully specified behaviors have proved quite useful and enjoy continued use.

2. The scales developed by Rogers's students (mainly Truax and Carkhuff) have many problems associated with their use. Consideration should be given to the discontinuation of their frequent application in research studies. They are time-consuming and expensive to employ properly. They require considerable inference on the part of judges and quite possibly are not measuring the same dimensions when used by different experimenters. Finally, they do not have a strong relationship with psychotherapy outcome despite frequent use in the past.

3. The most convincing procedure has been the evaluation of training through criteria from several sources. This is considered absolutely necessary in psychotherapy outcome research and seems desirable in the domain of supervisory research. Frequency counts of specified therapist behaviors provide a valuable source of information from the point of view of ideal therapist behavior. It seems desirable to collect data about the therapist-

trainee from clients and from the trainees themselves. The Barrett-Lennard Relationship Inventory has the advantage of having been used in numerous outcome studies and it has been shown to have a modest relationship to psychotherapy outcome. It has several shortcomings but, at this time, is perhaps the best measure of the therapeutic relationship as it is perceived by the client. The trainee, of course, can provide valuable information about learning. This can be obtained through a variety of self-report measures such as the Trainee Value of Cues Scale (McClure and Vriend, 1976).

4. *Devices that are based on simulations of psychotherapy, especially those that rely on a fixed client role and fixed therapist responses, but also those that leave the trainee free to construct his own response, are not yet acceptable and convincing training criteria.* In part, their use depends upon the extent to which researchers and supervisors wish to generalize their results. As long as no inference is made suggesting that changes on these measures reflect similar changes in other situations, such as actual therapy sessions, their use is acceptable but of limited value. However, there is at present little information to allow generalization to actual performance and much information to the contrary.

5. The most persuasive studies of the effects of training and supervision will include an analysis of trainee *behaviors* with actual clients, as well as a measure of the effects of these behaviors on clients. If, for example, a trainee is being supervised specifically on variables that are supposed to affect the therapist-client relationship, then not only is a measure of those variables necessary, but some measure of the quality of the relationship is also called for. It would also be ideal to test the effects of supervision by examining patient outcome. Given the state of empirical findings in this area, however, this remains an ideal that will not be achieved in the near future.

SUMMARY AND CONCLUSIONS

A survey of research on supervision of counselors and psychotherapists suggests a number of conclusions and recommendations.

Despite the agreed-upon importance of the supervisor relationship, very few studies have actually focused upon supervision. More studies are clearly needed.

Most research in the area has focused on the complete novice, or even paraprofessionals. Thus, the issues studied have usually centered on the acquisition of elementary interviewing skills. Some research needs to be done on the outcome of supervision with the more experienced student or practicing psychotherapist. Also, much more research on variables other than basic facilitative interpersonal skills is needed.

The clear specification of the goals of supervision has resulted in training methods that speed up the acquisition of knowledge actual performance. Thus, it has been found that trainees can learn to be empathic with their clients more quickly when they are systematically trained than when they are provided with "traditional supervision." This suggests that supervision will become less necessary and important as more and more of the causal components in psychotherapy become known. The goals of supervision will change over time and, therefore, so will research questions. Still, a technology of helping is more of a hope than a reality.

Research studies have generally not dealt with the personal characteristics of the supervisor, or techniques of supervision in *interaction* with the personal qualities of trainees. Thus, future research will need to identify in a prescriptive sense the ideal learning environment for given students at particular times. Knowledge of the ideal combination of these variables may never be fully realized, but will certainly not be realized without empirical study. The possibility of prescriptive supervision should be explored. Some comparisons that come to mind are those that involve varying the level of experience of trainees and type of supervisor focus, such as didactic versus affective. In addition to trainee experience, these trainee variables might be worth exploring in a prescriptive design: anxiety level, open-mindedness, defensiveness, cognitive flexibility, and locus of control. In order to avoid some of the unpredictive results obtained in psychotherapy research it is suggested that these variables be assessed by means of situation specific measures. The literature on the supervisor suggests a number of experimental procedures: High versus low structure, trainee focus versus client focus, and didactic versus experiential, to mention but a few.

The success we have in measuring the outcome of supervision is obviously dependent on our ability to sense the differential effects of the supervisor. Many criterion measures have been developed and used in research studies. Far too many research reports have used criteria of dubious validity. The most acceptable outcome measures are those that are made to be used in the actual counseling relationship. Many psychotherapy process measures can be used for this purpose and are preferable to devices that rely on a simulation of the counseling relationship. Research that does not show that trainee learning actually generalizes to live interviews is, at best, of limited value.

While the above conclusions and recommendations focus on the problems and difficulties of research on supervision, this is not meant to detract from the progress that has been made in this area. We are much closer to understanding the many effective processes that ultimately affect the well being of both trainees and the clients who they serve.

ACKNOWLEDGMENTS

I would like to thank Lorraine Morris and Pat Lowry for their helpful comments on this chapter. I also employed several ideas offered by Professors Norma Rohde, and Burton Kelly, who read an early draft of this manuscript.

REFERENCES

Amidon, E. J. A technique for analyzing counselor-counselee interaction. In J. F. Adams (Ed.), *Counseling and Guidance: A summary view.* New York: Macmillan, 1965.

Anderson, R. P., and Anderson, G. V. Development of an instrument for measuring rapport. *Personnel and Guidance Journal,* 1962, *41,* 18–24.

Aspy, D. N. Reaction to Carkhuff's articles. *Counseling Psychologist,* 1972, *3,* 35–41.

Aspy, D. N. Empathy: Let's get the hell on with it. *Counseling Psychologist,* 1975, *5,* 10–14.

Authier, J., and Gustafson, K. Application of supervised and nonsupervised microcounseling paradigms in the training of paraprofessionals. *Journal of Counseling Psychology,* 1975, *22,* 74–78.

Bales, R. F. *Interaction Process Analysis: A method for the study of small groups.* Reading, Mass.: Addison-Wesley, 1950.

Barrett-Lennard, G. T. Dimensions of perceived therapist response as causal factors in therapeutic change. *Psychological Monographs,* 1962, *76* (43, Whole No. 453).

Barrington, B. Changes in psychotherapeutic responses during training in therapy. *Journal of Counseling Psychology,* 1958, *5,* 120–125.

Berenson, B. G., Carkhuff, R. R., and Myrus, P. The interpersonal and training of college students. *Journal of Counseling Psychology,* 1966, *13,* 441–446.

Bergin, A. E., and Suinn, R. M. Individual psychotherapy and behavior therapy. *Annual Review of Psychology,* 1975, *26,* 509–556.

Biasco, F., and Redfering, D. C. Effects of counselor supervision on group counseling: Client perceived outcomes. *Counselor Education and Supervision,* 1976, *16,* 216–220

Blocksma, D. D., and Porter, E. H., Jr. A short term training program in client centered counseling. *Journal of Consulting Psychology,* 1947, *11,* 55–60.

Boyd, J. D., II. Microcounseling for a verbal response set: Differential effects of two methods of supervision. *Journal of Counseling Psychology,* 1973, *20,* 97–98.

Bozarth, J. D., and Grace, D. P. Objective ratings and client perception of therapeutic conditions with university counseling center clients. *Journal of Clinical Psychology,* 1970, *26,* 117–118.

Buber, M., and Friedman, M. *The knowledge of man.* New York: Harper and Row, 1965.

Butler, E., and Hansen, J. Facilitative training: Acquisition, retention, and modes of assessment. *Journal of Counseling Psychology,* 1973, *20,* 60–65.

Campbell, R., Kagan, N., and Krathwohl, D. The development and validation of a scale to measure affective sensitivity (empathy). *Journal of Counseling Psychology,* 1971, *18,* 407–412.

Canada, R. M. Immediate reinforcement vs. delayed reinforcement in teaching a basic interview technique. *Journal of Counseling Psychology,* 1973, *20,* 395–398.

Caracena, P., and Victory, J. Correlates of phenomenological and judged empathy. *Journal of Consulting Psychology,* 1969, *16,* 510–515.

Carkhuff, R. R. *Helping and Human Relations* (Vol. 1). New York: Holt, Rinehart, and Winston, 1969.(a)

Carkhuff, R. R. *Helping and Human Relations* (Vol. 2). New York: Holt, Rinehart, and Winston, 1969.(b)

Carkhuff, R. R. Rejoinder: What's it all about any way? Some reflections on helping and human resource development models. *Counseling Psychologist,* 1972, *3,* 79–87.

Carkhuff, R. R., and Burstein, J. Objective therapist and client ratings of therapist-offered facilitative conditions of moderate to low functioning therapists. *Journal of Clinical Psychology,* 1970, *26,* 394–395.

Carkhuff, R. R., and Truax, C. B. Training in counseling and psychotherapy: An evaluation of an integrated didactic and experiential approach. *Journal of Consulting Psychology,* 1965, *29,* 333–336.

Collingwood, T. Retention and retraining of interpersonal communications skills. *Journal of Clinical Psychology,* 1971, *27,* 294–296.

Cormier, L. S., Hackney, H., and Segrist, A. Three counselor training models: A comparative study. *Counselor Education and Supervision,* 1974, *14,* 95–104.

Dalton, R. F., Jr., and Sundblad, L. M. Using principles of social learning in training for communication of empathy. *Journal of Counseling Psychology,* 1976, *23,* 454–457.

Dellis, N. O., and Stone, H. K. (Eds.). *The training of psychotherapists: a multi-disciplinary approach.* Baton Rouge, La.: Louisiana State University Press, 1960.

Demos, G. D. The application of certain principles of client-centered therapy to short-term vocational-educational counseling. *Journal of Counseling Psychology,* 1964, *11,* 280–284.

Demos, G. D., and Zuwaylif, F. H. Counselor movement as a result of an intensive six-week training program in counseling. *Personnel and Guidance Journal,* 1963, *42,* 125–128.

Deshaies, G. The effects of group sensitivity training and group didactic-experiential training on the accurate empathy of counselor trainees. (Doctoral dissertation, Boston University, 1974). *Dissertation Abstracts International,* 1974, *35,* 3421A–3422A (University Microfilms No. 74–26, 440).

Doster, J. Effects of instruction, modeling and role rehearsal on interview verbal behavior. *Journal of Consulting and Clinical,* 1972, *39,* 202–209.

Dowall, R. L. *An experimental study of systematic prepracticium counselor training.* Unpublished doctoral dissertation, Boston University, 1973.

Dowling, T. H., and Franz, T. T. The influence of facilitative relationship on imitative learning. *Journal of Counseling Psychology,* 1975, *22,* 259–263.

Ekstein, R., and Wallerstein, R. S. *The teaching and learning of psychotherapy.* New York: Basic Books, 1958.

Fish, J. M. Empathy and the reported emotional experiences of beginning psychotherapists. *Journal of Consulting and Clinical Psychology,* 1970, *35,* 64–69.

Forestandi, R. N. The supervision of pre-practicum counseling experiences; development of a counselor verbal response set in neophyte counselors. (Doctoral dissertation, West Virginia University, 1973). *Dissertation Abstracts International,* 1973, *34,* 1613A (University Microfilms No. 73–23, 866).

Forge, H. L. Comparison of three variations of microtraining in teaching basic interviewing skills to counselor trainees. (Doctoral dissertation, University of Missouri, 1973). *Dissertation Abstracts International,* 1974, *35,* 3867A (University Microfilms No. 74–1746).

Fry, P. S. Effects of desensitization treatment on core-condition training. *Journal of Counseling Psychology,* 1973, *20,* 214–219.

Gelso, C. J. Inhibition due to recording and clients' evaluation of counseling. *Psychological Reports,* 1973, *31,* 675–677.

Gerkin, C. An objective method for evaluating training programs in counseling psychology. *Journal of Counseling Psychology,* 1969, *16,* 227–237.

Gormally, J., Hill, C. E., Gulanick, N., and McGovern, T. The persistence of communication skills for undergraduate and graduate trainees. *Journal of Clinical Psychology,* 1975, *31,* 369–372.

Gottman, J., and Markman, H. J. Experimental designs in psychotherapy research. In S. Garfield and A. E. Bergin (Eds.), *Handbook of psychotherapy and behavior change* (2nd ed.). New York: Wiley, 1978.

Grzegorek, A. E., and Kagan, N. A study of the meaning of self-awareness in correctional counselor training. *Criminal Justice and Behavior,* 1974, *1,* 99–122.

Guttman, M. A. J. Reduction of defensive behavior of counselor trainees during counseling supervision. *Counselor Education and Supervision,* 1973, *13,* 294–299.

Haase, R. F., Dimattia, D., and Guttman, M. Training of support personnel in three human relations skills: A systematic one year follow-up. *Counselor Education and Supervision,* 1972, *11,* 194–199.

Hackney, H. L., and Nye, S. *Counseling stratagies and objectives.* Englewood Cliffs, N. J.: Prentice Hall, 1973.

Hansen, J. C., and Barker, E. N. Experimenting and the supervisory relationship. *Journal of Counseling Psychology,* 1964, *11,* 107–111.

Hansen, J., Moore, G., and Carkhuff, R. The differential relationships of objective and client perceptions of counseling. *Journal of Clinical Psychology,* 1968, *24,* 244–246.

Hart, G. A programmed approach to increased open-mindedness. *Journal of Counseling Psychology,* 1973, *20,* 569–570.

Harway, N. E., Dittmann, A. T., Raush, H. L., Bordin, E. S., and Rigler, D. The measurement of depth of interpretation. *Journal of Consulting Psychology,* 1955, *19,* 247–253.

Hefele, T., and Hurst, M. W. Interpersonal skill measurements: Perception, validity and utility. *Counseling Psychologist,* 1972, *3,* 62–69.

Hester, L. R., Wertz, L. J., Anchor, K. N., and Roback, H. B. Supervisor attraction as a function of level of supervisor skillfulness and supervisees' perceived similarity. *Journal of Counseling Psychology,* 1976, *23,* 254–258.

Hill, W. F. *Hill Interaction Matrix.* Los Angeles: University of Southern California, Youth Study Center, 1965.

Hill, C. E. A comparison of the perceptions of a therapy session by clients, therapists, and objective judges. *JSAS Catalog of Selected Documents in Psychology,* 1974, *4,* 16. (Ms. No. 564)

Hoch, E. C., Ross, A. D., and Winder, C. G. Conference on the professional preparation of clinical psychologists; A summary. *American Psychologist,* 1966, *21,* 42–52.

Hogan, R. Development of an empathy scale. *Journal of Consulting and Clinical Psychology,* 1969, *33,* 307–316.

Howe, E. S., and Pope, B. An empirical scale of therapist verbal activity level in the initial interview. *Journal of Consulting Psychology,* 1961, *25,* 510–520.

Ivey, A. E. *Microcounseling: Innovations in interviewing training.* Springfield, Ill.: Charles C. Thomas, 1971.

Ivey, A. E., Normington, C. J. Miller, D. C., Merrill, W.H., and Haase, R. F. Microcounseling and attending behavior: An approach to prepracticium counselor training. *Journal of Counseling Psychology, Monograph Supplement,* 1968, *15,* (5), 1–12.

Kagan, N., Krathwohl, D. R., et al. Studies in human interaction: Interpersonal process recall stimulated by video-tape. Final Report, U. S. Office of Education, Project No. 5-0800. East Lansing: Michigan State University Educational Publication Series, 1967.

Kepecs, J. G. Teaching psychotherapy by use of brief typescripts. *American Journal of Psychotherapy,* 1978, *20,* 383–393.

Kiesler, D. J. Some myths of psychotherapy research and the search for a paragigm. *Psychological Bulletin,* 1966, *65,* 110–136.

Kingdon, M. A. A cost/benefit analysis of the interpersonal process recall technique. *Journal of Counseling Psychology,* 1975, *22,* 353–357.

Kuna, D. J. Lecturing, reading, and modeling in counselor restatement training. *Journal of Counseling Psychology,* 1975, *22,* 542–546.

Kurtz, R., and Grummon, D. Different approaches to the measurement of therapist empathy and their relationship to therapy outcomes. *Journal of Consulting and Clinical Psychology,* 1972, *3,* 106–116.

Lambert, M. J., and Beier, E. G. Supervisory and counseling process: A comparative study. *Counselor Education and Supervision,* 1974, *14,* 54–60.

Lambert, M. J., and DeJulio, S. S. Outcomes in Carkhuff's human resource development: Where's the donut? *Counseling Psychologist,* 1977, *6,* 79–86.

Lambert, M. J., DeJulio, S. S., and Stein, D. M. Therapist interpersonal skills: Process, outcome, methodological considerations, and recommendations for future research. *Psychological Bulletin,* 1978, *85,* 467–489.

Lane, R. G. *The influence of supervision on the trainee's development of facilitative skills in counseling.* Unpublished doctoral dissertation, Arizona State University, 1974.

Lee, D. Y., Zingle, H. W., Patterson, J. G., Ivey, A. E., and Haase, R. F. Development and validation of a Microcounseling Skill Discrimination Scale. *Journal of Counseling Psychology,* 1976, *23,* 468–472.

Lennon, W. J. *A study of the effects of counseling practicium supervisor offered facilitative conditions on supervisee self-exploration.* Unpublished doctoral dissertation, University of Florida, 1972.

Linden, J. D., Stone, S. C., and Shertzer, B. Development and evaluation of an inventory for rating counseling. *Personnel and Guidance Journal,* 1965, *44,* 267–276.

Lister, J. L. Development of a scale for the measurement of empathic understanding. *Journal of Counseling Psychology,* 1970, *17,* 360–366.

London, P. *The modes and morals of psychotherapy.* New York: Holt, Rinehart and Winston, 1964.

Luborsky, L., Singer, B., and Luborsky, L. A comparative study of psychotherapies: Is it true that "everyone has won and all deserve prizes"? *Archives of General Psychiatry,* 1975, *32,* 995–1008.

McClure, W. J., and Vriend, J. Training counselors using absentee-cuing system. *Canadian Counselor,* 1976, *10,* 120–126.

McWhirter, J. J. Two measures of the facilitative conditions: A correlation study. *Journal of Counseling Psychology*, 1973, *20*, 317–320.

Matarazzo, R. G. Research on the teaching and learning of psychotherapeutic skills. In S. Garfield and A. E. Bergin (Eds.), *Handbook of Psychotherapy and Behavior Change* (2nd ed.), New York: Wiley, 1978.

Matarazzo, J. D. and Wiens, A. N. Speech correlates of empathy and outcome. *Behavior Modification* (in press).

Matarazzo, R. G., Phillips, J. S., Wiens, A. N., and Saslow, G. Learning the art of interviewing: A study of what beginning students do and their pattern of change. *Psychotherapy: Theory, Research and Practice*, 1965, *2*, 49–60.

Mitchell, K. M., Bozarth, J. D., and Krauft, C. C. A reappraisal of the therapeutic effectiveness of accurate empathy, nonpossesive warmth, and genuineness. In A. S. Gurman and A. M. Razin (Eds.), *Effective Psychotherapy*. New York: Pergamon, 1977.

Moreland, J. R., Ivey, A. E., and Phillips, J. S. An evaluation of microcounseling as an interviewer training tool. *Journal of Consulting and Clinical Psychology*, 1973, *41*, 294–300.

Munger, P. F., and Johnson, L. A. Changes in attitudes associated with an NDEA counseling and guidance institute. *Personnel and Guidance Journal*, 1960, *38*, 751–753.

Myrick, R. D., and Kelly, F. D. A scale for evaluating practicium students in counseling and supervision. *Counselor Education and Supervision*, 1971, *10*, 330–336.

Olson, L. R. *The effects of immediate and delayed feedback on counselor trainees' acquisition of two interview behaviors.* Unpublished doctoral dissertation, East Texas State University, 1973.

Orlinsky, D. E., and Howard, K. I. *Varieties of Psychotherapeutic Experiences: Multivariate analysis of patients' and therapists' reports.* New York: Teachers College Press, 1975.

Parker, C. A. (Ed.). *Counseling Theories and Counselor Education.* Boston: Houghton Mifflin, 1968.

Payne, P.A., and Gralinski, D. M. Effects of supervision style and empathy upon counselor learning. *Journal of Counseling Psychology*, 1968, *15*, 517–521.

Payne, P.A., Weiss, S. D., and Kapp, R. A. Didactic, experiential, and modeling factors in the learning of empathy. *Journal of Counseling Psychology*, 1972, *19*, 425–429.

Perry, M. A. Modeling and Instructions in training for counselor empathy. *Journal of Counseling Psychology*, 1975, *22*, 173–179.

Peters, G. A., Cormier, L. S., and Cormier, W. H. Effects of modeling, rehearsal, feedback, and remediation on acquisition of a counseling strategy. *Journal of Counseling Psychology*, 1978, *25*, 231–237.

Pierce, R. M., Carkhuff, R. R., and Berenson, B. G. The effects of high and low functioning counselors upon counselors in training. *Journal of Clinical Psychology*, 1967, *23*, 212–215.

Pierce, R. M., and Schauble, P. G. Graduate training of facilitative counselors: The effects of individual supervision. *Journal of Counseling Psychology*, 1970, *17*, 210–215.

Pierce, R. M., and Schauble, P. G. Study on the effects of individual supervision in graduate school training. *Journal of Counseling Psychology*, 1971, *18*, 186–187.

Porter, E. H., Jr. A simple measure of counselor attitudes. In E. G. Williamson (Ed.), *Trends in Student Personnel Work.* Minneapolis: University of Minnesota Press, 1950.

Richardson, J. E., Jr. The effectiveness of a group process module on the counselor trainee's empathic understanding. (Doctoral dissertation, Texas A & M University 1974). *Dissertation Abstracts International,* 1974, *35,* 1989A–1990A (University Microfilms No. 74–21, 217).

Robinson, V. P. *The dynamics of supervision under functional controls.* Philadelphia: University of Pennsylvania, 1949.

Rogers, C. R. A theory of therapy, personality, and interpersonal relationships, as developed in the client-centered framework. In S. Koch (Ed.), *Psychology: A Study of a Science. Vol. 3: Formulations of the person and the social context.* New York: McGraw-Hill, 1959.

Rogers, C. R. Empathic: An unappreciated way of being. *Counseling Psychologist,* 1975, *5,* 2–10.

Rogers, C. R., Gendlin, E., Kiesler, D., and Truax, C. B. *The therapeutic relationship and its impact.* Madison, Wis.: University of Wisconsin Press, 1967.

Ronnestad, M. H. Effects of modeling, feedback, and experiential supervision on beginning counseling students' communication of empathic understanding. (Doctoral dissertation, University of Missouri, 1973). *Dissertation Abstracts International,* 1974, *35,* 6985A–6985A (University Microfilms No. 74–9982).

Rosenthal, N. R. A prescriptive approach for counselor training. *Journal of Counseling Psychology,* 1977, *24,* 231–237.

Ross, G. N. *A comparison of three treatment methods on the counseling effectiveness of counseling candidates in the counseling practicium.* Unpublished doctoral dissertation, University of Georgia, 1973.

Silverman, M. S. Practicium perceptions of initial interviews: Client counselor divergence. *Counselor Education and Supervision,* 1973, *13,* 158–161.

Silverman, M. S., and Guinn, P. F. Co-counseling supervision in practicium. *Counselor Education and Supervision,* 1974, *14,* 256–260.

Silvers, D. L., III. Effects of differential supervisor-trainee dominance pairings on two dimensions of counselor trainee behavior. (Doctoral dissertation, University of Maryland, 1974). *Dissertation Abstracts International,* 1974, *35,* 3435A–3436A. (University Microfilms No. 74–29, 110)

Spooner, S. E., and Stone, S. C. Maintenance of specific counseling skills over time. *Journal of Counseling Psychology,* 1977, *24,* 66–71.

Sprinthall, N. Human resource training: A response. *Counseling Psychologist,* 1972, *3,* 57–61.

Stone, G. L., and Vance, A. Instructions, modeling and rehearsal: Implications for training. *Journal of Counseling Psychology,* 1976, *23,* 272–279.

Strupp, H. H., and Hadley, S. W. Specific versus nonspecific factors in psychotherapy: A controlled study of outcome. *Archives of General Psychiatry,* (in press).

Sundland, D. M., and Barker, E. N. The orientations of psychotherapists. *Journal of Consulting Psychology,* 1962, *26,* 201–212.

Tentoni, S. C., and Robb, G. P. Improving the counseling practicum through immediate radio feedback. *College Student Journal,* 1977, *12,* 279–283.

Tosi, D. J., and Eshbaugh, D. M. A cognitive-experiential approach to the interpersonal and intrapersonal development of counselors and therapists. *Journal of Clinical Psychology,* 1978, *34,* 494–500.

Toukmanian, S. G., and Rennie, D. L. Microcounseling versus human relations training: Relative effectiveness with undergraduate trainees. *Journal of Counseling Psychology,* 1975, *22,* 345–352.

Truax, C. B. Therapist empathy, warmth, and genuineness and patient personality change in group psychotherapy: A comparison between interaction unit measures, time sample measures, and patient perception measures. *Journal of Clinical Psychology,* 1966, *22,* 225–229.

Truax, C. B., and Carkhuff, R. R. *Toward Effective Counseling and Psychotherapy.* Chicago: Aldine, 1967.

Uhleman, M. R., Lea, G. W., and Stone, G. L. Effects of instructions and modeling on trainees low in interpersonal-communications skills. *Journal of Counseling Psychology,* 1976, *23,* 509–513.

Van Der Veen, F. Client perception of therapist conditions as a factor in psychotherapy. In J. T. Hart and T. M. Tomlinson (Eds.), *New Directions in Client-Centered Therapy,* Boston: Houghton Mifflin, 1970.

Vander Kolk, C. J. Comparison of two mental health counselor training programs. *Community Mental Health Journal,* 1973, *9,* 260–269.

Wallace, W. G., Horan, J. J., Baker, S. B., and Hudson, G. R. Incremental effects of modeling and performance feedback in teaching decision-making counseling. *Journal of Counseling Psychology,* 1975, *22,* 570–592.

Waltz, G. R., and Johnston, J. A. Counselors look at themselves on videotape. *Journal of Counseling Psychology,* 1963, *10,* 232–236.

Wolberg, L. R. *The Technique of Psychotherapy.* New York: Grune and Stratton, 1954.

PART EIGHT

Professional Considerations

Part VIII, "Professional Considerations," examines certain contextual factors that are all too often overlooked in the practice of psychotherapy and its supervision.

Chapter 28, *Legal Issues in Psychotherapy Supervision* by Ralph Slovenko, presents the developing legal framework regarding responsibility for client welfare and therapist and supervisor conduct. The legal and ethical implications for various parties are reviewed.

Chapter 29, *Racial, Ethnic, and Social Class Considerations in Psychotherapy Supervision* by LaMaurice H. Gardner, examines the racial, ethnocentric, and sociocentric biases that can thwart the psychotherapeutic encounter. The ways in which the supervisory relationship can use racial, ethnic, and social class differences to effect growth are discussed.

Chapter 30, *Sex Role Issues in the Supervision of Therapy* by Annette M. Brodsky, describes the various forms that sex role bias can take in the clinical situation. This chapter specifies how supervisors and therapists can benefit from exploring their gender based images of themselves and others.

CHAPTER 28

Legal Issues in Psychotherapy Supervision

RALPH SLOVENKO

One may be held legally responsible not only for one's own faulty conduct but also for that of others. By reason of certain relationships that may exist between parties, the negligence of one may be charged against the other, though the latter has played no part in it, has done nothing whatever to aid or encourage it, and in fact has done all that he possibly can to prevent it (Prosser, 1971, p. 458). Under this doctrine, called "vicarious liability" or "imputed negligence," an employer, for example, would be liable for the tortious conduct of an employee committed in the scope of his employment.

Historically, to contain revenge, it was found necessary to state expressly in the Mosaic Code, and in Plato's laws, that each man should be punished only for his own sin and not for that of his father or son. By the year 1300 the theory was established in the common law that a master is liable only for those acts which he commanded or to which he expressly assented. This responsibility was later expanded to include acts of implied command or authority and eventually to acts within the scope of employment. In 1852 the United States Supreme Court ruled that vicarious liability does not depend on a "chain of command" between the employer and employee, but simply on whether the employee's acts were within the scope of employment (Philadelphia & R.R.R. v. Derby, 1852). Evolving with the growth of industry and commerce, the modern theory makes a metaphysical identification of the employer and employee as a single "persona" jointly liable for the injury. The employer is made to carry the risk as his enterprise benefits economically, in general, by the acts of the employees, and he is best able to carry the financial burden.

The employer would, of course, be subject to direct liability for any personal fault, such as lack of care. In such case, there would not be the necessity of involving the "vicarious liability" theory even though the act is that of the employee. Thus, the entrustment of a vehicle to an incompetent driver would constitute negligence on the part of the owner. It is possible for one to be primarily responsible for the act of another, though the other is legally faultless, as in the case where an adult gives a young child a gun or other instrument which would involve an unreasonable risk of harm to others (Johnson v. Krueger, 1975).

Under these principles, a physician employing another physician, nurses, or paramedical personnel is vicariously liable for the torts that they commit in the course of employment (Heimlich v. Harvey, 1959), and he would be primarily liable in entrusting a task to one who is incompetent to undertake it (Hoppe, 1977). Delegating an unlicensed person to carry out a licensed activity, unless that individual is educationally qualified and is merely establishing residency to obtain a license, may also result in criminal and professional penalties for aiding and abetting unlawful practice (Peterson, 1971; Michigan Compiled Laws §333.-16215). Most licensing statutes, such as those applicable to automobile drivers, are construed as intended for the protection of the public against injury at the hands of incompetents, and to create no civil liability where the actor is in fact competent but unlicensed (Prosser, 1971, p. 196), but breach of a licensing statute is some evidence of negligence (Gregory, 1951). A judgment arising out of an activity carried out by an unlicensed or otherwise incompetent employee might not be covered by the employer-physician's malpractice insurance, since most policies provide coverage only for negligence of "duly qualified" assistants (Holder, 1975, p. 201).

Licensing serves to clarify, as well as control, areas of practice. Thus, there may be controversy over whether or not the use of biofeedback techniques is solely a function of the medical profession or may also be performed by others. In recent Michigan legislation on the licensing of psychologists, the "practice of psychology" is defined as

the rendering to individuals, groups, organizations, or the public of services involving the application of principles, methods, and procedures of understanding, predicting, and influencing behavior for the purposes of the diagnosis, assessment related to diagnosis, prevention, amelioration, or treatment of mental or emotional disorders, disabilities or behavioral adjustment problems by means of psychotherapy, counseling, behavior modification, hypnosis, biofeedback techniques, psychological tests, or other verbal or behavioral means.

It adds, "The practice of psychology shall not include the practice of medicine such as prescribing drugs, performing surgery, or administering electro-convulsive therapy." [Michigan Compiled Laws §333.18201(1)(b)]

Within the hospital context, fanciful terminology developed during the 1940s and 1950s to describe the responsibility of the private physician performing surgery; he was called "the captain of the ship" because allegedly he had a right of control over what transpired in the operating room (McConnell v. Williams, 1949). Vicarious liability might be imposed on a physician for negligent acts committed in the hospital setting not only by paramedical personnel under his supervision but also by professionals such as anesthesiologists.

Physicians complained that the "right of control" underlying the "captain of the ship" doctrine was a fiction. At trial, they argued that they had no true power to control who would be assigned to the operating room, and that if they attempted to supervise the tasks of others too closely they might negligently discharge their own work. With the demise of charitable and governmental immunity, hospitals are more open to suit and the doctrine has been limited somewhat in many jurisdictions to the time that surgery takes place. Broadly applied, it would have a deterrent effect on the use of paraprofessional personnel (Kinkela and Kinkela, 1969; Young, 1974).

Applying these principles in mental hospitalization, one finds the hospital and attending physician being held responsible for an aide's faulty act (or omission to act) in the administration of electro-shock therapy (ECT) or in the supervision and attendance of a suicide-prone patient (Tancredi, Lieb and Slaby, 1975, p. 132). These are the types of cases which have been observed with relative frequency in malpractice suits involving psychiatric care (Trent and Muhl, 1975). They include cases in which the evidence shows the patient had a suicidal proclivity of which the psychiatrist knew or should have been aware. The psychiatrist did not give proper attention to that history, failed to give appropriate orders to the hospital staff, or the hospital staff failed to carry out the orders (Slovenko, 1973, p. 395).

In frequency of suits against medical specialties, psychiatry ranks eighth. The smaller number of suits against psychiatrists, in comparative or absolute terms, are said to be due to a patient's reluctance to expose a psychiatric history, the skill of the psychiatrist in dealing with the negative feelings of the patient, and the difficulty in linking injury with treatment.

The areas of litigation, apart from the electroshock and suicide cases, have mainly involved faulty diagnosis or screening, improper certification in commitment, harmful effects of psychotropic drugs, improper divulgence of information, and sexual intimacy with patients (Slovenko, 1973, p. 395). In almost every suit for psychiatric malpractice in which liability was imposed, tangible physical injury was demonstrated, and most of these cases involved hospital care. In the hospital situation, the supervisor or administrator is usually joined as a party defendant, but in the non-hospital situation, the supervisor (or consultant) is rarely a party defendant. This may be due, more than anything else, to oversight on the part of the claimant's attorney.

Psychotherapy itself has been the subject of even fewer malpractice suits. It is a formidable, if not well-nigh impossible, task to establish bad psychotherapy, and a causal nexus between that therapy and the alleged harm. In view of that difficulty in establishing primary liability on the part of the therapist, it may be purely academic to talk about vicarious responsibility of the supervisor. Vicarious liability is a second-story superstructure built upon another's liability. It may likewise be difficult to establish primary liability on the part of the supervisor in cases where it is alleged that supervision was faulty. A psychoanalyst or psychotherapist is in law like an educator, who owes no legal duty of care to students to support a negligence action for "educational malpractice." Thus, a student may not recover damages in tort alleging that, after graduation, he was unable to read and write simple basic English and had no understanding of the other subjects covered in his courses (Donohue v. Copiague Union Free School District, 1978).

In recent years, however, there has been growing attention to the nature of psychotherapy, and to "mal-psychotherapy" (Bergin, 1971; Kazdin, 1978; Strupp et al., 1977; Stuart, 1970; Tennov, 1975). Inherent in the words that describe the psychoanalytic or psychotherapy situation is the idea that the analyst or therapist exerts an influence, therapeutic or otherwise, on his patient (Szasz, 1963). Abrahm Kardiner (1977, p. 69) wrote in *My Analysis with Freud,* "Freud was always infuriated whenever I would say to him that you could not do harm with psychoanalysis. He said, 'When you say that, you also say that it cannot do any good. Because if you cannot do any harm, how can you do good?' " Some say the chief danger is wasting the patient's time and money. Schimel (1978) says that to harm a patient the therapist has to be diligent, destructive, and talented, and, he finds, very few therapists meet these three criteria.

The growing demand for accountability is one of the most widespread recent phenomena in the field of medicine, including mental health. The development of third-party payment, the pressure for insurance reimbursement for psychotherapy, and Federal and State supervision of mental health programs have sharpened the issue. Increasingly, those in the mental health field are being asked to demonstrate through extensive forms what it is that is being treated, what kind of treatment is being offered, what the outcome of the treatment is, and who is doing the treating. Dr. Gerald Klerman, Director of the Alcohol, Drug Abuse, and Mental Health Administration, has called for controlled clinical trials of the sort used in drug testing to develop "clear and compelling" evidence of the efficacy of the psychotherapies. Wondering whether the country needs an "FDA for psychotherapy," he noted: "Appeals to usual and customary practice, or to what is generally regarded as effective no longer suffice. . . . The failure to generate evidence of efficacy over the past few decades is now hindering the mental health field in its attempts to strengthen its position in the mainstream of health policy and programs." [*Psychiatric News,* Oct. 6, 1978, p. 3]

Recent legislation mandates specific physician disclosure standards prior to treatment; pretreatment peer review and claims review or retrospective review; record-keeping systems; additional consent. Legislation or judicial decisions also regulate the administration of "intrusive therapies" (Plotkin, 1977). Peer review as now practiced, however, leaves much to be desired in that it is a review of records, not patients—it is thus very much a measure of how well one writes a record.* Like a statement of expenses, the preparation of such reports is often

*The 1972 amendments to Title XI of the Social Security Act provide for the establishment of Professional Standards Review Organizations (PSROs) "to promote the effective, efficient and economical delivery of health care services of proper quality" under fully or partially federally funded programs. The duty and function of each local PSRO is to review the practices of physicians, other health care practitioners, institutional and noninstitutional providers of health care services which may be paid for with federal funds, in order to determine whether: (a) such services and items are or were medically necessary; (b) the quality of such services meets professionally recognized standards of health care; and (c) in case such services and items are proposed to be provided in a hospital or other health care facility on an inpatient basis, such services and items could . . . be effectively provided on an outpatient basis or more economically in an inpatient health care facility of a different type." The local PSRO is intended to be, with minor qualifications, a nonprofit, voluntary, professional association of licensed physicians, and open to all. Each PSRO is to investigate and compile profiles on care provided to various types of patients by each health care practitioner and facility. Moreover, it is authorized to develop "norms of care, diagnosis and treatment based upon typical patterns of

creative writing at its best. Fiction aside, peers generally tend not to say that a colleague's treatment is unnecessary or inappropriate, particularly as that might suggest an action in malpractice (Comment, 1974). The PSRO is subject to the disclosure provisions of the Freedom of Information Act (Chayet, 1979).

Tangentially, we may note, recent legislation also seeks to make every physician something of a supervisor over other physicians, though they are not in his employ (the development is on the horizon for other professions as well). A number of states have enacted mandatory reporting statutes requiring a physician to report a colleague's professional misconduct, subject to being charged with misconduct should he fail to report witnessed acts. Several states make it unlawful to withhold information about doctors with debilitating problems from licensing boards, and make those who knew or should have known liable for the actions of their colleagues. In exchange for a monopoly privilege (Illich, 1974; Hodgson, 1977), members of a profession, after all, are supposed to police one another. While these reporting statutes do provide immunity from suit for the complaining doctor, it remains to be seen whether they, like peer review, will prove to be of much consequence. Surveys indicate that while 38% of physicians could identify colleagues who were experiencing debilitation problems, very few said they would discuss this with the individual involved or report the problem to the appropriate authority (Rensberger, 1976).

Traditionally, to avoid a claim of battery, the doctor or other therapist needed to relate what he proposed to do and obtain the patient's consent thereto. However, simultaneously with the advent of product liability and consumer law generally, the courts began to require that the doctor also relate sufficient information to allow the patient to decide whether such a procedure is acceptable in light of its risks and benefits and the available alternatives, including no treatment at all. The burden is not put on the client or patient to ask questions, but rather on the therapist to volunteer information. This duty of full disclosure gave rise to the phrase, "informed consent"; uninformed consent is deemed no consent. Since there is no touching (an essential of battery) in purely verbal therapy, there is no need to consider informed consent or other defense. It is necessary to consider defenses only when there is a cause of action.

But beginning in the 1960s, failure to disclose has become an element of negligence law, where the element of touching is not of the essence. The standard of disclosure, or the information that must be given, is in dispute. Some courts say that there is no need to prove what other doctors might tell their patients in similar circumstances. According to this line of jurisprudence, as one court put it:

The jury is capable of deciding whether the doctor did not tell the patient about something that should have been revealed. The jury does not need testimony from physicians about the norm of disclosure in the community. The usual conduct of doctors in this matter is not relevant to the establishment of the liability which is imposed by law. The jury, as lay people, are equipped to place themselves in the position of a patient and decide

---

care in its region." Peer review in psychiatry is examined in Gibson (1977).

whether under the circumstances, the patient should have been told (Miller v. Kennedy, 1975).

Other courts say that the standard of disclosure is that of the "reasonable and prudent doctor" (Trogun v. Fruchtman, 1973). In any event, it may be noted that Freud advised against "lengthy preliminary discussions before the beginning of the analytic treatment," but he did recommend that the patient be told of the difficulties and sacrifices which analytic treatment involves so that the patient would be deprived "of any right to say later on that he has been inveigled into a treatment whose extent and implications he did not realize" (Freud, 1913). Ancient wisdom teaches the healer: "Always warn the patient that the cure will take a long time, in fact make it twice as long as you really think it will be" (quoted in Burns, 1977, p. 212).

In the case of ongoing treatment, as occurs in psychiatry, consent as to the mode of procedure at least may be implied from the patient's voluntary return. He has had a sample. As to other matters, a psychotherapist may be obliged, among other things, to point out the risk involved in the working through of transference feelings. Moreover, considering that informed consent is an issue about which the public has become sensitized, it could conceivably involve psychotherapy supervision. How much should patients be told about the supervisory process? Do they have a right to know who the supervisor is? Consent is obtained for the dissemination of information to another physician or to an insurance carrier, so it may likewise be deemed necessary to advise about the disclosure of information in supervision, and also the identity of the supervisor. In the case of medical records in a hospital, a patient gives permission by implication for all hospital personnel directly involved in the treatment to see the records, and they may also be viewed by hospital committees involved in monitoring quality of care. Supervision in psychotherapy, however, is not common knowledge and hence permission may not be assumed by implication. In the business world, companies are now being obliged to disclose information to shareholders about the quality and effectiveness of corporate boards of directors. Should this practice be extended to the medical or psychotherapy profession? The American Hospital Association's "Patient's Bill of Rights" (1975) says that the patient "has the right to know, by name, the physician responsible for coordinating his care."

In general, the professions are now all under siege (Barzun, 1978; Glazer, 1978); the public is demanding openness and accountability. In the health care field, there are renewed attempts to achieve this surveillance by means of citizen participation in regulation by licensing or certification, by limited licensure and required relicensure, by increased monitoring through PSRO-type agencies, and by the tort or contract suit (Slovenko, 1978). In a program that has received some commendation (notably among professionals), California's medical association attempts to deal with the problem of the impaired physician through its Physicians Health and Effectiveness Committee; the emphasis in the program is to be nonpunitive, confidential, and to offer a reentry procedure for doctors brought to the Committee's attention. The American Medical Association in 1975 held its first of several national conferences on "The Impaired Physician," and suggested a model Disabled Physicians Act, which has been enacted, with some variation, by some 28 states to date (AMA, 1975, 1976).

To be sure, one cannot be responsible for everything done by one's colleagues, clients or patients,* but one (and one's supervisor) might be responsible for some things that they do. However, in any system of accountability the obtaining of evidence is essential. In this regard note must be taken of the physician-patient or psychotherapist-patient shield law, which is designed to protect the confidentiality of what is said in the relationship. Not infrequently, when this law (providing a privilege to remain silent in the face of a subpoena) is urged by the therapist (theoretically on behalf of the patient), the effect is to shield the therapist from the kind of independent observation essential for accountability. If a therapist consistently has more patients getting a divorce, failing at work, or committing suicide than others, "mal-therapy" may well be the cause; but to establish it, a study showing a pattern would have to be done that would invade privacy to some degree. In 1978, a Chicago hospital (and some of its former psychiatric patients) won a court ruling on the basis of privilege to keep a grand jury from looking at hospital records—without patient consent—for evidence of insurance fraud and abusive treatment [*Psychiatric News,* May 19, 1978, p. 1]. While the privilege may be urged on behalf of the patient, it belongs to the patient and can be waived by the patient at his discretion. In such investigations, though, a hospital or therapist can readily obtain a few patients among the population to object to disclosure of records that would frustrate inquiry into a system of operation. A Confidentiality Act enacted in 1978 in Illinois, containing most of the provisions of a model law on confidentiality recommended by the American Psychiatric Association, provides access to the state's attorneys for investigative purposes, but with the proviso that unauthorized redisclosure is prohibited. The exercise of the privilege must be "in the interests of the patient" (Beigler, 1979).

Apparently unrecognized, or at least not commented upon, are the implications of developing accountability for the supervisor in psychotherapy as teacher or manager. Questions abound, such as: what is the role, if any, of the supervisor in the success or failure of psychotherapy? It is commonly assumed, we have noted, that a therapist exercises influence on his client or patient; the supervisor in turn, by hypothesis, exercises influence on the therapist. What, then, is the responsibility of the supervisor for maintaining the treatment relationship, or for assuring satisfactory outcomes? Studies suggest that continuance of the therapeutic relationship is more the responsibility of a clinician than of the patient (Duehn and Proctor, 1977). A fundamental axiom of psychotherapy is that feelings related to countertransference, the therapist's conscious or unconscious emotional reaction to a patient, strongly influence the therapist's work, and that one of the tasks of a supervisor is to explore its implications and effects (Schwartz, 1978). Ekstein and Wallerstein (1972) develop the theme that at times the trans-

---

*Different theoretical persuasions on which various forms of psychotherapy are based, we may note, vary in whether the individuals seen are referred to as "patients" or "clients."

ference which develops between patient and therapist is paralleled by one that develops between therapist and supervisor.

As a matter of practice, it is assumed that the supervisor in psychotherapy, like the supervisor in business, knows or should know what is going on, and also that the supervisor has an impact on the quality of work that is done (Benedek, Barton, and Bieniek, 1977). True to the "self-fulfilling prophecy," an individual who is expected to perform at a certain level will perform at that level (Gschwend, 1977). In the business world, apprentices report that they are stimulated to higher levels of performance by constructive criticism of their assignments, and by evaluations that are precise and thought-provoking (Scott, 1978). Maccoby (1976) reports in his book, *The Gamesman,* that male supervisors often withhold needed encouragement from young women because they are fearful of appearing to be "too intimate" with them. Women executives, too, may fail in their teaching function because of a reluctance to be cast in a mothering role (Scott, 1978).

In general, the legal responsibility imposed on a supervisor is linked to the actual or apparent control, *de facto* or *de jure,* that he exercises. There are, we know, in psychotherapy two types of supervision (possibly combined in one supervisor)—"administrative supervision" and "therapy supervision." In administrative supervision, the supervisor assumes a position of official power over the supervisee. In therapy supervision, where the goal is learning how to do therapy, the supervisor is like a teacher who uses his expertise to influence in a verbal, confidential, nonauthoritarian manner. To be sure, where the supervisee is highly dependent on the supervisor, the supervisor practically becomes the therapist *in absentia* (Book, 1973); like Cyrano de Bergerac who spoke on behalf of inept lovers. In therapy supervision, as a rule, a supervisor does not interfere in the therapy by exercising his rank, even when he does not agree with the course taken by the supervisee, unless such a course constitutes malpractice or violates professional ethics (Hassenfeld and Sarris, 1978). In some clinic operations as well as in residency training, the supervisor has a dual role of evaluating and teaching the resident.

There are novelties in psychotherapy supervision that may differ from supervision in the business world. In psychotherapy supervision, a supervisor may be one of several; there may be a frequent change of supervisors; there may be discussion of only one case (the troublesome or the most interesting one). With few exceptions, a therapy supervisor is posted on what is going on through the reports of the supervisee, he never sees what is done firsthand, he rarely if ever interviews the patient or client. He is not like a supervisor in surgery, or the mentor in driver training, who is alongside the trainee ready to intervene at a moment's notice. Questions have been raised about the effects of videotapes, one-way mirrors, audiotapes, and direct observation of the therapist and patient. Fear of artifactual interference with the therapeutic process has been expressed. As a consequence, these devices are not extensively used, but misgivings have been expressed about that, as well as about the aims of supervision in psychotherapy (Grotjahn, 1955; Schuster et al., 1972). Increasingly, videotape replays are being employed in supervision, and direct observation is becoming more common in family therapy.

There are many definitions in the decisional and statutory law of the term "supervision," appearing in various contexts. It is another example of the same word meaning different things in different contexts. In a case involving the responsibility of a corporate officer to oversee the activities of company employees, the court said: "Turning to an old friend, Webster's Third International Dictionary, one finds that 'supervise' means 'to co-ordinate, direct, and inspect continuously and at first hand the accomplishment of another, or to 'oversee with the powers of direction and decision the implementation of one's own or another's intentions' " (Saxton v. St. Louis Stair Co., 1966). In a case where a contracting party agreed to supervise the performance of a contract, the court said: "To supervise does not mean to do the work in detail, but to see that it is done. It means to oversee, with power of direction" (Egner v. States Realty Co., 1947). The term "supervision of construction" or "general supervisory services" in an architect's contract of employment is held not to be a word of art, that is to say, a word which has a particular meaning to a particular area, and thus evidence of the profession may be excluded as to what constitutes due care in the carrying out of that supervision (Aetna Ins. Co. v. Hellmuth, Obata & Kassabaum, 1968). The State Attorney General has the duty of "direct supervision" over every district attorney and sheriff and other law enforcement officers but such power "does not contemplate absolute control and direction of such officials" (People v. Brophy, 1942). Probation officers must "take charge of and watch over" those placed on probation. This includes inquiries into probationer employment status on such matters as job performance and relationships with other employees and supervisors; interviews with probationers and their families and acquaintances; and other forms of inquiry to determine if probation conditions are being complied with [George, 1978, §11.10(b)]. Recent court decisions involving the liability of parole and probation officers have greatly stimulated an interest in the legal responsibility of probation officers to employers or prospective employers of persons under their supervision, and to the community (Kutcher, 1977).

The Michigan legislature in 1978 set out the following definition of psychology supervision [Michigan Compiled Laws §333.16109(2)]:

"Supervision" means the overseeing of or participation in the work of another individual by a health professional licensed under this article in circumstances where at least all of the following conditions exist:
(a) The continuous availability of direct communication in person or by radio, telephone, or telecommunication between the supervised individual and licensed health professional.
(b) The availability of a licensed health professional on a regularly scheduled basis to review the practice of the supervised individual, to provide consultation to the supervised individual, to review records, and to further educate the supervised individual in the performance of the individual's functions.
(c) The provision by the licensed supervising health professional of predetermined procedures and drug protocol.

In general, "due care" in the discharge of one's duties is defined in law as that "degree of diligence, care and skill that ordinarily prudent men would exercise under similar circumstances in like position." This is a flexible standard (some say an unstandard standard) to meet the varied factual contexts. Unless the fact patterns are clearly distinguishable, the lawyer's argument is usually by analogy. One analogy that might be considered here is that of directors and officers of corporations. It is interesting to note that historically businessmen have tended to welcome invitations to join the board of a corporation, but, as recent studies point out, businessmen in many instances are now viewing such invitations with considerable caution. A primary reason for this change is the legal environment in which corporate boards now operate. They must now conduct their business in the glare of publicity, and may be exposed to substantial personal liability. Government regulatory agencies have increased their policing roles, and shareholders are not reluctant to sue directors for grievances they believe the board has committed. The courts have ruled that corporate directors—inside and outside, new and old—are responsible for conducting reasonable investigations and surveillances of corporate activities. They cannot rely purely and simply on reports and financial statements provided about the company's operations by the company and its management (INA, 1978).

Like the clinical supervisor, the psychotherapy supervisor assumes, in general, clinical responsibility much as if the patient were under his own personal care (Hassenfeld, 1978). This proposition is least contestable where the student is a preprofessional (e.g., medical student, psychology graduate student). In the case of psychiatric residents who are licensed physicians, the supervisor's total clinical responsibility still holds, since the resident cannot be expected to have mastered the skills and techniques of psychotherapy before completing the training program. Without the locus of clinical responsibility resting squarely on the supervisor's shoulders, there would be little justification for troubled people being assigned to partially trained students (by definition any person in the process of training is only partially trained). Nursing students must perform their tasks with the same skill as licensed nurses.

Thus considered, it is a heavy responsibility that clinicians assume when they take on a supervisory role, especially in light of more or less common problematic situations: (1) the supervisee engaging in unethical conduct with the patient which is not reported to the supervisor; (2) the supervisee not carrying out the supervisor's recommendations but saying that he did; and (3) the incomplete learning of psychotherapy techniques. A graduate student or resident requires the freedom to make clinical judgments, but because of inexperience he may (often) be mistaken.

More specifically, potential areas of malpractice are here suggested where the supervisor in a psychotherapeutic situation might be held liable. This is not to suggest that all circumstances involving similar facts will lead to liability, but rather to peer into the uncertain future and to suggest that given a similar fact situation, a litigious client, and a creative or pugnacious lawyer, a suit might be filed, the issue submitted to a jury and an action for malpractice stated. In the following examples one can assume in each case that the actions of the supervisor or trainee proximately caused injury or damage to the client or patient:

1. The supervisor or the agency promulgates an intake form to be used by the trainee, it omits relevant questions (homocidal tendencies, suicidal tendencies, previous therapy). The client receives improper treatment and injures himself or others.

2. The trainee takes relevant notes during therapy, the supervisor does not study these notes and does not realize that the notes indicate a therapy method other than that offered or available.

3. The trainee even with the supervisor's help is incapable of offering proper therapy. There is a need to refer to a more competent professional.

4. There is a need to consult a specialist, but the supervisor does not realize the need because certain facts are not discussed during the supervisory sessions.

5. There is a medical problem which would be discovered by a person with more training, but which is not discovered by the trainee. A medical doctor is not consulted. The psychological problem is caused by a hearing loss, a vitamin deficiency, or other physical imbalance.

6. The diagnosis is improper, the prognosis faulty, or the treatment plan ineffective. The supervisor does not discover the error in any of the three areas or the interrelationship of one to the other, and therapy continues inappropriately.

7. Written progress notes are inadequate or do not support the treatment plan.

8. The trainee and patient (or trainee and supervisor) have a conflict of personalities, yet the treatment continues.

9. The trainee becomes socially involved with the client, but cleverly hides the involvement from the supervisor. The supervisor should have known by more complete supervisory sessions.

10. The trainee goes on vacation, there is no adequately prepared relief therapist.

11. The trainee breaches confidentiality and shares a particularly intriguing story with a co-trainee or friend, word gets back to the client. The supervisor had not warned the trainee of the importance and meaning of confidentiality.

12. The client consents to treatment but does not know it is by a trainee. He assumes it is on a regular professional level.

13. The trainee is subpoenaed to testify in court and is improperly prepared by training or experience for courtroom testimony.

There are apparently no safeguards in the situations where the supervisee engages in unethical conduct with the patient which is not reported to the supervisor, or where the supervisee does not carry out the supervisor's recommendations but says that he did, except the supervisor's ongoing assessment of the quality of the supervisory relationship (Hassenfeld and Sarris, 1978). The situation involving miscues while learning psychotherapy techniques assumes that supervisors are able to make distinctions between errors in techniques and truly psychonoxious interventions. (Needless to say, it would be interesting to find out whether experienced supervisors can agree on which is which.) Where "psychonoxious" interventions occur, the supervisor must actively protect the patient. Those who assume responsibility in this back-up model must "have a sure sense of when it is necessary to intervene, and have a good system of supervision and accountability" (Heiman, 1978).

The manifold problems of teaching hospitals appear within the setting of psychotherapy and psychoanalysis. In analytic work, it is not unusual to find exceptionally bright and gifted therapists who adequately understand what is transpiring both in the patient and manifestly in the transference, but their psychotherapeutic effectiveness is interfered with both by an intellectual misunderstanding of their task and by personal inhibitions. To what extent can a supervisor deal with such a problem? And to whom does the supervisor owe primary responsibility—the supervisee or the supervisee's patient? In practice, some supervisors would concentrate on the supervisee's own intrapsychic dynamics, while others would focus on therapeutic techniques and the patient.

Among troublesome experiences, veteran psychoanalysts report that at times they are asked for supervision by interested young mental health professionals who are not in analytic training and who practice a less intensive, more superficial kind of psychotherapeutic work. This young therapist might present a patient or client who is successful, by conventional social standards, and who has the type of neurotic problems for which psychoanalysis may well be the treatment of choice. If the supervisor views himself as simply offering a specialized type of expertise to enhance the education of the young therapist, then he presents his experience and knowledge for whatever it may offer in enriching psychotherapy. On the other hand, the supervisor may have the responsibility to point out that the patient or client would best be served by the type of treatment which the therapist is not able to provide. Ironically, younger therapists have great difficulty resolving what seems to be implied in such a case, that is, that whenever they are fortunate enough to have a "good" patient, they should be referring him to someone else. This situation has mainly ethical implications, but there is increasing concern about its legal implications (Poland, 1978).

The underlying premise of mental health and other health agencies in seeking to extend care to a larger number of people is that "supervision" safeguards or improves the standard of care (Bell, 1978); even paraprofessionals can play an important and increasing role in health care if they have "appropriate training and supervision" (Bourne, 1978). The supervisor should establish the overall tone and direction of the agency, develop new treatment programs, and work closely with staff to make sure patients are properly evaluated and treated. With national health insurance a possibility, the prevailing practice in Michigan (though it may change there) warrants close examination as it might become a national pattern. Whatever the source of third-party payment—whether national health insurance or private commercial insurance, Medicare or Medicaid, community mental health centers, or various kinds of public or private clinics—the issue of good quality care, cost effectiveness, and the qualifications of those who provide it is a significant and pressing concern. Interdisciplinary differences, lack of peer review, questions of responsibilities, and dissension over hierarchy or authority have become battlegrounds on which guild wars are waged (Hartocollis, 1978).

The nature and structure of the Out-patient Psychiatric Clinic (OPC) in Michigan, as it may be a harbinger of things to come, warrants examination regarding standards and potential abuses to be found in that pattern. The OPC in Michigan was largely generated by the United Automobile Workers' attempt to expand the number of mental health personnel available to their members. Blue Cross-Blue Shield, the primary insurer of OPCs, pursuant to its agreement with the UAW requires for their approval that three professions—the triad of psychiatry, psychology, and social work—be represented in the out-patient clinic; at least one physician who specializes in psychiatry, one psychologist certified at the consulting level, and one certified social worker. In addition, the BC/BS requires that there be a psychiatric medical director (a psychiatrist) and a clinic director (a person representing any one of the mental health professions). Periodic case reviews are to be held at which all professions are represented. Recent additional requirements call for a governing board and a utilization review committee. The OPC program was patterned on the child guidance clinics, where a psychiatrist directs a "mental health team" of psychologists and social workers (Sargent, 1977).

Each profession of the triad acknowledges awareness of numerous abuses, including rake off of fees, low quality care, and dumping of patients. These abuses are not specifically spelled out in public, but the lower members of OPC hierarchy complain about them in private and some of them have received adverse publicity in the press (Katz, 1978). Under the program, the services of psychologists and social workers are reimbursable only if they are "supervised" by psychiatrists. Psychiatrists, reasonably enough, expect payment for their services. In many cases, however, what this means is that the psychologist or social worker treats the patient while the psychiatrist, though spending little time supervising, obtains on the average a 50% portion of the fee that BC/BS pays for the therapy. Some call it duplicity, others call it "fraud and abuse" (Towery and Sharfstein, 1978), still others call it "protection money." For the fee, the psychiatrist signs payment forms and participates in periodic discussions of the patient's case. Where the psychiatrist owns the clinic, he also covers the overhead. The psychiatrist makes a tidy profit from his "stable" of psychologists and social workers, apart from what he earns treating his own patients. In other clinics, now under fire, the psychiatrist acts very much like a consultant, having his own office in another location, and dropping into the clinic periodically to sign forms and prescribe medication, if necessary (Katz, 1978). The advisory board, consisting of 25 to 50 citizens, meets periodically, usually at a banquet, where they hear a report, and receive a fee equivalent to a psychiatry hour for their attendance.

In a statement to its members (April 1975), the Michigan Psychiatric Association reported that there have been "many abuses" in the operation of the OPC. It suggested standards to be implemented by the ethics committee and the committee on peer review. Some of the abuses have been checked, one apparent change being a switch from (clearly unethical) fee-splitting to a salaried position (often a disguise for a fee-splitting system) for lower members of the OPC hierarchy. The UAW blames the abuses on shoddy administration of its program by BC/BS, but it is questionable whether a fiscal third-party ought to set out standards and maintain supervision (Mount Sinai Hospital of Greater Miami v. Weinberger, 1975).

But even assuming that the psychiatrist indeed acts as a real supervisor, one might ask why his supervision is needed at all. The Michigan Psychiatric Society takes the position that there must be a psychiatrist as medical director who has responsibility for all patients as well as for the quality of their care. On the other hand, the psychologists and social workers take the position that each profession should be independently responsible for the mental health personnel in their disciplines (News and Comment, 1973). They contend that supervision by one who merely carries the title of psychiatrist would serve no useful purpose; they would actually prefer the facade of supervision to supervision in fact, which they claim would be a waste of time. In the best operating OPCs, the arrangement in practice is collegial, not hierarchial; supervision in such cases is essentially an exchange of ideas.

The position of a resident in training changes gradually from that of a novice to that of a professional colleague, and in the latter role he is free to use his own style and orientation (Greben, Markson, and Sadovoy, 1973). Completion of residency training is something like a Bar Mitzvah, where the rabbi tells the young lad: "Beginning today you are old enough to be responsible for your own sins. Your father no longer takes them on his shoulders. Today you are a man." In law, a parent is not responsible for the acts of a child arising out of failure of supervision when the child is capable of appreciating a duty of care (Lubitz v. Wells, 1955). But those supervised in the OPC, professionals and paraprofessionals alike, never achieve this level of freedom; they remain supervisees forever. In a psychiatric residency training program, a psychologist may be teacher or supervisor, but upon completion of the training, the psychiatrist ranks over the psychologist in the OPC hierarchy. Psychologists in Michigan have been lobbying for legislation that would require insurance companies to pay them on the same basis as they pay psychiatrists. Such laws, called "freedom of choice" laws, have been enacted in a number of states. Licensed psychologists have been recognized as independent providers in CHAMPUS, CHAMPVA, FEHBA, Aetna insurance programs, Medicaid (17 states), some Blue Cross/Blue Shield plans, and so on. (Dörken, 1976). The impact of the antitrust laws on the practice of psychiatry may be affected significantly by the outcome of investigations by the Federal Trade Commission and by private or nongovernmental antitrust actions that have been brought against psychiatric organizations (Klein, 1978).

The UAW, in requiring psychologists and social workers to work with or under psychiatrists, has taken the position that professionals who work together in groups provide more comprehensive care than practitioners who work alone, and that the medical model would contain costs. It is the hierarchy that is set up, however, that is the source of controversy. Even more disconcerting is the inadequacy of guidelines and statements concerning the actual providers of services. There is want of delineation of the educational preparation, amount of experience, and kind and quality of training of the providers of services. Within this structure some service providers may be prepared, while others are not. Inadequately trained persons are allowed to perform services on the theory that supervision will remedy any deficiencies. This expectation places the supervisor in the role of an educator, a role for which the supervisor may or may not be prepared.

Assuming that providers of services have sufficient training to perform their tasks or that the supervisor has expertise in the field in which he is supervising, there are several important questions left unanswered. They include: How much supervision is necessary per case in terms of frequency and amount? How much seminar time should be required? How should such training be adjusted to the previous education, experience, and training level of the supervisee, the direct service provider? Whether recognized by the planner or not, the OPC is set up as a possible training institute but without the kinds of standards that would be required of other kinds of training institutions. To say that each supervisor—for example, each psychiatric physician—bears the responsibility for the clinical operation and thus must answer to himself for such questions as these and others which bear so strongly on quality of patient care is to beg the issue (Report, 1977).

Ambiguous standards and guidelines leave loopholes which do not prevent poor patient care and inadequate cost effectiveness; this can readily occur under a set-up that does not prevent "fronting" practices. Although a qualified psychiatrist, psychologist, and social worker must be members of the staff in order to fulfill the requirements of the OPC, there is not adequate restriction as to who, in addition, may be members of the staff, and as a consequence, the client or patient may be turned over to a substandard therapist and the third-party payment still made. The ambiguities in the clinic organization make it difficult for the patient to assess the quality of his treatment or the person rendering it. It may also be noted that there is the possibility that when the patient's insurance runs out, he may be "transferred" to a public agency or simply "dumped". Certainly, substandard patient care and poor cost effectiveness is the opposite of what the originators intended.

The Michigan OPC operation points out the potential impact of third-party payment programs. It makes for exploitation of mental health professionals and paraprofessionals, and for poor quality care. It is not a happy picture of cost effectiveness. It sharply poses several questions that have been raised for some time (Chodoff, 1978; Sharfstein, 1978): (1) Who shall be considered a mental health professional? (2) Should there be a hierarchy among the mental health professions? (3) What are the practical guidelines that might be offered insurance carriers? (4) Without practical or just guidelines should there be insurance coverage of out-patient psychotherapy at all? (5) Is hospitalization the alternate to out-patient psychotherapy (hospital practice has the economic attraction—for the physician—of allowing "head in the door" visits)? (6) What is truly the best way of containing costs yet providing best care? Considering, as data seems to suggest, that the mental health professions themselves are not clearly differentiated in terms of professional functions when it comes to psychotherapy, it seems predictable that funding agencies and administrators at all levels will have difficulty deciding which professional should engage in which function (House, Miller, and Schlachter, 1978).

Psychiatrists say that as physicians, only they are capable of recognizing physical illnesses that mimic mental disorders; a person with a physical illness seen by a psychologist might be in useless therapy while the real disease goes untreated. Moreover, only they, as physicians, can prescribe medication that is sometimes needed in the treatment of mental illness. Psychologists, on the other hand, argue that the overwhelming majority of people with symptoms of mental illness do not have physical diseases and that requiring psychiatric supervision to screen out the few is an unwarranted expense. Furthermore, they contend, the problem can be solved more cheaply and more effectively by having the client get a physical examination from an internist before psychotherapy begins; a client who needs drugs can be referred to a psychiatrist or family doctor for a prescription and can return to the psychologist for continued therapy.

The controversy continues (Brady and Brodie, 1978), the class system prevails, and with it, the concept of supervision. With that regime prevailing, litigation involving supervisors may be called the "suit of the future." Profiting from an enterprise, the supervisor—like a corporate officer or director—must also bear its perils. That is the underlying principle of vicarious responsibility—"let the superior reply."

This doctrine, we may point out, allows the joining of several defendants in one lawsuit. Each being liable for all, the plaintiff may look to any one of the defendants and recover his damages in full from any of them. As a consequence, joinder improves a claimant's chances of recovery either in settlement or at trial. However, as a matter of trial tactic, there may be times when it would not be prudent to join various parties in one suit, as when joinder would blur the responsibility of the primary actor and thus weaken the case.

Some cases may be noted. In the much publicized case of *Tarasoff v. Regents of University of California* (1974), the California Supreme Court ruled that a psychotherapist who has reason to believe that a patient may injure or kill another must notify the potential victim, his relatives, or the authorities; the court held that a cause of action was stated against the parties sued, namely, the treating psychotherapist (a psychologist), the clinic supervisor (a psychiatrist), and the institution. On the supervisor's responsibility in the case, the attorney (McKray, 1978) for Tarasoff observed: "It is my view that if [the supervisor of the clinic] had personally examined the patient Poddar and made an independent decision that the patient Poddar was not dangerous to himself or his victim, Tatiana Tarasoff—there would be no cause of action based upon foreseeability. However [the supervisor] never saw the patient Poddar and ignored the medical records developed by his staff."

In a case in New Jersey, the court referred a person to a clinic for evaluation. A social worker did the interviewing, found that he was without mental disorder, and the supervising psychiatrist signed the report without interviewing him. A few days later he killed his wife and children. The supervisor was sued in a malpractice action; the case was settled (Trent, 1978; Trent and Muhl, 1975).

In New York (Cohen v. State of New York, 1976), a 23-year-old married male in his third year of medical school voluntarily entered the Downstate Medical Center psychiatric department for a condition diagnosed as paranoid schizophrenia. The admission record contained a statement that he had shown suicidal potential and he was placed on an open-door ward organized around the concept of a therapeutic community. Four months later, the treating physician, a first-year resident, made a determination that the patient should not be restricted to the ward. The same day the patient committed suicide.

The issue before the court in this case was whether the doctors had made a careful examination of the decedent and then exercised reasonable care in determining that he should not be restricted to the ward. The essential factual issue, however, was whether a qualified psychiatrist was actively supervising the care of the decedent. Ruling for the plaintiff in this wrongful death action, the court said that the resident "did not, at this point in his medical career, possess the requisite skill or trained psychiatric judgment to, essentially unsupervised, provide ordinary and reasonable psychiatric medical treatment and care to this decedent." The court went on to say: "In the case at bar, there was much more than a mere error of judgment. There was not one but many errors of judgment made by a doctor not qualified in an unsupervised status to make a judgment; made by those in supervisory capacity; and, all made without careful examination."

CONCLUSION

The supervisory concept is presented to the public as a means of offering responsible health care, while at the same time allowing the supervisor to profit as an entrepreneur. Under the law, an entrepreneur must bear vicarious responsibility for what takes place in the enterprise. At times there is primary responsibility. The law says that an accountant must be a watchdog, if not a bloodhound (In re Cotton, 1896). Is less to be expected of a psychotherapy supervisor?

The crucial issue at law is whether "supervision" will be regarded as a term of art so as to allow evidence of the profession as to its meaning. Otherwise, it may be well for the profession to use a different term.

REFERENCES

American Hospital Association. *A patient's bill of rights.* 1973; reprinted in Annas, G. J. *The Rights of Hospital Patients.* New York: Avon, 1975, pp. 25–27.

AMA Department of Mental Health. *The impaired physician* (Report of Conference). Chicago: American Medical Association, 1975.

AMA Legislative Department. *An act relating to the improvement of medical discipline: To require hospitals, medical societies, and insurers to report certain information relating to medical incompetence; and to provide for the maintenance of records regarding medical incompetence.* Chicago: American Medical Association, 1976.

Aetna Ins. Co. v. Hellmuth, Obata & Kassabaum (1968), 392 F.2d 472 (8th Cir.).

Barzun, J. The professions under seige. *Harper's,* October 1978, pp. 61–68.

Beigler, J. S. Editorial/The APA Model Law on Confidentiality. *American Journal of Psychiatry,* 1979, *136,* 71.

Bell, W.S. Medico-legal implications of recent legislation concerning allied health practitioners. *Loyola of Los Angeles Law Review,* 1978, *11,* 379–398.

Benedek, E.P., Barton, G., and Bieniek, C. Problems for women in psychiatric residency. *American Journal of Psychiatry,* 1977, *134,* 1244–1248.

Bergin, A. The evaluation of therapeutic outcomes, in Bergin, A., and Garfield, S. (Eds.). *Handbook of psychotherapy and behavior change.* New York: Wiley, 1971.

Book, H.E., On maybe becoming a psychotherapist, perhaps. *Canadian Psychiatric Association Journal,* 1973, *14,* 487–493.

Bourne, P.G. Letter. *American Journal of Psychiatry,* 1978, *135,* 1113.

Brady, J.P., and Brodie, H.K.H. (Eds.). *Controversy in psychiatry.* Philadelphia: Saunders, 1978.

Burns, C.R. (Ed.). *Legacies in ethics and medicine.* New York: Science History Publications, 1977.

Chayet, N. Reviewing PSRO review. *Medical Tribune,* Feb. 7, 1979, p. 8.

Chodoff, P. Psychiatry and the fiscal third party. *American Journal of Psychiatry,* 1978, *135,* 1141–1147.

Comment, PSRO: Malpractice liability and the impact of the Civil Immunity Clause. *Georgetown Law Journal,* 1974, *62,* 1499–1513.

Cohen v. State of New York (1976), 382 N.Y.S.2d 128.

Donohue v. Copiague Union Free School District (1978), 407 N.Y.S.2d 874.

Dörken, H., et al. *The professional psychologist today/New developments in law, health insurance, and health practice.* San Francisco: Jossey-Bass, 1976.

Duehn, W.D. and Proctor, E.K. Initial clinical interaction and premature discontinuance in treatment. *American Journal of Orthopsychiatry,* 1977, *47,* 284–290.

Egner v. States Realty Co. (1947), 223 Minn. 365, 26 N.W.2d 464.

Ekstein, R., and Wallerstein, R.S. *The teaching and learning of psychotherapy.* New York: International Universities Press, 1972.

Freud, S. On beginning the treatment [Further recommendations on the technique of psycho-analysis I], in Strachey, J. (Ed.), *Complete Psychological Works of Sigmund Freud.* London: Hogarth Press, 1958, pp. 121–144.

George, B.J. *Michigan criminal procedure.* Ann Arbor: Institute of Continuing Legal Education, 1978.

Gibson, R.W. (Ed.). *A conference report/Professional responsibilities and peer review in psychiatry.* Washington, D.C.: American Psychiatric Association, 1977.

Glazer, N. The attack on the professions. *Commentary,* November 1978, pp. 34–41.

Greben, S.E., Markson, E.R., and Sadavoy, J. Resident and supervisor: An examination of their relationship. *Canadian Psychiatric Association Journal,* 1973, *18,* 473–479.

Gregory, C.O. Breach of criminal licensing statutes in civil litigation. *Cornell Law Quarterly,* 1951, *36,* 622–642.

Grotjahn, M. Problems and techniques of supervision. *Psychiatry,* 1955, *18,* 9–15.

Gschwend, B.L. The self-fulfilling prophecy in supervision. *American Journal of Occupational Therapy,* 1977, *31,* 612–613.

Hartocollis, P. The hospital team and the conflict of professional disciplines: Psychologists versus psychiatrists. *Journal of the National Association of Private Psychiatric Hospitals,* 1978, *9,* 42–43.

Hassenfeld, I.N. Personal communication, October 26, 1978.

Hassenfeld, I.N., and Sarris, J.G. Hazards and horizons of psychotherapy supervision. *American Journal of Psychotherapy,* 1978, *32,* 393–401.

Heiman, E.M. The future relationship of psychiatrists with other mental health professionals. *Psychiatric Opinion,* 1978, *15,* 27–30.

Heimlich v. Harvey (1949), 255 Wis. 471, 39 N.W.2d 394.

Hodgson, E.L. Restrictions on unorthodox health treatment in California: A legal and economic analysis. *UCLA Law Review,* 1977, *24,* 647–696.

Holder, A.R. *Medical malpractice law.* New York: Wiley, 1975.

Hoppe, W.G. Physicians' liability for negligence of office assistants and hospital employees. *Journal of the American Medical Association,* 1979, *238,* 1485–1486.

House, W.C., Miller, S.I., and Schlachter, R.H. Role definitions among mental health professionals. *Comprehensive Psychiatry,* 1978, *19,* 469–476.

INA. *Insurance decisions/Directors' and officers' liability.* Philadelphia: Insurance Company of North America, 1978.

Illich, I.D. *Energy and equity.* London: Calder and Boyars, 1974.

In re Cotton (1896), 2 Ch. Div. 279.

Johnson v. Krueger (Colo. App. 1975), 539 P.2d 1296.

Kardiner, A. *My Analysis with Freud.* New York: Norton, 1977.

Katz, D. The UAW, mental patients and a concept gone awry. *Detroit Free Press,* May 14, 1978, p. 4-B.

Kazdin, A.E. Criteria for evaluating psychotherapy. *Archives of General Psychiatry,* 1978, *35,* 407–416.

Kinkela, G.G., and Kindela, R.V. Hospital nurses and tort liability. *Cleveland-Marshall Law Review,* 1969, *18,* 53–69.

Klein, J. Judicial Action Report. *Psychiatric News,* November 3, 1978, p. 23.

Kutcher, J.D. The legal responsibility of probation officers in supervision. *Federal Probation,* March 1977, pp. 35–38.

Lubitz v. Wells (1955), 19 Conn. Supp. 322, 133 A.2d 147.

Maccoby, M. *The gamesman.* New York: Simon and Schuster, 1976.

McConnell v. Williams (1949), 361 Pa. 355, 65 A.2d 243.

McKray, G.A. Personal communication, November 28, 1978.

Miller v. Kennedy (1975), 11 Wash. App. 272, 522 P.2d 852, affirmed, 85 Wash.2d 151, 530 P.2d 334.

Mount Sinai Hospital of Greater Miami v. Weinberger (1975), 517 F.2d 329 (5th Cir.).

News and Comment, Psychology: Clinicians seek professional autonomy. *Science,* 1973, *181,* 1147–1150.

People v. Brophy (1942), 49 Cal. App.2d 15, 120 P.2d 946.

Peterson, I. 2 L.I. doctors reported indicted; salesman allegedly aided surgery. *The New York Times,* November 2, 1977, p. 1.

Philadelphia & R.R.R. v. Derby (1852), 55 U.S. (14 How.) 467.

Plotkin, R. Limiting the therapeutic orgy: Mental patients' right to refuse treatment. *Northwestern University Law Review,* 1977, *72,* 461–525.

Poland, W.S. Personal communication, October 4, 1978.

Prosser, W.L. *Handbook of the law of torts* (4th ed.). St. Paul, Minn.: West, 1971.

Rensberger, B. Few doctors ever report colleagues' incompetence. *New York Times,* January 29, 1976, p. 1.

Report, Co-Chair (Slovenko, R., and Zemon-Gass, G.), Task force on third-party payment and its effect on quality patient care, American Orthopsychiatric Association, New York, N.Y., 1977.

Sargent, D.A. The BCBSM Outpatient Psychiatric Clinic program: Criticisms and recommendations. *Michigan Psychiatric Society Newsletter,* 1977, *20,* 5, 7–8.

Saxton v. St. Louis Chair Co. (1966), 410 S.W.2d 369 (Mo. App.).

Schimel, J.L. Personal communication, November 28, 1978.

Schuster, D.B., Sandt, J.J., and Thaler, O.F. *The clinical supervision of the psychiatric resident.* New York: Brunner/Mazel, 1972.

Schwartz, M.C. Helping the worker with counter-transference. *Social Work,* 1978, *23,* 204–209.

Scott, C.H. Managers as teachers. *Wall Street Journal,* October 9, 1978, p. 20.

Sharfstein, S.S. Third-party payers: To pay or not to pay. *American Journal of Psychiatry,* 1978, *135,* 1185–1188.

Slovenko, R. *Psychiatry and law.* Boston: Little, Brown, 1973.

Slovenko, R. Psychotherapy and informed consent: A search in judicial regulation. In Barton, W.E., and Sanborn, C.J. (Eds.), *Law and the mental health professions/Friction at the interface.* New York: International Universities Press, 1978.

Strupp, H.H., Hadley, S.W., and Gomes-Schwartz, B. *Psychotherapy for better or worse: The problem of negative effects.* New York: Jason Aronson, 1977.

Stuart, R.B. *Trick or treatment.* Champaign, Ill.: Research Press, 1970.

Szasz, T.S. Psychoanalytic Treatment as Education. *Archives of General Psychiatry,* 1963, *9,* 46–52.

Tancredi, L.R., Lieb, J., and Slaby, A.E. *Legal issues in psychiatric care.* New York: Harper and Row, 1975.

Tarasoff v. Regents of University of California (1974), 529 P.2d 342, 118 Cal. Rptr. 129, vacated, 17 Cal.3d 425, 551 P.2d 334, 131 Cal. Rptr. 14 (1976).

Tennov, D. *Psychotherapy: The hazardous cure.* New York: Abelard-Schuman, 1975.

Towery, O.B., and Sharfstein, S.S. Fraud and abuse in psychiatric practice. *American Journal of Psychiatry,* 1978, *135,* 92–94.

Trogun v. Fruchtman (1973), 58 Wis.2d 569, 207 N.W.2d 297.

Trent, C.L. Personal communication, October 20, 1978.

Trent, C.L., and Muhl, W.P. Professional liability insurance and the American psychiatrist. *American Journal of Psychiatry,* 1975, *132,* 1312–1314.

Young, J.T. Separation of responsibility in the operating room: The borrowed servant, the captain of the ship, and the scope of surgeons' vicarious liability. *Notre Dame Lawyer,* 1974, *49,* 933–947.

CHAPTER 29

Racial, Ethnic, and Social Class Considerations in Psychotherapy Supervision

LA MAURICE H. GARDNER

> I find myself suddenly in the world and I recognize that I have one right alone: that of demanding human behavior from the other.
>
> Frantz Fanon
> *Black Skin, White Masks*

INTRODUCTION

Evidence of widespread difficulty among mental health professionals in treating the poor and disadvantaged minorities abounds in the literature of psychotherapy; and despite massive efforts at rationalizing failures, it has become apparent to a number of investigators (Everett, 1977; Gardner, 1971; Griffith, 1977; Jones and Seagull, 1977; B. Lerner, 1972; Lorion, 1974, 1978; Sattler, 1970; Smith, Burlew, Mosley and Whitney, 1978; Thomas and Sillen, 1972) that ethnocentric and sociocentric bias play a most substantial role in accounting for the observed problems. For numerous reasons disadvantaged patients have come to have increasingly greater amounts of contact with mental health professionals since the 1960s. But the extent to which they have failed to find such contacts useful and therapeutic would seem to indicate that traditional training programs in universities and clinics have failed to produce professionals with sufficient ethnohistorical perspective to truly understand or effectively ameliorate the psychosocial problems of nontraditional patient populations (Gardner, 1975).

This contribution to the theory and practice of psychotherapy supervision attends to the important but largely neglected topic of the complex and not easily resolved problems encountered by therapists—neophyte and seasoned alike—when they attempt to treat the psychosocial problems of individuals who differ from themselves and their more traditional patients in terms of race, ethnicity, or social class (e.g., the poor in general, Blacks, Latinos, Native Americans, Mexican Americans, Appalachian Whites, etc.). Its specific focus is upon the role of clinical supervision in assisting developing professionals come to better identify, understand, and resolve those psychodynamic, culturally conditioned, and-/or academically induced sources of bias which all too often attenuate therapeutic success with nontraditional patient populations.

But before attempting to discuss tactics, strategies, and technical recommendations for use by supervisors in training students to achieve greater success in treating disadvantaged patients, it seems entirely necessary to review the history of difficulties and failures, to discuss the major explanations which have been offered to account for the observed problems, and to present evidence and arguments suggesting that the phenomena are explained best in terms of the ethnocentric and sociocentric bias so characteristic of western society. In essence it will be proposed that the professionally embarrassing history of psychotherapeutic efforts with nontraditional groups provides excellent material for demonstrating the relevance of the emerging discipline of the sociology of psychological knowledge to understanding and correcting problems in treating the poor and disadvantaged minorities.

DIDACTICS FOR SUPERVISORS AND STUDENTS

Sociological Aspects of Psychological Knowledge about the Poor and Disadvantaged Minorities

There is a long history of ethnocentric and sociocentric bias among Western European and American social and behavioral scientists (Berry and Dasen, 1974; Cole and Scribner, 1974; Kamin, 1974; Thomas and Sillen, 1972). These attitudes are deeply entrenched in western society and reflect prevailing ideological, social, and political perspectives. Even in today's overtly liberal societies it can still be maintained that in the course of each individual's socialization clear notions are absorbed concerning differences between human groups. These notions carry with them a strong affective charge and condition individuals to repudiate characteristics considered alien and undesirable and to revere those considered desirable. Indeed, as the poet, Walter Benton (1943), once wrote ". . . hate is legislated, written in the primer and testament, shot into our blood and brain like vaccine and vitamin." It is difficult to rid one's self of attitudes which saturate one's social environment and are constantly reinforced by the social institutions with which we daily interact. It should come as no surprise, then, that men of science, being no less social creatures than the average man, often demonstrate the influence of collective prejudices in their professional contributions to understanding the psychosocial behavior of groups not quite acceptable to their own reference group.

The source of the propensity toward bias in western society appears to reside in a set of values which Max Weber (1958) called *the protestant ethic.* Bakan (1966) has subjected Weber's description of this ethic to psychological analysis with particular interest in its implications for personality development and social functioning. Bakan saw in the protestant ethic aspects of what he has come to call "agency." Agency is described as representing (1) concern with the individual rather than some larger organism of which the individual is a part, (2) emphasis on self-protection, self-assertion, and self-expansion, along with manifestations of isolation, alienation, and aloneness, as opposed to contact, openness, and union, and (3) the repression of thought, feeling, and impulse. Comparing his conceptualization of agentic modes of functioning with Weber's formulation of the protestant ethic, Bakan notes that:

> ... Weber pointed out how concern with salvation among Calvinists is associated not with neglect but devotion to secular affairs; ascetism is associated not with eschewing wealth but with its increase; predestination by God is associated not with the surrender of initiative but with its heightening; and the alienation of man from man is associated with superiority in social organization [p.17]. ... Within Protestantism, he identified predestination and preoccupation with personal salvation, the idea of the calling, and the ascetic ideal. In the personality he identified directed activity, social and personal organization, the pursuit of vocation with little thought to its extrinsic consequences, saving and profit-making, uniformity, regularity, personal reliability, self-control, the eschewing of sociability, the eschewing of magic and mystery, the pursuit of physical science, suspicion of emotion and feeling, great loneliness, and impersonality and distrust in interpersonal relations (pp. 19–20).

The attitudes and values described by Weber and Bakan provide a fitting reference point for understanding the sources of the many negative attributions made by therapists in relation to their nontraditional patients, as well as the aversive tendencies they demonstrate toward them. Closely associated with the protestant ethic was social Darwinism, a pseudoscientific application of evolutionary constructs and theories to understanding human cultural diversity.

Herbert Spencer, a leading figure in British scientic and intellectual circles in the latter half of the nineteenth century, taught a theory of social evolution which assumed that better adapted human groups had acquired higher physical and mental traits and thereby had made the greatest social advances. For him nineteenth-century Englishmen possessed the highest mentality and lived in the most advanced society. Thus the norms, social organization, and life-styles prevalent in England became the standards against which other people were to be measured. Groups living at lower socioeconomic levels were considered arrested at earlier stages of the evolutionary process and characterized as primitive, savage, and uncivilized. Their thought processes were said to demonstrate the absence of a conception of general facts, an inability to anticipate future events, the absence of abstract ideas, and the absence of the idea of causality (Cole and Scribner, 1974).

The problem with all ethnocentric thinking is its obvious lack of ethnohistorical perspective. What British social scientists had to say about other groups and nations was at one time said of British subjects. Thomas and Sillen (1972) report that two thousand years ago Cicero, the Roman orator, advised a friend: "do not obtain your slaves from Britain because they are so stupid and so utterly incapable of being taught." In relation to Europeans in general, the Moorish savant Said of Toledo declared, a thousand years later, that "races north of the Pyrenees are of cold temperament and never reach maturity; they are of great stature and of a white color. But they lack all sharpness of wit and penetration" (p.23).

Within the United States the poor and disadvantaged have varied considerably over time in terms of ethnicity and national origin. Attitudes of prejudice and acts of discrimination were directed not only toward Africans, Mexicans, Asians, and Native Americans, but also toward southern and eastern European groups. Kamin (1974), writing on *The Science and Politics of IQ,* demonstrated how prominent psychologists used their science of mental measurement to support and reinforce popular prejudices in relation to these groups and to foster legislation which would limit their immigration to this country. Among the psychologists most active in these efforts were Goddard, Terman, Yerkes, and Brigham. On the basis of the administration of IQ tests to immigrants at Ellis Island, Goddard concluded that 83% of the Jews, 80% of Hungarians, 79% of Italians, and 87% of the Russians were "feeble-minded." Kamin discloses other interesting facts about this early group of psychologists. Most of them were actively involved in the eugenics movement and strongly opposed the propagation of those they judged to be inferior. The comments made by Dr. Chester Carlisle in 1918 sound very similar to what one often finds in contemporary social science literature on the characteristics of disadvantaged groups. He stated that

... those lacking in intelligence capacity drift into the lower levels of our social life and come to be the denizens of city slums. . . . The more active and higher types among them leave their more defective kin. Hence their progeny show . . . gross intellectual defects. ". . . Pauper," dreaded word in every land, has epitomized the dregs of failure. . . . There often remains a residue of families who . . . cannot find work. . . . The old doctrine of predestination now dressed in terms of modern psychology reasserts itself (Kamin, p.2).

How much more powerful and influential can prejudices and self-serving ideologies be than when they are wrapped in the mantle of science? The tendency is no less prevalent in contemporary social science research and scholarship, although its expression has assumed a less explicit and more subtle form. Conspicuous examples are to be found in the resuscitation of the nature-nurture debate around observed differences across race (Jensen, 1969) and social class (Herrnstein, 1971) in measured intelligence.

Among the more important revelations emerging from excursions into the sociology of science and knowledge have been realizations that the concept of objectivity in science is highly overrated (Polanyi, 1958) and that claims that progressions and shifts in the paradigms of science are the hard-won consequences of linear accretions of empirical data and related theory construction are historical myths (Kuhn, 1962). The true nature of the scientific enterprise is far more complex and human; for science is shaped by its sociohistorical context which includes economic motivations and political priorities (Toulmin, 1977). The sciences of individual and collective human behavior are particulary prone to influence from nonrational sources. The scholarly activities of social scientists abound in intellectual snares and class prejudices that insidiously bias research and policy (Guttentag, 1970).

Buss (1975) makes the point that psychology as practiced by professional academicians occurs within a social context which contributes substantially to its prevailing ideas, ideologies, dominant research paradigms, and technology. Quoting Karl Marx, he states that it is the ideas of the ruling class that become the dominant ideas in a society and that such ideas are nothing more than the mental expression of material relationships. In this way, ideologies emerge that serve the purpose of legitimizing the existing class structure (p. 989).

Empirical evidence of the operation of this social dynamic in recent psychological research may be found in an investigation by Sherwood and Nataupsky (1968), who found that they were able to predict conclusions of black-white intelligence research from seven biographical characteristics of the investigators. These characteristics included: (1) age when the research was published, (2) birth order, (3) whether grandparents were American or foreign born, (4) mother's educational level, (5) father's educational level, (6) childhood in rural or urban community, and (7) undergraduate scholastic standing. Generally, investigators who concluded that blacks are innately intellectually inferior were from higher socioeconomic backgrounds, as might be predicted from principles inherent in the sociology of knowledge.

In a review of developments within the domain of psychology and culture, Triandis, Malpass, and Davidson (1973) found progress severely hampered by ethnocentric contamination in the design and execution of research. They made the important observation that most of the studies comparing abilities across racial groups were methodologically so poor that they should never have been published. But more serious and sociologically most revealing was the fact that not only were they published in large numbers, they were also uncritically and favorably reviewed and employed as a basis for public policy. M. Lerner (1969) has suggested that the field of academic psychology is one of the strongest supports of upper-class respectable bigotry and that much of what its practitioners choose to investigate and interpret is subtly influenced by this deeply embedded tendency.

What Flacks and Turkel (1978) have had to say of academic sociology seems equally applicable to academic and professional psychology, that is, that they appear to be institutionalized adjuncts of policy and management, with theoretical paradigms and research foci biased toward systems-maintenance. These observations and findings on the role of our universities and the professionals they produce are not a surprise in light of the fact that approximately 97% of our social scientists are white males from middle and upper-middle class backgrounds. This situation is perpetuated by university selection and admissions criteria, the character and content of our training programs, positions assumed and espoused by leadership in the profession, and role models of professional life styles and political priorities (Chesler, 1976). Scholars who support the prevailing beliefs of society get better press and greater reward than those who challenge them (Gordon and Green, 1974).

With these considerations in mind, we may turn now to a discussion of ways in which the prevailing social climate has affected the professional activities and scholarly contributions of psychotherapists in relation to the poor and disadvantaged minorities.

DIFFICULTIES IN THE TREATMENT OF NONTRADITIONAL PATIENTS

A critical review of the extensive literature on the psychotherapeutic treatment of the poor and disadvantaged minorities should convince the average reader of the need to revise hypotheses which have prevailed in the field that attribute responsibility for treatment difficulties and failures to deficits in the patient population. The literature suggests instead that the relevant explanatory variables are less technical than personal, less the problem of the victim (patient) than that of the perpetrator (therapist), and less the "deficits" of so-called "nonverbal" and intellectually "dull" patients than the arrogance and lack of sensitivity of professionals operating under the influence of systematically biased social and academic institutions. Professionals apparently possess strong negative attitudes toward treating certain populations, such as welfare clients, the retarded, and the severely disturbed (Wills, 1978). These attitudes stem apparently from their adherence to a value system which extolls the virtues of work, self-control, planning ahead, and achievement (McSweeny, 1977).

The earlier literature on the applicability of psychotherapy to the problems of nontraditional patients was developed primarily by psychiatrists. No doubt many of their preconceptions and theoretical biases may be attributed to their strong grounding in medical science with its emphasis on genetic and constitutional factors as central determinants of individual and racial differences in biological and social adaptation. Thomas and Sillen (1972) have provided a thorough and thoughtful review of this early literature, the largest proportion of which concerns itself with descriptions of the personality, character, and suitability for treatment of black Americans.

The ethnocentric and sociocentric nature of the attitudes and opinions expressed by contributors to this literature is documented by means of direct quotations from some of them who were distinguished and leading psychologists and psychiatrists (e.g., Francis Galton, G. Stanley Hall, William Alanson White, William McDougall, Carl G. Jung, etc.). Lauretta Bender (1939), for example, reported that the psychiatric problems of black youngsters, like others of their characteristic traits, such as laziness and the ability to dance, were reflections of specific brain impulse tendencies. A more modern version of this theory of the lack of neuropsychological differentiation was put forward by one Dr. A. Carothers who, in an address before the World Health Organization in 1954, shamelessly declared that Africans make very little use of their frontal lobes and that all the particularities of African psychiatry could be understood in terms of frontal laziness. For him the African was comparable to a lobotomized European (Fanon, 1966).

All too much of the early literature was cast in blatantly racist and sociocentric terms, suggesting that members of the lower-social classes and disadvantaged minorities were inherently lacking in the qualities and skills required to profit from existing forms of psychotherapy. Shortly after the end of World War II, the psychotherapy literature began to show an ever increasing interest in differences and difficulties experienced in the treatment of nontraditional segments of the population that had not been seen in private consultation rooms or clinics with any degree of frequency in prior years. While a small number of such patients had made limited contact with mainstream mental health professionals, few had received psychotherapeutic treatment. Most were discouraged from seeking professional care unless their problems had become so acute that they could no longer be managed or tolerated by family and community. When this point was reached they were most often consigned to public institutions where care was essentially custodial in nature (Hollingshead and Redlich, 1958).

While this neglect of the disadvantaged had not been so characteristic of the more community-oriented mental health programs of the century's first three decades, the arrival of psychoanalysis in America and the powerful influence its theory and practice came to exert upon the field in the 1930s and thereafter caused a dramatic shift in the service delivery paradigm. The mental health service atmosphere became more elitist and conservative (Levine and Levine, 1970). An unfortunate consequence of the extensive adoption of psychoanalytic guidelines for diagnosis and treatment was the generalization of its technically specific concept of analysability to criterion status for virtually every existing form of psychotherapy, and to some extent to the very definition of what constitutes a worthwhile human being (Szasz, 1961). These comments are not intended as a criticism of psychoanalysis per se, but rather as a demonstration of one important impact it had upon mental health service delivery systems in this county.

In his early writings on the psychoanalytic treatment of emotional disorders, Freud emphasized the favorable prognostic value of such factors as the severity and chronicity of a given disorder, the youthfulness, strength of character, and motivation of the patient, and the patient's ability and willingness to tolerate frustration (Strupp, 1973). These criteria, when applied generally to psychotherapy, resulted in exclusion of the poor and disadvantaged minorities who were considered traditionally as action-oriented rather than verbal, more extrospective than introspective, inclined to see their problems as physical rather than psychological (Heitler, 1976), impulsive and unreflective (Kardiner and Ovesey, 1951), and so on. As Schofield (1964) points out, traditional criteria of treatability favored the young, attractive, verbal, intelligent, and successful patient (YAVIS syndrome) and discriminated against the elderly, the severely disturbed, the poor, and certain minorities, many of whom would make substantial gains in psychotherapy if treated by better prepared and less doctrinaire therapists (Gardner, 1971; B. Lerner, 1972; Yamamoto et al., 1967).

The prevalence of the YAVIS syndrome appears to have remained fairly stable over the past several decades. It is a highly contagious, if not virulent disorder, which incubates in academic lecture halls and between the jackets of ever-so-sophisticated books and journals to be transmitted to susceptable hosts by "erudite" supervisors in the form of clinical lore and wisdom. Supervisors are often quite vocal in their pontifications on who is or is not a suitable candidate for psychotherapy. Not infrequently students are advised that attempts at using traditional forms of psychotherapy in the treatment of disadvantaged patients is no less than a waste of time (Lorion, 1978).

With the exception of the writings of a few discordant and challenging professionals (e.g., Adams, 1950; Heine, 1950; Sommers, 1953; Seward, 1956; and to some extent, Kardiner and Ovesey, 1951), published accounts of treatment experiences with black patients demonstrated that biased attitudes die hard and that psychotherapy as a social institution makes substantial contributions to the perpetuation of stereotypic racial attributions which not only distort perception and thought but also serve to reinforce the aversive and discriminative tendencies so rife in western society. Psychotherapists added to the lists of negative attributions which were said to characterize the poor and disadvantaged minorities. They described them as hostile and suspicious (Frank, 1947; Rosen and Frank, 1962; St. Clair, 1951), resistive to efforts at establishing rapport (St. Clair, 1951; Kadushin, 1972), defensive and inclined to conceal (Heine, 1950), untreatable and unreachable (Calnek, 1970), incapable of insight, and so on. Some would have us believe that the conditions of slavery were more favorable to the psychological security of blacks (Wilson and Lantz, 1957) and that their psychosocial problems are a natural consequence of their premature emancipation and separation from the symbiotic plantation-slave common membrane (Hunter and Babcock, 1967). Still others in the "cultural deprivation" idiom suggest that lower-class black families are becoming increasingly disorganized and that this is a major cause of pathology in the black community (Moynihan, 1965). Speaking of disadvantaged populations in general, Glazer and Moynihan (1963) declared that the principal causes of the plight of the poor are found in the internal deficiencies of their own way of life, and their total condition is seen not only as self-perpetuating, but essentially hopeless.

Paralleling the social action movements of the 1960s, mental health professionals began to take a new look at some of the operating assumptions employed in their approach to understanding and treating nontraditional patients. Civil rights demonstrations and the War on Poverty had already touched the consciences of many middle-class white professionals and sent them scurrying to prove themselves innocent of any contribution to the discriminatory practices that sustain the patently unfair distribution of opportunities, advantages, and services. National polls taken regularly since those times would have us believe that, with the exception of a few pathological groups, ethnocentric and sociocentric prejudices have been successfully purged from our society—another indication that paper never refused ink.

But it was not so easy for mental health professionals to deny complicity in active discrimination against the poor and disadvantaged minorities. Hollingshead and Redlich (1958) had already demonstrated their negligent, if not altogether callous, attitudes toward these groups. History was the most irrepressible and damning witness against them. At their hands disadvantaged patients had received the most severe diagnoses and the poorest quality of care. Seldom were they referred for either individual or group forms of psychotherapy (Yamamoto et al., 1967; Lorion, 1974; Pierce, 1974); and in the few instances where such referrals were made these patients were treated by the least experienced members of staffs (Hollingshead and Redlich, 1958; Albee, 1977).

Unfortunately, however, when mental health professionals were confronted directly with their culpability in relation to the negligence and mistreatment of nontraditional patients they could not tolerate the truth and associated feelings of guilt. As many would-be liberals are wont to do, they found new and more subtle rationalizations with which to assuage their guilt. The illusion of new insight found its way into the literature along with suggestions that promising new technical solutions were developing which would help resolve previous dificulties in treating the disadvantaged. Again there emerged a paradigm shift, this time specifically in relation to theory and practice in the treatment of the poor. To wit, while the earlier literature had found disadvantaged populations unsuitable for dynamic psychotherapy, the new, more progressive literature found dynamic psychotherapy unsuited to the needs of the disadvantaged.

Interestingly this turnabout appealed to a very large segment of mental health professionals and for a variety of reasons. But regardless of the motives underlying acceptance of the new formulation, it operated effectively to justify the continued exclusion of the poor and disadvantaged minorities from easy access to dynamic psychotherapy. The new formulations on the inappropriateness of traditional psychotherapy for the problems of nontraditional patients reached the status of official mental health ideology with the publication of the findings of the Joint Commission on Mental Illness and Health (1961) and the passage of federal legislation establishing the community mental health movement in 1963. These developments, while valuable in their own right, reinforced the bifurcation of service delivery along lines of social class and ethnicity. The affluent continued to receive dynamic psychotherapy, often in publicly supported clinics and community mental health centers, while the disadvantaged received short-term, crisis-oriented treatment or maintenance-oriented after care (Albee, 1977).

In a recent paper on national health insurance and mental health service delivery systems, Albee (1977) restated his long standing belief that psychotherapy was invented for and best suits the needs of the affluent. In the same publication McSweeny (1977) argued that psychotherapy is not suited to the needs of the poor because it requires of the patient expectations, values, and verbal skills which the poor do not possess. This sounds like a return to the earlier paradigm which blamed the victim for the failures of psychotherapists, but it is actually a mixed paradigm. Psychotherapy is unsuitable as a treatment of the poor because the poor are not suitable candidates for psychotherapy. The notion that the poor are largely nonverbal or at least lacking in adequate verbal skills for psychotherapy, has origins quite old in western thinking. A contemporary academic expression of this belief is clearly represented in the sociolinguistic theory of Bernstein (1961), who taught that the poor have a low level of language ability which is concrete, impersonal, and reflective of social rather than personal identity. The language style of the poor was seen as restricted and associated with an inability or unwillingness to defer gratification, apathy and hopelessness, hostility toward the greater society, and a tendency to retreat into primitive life styles (Panzetta and Stunkard, 1974). These notions, however, were called into serious question by Labov (1972), who used methods of participant observation to overcome reactance variables in his investigation of Black English Vernacular among inner city youth. When his subjects became sufficiently acquainted and at ease with him they demonstrated quite well-developed verbal skills within their nonstandard dialect which showed equivalent ways of expressing the same logical content as standard English.

Labov's work on and interpretation of the structure and functional value of lower-social class linguistic styles represents an important new trend in the social and behavioral sciences. Whereas divergences from middle-class norms, values, achievement motivation, IQ scores, and so on among disadvantaged subjects were once described as deficits, it is now considered less ethnocentric and more sophisticated to view them as *differences* related to variations in the adaptive demands of differing environments.

INNOVATIONS IN THE TREATMENT OF THE DISADVANTAGED

Adopting the *difference* paradigm to account for difficulties and failures in the application of traditional psychotherapies to the problems of disadvantaged patients, mental health professionals now argue that the demands of expressive psychotherapy run counter to both the expectations and the typical modes of problem solving found in lower-class, unsophisticated patients (Heitler, 1976). As evidence they cite data indicating that the poor often reject psychotherapy as irrelevant to their expectations and needs (Korchin, 1976), that they are likely to drop out of therapy prematurely (Poussaint, 1975; Heitler, 1976; Korchin, 1976), that they tend to seek rapid relief of symptoms with minimal commitment to the therapeutic situation (Korchin, 1976), and that they prefer medication and occasional advice to regularly scheduled talks about their problems (Hornstra, Lubin, Lewis and Willis, 1972). These observations have led some therapists to suggest alternative ways of solving these problems so that more effective treatment services may be provided for the poor and disadvantaged minorities. Korchin (1976) proposes the alternatives of (1) abandoning individual psychotherapy in favor of community-oriented interventions, (2) abandoning verbal therapy in favor of behavioral methods which the poor can better comprehend and respond to; and (3) adapting psychotherapy so that it is more responsive to the psychosocial skills and needs of the poor. To this list we would add a fourth alternative: modifying therapist thought and behavior so that bias, misunderstanding, and unnecessary technical rigidity are overcome and disadvantaged patients can seek assistance in a truly therapeutic atmosphere.

Recent work by Goldstein (1973) represents the most fully developed version of the alternative calling for the abandonment of psychotherapy in favor of behavioral methods which disadvantaged populations will supposedly better comprehend and respond to. Goldstein's approach, known as "structured learning therapy," is ground in modern social learning theory which places special emphasis on the cognitive processes of imitation, role playing, modeling and social reinforcement in the acquisition and extinction of simple and complex patterns of behavior. Rappaport's (1977) analysis of the potential advantages of structured learning therapy in the treatment of the poor and disadvantaged minorities emphasizes its relative simplicity and effectiveness in teaching desired skills to normal and abnormal subjects from a variety of social class backgrounds.

The methods of structured learning therapy are discribed by Goldstein and his co-workers (cited by Rappaport) as involving a situation in which patients are provided with numerous, specific, detailed, and vivid displays of interpersonal or personal skills therapists want to teach them through behavioral examples. Following the modeling behavior of the therapist, the patient is given the opportunity, training, and encouragement to practice the modeled behavior in the context of positive feedback and reward as his/her behaviors increasingly approximate those of the model (Gutride, Goldstein, and Hunter, 1973). It is assumed that social learning approaches to the treatment of the poor and disadvantaged minorities have the advantage of requiring only the most basic language skills and are value free. In addition to the specificity of the treatment, the program requires that it be tailored to fit the needs and life style of the individual patient—unlike the procrustean couch of psychoanalysis and the techniques of related dynamic psychotherapies. But as Rappaport (1977) points out, this technique-oriented approach does not provide safeguards against the intrusion of the negative expectations and self-fulfilling prophecies that may arise from the fact of the therapist's membership and socialization in middle-class society. Therapist personality variables may be as damaging in behavior therapy as in traditional psychotherapy.

Bergin and Suinn (1975), after reviewing the relevant research, have declared behavior therapies to be as loaded with affective and cognitive variables as traditional therapies. Patients who improved when treated with behavior therapy in the Temple study (Sloane et al., 1975) identified as the most helpful component in their treatment the interpersonal characteristics of the therapist, not a given technical procedure. Bergin and Suinn also cite an interesting report by Lazarus (1971) on where behavior therapists take their own troubles for treatment. In a survey of 20 behavior therapists who sought treatment, 10 were found to be in psychoanalysis, 5 in Gestalt therapy, 3 in bioenergetics, 4 in existential therapy, and 1 in group dynamics (sic!). Not one had sought out behavioral therapy. This rather amusing finding should give us pause in recommending the wholesale substitution of behavior therapy for psychotherapy with the poor. If a treatment's practitioners consider it second rate where their own needs are concerned it will not take long before it is identified as second class and worthy of only second-class citizens.

The third alternative—adapting psychotherapy so that it is more responsive to the psychosocial skills and needs of the poor—is one that is receiving increasing amounts of attention. Many investigators have attributed difficulties in the treatment of the poor and disadvantaged minorities to striking discrepancies between what patient and therapist believe to constitute the appropriate method of resolving an emotional disorder or behavior problem. While therapists expect verbal, cooperative, and psychologically-minded patients, interested in and willing to discover the psychodynamic basis of their difficulties, lower-class patients tend to focus more on possible physical causes, to expect rapid relief from symptoms, to be rather unsophisticated about the relevance of standard "talking" techniques to resolving their problems, and generally to be impatient with what appears to them to be psychodynamic "mumbo jumbo."

The recognition of a need to reduce the amount of incongruity between the expectations of therapists and patients led to recommendations that before therapy begins patients should be encouraged to openly and frankly discuss their conceptions of how therapy would best help in the relief of their problems. With such information and understanding at hand it was expected that the therapist could discuss differences and begin direct efforts at training patients for actual role-relationships with the therapist as they typically occur in psychotherapy (Overall and Aronson, 1963). In one respect this may be viewed as a method of socializing the patient for the psychotherapeutic role he/she is to assume and manipulating his expectations. As Frank (1961) argues, the induction of favorable therapeutic expectations makes patients more susceptible to desired change. In some respects role-induction, witting or unwitting, is an important aspect of all successful treatment, regardless of school or method. Such valuable procedures should not be left to chance or at the peripherally conscious level of unintentional suggestion. Patients have a strong need to understand what is to happen to them and to sense the logic of the therapist's method. Meichenbaum (1976) has recognized the importance of these principles and points out that it is the plausibility of a particular conceptualization of effective therapy rather than its scientific validity that convinces patients of the value of a given therapeutic procedure and facilitates successful outcome. He recommends as a general treatment strategy the sharing with the patient, in terms he can readily understand, of the rationale that led to the present treatment approach. It is the mutually understood working roles of patient and therapist that fosters the working alliance in psychotherapy; and it is on this basis that the therapist is able to elicit the patient's reasonable cooperation in achieving relief and change (Heitler, 1976).

A number of valuable techniques have been developed for the purpose of assisting disadvantaged patients to understand and adopt roles more consistent with the requirements of traditional forms of psychotherapy. Excellent reviews of these pretreatment parameters and their positive affects on process and outcome in the treatment of poor and disadvantaged minority patients may be found in works by Heitler (1976) and Lorion (1974, 1978). Available evidence indicates that role induction techniques, using such strategies as direct instruction, informational interviews, role playing, or modeling, prior to beginning treatment proper, greatly enhance appropriate patient role behavior and maximize opportunities for successful outcome. Prepared disadvantaged patients reported greater satisfaction with psychotherapy, while their therapists found them more attractive and interesting than their unprepared cohorts.

The fourth alternative offered here involves modifying therapist thought and behavior in such a way as to reduce the bias, misunderstanding, and unnecessary technical rigidities which frequently come into play in the treatment of disadvantaged patients. In light of the frequency with which therapists have described disadvantaged patients in strongly negative terms and have reported negative therapeutic results, discerning investigators could not help but suspect that powerful affective factors of an aversive nature might be operating in them and contributing to self-fulfilling prophecies.

More direct investigations of therapist's experiences and affective reactions to poor and disadvantaged minority patients have revealed that many therapists are aware of strong conscious aversive ideas and feelings in relation to them. Recognizing this, several authors have seriously questioned the extent to which therapists from white middle- and upper-income groups can have any capacity to empathize with the needs and experiences of such groups (Lorion, 1978). Clearly, psychotherapy is not a value-free social institution; and Griffith (1977) argues that cultural variables enter into treatment in ways that parallel their operation in society. There is a series of studies which indicates that the role of therapist competence and comfort in dealing with racial and class differences plays a central role in determining the quality of outcome. Not infrequently therapists who have worked with disadvantaged patients report strong feelings of discomfort with them and low expectations of improvement (Gomes-Schwartz, Hadley, and Strupp, 1979). Krebs (1971) found the white therapists he studies unable to work successfully with black patients, while Davis, Sharfstein, and Owens (1974) found rather striking indifference manifested by white mental health staff toward black patients. The major problem appears to lie in the shock and anxiety aroused by value differences. Middle-class white therapists know their own values and are conditioned to believe there are no others of substance or validity (Smith and Gundlach, 1974; Billingsley, 1968).

Lorion (1978) summarized major negative attitudes reported by therapists in relation to work with disadvantaged patients. These included: (1) a felt lack of rapport, (2) a conviction that these patients were too hostile and suspicious to enter a working alliance with them, (3) difficulty with being empathic or genuinely concerned with these patients, (4) disapproval of their sexual and aggressive behaviors, crude language, violent outbursts, and apparent apathetic response to treatment, and (5) the greater amounts of dysphoric affect experienced while treating this class of patients compared to more traditional ones. Siegel (1974) sums all of this up succinctly when he states that therapists generally prefer treating traditional white middle-class patients. The problem is clearly more severe with disadvantaged minorities than disadvantaged white patients, the protestations of Abramowitz and Dokecki (1977) not withstanding. White therapists appear to have accepted the popular notion that they will not come across positively or be of help to the black patient (Mullozzi, 1973).

Additional insight into why maximizing the value of traditional psychotherapy with disadvantaged patients might come through altering therapist behavior, thought, and affect in relation to them may be gained from attending to patient reports of how therapists typically perceive and react to them. Everett (1977) reports that disadvantaged patients frequently perceive therapists, particularly those with a psychodynamic orientation, as cold, distant, rejecting, paternalistic, condescending, and insensitive. Peck (1974) reports that lower-class patients frequently leave treatment after less than five sessions because of disappointment in the methods used by therapists. They failed to receive practical advice on how to solve their problems, lacked confidence in talking treatment, and did not find realized in the therapeutic relationship their expectations of an active, warm, and sympathetic professional. Yamamoto and his co-workers (1968) report that 61% of the black patients studied in their sample were particularly sensitive to and often found evidence of racial prejudice in their white therapists, while Warren et al. (1973) report data indicating that they felt less helped, less understood, less liked, and more alienated than white patients receiving treatment in the same facility.

The mutual distrust, lack of understanding, and even aversion that exists in many inter-class and inter-racial therapeutic dyads have placed great limits on the psychotherapeutic process. These can be overcome through specific didactic and experiential programs, as patient preparation experiments are beginning to demonstrate. Modification of therapist attitude and behavior may be accomplished through clinical instruction and supervision. Baum and Felzer (1964) have demonstrated that when psychiatric residents were given information about the life-styles, needs, and expectations of their disadvantaged patients, attrition rates declined sharply with 65% of these patients remaining in treatment. Analysis of process data from treatment showed increased communication and understanding, and generally improved therapist empathy and effectiveness. Mayer and Timms (1970) found that working class patients in England preferred therapists with better interpersonal skills and a capacity to intervene directly. Lerner and Fiske (1973) showed that the poor prognosis for lower class patients has more to do with therapist attitudes than patient attributes.

SUPERVISION PROPER

Psychotherapy is an exquisitely human enterprise. It is a deeply personal encounter—of necessity contractual—wherein a trained professional attempts to assist a suffering fellow human to resolve the psychosocial problems and conflicts that place unacceptable limits on the quality of subjectively experienced living. Beyond issues of formal training, theoretical orientation, and technical skill, the effective practice of psychotherapy will be seriously hampered unless the therapist's relation to his patients is first and foremost determined by love (Braatoy, 1954). The Scandanavian psychoanalyst Trygve Braatoy has written a guide to the practice of psychoanalysis and psychotherapy that is one-of-a-kind. The text is filled with clinical wisdom and focuses intently upon the role of therapeutic relationship factors in setting the course and determining the outcome of psychotherapy. It is an excellent source book for supervision where difficulties arise between therapist and patients due to differences in race, class, or ethnicity.

Braatoy views "nervous patients" as individuals who are thwarted in their ability to love and to give warmth. What they require above all else is a corrective emotional experience which will reduce their interpersonal anxieties and restore the trust necessary to endure the risks associated with opening themselves to learning that love and warmth do not inevitably lead to frustration and pain. For Braatoy successful change in psychotherapy will never develop or occur unless the therapist from the beginning possesses a surplus of warmth. This seems to apply particularly to the poor and disadvantaged minority patients who are not likely to respond to what he describes as classical therapist characteristics of fixed time schedules and detached, chair-sitting interest in "psycho-*logical*" problems. Knowledge of technique is, of course, essential, but enslavement to it is deadly. Braatoy believes that a reliable correspondence exists between love and technical wisdom. Addressing himself to difficulties often encountered when therapists attempt to treat nontraditional patients, he wrote:

> In such a community his ability to adapt himself to the demands of the patient, conditioned by local factors, his ability to improvise in situations not described in books or discussed in seminars, will be his most important asset. If he is an oral-intellectual . . . sucker, this unprepared food will disturb him very much. He will be steadily distracted by the lack of understanding he . . . still has to face and he will long for the meat balls chewed and regurgitated and ruminated on in New York (Berlin, Vienna, Egypt) [p. 52]. . . . If his attitude is that personal psychotherapy starts *with the adaptability of the therapist* he will have fascinating work wherever he goes (p. 53).

The ability to practice psychotherapy effectively cannot be acquired solely from classroom lectures and readings. Its proper practice relates to its status as a skill or art which combines knowledge of the science of human behavior with successful apprenticeship under a master practitioner. The role of the supervisor is, then, crucial in determining how well a given supervisee will internalize standards and attitudes of a truly therapeutic nature which can be applied to diverse racial, ethnic, and socioeconomic groups. Polanyi (1958), in discussing the nature of skillful performance, shows that a practical art which cannot be specified in detail cannot be transmitted by prescription. No prescription for it exists. It can be passed on only by example from master to apprentice. Supervisors must be selected with a great deal of care since their responsibility to students is so grave. As Polany puts it:

> To learn by example is to submit to authority. You follow your master because you trust his manner of doing things even when you cannot analyse and account in detail for its effectiveness. By watching the master and emulating his efforts in the presence of his example, the apprentice unconsciously picks up the rules of the art, including those which are not explicitly known to the master himself. These hidden rules can be assimilated only by a person who surrenders himself to that extent uncritically to the imitation of another. (p. 53)

Selection and Training of the Ideal Therapist

If we were to take quite seriously the characterizations of the ideal therapist that have appeared in the literature (Mintz, Luborsky, and Auerbach, 1971; Swensen,

1971; Truax, 1971; Strupp, 1973; Bordin, 1974; Bergin and Suinn, 1975) it would be necessary to look for him in the Platonic world of pure essences or forms–surely not within the space-time conditions and material limits of actual existence. Consider, for example the array of "virtues" required:

warmth	intelligence	curiosity	sensitivity
empathy	genuiness	interest in people	integrity
relaxed style	congruence	self-insight	self-control
spontaneity	understanding	tolerance	devotedness
skillfulness	originality	responsibility	broad learning
perceptiveness	industriousness	tactfulness	

While one would not anticipate finding all of these attributes combined in any single person, they do provide ideal standards for use in the selection of individuals to be trained for work as psychotherapists. But, as far as it can be determined, existing selection methods have failed to maximize the likelihood that the majority of candidates admitted to training programs will demonstrate high potential for successful functioning as therapists (Matarazzo, 1978). This may be due to the fact that potential therapists are drawn from highly competitive training programs (medicine, social work, and psychology) that make their selections on bases (e.g. grade point average, national competitive examinations, Miller Analogies, etc.) which may be fine predictors of academic success, but poorly related to the practice of psychotherapy. Braatoy (1956) has complained that we may too often choose the cool schizoid character with an IQ of 145 over the lively, warm person with an IQ of 115. Observing the professional styles and the generalized "affective neutrality" of many highly trained psychotherapists could lead one to wonder if the world would not be a better and safer place if they were to limit their contributions to the art and science of psychotherapy to academic lectures and systematically avoid its practice.

The strongest indictment of existing selection criteria used by the professions to supply the nation's mental health manpower needs has come from Albee (1977), who contends that the personality characteristics of most psychotherapists make them particularly unqualified to deal with other than middle and upper-middle class patients with relatively mild disorders. He views these professionals as obsessive high-achievers who are indoctrinated and rigid about the importance of time, inner control, and research. Patients, on the other hand, prefer and feel helped most by therapists who are keenly attentive, interested, benign, concerned listeners, warm and natural, not averse to giving advice, and who are able to "speak the patient's language" (Swensen, 1971). Bergin and Suinn (1975) report that the most frequent reason patients—traditional and disadvantaged—give for leaving therapy is the inexperience or incompetence of their therapists. It seems unlikely that such judgments are based on considerations of technique rather than on therapist interpersonal skill. Levine and Kozloff (1978) indicate that even in the absence of patient understanding of the relevance of technical competence to the achievement of their goals, a major determinant of satisfaction is the quality of the therapeutic relationship and "expressed affectivity" of the therapist. Examples of "expressed affectivity" include spending time to talk with patients, showing interest, and demonstrating devotion.

Research on the characteristics of successful therapists does seem to indicate that they share in common such traits as psychological good health, flexibility, open-mindedness, positive attitudes toward others, and interpersonal skill (Matarazzo, 1978). These are not the attributes of therapists who demonstrate persistent anti-therapeutic attitudes, the number of whom may constitute as much as one-third of the profession (Bergin, 1971). And yet, the difficulties and failures experienced by a majority of therapists when they attempt to treat poor and disadvantaged minority patients indicate that the characteristics we have come to believe to be necessary to the effective practice of psychotherapy may be facilitated or inhibited by such situational or stimulus variables as race and class.

While it seems clear that continued progress in the development and refinement of the scientific aspects of psychotherapy requires that it remain associated with graduate and professional school training programs, far greater effort must be directed toward the recruitment of candidates who demonstrate, in addition to the usual academic qualification, the personal warmth, open-mindedness, freedom of bias, and integrity necessary to forecast reasonable therapeutic effectiveness with patients regardless of racial, ethnic, or class differences. This would require that admissions standards be expanded to include more intensive investigations of the attitudes, beliefs, dominant traits and dispositions, and general personality patterns of white, middle-class individuals who are otherwise qualified applicants. It goes without saying, of course, that personality inventories, situational tests, and clinical interviews are not infallible. But, no doubt, their standard use would help in maximizing the selection of students more adept at working with people.

A much more difficult problem for the mental health professions is attracting and recruiting candidates with lower-social class and disadvantaged minority backgrounds who possess the necessary intellectual and personal resources noted above. Many such individuals exist. But for any number of reasons they either fail to be recruited or admitted to graduate programs, or they fail to consider the prospects of such a career and do not apply. Whatever the phenomemological reasons, there can be little doubt that a long history of tacit and systematic discrimination has created a situation in which the poor and disadvantaged minorities have very limited opportunities to acquire quality education. Considerable evidence indicates that therapists from disadvantaged backgrounds tend to be effective in the psychotherapeutic treatment of patients who vary extensively in racial and social class characteristics (Gardner, 1971; Lorion, 1974; Smith, Burlew, Mosley, and Whitney, 1978).

Effective psychotherapists demonstrate far more flexibility and willingness to introduce parameters or modifications in standard technique when necessary in order to suit the treatment to the patient rather than the reverse. Basic to this flexibility is the therapist's ability to provide a nonthreatening, safe, trusting, or secure atmosphere through his own acceptance, positive regard, love, valuing, or nonpossessive warmth for the patient (Truax, 1971). Among the modifications such therapists have introduced with success are pre-therapy role induction interviews (Albronda, Dean, and Starkweather, 1964; Hoehn-Saric, Frank, Imber, Nash, Stone, and Battle, 1964; Orne and Wender, 1968), the use of specially prepared film demonstrating typical therapist and patient roles in traditional psychotherapy (Strupp and Bloxom, 1973), offering treatment in a direct, simple manner with minimal emphasis on social distance between patient and therapist (Gould, 1967), readiness to use more directive approaches when indicated, making sessions less formal, using role playing techniques during therapy to clarify issues, and the willingness to introduce educational and guidance materials to enhance patient's understanding (Peck, 1974).

In relation to the poor and disadvantaged minorities, the ideal therapist acknowledges the existence of real differences in life-style and value orientation. He/she uses his/her well-developed capacities for open-mindedness and empathy to comprehend the functional and adaptive nature of the patient's differences and thereby gains insight into what, for this patient, constitutes effective coping and how best to diagnose psychopathology in psychosocial environments which differ substantially from his/her own. The effective therapist understands the nature of prejudice and its ubiquity. Forearmed, he/she is sensitive to the movement of its currents both within himself/herself and in his/her patient. Such therapists can directly confront racial and class issues in psychotherapy and open sessions to their frank discussion, while at the same time encouraging the patient to honestly explore feelings, fantasies, fears, and expectations related to racial or social class differences (Everett, 1977). This kind of therapist is in all manner accepting of the patient as an equal and respecting of his/her personhood and individuality. Most of all, he/she lacks the defensive attitudes that lead so many therapists to explain away difficulties and failures in terms of the patient's negative transference reactions; for this kind of therapist understands that these reactions in patients may in many instances be as justifiably labeled countertransference as transference (Braatoy, 1956).

Along with didactic instruction in matters of therapeutic technique and careful analysis of process variables in a continuing case, a major goal of psychotherapy supervision must be the activation of those cognitive and emotional elements within the student which approximate characteristics of the ideal therapist and maximize the likelihood of therapeutic efficacy with a wide variety of patients. This is a large, important, and not easily accomplished task. At times it may be rather lengthy and require that a given supervisor-supervisee relationship have stability of a year or more. Most important, however, is that the supervisor possess the knowledge, technical skill, and personal qualities to be developed in the supervisee, and that the supervisee demonstrate the potential necessary to reach the desired goal. One can no more make a silk purse out of a sow's ear than a sow can make a silk purse. Hence, the issue of selection applies equally to students and supervisors. All too often professionals are elevated to the status of supervisor on the basis of seniority or longevity rather than, more rationally, on the basis of recognized excellence as practicing therapists. This practice must be ended if we are to improve the overall quality of manpower in this important field of human service.

The ideal supervisor possesses many of the attributes of the ideal therapist. In addition he/she will have demonstrated superior competence as a therapist with treatable patients from a wide variety of racial, ethnic, and social class backgrounds. He/she will have a special appeal to students and colleagues as a role model because of his/her skill, knowledge, and clinical wisdom; his/her demonstrated effectiveness as a teacher, his/her interest in the understanding of variations in behavior and their adaptive significance, his/her personal warmth and humanity, and his/her noteworthy devotion to the profession. The average supervisor can hope only to approximate this ideal image and those responsible for the clinical training of students might use it as a standard in the selection and assignment of supervisors. It is this kind of supervisor who serves best and accomplishes most in helping developing psychotherapists actualize their potential as agents of constructive behavioral change.

Characteristics of the Novice Therapist

The student who has entered his/her novitiate as a psychotherapist is typically filled with complex and conflicting ideàs and emotions. On the one hand he/she may be quite excited about the opportunity finally to apply his/her theoretical knowledge and put to test long-nurtured fantasies of achieving recognition by peers and supervisors as an exceptionally talented and competent psychotherapist. He/she will welcome the opportunity to learn more about human psychodynamics and will eagerly take to supervision as disciple to master. On the other hand, however, the novice therapist will approach these opportunities with trepidation and depressive anxiety, fearing that his/her performance may fall well beneath the expected standard and that, at best, he/she will be considered mediocre and, at worst, totally incompetent. Empathic understanding of the novice's dilemma should guide supervisory technique. The trainee's anxiety constitutes the greatest obstacle to his/her learning and effective use of the supervisory process. Hence the atmosphere of supervisory sessions should resemble the atmosphere of psychotherapy which is, after all, no less than an ideal condition for learning (Matarazzo, 1978; Porter, 1979). While novice therapists will be taxed and challenged in learning to practice psychotherapy effectively with traditional patients, they are likely to experience special difficulties in the treatment patients who are poor or members of disadvantaged minority groups. As noted in an earlier paper (Gardner, 1975) mental health professionals from traditional backgrounds frequently experience massive frustration and feelings of impotence when they attempt to diagnose and treat nontraditional patients. These patients bring psychosocial problems of a complexity not at all discussed or predicted during the trainee's graduate studies. Aside from relative ignorance of the values, life-styles, coping patterns, and goals of these nontraditional patients, the novice therapist has to face the difficult task of recognizing and coming to terms with the many distortions, myths, misunderstandings, and outright prejudices about them that he/she has internalized in the course of his/her familial, cultural, and academic socialization. The frustration and shock of initial experiences in the treatment of the nontraditional patient may be buffered by supervisors through a process of anticipatory preparation involving a more positive presentation of the personality structures, life styles, and potentials of the group to which the patient belongs.

The supervisor, of course, should have a reservoir of positive therapeutic experiences with nontraditional patients from which he can draw instructive, anxiety-reducing, and insight-inducing examples. If the supervisor has had no such experiences he/she will probably not be of much help to his trainee and should probably disqualify himself/herself from supervising the treatment. It is of critical importance that a supervisor have special knowledge of and empathy for the class of patients whose treatment he/she is to supervise. Otherwise the student runs the risk of internalizing erroneous beliefs, faulty dynamic formulations, and alienating biases. In terms of outcome in the treatment of nontraditional patients by novice therapists, there is a complex interaction of variables (supervisor $\times$ therapist $\times$ patient $\times$ race $\times$ ethnicity $\times$ class $\times$ sex) which will determine the nature and quality of the therapeutic process. Since these interactions may either enhance or seriously impede therapeutic progress they deserve the most careful consideration.

Training Therapists to Work Effectively with Nontraditional Patients

A careful study of comparative psychotherapy from historical (Ellenberger, 1970) and cross-cultural (Davidson, 1969; Doob, 1965) vantage points demonstrates that the diverse psychological methods that have been employed to diagnose and treat psychosocial disorders bear striking formal similarities despite great variations in content conditioned by historical era and geographic location. Indeed, dynamic psychotherapy appears to have found effective use with almost every known human group (Ellenberger, 1970). We have yet, however, to determine the generic components of psychotherapy; and as we may infer from the published literature, local commitments and preoccupations in terms of technique and definitions of suitable patient characteristics operate not only to impede progress toward this goal, but also to place unnecessary limits on the range of application of available methods.

We have seen in the literature reviewed thus far that very little effort has been directed toward the development of systematic training programs to prepare psychotherapists to work more effectively with the poor or with disadvantaged minorities; and only in recent years have there appeared efforts at experimenting with and modifying traditional treatment approaches to make them more relevant to the expectations and needs of nontraditional groups (Heitler, 1976; Lorion, 1978). The time has come to begin programmatic research on methods of assisting therapists to acquire the special cognitive and emotional orientations necessary for effectively treating such patients. Without scientifically tested procedures those who would teach methods of supervision or engage in the direct supervision of work with nontraditional patients will have to rely upon an underdeveloped literature, unvalidated personal experience and knowledge, and a variety of trial-and-error experiences guided by keenly attuned empathy and clinical wisdom.

Since much of the empirical evidence indicates that race, ethnicity, and social class bear no direct relationship to outcome in traditional psychotherapy (Bergin and Suinn, 1975), but rather that ethnocentricity (Yamamoto et al, 1967) and the lack of democratic attitudes and values (B. Lerner, 1972) are strongly implicated in the observed difficulties and failures, supervision of therapists treating nontraditional patients must give particular attention to the interpersonal aspects of the therapeutic interaction process. Clearly the personality of the therapist—the kind of person he is, beyond his specific preparation—influences his treatment behaviors and effectiveness (Strupp, 1973).

Frank (1972) has proposed that all forms of psychotherapy share in common the following characteristics: (1) an emotionally charged, confiding relationship; (2) a therapeutic rationale shared by therapist and patient; (3) the provision of new and corrective information by precept, example, and self-discovery; (4) reinforcement of the patient's expectation of help; (5) providing the patient with experiences of success; and (6) the facilitation of emotional arousal. These aspects of the therapeutic process become effective in relationships marked by warmth, closeness, and the sense that the therapist genuinely cares about the patient and conducts the treatment with relaxed rapport and open communication (Bergin and Suinn, 1975).

Reviews of theoretical and empirical literature on the nature and efficacy of training and supervision in psychotherapy (Matatazzo, 1978; Porter, 1979) provide valuable information on procedures most likely to be successful in assisting trainees develop desirable therapeutic attitudes and skills. These, of course, include didactic instruction, supervisor modeling of empathy, warmth, and respect, and live experience with cases followed by supervisory feedback after sessions. The aims of these procedures are the development of interviewing skills which facilitate communication and elicit relevant information, initiating, observing, and understanding the emergence of a positive therapeutic alliance, strengthening capacities for empathy, and improving the accuracy of the student's conceptualization of the patient's dynamics. These procedures and achievements are essential in supervisory work where patients are either traditional or nontraditional. Let us consider them, however, in terms of work with nontraditional patients.

Didactic Instruction

DeBell (1963) defines the purposes of psychotherapy supervision as teaching and testing. The supervisor has the responsibility of imparting theoretical and empirical knowledge of psychodynamics and the therapeutic process to students, along with the systematic monitoring of student progress toward approximating standards of excellence in both domains. Experienced therapists know well and often bemoan the fact that trainees vary extensively in the amount and quality of personal and academic preparation they demonstrate for sucessful work as psychotherapists. A perennial problem has been the gap—bridged with some difficulty—between formal classroom preparation (lecture/seminar) and the kinds of knowledge required for effective work with real people in the real world, especially in relation to disadvantaged populations dwelling in large urban centers.

The main deficit in the average program of didactic instruction is the lack of adequate opportunities to develop the cross-cultural and ethnohistorical frames of reference which facilitate work with the poor and disadvantaged minorities. Clearly students in preparation to become psychotherapists should receive substantial training in such areas as urban and ethnic studies, the methodology and findings of cross-cultural research, and the fascinating new insights into behavior emerging in the field of ecological psychology. This diverse but interrelated body of knowledge might easily be synthesized and taught in a required course on racial and cultural factors in mental health practice (Gardner, 1975).

In the case of students who lack preparation in understanding differences in behavior, coping, personality organization, styles of relating, and attitudes toward mental disorder and its treatment from ethnohistorical and cross-cultural perspectives, clinical training facilities will be required to develop appropriate didactic programs and lobby for their inclusion in the academic departments from which they draw their trainees. Once the supervisor is certain that the student has mastered the basic intellectual knowledge necessary for practice, he/she is then free to use supervisory sessions to assist him/her in verbalizing material from therapeutic transactions, in organizing it mentally so as to discern its structural and process characteristics, and in providing an opportunity for the student to review his/her specific understanding and technical interventions with his/her patients—traditional or nontraditional. It must be understood that a knowledge base is required for understanding life styles, correctly diagnosing problems, and developing accurate empathy.

Where a supervisor encounters students with substantial ignorance of the typical psychosocial patterns and culturally conditioned life-styles of the nontraditional patients he/she is to treat, it will be of special importance that he/she be able to provide the student with informative input and guide his/her readings so that the student may achieve optimal understanding of the sociohistorical context of the patient's personality and problems. Aside from the supervisor's personal knowledge and experience in relation to the patient's reference group, he/she will need to have an especially well-informed and reliable grasp of existing social and behavioral science literature on the group so as to be able to help the student in selecting the less biased and less distorted contributions.

In view of the fact that trainees are often defensive and fail to disclose aspects of therapeutic interaction which might make them uncomfortable or cause embarrassment in supervision, the use of videotaping of therapeutic sessions has been found to be of great value (Matarazzo, 1978). One would suspect that it would be of even greater value in instances where the operation of ethnocentric and sociocentric bias can seriously impede therapeutic progress. In today's liberal atmosphere it is difficult for sophisticated individuals to acknowledge the existence of attitudes of prejudice in themselves (Gaertner, 1976). Videotaping, then, will permit relating actual therapist behaviors and transactions to classical examples described in the literature of inter-racial and inter-class psychotherapy (Gardner, 1971; Lorion, 1978).

Another approach to enhancing therapist effectiveness through the supervisory process that is essentially didactic in nature is the use of pre-therapy preparation techniques with trainees. Herein the supervisor discusses in detail with the trainee, prior to the treatment beginning, diagnostic and social history information available along with what attitudes, defensive styles, cultural differences, and therapeutic expectations, may be anticipated in relation to the patient's reference group (Baum and Felzer, 1964). I have often found it useful to inquire of the student the specific geographic area in which the patient was socialized and educated. This information is of particular value in helping students realize the contribution of specific social ecologies to shaping a patient's values, life styles, and favored coping mechanisms, as well as his/her definitions of what constitutes normal or abnormal patterns of behavior. Whatever variables are selected for purposes of assisting students to obtain essential knowledge, the existence of such knowledge in the therapist contributes to increased rapport, the elimination of tactless phraseology, and the development of more effective communication and comprehension of the social realities of nontradition patients (Griffith, 1977).

The Role of Modeling in the Teaching and Learning of Psychotherapy

It would appear from what little empirical data are available that the use of modeling techniques in the supervisory process is most productive of clinical learning and skill when it follows a period of didactic instruction. With a conceptual frame of reference the student seems better able to discern the most relevant and significant aspects of the supervisor's (model's) behavior (Uhleman, Leo, and Stone, 1976). As social learning theorists have demonstrated in recent years (Bandura, 1969), much of the most significant learning that occurs in humans, that is, the acquisition of new modes of behavior or the modification of existing patterns, takes place as a consequence of observing the behaviors of others and their outcome. The processes involved have been referred to variously as observational learning, vicarious learning, modeling, imitation, and identification. Bandura boasts that such procedures are "ideally suited for effecting diverse outcomes including elimination of behavioral deficits, reduction of excessive fears on inhibitions, transmission of self-regulating systems, and social facilitation of behavioral patterns on a group-wide scale" (Bandura, 1969, p. 118).

Virtually all the potential achievements attributed to the robust quality of modeling processes are relevant to what the supervisor wants to achieve in his/her work with student psychotherapists. But such knowledge is not really new. The power of the supervisor's potential role as a model in facilitating the learning of psychotherapeutic skills has been known and discussed in psychoanalytic literature for several decades (see DeBell, 1963). Kohut (1962) described these processes in terms of the psychoanalytic construct of identification and points out its central importance in shaping the professional identity and therapeutic styles of analysts in training. The process of modeling effective therapeutic attitudes and technical procedures is accomplished best when the supervisory relationship itself has "therapeutic" characteristics. For Porter (1979) this means that student learning is facilitated when the supervisor is able to (1) establish a positive relationship with the student, (2) make use of his or her emotional reactions to the student to help him or her discern current problems in the therapy, (3) demonstrate accurate empathy for the anxieties and difficulties experienced by the student in the treatment situation, and (4) show genuine interest in and devotion to the student's increase in knowledge and insight, as well as his or her growth and development as a professional psychotherapist.

In relation to the supervision of a student's treatment of patients from racial, ethnic, and social class backgrounds different from his or her own, modeling processes will be far more effective in promoting appropriate learning than didactic instruction. This is true because distortions, prejudices, misinformation, and deeply embedded anxieties were internalized originally through similar processes of social learning from powerful and prestigious models. It is well known that such deeply rooted attitudes are refractory to mere instructional methods. The supervisor must possess the attitudes to be modeled as a natural dimension of his/her personality and psychosocial behavior and must be able to communicate the genuine sense of comfort, mutuality, and empathy he/she experiences with nontraditional patients. This will almost certainly come through in his discussions of the case material—his/her ability to sense the nontraditional patients's needs, goals, and aspirations, his/her sensitivity to the patient's values and psychosocial outlook, and his seemingly clairvoyant ability to forecast the direction of the patient's associations and transferences.

The instructional film developed by Strupp and Bloxom (1973) suggests an excellent approach to enhancing learning through the modeling process. There would be obvious value in developing a series of such films depicting prestigious therapists engaged in psychotherapy with specific patients representing one of the several groups of the poor or disadvantaged minorities. The availability of such film for pre-therapy training with student therapists would contribute substantially to enhancing understanding and empathy for the disadvantaged patient and would, no doubt, correct many existing negative expectations in relation to his/her suitability for psychotherapy.

Yet other approaches to teaching effective psychotherapy with disadvantaged patients through the modeling process would involve the use of prestigious supervisors who themselves have origins in and continuing connections with nontraditional groups. These supervisors have the advantage of being able to speak authoritatively from experiences both as a group member and as a therapist successful in the treatment of that group. If such supervisors are too few in number to supervise the number of cases to be handled, they may at least be available for consultation or occasional seminars. The presence among trainees of individuals from disadvantaged groups may also be of value, especially in group supervision, since they have the potential for acting as interpreters of patients' language, metaphors, values, and life-styles. They provide also a direct basis for white middle-class students to have an opportunity to gain first hand experience of the common cognitive and emotional bases of behavior which transcend the accidental differences between groups conditioned by cultural factors.

Direct Experience in Treating Disadvantaged Patients

After the supervisor has worked with the student to determine that the patient selected for treatment meets basic criteria of motivation for treatment, at least average intelligence, freedom from brain pathology, and a reasonable degree of ego strength, and has discussed with the student unique aspects of the patient's disadvantaged psychosocial background, the student is prepared to begin regular therapeutic sessions. At this point the supervisor will want to direct the student's attention to aspects of the initial phase of therapy and what he/she must attempt to foster in it. In the initial phase of psychotherapy the student's task is essentially that of laying the ground-work for the future successful course of the treatment. Establishing a working alliance with the patient based upon mutual respect, confidence, and an understanding of the therapeutic process provides the basis for continuing the important work of understanding and changing maladaptive behavior patterns even in the face of great discomfort and anxiety. Here the supervisor assists the student to enter the world of the disadvantaged patient with special kinds of listening skills which involve understanding the sub-group's particular language, metaphors, and idioms.

Once the student-therapist is familiar with the patient's language and its cognitive and physiognomic meaning (Werner and Kaplan, 1963) he/she can learn to achieve the state of free-floating attention so necessary to grasping the underlying structure of the strivings and inhibitions responsible for his/her emotional difficulties. The importance of understanding the disadvantaged patient's "language" and frame of reference can hardly be overestimated; Such understanding will assist the student in making inferential interpretations that are explanatory, in accurately estimating the patient's level of anxiety and resistance, and in having the clinical wisdom which will determing the timing of confrontations and interpretations (Keiser, 1969).

Ekstein (1969) provides a framework for supervisors in detecting areas in which the student may be experiencing difficulty in learning to work effectively with patients. He speaks of the student's dumb spots, blind spots, and deaf spots. Dumb spots involve areas where the student lacks proper knowledge and skill related to therapeutic intervention. The novice therapist is certain to demonstrate dumb spots in the treatment of poor and disadvantaged minority patients where sharp differences exist in their respective backgrounds. It will be through studying process aspects of the treatment that the supervisor may test the student's knowledge of both the theory of therapeutic technique and specific awareness of the patient's psychosocial background.

When it comes to the student's blind spots the problem is more complicated and relates directly to his/her own psychodynamics as these are engaged in his encounter with a specific patient. Gardner (1971) has discussed this aspect of the therapeutic relationship in relation to the white therapist and black patient; and judging from the literature on disadvantaged patients in general, his observations may have substantial potential for generalization to problems in the treatment of other disadvantaged groups. Blind spots to be detected, monitored, and resolved, according to Gardner, include:

1. Culturally conditioned interaction tendencies which influence transference and countertransference phenomena, but are actually independent of them.

2. Defensive avoidance tendencies reactive to unconscious conflicts aroused in the therapists due to racial or social class aversion.

3. Failure to deal with subcultural differences that play a role in the patient's conflicts due to a need to deny such differences.

4. Assuming the "I love everyone. I'm not prejudiced" posture as an unconscious reaction formation against race or class aversion and/or hostility, which will frequently cause the therapist to be oversympathetic and overindulgent with his disadvantaged patient and inhibit the use of confrontations and interpretations even remotely associated with the patient's racial or class status when proper technique requires them.

5. Minimizing or overlooking severe psychopathology in the patient due to a tendency to attribute the source of the disadvantaged patient's problems to environmental stress, institutionalized discriminatory practices, and intercultural conflict.

Gardner's (1971) paper is an important one for understanding the complexities and consequences of the emotional and defensive aspects of therapist blinds spots and how they affect therapeutic interaction with dasadvantaged patients. It should be studied by students and supervisors.

Deaf spots may be defined in terms of the student's inability to listen either to patient or teacher due to conscious or unconscious conflicts within himself/herself. In relation to the disadvantaged patient, not listening and not hearing may represent either a form of rejecting the patient or a wish not to hear material that threatens to arouse guilt, anxiety, or otherwise unpleasant and disruptive affects. In relation to listening to and learning from the supervisor, student resistance may betray the existence of an unresolved hostility toward authority on the one hand, or a regressive desire for submissive acceptance of information from an overidealized source of knowledge (Ekstein, 1969). In this latter scheme lack of knowledge is associated with deprivation and hunger, and information is associated with food to be repetitively administered by a nurturant parental figure.

It is not easy for traditional psychotherapists to enter into or deal effectively with the kinds of problems and therapeutic behaviors disadvantaged patients are likely to bring to the treatment situation. Particularly troublesome from the middle-class therapist's orientation and value system are disadvantaged patients' tendencies to deny the psychological bases of their symptoms, the intrusion of transient paranoid feelings in relation to social issues, frequent and conspicuous silences, claims of being passive victims of life, recurrent lateness for therapeutic appointments, nonpayment of bills, missed appointments, and premature termination (Poussaint, 1975). This often observed configuration of behaviors may make therapists rather frustrated and impatient and they may become angry with the disadvantaged patient's different mode of responding to rules and regulations. Even more problematic is the situation in which the therapist has so thoroughly internalized standardized inter-class and inter-caste relationship patterns that he cannot be himself/herself with disadvantaged patients (Calnek, 1970).

The interactional complexities of cross-racial and cross-class psychotherapy may cause therapists to assume such negative countertransference defenses as coldness, distance, rejecting attitudes, paternalism, condescension, and insensitivity (Everett, 1977). These will be easy for the supervisor to detect when sessions are presented by means of audio- or videotape, but will be more difficult to detect from the student's presentation from written notes. Hence it is of particular importance to make use of these technologies in supervision where matters of race, ethnicity, and class are involved in treatment.

Strupp (1973, pp. 44–45) has provided several guidelines that will be of use to supervisors in detecting more or less subtle evidence of ways in which therapists may be unconsciously rejecting their patients. These seem important enough to list here.

1. The therapist harbors the conviction that he needs to be stricter than usual with the patient and consequently makes greater demands on him.

2. The therapist's activity level is increased to the point of discouraging the patient's free expression of thought and feeling.

3. The therapist decides the prognosis is poor and thereby justifies his lack of interest and his feeling that the patient is not worth helping.

4. The therapist gives less energy to creating a favorable emotional context for psychotherapy, viewing it as a waste of time.

5. The therapist recommends brief psychotherapy rather than more intensive psychotherapy.

6. The therapist comes to rationalize that the patient does not really need psychotherapy.

7. The therapist manipulates the transference in order to direct the patient in how he should lead his life.

8. The therapist encourages the patient in the avoidance of discussing certain topics.

9. The therapist shows evidence of not wanting to treat the patient and makes an effort to refer him elsewhere.

One cannot help recognizing in the guidelines suggested by Strupp (1973) many of the findings presented in the earlier review of the literature on the treatment of disadvantaged patients.

The supervisor will be of greatest assistance to the student treating disadvantaged patients when he/she can therapeutically bring the student to an awareness that ethnocentric and sociocentric biases are ubiquitous, that they play a significant role in all inter-class and inter-ethnic relationships and that they operate in specific and identifiable ways in the treatment process being supervised. The student must be shown that the first step in preparing himself/herself for work with disadvantaged patients will be acknowledgement of the existence of such biases in himself despite reluctance to do so (Yamamoto, 1971). On the basis of this first important step, the average student should then be able to move in the direction of ease in establishing a trusting therapeutic relationship with patients where race and class are sources of information about the context of patient behavior and adjustment rather than impediments to understanding and empathy (O'Shea, 1972).

Supervision, effectively conducted, will facilitate the student's understanding and overcoming of prejudices, will enhance learning about a variety of nontraditional patient groups, augment appreciation of the patient's individuality, and generally heighten the therapist's dedication to the goals of his patient (Boyer, 1964). It is on the basis of such understanding and empathy that student therapists will be able to be more flexible in their technical approach to treating their patient's problems. Modes of scheduling appointments, duration of sessions, and the use of educational and even directive techniques, where appropriate, will all lend themselves to flexible use to the advantage of the therapeutic process.

Handling Recalcitrant Problems in the Treatment of Disadvantaged Patients

While difficulties in understanding and empathy, along with fairly common countertransference problems, are likely to occur in the average therapist's initial work with patients who are poor or who are members of disadvantaged minority groups, most of these difficulties will lend themselves readily to resolution when the supervisor makes effective use of the didactic, modeling, and experiential procedures discussed above. But there will be instances, usually few in number, wherein, despite careful efforts in patient selection and pre-treatment preparation of the therapist, the supervisor will find that the student—due to deeply embedded neurotic conflicts and defenses—seems relatively incapable of creating a truly therapeutic climate in his/her work with nontraditional patients. In such instances the therapist may affect the patient in a psychonoxious manner and cause deterioration rather than salutary effects on his/her patient. Where the supervisor becomes aware of such developments he/she is duty-bound to intervene and, if necessary, to advise the therapist of the need to protect the patient's interests by dissolving the treatment relationship and arranging for the patient's transfer to a therapist with demonstrated competence in treating members of the racial, ethnic, and/or social class group to which the patient belongs.

The problem of psychonoxious therapeutic influence upon a patient that is based on ethnocentric and sociocentric therapist bias is less likely to occur in the consciously biased therapist than in the self-deceiving and self-protective therapist who delusionally believes that to be competent and worthwhile he/she must be all things to all people. Individual therapists with such problems may be placed on a continuum in relation to the extent to which their problem is more or less resolvable. The gradients of resolvability may be judged in such terms as the intensity of the antipathy, the relative location of the individual therapist on a scale ranging from the unconscious to the conscious realization of his or her antipathy, and the over-all openness to experience and new learning of which the therapist is capable.

Where the therapist has very intense and conscious antipathies of either an ethnocentric or sociocentric nature, it is best to restrict his involvement in the treatment of relevant patients. Therapists with milder and less conscious biases may more readily lend themselves to corrective influences; and while space does not allow a detailed discussion of the various methods that have been investigated in relation to the reduction or elimination of bias, recent reviews (Katz, 1976) suggest that some methods are distinctly superior to others. Weissback (1976), for example, interprets the empirical literature to indicate that such factors as belief similarity, equal status experiences, a favorable social climate, social and interpersonal intimacy, and the experience of inter-group successful cooperation in the attainment of superordinate goals are most productive of prejudice reduction.

Yehuda (1976) provides a similar list of conditions favorable to the reduction of inter-group prejudice which may be utilized in imaginative-creative ways to enhance therapist growth in the direction of reduced racial, ethnic, and class bias. These include: (1) equal status contact between members of various ethnic groups (e.g., the opportunity to meet and share experiences with fellow professionals from various ethnic groups), (2) contact (professional and otherwise) with high status members of disadvantaged groups, (3) involvement in projects requiring intergroup cooperation to achieve significant objectives; and (4) exposure to intergroup contact experiences that are intrinsically pleasant and rewarding.

In general the methods of altering ethnocentric and sociocentric bias in psychotherapists differ in no substantial ways from those proven effective with the general population. They may include intensive psychotherapy, self-insight and-/or sensitivity training, catharsis, humor (based on the obvious incongruence of biased versus objective evaluations of situations), training for appreciation of routinely experienced psychosocial and cultural complexity, role playing, and so on. A number of studies have suggested that group therapy may be quite effective in reducing prejudices among graduate level clinicians in training (Weissback, 1976), but this writer is not aware of reports on the outcome on similar efforts using individual therapy approaches. This is likely the result of one method (group) being experimental and intentional, while the other (individual) is probably ad hoc or incidental. Using either method, the findings accord with the reasonable expectation that the more severe the problem the more resistive it is likely to be to existing ameliorative procedures.

Although there may be a few and occasional positive surprises, supervisors may frequently be able to predict from observed therapeutic interactions the extent to which given trainees can overcome their ethnic and/or social class biases to the extent necessary to allow therapeutic efficacy with nontraditional patients. The supervisor, when he/she observes therapeutic potential in the trainee, should exhaust all methods available to assist the trainee in removing obstacles. When none of these work the supervisor should probably revise his/her judgment of the trainee and accept the likelihood that he/she has been deceived by the trainee's conscious sophistication and his/her ability to mask his/her biased racial and social attitudes.

REFERENCES

Abramowitz, C.V., and Dokecki, P.R. The politics of clinical judgment: Early empirical returns. *Psychological Bulletin,* 1977, *84,* 460–476.

Adams, W.A. The negro patient in psychiatric treatment. *American Journal of Orthopsychiatry,* 1950, *20,* 305–310.

Albee, G. Does including psychotherapy in health insurance represent a subsidy to the rich from the poor? *American Psychologist,* 1977, *32,* 719–721.

Albronda, H.F., Dean, R.L., and Starkweather, J.A. Social class and psychotherapy. *Archives of General Psychiatry,* 1964, *10,* 276–283.

Bakan, D. *The duality of human existence: Isolation and communion in western man.* Boston: Beacon Press, 1966.

Bandura, A. *Principles of behavior modification.* New York: Holt, Rinehart and Winston, 1969.

Baum, O.E., and Felzer, S.B. Activity in initial interviews with lower-class patients. *Archives of General Psychiatry,* 1964, *10,* 345–353.

Benton, W. This is my beloved. New York: Knopf, 1943.

Bender, L. Behavior problems in negro children. *Psychiatry,* 1939, *2,* 213.

Bergin, A.E. The evaluation of therapeutic outcomes. In A.E. Bergin and S. L. Garfield (Eds.), *Handbook of Psychotherapy and behavior change: An empirical analysis.* New York: Wiley, 1971.

Bergin, A.E., and Suinn, R.H. Individual psychotherapy and behavior therapy. *Annual Review of Psychology,* 1975, *26,* 509–556.

Bernstein, B. Social class and linguistic development: A theory of social learning. In A.H. Halsey, J. Floyd, and C.A. Anderson (Eds.), *Education, economy and society.* Glencoe, Ill.: Free Press, 1961.

Berry, J.W., and Dasen, P.R. *Culture and cognition: Readings in cross-cultural psychology.* London: Methuen and Co., Ltd., 1974.

Billingsley, A. *Black families in white America.* Englewood Cliffs, N.J.: Prentice-Hall, 1968

Bordin, E.S. *Research strategies in psychotherapy.* New York: Wiley, 1974.

Boyer, L.B. Psychoanalytic insights in working with ethnic minorities. *Social Casework,* 1964, *45,* 519–526.

Braatoy, T. *Fundamentals of psychoanalytic technique.* New York: Wiley, 1954.

Buss, A.R. The emerging field of the sociology of psychological knowledge. *American Psychologist,* 1975, *30,* 988–1002.

Calnek, M. Racial factors in the countertransference. *American Journal of Orthopsychiatry,* 1970, *40,* 39–46.

Chesler, M. Contemporary sociological theories of racism. In P. Katz (Ed.), *Towards the elimination of racism.* New York: Pergamon Press, 1976.

Cole, M., and Scribner, S. *Culture and thought.* New York: Wiley, 1974.

Davidson, B. *The African genius.* Boston: Little, Brown, 1969.

Davis, M.I., Sharfstein, S., and Owens, M. Separate and together: All-black therapy group in the white hospital. *American Journal of Orthopsychiatry.* 1974, *44,* 19–25.

DeBell, D. A critical digest of the literature on psychoanalytic supervision. *Journal of the American Psychoanalytic Association,* 1963, *11,* 546–575.

Doob, L.W. Psychology. In R.A. Lystad (Ed.) *The African world: A survey of social research.* New York: Praeger, 1965.

Ekstein, R. Concerning the teaching and learning of psychoanalysis. *Journal of the American Psychoanalytic Association,* 1969, *17,* 312–332.

Ellenberger, H.F. *The discovery of the unconscious.* New York: Basic Books, 1970.

Everett, M.L. *Race relations, racism and interracial psychotherapy.* Unpublished manuscript. Department of Psychology, University of Michigan, 1977.

Fanon, F. *Black skin, white masks.* New York: Grove Press, 1967.

Fanon, F. *The wretched of the earth.* New York: Grove Press, 1966.

Flacks, R., and Turkel, G. Radical sociology: The emergence of neo-marxian perspectives in U.S. sociology. *Annual Review of Sociology,* 1978, *4,* 193–238.

Frank, J.D. Adjustment problems of selected negro soldiers. *Journal of Nervous and Mental Disease,* 1947, *105,* 647–660.

Frank, J.D. *Persuasion and healing: A comparative study of psychotherapy.* New York: Schocken Books, 1961.

Frank, J.D. Therapeutic factors in psychotherapy. In. J.D. Matarazzo et al. (Eds.), *Psychotherapy 1971.* New York: Aldine-Atherton, 1972.

Gaertner, S.L. Nonreactive measures in racial attitude research: A focus on liberals. In P. Katz (Ed.), *Towards the elimination of racism.* New York: Pergamon Press, 1976.

Gardner, L.H. The therapeutic relationship under varying conditions of race. *Psychotherapy: Theory, Research and Practice,* 1971, *8,* 78–87.

Gardner, L.H. Clinical psychology and the urban scene: Retrospect and prospect. *The Clinical Psychologist,* 1975, *28,* 12–14.

Glazer, N., and Moynihan, D.P. *Beyond the melting pot.* Cambridge, Mass.: M.I.T. Press, 1963.

Goldstein, A.P. *Structured learning therapy: Toward a psychotherapy for the poor.* New York: Academic, 1973.

Gomes-Schwartz, B. Hadley, S.W., and Strupp, H.H. Individual psychotherapy and behavior therapy. *Annual Review of Psychology,* 1978, *28,* 435–472

Gordon, E.W., and Green, D. An affluent society's excuses for inequality: Developmental, economic, and educational. *American Journal of Orthopsychiatry,* 1974, *44,* 4–18.

Gould, R.E. Dr Strangeclass: Or how I stopped worrying about theory and began treating the blue-collar worker. *American Journal of Orthopsychiatry,* 1967, *37,* 78–86.

Griffith, M.S. The influence of race on the psychotherapeutic relationship. *Psychiatry,* 1977, *40,* 27–40.

Gutride, M.E., Goldstein, A.P., and Hunter, G.F. The use of modeling and role playing to increase social interaction among asocial psychiatric patients. *Journal of Consulting and Clinical Psychology,* 1973, *40,* 408–415.

Guttentag, M. The insolence of office. *Journal of Social Issues,* 1970, *26,* 11–17.

Heine, R.W. The negro patient in psychotherapy. *Journal of Clinical Psychology,* 1950, 16, 373–376.

Heitler, J.B. Preparatory techniques in initiating expressive psychotherapy with lower-class, unsophisticated patients. *Psychological Bulletin,* 1976, 83, 339–352

Herrnstein, R.J. I.Q., *Atlantic Monthly,* September, 1971, p. 57.

Hoehn-Saric, R., Frank, J.D., Imber, S.C., Nash, E.H., Stone, A.R., and Battle, C.C. Systematic preparation of patients for psychotherapy: 1. Effects of therapy behavior and outcome. *Journal of Psychiatric Research,* 1964, *2,* 267–281.

Hollingshead, A.B., and Redlich, F.C. *Social class and mental illness.* New York: Wiley, 1958

Hornstra, R., Lubin, B., Lewis, R., and Willis, B. Worlds apart: Patients and professionals. *Archives of General Psychiatry,* 1972, *27,* 553–557.

Hunter, D.M., and Babcock, C.G. Some aspects of the intropsychic structure of certain American negroes as viewed in the intercultural dynamic. In W. Muensterberger and S. Axelrad (Eds.), *The Psychoanalytic Study of Society.* New York: International Universities Press, 1967.

Jensen, A.R. How much can we boost IQ and scholastic achievement? *Harvard Educational Review,* 1969, *39,* 1–123

Joint Commission on Mental Illness and Health. *Action for mental health.* New York: Basic Books, 1961.

Jones A. and Seagull, A.A. Dimensions of the relationship between the black client and the white therapist. *American Psychologist,* 1977, 32, 850–855.

Kadushin, A. The racial factor in the interview. *Social Work,* 1972, *1,* 88–98.

Kamin, L.J. *The science and politics of I.Q.* New York: Wiley, 1974.

Kardiner, A., and Ovesey, L. *The mark of oppression.* New York: Norton, 1951.

Katz, P.A. (Ed). *Towards the elimination of racism.* New York: Pergamon Press, 1976.

Keiser, S. Psychoanalysis—taught, learned, and experienced. *Journal of the American Psychoanalytic Association,* 1969, *17,* 238–267.

Kohut, H. The psychoanalytic curriculum. *Journal of the American Psychoanalytic Association,* 1962, *10,* 153–163.

Korchin, S.J. *Modern clinical psychology.* New York: Basic Books, 1976.

Krebs, R.L. Some effects of a white institution on black outpatients. *American Journal of Orthopsychiatry,* 1971, *41,* 589–596.

Kuhn, T.S. *The structure of scientific revolutions.* Chicago: University of Chicago Press, 1962.

Labov, W. *Language in the inner city.* Philadelphia: University of Pennsylvania Press, 1972.

Lazarus, A.A. Where do behavior therapists take their troubles? *Psychological Reports,* 1971, *28,* 349–350.

Lerner, B. *Therapy in the ghetto.* Baltimore: Johns Hopkins University Press, 1972.

Lerner, B.A., and Fiske, D.W. Client attributes and the eye of the beholder. *Journal of Consulting and Clinical Psychology,* 1973, *40,* 272–277.

Lerner, M. Respectable bigotry. *American Scholar,* 1969, *38,* 606–617.

Levine, S., and Kozloff, M.A. The sick role: Assessment and overview. *Annual Review of Sociology,* 1978, *4,* 317–343.

Levine, M., and Levine, A. The more things change: A case history of child guidance clinics. *Journal of Social Issues,* 1970, *26,* 19–34.

Lorion, R.P. Patient and therapist variables in the treatment of low-income patients. *Psychological Bulletin,* 1974, *81,* 344–354.

Lorion, R.P. Research on psychotherapy and behavior change with the disadvantaged: Past, present, and future directions. In S.L. Garfield and A.E. Bergin (Eds.), *Handbook of psychotherapy and behavior change.* New York: Wiley, 1978.

Matarazzo, R.G. Research on the teaching and learning of psychotherapeutic skills. In S.L. Garfield and A.E. Bergin (Eds.), *Handbook of psychotherapy and behavior change.* New York: Wiley, 1978.

Mayer, J.E., and Timms, N. *The client speaks: Working class impressions of casework.* London: Routledge, and Kegan Paul, 1970.

McSweeny, A.J. Including psychotherapy in national health insurance. *American Psychologist,* 1977, *32,* 722–730.

Meichenbaum, D. Toward a cognitive theory of self-control. In G.E. Schwartz and D. Shapiro (Eds.), *Consciousness and Self-Regulation.* New York: Plenum, 1976.

Mintz J., Luborsky, L., and Auerbach, A.H. Dimensions of psychotherapy: A factor-analytic study of ratings of psychotherapy sessions. *Journal of Consulting and Clinical Psychology,* 1971, *36,* 106–120.

Moynihan, D.P. *The negro family: The case for national action!* Washington, D.C.: U.S. Department of Labor, 1965.

Mullozzi, A. *Interracial counseling: Client's ratings and counselor's ratings in the first session.* Unpublished doctoral dissertation, Southern Illinois University, 1973.

Orne, M., and Wender, P. Anticipatory socialization for psychotherapy: Method and rationale. *American Journal of Psychiatry,* 1968, *124,* 88–98.

O'Shea, C. Two gray cats learn how it is in a group of black teenagers. In I. Berkowitz (Ed.), *Adolescents grow in groups.* New York: Brunner/Mazel, 1972.

Overall, B., and Aronson, H. Expectations of psychotherapy in patients of lower socioeconomic class. *American Journal of Orthopsychiatry,* 1963, *33,* 421–430.

Panzetta, A.F., and Stunkard, A.J. Planning the delivery of mental health services to seriously disadvantaged populations. In S. Arieti (Ed.), *American Handbook of Psychiatry* (Vol. 6). New York: Basic Books, 1974.

Peck, H.B. Psychiatric approaches to the impoverished and under privileged. In Arieti, S. (Ed.), *American Handbook of Psychiatry* (Vol. 6). New York: Basic Books, 1974.

Pierce, C.M. Psychiatric problems of the black minority. In S. Arieti (Ed.). *American Handbook of Psychiatry* (Vol. 2). New York: Basic Books, 1974.

Polanyi, M. *Personal knowledge: Towards a post-critical philosophy.* New York: Harper Torchbooks, 1958.

Porter, M. *The effects of the nature of the supervisory relationship on participants' ability to give accurate descriptions of the client.* Unpublished doctoral dissertation, University of Detroit, 1979.

Poussaint, A. Interracial relations. In A. Freedman, H. Kaplan, and B. Sadock (Eds.), *Comprehensive Textbook of Psychiatry/II.* Vol. 2 Baltimore: Williams and Wilkins, 1975.

Rappaport, J. *Community psychology: Values, research, and action.* New York: Holt, Rinehart and Winston, 1977.

Rosen, H., and Frank, J.D. Negro patients in psychotherapy. *American Journal of Psychiatry,* 1962, *119,* 456–460.

Sattler, J.M. Racial "experimenter effects" in experimentation, testing, interviewing, and psychotherapy. *Psychological Bulletin,* 1970, *73,* 137–160.

Schofield, W. *Psychotherapy, the purchase of friendship.* Englewood Cliffs, N.J.: Prentice-Hall, 1964.

Seward, G. *Psychotherapy and cultural conflict.* New York: Ronald Press, 1956.

Sherwood, J.J., and Nataupsky, M. Predicting the conclusions of Negro-white intelligence research from biographical characteristics of the investigator. *Journal of Personality and Social Psychology,* 1968, *8,* 53–58.

Siegel, J.M. A brief review of the effects of race in clinical service interactions. *American Journal of Orthopsychiatry,* 1974, *44,* 555–562.

Sloane, R.B., Staples, F.R., Cristol, A.H., Yorkston, N.J., and Whipple, K. *Psychotherapy versus behavior therapy.* Cambridge, Mass: Harvard University Press, 1975

Smith, W.D., Burlew, A.K., Mosley, M.H., and Whitney, W.M. *Minority issues in mental health.* Reading, Mass.: Addison-Wesley, 1978.

Smith, O.S., and Gundlach, R.H. Group therapy for blacks in a therapeutic community. *American Journal of Orthopsychiatry,* 1974, *44,* 26–36.

Sommers, U.S. An experiment in group psychotherapy with members of mixed minority groups. *International Journal of Group Psychotherapy,* 1953, *3,* 254–269.

St. Clair, H.R. Psychiatric interview experience with negroes. *American Journal of Psychiatry,* 1951, *108,* 113–119.

Strupp, H.H. *Psychotherapy: Clinical, research and theoretical issues.* New York: Jason Aronson, 1973

Strupp, H., and Bloxom, A. Preparing lower-class patients for group psychotherapy: Development and evaluation of a role induction film. *Journal of Consulting and Clinical Psychology,* 1973, *41,* 373–384

Swensen, C.H. Commitment and the personality of the therapist. In J.D. Matarazzo et al. (Eds.), *Psychotherapy, 1971.* New York: Aldine-Atherton, 1972.

Szasz, T.S. The use of naming and the origins of the myth of mental illness. *American Psychologist,* 1961, *16,* 59–65.

Thomas, A., and Sillen, S. *Racism and Psychiatry.* New York: Brunner/Mazel, 1972.

Toulmin, S. From form to function: Philosophy and history of Sciences in the 1950's and now. *Daedalus,* 1977, *106,* 143–162.

Triandis, H., Malpass, R., and Davidson, A. Psychology and culture. *Annual Review of Psychology,* 1973, *24,* 355–378.

Truax, C.B. The outcome effects of counselor or therapist accurate empathy, nonpossessive warmth and genuineness. In J. D. Matarazzo et al. (Eds.), *Psychotherapy 1971.* New York: Aldine-Atherton, 1972.

Uhleman, M.R., Leo, G.W., and Stone, G.L. Effects of instructions and modeling on trainees low in interpersonal-communications skills. *Journal of Counseling Psychology,* 1976, *23,* 509–513.

Warren, R.C., Jackson, A.M., Nugaris, J., and Farley, G.K. Differential attitudes of black and white patients toward treatment in a child guidance clinic. *American Journal of Orthopsychiatry,* 1973, *43,* 384–393.

Weber, M. *The protestant ethic and the spirit of capitalism.* New York: Charles Scribner's Sons, 1958.

Weissback, T.A. Laboratory controlled studies of change of racial attitudes. In P. Katz (Ed.), *Towards the Elimination of Racism.* New York: Pergamon Press, 1976.

Werner, H. and Kaplan, B. *Symbol Formation.* New York: Wiley, 1963.

Wills, T.A. Perceptions of clients by professional helpers. *Psychological Bulletin,* 1978, *85,* 968–1000.

Wilson, D.C., and Lantz, E.M. Effect of culture change on the negro race in Virginia. *American Journal of Psychiatry,* 1957, *114,* 25

Yamamoto, J. Optimal treatment for patients of all races and social classes in a Los Angeles clinic. *International Psychiatric Clinics,* 1971, *8,* 143–166.

Yamamoto, J., James, Q.C., Bloombaum, M., and Hattem, J. Racial factors in patient selection. *American Journal of Psychiatry,* 1967, *124,* 630–636.

Yamamoto, J., James, Q. C.; and Palley, N. Cultural problems in psychiatric therapy. *Archives of General Psychiatry,* 1968, *19,* 45–49.

Yehuda, A. The role of intergroup contact in change of prejudice and ethnic relations. In P. Katz (Ed.), *Towards the Elimination of Racism.* New York: Pergamon Press, 1976.

CHAPTER 30

Sex Role Issues in the Supervision of Therapy

ANNETTE M. BRODSKY

We live in a time of rapidly changing sex roles. The options for appropriate behavior for men and women are expanding considerably and many individuals, including therapists, find themselves confused and uncertain about the parameters of expected and acceptable behavior for men and women. Years ago male and female clients seemed to operate on separate tracks. We could anticipate that the typical middle class 25-year-old woman was married and staying at home full-time caring for her young children (Bem and Bem 1976). Her male counterpart was less easily pigeonholed, but he was not expected to have a major involvement in the childcaring, nurturing role in the family. Should a marriage end in divorce, we assumed that (unless she was very disturbed) the mother would get custody of the children and most likely would need to find a job to subsidize the child support that often was not regularly forthcoming (National Commission, 1976). Her husband was more inclined to engage in extra-marital affairs (Kinsey et al., 1953), and did not find himself in a vastly different occupational role after divorce. Thus, he could expect less sympathy for any emotional sequelae.

Indeed, men have been described as relatively less rewarding therapy clients compared to their female counterparts. Men were noted to be uncommunicative, repressing their emotions and failures, and resenting weakness by the display of dependency on an authority such as a therapist. Women have typically been the "good" clients on the other hand; they are highly verbal, open about their weaknesses, and eager to appeal to the authority of the therapist. They have been characterized as readily accepting the blame for their problems and accustomed to the role of a dependent, help-seeking, and approval-seeking individual (Chesler, 1972).

The typical therapy dyad involved a male therapist and a female client (Chesler, 1971; Fabrikant, 1974). This was sex role consonant with the authority pattern established in our culture and, as noted by Phyllis Chesler (1971), the relationship was likely to parallel the role of the sexes in a typical middle class American marriage. As long as each party accepted his or her own place and the therapist continued to be male while the client was female, very few questioned the influence of sex roles on psychotherapy.

However, many of these stereotyped situations no longer exist as unquestioned norms. As Eleanor Maccoby noted (1971), "Our sex role free ego space has expanded." There has been an exponential increase in the number of new opportunities in careers, new life-styles, new modes of relationships between the sexes. Today, more than half of all women are in the labor force (U.S. Department of Commerce, Bureau of the Census, 1976), including the majority of mothers of school age children. Women no longer automatically get custody of the children in a divorce. While women's salaries are not even close to men's salaries yet (National Commission, 1976), women have increased their pursuit of professional careers in previously male-dominated occupations. Women were no longer willing to accept a subordinate role in relationship to men (Bird, 1968; Friedan, 1963), and this change, fostered by the women's movement, affected the institution of psychotherapy through the development of the feminist therapies (Brodsky et al., 1978) and the popularization of assertive training programs specifically geared to women (Jakubowski-Spector, 1973).

The movement toward male awareness of the effects of traditional sex roles on their lives has been more recent, but there is increasing evidence that men are rejecting the demandingly macho, strong, silent life-styles and are entering into relationships with their families and friends that include more involvement and expressiveness. Corporations must deal with men who refuse to uproot families for a promotion, and male students increasingly demonstrate that "fear of success" is not just a female phenomemon (Tresemer, 1974). While women are becoming attracted to masculine occupations for the money, men are entering more feminine domains such as nursing, elementary school education, and dietetics out of a new freedom to choose these options. Couples are entering into individualized marriage contracts, and the division of labor within marriages is not as rigidly assigned along sex role lines as it once was. Where divorce occurs (and the option to choose divorce is much more readily available as evidenced by its frequency, and the ease of "no fault" divorce), it is now likely to result in joint custody (Tresemer, 1974), with alimony going to either sex, and women as well as men paying child support.

SEX BIAS IN PSYCHOTHERAPY

Clients are coming to therapy with problems that reflect this age of transition in the sex roles for men and women. Many women specifically seek out female therapists, and others specifically request feminist therapists (Brodsky et al., 1978). Women no longer seem to consider male psychotherapists as more competent (Kirshner, et al., 1978). Male therapists are becoming aware of this shift in demand to female therapists and expressing concern with the consequences for their practices (Lasky, 1978).

The issue of which sex therapist is appropriate for which sex client became a sensitive issue in the early 1970s when it was suggested that only women should see female clients because of the great potential for sexism among male therapists (Chesler, 1972). The empirical data has not been particularly supportive of sex of therapist as a major difference in the satisfaction in therapy by clients (Brodsky et al., 1978), but more circumscribed studies of pairing of therapists and clients regarding attitudes toward sex roles has had more fruitful results in indicating the same-sex therapist-client dyads may show more empathy (Olesker and Balter, 1972; Kirshner, et al., 1978) than cross-sex dyads, particularly for women clients. Orlinsky and Howard (1976) demonstrated that sex of therapist and client interact in complex ways that single variable studies miss, so that young unmarried women clients are most likely to feel comfortable and helped by women therapists, while older, married women clients are equally or even more likely to report high levels of satisfaction from male therapists. Based on a survey by Kenworthy, Koufacos, and Sherman (1978), therapists today report less bias against women than previous complaints would indicate, but are still inadequately knowledgeable about women's situations regarding their psychological and physiological functioning.

The question of actual discrimination against women in psychotherapy has been raised in the context of the domination of therapy theory and practice by males, starting with Freud and his explanation of female inferiority as a result of the anatomical distinction between the sexes (Freud, 1924). Current charges of sexism in psychotherapy were examined by the Task Force on Sex Bias and Sex Role Stereotyping in Psychotherapeutic Practices of the American Psychological Association (APA) (APA, 1975). This task force surveyed women psychologists for examples of sexist practices. From the survey the task force derived four major categories of complaints:

1. Fostering traditional sex roles (e.g., encouraging the roles of wife and mother regardless of the goals of the client).

2. Bias in expectations and devaluation of women (e.g., quickness to label women as manipulative, seductive, and hysterical).

3. Sexist use of psychoanalytic concepts (e.g., use of penis envy to explain a client's frustration with discrimination on the job).

4. Responding to women as sex objects, including seduction of female clients (e.g., focusing on a woman's sexuality regardless of the presenting complaint).

As a result of these complaints from women psychologists reflecting on their roles as therapists, patients, and colleagues of other therapists, the task force developed recommendations to the various boards, committees, and divisions of the APA, including recommendations for the training of psychotherapists. Essentially, there was felt a need for sensitizing therapists to the issues of sex bias and sex role stereotyping through education in practicum settings and through postgraduate workshops and consciousness raising seminars (APA, 1975). Direct guidelines for positive approaches to working with women clients were also produced, as a guide to educational efforts (APA, 1978).

No comparable study has been done to identify the issues that male clients raise about their female therapists, but we can assume that this combination has not been as prominent and we can also assume that in most cases, the guidelines developed for women could probably be applied to men with equal success. The 13 guidelines for therapy with women were stated in nonsex specified language with only a few that need be interpreted exclusively for women. Thus, most of these guidelines that address sex role issues are relevant for both sexes:

Table 1[a]

1. The conduct of therapy should be free of constrictions based on gender-defined roles, and the options explored between client and practitioner should be free of sex role stereotypes.
2. Psychologists should recognize the reality, variety, and implications of sex discriminatory practices in society and should facilitate client examination of options in dealing with such practices.
3. The therapist should be knowledgeable about current empirical findings on sex roles, sexism, and individual differences resulting from the client's gender-defined identity.
4. The theoretical concepts employed by the therapists should be free of sex bias and sex role stereotypes.
5. The psychologist should demonstrate acceptance of women as equal to men by using language free of derogatory labels.
6. The psychologist should avoid establishing the source of personal problems within the client when they are more properly attributable to situational or cultural factors.
7. The psychologist and a fully informed client mutually should agree upon aspects of the therapy relationship such as treatment modality, time factors, and fee arrangements.
8. While the importance of the availability of accurate information to a client's family is recognized, the privilege of communication about diagnosis, prognosis, and progress ultimately resides with the client, not with the therapist.
9. If authoritarian processes are employed as a technique, the therapy should not have the effect of maintaining or reinforcing stereotypic dependency of women.
10. The client's assertive behaviors should be respected.
11. The psychologist whose female client is subjected to violence in the form of physical abuse or rape should recognize and acknowledge she is the victim of a crime.
12. The psychologist should recognize and encourage exploration of a woman client's sexuality and should recognize her right to define her own sexual preferences.
13. The psychologist should not have sexual relations with the client, nor treat her as a sex object.

TRAINING ISSUES

In order to transfer these guidelines into training situations, it is necessary to consider the following two points. First, there is usually no recognition in oneself of one's particular biases. Prejudice against women or men or any other defined group implies an unawareness of this aspect of one's personality. Therefore, the training to remove such biases involves the identifying of the particular practices that are high risk for bias by someone other than the individual in question.

Second, in a training situation, the supervisor is also likely to have certain prejudices and biases, and he or she brings these traits to the supervisory sessions. Thus it is possible in all earnestness and with all good intentions for practices

[a]From "Guidelines for Therapy With Women," Task Force on Sex Bias and Sex Role Stereotyping in Psychotherapeutic Practice, October 1, 1976. Copyright 1978 by the American Psychological Association. Reprinted by permission.

noxious to women or men to be perpetuated through a training situation in which neither party is aware that biases exist. On the other hand, when either or both parties are educated to the common stereotypes and biases in psychotherapeutic situations, growth is experienced by all involved: the supervisor, the trainee, and the client.

THE MALE SUPERVISOR

I have maintained that one of the experiences necessary for training students to recognize their sex role biases is that they receive at least one segment of the total training experience in which the supervisor is the opposite sex of the trainee (Brodsky, 1977). In the traditional supervisory dyad, the supervisor is male and the trainee is also male. With the greater percentage of female trainees in recent years, it is now more likely that a male supervisor will have a female trainee and most typically with a female client. In this situation, while the male supervisor is in a position to help the female with therapy issues in general, it may well be that the female trainee can offer some positive learning experiences for the male supervisor by her personal insights in dealing with a female client.

This situation is particularly advantageous if the male supervisor has not had a female supervisor in his student days. His clinical experiences with women clients may have taught him much about psychotherapy techniques, but there is a good possibility that he has not become knowledgeable about the special needs of women in therapy, such as rape victimization, pregnancy, mothering of small children, widowhood, and so on. While the female trainee may not have experienced any of these situations herself, the possibility that these issues could affect her personally gives her an edge on empathizing with the client. A rape victim may more easily relate her experience to someone who she thinks has already faced or may have to face the same trauma. More directly, individuals can be helpful to their clients by virtue of having survived similar situations and sharing this information. The mother of small children has a much more explicit understanding of the frustrations, responsibilities, and intense involvement with an infant than does the typical father in our culture. I have seen male colleagues shake their heads with disbelief in seeing an otherwise calm, mature female colleague, client, or relative shout at her youngster or ignore her child's demands. However, I have never seen a woman therapist who is or has been the mother of young children fail to understand the normality of such behavior on appropriate occasions. While the nature of mothering young children can be communicated in course work and in supervision hours to trainees of both sexes, the academic learning is never quite as immediately useful as the experience.

I try to encourage female students of psychotherapy to use their supervisory hours with male supervisors as an opportunity to enlighten the supervisor as well as to learn from him. This advice came after hearing many stories by female trainees whose gut-level feelings told them that the advice provided by their supervisors did not meet the client's needs, although they hesitated to suggest that this advice was inadequate. In actuality, many of the male supervisors that they talked about were not insensitive men who did not understand women. Rather, they were very sensitive, competent supervisors with the lapses of consciousness we all have in areas in which we have not had specific training. Viewing their supervisors in this framework, female trainees feel much freer to discuss their own experiences that parallel the client's problem areas.

Most male supervisors are usually quite receptive and respectful of female trainees' insights about a woman client. Where the male supervisor is not receptive in such a relationship, one can anticipate the abuse of power. Some men, even accomplished therapists, are unable to tolerate allusions to their incompetence in even a very specific sex role area. They suffer from the insecurity that as a supervisor they must be more knowledgeable than the trainee—especially if she is a woman. Of course, this must be qualified by mentioning that it is possible that a male supervisor has met with a particular situation about women often enough and emphatically enough to have some very good insights about what may be occurring based both on clinical experience and by feedback from his female clients.

The female trainee can be wrong in her supposition about the female client, overinterpreting the client's dynamics based on the trainee's very personal but atypical experience. After all, women are not all alike. A "seductive" female client will be perceived quite variably by males and females who respond according to their own standards of conduct. As an example, one male supervisor told his female student that the woman client in a marital pair could not be trusted at a social event in the company of a certain male known in the community for his female conquests. The student remained silent but found the supervisor's suggestion appallingly sexist, especially when the supervisor implied he would not trust his own wife around such a man. However, upon consultation with other female trainees, the student realized that her client's impulses were abnormally out of control. She was able to accept that a woman could need external controls in such a situation, but she could also challenge the supervisor on his perception that his own wife might need such controls! I find that such controversial situations are relatively rare, and where conflicts of such a nature occur between a male supervisor and a female trainee, they should both be willing to consult an additional opinion regarding the client, as well as to investigate the nature of their relationship in terms of willingness of the trainee to communicate disagreement.

THE FEMALE SUPERVISOR

In the opposite situation, where the male is the trainee and the female the supervisor, some parallels may occur. When the client is male, the male trainee is in a position to help the female supervisor understand the dynamics at a personal level. In fact, it is often very fruitful for cross-sex dyads to explore their perspectives about the client's problems from their own sex role vantage point. I have learned much from my male trainees about difficulties with the male sex role. In fact, occasionally what I have learned from one male trainee, I then proceed to teach to another male trainee who has not had the particular experiences of the previous trainee. Thus, in discussing the prospects of behavioral assignments for the male client who is socially inept with women, it is very valuable to me to have the male trainees reminisce about the kinds of fears and fantasies that an adolescent male engages in before mustering the courage to ask a girl on an important date.

For both sexes, learning to treat male and female trainees equally is something that does not come naturally. The stereotypes with which we have been raised are always lurking beneath the surface, even when one makes a concerted effort not to expose them. As an example, it was recently brought to my attention by some male trainees that I was not nurturant enough as a supervisor. On reflection, the vicissitudes of the specific situation were complex, but nevertheless, at least one factor appeared to be some subliminal feeling on my part that male trainees do not need or want the same degree of praise, particularly from a woman. I think that at some level I assumed that they would resent direct and obvious praise and consider it patronizing. After all, my female trainees and I have discussed how patronized we have felt when a male supervisor makes too much of what we considered rather ordinary efforts and successes.

I now believe that just the opposite may be true. That is, it may be more necessary for the female supervisor to compliment and to reassure her male trainees than her female trainees that they are recognized as adequate. Alternately, the male supervisor often needs to tone down his praise to genuine feedback with female trainees. I hope these attitudes may counteract our stereotyped notions that women need to be patted on the head for little efforts and that men who are strong and independent would resent mothering by a female authority figure.

SEXUAL INVOLVEMENT OF SUPERVISOR AND TRAINEE

At this point, a discussion is in order about the most sensitive issue in any cross-sex professional relationship—that of the sexual relationship between the individuals. Obviously, the professional relationship between therapist and client excludes a personal relationship of any degree of intimacy. The revised American Psychological Association ethical code (APA, 1977) clearly states that dual relationships are not permitted between therapists and clients, and more specifically, that sexual intimacy with a client is unethical. However, it is not as explicitly stated that sexual relationships between the student and professor or student and supervisor are unethical. While there has been a great deal of discussion of sexual harassment in employment (Lindsey, 1977), sexual involvement between students and professors in psychology is just beginning to be studied (Division 35 of the American Psychological Association has formed a Task Force to investigate the issues). Much of the concern about the relationship between trainees and supervisors has been brought forward from cases of female trainees discussing these issues years after the incidents (APA, 1975; Brodsky, 1977).

The major issue with seduction, of course, is not a sexual issue, but one of the abuse of power. Where one person in a relationship has a position of power over the other, there is no true informed consent for the acceptance of a personal relationship. In the therapeutic relationship, this inequality of power is more obvious. The therapist, by virtue of his or her influential position, cannot assume that the client is participating out of his/her own free will; the client must weigh the threat of losing the therapist by protesting the "treatment," or may trust the therapist's judgment more than a confused self, or feel embarrassment in refusal, or experience a great sense of personal weakness and vulnerability at the time, negating the usual restraints on behaviors considered immoral or inappropriate under more ordinary circumstances.

But the situation between supervisor and trainee is less clear. The trainee is supposed to be a mature adult in stable psychological condition. Such a person should be able to make a free choice regarding a sexual involvement, but the danger in the situation is of losing sight of a trainee's needs for therapy supervision. In one case reported to me (Brodsky, 1977), a female trainee revealed that due to fear of her supervisor's advances she was unable to freely discuss the information she needed about a particular client's sexuality. Her fear was that any discussion of sexuality of the client would lead to a parallel discussion of her sexuality with her supervisor. Apparently, the supervisor did not recognize her discomfort, and thus, one major aspect of the therapy was never supervised.

The issue in these cases is not so much to point out what is and what is not ethical. Such facts are readily recognizable by the individuals involved even if they choose to flout them. The critical factor is that supervision suffers because the supervisor is not free to explore the effect of the client's transference on the trainee with any objectivity. We know that sex between therapists and clients continues even in the face of the formalizing of negative sanctions by professional ethical codes (American Psychological Association, 1977; American Psychiatric Association, 1973). In fact, one study (Holroyd and Brodsky, 1977) has shown that therapists who admit to becoming sexually involved with their clients and who recognize that the results have had negative consequences for themselves and/or their clients, frequently repeat the unethical behavior.

Current research is beginning to look at the characteristics of the therapist who engages in such activity. One recent study (Holroyd and Brodsky, 1978) has discovered that those therapists who have intercourse with their clients are not necessarily from the same population as those who engage in erotic touching of clients but not sexual intercourse. So we do not yet know the relationship between other forms of erotic behavior and actual sexual intercourse, nor do we know what this means for supervision. We also suspect that therapists who engage in touching behavior as part of their therapeutic method run a high risk for potential sexual abuse of their clients if they touch only clients of the opposite sex (Holroyd and Brodsky, in press).

I would contend that the very behaviors that are at high risk for occurring in the therapy hour (such as a very strong sexual countertransference by the therapist) are the most needed issues to be covered while the therapist is still in training. Sexual feelings toward clients are still taboo and sources of embarrassment in therapists. Thus, they are not often discussed seriously among colleagues in consultation after formal training. But, if the therapist is to learn how to handle himself or herself when such a situation arises, his/her training experience should specifically include such topics of discussion and, after formal training, consultation with opposite sex colleagues should be readily available to independent practitioners. I know that my trainees are often reluctant to share their sexual feelings toward clients with their peers, and yet when students present case conferences which explore the issues in question, their peers are extremely appreciative and supportive of the trainees who are willing to reveal their struggles.

OTHER CROSS-SEX SUPERVISION ISSUES

Although sexuality may be the most obvious and prominent of the issues for cross-sex dyads, other issues also warrant mention. What the supervisor models by his or her interaction with the trainee in the supervision hour is assumed to be paralleled at some level in the interaction between the therapist and client. Likewise, the stereotypes that clients have about their expectations of the therapist can have parallels in the stereotypes that trainees have of their supervisors.

As some clients assigned to female therapists have felt that they were being short-changed (Brodsky et al., 1978), it has been suggested by Alonzo and Rutan (1978) that female supervisors are not always accepted readily by male trainees. They noted male trainees to be reluctant to discuss sex bias and other sensitive materials with their female supervisors and to admit various concerns about the expression of healthy aggression in the female patient. Alonzo and Rutan (1978) suggest dealing with such situations indirectly. They provide an example of behavior that the female supervisor might share with the trainee to model appropriate responses of women to sexist practices: the supervisor makes an obvious effort to express her anger at receiving a cramped, inadequate office in the clinic, smaller than anyone else's, in response to the trainee's talking about an angry female client who did not feel that she got what she needed on her job. Thus, the female supervisor becomes a role model for the male trainee of appropriate anger to classical frustrations experienced by women in the patient's situation, a situation that is not so likely to be experienced by men and thus not likely to elicit empathy.

Alonzo and Rutan suggest that there is a potential for the female patient and the male therapist to misally from a need of both to defend against one or more sexist aspects. They offer the example of the female client feeling comforted by having a paternalistic male therapist watch over her, and in return the male therapist receives an important source of esteem from the nurturing of the client. Galinas (1977) cautions that such a collusion of the client and therapist in a distortion of reality can be persuasive and destructive, particularly if it concerns the self-esteem of the client. However, when the female supervisor tries to confront such issues, Galinas notes that she risks the danger of calling the male trainee prejudiced or narcissistic, in which case he may experience humiliation rather than learning.

While the face-saving of the trainee is needed to maintain self-confidence, it is the responsibility of the supervisor to see that the client is not hurt by prolonging the biased practices of the trainee during the working through of the dynamics of the therapist in the supervision sessions. The primary responsibility of both supervisor and therapist is that the client receive adequate therapy. The client's right to protection from biased therapy supercedes the desirability of a more time consuming development of insight by the therapist where the supervisor detects a conflict between the two goals.

EFFECTS ON CLIENTS OF BIASES

Sex role stereotyped therapy can have devastating results for a client (APA, 1975). Without systematic training in academic programs and internships on the psychology of sex roles, a major gap in training will continue to exist. We can conclude that sex role stereotyping and sex bias represent one area of incompetence limiting the scope of psychotherapy by placing restrictions on the therapist's ability to help the client achieve the full range of his/her potential growth. Limitations also exist for the supervisor who cannot recognize the potential of trainees and/or clients, but of most concern is that stereotyping may unwittingly contribute to a deterioration effect of therapy as noted in cases where clients have reported negative experiences in previous therapy due to sex bias of therapists (APA, 1975).

TRAINING TECHNIQUES FOR GROUPS

With these potential problems in mind, feminist therapists have sought to develop techniques for reducing sex role stereotyping in the training and practice of psychotherapists. In the past few years we have seen the development of workshops and training materials to identify and remediate these difficulties (APA, 1977; Brodsky, 1977; Sargent, 1977). The task is a difficult one, as criterion measures are not defined. Assessing an individual's attitude toward sex roles is a new concept.

The Attitude Toward Women Scale (Spence and Helmreich, 1972) has been used in research, along with a variety of lesser-known scales on women's issues (Dempewolff, 1974; Kirkpatrick, 1936; Brodsky, Elmore, and Naffziger, 1976) but none of them have as yet resulted in any valuable and reliable indices warranting our clinical use.

The Bem Sex Role Inventory (Bem, 1974) measures androgyny, or the freedom of members of both sexes to use the advantageous traits associated with the opposite sex role, as well as their own. This scale has been used to evaluate success in psychotherapy as related to sex-role free behavior. Unfortunately it is not clear that the androgynous person is more mentally healthy (Kaplan, 1976). It appears that in our culture, "masculine" traits are considered mentally healthy and therapists of both sexes endorse them over those considered "feminine" (Broverman et al., 1970).

Techniques for raising the awareness of therapists toward their sex role biases need not wait for such measures. Workshop exercises to sensitize therapists working with opposite sex clients have, been used successfully (Brodsky, Hare-Mustin, and Gilbert, 1977).

I have found a variety of awareness techniques to be useful in exploring the stereotypes and biases we all have with regard to opposite sex clients. One particular favorite is the guided fantasy into the body and mind of a person of the opposite sex (Estrup and Taylor, 1972). Nothing appears to be more productive for physical and psychological empathy with the opposite sex than a simulated experience of living in another body complete with clothing, posture, a change in childhood and adulthood history, and the visualizing of growing old as a member of the opposite sex. Any idealization of or envy of the opposite sex is soon tempered by the recognition of vulnerabilities such as a woman considering having to protect external genitals or a male considering not being tall enough or strong enough to count on his body to protect him from human aggression.

On the other hand, the positive features such as the grace of moving with a female body, or the dominance feeling of being larger and more imposing as a male is experienced, also. Psychological insights into the difficulty of men being expected to pursue women in courting with its attendant risks of rejection, versus the comfort of waiting to be approached, are countered by trying on the female role of having no control over selection of partners. Growing older has different but equally fearful consequences. Women lose their beauty, men their physical prowess. Women can more easily accept dependency, men more easily maintain the respect of others.

Other techniques include sex role reversals, with participants trying to play assigned opposite sex roles, or having to guess what role they have been assigned (on a card on one's back) by considering how others are reacting to them in a simulated party scene. Ultimately to be trained for nonsexist therapy, the use of therapy simulations or training materials must be included. Videotaped scenes that encompass situations at high risk for sexist practices are helpful (Brodsky, 1977). These scenes are used as stimuli for trainees to discuss their initial reactions to the following four questions: What is the client trying to tell you, the therapist? What do you think the client is thinking or feeling? What do you feel toward the client at this moment? What do you say or do now? Eventually, training materials will be developed from experiences from supervision sessions. The use of group supervision enhances sex-role training as interactions between individuals can be observed by others. Some topics of particular relevance are: relationship issues between therapist and client, particularly regarding transference and counter-transference; unique problem situations for one sex only such as rape, abortion, and childbirth for women, or sexual performance anxiety, aggressive challenges, and emotional expression for men. Having both sexes present for such training facilitates discussion by pointing out the differences in viewpoint that polarize the sexes due to differing perspectives and experiences with the subject matter. In fact, if there is one message for all participants in the supervisory situation regarding sex bias and sex role stereotyping it is that the training of most value is by a person of the opposite sex. Nowhere is sex role modeling more important than in the handling of clients with problems relating to their sex roles.

CONCLUSION

The insight that we learn much from our students in the process of teaching them is the basis of the model I propose for supervisors with regard to sex role issues. As long as we live in a world that continues to differentiate individuals by their sex and insists on assigning personality traits, social and economic status, and images of competence as part of gender roles, then we will need to develop remedial techniques to minimize our prejudices based on these pervasive stereotypes.

The use of a close, professional relationship with a colleague, trainee, or supervisor of the opposite sex is one major asset in overcoming our biases toward our own as well as our opposite sex clients. However, this insurance of consulting with opposite sex supervisors or colleagues is not sufficient. The formalization of training future therapists to be sensitive to sex bias and sex role stereotyping is just beginning to be explored by the psychological professions in response to a demand by an increasing number of women. Workshops and professional articles and books will continue to be necessary as an adjunct to direct experience in training. Complacency due to any one type of experience or information is the danger in training therapists. Continuing education will always be a factor for an area that is subject to rapid changes in values.

REFERENCES

Alonso, A., and Rutan, J. Cross-sex supervision for cross-sex therapy. *American Journal of Psychiatry,* 1978, *135,* 928–931.

American Psychiatric Association. The principles of medical ethics with annotations especially applicable to psychiatry. *American Journal of Psychiatry,* 1973, *130,* 1057–1064.

American Psychological Association. Report of the Task Force on Sex Bias and Sex Role Stereotyping in Psychotherapeutic Practice. *American Psychologist,* 1975, *30,* 1169–1175.

American Psychological Association. Ethical standards of psychologists. *APA Monitor,* 1977, *3,* 22–23.

American Psychological Association. Guidelines for therapy with women. *American Psychologist,* 1978, *33,* 1122.

Bem, S.L. The measurement of psychological androgyny. *Journal of consulting and clinical psychology,* 1974, *42,* 155–162.

Bem, S.L., and Bem, D.J. Case study of a nonconscious ideology: training the woman to know her place. In S. Cox (Ed.), *Female psychology: the emerging self.* Chicago: Science Research Associates, 1976.

Bird, C. *Born female: The high cost of keeping women down.* New York: McKay, 1968.

Brodsky, A.M. Countertransference issues and the woman therapist: Sex and the student therapist. *The Clinical Psychologist,* 1977, *30,* 12–14.

Brodsky, A.M. A decade of feminist influence on psychotherapy. *Psychology of women quarterly,* in press.

Brodsky, A.M., Elmore, P., and Naffziger, N. Development of the Attitudes Toward Feminist Issues Scale. *Measurement and Evaluation in Guidance,* 1976, *9,* 140–145.

Brodsky, A.M., Hare-Mustin, R., and Gilbert, L. *Using videotapes in training of non-sexist therapy.* Workshop presented at the Conference on Feminist Therapy, Colorado Women's College, Denver, 1977.

Brodsky, A.M., Holroyd, J.C., Payton, C.R., Rubinstein, E.A., Rosenkrantz, P., Sherman, J., Zell, F., Cummings, T., and Suber, C.J. Source materials for non-sexist therapy. *JSAS Catalog of Selected Documents in Psychology,* 1978, *3,* 40. (Ms. No. 1685)

Broverman, I.K., Broverman, D.M., Clarkson, F., Rosenkrantz, P., and Vogel, S.R. Sex-role stereotypes and clinical judgments of mental health. *Journal of Consulting Psychology,* 1970, *34,* 1–7.

Chesler, P. Patient and patriarch: Women and the psychotherapeutic relationship. In V. Gornick and B.K. Moran (Eds.), *Woman in sexist society.* New York: Basic Books, 1971.

Chesler, P. *Women and madness.* New York: Doubleday, 1972.

Dempewolff, J.A. Development and validation of a feminism scale. *Psychological Reports,* 1974, *34,* 651–657.

Estrup, L., and Taylor, L. *Sugar 'n spice and puppy-dog tales.* Unpublished manuscript, 1972. (Available from Consciousness Raising of Women—CROW, Los Angeles)

Fabrikant, B. The psychotherapist and the female patient: Perceptions and change. In V. Franks and V. Burtle (Eds.), *Women in therapy.* New York: Brunner/Mazel, 1974.

Freud, S. 1924. Some psychical consequences of the anatomical distinction between the sexes. In J. Strachey (Ed.), *Standard edition of the complete psychological works of Sigmund Freud.* London: The Hogarth Press and the Institute of Psycho-Analysis, XIX, 1964.

Friedan, B. *The feminine mystique.* New York: Dell, 1963.

Galinas, D. *The psychotherapy supervisor's dilemma: Problematic client-therapist interaction patterns.* Unpublished manuscript, University of Massachusetts, 1977.

Holroyd, J.C., and Brodsky, A.M. Psychologists' attitudes and practices regarding erotic and non-erotic physical contact with patients. *American Psychologist,* 1977, *32,* 843–849.

Holroyd, J.C., and Brodsky, A.M. Does touching lead to sexual intercourse between therapist and client? *Professional Psychology,* in press.

Jakubowski-Spector, P. Facilitating the growth of women through assertive training. *The Counseling Psychologist,* 1973, *4*(1), 75–86.

Kaplan, A.G. Clarifying the concept of androgyny: Implications for treatment. In A. Brodsky (Chair), *Applications of Androgyny to the Theory and Practice of Psychotherapy.* Symposium presented at the meeting of the American Psychological Association, Washington, D.C., 1976.

Kenworthy, J., Koufacos, C., and Sherman, J. Therapists: Their attitudes and information about women. *Psychology of Women Quarterly,* 1978, *2,* 300–313.

Kinsey, A.C., Pomeroy, W.B., Martin, C.E., and Gebhard, P.H. *Sexual Behavior in the Human Female.* Philadelphia: Saunders, 1953.

Kirkpatrick, C. The construction of a belief-pattern scale for measuring attitudes toward feminism. *Journal of Social Psychology,* 1936, *7,* 421–437.

Kirshner, L.A., Genack, A., and Hauser, S.T. Effects of gender on short-term psychotherapy. *Psychotherapy: Theory, Research and Practice,* 1978, *15,* 158–167.

Lasky, E. (Chair). *Threat to the male therapist: Decreasing patient load.* Symposium presented at the meeting of the American Psychological Association, Toronto, 1978.

Lindsey, K. Sexual harassment on the job. *Ms. Magazine,* 1977, *6,* 47–48.

Maccoby, E. *Sex differences and their implications for sex roles.* Paper presented at the meeting of the American Psychological Association, Washington, D.C., 1971.

National Commission on the Observance of International Women's Year, 1976. *To form a more perfect union: Justice for American Women,* 57–67.

Olesker, W., and Balter, L. Sex and empathy. *Journal of Counseling Psychology,* 1972, *19,* 559–562.

Orlinsky, D., and Howard, K. The effects of sex of therapist on the therapeutic experiences of women. *Psychotherapy: Theory, Research and Practice,* 1976, *13,* 82–88.

Sargent, A.G. *Beyond Sex Roles.* New York: West Publishing Company, 1977.

Spence, J.T., and Helmreich, R. The Attitudes Toward Women Scale: An objective instrument to measure attitudes toward the rights and roles of women in contemporary society. *JSAS Catalog of Selected Documents in Psychology,* 1972, *2,* 66.

Tresemer, D. Fear of success: Popular, but unproven. *Psychology Today,* 1974, *7,* 82.

U.S. Department of Commerce, Bureau of the Census. *A Statistical Portrait of Women in the U.S.* Current Population Reports, Special Studies, Series P-23, No. 58, 1976.

PART NINE

Conclusion

Part IX, "Conclusion," consists of Chapter 31, *Summing Up and Moving Forward in Psychotherapy Supervision,* by Allen K. Hess. This is a brief review of issues covered in prior chapters, a discussion of supervision as a professional activity, and a survey of developments that will likely occur in the area of psychotherapy supervision.

CHAPTER 31

Summing Up and Moving Forward in Psychotherapy Supervision

ALLEN K. HESS

The area of psychotherapy supervision can be characterized by Ebbinghaus' quote about psychology: "It has a long past but a short history" (Boring, 1950, p. 392). If one sees supervision as a form of teaching, then its path winds back into unrecorded time. Supervision as teaching can be dated to the Grecian academy where the teachings of men like Aristotle (as known through his student, Plato) extended beyond specific content into areas of ethics, personal conduct, ways of construing the world, and ways of thinking or reasoning through problems. In more recent times, in the area of human services and psychiatric care, the teachings of Charcot, Bleuler, and others (Ellenberger, 1970) follow the traditional tutorial model with lectures, demonstrations, and monitoring of student-conducted patient care. The definition of teaching psychotherapeutic treatment was drawn more clearly with the advent of psychoanalysis. The training institute with training and control analysis procedures became part of the model of supervision that has continued through the present day. The shift from a didactic emphasis on "teaching" to a more personally involved type of teaching and learning can be seen by both (a) the tracing of an analyst's lineage through his or her analyst back to his or her training analyst's training analyst, and (b) a notable quote by Freud: "I do not believe that one can give the method of technique through papers. It must be done by personal teaching. Of course, beginners probably need something to start with. Otherwise they would have nothing to go on. But if they follow the directions conscientiously, they will soon find themselves in trouble. Then they must learn to develop their own technique" (Blanton, 1971, p. 48).

As other "schools" of psychotherapy developed, each has had strong components—and space in its journals—devoted to teaching and promulgating its own techniques. As can be seen in chapters preceding this one, the "schools" as a rule have used their own techniques as the training model (see Rice's Chapter 12, Linehan's Chapter 13, Wessler and Ellis' Chapter 14, Beier and Young's Chapter 15, and Dies' Chapter 23 as exemplars). This development of training within "schools" of therapy perhaps is one reason a specified focus or set of theories regarding psychotherapy supervision has not emerged. A second factor seems to be the somewhat abstract, amorphous, and undefined nature of supervision as it has existed. Several recent trends have converged to cause psychotherapy supervision to merit better definition.

DEFINITIONS

At least five elements of psychotherapy supervision require specification in order to arrive at a satisfactory definition. These are the constructs or ideas: supervisee, supervisor, what is learned, how it is accomplished, and what is particular to supervision distinguishing it from more generic relationships such as "teaching," administrative control, and consultation.

Part of the amorphous quality of psychotherapy supervision may come from the difficulty in defining its participants. The *supervisee* may be anyone ranging in training from a lay volunteer to a senior psychotherapist who supervises others him or herself. What all seem to have in common is that, whether their primary role is that of a student or a private practitioner, the person is an actual or potential deliverer of mental health service, particularly psychotherapy. The person can be described as in need of skill refinement as judged by him or herself (most optimally), by a more senior or higher ranking person in an agency, or by an agency policy. Interestingly, this approximation toward a definition is resisted by some more senior professionals for whom entering supervision is construed as requiring the one in the supervisee role essentially to proclaim a deficiency. Yet senior practitioners can use supervision as self-improvement, as a check against human blind spots, to continue their sensitivity as to what the supervisee role requires of their own supervisees, and to secure the consultation of colleagues as a way of keeping one's skills honed. In this regard, a recently divorced colleague decided not to accept marital cases, and entered into both a peer consultation and a group supervision arrangement which involved male and female therapists discussing their sexual and marital value structures and how it affects their treatment of clients.

Thus, the supervisee can not be defined as being at a particular stage in training, but as being in training.

The *supervisor,* similarly, is difficult to define. While the supervisor often has more skill, experience, knowledge, or acumen, this need not be the case in some forms of productive supervision. As Gardner's Chapter 29 and Brodsky's Chapter 30—on racial, ethnic, and social class considerations, and on sex role issues respectively—illustrate, a corrective influence can flow from the supervisee to the supervisor, or might consist of learning based on noncognitive issues. If the learning is relational or interpersonal in nature, then traditional academic-related credentials are less helpful (although still necessary) in defining the supervisor. Much like the supervisee role, the supervisor role can be defined from a functional position; the supervisor is someone whom an actual or potential psychotherapist sees as a resource for knowledge or skill development so the psychotherapist can do psychotherapy more effectively. The definition can have structural tones, too, as when a supervisor is defined by an agency job description, or as in the case with faculty appointments in universities, training institutes, and clinics. There is no guarantee that those people who are appointed have any demonstrated supervisory expertise. Unfortunately, too, these definitions require further clarification, since a motion picture—such as *Diary of a Mad Housewife* or Woody Allen's

Interiors—can be as instructive about marital and family dynamics as a semester-long seminar for an individual, yet a movie can hardly be classified as a supervisor. Thus the use of an effect cannot be the key to defining a supervisor. Nor can the assignment to that role by an agency be the sole defining characteristic. Many agencies might assign a person to the supervisory role based on the person's accomplishments as a skilled therapist. Yet, if we could identify a person as a skilled therapist, across clients, modalities of therapy, and client disorders, it is still debatable as to whether the person would be a skilled supervisor. The "good supervisor" quest may be somewhat illusory; the question can be better conceptualized as which supervisor under what conditions with which kind of cases with which supervisees will be effective on particular outcome measures. Essentially, Kiesler's (1966) "uniformity myths"—warning us of the fallacies that there is a "patient" treated by a "therapist" to produce an "outcome" with little regard to the heterogeneity of each element—ought not be repeated in the supervision area (see also Lambert's Chapter 27 on this point).

Defining supervision by *what is learned* leads to several interesting questions. Perhaps the most profound is whether something is learned at all. Styczynski's Chapter 3 and Barnat's Chapter 5, as well as a number of other chapters, illustrate the problem of defining what, if anything, cognitive is acquired. Most likely, noncognitive changes occur. Typically they include experientially based changes such as being more "confident," more "comfortable" and "congruent," more "open" to the client's and one's own experiences, more aware of family, group, and age related dimensions, and more cognizant of one's blind spots or biases, to mention a few. Much of the change may occur in sudden shifts rather than in the incremental steps that the term "learning" suggests. Burkhart's point, in Chapter 26, is that understanding and working within a client's metaphoric system as a key to successful behavior change illustrates the problem of defining the supervisee's task in "learning" how to deliver human service. Thus "what is learned" may be more aptly phrased: Is the change agent's (supervisee's) experiential construct system more effectively apprehending and modifying the client's experiential construal processes and subsequent behavior?

Once one has clarified the content of supervision (which is still a moot question) the cognate question arises: *How this is achieved* ("how 'learning' is accomplished")? Paradoxically, it seems that we have a variety of technologies by which we can teach psychotherapy better than we can define what it is that we are teaching. Most notably Akamatsu's Chapter 16, Glenwick and Stevens' Chapter 17, Forsyth and Ivey's Chapter 18, Kagan's Chapter 19, Dies' Chapter 23, and Lambert's Chapter 27, among others, provide ways of understanding how supervision is accomplished. Yet, as there are heterogeneous experiences or skills that one acquires in supervision, so there are different ways to acquire them. It seems, then, that supervision could not be definitively stated as requiring a particular set of techniques.

Moreover, none of the skills to be acquired or techniques of acquisition are *unique to supervision*. Many—if not all—of the skills to be acquired and methods of acquisition are common to psychotherapy. Also, both teaching in a larger sense, and humanistically oriented administration are difficult to distinguish from a definition of psychotherapy supervision.

Reisman (1971) reviewed definitions of psychotherapy in terms of goals, processes, the practitioner, and the relationship, finding these elements, used singly, to be unduly restrictive or indefinitely broad. The same problems beset definitions of psychotherapy supervision in terms of the five elements reviewed above. Mindful of the pitfalls attendant on defining such an abstract activity, we tentatively offer the definition that psychotherapy supervision is: a relationship where one or more person's skills in conducting psychotherapy or mental health services are intentionally and potentially enhanced by the interaction with another person. G. K. Chesterton said, "I like getting into hot water, it keeps me clean." Similarly, defining psychotherapy supervision should generate some discussion, with subsequent attention given to the various supervisory roles that abound, the development of the parties, the boundary conditions or parameters of psychotherapy supervision, its techniques, and its effects.

RESEARCH AND DEVELOPMENT

Lambert's Chapter 27, and to some extent Akamatsu's Chapter 16, Rice's Chapter 12, Linehan's Chapter 13, Forsyth and Ivey's Chapter 18, Kagan's Chapter 19, and Dies' Chapter 23 review research pertinent to psychotherapy supervision. These chapters show that there has been a quiet but active accumulation of research, in diverse professional journals. As more attention is given to training in mental health, particularly with the growth of continuing education programs, more research will be needed and conducted.

Among the areas of research that will develop are psychometrically sound rating scales. Attention can be invested with profit in rating both the supervisor and the supervisee. This will help lead to finer definitions of these roles. Also, the content and process of supervision, and supervision's effects on both the psychotherapist and the client (outcome studies) will be conducted. I would expect that this should include the harmful effects of clinical training (Layne, 1978), as well as the vagaries of the effects of the supervisor and supervisee personalities on each other (Hassenfeld and Sarris, 1978). As psychotherapy research discovered the therapist-client match to be important, I expect that the supervisor and therapist match on critical dimensions such as "openness to experience," or "cognitively differentiated" or "pragmatic," will emerge as important in "successful" supervision. One interesting example of the question of supervisor-supervisee matching is Munson's (1979) study of the functioning of male and female supervisors as rated by both male and female supervisee-practitioner's perceptions. Mead and Crane (1978) attempt to disentangle what reward and punishment contingencies by the client, the counselor's history, the setting, the supervisor, and the administration contribute to determining the counselor's therapy behavior.

While Ivey's model (see Chapter 18) describes different theoretical orientations as having potentially different styles of communicating, Markowitz's (1958) study

—in which he entered into supervision with a number of his colleagues—concluded that intrapersonal needs, not differential schooling, determined the nature of supervision. Reiss (1960) suggests that acceptance of the supervisee's orientation (and vice versa, I may add) is fundamental, and that there is ample room for "personal predilections" of both the supervisor and trainee.

NEEDS FOR SUPERVISION

As mentioned in the Preface, psychotherapy supervision is both a frequent activity and one that continues to increase. In a sample of academic clinicians, Shemburg and Leventhal (1978) show that 55% described themselves as spending between 10 and 29% of their time doing clinical supervision, and 7% claimed to spend more than 30% of their time in supervision. Thus it seems that supervision occurs frequently. Each American Psychological Association training conference, including those at Boulder, Northwestern, Thayer, Miami, Chicago, Vail, and Austin, among others [and the Shakow report (American Psychological Association, 1947) preceding them], has focused on psychotherapy training, practica, and staff training, all recognizing the need for such training. The APA's Division of Psychotherapy, in its recommended standards for doctoral education, suggests: (a) in principle 1, that faculty be hired and promoted for excellence in psychotherapy supervision as well as for excellence in research and didactic teaching, (b) in principle 3, that the complexity of clinical teaching requires regulation of other duties to allow ample time for supervision, (c) in principle 9, that faculty be competent in supervision having had course work on the theory and practice of supervision and having had supervised practica in psychotherapy supervision, and (d) in principle 20, that students receive training in the supervision of psychotherapy (Division of Psychotherapy, 1971).

The increase in third party payers and a more consumer-oriented stance on the part of clients will result in the need for more quality control (see Hess' Chapter 2 and Slovenko's Chapter 28). One approach the private practice therapist judiciously may decide to use is to have a supervisor review cases at least every six months to help the psychotherapist assess the progress of the case, and to ensure that he or she does not become isolated in his or her practice and adrift in conceptualizing the client problems faced continually.

Additionally, as more diverse programs are granting degrees in one or another area of mental health services, some ongoing credentialing procedures must develop. These should necessarily involve supervision.

As supervision develops, more attention must be given to the definition (as mentioned above), training, and possibly credentialing of supervisors. While it is likely that supervisors will continue to be defined by the training institute, academic department, or clinic, professional standards will be developed for supervisor education. These developments make the need for definition and research on the supervisory processes even more urgent.

In our quest for developing ourselves and each other a tale from the Hasidim seems relevant:

The Maggid of Zlatchov was asked by one of his disciples: "in the book of Elijah we read: 'Everyone in Israel is in duty bound to say: When will my work approach the works of my fathers, Abraham, Isaac, and Jacob.' How are we to understand this? How could we venture to think that we could do what our fathers could?"

The rabbi expounded: "Just as our fathers invented new ways of serving, each a new service according to his own character: one the service of love, the other that of stern justice, the third that of beauty, so each one of us in his own way shall devise something new in the light of the teachings and of service, and do what has not yet been done." (Buber, 1947).

REFERENCES

American Psychological Association, Committee on Training in Clinical Psychology. Recommended graduate training program in clinical psychology. *American Psychologist,* 1947, *2,* 539–558.

Blanton, S. *Diary of my analysis with Sigmund Freud.* New York: Hawthorn Books, 1971.

Boring, E. G. *A history of experimental psychology* (2nd ed.). New York: Appleton-Century-Crofts, 1950.

Buber, M. *Tales of the Hasidim: The early masters.* New York: Shocken Books, 1947.

Division of Psychotherapy, American Psychological Association. Recommended standards for psychotherapy education in psychology doctoral programs. *Professional Psychology,* 1971, *2,* 148–154.

Ellenberger, H. F. *The discovery of the unconscious.* New York: Basic Books, 1970.

Hassenfeld, I. N., and Sarris, J. G. Hazards and horizons of psychotherapy supervision. *American Journal of Psychotherapy,* 1978, *32,* 393–401.

Kiesler, D. J. Some myths of psychotherapy research and the search for a paradigm. *Psychological Bulletin,* 1966, *65,* 110–136.

Layne, C. Harmful effects of clinical training upon students' personalities. *Perceptual and Motor Skills,* 1978, *47,* 777–778.

Markowitz, M. A supervisor supervised: A subjective eclective experience. *American Journal of Psychotherapy,* 1958, *12,* 488–492.

Mead, E., and Crane, D. R. An empirical approach to supervision and training of relationship therapists. *Journal of Marriage and Family Counseling,* 1978, *4*(4), 67–75.

Munson, C. E. Evaluation of male and female supervisors. *Social Work,* 1979, *24,* 104–110.

Reisman, J. M. *Toward the integration of psychotherapy.* New York: Wiley, 1971.

Reiss, B. F. The selection and supervision of psychotherapists. In N. P. Dellis and H. K. Stone (Eds.), *The training of psychotherapists.* Baton Rouge: Louisiana State University Press, 1960.

Shemberg, K. M., and Leventhal, D. B. A survey of activities of academic clinicians. *Professional Psychology,* 1978, *9,* 580–586.

AUTHOR INDEX

SUBJECT INDEX

ABC theory of personality, 181–183
Abuses, patient care and legal issues, 465
Accountability, demand for, 456
Adaptive contexts, 104
Administration, and community psychology, 386
Administrative supervision, and legal issues, 460
Adolescence
  concerns of
    biological, 307–308
    cognitive, 308–309
    differentiation, 309
    identity formation, 310–311
    individuation from family, 309
    orientation to action, 308, 313
    separation from family, 309
    ultimatums, 308, 312–313
    vocational choices, 309
  definitions of, 306–307
  theories of, 307
Adolescent psychotherapy
  decisions about individual and long-term
    treatment, 316
  group treatment, 316–317
  resistance in, 314
  sex of therapist, client, and supervisor,
    315–316
  therapist's use of youthful argot, attire, and
    adornments, 315
Adolescents
  confidentiality and, 317–318
  consent to treatment, 318–319
  right to treatment, 318–319
Aged
  and modifications of regular therapy, 331
    therapy with
    techniques, 328–329
    therapist characteristics, 329–330
Agency, 475–476
Aging
  attitudes toward, 323
  and crises, 325–327
  definitions of, 323–324
  and organic brain syndrome, 325–326
  pathology of, 324–327
  and problems from earlier years, 325–326
  and special life crises, 325–327
American Group Psychotherapy Association,
  training guidelines, 338
APA (American Psychological Association)
  Division for Psychotherapy, 529
  Taskforce on Sex Bias and Sex Role
    Stereotyping in Psychotherapeutic Practices,
    511, 515

Training Conferences, 529
Attitudes
  toward human nature and change, 138–140
  toward the self, 138, 140–141
Authenticity, integrating treatment techniques
  with, 41–43

Beginning supervisors; see Novice supervisors
Behavior therapy
  characteristics of, 150–154
  content of, 150–151
  definitions of, 154
  methodological approach of, 152
  therapeutic focus of, 151–152
Behavioral counseling approach, 156
Behavioral functioning, model of, 158
Behavioral role play assessment, 211
Behavioral supervision
  cognitive skills, 162–166
  overt motor skills, 166–169
  physiological/affective skills, 168–170
  procedures and techniques, 170–174
  skill training in, 155
  target systems and skills, 159–170
Behavioral systems approach, 156
Beliefs
  irrational (iBs), 182, 186, 187
  rational (rBs), 182
Bias
  overcoming trainee-based, 501–503
  in psychotherapy, 478, 491
  see also Sex bias
Bipersonal field, 103
  Type One derivatives, 104
  Type Two derivatives, 104
Bipersonal predictive validational model, 107,
  113
Bug-in-the-ear, 436

Catastrophe theory, cusp model, 8–9
Child psychotherapist
  qualifications of, 292–293
  training of, 292–293
Child psychotherapy
  approaches to supervisee's task, 294–297
  definitions of, 290–292
  early practices, 287–288
  harmful effects of, 293
  limit setting, 297–299
  and parental involvement, 299–302
Client-centered relationship, 138–140
  self attitudes in, 140–141
Client-centered theory, 137

545

Handbook of Infant Development
edited by Joy D. Osofsky

Understanding the Rape Victim: A Synthesis of Research Findings
by Sedelle Katz and Mary Ann Mazur

Childhood Pathology and Later Adjustment: The Question of Prediction
by Loretta K. Cass and Carolyn B. Thomas

Handbook of Minimal Brain Dysfunctions
edited by Herbert E. Rie and Ellen D. Rie

Intelligent Testing with the WISC-R
by Alan S. Kaufman

Handbook of Adolescent Psychology
edited by Joseph Adelson

Adaptation in Schizophrenia: The Theory of Segmental Set
by David Shakow

Psychotherapy: An Eclectic Approach
by Sol L. Garfield

Handbook of Behavioral Interventions: A Clinical Guide
edited by Edna B. Foa and Alan Goldstein

Art Psychotherapy
by Harriet Wadeson

Restricted Environmental Stimulation: Research and Clinical Applications
by Peter Suedfeld

Psychotherapy Supervision: Theory, Research and Practice
edited by Allen K. Hess

Psychology and Psychiatry in Courts and Corrections: Controversy and Change
by Ellsworth A. Fersch, Jr.